Monetary Economics

✓ **W9-AWO-227**

The New Palgrave Economics Collection
Editors: Steven N. Durlauf, University of Wisconsin-Madison, USA & Lawrence E. Blume, Cornell University, USA

Also in the series:
Behavioural and Experimetal Economics
Economic Growth
Game Theory
Macroeconometrics and Time Series Analysis
Microeconometrics

Series Standing Order ISBN 978-0-230-24014-8 hardcover
Series Standing Order ISBN 978-0-230-24013-1 paperback

To receive future titles in this series as they are published quote one of the ISBNs listed above to set up a standing order: contact your bookseller; write to Customer Services Department, Macmillan Distribution Ltd, Houndmills, Basingstoke, Hampshire, RG21 6XS; or email orders@palgrave.com.

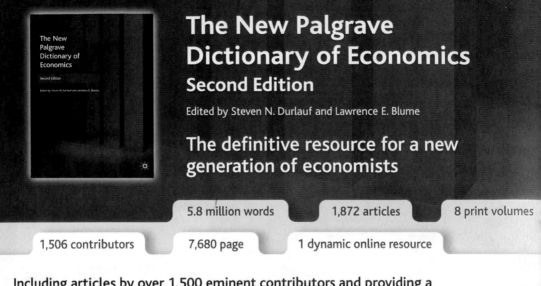

The New Palgrave Dictionary of Economics
Second Edition

Edited by Steven N. Durlauf and Lawrence E. Blume

The definitive resource for a new generation of economists

| 5.8 million words | 1,872 articles | 8 print volumes |

| 1,506 contributors | 7,680 page | 1 dynamic online resource |

Including articles by over 1,500 eminent contributors and providing a current overview of economics, this second edition of *The New Palgrave* is now available both in print and online.

The online *Dictionary* is a dynamic resource for economists which:

- Is regularly updated with new articles and updates to existing articles, along with new features and functionality

- Allows 24x7 access to members of subscribing institutions, outside library opening hours, on the move, at home or at their desk

- Offers excellent search and browse facilities, both full text and advanced, which make it possible to explore the Dictionary with great speed and ease

- Contains hyperlinked cross-references within articles, making it an indispensable tool for researchers and students

- Features carefully selected and maintained links to related sites, sources of further information and bibliographical citations

- Enables users to save searches, make personal annotations and bookmark articles they need to refer to regularly by using 'My Dictionary'

Experience the world of economics at your fingertips!

Why not see for yourself how valuable the online *Dictionary* is by encouraging your librarian to request a trial today?

Free 2 week trials of *The New Palgrave Dictionary of Economics Online* are now available to prospective institutional subscribers worldwide. Your librarian can register today at www.dictionaryofeconomics.com.

www.dictionaryofeconomics.com

Monetary Economics

Edited by
Steven N. Durlauf
University of Wisconsin-Madison, USA

Lawrence E. Blume
Cornell University, USA

palgrave
macmillan

First published 2010 by
PALGRAVE MACMILLAN

Palgrave Macmillan in the UK is an imprint of Macmillan Publishers Limited,
registered in England, company number 785998, of Houndmills, Basingstoke,
Hampshire RG21 6XS.

Palgrave Macmillan in the US is a division of St Martin's Press LLC,
175 Fifth Avenue, New York, NY 10010.

Palgrave Macmillan is the global academic imprint of the above companies
and has companies and representatives throughout the world.

Palgrave® and Macmillan® are registered trademarks in the United States,
the United Kingdom, Europe and other countries.

ISBN 978-0-230-23887-9   hardback
ISBN 978-0-230-23888-6   paperback

This book is printed on paper suitable for recycling and made from fully
managed and sustained forest sources. Logging, pulping and manufacturing
processes are expected to conform to the environmental regulations of the
country of origin.

A catalogue record for this book is available from the British Library.

A catalog record for this book is available from the Library of Congress.

10   9   8   7   6   5   4   3   2   1
19   18   17   16   15   14   13   12   11   10

Printed and bound in the United States of America

Contents

List of Contributors

THEO BALDERSTON
The University of Manchester, UK

WILLIAM A. BARNETT
University of Kansas, USA

MICHAEL BINDER
University of Maryland, USA

MICHAEL D. BORDO
Rutgers University, USA

J. H. BOYD
University of Minnesota, USA

PHILLIP CAGAN
Professor Emeritus, Columbia University,
USA

CHARLES W. CALOMIRIS
Columbia University, USA

SATYAJIT CHATTERJEE
Federal Reserve Bank of Philadelphia, USA

P. DEAN CORBAE
University of Texas, USA

ROBERT W. DIMAND
Brock University, Canada

GAUTI B. EGGERTSSON
Federal Reserve Bank of New York, USA

CHRISTOPHER J. ERCEG
Federal Reserve Board, Washington DC, USA

BENJAMIN M. FRIEDMAN
Harvard University, USA

MILTON FRIEDMAN
Hoover Institution, Stanford University, USA

TIMOTHY S. FUERST
Bowling Green State University, USA

DOUGLAS GALE
New York University, USA

MIKHAIL GOLOSOV
Massachusetts Institute of Technology,
USA

CHARLES A.E. GOODHART
London School of Economics, UK

CHRISTIAN HELLWIG
University of California Los Angeles, USA

DONALD D. HESTER
University of Wisconsin-Madison, USA

PETER N. IRELAND
Boston College, USA

PAUL KLEIN
University of Western Ontario, Canada

NARAYANA R. KOCHERLAKOTA,
Federal Reserve Bank of Minneapolis, USA

RICARDO LAGOS
New York University, USA

ERIC M. LEEPER
Indiana University, USA

JAMES M. NASON
Federal Reserve Bank of Atlanta, USA

JUAN PABLO NICOLINI
Universidad Torcuato di Tella, Argentina

LAWRENCE H. OFFICER
University of Illinois at Chicago, USA

ATHANASIOS ORPHANIDES
Federal Reserve Board, Washington DC, USA

DON PATINKIN
Hebrew University of Jerusalem, Israel

ADAM S. POSEN
Peterson Institute for International
Economics, USA

WILLIAM ROBERDS
Federal Reserve Bank of Atlanta, USA

ARTHUR J. ROLNICK
Federal Reserve Bank of Minneapolis, USA

LARS E. O. SVENSSON
Princeton University, USA

JAMES TOBIN
Former Sterling Professor of Economics,
Yale University, USA

ALEH TSYVINSKI
Yale Department of Economics, USA

FRANÇOIS R. VELDE
Federal Reserve Bank of Chicago, USA

NEIL WALLACE
Pennsylvania State University, USA

CARL E. WALSH
University of California Santa Cruz, USA

WARREN E. WEBER
Federal Reserve Bank of Minneapolis, USA

VOLKER WIELAND
Goethe University, Germany

RANDALL WRIGHT
University of Pennsylvania, USA

General Preface

All economists of a certain age remember the "little green books". Many own a few. These are the offspring of *The New Palgrave: A Dictionary of Economics*; collections of reprints from *The New Palgrave* that were meant to deliver at least a sense of the *Dictionary* into the hands of those for whom access to the entire four volume, four million word set was inconvenient or difficult. *The New Palgrave Dictionary of Economics, Second Edition* largely resolves the accessibility problem through its online presence. But while the online search facility provides convenient access to specific topics in the now eight volume, six million word *Dictionary of Economics*, no interface has yet been devised that makes browsing from a large online source a pleasurable activity for a rainy afternoon. To our delight, *The New Palgrave's* publisher shares our view of the joys of dictionary-surfing, and we are thus pleased to present a new series, the "little blue books", to make some part of the *Dictionary* accessible in the hand or lap for teachers, students, and those who want to browse. While the volumes in this series contain only articles that appeared in the 2008 print edition, readers can, of course, refer to the online *Dictionary* and its expanding list of entries.

The selections in these volumes were chosen with several desiderata in mind: to touch on important problems, to emphasize material that may be of more general interest to economics beginners and yet still touch on the analytical core of modern economics, and to balance important theoretical concerns with key empirical debates. The 1987 Eatwell, Milgate and Newman *The New Palgrave: A Dictionary of Economics* was chiefly concerned with economic theory, both the history of its evolution and its contemporary state. The second edition has taken a different approach. While much progress has been made across the board in the 21 years between the first and second editions, it is particularly the flowering of empirical economics which distinguishes the present interval from the 61 year interval between Henry Higgs' *Palgrave's Dictionary of Political Economy* and *The New Palgrave*. It is fair to say that, in the long run, doctrine evolves more slowly than the database of facts, and so some of the selections in these volumes will age more quickly than others. This problem will be solved in the online *Dictionary* through an ongoing process of revisions and updates. While no such solution is available for these volumes, we have tried to choose topics which will give these books utility for some time to come.

Steven N. Durlauf
Lawrence E. Blume

Introduction

Monetary economics is one of the most venerable fields of study in all of economics. As such, the entries in this collection span an enormous range of topics and include entries that originally appeared in the 1987 edition of *The New Palgrave*, notably 'money' by James Tobin, 'neutrality of money' by Don Patinkin, and 'quantity theory of money' by Milton Friedman. These entries are representative of a strategy pursued in the 2008 edition of preserving iconic entries whose content captured a vision of ideas circa 1987, with other entries capturing recent developments on the topic. Hence we also include entries on fiat and commodity money and a comparison of the quantity theory and real bills doctrine which embody contemporary perspectives.

The 2008 edition expanded the domain of coverage of monetary economics in two important directions. First, new approaches to monetary economics such as the increasing use of search-theoretic models to study money demand, is now part of the *Dictionary*. More importantly, the current edition gives much more extensive coverage to issues on monetary policy. Conceptual issues involving commitment and the time consistency of monetary policy are now included. Further, the renaissance of study of monetary policy rules, whether simple Taylor style rules or sophisticated monetary targeting practices, receives substantial attention.

In addition to theoretical articles, this collection contains much historical and institutional content. Entries appear on both the Bank of England and the Federal Reserve, which are the exemplars of monetary authorities. We have also included entries on hyperinflation and monetary forces in the Great Depression. These are reminders of how much damage bad monetary policy can produce, as well as laboratories for understanding how money affects the economy.

Steven N. Durlauf
Lawrence E. Blume

Bank of England

The primary motivation for the establishment of the Bank of England was the need to raise funds to help the government finance the then current war against France, although the view had also developed that a bank could help to 'stabilize' financial activity in London given periodic fluctuations in the availability of currency and credit. An original proposal by William Paterson in 1693 for a government 'fund of perpetual interest' was turned down in favour of another proposal by Paterson in 1694 to establish a company known as the Governor and Company of the Bank of England, whose capital, once raised, would be lent in its entirety to the government.

An ordinary finance act, now known as the Bank of England Act (1694), stipulated that the Bank was to be established via stock subscriptions which were to be lent to the government. A governor, deputy governor and 24 directors were to be elected by stockholders (holding £500 or more of stock).

The evolution of the Bank's objectives and functions, 1694–1914

Under its original charter the Bank was allowed to issue bank notes, redeemable in silver coin, as well as to trade in bills and bullion. The notes of the Bank competed with other paper media of exchange, which comprised notes issued by the Exchequer and by private financial companies. In addition, customers could maintain deposit accounts with the Bank, which were transferable to other parties via notes drawn against deposit receipts (known as accomptable notes), thus providing an early form of cheque.

An early customer of the Bank was the Royal Bank of Scotland, which made arrangements to keep cash at the Bank from its outset in 1727. Loans were extended, predominantly in the form of discounting of bills, to individuals and companies, and the Bank undertook a large amount of lending (often via overdrafts) to the Dutch East India Company and, from 1711, to the South Sea Company. The Bank also acted as a mortgage lender, although this business never took off, and ceased some years later. Finally, an important function of the Bank was the remittance of cash to Flanders and elsewhere for the wars against Louis XIV, which was facilitated through correspondent arrangements with banks in Holland.

In 1697 the renewal of the Bank's charter for another ten years involved the passage of a second Bank Act, which increased the capital of the Bank and prohibited any other banks from being chartered in England and Wales. This monopoly was strengthened at the next renewal of the Bank's charter in 1708, when any association of six or more persons was forbidden to engage in banking activity, thereby precluding the establishment of any other joint stock banks. The Bank's position as banker to the government was consolidated in 1715 when it was decided that subscriptions for government debt issues would be paid to the Bank, and further that the Bank was to manage the government debt (the Ways and Means Act). The Bank then acted as manager of the government's debts from that date until 1997.

The Bank also encouraged the use of its own notes in preference to other media of exchange by persuading the Treasury to increase the denomination of Exchequer bills. By 1725 the Bank's notes had become sufficiently widely used as to be pre-printed for the first time. Although a number of private banks had developed by 1750, both within and outside London, none competed seriously with the Bank in the issue of notes. By 1770 most London bankers had ceased to issue notes, using Bank of England notes (and cheques) to settle balances among themselves in what had become a well-developed clearing system. Furthermore, in 1775 Parliament raised the minimum denomination for any non-Bank of England notes to one pound and, two years later, to five pounds, effectively guaranteeing the use of Bank of England notes as the dominant form of currency. Problems relating to counterfeiting, and to the harsh treatment of those caught in the act, were, however, perennial.

In Scotland, by contrast, no note issuing monopoly existed, and banks were free to issue notes, although two banks dominated, namely, the Bank of Scotland and the Royal Bank of Scotland. Furthermore, several private note-issuing banks were in business in Ireland, and the Bank of Ireland was established in 1783. These banks relied on the Bank of England to obtain silver and gold, particularly during times of financial stress, such as 1783 and 1793.

Following a dramatic rise in government expenditures after 1793 due to the war against France, which caused a large rise in the Bank's note issue, the Bank's gold holdings fell sharply. After a scare about a French invasion convertibility was suspended in 1797, and resumed only in 1821. In view of the financial exigencies of the war, and the fact that there was in such circumstances no limit to the expansion of its note issue, now effectively legal tender, by the Bank, a privately owned company, what is in retrospect surprising about the period of suspension is how comparatively low the resulting inflation was. Even so, it was high enough to set off a major debate on its causation, for example in the Parliamentary Committee on the High Price of Bullion (1810). This period saw a further consolidation of the Bank as a note issuer, since it began to issue small denomination notes (given the shortage of silver and gold coin), which became legal tender in 1812. Furthermore, in 1816 silver coin ceased to be legal tender for small payments. The government also moved most of its accounts to the Bank in 1805 (in 1834 all government accounts were finally moved to the Bank).

During the 18th century and early part of the 19th century, smaller country banks had proliferated throughout England and Wales, many issuing their own notes. Given the prohibition on joint stock banking, the capital of these banks was usually small, and they regularly became insolvent, especially when the demand for cash (coin) became strong. This contrasted sharply with Scotland, where joint stock banking and branch banking were permitted, and relatively few failures occurred. Following a severe banking crisis in 1825, during which many English country banks failed, an Act renewing the Bank's charter (in 1826) abolished the restrictions on banking activity more than 65 miles outside of London. This led to the establishment of several joint stock banks, while the Bank countered by opening several branches throughout England.

Thus, a semblance of a banking 'system' began to emerge by 1830, with the Bank of England as the 'central' bank. By far the best book on such nascent central banking at this time was that written by Henry Thornton, *An Enquiry into the Nature and Effects of the Paper Credit of Great Britain* (1802). The practice of banks placing surplus funds with bill brokers also developed, with the Bank beginning to extend secured loans to these brokers on a more or less regular basis. In 1833 joint stock banks were finally allowed to operate in London, although they were not permitted to issue notes and thus were essentially deposit-taking banks only. The same Act specified that Bank of England notes were legal tender, and the Bank was also given the freedom to raise its discount rate freely (until then usury laws had placed a ceiling on interest rates) in response to cash outflows. The Bank's reaction (an early reaction function), in varying its interest rate, to cash inflows and outflows became codified around this time in what became known as the Palmer rule, after Horsley Palmer, Governor 1830–33, though the rule itself is usually dated from 1827.

The position of Bank of England notes was consolidated in an important Act, passed in 1844, generally known as the Bank Charter Act, preventing all note issuers from expanding their note issue above existing levels, and prohibiting the establishment of any new note-issuing banks. The 1844 Act also separated the issue and banking functions of the Bank into different departments, and required the Bank to publish a weekly summary of accounts.

Given that it did not pay interest on its deposits, the deposit activity of the Bank could never really compete with that of other banks, which expanded rapidly from 1850 onwards. In 1854, joint stock banks in London joined the London Clearing House, and it was agreed that clearing by transfer of Bank of England notes would be abandoned in favour of cheques drawn on bank accounts held at the Bank. Ten years later the Bank of England itself entered this clearing arrangement, and cheques drawn on bankers' accounts at the Bank became considered as paid.

Although the Bank had, from the beginning of the 19th century, periodically bought or sold exchequer bills to influence the note circulation, explicit open-market borrowing operations to support its discount rate began in 1847. From 1873 until 1890 the Bank almost always acted as a borrower rather than a lender of funds, as there were typically cash surpluses. As a result, the Bank introduced the systematic issue of Treasury bills via a regular tender offer in 1877. Treasury bills had a much shorter maturity (three to twelve months) than Exchequer bills (five or more years), and were to play an important role in raising funds from the outset of the First World War onwards.

By 1890, the Bank's role as lender of last resort became undisputed when it orchestrated the rescue of Baring Brothers and Co., a bank whose solvency had become suspect, threatening to cause systemic problems. Earlier, in 1866, the failure of a discount house, Overend, Gurney and Co., had precipitated a financial panic, during which the Bank discounted large amounts of bills and extended considerable loans.

The Bank, however, was criticized for not doing more to prevent the onset of such a panic, not least by Walter Bagehot in his famous book *Lombard Street* (1873).

Throughout the 19th century, the Bank streamlined its discount facilities. In 1851 it overhauled its discount rules, stipulating that only those parties having a discount account could present bills, and that these bills had to have a maturity of fewer than 95 days and be endorsed by two creditworthy firms. In the latter part of the century, however, the Bank gradually came to favour discount houses, often by presenting them with better rates of discount, and the range of firms doing discount business with the Bank declined. Discount houses were favoured because there was tension then between the Bank and the rapidly growing commercial banks – there was much banking consolidation via mergers between the 1870s and 1914 – and dealing via the intermediation of the discount houses enabled the Bank to influence market rates without having to interact directly with the joint-stock banks as counterparties.

Until the First World War the Bank pursued a discount policy which was primarily aimed at maintaining its gold reserves (as noted earlier) and which was conducted largely independently of the government. During the First World War, however, a clash occurred between the Bank Governor (Cunliffe) and the Chancellor (Law), during which the government made clear that it bore the ultimate responsibility for monetary policy, and that the Bank was expected to act on its direction.

A subservient Bank, 1914–1992

The First World War was a major watershed not only in the history of the Bank but in the world more widely. It ushered in a half-century of increasing government intervention in every country, of a move towards socialist economies in most, and of communism in a wide swathe of countries. Under these circumstances the Bank became increasingly subservient to the government, in practice to the Chancellor of the Exchequer and to the Treasury, in the conduct of macro-monetary policy, its previous primary function.

Initially, however, there was little perception that the war and the rise of socialist ideas had irretrievably altered the context for policy. There was a desire to return to the previous regime, the gold standard, with its tried and true verities, as expressed in the Cunliffe Committee Report (the first report of the Committee on Currency and Foreign Exchange, 1919). That was probably inevitable under the circumstances, but a much more questionable decision was to return at the pre-war parity (against gold) despite the war-induced loss of markets (especially for the UK's main staples, textiles, coal, and iron and steel) and of competitiveness. Several of the other belligerent states, notably France, had inflated, and allowed their exchange to float downwards by so much that they did not seek to re-peg at the previous parity, but could choose a more suitable and competitive rate. While the decision to return to gold at the pre-war parity, steadfastly supported by the Bank, has been much criticized, the modern theory of time inconsistency provides some defence, namely, if the Bank had started to change the chosen rate to suit the immediate conjuncture it would have been expected to do so again in future, making commitment to the regime less credible.

Be that as it may, conditions after the First World War, with a weak balance of payments and a massively inflated money stock and floating debt, were hardly conducive to the re-establishment of gold standard conditions. Indeed, the authorities initially felt forced to move in the other direction, to unpeg the sterling–dollar rate that had been established since 1916 and formally to leave the gold standard in March 1919. The ending of the war led then to an extremely sharp and short boom and bust, in which tight monetary policy played a major role in the subsequent deflation (see Howson, 1975). From then until the return to gold at the pre-war parity of $4.86 to the pound in 1925, the Bank advocated keeping the Bank rate high enough to facilitate that regime change, but decisions on Bank rate and on the conduct of monetary policy were joint, in that no proposal by the Bank could be activated without the agreement of the Chancellor and HM Treasury; the Treasury view, however, then was in line with classical thought, namely, that monetary policy could and should impinge primarily on nominal prices, with real output affected by real factors.

Despite the boom in the USA, growth in the UK was perceived as remaining low and unemployment high, at least as compared with its main comparator countries, in the 1920s. This was in part due to the continuing problems of restoring a successful economic regime in Europe, wherein German reparations had a malign effect. Although the Bank had lost much of its power to direct domestic monetary policy (to Whitehall), the Bank and its Governor, Montagu Norman, played a leading role in the various international exercises to try to restore Europe to normality and to the gold standard, (Sayers, 1976, ch. 8); and Sir Otto Niemeyer, a top Bank official, spread the gospel of establishing central banks to maintain price stability to the Dominions.

This whole structure came apart in the crisis that started in the USA in 1929 and then engulfed the rest of the world progressively through the subsequent four years. How far that collapse was itself exacerbated by the attempt to restore the gold standard has been explored by Eichengreen (1992). The UK was not in a strong economic position to avoid the world recession, but suffered a much smaller decline in output than in the USA or much of Continental Europe. The struggle to maintain the gold standard had required the maintenance of high interest rates, despite the imposition of controls on new issues in sterling by foreign governments. Despite high unemployment, wages and prices remained too sticky to allow the restoration of international competitiveness, though quite why this was so remains a debated issue.

With the gold standard collapsing in Europe and social pressures rising in the UK, there was diminishing political will to take the measures that appeared necessary to maintain the gold standard. The government decided to abandon it (in Norman's absence) in September 1931. From that moment onwards, until May 1997, the decision to alter the Bank rate moved decisively to Whitehall, effectively into the hands of the Chancellor, advised by HM Treasury. Of course, the Bank could, and did, make suggestions and played a major role in all the discussions, but the Chancellor took the decisions. Indeed, from June 1932 until November 1951 a policy of cheap money was followed whereby Bank rate was held constant at two per cent. Norman stated in 1937, 'I am an instrument of the Treasury'.

Meanwhile, the Bank was becoming more professional. The old system of circulating the Governor's chair in turn among the directors of the Bank, who were appointed from city (but not commercial bank) institutions, was superseded by the continuing governorship of Montagu Norman from 1920 until 1944. While this arose by happenstance rather than intention (see Sayers, 1976, ch. 22), it gave the Bank highly skilled, even if also highly idiosyncratic, leadership. Moreover, Norman introduced economists and other able officials into both the staff and the Court (the largely ceremonial board) of the Bank, although it is (apocryphally) recorded that Norman told one such economist, 'You are not here to tell me what to do, but to explain why I have done what I have already decided to do.'

In effect, the Bank had already become nationalized by the end of the Second World War. So the formal act of nationalization in 1946 brought about no real substantive changes, except that the Governor and his deputy (there has as yet been no woman Governor, although Rachel Lomax became the first female Deputy Governor in 2003), were appointed by the government for five years, renewable once more in most cases. Indeed, the more profound changes were brought about by Governor Gordon Richardson (1973–83) in the early 1980s. Until then, the Governor had been rather akin to a chairman, with the deputy and other internal directors as members of the board, setting strategy. Much of the executive power still lay with the Chief Cashier, who acted as leader of the heads of department, who ran the Bank. There was a clear break, a division, between the staff in the departments on the one hand and the Governors and Directors on the other. Richardson changed all that, concentrating power in the Governors' hands, sharply demoting the role of Chief Cashier, and underlining the precedence of (internal) directors over heads of department in all policy matters.

So, as power to decide the course of monetary policy – and to set the Bank rate – passed to Whitehall, what did these professional central bank officials do? The Bank came to have three main areas of responsibility. The first was the management of markets, notably the money market, the bond (gilts) market and the foreign exchange market. The UK had come out of the Second World War with a massively inflated ratio of debt to GDP, and its management had remained difficult and delicate, at least until after the War Loan Conversion of 1932. No sooner, however, had debt management been thereby put on a sounder foundation than the Second World War led to a further upsurge in the debt ratio, which led once again to debt management becoming a major preoccupation of policy. Thereafter, a combination of generally prudent fiscal policies, so that the debt ratio fell steadily, and then unexpected inflation in the 1970s, which accelerated the decline in the debt ratio, and market reforms in the 1980s, enabled the procedures of debt management to become simpler and standardized. Similarly, the floating exchange rate in the 1930s, followed by attempts to maintain pegged exchange rates both during the Second World War and thereafter under the Bretton Woods system, against a background of perennially weak balance of payments conditions, made the management of the UK's foreign exchange reserves and intervention on the foreign exchange market a crucial function of the Bank until 1992, when the UK was forced out of the European exchange rate mechanism. During crises the officials in charge of such foreign exchange operations were in telephone communication with the Chancellor and, occasionally, the Prime Minister at frequent intervals.

The Bank held that such market operations required a special professional expertise (though HM Treasury remained sceptical). The Bank threw itself into such activities with enthusiasm, and defended its pre-eminent role in this respect stoutly against all outside encroachment or criticism. Indeed, its market 'savvy' was its most powerful lever to persuade the Chancellor to its views in any debate; 'I am sorry, Chancellor, but the market will not accept that policy' was the strongest card it had to play, and that card was played often and with alacrity.

Although ultra-cheap money, with Bank rate held at two per cent, was abandoned in 1951, when the Conservative Party was returned to office, monetary policy in general, and interest rates in particular, were still seen as both more ineffective and uncertain in their impact on domestic demand than the supposedly more reliable fiscal policy, a conclusion upheld by the controversial Radcliffe Report (1959). Consequently, fiscal policy was used to try to steer domestic demand while interest rates were raised to protect the balance of payments during the regular bouts of external weakness, and otherwise held low both to ease government finance and to support fixed investment. The outcome was a system in which inflationary pressures regularly threatened both the internal and external value of the currency. The chosen solution was to supplement market measures by direct interventions, in the case of external pressure via exchange controls, in the case of monetary expansion via direct controls on bank lending to the private sector. In both instances the Bank acted as the administrative agent of HM Treasury.

Such direct controls were introduced (on bank lending), or greatly extended and tightened (exchange controls), with the onset of the Second World War in 1939, but were continued, for the reasons outlined above, until 1971 for bank lending and 1979 for exchange controls. The administration of exchange controls required a large staff, but, unlike with its market operations, the Bank had little enthusiasm for acting in this guise. The Bank hoped to restore London to its former role as an international financial centre. While it succeeded in this through its encouragement of the Eurodollar market, aided by inept US policies, the continued administration of exchange controls remained an unwelcome burden. The same was true for direct controls on bank lending. Such controls were regarded by politicians as a comparatively painless way of dampening demand and inflation, while they were resented by commercial bankers. The Bank found itself in the middle of these disputes, and grew painfully aware of such controls' stultifying effect on efficiency, dynamism and growth. The Bank, inspired by John Fforde (the then executive director in charge of domestic finance, and subsequent Bank historian), pressed hard for these controls to be dismantled, and succeeded with the liberalizing reform of Competition and Credit Control (Bank of England, 1971).

As with many other cases of banking liberalization, such as in Scandinavia at the end of the 1980s, this was followed by an expansionary boom and then a bust, the fringe (secondary) bank crisis of 1973/74 (Reid, 1982). While there remain questions about how monetary policy could have been better applied to prevent the prior monetary boom (1972/73), there was no question but that the financial crisis found both the Bank and the banks unskilled in risk management and unprepared for adverse shocks to financial stability. The long period of financial repression – that is, controls on bank lending to the private sector and force-feeding with government debt – had had the by-product of making the (core) commercial banking system safe between the mid-1930s and the early 1970s. The central banking function of maintaining financial stability, via regulation and supervision, had atrophied.

This had not been so earlier, and the Bank had been closely involved in the rescue of Williams Deacon's Bank by the Royal Bank of Scotland in 1930 (Sayers, 1976, ch. 10), and in helping to shape the structure of both the commercial banking system and the London Discount Market Association. Williams Deacon's had got into trouble largely because of bad debts from Lancashire cotton companies. Norman, and the Bank, extended their structural interventions beyond banking to try to encourage strategic amalgamations to shore up the positions of weakened companies in a variety of industries, such as cotton, steel, shipping, armaments (Sayers, 1976, ch. 14). The Bank's involvement in structural matters outside of banking itself was episodic depending on both circumstances and personalities. Another example of such Bank involvement was the considerable role it played in the reform of the UK capital market in the 1980s, more familiarly known as 'Big-Bang'. But views on whether the Bank has any locus in such wider structural issues vary over time; the early 2000s saw a major withdrawal by the Bank from any such involvement.

The fringe bank crisis in the early 1970s was, however, a clarion call to put more emphasis on its third main function, bank supervision and regulation. The immediate result was a reorganization in the Bank. Initially a nucleus of a new specialized department was established in the Discount Office where the limited staff assigned to this role had sat, which rapidly absorbed staff and resources. Thereafter this became a separate department devoted to banking supervision and regulation (its first head was George Blunden, later to become Deputy Governor, who handed it on to Peter Cooke in 1976). Its position was regularized in the Banking Act (1979) which gave formal powers to the Bank to authorize, monitor, supervise, control and, under certain circumstances, withdraw prior authorization (tantamount to closure) for banks. No such powers had been available before that date. Meanwhile, other financial intermediaries, such as building societies or insurance companies, remained (lightly) regulated by various government departments.

The fringe bank crisis was almost entirely domestic, confined to British headquartered companies. Meanwhile, however, the onwards march of liberalization (involving the removal of direct controls, notably exchange controls in 1979) and of information technology were leading to a growing internationalization of financial business. For a variety of reasons, mostly relating to the innovation of the Eurodollar and Euro-markets, London regained its role as an international financial centre in the 1960s, and thus international monetary problems became of particular importance to the Bank, which took a leading role in such matters from the 1970s onwards.

Central bankers had met regularly at the headquarters of the Bank for International Settlements (BIS) in Basel for many years. It was, therefore, a logical step for supervisory officials also to come together at Basel on regular occasions to discuss matters of common interest. Thus was born (in 1974), as a result of an initiative from Gordon Richardson, the Basel Committee on Banking Regulation and Supervisory Practices. For the first 15 years of its existence it was chaired by the participant from the Bank of England, and was usually known by his name; thus, the Blunden Committee (1974–77) gave way in due course to the Cooke Committee (1977–88). The failures of Franklin National and Herstatt prompted the First Basel Concordat, which allocated responsibility for supervising internationally active banks to home and host authorities.

So by the mid-1970s, a need was perceived for banking supervision at both the domestic and, via consolidation, at the international levels. The purpose of these initiatives was to clarify where responsibility lay for the supervision of international banks, to prevent fragile, and possibly fraudulent, banking leading to avoidable failures and potential systemic crises.

Despite the growing number of bank supervisors, and notable success in reversing prior declines in capital ratios, the history of banking in the subsequent decades in the UK was spotted by occasional bank failures. Unlike the fringe bank crisis, none was, or was allowed to become, systemic, nor did individual depositors lose any money, except in the case of Bank of Credit and Commerce International (BCCI), and even in that case the deposit protection scheme provided some relief. The failures of Johnson–Matthey (in 1984), BCCI (in 1991) and Barings (in 1995) were all isolated cases of bad, in some respects fraudulent, banking.

The main problem of the 1970s and 1980s was, however, that of combating inflation, which soared to heights previously unknown, not only in peacetime but even in wartime, during the 1970s, up to 25 per cent per annum. There were three main theories, though divisions between them were never completely distinct. The first was the cost-push theory, that inflation was driven by over-mighty trade unions, seeking to increase the relative real pay of their members; the appropriate remedy was then prices and incomes policies plus reform (and constraint) of trades unions. The second was the (vertical) Phillips curve analysis; the remedy here was to raise unemployment above the 'natural' rate to reduce inflation. The third was that inflation was a monetary phenomenon; the remedy was to control the rate of growth of the (appropriate) monetary aggregate.

Until the mid-1970s, both major political parties, the Bank and HM Treasury all professed some combination of theories 1 (cost-push) and 2 (Phillips curve). Left-leaning politicians, academics and officials tended to put more weight on cost-push.

In the 1960 and 1970s the third, monetarist, view seemed to explain events better and gained strength, not only in the USA (Milton Friedman) but also in the UK. In particular, the surge in inflation in the UK in 1973–75 followed closely behind the rapid expansion of broad (but not narrow) money in 1972–73. So, when in opposition, the leading Conservative politicians Keith Joseph and Margaret Thatcher embraced a version of monetarism.

When they came to power in 1979, they tried to commit monetary policy to follow a target for broad money, via the Medium Term Financial Strategy. In order to achieve this, nominal, and real, interest rates were kept high, and the exchange rate appreciated sharply, partly under the influence of North Sea oil and confidence in Thatcherite policies. Inflation duly declined, as planned, but broad money growth did not. This latter was partly due to the abolition of the 'corset' in 1980. The 'corset' was a reformulated, and somewhat disguised, direct control over commercial bank expansion that had been pressed into service on several occasions during the 1970s. The Bank was glad to see the end of exchange controls and direct controls over bank lending, but had never shared the government's monetarist faith in trying to set, and stick to, targets for the growth of (the various) monetary aggregates.

The empirical demonstration of the unpredictability of the relationship between (broad) money and nominal incomes in the early 1980s soon weakened the government's own faith. After moving from one monetary target to several joint targets, and an attempt to hit the broad money target by 'overfunding', an exercise criticized by many as artificial, the government abandoned its monetary targetry in 1986.

That left the question of how monetary policy, and with it control of inflation, was to be managed or, in the standard phrase, 'anchored'. The then Chancellor, Nigel Lawson, wanted to 'anchor' by joining the exchange rate mechanism (ERM) of the European Monetary System and leaving the steering of monetary policy to the Bundesbank. The Prime Minister, Mrs Thatcher, and her adviser, Alan Walters, were opposed, both on economic grounds (that such a pegged system was 'half-baked') and for wider political reasons. There was a battle royal in which the Bank was left on the sidelines. Lawson was sacked, but eventually Mrs Thatcher was, grudgingly, persuaded to allow the UK to join the ERM in October 1990.

This was in the aftermath of German reunification, and the expenditures connected with that led the Bundesbank to keep interest rates higher than was tolerable for the UK (or Italy). The UK was in the throes of a sharp downturn in housing prices, following an unstable housing boom in the late 1980s. With the Conservatives having become politically weaker, there was just no stomach to raise interest rates to the levels necessary to sustain the ERM. The UK was forced out in September 1992.

Independent and focused, 1992–

The ejection of the UK from the ERM left the government and HM Treasury with the recurrent problem of how to manage, to 'anchor', monetary policy. Both monetary and exchange rate targets had been tried, and both had been found wanting.

While the economic experience of the 1980s was better than that of the stagflationary 1970s, it was hardly stellar, with a boom–bust cycle at the end of the decade.

Meanwhile, a new approach had been adopted in New Zealand, whereby the central bank was given administrative freedom to vary interest rates for the purpose of hitting a target for the inflation rate, jointly set by the government and the central bank: that is, inflation targetry. This obviated one of the shortcomings of monetary targetry, namely, the unpredictability of the velocity of money; it left setting the goals of policy, the overall strategy, in the hands of government, but shifted the (constrained) discretion to vary interest rates to the professional and technical judgement of the central bank. This procedure soon generated a strong body of academic support (for example, Fischer, 1994).

Although Conservative Chancellors (both Lawson and Lamont) had toyed with the idea of giving the Bank operational independence, consecutive Prime Ministers (Thatcher and Major) refused, primarily on political grounds. Nevertheless Lamont wanted to move to an inflation target. But there was a problem of governmental credibility. To foster credibility, Lamont now encouraged (in 1992/93) the Bank to prepare and to publish an independent forecast of the likely projection for inflation, the *Inflation Report* (on the assumption of unchanged policies); this was a reversal of prior habits whereby HM Treasury and Ministers customarily censored Bank publications and discouraged any publication of internal Bank forecasts. The process of gradually giving the Bank a more independent role in setting monetary policy took a step further when the next Chancellor, Clarke, not only held a meeting with the Governor, and the Bank, to discuss future changes in interest rates, but published the minutes of the meeting, including the Governor's initial statement, verbatim; this was termed the Ken (Clarke) and Eddie (George) show. That said, Clarke had strong views on the appropriate policy and on a couple of occasions overruled the Governor's suggestions.

At that time – the mid-1990s – there were still question marks over the Labour Party's ability to manage the economy; financial markets are inherently suspicious of left leaning governments. So Labour had more to gain (than the Conservatives), in terms of confidence and lower interest rates, by granting operational independence (back) to the Bank. In advance of the 1997 election the then shadow Chancellor, Gordon Brown, was cautious; while indicating general support for both inflation targetry and operational independence, he stated that he wanted time to see how well the Bank performed before granting such independence. But, within days of winning the election, he made that strategic change to the monetary regime.

This was, of course, a great prize for the Bank, but it did not come without cost. In the same month as operational independence was awarded to the Bank, both debt management and banking supervision were hived off, to a separate Debt Management Office (DMO) and Financial Services Authority (FSA) respectively. With the government debt to GDP ratio having declined and capital markets strengthened, debt management had become more of a routine and standardized exercise. Nevertheless, its departure to the DMO, and the fact that the float of the exchange rate after 1992 was kept 'clean', that is, without intervention, meant that much of the market operations which had been so central to the Bank in the post-Second World War period disappeared, though its money market operations, of course, continued. The administration of direct controls had gone at the beginning of the 1980s. And now banking supervision was also taken away. This meant that almost *all* the prime functions that the Bank had undertaken in its post-Second World War period of subservience had now gone. Instead, the Bank was now focused on varying interest rates to achieve the inflation target set for it by the Chancellor.

There are numerous arguments, quite evenly balanced, for whether bank supervision should be kept within a central bank or put with a separate Financial Services Authority (FSA), covering both banks and other financial intermediaries (see Goodhart, 2000). Be that as it may, there are various aspects of the financial system, such as oversight of the payments' system, and of crisis management, such as lender of last resort functions, which cannot be delegated to an FSA. Moreover, the achievement of price stability is likely to be seriously compromised by any serious bout of financial instability – and vice versa, with financial stability adversely affected by price instability. So the removal of individual bank supervision does not absolve the Bank from concern with financial stability issues more widely; indeed, the Bank is specifically charged with maintaining overall systemic stability in the financial system. But exactly what that means when responsibility for the conduct of individual bank supervision is located elsewhere is not yet entirely clear.

What it certainly does mean is that the FSA, the Bank, and the political authorities as the ultimate source of any needed fiscal support have to work extremely closely together, in advising on any new regulations (whether domestic or international), in monitoring developments (as in the Financial Stability Review), and in crisis management. This latter task would be done via the Tripartite Standing Committee (FSA, Bank, and HM Treasury), set up in 1997, although so far no such financial (as contrasted with simulated 'war games') crisis has occurred, though the Committee did meet after the terrorist attacks on 7 July 2005. How successful crisis management by such a committee may be has yet to be seen.

The monetary policy function of the Bank, now its central preoccupation, has, however, been very successful by all the usual criteria. In several papers Luca Benati (for example, Benati, 2005) has demonstrated that the variance of both GDP and of inflation around its target has been lower under the inflation targetry regime (whether taken as starting in 1992 or in 1997) than under any previous historical regime. The procedures of having a Monetary Policy Committee consisting of five senior Bank officials and four outside experts (appointed by the Chancellor), with the Committee serviced by Bank staff, has worked generally smoothly and well. So the Bank's reputation and credibility have rarely been higher, although now tightly focused on one main function.

CHARLES A.E. GOODHART

See also **banking crises; gold standard; inflation targeting; monetary policy, history of.**

Bibliography

Acres, W. 1931. *The Bank of England from Within*. London: Oxford University Press.
Andréadès, A. 1909. *A History of the Bank of England*. London: P. S. King and Sons.
Bagehot, W. 1873. *Lombard Street*. London: Kegan, Paul and Co.
Bank of England. 1971. *Competition and Credit Control*. London: Bank of England.
Bank for International Settlements. 1963. 'Bank of England', in *Eight European Central Banks*. Basle: Bank for International Settlements.
Benati, L. 2005. The Inflation-targeting framework from an historical perspective. *Bank of England Quarterly Bulletin* 45(2), 160–8.
Bowman, W. 1937. *The Story of the Bank of England: From its Foundation in 1694 until the Present Day*. London: Herbert Jenkins.
Chapham, R. 1968. *Decision Making: A Case Study of the Decision to Raise the Bank Rate in September 1957*. London: Routledge and Kegan Paul.
Clapham, J. 1944. *The Bank of England: A History*. Cambridge: Cambridge University Press.
Clay, H. 1957. *Lord Norman*. London: Macmillan.
Committee on Currency and Foreign Exchange After the War (Cunliffe Committee). 1918. *First Interim Report*, Cmnd. 9182; and 1919. *Final Report*, Cmnd 464, London: HMSO.
Eichengreen, B. 1992. *Golden Fetters: The Gold Standard and the Great Depression*. New York: Oxford University Press.
Feavearyear, A. 1963. *The Pound Sterling: A History of English Money*, 2nd edn, rev. E. Morgan. Oxford: Clarendon.
Fforde, J. 1992. *The Bank of England and Public Policy 1941–1958*. Cambridge: Cambridge University Press.
Fischer, S. 1994. 'Modern central banking', in F. Capie, C. Goodhart, S. Fischer and N. Schnadt, *The Future of Central Banking*. Cambridge: Cambridge University Press.
Geddes, P. 1987. *Inside the Bank of England*. London: Boxtree.
Giuseppi, J. 1966. *The Bank of England: A History from its Foundation in 1694*. London: Evans Brothers Limited.
Goodhart, C. 2000. The organisational structure of banking supervision. Special Paper No. 127. London: Financial Markets Group Research Centre, London School of Economics. Subsequently published in *Economic Notes* 31, 1–32.
Hennessey, E. 1992. *A Domestic History of the Bank of England 1930–1960*. Cambridge: Cambridge University Press.
Howson, S. 1975. *Domestic Monetary Management in Britain, 1919–38*. Cambridge: Cambridge University Press.
Radcliffe Report. 1959. *Report: Committee on the Working of the Monetary System*. Cmnd 827. London: HMSO.
Reid, M. 1982. *The Secondary Banking Crisis, 1973–75: Its Causes and Course*. London: Macmillan.
Richards, R. 1929. *The Early History of Banking in England*. London: Frank Cass and Co.
Rogers, J. 1887. *The First Nine Years of the Bank of England*. Oxford: Clarendon.
Sayers, R. 1936. *Bank of England Operations, 1890–1914*. London: P.S. King and Son.
Sayers, R. 1957. *Central Banking After Bagehot*. Oxford: Clarendon.
Sayers, R. 1976. *The Bank of England, 1891–1944*. Cambridge: Cambridge University Press.
Smith, V. 1936. *The Rationale of Central Banking*. London: P.S. King and Son.
Steele, H. and Yerbury, F. 1930. *The Old Bank of England*. London: Ernest Benn.
Stockdale, E. 1967. *The Bank of England in 1934*. London: Eastern Press.
Thornton, H. 1802. *An Enquiry into the Nature and Effects of the Paper Credit of Great Britain*. New York: Kelley, 1962.
Ziegler, D. 1990. *Central Bank, Peripheral Industry: The Bank of England in the Provinces 1826–1913*. London: Leicester University Press.

banking crises

There are two distinct phenomena associated with banking system distress: exogenous shocks that produce insolvency, and depositor withdrawals during 'panics'. These two contributors to distress often do not coincide. For example, in the rural United States during the 1920s many banks failed, often with high losses to depositors, but those failures were not associated with systemic panics. In 1907, the United States experienced a systemic panic, originating in New York. Although some banks failed in 1907, failures and depositor losses were not much higher than in normal times. As the crisis worsened, banks suspended convertibility until uncertainty about the incidence of the shock had been resolved.

The central differences between these two episodes relate to the commonality of information regarding the shocks producing loan losses. In the 1920s, the shocks were loan losses in agricultural banks, geographically isolated and fairly transparent. Banks failed without resulting in system-wide concerns. During 1907, the ultimate losses for New York banks were small, but the incidence was unclear *ex ante* (loan losses reflected complex connections to securities market transactions, with uncertain consequences for some New York banks). This confusion hit the financial system at a time of low liquidity, reflecting prior unrelated disturbances in the balance of payments (Bruner and Carr, 2007).

Sometimes, large loan losses, and confusion regarding their incidence, occurred together. In Chicago in mid-1932 losses resulted in many failures and also in widespread withdrawals from banks that did not ultimately fail. Research has shown that the banks that failed were exogenously insolvent; solvent Chicago banks experiencing withdrawals did not fail. In other episodes, however, bank failures may reflect illiquidity resulting from runs, rather than exogenous insolvency.

Banking crises can differ according to whether they coincide with other financial events. Banking crises coinciding with currency collapse are called 'twin' crises (as in Argentina in 1890 and 2001, Mexico in 1995, and Thailand, Indonesia and Korea in 1997). A twin crisis can reflect two different chains of causation: an expected devaluation may encourage deposit withdrawal to convert to hard currency before devaluation (as in the United States in early 1933); or, a banking crisis can cause devaluation, either through its adverse effects on aggregate demand or by affecting the supply of money (when a costly bank bail-out prompts monetization of government bail-out costs). Sovereign debt crises can also contribute to bank distress when banks hold large amounts of government debt (for example, in the banking crises in the United States in 1861, and in Argentina in 2001).

The consensus views regarding banking crises' origins (fundamental shocks versus confusion), the extent to which crises result from unwarranted runs on solvent banks, the social costs attending runs, and the appropriate policies to limit the costs of banking crises (government safety nets and prudential regulation) have changed dramatically, and more than once, over the course of the 19th and 20th centuries. Historical experience played a large role in changing perspectives toward crises, and the US experience had a disproportionate influence on thinking. Although panics were observed throughout world history (in Hellenistic Greece, and in Rome in AD 33), prior to the 1930s, in most of the world, banks were perceived as stable, large losses from failed banks were uncommon, banking panics were not seen as a great risk, and there was little perceived need for formal safety nets (for example, deposit insurance, or programmes to recapitalize banks). In many countries, ad hoc policies among banks, and sometimes including central banks, to coordinate bank responses to liquidity crises (as, for example, during the failure of Barings investment bank in London in 1890), seemed adequate for preventing systemic costs from bank instability.

Unusual historical instability of US banks

The unusual experience of the United States was a contributor to changes in thinking that led to growing concerns about banks runs, and the need for aggressive safety net policies to prevent or mitigate runs. In retrospect, the extent to which US banking instability informed thinking and policy outside the United States seems best explained by the size and pervasive influence of the United States; in fact, the US crises were unique and reflected peculiar features of US law and banking structure.

The US panic of 1907 (the last of a series of similar US events, including 1857, 1873, 1884, 1890, 1893, and 1896) precipitated the creation of the Federal Reserve System in 1913 as a means of enhancing systemic liquidity, reducing the probability of systemic depositor runs, and mitigating the costs of such events. This innovation was specific to the United States (other countries either had established central banks long before, often with other purposes in mind, or had not established central banks), and reflected the unique US experience with panics – a phenomenon that the rest of the world had not experienced since 1866, the date of the last British banking panic (Bordo, 1985).

For example, Canada did not suffer panics like those of the United States and did not establish a central bank until 1935. Canada's early decision to permit branch banking throughout the country ensured that banks were geographically diversified and thus resilient to large sectoral shocks (like those to agriculture in the 1920s and 1930s), able to compete through the establishment of branches in rural areas (because of the low overhead costs of establishing additional branches), and able to coordinate the banking system's response in moments of confusion to avoid depositor runs (the number of banks was small, and assets were highly concentrated in several nationwide institutions). Outside the United States, coordination among banks facilitated systemic stability by allowing banks to manage incipient panic episodes to prevent widespread bank runs. In Canada, the Bank of Montreal would occasionally coordinate actions by the large Canadian banks to stop crises before the public was even aware of a possible threat.

The United States, however, was unable to mimic this behaviour on a national or regional scale (Calomiris, 2000; Calomiris and Schweikart, 1991). US law prohibited nationwide branching, and most states prohibited or limited within-state branching. US banks, in contrast to banks elsewhere, were numerous (for example, numbering more than 29,000 in 1920), undiversified, insulated from competition, and unable to coordinate their response to panics (US banks established clearing houses, which facilitated local responses to panics beginning in the 1850s, as emphasized by Gorton, 1985).

The structure of US banking explains why the United States uniquely had banking panics in which runs occurred despite the health of the vast majority of banks. The major US banking panics of the post-bellum era (listed above) all occurred at business cycle peaks, and were preceded by spikes in the liabilities of failed businesses and declines in stock prices; indeed, whenever a sufficient combination of stock price decline and rising liabilities of failed businesses occurred, a panic *always* resulted (Calomiris and Gorton, 1991). Owing to the US banking structure, panics were a predictable result of business cycle contractions that, in other countries, resulted in an orderly process of financial readjustment.

The United States, however, was not the only economy to experience occasional waves of bank failures before the First World War. Nor did it experience the highest bank failure rates, or bank failure losses. None of the US banking panics of the pre-First World War era saw nationwide banking distress (measured by the negative net worth of failed banks relative to annual GDP) greater than the 0.1 per cent loss of 1893. Losses were generally modest elsewhere, but Argentina in 1890 and Australia in 1893, where the most severe cases of banking distress occurred during this era, suffered losses of roughly ten per cent of GDP. Losses in Norway in 1900 were three per cent and in Italy in 1893 one per cent of GDP, but with the possible exception of Brazil (for which data do not exist to measure losses), there were no other cases in 1875–1913 in which banking loss exceeded one per cent of GDP.

Loss rates tended to be low because banks structured themselves to limit their risk of loss, by maintaining adequate equity-to-assets ratios, sufficiently low asset risk, and adequate asset liquidity. Market discipline (the fear that depositors would withdraw their funds) provided incentives for banks to behave prudently. The picture of small depositors lining up around the block to withdraw funds has received much attention, but perhaps the more important source of market discipline was the threat of an informed (often 'silent') run by large depositors (often other banks). Banks maintained relationships with each other through interbank deposits and the clearing of public deposits, notes and bankers' bills. Banks often belonged to clearing houses that set regulations and monitored members' behaviour. A bank that lost the trust of its fellow bankers could not long survive.

Changing perceptions of banking instability

This perception of banks as stable, as disciplined by depositors and interbank arrangements to act prudently, and as unlikely to fail was common prior to the 1930s.

The banking crises of the Great Depression changed this perception. US Bank failures resulted in losses to depositors in the 1930s in excess of three per cent of GDP. Bank runs, bank holidays (local and national government-decreed periods of bank closure to attempt to calm markets and depositors), and widespread bank closure suggested a chaotic and vulnerable system in need of reform. The Great Depression saw an unusual raft of banking regulations, especially in the United States, including restrictions on bank activities (the separation of commercial and investment banking, subsequently reversed in the 1980s and 1990s), targeted bank recapitalizations (the Reconstruction Finance Corporation), and limited government insurance of deposits.

Academic perspectives on the Depression fuelled the portrayal of banks as crisis-prone. The most important of these was the treatment of the 1930s banking crises by Milton Friedman and Anna Schwartz in their book, *A Monetary History of the United States* (1963). Friedman and Schwartz argued that many solvent banks were forced to close as the result of panics, and that fear spread from some bank failures to produce failures elsewhere. They saw the early failure of the Bank of United States in 1930 as a major cause of subsequent bank failures and monetary contraction. They lauded deposit insurance: 'federal deposit insurance, to 1960 at least, has succeeded in achieving what had been a major objective of banking reform for at least a century, namely, the prevention of banking panics'. Their views that banks were inherently unstable, that irrational depositor runs could ruin a banking system, and that deposit insurance was a success, were particularly influential coming from economists known for their scepticism of government interventions.

Since the publication of *A Monetary History of the United States*, however, other scholarship (notably, the work of Elmus Wicker, 1996, and Charles Calomiris and Joseph Mason, 1997; 2003a) has led to important qualifications of the Friedman–Schwartz view of bank distress during the 1930s, and particularly of the role of panic in producing distress. Detailed studies of particular regions and banks' experiences do not confirm the view that panics were a nationwide phenomenon during 1930 or early 1931, or an important contributor to nationwide distress until very late in the Depression (that is, early 1933). Regional bank distress was often localized and traceable to fundamental shocks to the values of bank loans. Not only does it appear that the failure of the Bank of United States had little effect on banks nationwide in 1930, one scholar has argued that there is evidence that the bank was, in fact, insolvent when it failed (Lucia, 1985).

Other recent research on banking distress during the pre-Depression era has also de-emphasized inherent instability, and focused on the historical peculiarity of the US banking structure and panic experience, noted above. Furthermore, recent research on the destabilizing effects of bank safety nets has been informed by the experience of the US Savings and Loan industry debacle of the 1980s, the banking collapses in Japan and Scandinavia during the 1990s, and similar banking system debacles occurring in 140 developing countries in the last quarter of the 20th century, all of which experienced banking system losses in excess of one per cent of GDP, and more than 20 of which experienced losses in excess of ten per cent of GDP (data are from Caprio and

Klingebiel, 1996, updated in private correspondence with these authors). Empirical studies of these unprecedented losses concluded that deposit insurance and other policies that protect banks from market discipline, intended as a cure for instability, have become instead the single greatest source of banking instability.

The theory behind the problem of destabilizing protection has been well known for over a century, and was the basis for US President Franklin Roosevelt's opposition to deposit insurance in 1933 (an opposition shared by many). Deposit insurance was seen as undesirable special interest legislation designed to benefit small banks. Numerous attempts to introduce it failed to attract support in Congress (Calomiris and White, 1994). Deposit insurance removes depositors' incentives to monitor and discipline banks, and frees bankers to take imprudent risks (especially when they have little or no remaining equity at stake, and see an advantage in 'resurrection risk taking'). The absence of discipline also promotes banker incompetence, which leads to unwitting risk taking.

Empirical research on late 20th-century banking collapses has produced a consensus that the greater the protection offered by a country's bank safety net, the greater the risk of a banking collapse (see, for example, Caprio and Klingebiel, 1996, and the papers from a 2000 World Bank conference on bank instability listed in the bibliography). Empirical research on prudential bank regulation emphasizes the importance of subjecting some bank liabilities to the risk of loss to promote discipline and limit risk taking (Shadow Financial Regulatory Committee, 2000; Mishkin, 2001; Barth, Caprio and Levine, 2006).

Studies of historical deposit insurance reinforce these conclusions (Calomiris, 1990). The basis for the opposition to deposit insurance in the 1930s was the disastrous experimentation with insurance in several US states during the early 20th century, which resulted in banking collapses in all the states that adopted insurance. Government protection had played a similarly destabilizing role in Argentina in the 1880s (leading to the 1890 collapse) and in Italy (leading to its 1893 crisis). In retrospect, the successful period of US deposit insurance, from 1933 to the 1960s, to which Friedman and Schwartz referred, was an aberration, reflecting limited insurance during those years (insurance limits were subsequently increased), and the unusual macroeconomic stability of the era.

Models of banking crises followed trends in the empirical literature. The understanding of bank contracting structures, in light of potential crises, has been a consistent theme. Banks predominantly hold illiquid assets ('opaque,' non-marketable loans), and finance those assets mainly with deposits withdrawable on demand. Banks are not subject to bankruptcy preference law, but rather, apply a first-come, first-served rule to failed bank depositors (depositors who are first in line keep the cash paid out to them). These attributes magnify incentives to run banks. An early theoretical contribution, by Douglas Diamond and Philip Dybvig (1983), posited a banking system susceptible to the constant threat of runs, with multiple equilibria, where runs can occur irrespective of problems in bank portfolios or any fundamental demand for liquidity by depositors. They modelled deposit insurance as a means of avoiding the bad (bank run) equilibrium. Over time, other models of banks and depositor behaviour developed different implications, emphasizing banks' abilities to manage risk effectively, and the beneficial incentives of demand deposits in motivating the monitoring of banks in the presence of illiquid bank loans (Calomiris and Kahn, 1991).

The literatures on banking crises also rediscovered an older line of thought emphasized by John Maynard Keynes (1931) and Irving Fisher (1933): market discipline implies links between increases in bank risk, depositor withdrawals and macroeconomic decline. As banks respond to losses and increased risk by curtailing the supply of credit, they can aggravate the cyclical downturn, magnifying declines in investment, production, and asset prices, whether or not bank failures occur (Bernanke, 1983; Bernanke and Gertler, 1990; Calomiris and Mason, 2003b; Allen and Gale, 2004; Von Peter, 2004; Calomiris and Wilson, 2004). New research explores general equilibrium linkages among bank credit supply, asset prices and economic activity, and adverse macroeconomic consequences of 'credit crunches' that result from banks' attempts to limit their risk of failure. This new generation of models provides a rational-expectations, 'shock-and-propagation' approach to understanding the contribution of financial crises to business cycles, offering an alternative to the endogenous-cycles, myopic-expectations view pioneered by Hyman Minsky (1975) and Charles Kindleberger (1978).

CHARLES W. CALOMIRIS

Bibliography

Allen, F. and Gale, D. 2004. Financial fragility, liquidity, and asset prices. *Journal of the European Economic Association* 2, 1015–48.

Barth, J.R., Caprio, G. and Levine, R. 2006. *Rethinking Bank Regulation: Till Angels Govern.* Cambridge: Cambridge University Press.

Bernanke, B.S. 1983. Nonmonetary effects of the financial crisis in the propagation of the great depression. *American Economic Review* 73, 257–76.

Bernanke, B.S. and Gertler, M. 1990. Financial fragility and economic performance. *Quarterly Journal of Economics* 105, 87–114.

Bordo, M. 1985. The impact and international transmission of financial crises: some historical evidence, 1870–1933. *Revista di Storia Economica* 2(2d), 41–78.

Boyd, J., Gomis, P., Kwak, S. and Smith, B. 2000. A user's guide to banking crises. Conference paper. Washington, DC: World Bank.

Bruner, R.F. and Carr, S.D. 2007. *Money Panic: Lessons from the Financial Crisis of 1907.* New York: Wiley.

Calomiris, C.W. 1990. Is deposit insurance necessary? A historical perspective. *Journal of Economic History* 50, 283–95.

Calomiris, C.W. 2000. *U.S. Bank Deregulation in Historical Perspective.* Cambridge: Cambridge University Press.

Calomiris, C.W. and Gorton, G. 1991. The origins of banking panics: models, facts, and bank regulation. In *Financial Markets and Financial Crises*, ed. R.G. Hubbard. Chicago: University of Chicago Press.

Calomiris, C.W. and Kahn, C.M. 1991. The role of demandable debt in structuring optimal banking arrangements. *American Economic Review* 81, 497–513.

Calomiris, C.W. and Mason, J.R. 1997. Contagion and bank failures during the great depression: the June 1932 Chicago banking panic. *American Economic Review* 87, 863–83.

Calomiris, C.W. and Mason, J.R. 2003a. Fundamentals, panics and bank distress during the depression. *American Economic Review* 93, 1615–47.

Calomiris, C.W. and Mason, J.R. 2003b. Consequences of bank distress during the great depression. *American Economic Review* 93, 937–47.

Calomiris, C.W. and Schweikart, L. 1991. The panic of 1857: origins, transmission, and containment. *Journal of Economic History* 51, 807–34.

Calomiris, C.W. and White, E.N. 1994. The origins of federal deposit insurance. In *The Regulated Economy: A Historical Approach to Political Economy*, ed. C. Goldin and G. Libecap. Chicago: University of Chicago Press.

Calomiris, C.W. and Wilson, B. 2004. Bank capital and portfolio management: the 1930s 'capital crunch' and scramble to shed risk. *Journal of Business* 77, 421–55.

Caprio, G. and Klingebiel, D. 1996. Bank insolvencies: cross country experience. Working Paper No. 1620. Washington, DC: World Bank.

Cull, R., Senbet, L. and Sorge, M. 2000. Deposit insurance and financial development. Conference paper. Washington, DC: World Bank.

Demirguc-Kunt, A. and Detragiache, E. 2000. Does deposit insurance increase banking system stability? Conference paper. Washington, DC: World Bank.

Demirguc-Kunt, A. and Huizinga, H. 2000. Market discipline and financial safety net design. Conference paper. Washington, DC: World Bank.

Diamond, D. and Dybvig, P. 1983. Bank runs, deposit insurance, and liquidity. *Journal of Political Economy* 91, 401–19.

Fisher, I. 1933. The debt deflation theory of great depressions. *Econometrica* 1, 337–57.

Friedman, M. and Schwartz, A.J. 1963. *A Monetary History of the United States, 1867–1960*. Princeton, NJ: Princeton University Press.

Gorton, G. 1985. Clearing houses and the origin of central banking in the United States. *Journal of Economic History* 45, 277–83.

Honohan, P. and Klingebiel, D. 2000. Controlling fiscal costs of banking crises. Conference paper. Washington, DC: World Bank.

Keynes, J.M. 1931. The consequences to the banks of the collapse of money values. In *Essays in Persuasion*. New York: W.W. Norton, 1963.

Kindleberger, C.P. 1978. *Manias, Panics, and Crashes: A History of Financial Crises*. New York: Basic Books.

Lucia, J.L. 1985. The failure of the bank of United States: a reappraisal. *Explorations in Economic History* 22, 402–16.

Minsky, H.P. 1975. *John Maynard Keynes*. New York: Columbia University Press.

Mishkin, F.S. 2001. *Prudential Supervision: What Works and What Doesn't*. Chicago: University of Chicago Press.

Shadow Financial Regulatory Committee. 2000. *Reforming Bank Capital Regulation*. Washington, DC: American Enterprise Institute.

Von Peter, G. 2004. Asset prices and banking distress: a macroeconomic approach. BIS Working Paper No. 167. Basel: Bank of International Settlements.

Wicker, E. 1996. *The Banking Panics of the Great Depression*. Cambridge: Cambridge University Press.

central bank independence

Central bank independence refers to the freedom of monetary policymakers from direct political or governmental influence in the conduct of policy.

During the 1970s and early 1980s, major industrialized economies experienced sustained periods of high inflation. To explain these periods of inflation, one must account for why central banks allowed them to happen. One influential line of argument pointed to the inflation bias inherent in discretionary monetary policy if the central bank's objective for real output (unemployment) is above (below) the economy's natural equilibrium level or if policymakers simply prefer higher output levels (Barro and Gordon, 1983). Under rational expectations, the public anticipates that the central bank will attempt to expand the economy; as a consequence, real output is not systematically affected but average inflation is left inefficiently high.

This explanation for inflation raises the question why central banks might prefer economic expansions or have unrealistic output goals. Economists have frequently pointed to political pressures as the answer. Elected officials may be motivated by short-run electoral considerations, or may value short-run economic expansions highly while discounting the longer-run inflationary consequences of expansionary policies. If the ability of elected officials to distort monetary policy results in excessive inflation, then countries whose central banks are independent of such pressure should experience lower rates of inflation. Beginning with Bade and Parkin (1988), an important line of research focused on the relationship between the central bank and the elected government as a key determinant of inflation.

This empirical research found that average inflation was negatively related to measures of central bank independence. Cukierman (1992) provides an excellent summary of the empirical work; references to the more recent literature can be found in Eijffinger and de Haan (1996) and Walsh (2003, ch. 8). The empirical findings led to a significant body of work addressing the following questions: what do we mean by central bank independence? How should central bank independence be measured? What causal interpretation should be placed on the empirical correlations between central bank independence and macroeconomic outcomes discovered in the data? What is the theoretical explanation for these correlations?

The meaning of independence

The historical, legal and de facto relationships between a country's government and its central bank are very complex, involving many difference aspects. These include, but are not limited to, the role of the government in appointing (and dismissing) members of the central bank governing board, the voting power (if any) of the government on the board, the degree to which the central bank is subject to budgetary control by the government, the extent to which the central bank must lend to the government, and whether there are clearly defined policy goals established in the central bank's charter.

Most discussions have focused on two key dimensions of independence. The first dimension encompasses those institutional characteristics that insulate the central bank from political influence in defining its policy objectives. The second dimension encompasses those aspects that allow the central bank to freely implement policy in pursuit of monetary policy goals. Grilli, Masciandaro and Tabellini (1991) called these two dimensions 'political independence' and 'economic independence'. The more common terminology, however, is due to Debelle and Fischer (1994), who called these two aspects 'goal independence' and 'instrument independence'. Goal independence refers to the central bank's ability to determine the goals of policy without the direct influence of the fiscal authority. In the United Kingdom, the Bank of England lacks goal independence since its inflation target is set by the government. In the United States, the Federal Reserve's goals are set in its legal charter, but these goals are described in vague terms (for example, maximum employment), leaving it to the Fed to translate these into operational goals. Thus, the Fed has a high level of goal independence. Price stability is mandated as the goal of the European Central Bank (ECB), but the ECB can choose how to interpret this goal in terms of a specific price index and definition of price stability.

Instrument independence refers only to the central bank's ability to freely adjust its policy tools in pursuit of the goals of monetary policy. The Bank of England, while lacking goal independence, has instrument independence; given the inflation goal mandated by the government, it is able to set its instruments without influence from the government. Similarly, the inflation target range for the Reserve Bank of New Zealand is set in its Policy Targets Agreement (PTA) with the government, but, given the PTA, the Reserve Bank has the authority to sets its instruments without interference. The Federal Reserve and the ECB have complete instrument independence.

Measuring independence

The most widely employed index of central bank independence is due to Cukierman, Webb and Neyapti (1991), although alternative measures were developed by Bade and Parkin (1988) and Alesina, Masciandaro and Tabellini (1991), among others.

The Cukierman, Webb and Neyapti index is based on four legal characteristics as described in a central bank's charter. First, a bank is viewed as more independent if the chief executive is appointed by the central bank board rather than by the government, is not subject to dismissal, and has a long term of office. These aspects help insulate the central bank from political pressures. Second, independence is greater the more policy decisions are made independently of government involvement. Third, a central bank is more independent if its charter states that price stability is the sole or primary goal of monetary policy. Fourth, independence is greater if there are limitations on the government's ability to borrow from the central bank.

Cukierman, Webb and Neyapti combine these four aspects into a single measure of legal independence. Based on data from the 1980s, they found Switzerland to have the highest degree of central bank independence at the time, closely followed by Germany. At the other end of the scale, the central banks of Poland and the former Yugoslavia were found to have the least independence.

Legal measures of central bank independence may not reflect the actual relationship between the central bank and the government. In countries where the rule of law is less strongly embedded in the political culture, there can be wide gaps between the formal, legal institutional arrangements and their practical impact. This is particularly likely to be the case in many developing economies. Thus, for developing economies, it is common to supplement or even replace measures of central bank independence based on legal definitions with measures that reflect the degree to which legally established independence is honoured in practice. Based on work by Cukierman, measures of actual central bank governor turnover, or turnover relative to the formally specified term length, are often used to measure independence. High actual turnover is interpreted as indicating political interference in the conduct of monetary policy.

Empirical evidence

The 1990s saw many countries, both developed and developing, adopt reforms that increased central bank independence. This trend was strongly influenced by empirical analysis of the relationship between central bank independence and macroeconomic performance. Among developed economies, central bank independence was found to be negatively correlated with average inflation. The estimated effect of independence on inflation was statistically and economically significant. Based on data from the high inflation years of the 1970s, for example, moving from the status of the Bank of England prior to the 1997 reforms that increased its independence to the level of independence then enjoyed by the Bundesbank would be associated with a drop in annual average inflation of four percentage points.

The form of independence may also matter for inflation. Debelle and Fischer (1994) report evidence that it is the combination of goal *dependence* and instrument *independence* that produces low average inflation, although their empirical results were weak.

Even if central bank independence leads to lower inflation, the case for independence would be greatly weakened if it also leads to greater real economic instability. However, little relationship was found between measures of real economic activity and central bank independence (Alesina and Summers, 1993). In other words, countries with more independent central banks enjoyed lower average inflation rates yet suffered no cost in terms of more volatile real economic activity. Central bank independence appeared to be a free lunch.

While standard indices of central bank independence were negatively associated with inflation among developed economies, this was not the case among developing economies. Developing countries that experienced rapid turnover among their central bank heads tended to experience high rates of inflation. This is a case, however, in which causality is difficult to establish; is inflation high because of political interference that leads to rapid turnover of central bank officials? Or are central bank officials tossed out because they can't keep inflation down?

The empirical work attributing low inflation to central bank independence has been criticized along two dimensions. First, studies of central bank independence and inflation often failed to control adequately for other factors that might account for cross-country differences in inflation experiences. Countries with independent central banks may differ in ways that are systematically related to average inflation. After controlling for other potential determinants of inflation, Campillo and Miron (1997) found little additional role for central bank independence.

Second, treating a country's level of central bank independence as exogenous may be problematic. Posen (1993) has argued strongly that both low inflation and central bank independence reflect the presence of a strong constituency for low inflation. Average inflation and the degree of central bank independence are jointly determined by the strength of political constituencies opposed to inflation; in the absence of these constituencies, simply increasing a central bank's independence may not cause average inflation to fall.

Theoretical models of independence

Central bank independence has often been represented in theoretical models by the weight placed on inflation objectives. When the central bank's weight on inflation exceeds that of the elected government, the central bank is described as a Rogoff-conservative central bank (Rogoff, 1985). This type of conservatism accorded with the notion that independent central banks are more concerned than the elected government with maintaining low and stable inflation. Rogoff's formulation reflects a form of both goal independence – the central bank's goals differ from those of the government – and instrument independence – the central bank is assumed to be free to set policy to achieve its own objectives. Because the central bank cares more about achieving its inflation goal, the marginal cost of inflation is higher for the central bank than it would be for the government. As a consequence, equilibrium inflation is lower.

One problem with interpreting independence in terms of Rogoff-conservatism is that Rogoff's model implies that a conservative central bank will allow output to be more volatile in order to keep inflation stable. Yet the empirical research finds no relationship between real fluctuations and measures of central bank independence.

An alternative way to model central bank independence is to view the central bank as having its own objectives, but the central bank must also take into account the government's objectives when deciding on policy. The central bank might have either a lower desired inflation target than the government or an output target that, unlike the government's target, is consistent with the economy's natural rate of output. If actual policy is set to maximize a weighted average of the central bank's and the government's objectives, the relative weight on the central bank's own objectives provides a measure of central bank independence. With complete independence, no weight is placed on the government's objectives; with no independence, all weight is placed on the government's objectives. If the objectives of the central bank and the government differ only in their desired inflation target, then the degree of central bank independence affects average inflation but not the volatility of either output or inflation. Such a formulation is consistent with the empirical evidence discussed above.

Often, theoretical approaches have not distinguished clearly between goal and instrument independence. Suppose independence is measured by the relative weight on the government's and the central bank's objectives. This can be interpreted as reflecting either goal dependence – the objectives of the central bank must put some weight on the goals of the government – or instrument dependence – the actual instrument setting diverges from what would be optimal from the central bank's perspective in order to reflect the government's concerns.

Independence and accountability

While many countries have granted their central banks more independence, the idea that central banks should be completely independent has come under criticism. This criticism focuses on the danger that a central bank that is independent will not be accountable. Although maintaining low and stable inflation is an important societal goal, it is not the only macroeconomic goal; monetary policy may have no long-run effect on real economic variables, but it can affect the real economy in the short run. In a democracy, delegating policy to an independent agency requires some mechanism to ensure accountability. For this reason, reforms have often granted central banks instrument independence while preserving a role for the elected government in establishing the goals of policy and in monitoring the central bank's performance in achieving these goals.

CARL E. WALSH

See also **inflation targeting; optimal fiscal and monetary policy (without commitment).**

Bibliography

Alesina, A. and Summers, L. 1993. Central bank independence and macroeconomic performance. *Journal of Money, Credit, and Banking* 25, 157–62.

Bade, R. and Parkin, M. 1988. Central bank laws and monetary policy. Working paper. Department of Economics, University of Western Ontario.

Barro, R. and Gordon, D. 1983. A positive theory of monetary policy in a natural-rate model. *Journal of Political Economy* 91, 589–610.

Campillo, M. and Miron, J. 1997. Why does inflation differ across countries? In *Reducing Inflation: Motivation and Strategy*, ed. C. Romer and D. Romer. Chicago: University of Chicago Press.

Cukierman, A. 1992. *Central Bank Strategy, Credibility, and Independence: Theory and Evidence.* Cambridge, MA: MIT Press.

Cukierman, A., Webb, S. and Neyapti, B. 1992. Measuring the independence of central banks and its effects on policy outcomes. *World Bank Economic Review* 6, 353–98.

Debelle, G. and Fischer, S. 1994. How independent should a central bank be? In *Goals, Guidelines and Constraints Facing Monetary Policymakers*, ed. J. Fuhrer. Boston: Federal Reserve Bank of Boston.

Eijffinger, S. and de Haan, J. 1996. The political economy of central-bank independence. Special Papers in International Economics, No. 19. Princeton University.

Grilli, V., Masciandaro, D. and Tabellini, G. 1991. Political and monetary institutions and public financial policies in the industrial countries. *Economic Policy* 6, 341–92.

Posen, A. 1993. Why central bank independence does not cause low inflation: there is no institutional fix for politics. In *Finance and the International Economy*, vol. 7, ed. R. O'Brien. Oxford: Oxford University Press.

Rogoff, K. 1985. The optimal commitment to an intermediate monetary target. *Quarterly Journal of Economics* 100, 1169–89.

Walsh, C. 2003. *Monetary Theory and Policy*, 2nd edn. Cambridge, MA: MIT Press.

commodity money

A commodity is an object that is intrinsically useful as an input to production or consumption. A medium of exchange is an object that is generally accepted as final payment during or after an exchange transaction, even though the agent accepting it (the seller) does not necessarily consume the object or any service flow from it. Money is the collection of objects that are used as media of exchange. Commodity money is a medium of exchange that may become (or be transformed into) a commodity, useful in production or consumption. This is in contrast to fiat money, which is intrinsically useless.

Commodity money can also be thought of as a medium of exchange that contains an option to consume a predetermined service flow at little or no cost. The option can be exercised in various ways, depending on the object. Coins can be melted down (at little cost) and the metal applied to non-monetary uses. In the case of paper or token money under a commodity money standard, the medium of exchange itself is intrinsically useless, but it is costlessly convertible into a specified quantity of the commodity on demand. Fiat money can also be converted into goods or services, but in quantities that will depend on market prices.

Commodity money is a thing of the past; countries worldwide now use fiat money standards. However, this is a relatively recent development. Commodity money, primarily in the form of coined metals, was the predominant medium of exchange for over two millennia. Although operating under a commodity money standard limits the scope for monetary policy, it does not eliminate it entirely. The history of commodity money is replete with numerous ways in which governments have altered the monetary system to achieve various goals.

From commodity money to fiat money

In early or primitive societies, it is often difficult to characterize the general patterns of trades and transactions, let alone determine how generally accepted a particular commodity might be. Nevertheless, a wide range of commodities have been reportedly used as money (cowry shells, wampum, salt, furs, cocoa beans, cigarettes and so on), perhaps the most exotic being the stone money of the island of Yap in Micronesia.

General acceptability of monetary objects is most clearly ascertained when the objects are standardized and exchanged repeatedly. With metallic commodities, the standardized objects are called coins. Coinage of metal began in the eastern Mediterranean region or the Middle East, India and China between the sixth and fourth centuries BC. Coinage has developed in parallel and broadly similar ways in these areas.

The metals most commonly used have been gold, silver and copper (in decreasing order of scarcity), in varying degrees of fineness (silver mixed with substantial amounts of copper, called billon). Lead, tin and various copper alloys (bronze, brass, potin) have also been used, although less frequently than the more common metals. The metal is either mined or acquired through trade. The most common method of coinage is striking with a die, although cast coins are also found. In many legal traditions the right of coinage is a prerogative of the public or central authority, although it may be delegated or leased to regional authorities or private parties. This prerogative may also extend to mining. In other words, the rules governing the supply of commodity money vary from government monopoly to minimal regulation.

In Europe and the Mediterranean, coinage – an invention mythically linked to Croesus, King of Lydia – began near the Aegean Sea in the sixth century BC. The use of money developed considerably in Greek and Roman times, leading to a three-tiered system of gold, silver, and copper denominations. In the Roman empire, the provision of coinage was a government monopoly. The collapse of the empire in the West led, after a long transition, to a purely silver-based monetary system, with a largely decentralized provision of minting. Uniformity of coinage was restored under Charlemagne but quickly disappeared along with political fragmentation. Gold returned in common use from the mid-13th century. By the 14th century, most mints in western Europe operated along similar lines, with more or less unrestricted coinage on demand provided by profit-making mints. A great multiplicity of monetary systems persisted, giving rise to both foreign exchange markets (the earliest financial markets) and money changers (the first financial intermediaries).

The first instances of token coinage (coins that are intrinsically useless but are claims to fixed amounts of the commodity) appeared in the 15th century in Catalonia. Notes convertible on demand appeared in the 17th century, in Sweden and later in England. For a more complete discussion of medieval European coinage, see Spufford (1988).

Coins appear to have been used in India in the early fourth century BC and were probably used before then. The earliest coins were so-called punch-marked coins and were adaptations of Greek prototypes. Coins were first used in China and the Far East about the same time as in India. The distinctive bronze coinage with the square hole in the middle first appeared in the third century BC. Early coins in eastern Islamic lands were copies of Byzantine gold and bronze coins; those in the East were copies of Sassanian silver coins. For more on coinage in India and the Far East, see Williams (1997).

Until the 19th century, coins typically bore no indication of face value, and their market value could fluctuate even relative to one another. From the late Middle Ages, governments increasingly sought to regulate the value of coins in some manner, in particular assigning face value or legal tender value by decree. It became desirable to turn the collection of objects used as a medium of exchange into a stable system with fixed exchange rates between the objects. This was achieved to a large degree with bimetallism, a system in which gold and silver coins remained concurrently in circulation at a constant relative price. Its heyday was the mid-19th century, but beginning in 1873 the system was quickly abandoned, and by the First World War countries were using either gold only or (in Africa and eastern Asia) silver only. (Bimetallism is discussed in more detail in Redish, 2000, and Velde and Weber, 2000.) The development of banking in the 19th century also led to increased use of (convertible) notes and other monetary instruments.

The First World War brought about the suspension of convertibility of the notes in many countries. Most countries returned to convertibility between 1926 and 1931, but the onset of the Great Depression reversed the movement. After the Second World War the only major country whose currency was in any way directly tied to a commodity was the United States under the Bretton Woods system: dollars were convertible by non-residents of the United States into gold on demand, while other currencies of the system were convertible into dollars. The link between gold and the dollar was severed in 1971. Fiat money standards are now universal.

The nature of commodity money

The definitions of commodity and fiat monies given above make it seem as if there is a clear distinction between the two. It is more helpful, however, to think of media of exchange along a continuum. An object serving a purpose as a medium of exchange has value above its intrinsic content, reflecting the value of the service as a medium of exchange.

Because the value of a commodity qua commodity and the value as a medium of exchange can differ, the value of all commodity monies has a fiat component. A pure fiat money is one for which this fiat component makes up its entire value. A nice theoretical discussion of commodity and fiat monies is given by Sargent and Wallace (1983).

Price-level determination

It is natural that the medium of exchange in an economy is what becomes the unit of account, the unit in which debt contracts and the prices of goods and services are expressed. It is natural because the money appears on one side of virtually every transaction.

Because commodity money has an intrinsic value apart from that which it obtains by being a medium of exchange, its relative price will not be zero. Thus, in a commodity money economy, the value of money (the inverse of the price level) is bounded away from zero. Moreover, in a canonical commodity money system (see below) with unlimited minting at a set price, the value of money and its quantity tend to remain within a band. If the value of money falls far enough, it becomes preferable to exercise the option and convert some of it into other, non-monetary uses, thus reducing the quantity and preventing the value from falling further. Conversely, if the value of money rises high enough, it becomes worthwhile for agents to turn metal into coins at the mint at the set price, thus increasing the quantity of money. Such a self-regulating commodity money system provides an anchor to the price level. This has been touted as one of the advantages of a commodity money system, particularly in the case of the gold standard.

The question of price-level determination becomes more complicated when multiple commodity monies are made out of different commodities. An example is the circulation of full-bodied gold and silver coins. Should the unit of account be the gold coin or the silver coin? This matters because under a commodity money system a monetary authority does not have the ability to set the exchange rate between monies of different commodities forever. Thus, to the extent that the unit of account is used in contracts to determine the amount of future payments, the choice of the unit of account can affect the allocation of goods and services. This was one of the issues surrounding the possible adoption of a bimetallic standard mentioned above.

The inability of the monetary authority to set the exchange rate between different monies goes away under a pure fiat money system. Because fiat money is (virtually) costless to produce, the monetary authority can costlessly exchange one money for another to maintain whatever exchange rate is desired between different monies that it issues.

Monetary policy

The fact that a commodity is used as money alters its value. This is because part of the total quantity of the commodity – namely, the metal locked up in the form of coins, or the reserves held by the monetary authority – is not available for non-monetary uses. The allocation between monetary and non-monetary uses is determined in equilibrium. Restrictions on the ability to change this allocation, such as restrictions on melting or exporting coins, or limitations on the minting of metal, will have an effect on the equilibrium value of the money even if it has no immediate effect on the allocation itself. (Since money is an asset, its valuation is forward looking.) Thus, there is scope for monetary policy under a commodity money standard, although what constitutes monetary policy is different from and more limited in scope than what holds under a pure fiat money standard.

Monetary policy consists in actions that tend to alter the value of money. In a commodity money system, the value of money is the value of the option we have described. (The strike price of the option is zero, since the commodity is the money.) Most aspects of monetary policy with commodity money consist in modifying this option, typically by modifying the institutions governing the exercise of the option rather than by modifying the quantity of money, which the authority usually cannot control directly. When the monetary authority is directly involved in the provision of the money, it may directly profit from its actions. Potential profit is often an important consideration of monetary policy.

The canonical form of a commodity money standard comprises the following. One or more commodities are chosen to be the standard to which the monetary system will be anchored. The monetary authority defines the specifications of the monetary objects (weight, fineness) and defines the unit of account in terms of these monetary objects. The conversion of commodity into commodity money and vice versa is as costless as possible. In particular, the monetary authority provides for unlimited (and even costless) conversion of the commodity into monetary objects (coins or notes). Conversely, it places no hindrances on the conversion of monetary objects into commodities (coins can be melted, notes are convertible on demand), nor does it place limitations on the consumption of the commodity or its service flow (free possession, unrestricted import and export of the commodity). The monetary objects are unlimited legal tender.

One type of monetary policy modifies the specifications of monetary objects and units of account. An example is debasement, which is reducing the commodity content of a monetary object (and, frequently, of the corresponding unit of account). The result of debasement is inflation, since nominal prices will be adjusted to maintain the relative prices of goods and money. And, just as occurs with fiat money, inflation has the effect of transferring wealth from nominal creditors to nominal debtors. Since governments generally tended to be debtors, debasements were used to reduce the amount of their debts. Historically, debasements also had the secondary effect of increasing seigniorage revenue, since the quantity of coins minted tended to increase significantly after debasements that involved the introduction of new coins (see Rolnick, Velde and Weber, 1996; Sargent and Smith, 1997). Debasements were also used by governments to remedy malfunctions of a multiple-denomination commodity money system (see Sargent and Velde, 2002).

A second type of monetary policy adds or modifies restrictions on the conversion of commodity into money or money into commodity. For example, minting might be restricted by quantity, in which case the authority decides how much to mint. Minting might be unlimited but subject to a fee, called seigniorage. Governments typically charged such a fee, both to cover the actual costs of minting (called brassage) and as a tax (England was the first, in 1666, to provide minting at no cost). The rate of this tax or, equivalently, the price paid by the mint for bullion might be changed. These restrictions tended to alter the allocation of the commodity between monetary and non-monetary uses, and hence the value of the commodity and the money.

A third type of monetary policy sets limits to the legal tender quality of certain coins, or changes their legal tender value. Since coins did not have face values until the 19th century, it was up to monetary authorities to set, and from time to time alter, the legal tender values of coins. Frequently, foreign coins were authorized as legal tender at rates set for domestic coins. Countries attempting to maintain bimetallism in the face of fluctuations in the relative price of gold and silver often had to adjust the face value of either their gold or silver coins. Changes in the legal tender values could also be motivated by fiscal considerations or by attempts to target a particular price level or exchange rate.

The physical nature of the medium of exchange led to a particular set of concerns. Coins, like anything else, depreciate with use, through wear and tear. Since coins of different values have different usage rates, the depreciation rate varied by denomination. Also, being roughly constant over time, depreciation depended on the age of the coin. Finally, imperfect minting technology as well as actions by the public (clipping, sweating) aggravated the disparities between coins. This factor introduced heterogeneity among coins and hindered the achievement of a stable and uniform monetary system. Improvements in coin production partially remedied the problem, as did periodic recoinages.

When the monetary objects consist not only of coins but also of paper currency or tokens that are demand promises to the commodity, a fourth type of monetary policy is available: suspension of convertibility. The monetary authority can refuse to honour the promise of convertibility for some period of time. An example is the suspension of convertibility by the Bank of England between 1797 and 1819 during the wars with France. During the 19th century suspensions were not uncommon during financial or fiscal emergencies, with the understanding that the suspension would end after the emergency and convertibility would be restored at the pre-existing parity. This understanding has been described as a state-contingent gold standard (see Bordo and Kydland, 1996).

When there is a central bank, an additional monetary tool is to change the discount rate, the interest rate at which the central bank lends reserves to the banking system. During the gold standard period, this was the primary means by which central banks affected the exchange rate of their money against the monies of other countries.

Conclusion

Commodity money is a thing of the past; countries worldwide now use fiat money standards. This practice has led to an efficiency gain in the sense that resources that were once tied up in coins are now available for consumption and production (perhaps prompting John Maynard Keynes to refer to gold as the 'barbarous relic'). It has also led to a greater scope for monetary policy because the supply of money can be changed almost costlessly. However, along with this greater scope has come the greater potential for governments to use inflation to collect seigniorage revenue or to reduce the real value of their debts. How to use the freedom that commodity money restricted is still a matter of debate.

FRANÇOIS R. VELDE AND WARREN E. WEBER

See also **fiat money; gold standard.**

Bibliography

Bordo, M. and Kydland, F. 1996. The gold standard as a commitment mechanism. In *Modern Perspectives on the Gold Standard*, ed. T. Bayoumi, B. Eichengreen and M. Taylor. Cambridge: Cambridge University Press.

Kiyotaki, N. and Wright, R. 1989. On money as a medium of exchange. *Journal of Political Economy* 97, 927–54.

Luschin von Ebengreuth, A. 1926. *Allgemeine Münzkunde und Geldgeschichte des Mittelalters und der neueren Zeit*. Munich: R. Oldenbourg.

Redish, A. 2000. *Bimetallism: An Economic and Historical Analysis*. Cambridge: Cambridge University Press.

Rolnick, A., Velde, F. and Weber, W. 1996. The debasement puzzle: an essay on medieval monetary history. *Journal of Economic History* 56, 789–808.

Sargent, T. and Smith, B. 1997. Coinage, debasements, and Gresham's laws. *Economic Theory* 10, 197–226.

Sargent, T. and Velde, F. 2002. *The Big Problem of Small Change*. Princeton, NJ: Princeton University Press.

Sargent, T. and Wallace, N. 1983. A model of commodity money. *Journal of Monetary Economics* 12, 163–87.

Spufford, P. 1988. *Money and Its Use in Medieval Europe*. Cambridge: Cambridge University Press.

Sussman, N. and Zeira, J. 2003. Commodity money inflation: theory and evidence from France in 1350–1436. *Journal of Monetary Economics* 50, 1769–93.

Velde, F. and Weber, W. 2000. A model of bimetallism. *Journal of Political Economy* 108, 1210–34.

Williams, J., ed. 1997. *Money: A History*. New York: St Martin's Press.

euro

The launch of the euro, the European Union's currency (at least for 12 of the 27 current members), on 1 January 1999, was a birth long foretold. From at least the 1992 Maastricht Treaty onwards, its creation was at the forefront of the European overall integration agenda, and the meeting of criteria for eurozone entry dominated macroeconomic policymaking in Western Europe. The academic and policy discussion of European Monetary Union's (EMU) potential advantages and disadvantages began even earlier (see Canzoneri, Grilli and Masson, 1992; De Cecco and Giovannini, 1989; De Grauwe, 2000; Cecchini, 1988; as well as the seminal European Commission, 1990. Most of these studies concerned how best to make EMU work, taking the goal as a given, or assessing the optimality of the EU as a currency area). New international reserve currencies, as the euro has begun to be, do not come along every day, or even every century. New currencies in general are launched usually out of need, due to replacement of a currency of hyperinflation-eroded value or to political fragmentation or secession; when currency unions are formed, they are usually done as pegs to a previously existing anchor currency of the largest and/or most stable member economy. The voluntary adoption of the euro by sovereign but not politically unified nations, and its replacement of already stable currencies (notably the Deutschmark), is thus an extraordinary monetary experiment and policy undertaking.

While the euro certainly has had no shortage of champions among economists – including beyond Euroland's borders the economists Bergsten (1997), Eichengreen (1999), Mundell (1998), and Portes and Alogoskoufis (1991) – many monetary economists observing the euro have tended to be sceptical: first of the virtues of the goal of monetary integration in Europe itself, then of the project's political viability, and then of its economic sustainability, in turn asserting that the euro was a solely political project. (Notable examples of this scepticism include, on the political side, Currie, Levine and Pearlman, 1992; Walters, 1990; and, famously, Feldstein, 1997; and on the economic side Arestis and Sawyer, 2001; De Grauwe, 1996; Dornbusch, 1989; Giavazzi and Spaventa, 1990; and Weber, 1991. See also the essays by eurosceptics in the face of mounting contrary evidence collected in *Cato Journal*, 2004.) Only as the euro passed its eighth birthday in wide usage, remained well past parity with the US dollar (see Figure 1) and experienced a strong cyclical recovery in the eurozone has sentiment changed. Increasingly, the question is being raised whether the euro might appreciate against the dollar for an extended period, be the beneficiary of substantial international portfolio adjustments, or even begin to supplant the dollar as the dominant global reserve currency. (Recent examples include Chinn and Frankel, (2004, 2007); Obstfeld and Rogoff, 2004; and Summers, 2004.) The euro's viability in its own large economic area may not be sufficient to set it on a path to monetary

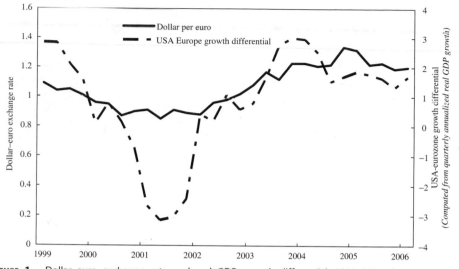

Figure 1   Dollar–euro exchange rate and real GDP growth differential, 1999–2006. *Source*: IMF, IFS Statistics.

leadership, but its existence now presents an alternative for capital markets to turn to should the dollar's own appeal diminish.

The waiting for US missteps for the euro to rise in importance, however, is a critical commentary on the limitations of the euro's importance to the eurozone member economies' performance in and of itself. When the euro was first proposed, a number of studies claimed that monetary integration would bring significant direct benefits to the economic performance of member states. Emerson, Gros and Italianer (1992) estimated that the elimination of transaction costs from moving to a single European currency would yield direct benefits of up to 0.4 per cent of EU GDP; the European Commission (1996) estimated cost savings of 1.0 per cent of GDP simply from eliminating transaction costs. The European Commission (1990) made the case that the reduction of nominal and real exchange rate uncertainty would lead to significant growth in intra-EU trade and investment. Financial markets in particular were expected to benefit from the introduction of the euro – McCauley and White (1997) and the European Commission (1997) forecast a rapid deepening and liquidity increase in European bond and lending markets, and perhaps even a 'decoupling' of European interest rates from those of the United States.

While empirical investigations to date of these effects remain mixed in interpretation, there is no question that the real economic effects of the euro's launch on the eurozone member countries have been something of a disappointment. In particular, European financial markets and trade integration are far deeper today than they were before the adoption of the euro, yet how much this represents the effect of the euro on EU integration as opposed to the broader international trends towards global integraton that benefited non-euro members as well is in doubt (see Forbes, 2005; Lane and Wälti, 2006; Mann and Meade, 2002; and Rey, 2005). The eurozone's interest rates remain asymmetrically affected by US interest rates, at least through the early 2000s, as established by Chinn and Frankel (2004). The effect of the euro on price convergence and on macroeconomic discipline cannot be all that substantial if on net there has been limited visible improvement in either of these areas (see the assessments of price convergence in Bradford and Lawrence (2003; 2004); and Rogers, 2003 and of macroeconomic discipline in Posen (2005a; 2005b). It seems that the euro has proven on net 'irrelevant' to real growth performance of large Continental European economies, neither a harm nor a boon to them, as Posen (1998) forecast it would be.

The external opportunities and shortfalls for the euro

The degree to which the euro comes into wider usage beyond intra-eurozone transactions, for example as an invoicing currency in world trade, is a major issue because of the eurozone's already large share of world output and trade (roughly comparable to that of the United States) and of the established 'domestic' monetary stability of the eurozone. Size does matter for international currency purposes. Yet insufficient integration and depth of European financial markets as well as lagging economic performance remain constraints on the euro's wider adoption and usage. Also important is the lack of coherent institutional representation for the eurozone in international monetary forums. Compared with the EU's one voice in global trade negotiations, the inability of the eurozone to speak as a single entity is striking, especially given the unconsolidated overrepresentation of the eurozone in the Bretton Woods institutions.

History also plays a role, however, in the global demand for currencies and their strength. Inertia and incumbency clearly contributed to the lingering of the British pound in a significant share of international reserves well after the Second World War. Yet the combination of macroeconomic mismanagement and growth underperformance in the United Kingdom from the 1920s to the 1980s eroded that role, and it is worth remembering that the passing of international monetary leadership from the pound to the dollar in the mid-20th century was in large part driven by these factors undermining the pound's reserve status. The steady accumulation of international debt by the United States since 1991 could contribute to a similar switch now that the euro is available. An extended dollar depreciation, the natural reaction to a multi-year series of widening US current account deficits, could induce a persistent portfolio diversification into euros by private and official holders of dollars.

In Washington, Frankfurt and Brussels, however, the widespread governmental opinion remains that the euro will not close the gap in usage with the dollar until the eurozone closes the gap with the US economy in per capita GDP growth and employment on a sustained basis (Figure 1 shows the growth differential of the USA over the eurozone). In a typical official expression of this sentiment, Quarles (2005, p. 40) finds that 'too much attention is being focused on exchange rate[s] … and too little on what seems … of far greater importance: namely, the more effective functioning of economies with regards to growth in output and employment'. Successive US governments have viewed both the short-term international adjustment process and the longer-term role of the euro vis-à-vis the dollar as driven by the gap in growth rates between the USA and Europe – with the burden on European economies to catch up by raising their growth rates. EU officials' disappointment with the degree of structural reforms catalysed by the introduction of the euro echoes this view, as does the promotion of the Lisbon Agenda announced in March 2000 for promotion of growth in the EU.

Such an external relative focus overlooks one achievement of the launching of the euro – ending the succession of devaluations, competitive depreciations and currency crises that had beset the members of the Exchange Rate Mechanism (ERM) prior to 1999. Certainly, the experiences of intra-European depreciations upon countries leaving the ERM, especially those of 1992–3, and their impact on economic performance and political outcomes in member states were in the forefront of European policymakers' minds when the run-up to the euro was under way in the late 1990s. And, despite the divergence in histories of some eurozone members, inflation and inflation expectations have remained stable and low in the eurozone. That could have been expected to assist in trade promotion among the already interdependent eurozone economies.

Still there has been little or no expansion in trade as a result of the adoption of the euro – among other evidence, the share of total eurozone exports destined for other members of the eurozone did not increase with the introduction of the currency, as would have been likely if the common currency had promoted trade (Baldwin, 2005 provides an excellent analytical summary of the evidence on this score). As shown in Rogers (2003), the bulk of convergence in traded-goods prices within the eurozone occurred between 1990 and 1994, in response to the creation of the single market, and not after 1999 and the introduction of the euro. As for the global dimension, there has been little change in the share of foreign exchange transactions denominated in euros globally from that previously denominated in Deutschmarks. Similarly, the use of the euro as an invoicing currency is somewhat higher than that for the eurozone home currencies prior to EMU, but remains far from universal within Europe or even comparable to the dollar's usage (with the regional exception of some of the newest members of the European Union).

Even the spreading use of the euro in the EU's new members in the east has been far less than many might have expected. A critical part of this outcome has been the insistence on the part of the European Central Bank (ECB) that all prospective eurozone members go through the full Maastricht Treaty-specified process for qualification, including not just fiscal discipline and nominal convergence but also a two-year period in the 'waiting room' of a new ERM-II mechanism. Early, expedited or unilateral adoption of the euro in EU member countries has in fact been discouraged by the ECB (with the exception of Estonia's pre-existing currency board with the euro). Arguably, this has as much to do with the ECB's desire for perceived control over monetary developments, given the ECB's Bundesbank-esque 'two pillar' strategy (of looking at both monetary growth and inflation goals when setting policy), and for keeping decision-making in the ESCB manageable, as with maintaining necessary discipline on eurozone members (see EUROPEAN CENTRAL BANK). The ECB has also been explicitly opposed to 'euroization' (dollarization with euros) by non-EU member countries, again partly for monetary control reasons, albeit acknowledging its contribution to stability in the post-conflict Balkan economies.

The limited impact of the euro on the eurozone financial integration and performance

The euro has delivered monetary stability in the face of a long list of economic shocks and a large initial decline against the dollar, only to rebound strongly since Autumn 2001 (see Figure 1). Europe has failed to follow the creation of the euro with the complementary policy reforms that were widely expected, however. This leaves an underlying tension between the constraints on national economic policy measures such as those in the Stability and Growth Pact on fiscal policy and the national frustrations with poor economic performance – a tension that raises recurrent doubts in eurosceptic financial markets about the sustainability of the euro itself, despite its lack of obvious vulnerabilities or viable exit options for any member country.

The euro was widely expected to transform two aspects of the eurozone economies: the integration and depth of their financial markets, and the conduct of their macroeconomic policies. Particularly with regard to the former, there has been beneficial change at least partly attributable to the euro's introduction and acceptance. Money market integration, which is critical to the implementation of a single monetary policy for the eurozone, given the need to transmit monetary policy in a decentralized fashion across the member economies, has succeeded. It took European money markets less than a month in 1999 to 'learn' how the new operational framework functioned, and to eliminate most of the volatility and cross-border dispersion in overnight interest rates. The evidence of integration in the unsecured lending rates in the European money market is similarly clear. Rey (2005) finds that government bond markets have seen intra-eurozone interest rate spreads virtually disappear, and benchmark securities of different countries have begun to emerge. Corporate bond markets went from 'almost non-existent' prior to EMU to 150 billion euro of issuance in 2003, and the euro swap market has become the largest financial market in the world.

Eurozone financial markets, however, still have a long way to go to become a global competitor with those based in London or New York. Factors in the non-financial economy, such as legal differences, obstacles to more rapid real growth, transaction costs, and institutional gaps in financial supervision combine to keep the eurozone from achieving truly deep, integrated financial markets, despite the removal of currency risk. Thus, there remains a striking contrast between the repo (repurchase of safe assets at central banks) and unsecured market in the degree of cross-national differences in interest rates due to the ongoing lack of harmonization in legal and procedural treatment of financial instruments in the eurozone countries. The costs of making cross-border securities transfers within the eurozone can still be ten times more than the cost of securities transfers within a given eurozone country.

Given the surge in capital flows across borders worldwide, following the recovery from the 1997–98 Asian financial crisis, almost half of which were in the form of portfolio investment, one would expect greater influence of market opinion about assets in a given currency or region upon the actual allocation of capital between regions. It seems that prospects for economic growth drive the relative demand for a region's assets, mostly by determining where trade and investment expands, which then in turn sets the pace of stock market integration of that region with the rest of the world. Given the medium-term outlook for European growth, this appears to militate against an increase in investment and therefore in integration (and influence) of European capital markets, which might be partially offset by some diversification incentives. In the long run, though, a slow growth rate in Europe would also translate into a smaller share of global GDP, and less incentive for central banks to hold euro-denominated reserves. In this context, Forbes (2005) and Lane and Wälti (2006) independently investigate whether the euro's launch prompted greater co-movement of stock prices within the eurozone across national borders, indicating greater financial integration as a result of EMU. Both investigations find that stock market correlations of eurozone member markets with the United States increased after the introduction of the euro more than those between the eurozone countries.

Prospects for the euro

The euro therefore occupies something of a halfway house. In terms of its purely technical functions it has been a resounding success, with no problems in acceptance at home or abroad, or in the payments system, and there has been convergence in key eurozone money market interest rates. There has also been evidence of stable low-inflation expectations for the varied eurozone membership as a whole, which remains an outstanding achievement of European central banking. None of the broader forecasts of economic doom or internal political conflict predicted by (mostly American) Chicken Littles came to pass, and those predictions look less credible than they ever did. European financial markets have significantly deepened and added liquidity since the advent of the euro, particularly for fixed-income securities. The sheer size of the eurozone economy as well as the ongoing adjustment of the world economy to US current account deficits propel the euro towards a prominent global role.

At the same time, however, European relative economic performance and growth potential will continue to fall short of that of many other advanced economies and large emerging markets for the foreseeable future. The adoption of the euro and the associated convergence process have failed to induce, let alone produce, the needed transformation in European economic structures, policies and performance. In most scenarios, a collapse of the dollar in coming years, or even an ongoing orderly adjustment involving higher US long-term interest rates and lower net imports, will have at least as great a contractionary effect on the eurozone as it will on the US economy – even if the Asian currencies take on their share of the adjustment burden. And if the Asian currencies, notably the Chinese yuan and Japanese yen, play their part, reserve switches accruing to euro-denominated securities, and their political benefits, will diminish along with the euro's share in the adjustment process. And as yet there has been little evidence of a change in global invoicing patterns from dollars to euros for traded good transactions.

In short, the euro has been a success within limits at home, but the eurozone economy is not yet strong enough – and is unlikely to be so for some time – to challenge the dollar as a global reserve currency or even to be widely utilized outside its borders. The euro, however, is not judged solely on its own merits, either by markets or by the international community, but rather is judged also in relative terms against developments in the dollar zone and elsewhere.

ADAM S. POSEN

See also **European Central Bank.**

Bibliography

Arestis, P. and Sawyer, M. 2001. Will the euro bring economic crisis to Europe? Economics Working Paper Archive: Washington University in St Louis.

Baldwin, R. 2005. The euro's trade effects. Presented at the ECB workshop: What effects is EMU having on the euro area and its member countries? Presented at the European Central Bank workshop. Frankfurt, 16 June.

Bergsten, F.C. 1997. The impact of the euro on exchange rates and international policy cooperation. In *EMU and the International Monetary System*, ed. M. Paul, T.H. Krueger and B. Turtelboom. Washington, DC: International Monetary Fund.

Bradford, S. and Lawrence, R.Z. 2004. *Has Globalization Gone Far Enough? The Costs of Fragmented International Markets*. Washington, DC: Institute for International Economics.

Canzoneri, M.B., Grilli, V. and Masson, P. 1992. *Establishing a Central Bank for Europe*. Cambridge: Cambridge University Press.

Cato Journal. 2004. *The Future of the Euro*, vol. 24 (Special Issue). Washington, DC: Cato Institute.

Cecchini, P. 1988. *Research on the 'Cost of Non-Europe': Basic Findings* (Cecchini Report). Luxembourg: EUR-OP.

Chinn, M.D. and Frankel, J.A. 2004. The euro area and world interest rates. Working Paper Series 1016. Center for International Economics, UC Santa Cruz.

Chinn, M.D. and Frankel, J.A. 2007. Will the euro eventually surpass the dollar as leading international reserve currency? In *G7 Current Account Imbalances: Sustainability and Adjustment*, ed. R. Clarida. Chicago: University of Chicago Press.

Currie, D., Levine, P. and Pearlman, J. 1992. European monetary union or hard EMS? *European Economic Review* 36, 1185–204.

De Cecco, M. and Giovannini, A. 1989. *A European Central Bank? Perspectives on Monetary Unification after Ten Years of the EMS*. Cambridge: Cambridge University Press.

De Grauwe, P. 1996. Monetary union and convergence economics. *European Economic Review* 40, 1091–101.

De Grauwe, P. 2000. *Economics of Monetary Union*. Oxford: Oxford University Press.

Dornbusch, R. 1989. The dollar in the 1990s: competitiveness and the challenges of new economic blocs. In *Monetary Policy in the 1990s: A Symposium*, sponsored by the Federal Reserve Bank of Kansas City, Jackson Hole, WY.

Eichengreen, B. 1999. Will EMU work? In *Euroen og den norske kronens skjebne*, ed. A.J. Isachsen and O.B. Roste. Bergen: Fagbokforlaget. English version online. Available at http://emlab. berkeley.edu/users/eichengr/policy/merrill.pdf, accessed 25 February 2007.

Emerson, M., Gros, D. and Italianer, A. 1992. *One Market, One Money: An Evaluation of the Potential Benefits and Costs of Forming an Economic and Monetary Union*. Oxford: Oxford University Press.

European Commission. 1990. One market, one money. *European Economy* 44.

European Commission. 1996. *Economic Evaluation of the Internal Market*. European Economy: Reports and Studies No. 4. Brussels.

European Commission. 1997. External aspects of economic and monetary union. Euro Papers No. 1. Brussels.

Feldstein, M. 1997. The political economy of the European economic and monetary union: political sources of an economic liability. *Journal of Economic Perspectives* 11(4), 23–42.

Forbes, K. 2005. The euro and financial markets. In Posen (2005a).

Giavazzi, F. and Spaventa, L. 1990. The 'new' EMS. Discussion Paper No. 369, CEPR.

Lane, P. and Wälti, S. 2006. The euro and financial integration. Discussion paper. Dublin: Institute for International Integration Studies.

Mann, C.L. and Meade, E.E. 2002. Home bias, transaction costs and prospects for the euro: a more detailed analysis. Working paper. Washington: Institute for International Economics.

McCauley, R.N. and White, W.R. 1997. The euro and European financial markets. Working Paper No. 41. Basle: BIS.

Mundell, R. 1998. What the euro means for the dollar and the international monetary system. *Atlantic Economic Journal* 26, 227–37.

Obstfeld, M. and Rogoff, K. 2004. The unsustainable US current account position revisited. Working Paper No. 10869. Cambridge, MA: NBER.

Portes, R. and Alogoskoufis, G. 1991. International costs and benefits from EMU. In *The Economics of EMU*. European Economy 1 (Special Issue), 231–45.

Posen, A.S. 1998. Why EMU is irrelevant for the German economy. Working Paper No. 1998/11, Center for Financial Studies, University of Frankfurt.

Posen, A.S., ed. 2005a. *The Euro at Five: Ready for a Global Role?* Washington, DC: Institute for International Economics.

Posen, A.S. 2005b. Can Rubinomics work in the eurozone? In Posen (2005a)

Quarles, R. 2005. Discussion of the euro and the dollar. In Posen (2005a).

Rey, H. 2005. The euro and financial markets. In Posen (2005a).

Rogers, J.H. 2003. Monetary union, price level convergence, and inflation: how close is Europe to the United States? International Finance Discussion Papers No. 740. Washington, DC: Board of Governors of the Federal Reserve System.

Summers, L.H. 2004. The United States and the global adjustment process. Third Annual Stavros S. Niarchos Lecture. Washington, DC: Institute for International Economics. Online. Available at http://www.iie.com/publications/papers/paper.cfm?ResearchID=200, accessed 25 February 2007.

Walters, A. 1990. Monetary constitutions for Europe. Speech at the 28th meeting of the Mont Pèlerin Society, Munich.

Weber, A.A. 1991. EMU and asymmetries and adjustment problems in the EMS: some empirical evidence. *European Economy* 44, 187–207.

European Central Bank

The European Central Bank (ECB) was established on 1 June 1998 and since 1 January 1999 has been responsible for the conduct of a single monetary policy for its member countries, namely, Austria, Belgium, Finland, France, Germany, Ireland, Italy, Luxembourg, the Netherlands, Portugal and Spain (with Greece subsequently becoming a member country on 1 January 2001 and Slovenia on 1 January 2007). Among European Union (EU) member countries Bulgaria, Czech Republic, Denmark, Estonia, Cyprus, Latvia, Lithuania, Hungary, Malta, Poland, Romania, Slovakia, Sweden and the United Kingdom are, as of 2007, not member countries of the ECB. These countries for the time being either have opted out of becoming member countries of the ECB (Denmark, Sweden and the United Kingdom) or have – according to the judgement of the EU Council – not yet achieved the necessary degree of economic convergence.

The launch of the ECB was the culmination of a process of monetary and economic integration that dates back at least to the efforts of the French government official Jean Monnet and others in the 1950s and gained decisive momentum with the April 1989 report of a committee headed by the then President of the European Commission, Jacques Delors, which drew up a blueprint for the progressive realization of the European Economic and Monetary Union (EMU). The establishment of the ECB and with it the launch of the euro (the currency of the ECB member countries for which banknotes and coins first went into circulation on 1 January 2002) has arguably been a unique endeavour in economic history, representing an experiment of hitherto unknown magnitude in central banking. In what follows, we shall describe the main aspects of the set-up and the responsibilities, strategy and operations of the ECB, discuss what appear to be the lessons learned from this experiment for monetary economics, and sketch some of the prospects for the ECB and the euro.

Lesson one: How to converge?

There can be little doubt that the European Council's June 1989 decision to pursue the Delors Committee's blueprint of a feasible path towards monetary union for its member countries was primarily driven by political considerations, viewing monetary union as a building block towards tighter political and economic integration of the member countries of the EU. However, given the broad consensus among economists and policymakers that, ideally, economic similarity rather than political boundaries should define the geographic area spanned by a common currency, the Delors report put considerable emphasis on realizing economic convergence before the establishment of a single European central bank. Key elements of the three stages to realization of the EMU as envisioned by the Delors Report were

- Stage 1 (1 July 1990): improvement of economic convergence; abolition of restrictions on cross-country flows of capital; increased cooperation between national central banks.
- Stage 2 (1 January 1994): strengthening of economic convergence; establishment of the European Monetary Institute (EMI) as predecessor of the ECB to strengthen cooperation between national central banks and increase coordination of monetary policy.
- Stage 3 (1 January 1999): completion of the necessary economic convergence; irrevocable fixing of currency conversion rates; single monetary policy to be conducted by the European System of Central Banks (ESCB).

It was envisioned in the Delors plan (and enacted in the Maastricht Treaty, which established the EU, as signed in February 1992) that only those countries should become member countries of the EMU that were successful in accomplishing economic convergence. The convergence criteria (Maastricht criteria) were meant to specify a sufficient degree of economic similarity of member countries with respect to price stability, sustainability of fiscal policy, exchange rate stability and the level of long-term interest rates. In particular, with respect to price stability member countries' average rate of inflation in the year preceding completion of the EMU was to fall within a one and a half per cent interval of average inflation in the three member countries displaying the highest degree of price stability. With respect to sustainability of fiscal policy, member countries were supposed not to carry an 'excessive deficit' – which would occur if the actual or planned government deficit to GDP ratio exceeded three per cent or if the ratio of government debt to GDP exceeded 60 per cent. Concerning exchange rate stability, member countries would in the two years preceding completion of the EMU have to keep the fluctuations of the value of their currency within the bands provided for by the European Exchange Rate Mechanism (ERM) and in particular not initiate any devaluation of their currency against that of any other member countries. Finally, with respect to the level of long-term interest rates, member countries' average long-term interest rates (on government bonds or comparable securities) in the year preceding completion of the EMU were to fall within a two per cent interval of average long-term interest rates in the three member countries displaying the highest degree of price stability.

Of course, economic similarities desirable for an optimal currency area do not end with these four criteria, but inter alia also include similarities in the monetary transmission mechanism, the coherence of the shocks and of the propagation mechanisms driving national business cycles as well as similarities in the prospects for trend output growth. These latter criteria were not part of the Maastricht criteria, though it was widely hoped that the economic convergence process prior to or immediately after the formation of the ECB would result in these latter criteria being approximately met as well.

Despite the relatively modest requirements for economic convergence in the Maastricht Treaty, the goal of EMU was jeopardized during the 1992–3 crisis of the ERM when foreign exchange market participants widely viewed the ERM's margins of fluctuation of two and a quarter per cent as not sustainable in the light of at best limited coordination of monetary policy, especially in Germany, with that in several other countries in the EU, specifically that in Italy and in the United Kingdom. The fact that despite the widening of the ERM's margins of fluctuation to 15 per cent in August 1993 the goal of EMU was maintained appears to have been due to the commitment of some of the then political leaders of the EU – perhaps most notably the then German Chancellor Helmut Kohl – who saw their vision of building a united Europe jeopardized. Owing to this political commitment as well as the fact that markets increasingly gave weight to complying with the Maastricht criteria as a signal for sound monetary and fiscal policy, convergence as outlined by the Maastricht criteria was sufficiently advanced in May 1998 for the heads of state and government of the EU to decide to proceed with Stage 3 of EMU as planned, if only for the 11 initial member countries of the ECB.

While it is a valuable lesson to have observed in the context of the establishment of the ECB that the prospect of a monetary union may itself help to induce partial economic convergence, it appears key to keep in mind that the process of formation of the ECB would probably not have been successful without the strong desire of the member countries' political leadership to see commonalities in cultural heritage also reflected in increasingly cohesive institutional entities, trusting that a common European currency would help the emergence of a single European identity.

Structural economic diversities between euro area member countries continue today (in 2007). Among these diversities perhaps most notable are persistent differences in trend output growth rates. The widely voiced hope expressed at the time of the signing of the Maastricht Treaty – that formation of the ECB would significantly spur convergence of trend output growth rates for euro area member countries through alignment of structural reforms of labour and product markets – has so far proven to be wishful thinking. While some critics of the ECB have argued that this is due to the mandate of the ECB being too narrowly focused on price stability, it may have been exactly this focus that allowed the ECB to successfully establish itself as a credible safeguard of price stability, an issue which we will discuss further below.

Lesson two: How to design and implement a monetary policy strategy
The starting point for any discussion of the ECB's monetary policy strategy has to be the mandate that the ECB was given by the Maastricht Treaty. Article 105 of that treaty specifies: 'The primary objective of the ESCB is to maintain price stability. Without prejudice to the objective of price stability the ECB shall support the general economic policies in the Community with a view to contributing to the achievement of the objectives of the Community as laid down in Article 2.' Article 2 specifies these objectives to be a high level of employment as well as sustainable and non-inflationary

growth. (The Maastricht Treaty refers to the ESCB rather than the ECB since it envisioned that all member countries of the European Union would eventually adopt the euro and that even before this was to happen all national central banks of member countries not part of the euro area would be bound by the same objectives.)

While the Maastricht Treaty does not specify a precise quantitative definition of price stability, the ECB, particularly on the basis of the argument that such quantification would strengthen its commitment to its primary objective as well as strengthen its accountability, in October 1998 defined price stability as a year-on-year increase in the Harmonized Index of Consumer Prices (HICP) for the euro area of below two per cent over the medium run. While this definition of price stability does exclude deflation as being consistent with price stability and leaves the ECB with no degree of freedom to potentially remove more volatile and/or temporary components of overall consumer prices in order to declare price stability, the definition does leave the ECB some flexibility in that a time horizon as to what would constitute the medium run was not established.

In its pursuit of price stability, the ECB decided to base its monetary policy framework on two pillars: 'monetary analysis' and 'economic analysis'. In declaring monetary aggregates as providing information valuable to the objective of price stability that should be separated from other economic and financial variables, the ECB has so far maintained that monetary aggregates do not just offer incremental information relative to such other variables for purposes of projecting inflation, but that at longer horizons (stretching beyond those typically adopted by central banks for the computation of their inflation projections but still essential for medium-run price stability) monetary aggregates provide information qualitatively different from that which other economic variables can provide. The ECB in this context has so far also maintained that money demand (as measured by the monetary aggregate M3) for the euro area has been stable at least over longer horizons, with some short-run instabilities being due to an exceptionally prolonged (but still temporary) period of high asset price volatility. Finally, the ECB has so far maintained that conventional macroeconomic analysis is not sufficiently advanced to combine the analysis of real economic phenomena with monetary trends within a single pillar framework. Driven by these considerations, the ECB therefore initially decided to announce annual reference values for the growth rate of M3 as a benchmark for keeping monetary growth in line with the objective of price stability.

The 'economic analysis' pillar of the ECB's monetary policy framework aims at identifying and quantifying short- to medium-term non-monetary risks to price stability. Variables entering this analysis include (a) gap measures of the discrepancy between actual output as well as its factors of production on the one hand and their medium- to long-run equilibrium values on the other hand; (b) labour cost measures; (c) exchange rates for the euro and international prices; and (d) asset prices other than exchange rates, particularly yield curve measures. Reflecting the sizeable degree of persistence of consumer price inflation in the euro area, considerable weight in the economic analysis is also given to recent consumer price dynamics.

The ECB's two-pillar strategy has been heavily criticized and remains controversial. Critics argue that monetary aggregates such as M3 – specifically due to the lack of sufficient stability of money demand – lack the degree of reliability needed to separate information in such monetary aggregates from other economic and financial variables. These critics inter alia also argue that, if the transparency and accountability of the ECB's decisions were to be improved, this would be helped most by the publication of inflation forecasts by the ECB as well as the publication of the minutes of the meetings of the ECB's Governing Council (for more on the latter, see below). The two-pillar strategy was reaffirmed in a broad internal assessment by the ECB in 2003, but two clarifications were provided. First, the Governing Council noted that it aims to maintain inflation rates below, but close to, two per cent over the medium run. A number of arguments in favour of tolerating a low rate of inflation – and not aiming at zero inflation – were acknowledged, among which the most important are the need for a safety margin against potential risks of deflation and the 'zero bound' on nominal interest rates. While this 'zero bound' renders central bank interest-rate management less effective at low rates of inflation, ECB studies argued that inflation rates below, but close to, two per cent would provide a sufficient safeguard against these risks. Second, the Governing Council emphasized that the 'monetary analysis' pillar was meant to serve mainly as a means of cross-checking, from a medium- to long-term perspective, the short- to medium-term indications provided by the 'economic analysis' pillar. To underscore the longer-term nature of the reference value for monetary growth, the practice of an annual review of the latter was discontinued.

It will be interesting to observe whether eventually the monetary pillar comes to be viewed as having been of importance only in the early years of operation of the ECB when the ECB had to establish its credibility by being as committed to price stability as the Deutsche Bundesbank (the German central bank) had been prior to 1999 and when the ECB was confronted with sizeable problems regarding the measurement of harmonized euro area-wide real economic aggregates, or whether ECB-style cross-checking by means of monetary analysis will become a common practice of central banks around the globe.

The operational framework used by the ECB to implement its monetary policy strategy is less controversial than the strategy itself and includes three main instruments: open market operations, standing facilities and reserve requirements. Among the open market operations of primary importance are the 'main refinancing options' that provide the bulk of refinancing to the financial sector and, through signalling the ECB's monetary policy stance, are supposed to steer market interest rates. The 'main refinancing options' are executed by the national central banks of the euro area member countries on a weekly basis through a tender procedure spanning three working days. 'Standing facilities' aim at providing and absorbing overnight liquidity, and 'minimum reserve requirements' (the ECB imposes minimum reserves on all credit institutions in the proportion of two per cent of the reserve base) aim at stabilizing market interest rates.

By way of evaluating the overall success of the ECB in terms of it being able to adhere to its price stability objective, we may observe that inflation rates in the euro area since 1999 have on an annual basis on average been slightly above two per cent (in the range of up to 30 basis points above two per cent). Also, given that surveys of average long-term inflation expectations in the euro area have consistently measured such expectations as below, but close to, two per cent, its track record has quite firmly established the ECB's credibility with regard to safeguarding price stability.

Lesson three: One central bank for many countries: how to organize decision-making

The most important decision-making body of the ECB is its Governing Council, which is made up of the Executive Board of the ECB (which in turn is made up of its president, vice-president and four other members) as well as the governors of all the national central banks of euro area member countries. It is the responsibility of the Governing Council to formulate monetary policy for the euro area, including decisions about intermediate objectives and key interest rates. The Executive Board is in charge of implementing the monetary policy decisions taken by the Governing Council, and to this purpose cooperates with the national central banks through open market activities. Each member of the Governing Council has one vote. Given that at present slightly more than two-thirds of the votes in the Governing Council, therefore, belong to national central banks, the latter have a strong influence on the ECB's monetary policy decisions.

This organizational structure implies an asymmetry between the economic size of euro area member countries and their influence on decisions arrived at by the Governing Council. Indeed, more than half the euro area member countries at present have an economic weight (as measured by the ratio of their national GDP to euro area GDP) that is smaller than their voting weight within the Governing Council. This is quite different from the structure of, say, the US Federal Reserve, which is significantly more centralized. While decentralization of the implementation of the ECB's monetary policy arguably is useful, particularly as long as there are important differences among national financial markets and institutions in the euro area, the decentralized institutional set-up of the ECB has risks, particularly during episodes of real divergence. It will be interesting to see whether the 'one person, one vote' principle for the Governing Council will be maintained after possible enlargement of the euro area to incorporate (some of) the EU member countries not presently member countries of the ECB. Even if the 'one person, one vote' principle is to be maintained, there appears to be considerable scope for future revision of the organizational system of the ECB, such as requiring approval of nominations of new central bank presidents by the Executive Board of the ECB.

Lesson four: Common currency and monetary policy: gains and losses

In general, the principal advantages of a common currency are widely held to include the reduction of transaction and information costs implied by the use of a common medium of exchange as well as the stimulus the common currency provides for the convergence of organizational principles used in business, in turn stimulating trade in goods and services and of cross-country flows of capital. The principal disadvantages of a common currency for multiple countries are widely held to include the loss of shock-absorber properties of flexible exchange rates and of independent national monetary policies. Furthermore, if a single monetary policy is accompanied by a diverse set of national fiscal policies, inappropriate fiscal policy in one country will – through its effect on interest rates – directly spread to other countries in the monetary union. Thus macroeconomic stability could be affected for the worse.

How has the euro area so far fared on these counts? Trade within the euro area increased from approximately 26.5 per cent of (euro area) GDP in 1998 to approximately 31 per cent of GDP in 2005; one and a half per cent of this increase was due to trade in services. Taking into account the limited time span, it is difficult to assess, however, to what extent this increase in trade was indeed driven by the creation of a single currency and to what extent it may instead have been driven by the process of economic globalization. We do know, in fact, that trade with trading partners outside the euro area over this same time period rose by a slightly larger margin than intra-euro area trade, from approximately 24 per cent of GDP in 1998 to approximately 30 per cent of GDP in 2005.

Regarding financial markets, for which the volume of transactions is probably still more sensitive to even small costs and risks associated with the use of multiple currencies, by a variety of measures deeper, broader and more liquid markets have emerged for the euro area member countries since establishment of the ECB. On the money market, issues of their interpretation aside, cross-country standard deviations for average overnight lending rates fell from 130 basis points in January 1998 to three basis points one year later, and since then have decreased to approximately one basis point. Cross-country standard deviations for rates at longer maturities (one and 12 months) for unsecured money market instruments have fallen to less than one basis point also, with the spreads still somewhat larger in the collateralized repurchase agreement (repo) market (due to continued differences in legal structures across euro area countries). In the interest rate derivatives market, the euro interest rate swap market at a daily volume of 250 billion euro was in 2006 one and a half times as large as the corresponding US dollar market. In the government bond market also, spreads have fallen to low levels, suggesting – in the likely absence of major changes in default risks – a significant fall of liquidity risk. The holdings of euro-denominated debt securities overall since 1999 have increased by well over ten per cent to approximately one-third of the global market (through holdings tend to be concentrated in countries neighbouring the euro area).

In the equity and retail banking markets integration has progressed more slowly. For example, despite a decrease in the number of credit institutions in the euro area member countries by almost 50 per cent between 1997 and 2006, less than one-third of the mergers and acquisitions driving this consolidation process have been cross-border. Also, the cross-country standard deviation of interest rates on consumer credit from 2004 to 2006 has still been close to one per cent.

While, just as for trade, it is difficult to disentangle the euro's contribution to the process of financial integration in euro area member countries from the global trend towards financial integration, the euro surely has greatly facilitated the task of bringing the European financial system closer to US standards in terms of market depth and liquidity. Further improvements in this direction, including the creation of a single payment system for the euro area member countries, are likely to intensify the debate about the potential role of the euro as a complement or competitor to the US dollar as an international reserve currency.

Finally, to turn to macroeconomic stability and the potential cost of losing flexible exchange rates and independent national monetary policies as shock absorbers, some such costs clearly have been observed since 1999. While the cross-country standard deviation of consumer price changes has fallen from approximately six per cent in the late 1990s to one per cent with the launch of the euro, and has been rather stable at this level in the following eight years, there have been persistent deviations from euro area average inflation rates for some countries, implying sizeable (and potentially destabilizing) differences in real interest rates. For example, for a sizeable part of the time period since 1999, real interest rates have been significantly lower in a booming Irish economy than in a German economy experiencing weak growth. When it comes to assessing the implications of the establishment of the ECB for macroeconomic stability, these costs have to be subtracted from benefits owed to factors such as the elimination of intra-euro area exchange rate crises and the fact that inflation rates for some euro area member countries have been falling sizeably in the eight years since 1999. However, a stronger degree of real convergence through aligned policies aimed at removing structural deficiencies in European product and labour markets would have helped to render the benefits yet larger.

Conclusion

While this article has suggested that on various counts (such as the monetary policy strategy and the organizational set-up) there is as of 2007 no consensus as to whether the ECB adheres to best international practice in central banking, it would appear rather questionable to label the establishment of the ECB and with it the introduction of the euro as anything but an enormous success. The ECB has successfully mastered the technical challenges of establishing a new common currency across a set of countries comprising one of the largest economic regions in the world, has in a short period of time established a strong track record of success in preserving price stability, and has on many counts, particularly in the area of financial markets, helped lead the way to a stronger integration of European markets. While it is undisputable that this integration of markets along with structural reforms needs to proceed much further, the key decisions that could facilitate such integration and structural reforms fall outside the core domain of responsibility of the ECB and, for that matter, should probably remain so for any central bank primarily entrusted with maintaining price stability.

MICHAEL BINDER AND VOLKER WIELAND

See also **euro; federal reserve system; inflation targeting.**

Bibliography

European Central Bank. 2004. *The Monetary Policy of the ECB.* Frankfurt am Main: ECB.

European Central Bank. 2006. *ECB Statistical Data Warehouse.* Online. Available at http://sdw.ecb.int, accessed 14 March 2007.

Issing, O. 2003. *Background Studies for the ECB's Evaluation of its Monetary Policy Strategy.* Frankfurt am Main: ECB.

Issing, O., Gaspar, V., Angeloni, I. and Tristani, O. 2001. *Monetary Policy in the Euro Area.* Cambridge: Cambridge University Press.

Padoa-Schioppa, T. 2004. *The Euro and Its Central Bank: Getting United after the Union.* Cambridge, MA: MIT Press.

Posen, A.S. 2005. *The Euro at Five: Ready for a Global Role?* Washington: Institute for International Economics.

Federal Reserve System

The Federal Reserve System of the United States was established on 23 December 1913, when President Woodrow Wilson signed the Federal Reserve Act. The need for a new federal banking institution became clear when a severe crisis occurred in 1907. In May 1908 the Aldrich–Vreeland Act established a bipartisan National Monetary Commission that proposed establishing a National Reserve Association with 15 locally controlled branches that would 'provide an elastic note issue based on gold and commercial paper' (Warburg, 1930, p. 59). The proposal was not enacted, nor was a subsequent proposal for a central bank with about 20 branches that would be controlled by a centralized Federal Reserve Board, consisting largely of commercial bankers. In the debate preceding the Federal Reserve Act, banking industry domination was rejected in favour of a board that had five members appointed by the President and two ex officio members, the Secretary of the Treasury and the Comptroller of the Currency. The appointed members had staggered terms and were to represent different commercial, industrial, and geographic constituencies. A sixth appointed member representing agriculture was added in 1923. The composition of the Board and its relation to Federal Reserve banks were drastically changed in 1935. Partly because of continuing disagreements about public versus commercial bank control, the new Board's powers were left ambiguous in the act.

The act mandated that all national banks become members of the new system and stockholders of Federal Reserve banks. Because reserves were to be concentrated in 12 Federal Reserve banks, the act substantially reduced reserve requirements at national banks. State chartered banks could join if they chose to and were judged to be financially strong. The first Board was sworn in on 10 August 1914 and the system opened for business on 16 November 1914. Federal Reserve notes that were backed 100 per cent by 'eligible paper' and, additionally, 40 per cent by gold began to circulate. Eligible paper was self-liquidating, short-term paper that arose in commerce and industry. The rationalization for eligible paper was the real bills doctrine, which held that credit extended for financing only the production and distribution of goods would not lead to inflation. The doctrine is invalid because of fungibility; there is no relation between paper acquired by Federal Reserve banks and loans the commercial banks are extending. In addition, all deposits at Federal Reserve banks had to be backed at least 35 per cent by gold. Subsequent amendments to the act effectively eliminated the supra-100 per cent collateralization of notes. A June 1917 amendment to the act forced all member banks to pool required reserves at Federal Reserve banks and further reduced reserve requirements to decrease the burden of membership on national banks and attract more state-chartered banks to the system.

The early years

The early years of the Federal Reserve System were marked by struggles to define the distribution of power between Federal Reserve banks and the Board, in the context of growing US involvement in the First World War. The Board gradually assumed more powers, but was unsuccessful in controlling open-market trading, which inevitably was concentrated in New York. Benjamin Strong, the New York bank governor, managed system trading. (Until 1935 the chief executives of Federal Reserve banks were called 'governors'. After 1935 their title was changed to 'president' and members of the Board were called 'governors'.) The Federal Reserve System was made fiscal agent for the Treasury in 1920, but the Treasury dealt directly with Federal Reserve banks, not the Board. Until 1922 the Board's statistical research office was located in New York, and arguably the Board was less informed than the New York bank about money market conditions.

Federal Reserve banks immediately sought earning assets in order to pay expenses and the six per cent required dividends on member bank capital subscriptions. As they expanded their portfolios of bills, US securities, discounted commercial paper, and acceptances, the breadth and liquidity of these markets increased. In early 1915 the New York bank was buying and selling for other Federal Reserve banks. Discount rates charged by reserve banks varied across Federal Reserve districts.

In anticipation of the US declaration of war on Germany in 1917, Federal Reserve banks became responsible for issuing and redeeming short-term Treasury debt certificates before and during Liberty Loan drives. There would be four large Liberty Loans and a Victory Loan in 1919 that required extensive Federal Reserve involvement. US bonds were sold to the public on an instalment plan by member banks; the interest rate banks charged on the unpaid balance on a bond was equal to the coupon rate on the bond. Member banks, in turn, discounted short-term US debt at Federal Reserve banks at an interest rate below the yield on the debt, which allowed them to recover their costs of instalment lending.

US government interest-bearing debt rose from $1.0 billion at the end of 1916 to $25.5 billion at the end of 1919, and would never again fall below $15 billion. This huge increase, and the fact that Federal Reserve banks offered preferentially low interest rates when member banks discounted government debt, had important lasting consequences on the money market. Before the war, Federal Reserve banks had schedules of discount rates that varied across the quality and maturity of discounted paper and the amount of borrowing by a member bank. Because of the low discount rate on government debt, member banks almost exclusively offered it as collateral when borrowing. The discount rate effectively became the rate charged on government debt. By 1922 each reserve bank effectively had a single discount rate, but rates still varied across Federal Reserve districts.

The November 1918 armistice brought new challenges. Continuing shortages of food and other goods in Europe and large increases in the stock of money led to inflation in the United States. The rate of inflation peaked in May 1920 and was followed by a sharp deflation in the following year of about 45 per cent in wholesale prices. In that year industrial production fell by about 30 per cent and unemployment soared. Until October 1919 Federal Reserve banks were obliged to keep the low wartime discount rates in order to allow banks and the public to absorb the 1919 Victory Loan. In November, Federal Reserve banks began raising their discount rates in an effort to combat inflation. In June 1920 four banks raised the rate to seven per cent. Amplifying the effects of the interest rate increases was an outflow of gold to Europe and a sharp reduction in discount window borrowing as Federal Reserve banks cut back on subsidizing the public's instalment purchases of US bonds.

The Boston bank lowered its rate from seven per cent to six per cent in April 1921, and was gradually followed by other reserve banks in an effort to respond to the slowdown. Deposits at all member banks reached a local maximum of $26.1 billion in the December 1919 call report and then fell to $22.8 billion in the April 1921 report. Discount window borrowings reached a year-end high of $2.7 billion in December 1920 and then fell to $0.6 billion at the end of 1922 as gold flows turned positive. As gold flowed in, reserve banks lowered their discount rates to 4.5 per cent in 1923 and early 1924.

While gold inflows slackened after 1923, it became apparent that new operating guidelines were needed. Governor Strong understood that the real bills doctrine was invalid and that many countries were not acting according to the old gold-standard rules. As interest rates fell, most reserve banks were again acquiring securities to augment their income. Strong, on the other hand, had begun to sterilize the New York bank's holdings of gold by selling its securities in the open market. The Treasury was concerned that reserve bank trading was upsetting securities markets when it was buying or selling debt. In May 1922 the reserve banks established the Governors Executive Committee consisting of the governors of the Boston, Chicago, Cleveland, New York, and Philadelphia banks to manage transactions for all 12 banks. The committee executed orders on behalf of the banks in the light of Treasury plans and made recommendations, but acted only as agents and had no executive power. In April 1923 it was renamed the Open Market Investment Committee (OMIC), which had the same membership as its predecessor but was required

> to come under the general supervision of the Federal Reserve Board; and that it be the duty of this committee to devise and recommend plans for the purchase, sale and distribution of open-market purchases of the Federal Reserve Banks in accordance with ... principles and such regulations as may from time to time be laid down by the Federal Reserve Board. (Chandler, 1958: 227–8)

Strong dominated the OMIC and began to understand the way open-market operations worked. He noted in particular that the sum of reserve bank open-market purchases and gold inflows almost equalled negative changes in member bank borrowing. He developed a case for active monetary policy and argued that restrictive monetary policy should be initiated with open-market sales and followed by increases in the discount rate. This was the likely origin of member bank borrowings and nominal interest rates as indicators of monetary policy. Policy instruments were open-market operations and the discount rate. While proposals to change discount rates originated with Federal Reserve banks, they required Board approval, which may explain why Strong preferred to lead with open-market operations. Strong was sensitive to the effects of monetary policy on prices, but objected to any legislated targeting of prices. His analysis was seriously incomplete when banks were not net borrowers from the Federal Reserve, and in such circumstances so were his policy tactics. Tragically, beginning in 1916 Strong suffered from recurrent attacks of tuberculosis and would die in October 1928, before such circumstances arose.

The 1923 Board Annual Report advocated an activist policy, but continued to support the real bills doctrine. In response to pressure from the Treasury and the Board, Federal Reserve banks sold most of their government securities in 1923; yearend holdings fell from $436 million to $134 million between 1922 and 1923. Federal Reserve notes and member bank reserves backed by such assets were unjustifiable under the doctrine, and the Treasury objected to Federal Reserve banks profiting from such assets. However, at the end of 1924 the banks held $540 million, and the banks' portfolio of government securities fluctuated considerably in the following years in response to changes in the volume of discounted bills and gold flows. Discount rates at Federal Reserve banks were lowered in the latter half of 1924 and 1925 before converging on four per cent at the beginning of 1926, largely following short-term interest rates in New York. Short-term market rates fell because of a sharp recession; the Federal Reserve index of industrial production ($1997 = 100$) fell from 7.84 in May 1923 to 6.43 in July 1924. Clearly policy was active, but not because of the real bills doctrine!

The discount rate was four per cent in June, when Federal Reserve banks began to cut the rate to 3.5 per cent and to make open-market purchases. At the beginning of 1928 discount rates were increased because of developing speculation in the stock market and continued to rise to as much as six per cent in October 1929, when the stock market crashed. In part, Federal Reserve discount rates were again responding to changes in industrial production, which had been quite sluggish until the end of 1927 and then began to grow rapidly until July 1929. In part, the 1927 rate cut reflected Federal Reserve efforts to help the United Kingdom maintain sales of gold at the pre-war sterling price, which had been restored in 1925. Governor Strong and Montagu Norman, the Governor of the Bank of England, were working to re-establish a gold standard that could restore order to international finance. To help the United Kingdom in 1925, the New York bank extended the Bank of England a $200 million gold credit and attempted to keep interest rates low in New York relative to those in London. By reopening gold sales at the pre-war price, Britain had effectively revalued the pound upward in 1925 by about ten per cent, with devastating consequences for its economy.

As Strong's health failed in 1928, a leadership vacuum developed. In an attempt to coordinate policy among all 12 reserve banks and the Board, the Board proposed in August 1928 that the five member OMIC be replaced by a new Open Market Policy

Committee (OMPC) that included all 12 reserve bank governors and was chaired by the Governor of the Federal Reserve Board. This proposal was rejected by bank governors, but a modified form was adopted in January 1930. Strong had been aware of growing stock market speculation and did not object to Federal Reserve open-market sales and the increase in the discount rate. These actions were reinforced by outflows of gold. In mid-1928 gold flows reversed, apparently attracted by high and rising short-term interest rates. Federal Reserve banks continued to sell bills and government debt, forcing member banks into the discount window to the extent of about $1 billion in the second half of 1928 and in the middle of 1929. At the end, Strong was aware of the danger of restrictive monetary policy actions over an extended period on the real economy, but remained reasonably optimistic that the situation could be controlled (Chandler, 1958: 460–3). After his death the struggle for control continued between his successor at the New York bank, George L. Harrison, and the Board; the latter argued that the real bills doctrine was not dead and that reserve banks should take direct action to penalize member banks making loans that supported security speculation. The Federal Reserve index of industrial production peaked in July 1929, Bureau of Labor Statistics (BLS) wholesale and consumer price indices had been slowly falling since 1926, and in October the stock market collapsed.

The Great Depression

Led by the New York bank, the Federal Reserve flooded the money market with cash by aggressively buying government securities. Discount window borrowing by member banks fell from $1,037 million in June 1929 to $632 million in December and to $271 million in June 1930. Further, discount rates at reserve banks were rapidly reduced; at the New York bank the rate was lowered from six per cent in October to 2.5 per cent in June 1930. The monthly average Standard and Poor common stock index (1935–1939 = 100) began to stabilize; it was 195.6 in January 1929, 237.8 in September, 159.6 in November, and 191.1 in April 1930. However, the index of industrial production continued to fall after the open-market purchases, and the BLS index of wholesale prices was ten per cent lower in 1930 than in 1929.

In mid-1930 reserve banks sharply reduced their purchases of government securities in the belief that monetary policy was adequately expansionary. The OMPC seems to have been guided by what Meltzer (2003: 164) calls the Riefler–Burgess Doctrine: 'If [discount window] borrowing and interest rates were low, policy was easy; if the two were high policy was tight.' An interpretation is that if member banks wanted to lend they could have inexpensive and relatively easy access to funds; if not, there was little more that the Federal Reserve could do. While total member bank discount window borrowing was positive, many banks were holding excess reserves. Conventional wisdom has it that the reserve banks should have continued buying securities. However, it is unclear even today whether continued large open-market purchases by the Federal Reserve would have had much of an impact on real economic activity in late 1930; the experiment was never tried. Rapid expansion of reserves and member bank deposits did occur in the late 1930s, with little effect on real economic activity.

On average about 600 bank failures a year occurred between 1920 and 1930; most failing banks were small and not members of the Federal Reserve System. The number of failing banks doubled in 1930 and increased by another 70 per cent in 1931. The total deposits of failing banks between 1920 and 1930 averaged less than $200 million a year, but more than quadrupled in 1930 and doubled again in 1931. Total deposits and currency had begun to fall after December 1928 and continued to fall after the stock market crash. Currency in circulation began to rise in November 1930, as bank failures increased. Industrial production and wholesale prices were falling at an accelerating rate. The directors of the New York bank counselled Governor Harrison to continue open-market purchases in 1930, but he encountered opposition in the OMPC and little was done. Net gold inflows were offset by open-market sales because the OMPC collectively believed monetary policy was expansionary. Reserve bank discount rates and money market interest rates trended down until 21 September 1931, when the United Kingdom suspended gold payments.

The British abandonment of gold led to very large withdrawals of gold and currency from the United States that were initially partially offset by open-market purchases of bills and increased discount window borrowing, which occurred at sharply higher interest rates as recommended by Bagehot (1873). However, Federal Reserve bank credit fell from $2.2 billion in October 1931 to $1.6 billion in March 1932. During this period of rising bank failures, rapidly declining economic activity, and falling prices, Harrison argued against open-market purchases for a number of reasons, but primarily because of the possibility of a shortage of 'free gold', that is, gold that was not required as collateral for Federal Reserve notes and reserves. The Glass–Steagall Act of 1932 authorized the Federal Reserve banks temporarily to use US government securities as collateral for Federal Reserve notes and thus largely solved the problem of a lack of free gold. In February 1932 Federal Reserve banks began aggressive open-market purchases of government securities that more than offset continuing gold losses and allowed member bank borrowings to fall about 50 per cent by August 1932. Discount rates at the New York and Chicago banks were lowered to 2.5 per cent in June 1932, but all other banks kept their rates at 3.5 per cent until the national banking 'holiday' that began on 5 March 1933 when President Roosevelt closed all US banks. Net free reserves (excess reserves minus discount window borrowing) had turned positive in September and thus signalled excessive ease to some individuals on the OMPC.

Restructuring the Federal Reserve System

It was obvious that the Federal Reserve had been ineffective in combating the collapse of the banking system and responding to the Great Depression. The banking system and the Federal Reserve needed to be restructured and strengthened. The Emergency Banking Act of 9 March 1933 authorized the Treasury to license and reopen national banks that were judged to be sound; state chartered banks that were sound would receive licences from state banking commissioners. Many reopening banks received capital injections by selling preferred stock to the Reconstruction Finance Corporation. At year-end 1929 there were 24,026 commercial banks of which 8,522 were members of the Federal Reserve System; at year-end 1933 there were 14,440 commercial banks of which 6,011 were member banks. For a period of one year all banks, whether members or not, could borrow on acceptable collateral from Federal Reserve banks.

Many of the reforms that were adopted would survive at least until late in the 20th century. Because of a belief that the collapse lay in undisciplined stock market trading, the Glass–Steagall Act of 1933 required that commercial banks divest themselves of investment banking activities. This act introduced deposit insurance that became effective in January 1934. It also banned interest payments on demand deposits and allowed the Board to impose ceilings on interest rates that banks could pay on time and savings deposits. Finally, the act renamed the OMPC the 'Federal Open Market Committee' (FOMC), but as in earlier incarnations its executive committee remained the same. The Securities Exchange Act of 1934 authorized the Board to impose margin requirements on stock market trades. Federal Reserve banks were authorized to make commercial and industrial loans to non-financial firms.

Having failed to expand reserve bank credit between July 1932 and February 1933, the Board found itself under extraordinary political pressure to expand resources to the banking system. As Meltzer (2003: 435–41) explains, President Roosevelt threatened to have the Treasury issue currency in the form of greenbacks if the FOMC failed to expand sufficiently. Net free reserves turned positive in May 1933 and rose to more than $3.0 billion by January 1936. The revaluation of gold in February 1934 together with subsequent large gold inflows from Europe and hesitancy to lend by member banks contributed to this surge in excess reserves.

The reconstruction of the Federal Reserve System continued with Roosevelt's nomination of Marriner Eccles to become Governor of the Federal Reserve Board in November 1934. Eccles had argued that system power should be concentrated in the Board and that reserve banks be prevented from undertaking open-market operations on their own accounts. Eccles's initiatives were opposed by Senator Carter Glass, many reserve bank governors, and the banking industry, but he largely succeeded in achieving his goals. The reforms were in the Banking Act of 1935, which restructured the Board to consist of seven appointed governors, each with a staggered 14-year term. The FOMC was restructured to consist of the seven governors and five reserve bank presidents. Two of the governors were to be appointed for four-year terms as chairman and vice-chairman of the Board by the president, with the advice and consent of the Senate. Eligible paper was no longer restricted to being short-term paper that originated in commerce and industry. The Board was empowered to vary reserve requirements; the upper limit was twice the percentages that were specified in the 1917 amendments to the Federal Reserve Act.

Members of the renamed Board of Governors of the Federal Reserve System took office in February 1936, with Eccles as chairman. For some time the FOMC had expressed concern about the inflationary potential of large excess reserves. In particular, because excess reserves exceeded reserve bank credit, the FOMC would not be able to absorb them without an increase in reserve requirements. Employing its new policy instrument, on 14 July 1936 the Board announced an increase in reserve requirements on August 15 of 50 per cent on all deposits at member banks. The increase was expected to absorb less than half of system excess reserves and was not expected to impinge on member bank lending or the economic recovery. In part because of continuing gold inflows, excess reserves were $3.0 billion at the end of July 1936, and averaged about $2.0 billion through the end of February 1937. Because excess reserves continued to be large, the Treasury began to sterilize gold inflows in December 1936, but not to the extent desired by the Board. At the end of January the Board announced a further two-step increase in reserve requirements of one-third to take place in March and May 1937. These actions took reserve requirements to their legal maxima and reduced excess reserves to below $800 million in summer months. In August and September reserve banks reduced their discount rates to one per cent or 1.5 per cent, levels that would last until December 1941. Coinciding with the May increase, the industrial production index (1997 = 100) reached a high of 10.4 and then decreased to 7.0 in May 1938. Continuing gold inflows and the Treasury's February 1938 abandonment of gold sterilization allowed excess reserves to increase to $1.5 billion in March 1938. Beginning after the Board's reduction in reserve requirements of more than ten per cent in April 1938, excess reserves began a rise to nearly $7 billion in late 1940; however, industrial production did not pass its 1937 peak until October 1939, after the Second World War had begun in Europe.

Second World War and recovery

As the war approached gold flowed into the United States, and the FOMC allowed its security holdings to fall and their maturity to lengthen. In response to inflationary pressures, the Board introduced consumer credit controls in September 1941 and again raised reserve requirements to their legal maxima in November. After the United States declared war, monetary policy was constrained to facilitate war finance. In April 1942 the FOMC set interest rate ceilings on treasury bills at 0.375 per cent and on long-term bonds at 2.5 per cent. The yield curve was upward-sloping and effectively 'pegged' by these two boundary conditions into the post-war period. Because capital gains could be earned by buying high coupon securities and selling as they approached maturity, the cost of intermediate term debt was higher than rates shown on the yield curve. Discount rates were lowered to one per cent by all reserve banks and were not raised again until 1948. A preferential discount rate of 0.5 per cent was charged for loans collateralized by short-term US debt. Reserve requirements for central reserve city member banks were lowered in 1942, causing interest-free reserves to disappear into interest-bearing US securities. Finally, a variety of selective credit controls were imposed during and after the war, which ended in August 1945.

Yearend deposits and government securities of member banks had risen from $61.7 billion and $19.5 billion in 1941 to $129.7 billion and $78.3 billion respectively in 1945. Because of the pegging of the yield curve, Federal Reserve bank yearend ownership of US securities rose from $2.3 billion in 1941 to $24.3 billion in 1945; treasury bills were $10 million in 1941 and $14.4 billion in 1946.

The preferential discount rate was eliminated in the spring of 1946. In July 1947 the FOMC relaxed the rate ceiling on treasury bills and the rate rose to about one per cent by yearend. Reserve banks raised the discount rate to 1.25 per cent in early 1948. Eccles's long term as chairman ended in February 1948, but he continued as a member of the Board. Reserve requirements were increased in 1948 as the Board sought to control inflation, although prices were actually falling at yearend when a recession occurred. Indeed, the reserve requirement policy instrument was used many times between April 1948 and February 1951 because it was perceived not to have a direct effect on treasury interest rates. A continuing struggle between the Board and the Treasury for an independent monetary policy would not be resolved until a spurt of inflation after the start of the Korean War led to an accord signed on 4 March 1951. It effectively freed the Board from pegging interest rates. Partly because of frictions leading to the accord, a new chairman, William McChesney Martin, Jr., was appointed in April.

Resumption of discretionary monetary policy

In the Martin era of discretionary monetary policy, new operating techniques were needed. In 1953 the FOMC settled on a policy of 'bills only', which meant that open-market operations would be largely confined to the market for treasury bills, because it was recognized that large policy actions in thin markets could impair market efficiency. Indicators of monetary policy continued to be net free reserves and market interest rates. Because evidence was lacking that interest rates had much effect on private sector investment, a new paradigm, the 'availability of credit' doctrine, was used to rationalize the transmission of policy actions to the real economy. It argued that banks rationed credit to marginal borrowers when restrictive policy led to rising interest rates or indebtedness at the discount window. With these adjustments the FOMC vigorously and unsuccessfully pursued goals of lowering inflation and combating unemployment in the turbulent decade of the 1950s. In that decade there were three business cycles, which were marked by successively rising peaks of interest rates, inflation, and unemployment. The reason for this failure was thought to be inflation-induced rising marginal rates of taxation, which were addressed by large tax cuts in the following decade.

As interest rates rose, the opportunity cost of holding excess reserves rose, which led to the reappearance of a federal funds market in which banks traded reserves. Because banks paid no interest on demand deposits, there was also rapid expansion of the market for commercial paper in which large firms with good credit ratings traded idle funds without the direct intervention of banks. Both markets had atrophied after the 1920s because of low interest rates, and served to change the relation between open-market operations and real economic activity. They were precursors of a wave of innovations that would have similar effects in the coming decade. These included large-denomination negotiable certificates of deposit, one-bank holding companies, offshore 'shell' branches, the Eurodollar market, and bank-related commercial paper.

Beginning in 1961, the Kennedy administration attempted to coordinate fiscal and monetary policy by proposing large tax cuts to encourage investment and economic expansion. A new problem was that the United States was experiencing large gold outflows as the world continued to recover from the world war. To cope with this new approach and problem, the FOMC was encouraged to abandon its bills-only policy and to attempt to twist the yield curve by buying long-term bonds and selling bills. As short-term rates rose the Board repeatedly raised the ceiling on interest rates that banks could pay on time and savings deposits. It was argued that lower long-term interest rates would encourage capital formation and that higher short rates would discourage foreign interests from converting dollars into gold, as they were entitled to under the Bretton Woods agreements. These efforts were not successful in discouraging gold outflows, but investment and the economy expanded strongly. In 1965 the Board introduced a Voluntary Foreign Credit Restraint programme, which discouraged banks from overseas lending that was not financing US exports. Nevertheless, gold continued to flow out and the requirement that Federal Reserve notes and reserves be backed by gold was cancelled in 1968. Large open-market purchases had been needed to offset gold losses.

Policy coordination between the Board and the new Johnson administration effectively ended in December 1965, when the Board approved an increase in the discount rate because of inflation arising from mobilizing for the Vietnamese War. Net free reserves had turned negative in 1965 and were increasingly so until late 1966. Short-term interest rates rose until October. Higher rates increased the cost of the mobilization and had devastating effects on residential construction and the savings and loan associations and mutual savings banks (hereafter thrifts) that financed it, because in September Congress passed legislation limiting interest rates that thrifts could pay on time and savings accounts. These limits meant thrifts would experience withdrawals of funds or 'disintermediation' because depositors switched funds to government securities, which had no limits. This policy transmission channel would soon disappear because Congress and the administration could not withstand the resulting political pressures. In 1968 the Federal National Mortgage Association was privatized and in 1970 the Federal Home Loan Mortgage Corporation was created. Both bypassed depository institutions by securitizing mortgage loans. Banks also responded to Board policies and restrictions on innovations by opening overseas offices that were not subject to them. A ten per cent income tax surcharge in 1967 was insufficient to stop inflation, and short-term interest rates rose to new highs in January 1970, when Chairman Martin's term ended. Net free reserves averaged about a negative $1 billion between May 1969 and July 1970. A decrease in short-term interest rates followed the then largest-ever US bankruptcy of the Penn Central Transportation

Company in June 1970, but led to large new capital outflows in 1971 that pressured the dollar. The FOMC responded by forcing short-term rates and net borrowed reserves up again.

Towards flexible exchange rates

The amplitude of changes in interest rates increased between 1965 and 1971, and the United States experienced a recession in 1970. As in the 1950s the Federal Reserve was unable simultaneously to achieve satisfactory unemployment, inflation, and exchange rate outcomes. Many of the Board's policy instruments, such as the discount rate, reserve requirement changes, and many regulations had effectively been disabled by innovations, so that only open-market operations were available to achieve multiple targets. For example, an increase in reserve requirements induced banks to resign from the system or to conduct more of their business overseas. One exception to this loss of powers was the 1970 amendments to the Bank Holding Company Act, which finally gave the Board regulatory authority over one-bank holding companies. In August 1971 the Nixon administration, with new Board Chairman Arthur F. Burns as an advisor, announced a 90-day freeze on prices and wages, suspension of gold sales, and several other major changes in the United States. The suspension of gold sales led to a floating exchange rate system, devaluation of the dollar, and sharp rises in dollar-denominated prices in international markets. The shift from a fixed to a floating exchange rate system is likely to have increased the potency of monetary policy, as was predicted by Mundell (1961). The FOMC responded to consequent high inflation by driving nominal short-term interest rates to very high levels in 1973 and 1974, which helped to induce a severe recession beginning in August 1973, but were inadequate because on average the real federal funds interest rate (calculated with the GDP deflator) was negative between the end of 1973 and 1978. Real estate and other durable goods prices rose relative to the GDP deflator, and the international value of the dollar fell. After the resignation of President Nixon in 1974, Congress required the Chairman to explain policy in semi-annual public hearings and report the FOMC's targets for two money stock measures: M1, a measure of transactions balances, and M2, a measure of liquid assets. Friedman and Schwartz (1963) had recommended using money as an indicator of monetary policy instead of interest rates or net free reserves.

Part of the explanation for the policy failure was continuing financial market innovation. Foreign banks operating in the United States grew rapidly and were unregulated until the 1978 International Banking Act, which placed them under Board supervision. The introductions of money market mutual funds (MMMFs) and negotiable order of withdrawal (NOW) accounts in 1972, the Chicago Board Options Exchange in 1973, and financial futures markets in 1975 again began changing the relation between financial and real markets. A more important change was the rapid expansion of repurchase agreements after 1970. In a repurchase agreement, a client's deposits are borrowed to finance a bank's or dealer's inventory of government securities, often only overnight. Large bank holdings of government securities often represented transactions balances of large corporations and state governments that could not easily be controlled.

The real federal funds rate turned distinctly positive in the third quarter of 1979 when Paul A. Volcker became chairman. In early October he announced that the FOMC would no longer limit fluctuations in short-term interest rates and would use open-market operations to control bank reserves. This was a major policy change from practices dating from the 1951 accord. Further, he imposed eight per cent marginal reserve requirements on non-deposit liabilities, that is, Eurodollar borrowing, federal funds purchased from non-member banks, and funds acquired through repurchase agreements. These vigorous actions together with large income tax cuts by the Reagan administration between 1981 and 1983 drove real short-term interest rates to levels not seen since the early 1930s and caused MMMFs to grow rapidly. In only two quarters between 1979 and 1986 was the average real federal funds less than five per cent. These high rates caused the trade-weighted value of the US dollar to appreciate by 87 per cent between July 1980 and February 1985, which savaged US exports and attracted imports with adverse consequences for US manufacturing.

Financial deregulation

The landmark Depository Institutions Deregulation and Monetary Control Act was signed by President Carter at the end of March 1980. It radically changed the Federal Reserve System by eliminating the significance of membership in the system. After an eight-year phase-in period, all depository institutions would be subject to uniform reserve requirements on demand and time deposits, although the requirement on the first $25 million of transactions deposits was less than that on other transactions deposits. The Board could vary reserve requirements. All depository institutions had access to reserve bank discount windows. This strengthened the system because banks could no longer threaten to leave it in order to get the lower requirements that many states imposed. Further, Federal Reserve banks were required to charge banks for the cost of services they provided. Before this act they had been giving away services as an inducement for banks to stay in the system. This pricing requirement in turn forced depository institutions to begin to charge their clients for services, which changed the way banking services were used. The act mandated that interest rate ceilings on time and savings accounts be eliminated after six years, increased deposit insurance, and had other important provisions that are beyond the scope of this discussion.

In late 1980 the Board announced that transfers from overseas branches to the United States could be treated as collected funds on the day they were transferred. Before then, transfers in a day were not 'good funds' until the following day. The expansionary effects of this change, rapidly growing repurchase agreements, and other innovations are evident in demand deposit turnover statistics that the Board reported from 1919 until August 1996. Turnover is the annualized value of all withdrawals from deposit accounts divided by aggregate deposit balances.

High interest rates were savaging thrift institutions, which had negative gaps (more fixed-rate assets than fixed-rate liabilities on most future dates), and allowed MMMFs to expand rapidly. Congress intervened in September 1982 by passing the Garn–St Germain Act, which provided temporary emergency assistance and among other changes introduced money market deposit accounts and super NOW accounts, which paid market interest rates. MMMF growth was slowed by this act, but the weakening condition of banks and thrift institutions would result in large numbers of failures as the decade wore on. Large banks also experienced large losses because the appreciating dollar had resulted in failures of sovereign states, especially in Latin America, to meet their loan obligations. Chairman Volcker was heavily involved in negotiating solutions for these defaults.

The restrictive monetary policy resulted in the deepest recession since the Depression; the unemployment rate was 10.8 per cent at the end of 1982. At the end of Volcker's term in August 1987 the unemployment rate had fallen to six per cent and the consumer inflation rate was less than two per cent. Real interest rates had fallen from 10.5 per cent in mid-1981 to four per cent, and the trade-weighted value of the dollar fell correspondingly. Volcker's February 1987 statement of monetary policy objectives to the Congress reported that M1 was not a reliable indicator of monetary policy and would be de-emphasized.

While his successor, Alan Greenspan, inherited a much improved economy, many problems remained from a rising wave of bank failures and the collapse of thrift institutions. Real estate markets were especially disorderly when the thrift crisis was resolved beginning in 1989 and were further distorted by provisions in the Tax Reform Act of 1986, which disallowed many interest tax deductions. After 1990 interest on home loans was effectively the only deductible interest on individual income tax returns. In addition, a collapse of stock prices in October 1987, strong foreign demand for US currency associated with the collapse of the Soviet Union, and a recession at the end of 1990 presented further challenges. The FOMC responded to these challenges by varying the real federal funds rate, defined using the contemporaneous GDP price deflator inflation rate. This rate fell sharply for two quarters after the stock market crash, rose before falling for two quarters after a second stock market dip in October 1989, and then began to fall in the fourth quarter of 1990. In July 1993 testimony before Congress, Greenspan disclosed that the FOMC was downgrading M2 as an indicator of monetary policy and, as could have been surmised from its actions, that an important guidepost was now real interest rates. The real federal funds rate averaged less than one per cent in 1993. In early 1995 it had risen to four per cent and held that value as an average until the collapse of a large hedge fund in September 1998. After the fallout from the hedge fund collapse had been resolved, the real federal funds rate was restored to an average of about four per cent in 2000. When a new recession appeared in 2001 together with a sustained large collapse in stock market prices, the real federal funds rate was lowered to near zero in the fourth quarter; the rate had averaged zero for 13 consecutive quarters as of March 2005.

Between December 1990 and April 1992 reserve requirements on time and demand deposits were reduced, which helped banks to increase net income. In January 1994 'retail sweep programmes' were introduced. In these programmes, a bank shifts funds from a depositor's transactions account to a synthetic time deposit account in the depositor's name in order avoid reserve requirements, usually without the depositor's knowledge. The Board does not measure the amount of funds swept, except at the time the programme was established. The Board estimated that as of August 1997 required reserves fell by one-third because of these programmes.

In November 1999 President Clinton signed the Financial Services Modernization (Gramm–Leach–Bliley) Act, which reversed the 1933 Glass–Steagall Act's ban on combining commercial and investment banking. The ban had been eroding since 1987, when some large bank holding companies were authorized by the Board to establish subsidiaries that could underwrite state and local government revenue bonds. The new act authorized the establishment of financial holding companies, which were to be regulated by the Board and could engage in an approved list of activities that included commercial banking, insurance, securities underwriting, merchant banking, and complementary financial undertakings. In 2003 there were more than 600 financial holding companies, which resemble the universal banks that exist in other countries.

In December 2002 the Federal Reserve discarded the discount rate as a policy instrument by replacing it with an interest rate on primary credit extended by the discount window that is one per cent above the FOMC target federal funds rate. Primary credits are collateralized loans to banks in sound financial condition.

As the foregoing dramatic institutional changes suggest, the Federal Reserve System is a work in progress. Its set of policy instruments and its dimensions have radically changed. Because of offshore banking facilities and retail sweep accounts, reserve requirement changes are no longer an effective policy instrument. As noted in the preceding paragraph, the discount rate has been discarded as an instrument; it is simply a penalty rate that is related to a bank rate, as is often the practice in other countries. Regulations on the interest rates banks pay on time and savings deposits have been discarded. Open-market operations are almost the sole policy instrument that can be used to achieve the Board's target nominal and real federal funds interest rates. While the FOMC has been able to control the overnight federal funds rate, the linkage between it and real economic activity is changing. First, the combined holdings of US government securities by foreign central banks have recently exceeded those of Federal Reserve banks. Foreign central bank holdings are partly a result of their efforts to manipulate exchange rates; their holdings are likely to change when FOMC policies change. Second, repurchase agreements and offshore transactions vary considerably over time and their volumes appear to be sensitive to US economic activity. Third, the outstanding stock of securitized mortgage and other debt has been growing rapidly; such debt is a close substitute for US government debt and its amount has real economic effects. Fourth, because of decreasing required reserves and growing offshore holdings of US currency, 89 per cent of Federal Reserve liabilities were in the form of Federal Reserve notes in December 2003; the corresponding share was 34 per cent in 1941, 57 per cent in 1970, and 79 per cent in 1989. In part, the Federal Reserve recently has become an institution for collecting seigniorage from the rest of the world. Finally, over the decade ending in 2003, the share of all credit market assets held by depository institutions in the Federal Reserve's flow of funds accounts fell. In the context of the most recent 13 quarters of a zero real federal funds interest rate, more changes could be expected.

DONALD D. HESTER

See also **Great Depression, monetary and finacial forces in; monetary and fiscal policy overview.**

Bibliography

Bagehot, W. 1873. *Lombard Street: A Description of the Money Market.* Homewood, IL: Richard D. Irwin, 1962.

Chandler, L. 1958. *Benjamin Strong: Central Banker.* Washington, DC: The Brookings Institution.

Chandler, L. 1970. *America's Greatest Depression 1929–1941.* New York: Harper and Row.

Crabbe, L. 1989. The international gold standard and US monetary policy from World War I to the New Deal. *Federal Reserve Bulletin* 75, 423–40.

Dykes, S. 1989. The establishment and evolution of the Federal Reserve Board: 1913–23. *Federal Reserve Bulletin* 75, 227–43.

Friedman, M. and Schwartz, A. 1963. *A Monetary History of the United States, 1867–1960.* Princeton: Princeton University Press.

Goldenweiser, E. 1951. *American Monetary Policy: A Research Study for the Committee for Economic Development.* New York: McGraw-Hill.

Greider, W. 1987. *Secrets of the Temple: How the Federal Reserve Runs the Country.* New York: Simon and Schuster.

Meltzer, A. 2003. *A History of theFederal Reserve, Volume I (1913–1951).* Chicago: University of Chicago Press.

Mundell, R. 1961. Flexible exchange rates and employment policy. *Canadian Journal of Economics* 27, 509–17.

Scott, I., Jr. 1957. The availability of credit doctrine: theoretical underpinnings. *Review of Economic Studies* 25(4), 41–8.

Warburg, P. 1930. *The Federal Reserve System: Its Origin and Growth,* vol. 1. New York: Macmillan.

fiat money

An object is often said to qualify as *money* if it plays one or more of the following roles: a unit of account, a medium of exchange, a store of value. The first and third seem insufficient. The Arrow–Debreu model with prices expressed in terms of either an abstract numeraire or one of the goods is not a model of a monetary economy. Neither is every model that contains an asset or durable good. That leaves the medium-of-exchange function: an object is a medium of exchange if it appears in many transactions – in the sense of a Clower (1967) transaction matrix.

As regards kinds of money, one distinction is between outside money, such as gold coins, and inside (private sector) money, such as demand deposits. (The quantity of outside money is unaffected by consolidation over the balance sheets of everyone in the economy, while the quantity of inside money disappears when that consolidation is performed – an inside money being someone's asset and someone else's liability.) Among outside monies, a distinction is usually made between commodity and fiat money. A commodity money is an object that has intrinsic value as a consumption good or as an input, while a fiat money does not.

One challenge is to construct models that depict the ancient notion that a medium of exchange is beneficial. (This notion goes back at least to the Roman jurist Paulus who said: 'Since occasions where two persons can just satisfy each other's desires are rarely met, a material was chosen to serve as a general medium of exchange' –Monroe, 1966.) Another is to construct models in which media of exchange are relatively poor stores of value, have low rates of return. And accompanying those challenges is a wide range of related policy questions. How, if at all, should inside money be regulated? How should a government monopoly on outside money be managed? Should there be country-specific outside monies?

Progress in meeting those challenges and in addressing policy questions has come about by taking seriously some old ideas: money is helpful when there are absence-of-double-coincidence difficulties that cannot be easily overcome with credit; and a good money has some desirable physical properties – recognizability, portability, and divisibility. In order to better appreciate the challenges and the progress, it is helpful to review the history of monetary theory.

The classical dichotomy

At the beginning of the 20th century, the dominant economic theory was a two-part model: a rudimentary Arrow–Debreu theory of relative prices and allocations; and a quantity-theory equation that was often interpreted as a supply-equals-demand for money equation. As was widely recognized, this model suffers from a blatant inconsistency. Everybody in the model is completely described in the theory of relative prices and allocations. Who, then, holds money, which is not one of goods in the relative price-allocation part of model? Patinkin (1951) called attention to this inconsistency by pointing out that the model fails to satisfy Walras's Law.

The model has other defects. Because the model does not describe transactions, it is silent about whether money is a medium of exchange. Whether it is or not, money is not helpful in the model because allocations are determined exactly as they would be in its absence. And, as was widely recognized, the real return on money in the model – determined entirely by the time path of the stock of money and its effect on the time path of the price level – could be less than, equal to, or greater than the real interest rate determined in the relative price part of the model. The third possibility was viewed as problematic because people would then, presumably, hold only money.

Notice, by the way, that money in the above model is implicitly fiat money and that holdings of it are minimized subject to being able to carry out transactions. Neither was an obvious feature of the economies to which the theory was applied for centuries. For most of that time, money was in fact a commodity and one that may not have been a poor store of value – if only because few alternatives were available. The distinction between commodity and fiat money may not be important because for some specifications of the intrinsic value of commodity money, the value of commodity money is determined in the same way as the value of fiat money (see, for example, Samuelson, 1968; Sargent and Wallace, 1983). The implicit assumption that money is a poor store of value is more significant because it means that money cannot be treated as an ordinary asset.

Real balances in utility or production functions

The first models to overcome the blatant inconsistency of the classical dichotomy and to, in some way, integrate value and monetary theory were models of fiat money in which its quantity and its price were arguments of utility or production functions (see Samuelson, 1961). Such models are consistent with individual endowments of money and have equilibria in which it has value.

The models were intended to overcome the inconsistency of the classical dichotomy, while preserving as much of the relative price part of the model as possible. However, not everything was preserved. After explaining why real balances, not nominal balances, are introduced as an additional argument of utility functions, Samuelson (1961, p. 119) says, 'This is not the only case in which economists have found it necessary to introduce prices into the indifference loci; there is also the example of goods which have snob appeal, or scarcity appeal...' Samuelson (1968) describes the welfare consequences of his formulation: the failure of the first welfare theorem. That failure should not be surprising; putting prices into utility or production functions is a back-door way of introducing externalities. The failure gave rise to the vast literature on the so-called Friedman rule: tax to support the payment of interest on money either explicitly or through deflation.

A desirable feature of these models is that money cannot have a higher pecuniary real return than other assets. The models treat real balances like clothing or refrigerators. Such assets throw off services and, therefore, in equilibrium have lower pecuniary rates of return than assets like bonds that do not throw off services.

Cash in advance and trading posts

Utility or production functions with real balances as arguments were always regarded as *indirect* functions. If so, then there ought to be a direct or underlying model. One suggestion for the underlying model is a model in which the Arrow–Debreu budget set is replaced by separate sets which insure that money will appear in many trades (see Clower, 1967). Some goods can be purchased only with money and the sellers of those goods who receive money can use that money only in subsequent trades. Such models, dubbed cash-in-advance models, are special cases of models of *incomplete markets* (see, for example, Magill and Quinzii, 2006).

Viewed that way, cash-in-advance models depart from the Arrow–Debreu model by amending its equilibrium concept. Shubik (1973) adopts that way of modelling money, but insists that trade be modelled as an explicit game. In particular, he suggests that it be modelled using what are called Shapley–Shubik trading posts, with each post defined by the pair of objects traded at the post. In static versions of that model in which the game is modelled as the simultaneous choice of quantities (a version of a Cournot quantity game), inactivity at any subset of posts (including all posts) is a Nash equilibrium. Such inactivity has been used as a rationale for selecting a subset of posts that produces the kind of transaction matrix we observe – for example, some goods cannot be traded for anything other than money and, in a multi-country context, some goods can be traded only for home money. However, Krishna (2005) questions the robustness of shutting down posts in which goods trade for assets that dominate money in rate of return.

Starr and Stinchcombe (1999) use a version of this model with fixed costs of operating a post to suggest that scale economies can imply that the efficient arrangement of posts when there are $n + 1$ objects, n goods and money is a monetary structure: at each of n active posts, money trades for one of the goods. Howitt (2005) uses an infinite-horizon version of that model with utility-maximizing agents who operate the posts to argue that there can be equilibria with that monetary structure of posts.

Imperfect monitoring and money

A different approach to modelling money is to depart from the environment of the Arrow–Debreu model – in particular, from its assumptions about commitment and information. Implicit in the absence-of-double-coincidence rationale for money is that the two persons cannot commit to future actions and are strangers. After all, a student in a class is more likely to say to a neighbouring student 'lend me a pencil' than 'sell me a pencil'. More generally, in order that absence of double coincidence be a basis for a beneficial role for money, it must be augmented by no-commitment and by informational assumptions that inhibit the use of credit in its most general sense – informational assumptions that in game theory are called *imperfect monitoring*.

One of the first discussions of the informational assumptions is in Ostroy (1973). Townsend (1989) uses imperfect monitoring in an explicit intertemporal model and Kocherlakota (1998) further formalizes it. This work treats fiat money as a mechanism whose only role is to provide evidence of previous actions that would otherwise not be known. Fiat money, a physical object, can play that role because, counterfeiting aside, others can say 'show me' if one tries to overstate ones holdings of it.

The potentially crucial role of imperfect monitoring can be illustrated by considering the well-known risk-sharing model in Green (1987) and the variant of it studied by Levine (1990). There is a non-atomic measure of people who have identical preferences and maximize expected discounted utility. The model is one of pure exchange with a single good at each date. At each date, each person receives an endowment realization from a two-point set (high or low), where realizations are i.i.d. among people at a date and over time and are private information. Green studies a version of this model with perfect monitoring: at each date, each person makes a report about the person's endowment realization, a report which in the future is associated with that person.

Levine (1990) studies a variant of this model, but assumes no monitoring at all. In his version, no announcement or action made by a person at a date is associated with that person in the future. Moreover, if endowments are treated as owned by individuals, then under Levine's assumption, there is a role for money even if endowment realizations are public information. If there is no way to remember in the future that a person with a high endowment surrendered some of it, then the person will not surrender it – except for something that the person can carry into the future. In a pure-exchange setting, that thing can only be fiat money.

Pairwise meetings

Absence of double coincidence is almost always described in terms of meetings between two people. That, of course, is very different from having everyone together or at least connected as in the Arrow–Debreu model. But, if the role of such pairwise meetings is only to prevent quid pro quo trade in commodities, then it is unnecessary. Such trade cannot happen in Green (1987), even in deterministic versions of it. So why bother with models of pairwise meetings?

One reason is that Paulus and others were reporting what they were seeing: namely, exchanges between two people. Another reason to study such models is to investigate their implications for transactions. Kiyotaki and Wright (1989) are the first to succeed in formulating and analysing such a model. In a world with many objects, they study the relationship between the intrinsic storage properties of objects – in particular, the (utility) cost of storing them – and their role in exchange. In order to make headway on that question, they adopt simplifying assumptions: objects are indivisible, each person can hold at most one unit of some object, and the intrinsic storage quality of an object is modelled as a utility cost which once realized does not become part of the state of the economy. Even with those simplifying assumptions, their model is not simple because the state of the economy is a distribution of holdings of the different objects. Nevertheless, they could show that there can be steady states in which objects other than the least costly-to-store object can play a medium-of-exchange role. (For the welfare properties of different equilibria in their model, see Renero, 1999.)

Still another reason for studying models with pairwise meetings is that such meetings can provide a rationale for imperfect monitoring. In a large economy, if people meet in pairs and, therefore, know only what they have experienced or what they have been told by people they meet, then imperfect monitoring emerges as an implication. This point of view is explored in non-monetary models in Kandori (1992) and in monetary models in Kocherlakota (1998) and Araujo (2004). Finally, models of pairwise meetings are attractive settings for exploring the consequences of imperfect recognizability and imperfect divisibility of money and other assets.

Models of pairwise meetings, however, also come with complications. One is the wide range of equilibrium concepts used to answer the old question: what do a pair who meet to trade do? One approach taken in the literature is descriptive – for example, the buyer and the seller make alternating offers, buyers make take-it-or-leave-it offers, or sellers commit to posted prices. Another approach explores all implementable outcomes subject either to individual defection or to such defection and cooperative defection by the pair in the meeting.

Another complication is the endogeneity of the distribution of assets. Such endogeneity also arises in models in which fiat money is the only durable object, in which people can hold more than one unit of money, and in which the meeting process gives rise to a distribution of outcomes – a person can end up buying, selling, or not trading. Obviously, in such models we do not expect to obtain simple closed-from solutions for equilibria or even steady states.

One response is to accept the endogeneity and to derive results for the model despite not having closed-form solutions (see Green and Zhou, 1998; Molico, 2006; Zhu, 2003; 2005). Another is to avoid it: by using the so-called *large-family* model (see Shi, 1997); by using a setting in which pairwise meetings alternate in some fashion with centralized meetings in which preferences are quasi-linear (see Lagos and Wright, 2005); or by using some other meeting process that lends itself to a simple or degenerate distribution of money.

Applications
New theoretical work should provide insights previously unavailable – insights about seemingly paradoxical observations or policies or both.

Outside money, credit and cashless economies
If we maintain the innocuous assumption that people cannot commit to future actions, then a model economy with perfect monitoring has no role for money, while one with no monitoring has no role for credit. Therefore, in order to find roles for

both money and credit, we should study models with some, but not perfect, monitoring.

Several alternative formulations of such imperfect monitoring have been studied. Kocherlakota and Wallace (1998) use the pairwise setting in Trejos and Wright (1995) and Shi (1995), and assume that there is a lag in updating the public record of individual actions. They show that the set of implementable allocations is larger the shorter the lag – an obvious result, but one that represents the sense in which technological improvements that allow better monitoring improve trade outcomes. Cavalcanti and Wallace (1999) use the same background model, but assume that some people are perfectly monitored and others not at all. They permit each person to issue perfectly recognizable durable objects that are specific to the person, objects that are best interpreted as transferable trade-credit instruments. They show that the set of implementable outcomes in which such instruments are not valued (or are prohibited) is a strict subset of those in which such instruments issued by monitored people are valued. (Kocherlakota, 2002, shows that there is a way to support efficient allocations in such models using only spot trade with money. However, his punishment scheme would not survive allowing either the defector or the non-defector to move first in a meeting.) Aiyagari and Williamson (2000) use an environment that is close to that of Green (1987), but assume that a report to the planner can be made with some probability less than 1. Their focus is on how competitive trade in money influences what the planner can achieve.

Obviously, limiting cases of the above formulations of imperfect monitoring give rise to what can be interpreted as cashless economies. Although there are many conceptions of cashless economies, one of which is the Arrow–Debreu model, the above formulations have the desirable property that the cashless limit is a limit of a cash economy in which a medium of exchange plays a beneficial role. Moreover, because the cashless economy is achieved by taking a limit with respect to monitoring while maintaining the no-commitment assumption, the cashless limit is not an Arrow-Debreu model.

In Cavalcanti and Wallace (1999) and Cavalcanti, Erosa and Temzelides (1999), the money issued by monitored people is used by and passed around among nonmonitored people. Wallace and Zhu (2007) use that idea to offer a new interpretation of the paradox concerning banknote issue pointed out by Friedman and Schwartz (1963). Toward the end of 19th century, many countries permitted banks to issue payable-to-the-bearer notes subject to redemption on demand and to collateral restrictions. In the United States and, presumably, in other countries, those systems seemed to give rise to a failure of an arbitrage condition: the yields on eligible collateral often seemed too high to be reconciled with their use as collateral for note issue. Put differently, those systems seemed not to produce currencies that were elastic with respect to the yield on eligible collateral. The explanation offered by Wallace and Zhu has two components. First, the profitability of note issue depends on the implied float. Second, note issuers face a menu of opportunities for issuing notes – a menu that displays an inverse association between the magnitude of possible note placements and the implied float. The paradox results from treating the observed float as if it applied to all possible uses of notes, rather than taking into account the fact that high-placement low-float opportunities – for example, in organized financial markets – are not chosen. In Wallace and Zhu, the low-placement, high-float opportunities are in pairwise meetings.

Physical properties of assets

Discussions of money have often described desirable physical properties of media of exchange: recognizability, portability and divisibility. Implicit in any such discussion is the idea that those properties are scarce, are not shared equally by all objects. However, only recently have the consequences of such scarcity been explored.

Recognizability

Freeman (1985) and Williamson and Wright (1994) use imperfect recognizability of alternatives to fiat money to produce models in which fiat money is helpful. In Freeman, the alternative to fiat money is a claim to long-lived capital. Under the assumption that such claims can be costlessly counterfeited, he argues that genuine claims cannot be traded competitively. Williamson and Wright use a model of pairwise matching *without* an absence-of-double-coincidence problem to show that imperfect recognizability of the (durable) goods is enough to make trade involving fiat money helpful.

In both of those models and many others, the holder of an asset knows more about it than at least some potential holders. (An exception is Huggett and Krasa, 1996.) Models of pairwise meetings are attractive for studying the role of such imperfect recognizability because it is in such meetings, rather than in 'large markets', that asymmetric information about quality ought to be important. Moreover, if, as in Freeman or Williamson and Wright, the low-quality asset is worthless, then it gets traded when subject to asymmetric information only if it masquerades as being genuine – that is, only in a *pooling* equilibrium.

However, pooling equilibria do not always exist – at least if refinements on beliefs about off-equilibrium actions are imposed. It remains to be determined whether such refinements could be used to strengthen the Freeman result. In particular, could a small difference in counterfeiting costs between two assets – between fiat money and claims to capital, or home money and foreign money, or outside money and inside money – be enough to generate trade in one of the assets and no trade in the other even if the less-costly-to-counterfeit asset, as in Freeman, has a large rate-of-return advantage?

Portability

Townsend (1989) and Smith (2002) build models based on portability of fiat money and the lack of portability of capital. However, as they emphasize, the mere lack of portability of real capital needs to be supplemented by imperfect monitoring. And when supplemented by sufficiently imperfect monitoring, such models give rise to a role for fiat money that is very similar to its role in other absence-of-double-coincidence settings.

To see the similarity, consider a version of those models in which people meet in pairs and in which there is one good per date. When two people meet, suppose that they have available to them some amount of the good that can either be consumed or used as an input (investment) that will give output at the next date, but only at the same location. Moreover, suppose that one and only one of the two people will be at the same location at the next date. If there is no monitoring, then fiat money, despite having a lower real return than investment, can have a beneficial role – the same role it has in other absence-of-double-coincidence settings with no monitoring. That is, the stayer retains all the capital, while the leaver takes some fiat money. The absence of monitoring prevents the leaver from retaining a claim to any of the capital.

Divisibility
Historians of monetary systems and others have often noted that money was generally not available in conveniently small denominations (see, for example, Redish, 2000; Sargent and Velde, 2002). However, until recently no models described how such absence would inhibit trade. Models of pairwise meetings are an obvious candidate: if neither the buyer nor the seller has small change, then trade (even if lotteries are permitted) is inhibited. If the model is to have implications for optimal divisibility, then it should also contain something to limit divisibility. Lee, Wallace and Zhu (2005) assume that there is a direct cost of carrying monetary items that is independent of denomination (that is, carrying thousands of pennies is very costly), while Lee and Wallace (2006) assume costs of producing and maintaining the stock of money that increase with divisibility.

Concluding remarks
Why is it better to make assumptions about meeting patterns, information, and the physical characteristics of potential assets than about which markets are open or the pattern of transaction costs over objects? First, the former lends itself to standard notions of incentive feasibility, which is what we ought to mean by integrating monetary economics with the rest of economics. Second, such an approach meets the proof-of-the-pudding criterion. Compare, for example, the results about inside money that can be obtained by working with the imperfect-monitoring point of view with what can be done with a cash-in-advance model.

But is such foundational work needed to deal with the nuts and bolts of monetary policy? It is generally agreed that open-market operations matter because the medium of exchange is a low-return asset and because the central bank has a monopoly on its supply. Can it be that beneficial management of that monopoly does not depend on how we explain the low return of the medium of exchange?

Finally, can we look forward to a monetary theory that in generality rivals the Arrow–Debreu model? Probably not. A need for a medium of exchange does not arise in every conceivable economy – think of Robinson Crusoe, even after he meets Friday, or of the Arrow–Debreu model. Such a need arises when there is some absence-of-double-coincidence difficulty that cannot be overcome with credit because people cannot commit to future actions and because there is imperfect monitoring. Those features may not lend themselves to a general formulation.

NEIL WALLACE

See also **inside and outside money; money; money and general equilibrium.**

Bibliography

Aiyagari, S. and Williamson, S. 2000. Money and dynamic credit arrangements with private information. *Journal of Economic Theory* 91, 248–79.

Araujo, L. 2004. Social norms and money. *Journal of Monetary Economics* 51, 241–56.

Cavalcanti, R., Erosa, A. and Temzelides, T. 1999. Private money and reserve management in a random matching model. *Journal of Political Economy* 107, 929–45.

Cavalcanti, R. and Wallace, N. 1999. Inside and outside money as alternative media of exchange. *Journal of Money, Credit and Banking* 31, 443–57.

Clower, R.W. 1967. A reconsideration of the microfoundations of monetary theory. *Western Economic Journal* 6, 1–8.

Freeman, S. 1985. Transaction costs and the optimal quantity of money. *Journal of Political Economy* 93, 146–57.

Friedman, M. and Schwartz, A. 1963. *A Monetary History of the United States.* Princeton: Princeton University Press.

Green, E. 1987. Lending and the smoothing of uninsurable income. In *Contractual Arrangements for Intertemporal Trade,* ed. E. Prescott and N. Wallace. Minneapolis: University of Minnesota Press.

Green, E. and Zhou, R. 1998. A rudimentary random-matching model with divisible money and prices. *Journal of Economic Theory* 81, 252–71.

Howitt, P. 2005. Beyond search: fiat money in organized exchange. *International Economic Review* 46, 405–29.

Huggett, M. and Krasa, S. 1996. Money and storage in a differential information economy. *Economic Theory* 8, 191–210.

Kandori, M. 1992. Social norms and community enforcement. *Review of Economic Studies* 59, 63–80.

Kiyotaki, N. and Wright, R. 1989. On money as a medium of exchange. *Journal of Political Economy* 97, 927–54.

Kocherlakota, N. 1998. Money is memory. *Journal of Economic Theory* 81, 232–51.

Kocherlakota, N. 2002. The two-money theorem. *International Economic Review* 43, 333–46.

Kocherlakota, N. and Wallace, N. 1998. Optimal allocations with incomplete record-keeping and no-commitment. *Journal of Economic Theory* 81, 272–89.

Krishna, R.V. 2005. Non-robustness of the cash-in-advance equilibrium in the trading-post model. *Economics Bulletin* 5, 1–5.

Lagos, R. and Wright, R. 2005. A unified framework for monetary theory and policy analysis. *Journal of Political Economy* 113, 463–84.

Lee, M. and Wallace, N. 2006. Optimal divisibility of money when money is costly to produce. *Review of Economic Dynamics* 9, 541–56.

Lee, M., Wallace, N. and Zhu, T. 2005. Modeling denomination structures. *Econometrica* 73, 949–60.

Levine, D. 1990. Asset trading mechanisms and expansionary policy. *Journal of Economic Theory* 54, 148–64.

Magill, M. and Quinzii, M. 2006. *Theory of Incomplete Markets, Volume I.* Cambridge, MA: MIT Press.

Molico, M. 2006. The distribution of money and prices in search equilibrium. *International Economic Review* 47, 701–22.

Monroe, A. 1966. *Monetary Theory Before Adam Smith.* New York: Kelley.

Ostroy, J. 1973. The informational efficiency of monetary exchange. *American Economic Review* 63, 597–610.

Patinkin, D. 1951. The invalidity of classical monetary theory. *Econometrica* 19, 134–51.

Redish, A. 2000. *Bimetallism: An Economic and Historical Analysis.* Cambridge: Cambridge University Press.

Renero, J. 1999. Does and should a commodity medium of exchange have relatively low storage costs? *International Economic Review* 40, 251–64.

Samuelson, P. 1961. *Foundations of Economic Analysis.* Cambridge: Harvard University Press.

Samuelson, P. 1968. What classical and neoclassical monetary theory really was. *Canadian Journal of Economics* 1, 1–15.

Sargent, T. and Velde, F. 2002. *The Big Problem of Small Change.* Princeton: Princeton University Press.

Sargent, T. and Wallace, N. 1983. A model of commodity money. *Journal of Monetary Economics* 12, 163–87.

Shi, S. 1995. Money and prices: a model of search and bargaining. *Journal of Economic Theory* 67, 467–98.

Shi, S. 1997. A divisible search model of money. *Econometrica* 65, 75–102.

Shubik, M. 1973. Commodity money, oligopoly, credit and bankruptcy in a general equilibrium model. *Western Economic Journal* 11, 24–38.

Smith, B. 2002. Taking intermediation seriously. *Journal of Money, Credit and Banking* 35, 1319–58.

Starr, R. and Stinchcombe, M. 1999. Exchange in a network of trading posts. In *Markets, Information and Uncertainty: Essays in Economic Theory in Honor of Kenneth J. Arrow,* ed. G. Chichilnisky. Cambridge: Cambridge University Press.

Townsend, R. 1989. Currency and credit in a private information economy. *Journal of Political Economy* 97, 1323–44.

Trejos, A. and Wright, R. 1995. Search, bargaining, money and prices. *Journal of Political Economy* 103, 118–41.

Wallace, N. and Zhu, T. 2007. Float on a note. *Journal of Monetary Economics* 54, 229–246.

Williamson, S. and Wright, R. 1994. Barter and monetary exchange under private information. *American Economic Review* 84, 104–23.

Zhu, T. 2003. Existence of a monetary steady state in a matching model: indivisible money. *Journal of Economic Theory* 112, 307–24.

Zhu, T. 2005. Existence of a monetary steady state in a matching model: divisible money. *Journal of Economic Theory* 123, 135–60.

financial intermediation

1. Preliminaries and introduction

Writing an article such as this requires making some tough decisions about what to include and what not. Many deserving topics in financial intermediation have not been mentioned at all and I cannot begin to cite all the good papers that deserve reference. Primarily, I rely on two excellent survey articles, one that focuses on theory (Gorton and Winton, 2003), and another that focuses on empirics (Levine, 2005). I received helpful comments from Doug Diamond, Jack Kareken, Ross Levine and Ed Prescott; however, they are totally absolved from any errors that remain.

It is the convention to distinguish between 'financial markets' and 'financial intermediaries'. A financial market is a market in which investors acquire direct claims against ultimate borrowers, usually in the form of debt or equity. A financial intermediary (FI) is a firm that substitutes its own liability for that of some ultimate borrower. That is, an investor lends to the FI and, in turn, the FI lends to an ultimate borrower. I adopt this standard convention even though the distinction is often imprecise. (For example, debt and equity claims are rarely traded directly between the ultimate claimants. Even these are 'intermediated'.) Next, let us turn to some facts about FIs.

The assets of FIs are almost exclusively financial claims. FIs do not have many physical assets, except buildings and computers, and they produce no physical products; thus they are service firms. Important and easily recognizable examples of FIs would include commercial banks, savings and loan associations, credit unions, life insurance firms, property and casualty insurers, consumer finance companies, and mortgage bankers.

Banks largest

Commercial banks (hereafter *banks*) are the most important class of FIs, and this has been true for centuries. In developing economies, banks often play a dominant role and may be, essentially, 'the only game in town'. Even in the United States, with its highly developed financial markets, banks accounted for about 14.2 per cent of financial intermediary assets, which is the largest private share, followed by mutual funds at 12.4 per cent (Board of Governors of the Federal Reserve System, 2005). This size factor helps explain why banks have been the most-studied class of FI by a wide margin. Banks are also especially important and heavily studied because they create money and thus are the conduit for monetary policy. This article follows the norm and devotes a disproportionate amount of its attention to banks.

Heavily regulated

FIs are heavily regulated relative to non-financial firms. Most of this regulation is advertised to promote 'safety and soundness', meaning that its stated intent is to reduce the frequency of failures and other problems in the industry. There are four basic forms of regulation: minimum capital requirements, examination by regulatory authorities, portfolio restrictions on asset holdings, and restrictions on who can own or manage an FI. In many countries, there has been a trend towards less intensive regulation of FIs since the mid-1990s, but in these four forms regulation remains obtrusive relative to most industries.

A large industry

The FI industry is relatively large. Especially in developed economies, the FI sector is a significant part of the economy, with a substantial share of measured output. In the United States, for example, the total value-added of financial intermediaries (essentially profits, wages and salaries) amounts to about 8.1 per cent of GDP. This makes the US FI sector much larger than (say) the agricultural sector, whose share of total value-added is about one per cent (Bureau of Economic Analysis, 2006). Across countries, there is a strong correlation between size and quality of the FI sector and the level of economic development. This relationship is an important topic in development economics but such issues are not considered here.

Organizational form

In most countries the dominant form of organization for FIs is the corporation; however, there are important exceptions. In particular, many FIs are organized as 'mutuals' or 'cooperatives'. With this alternative form of organization, there is no separate class of shareholders or equity owners, as would be the case in a corporation. For example, in mutual life insurance companies the policy holders are also the owners. In mutual savings and loan associations, the depositors are the owners. These alternative organizational forms are common in the United States, Europe and many other parts of the world.

Recent trends

Since the mid-1990s, the FI sector has experienced substantial change. The main trends worldwide are towards consolidation (a smaller number of larger firms), diversification (a larger set of financial activities or 'products' offered at the same FI), and internationalization (operating across borders). Almost every part of the world has participated in these developments, excepting sub-Saharan Africa (De Nicolò et al., 2004).

2. History of thought on financial intermediation

In the 1960s and 1970s, the economic analysis of *FI*s was largely focused on banks, and these were viewed essentially as 'black box' organizations that turned high-powered money (bank reserves) into money. At that time, most intellectual interest in banks derived from their role in creating money, and their being the conduits for monetary policy. In some sense, the study of banking was in those decades incidental to the study of monetary policy and macroeconomics. There had been an earlier literature on FIs that showed great depth of understanding, but in a non-mathematical, descriptive context. Scholars such as Bagehot, Goldsmith and Schumpeter wrote about, and clearly understood, information asymmetries, liquidity, and so forth. When ambitious scholars, such as Tobin (1969) or McKinnon (1973), tried to incorporate FIs into Keynesian models before the profession had invented the mathematical tools to formally model information and liquidity, the crucial intuitive insights about the role of FIs were absent from the models. Thus, finance became money, and money was simply a stock associated with real capital.

In the mid-1980s a new body of thought emerged and was largely attributable to the seminal work of Diamond (1984) and Diamond and Dybvig (1986). Other significant papers at about that same time included Williamson (1986) and Boyd and Prescott (1986). This new approach to studying financial intermediation stressed that FIs are firms that produce valuable economic services of a variety of kinds, and *explicitly modelled the nature of those services*. This literature was careful to model the profit, share price, or utility-maximizing behaviour of FIs subject to appropriate constraints, and much of this work was done in general equilibrium. More importantly, almost all this work and the large literature that followed featured environments with private information – private in the sense that different agents were endowed with different knowledge. This was a major deviation from the previously studied world of Arrow–Debreu, in which markets are frictionless and perfectly competitive, and all relevant information is common knowledge. It was a critical innovation because in the environment of Arrow–Debreu FIs are irrelevant (cannot increase welfare). In that world FIs are just not very interesting to study in a serious way, and they weren't.

Sequence was also very important in the development of the modern FI literature. Since the post-1983 FI literature almost exclusively employed models with private information, this meant that development of the literature depended on, and naturally followed, advances in information economics thanks to the pioneering work of Akerlof, Hurwitz, Stigler and others. Most likely, this is why earlier efforts to force FIs into Keynesian macro models were a failure; the required tools simply had not yet been invented.

In the next section, I briefly review some of the modern FI models developed in the 1980s and subsequently. Later, in Section 5, I discuss some areas in financial intermediation where, in my judgment, there remain important gaps in our knowledge.

3. The theory of financial intermediation

Banks and other FIs are firms that take in funds (FI liabilities) through a hypothetical front door, and put out funds (FI assets) through a hypothetical back door.

They produce no physical products. To survive, they must earn a profit, meaning that the average rate of return on their assets must exceed the average cost of their liabilities. This spread between asset returns and liability costs must be large enough to cover operating costs (primarily wages and salaries), and to earn a rate of return to equity investors. That FIs earn such positive profits has always troubled critics of the industry (of which there have always been many), who may conclude that FIs are somehow exploiting consumers or businesses. In fact, FIs are permitted to earn these positive interest rate spreads because they provide valuable economic services to the economy, and it is costly to provide these valuable economic services. Let us next consider these services.

One important function, offered by banks but not other FIs, is payment services. This is the 'creators of money' banking function that the old literature stressed, virtually to the exclusion of other FI functions. When we need to execute transactions, we use cash and coin, paper checks, credit cards, and wire transfers. All of these transaction tools are generally provided by banks and for obvious reasons they are economically important.

Another important function of FIs is that they are 'brokers' in the sense that they bring together large numbers of ultimate borrowers and lenders. When they bring these groups together, FIs substitute their own liabilities for those of ultimate borrowers, and this is what ultimately distinguishes FIs from financial markets. This process has been given many names in the literature ('asset transformation' is common) and understanding it is key to understanding what FIs actually do. Hypothetically, consider one single bank depositor, a wealthy individual, and one single bank borrower, a small business. The bank depositor might have lent directly to the small business through the stock or bond market. Instead, by assumption, he or she lends to the bank in the form of a deposit. In turn, by assumption, the small business borrows from the bank in the form of a commercial loan. The bank places itself in the middle of the exchange and becomes the counter-party to the others.

Why is this valuable? The answer is that bank liabilities typically have different attributes from ultimate borrower liability attributes, ones that are crafted to be desirable to the bank liability holders. If they are made better off, they are willing to lend at a lower rate than they would have required to lend directly. Thus, this process of asset transformation can, and usually does, make both borrowers and lenders better off.

For banks, the general direction of such asset transformation is well understood: bank liabilities will typically have shorter maturity than bank assets, and will be more liquid and less risky. As will become apparent, a key ingredient to this process is that the banks borrow from a large number of creditors, and lends to a large number of borrowers.

Shorter maturity
Bank liabilities often have shorter average maturity (or duration) than bank assets, and *ceteris paribus* this may make bank liabilities relatively more attractive to savers.

Such maturity mismatching exposes banks to an interest rate lottery and the risk that interest rates will increase, in which case they will suffer capital losses. Bank creditors are partially protected against interest rate risk by the bank's equity, at least until that is exhausted. The degree of interest rate risk exposure naturally depends on the magnitude of the asset–liability maturity mismatch, and on how volatile are interest rates. In the 1970s, the US savings and loan (S&L) industry experienced massive losses due to interest rate risk, losses so large as to bankrupt much of the industry as well as its government insurer, the Federal Savings and Loan Insurance Corp (FSLIC). The S&Ls' maturity mismatch was substantial, and interest rates had become extremely volatile by historical standards. However, the savings and loan industry should not be blamed for this sad experience. Government regulations essentially forced this industry to borrow short and lend long.

Since the mid-1990 banks and other FIs have become clever in finding ways to hedge interest rate risk in the forward, futures and swap markets. (Of course, someone still has to bear the aggregate risk.) Also, there is some evidence that, in the United States at least, FIs have in recent years become less willing to expose themselves to interest rate risk. As a practical matter, however, it is difficult to accurately measure the maturity mismatch of banks, and standard duration methods may not work very well for this industry. That's because a substantial proportion of bank liabilities are in the form of demand (checking) deposits. For these liabilities, the technical maturity is instantaneous but the true maturity is much longer, depends on economic conditions, and must be empirically estimated.

More liquid

Bank liabilities, especially deposits, are more liquid than bank assets. This is another desirable form of asset transformation since, *ceteris paribus*, lenders like to hold liquid assets. The liquidity provision function has been heavily studied by scholars, and the seminal reference on the topic is Diamond and Dybvig (1986). Now, liquidity is hard to define, let alone understand, and it may help to consider a simple theoretical environment, similar in some ways to the more complicated environment studied by Diamond and Dybvig (1986). Imagine a world in which there are only two assets: gold coins and land. By assumption, gold coins are perfectly liquid and can be spent at any time but earn no rate of return. Land, on the other hand, is highly productive but illiquid. It is hard to sell land in an emergency, and possibly it can't be sold at all. All agents in this economy have a known, say one per cent, chance of an 'emergency', the occurrence of which is independent across agents. In an emergency, agents desperately want to have all their wealth immediately so they can consume it. Now, consider the problem facing individual agents. If they put all their wealth in coins (land) they will do well 1 (99) per cent of the time; however, they will do very badly 99 (1) percent of the time. Common sense suggests that the best strategy will be to split up their holdings, and if you guessed that you would be right at least for most preferences. Even then, however, agents are not doing as well as they potentially could in either state of the world.

Next, assume a bank is organized, which offers each individual a deposit account that can be *redeemed in gold coins on demand*. Further, assume the bank puts 1 per cent of its assets in gold coins and 99 per cent in land. Now, if the bank deals with a sufficiently large number of depositors, it will have enough coins to just cover withdrawals and all the remaining can be invested in highly productive land. Everyone is better off than they could have done on their own account.

This kind of an arrangement is usually referred to as 'fractional reserve banking'. The key to its smashing success is diversification across a large number of depositors, and the fact that depositor withdrawal demands are independent. Now, as Diamond and Dybvig are quick to point out, this idealized solution may not always work out in practice. Suppose, for example, that emergency withdrawals become correlated, perhaps because there is a war. Then the bank can easily run out of coins, fail on its obligations, and land must be inefficiently liquidated. Even worse, just a false rumour of war could send too many depositors to the bank and cause it to fail. This sort of occurrence is called a 'bank run' and these have been quite common both historically and in recent times. In an imperfect world where withdrawals may be correlated and bank runs are possible, every bank faces a fundamental and unpleasant trade-off: if it holds a high fraction of gold coins (reserves) risk of insolvency will be low, but the average rate of return on its assets will be low. If it holds a high fraction of land (earning assets) its average rate of return on assets will be high, but its risk of insolvency will be high. There is a large literature on this topic, much of which is referenced in Gorton and Winton (2003).

Less risky
Bank liabilities are on average less risky than bank assets, and obviously this tends to make bank liabilities *ceteris paribus* more attractive. Now, bank liabilities can be less risky than the representative bank loan for a variety of reasons. One is that banks often place some fraction of their assets in default-risk-free government securities. A second reason is that banks raise part of their funds in the form of equity, and the bank's shareholders must suffer a total loss before liability holders lose. A third reason is that banks hold portfolios of different kinds of loans that are diversified by industry and geography, so that their loan portfolio is less risky than its individual components. A fourth reason is that in most countries bank deposits are fully or partially insured by government.

In addition, banks are very good at determining to whom to lend, and in setting loan terms for those who are funded. This topic has been heavily studied in the FI literature and the reader can find many studies under the headings 'adverse selection', 'sorting' and 'screening' in Gorton and Winton (2003). In most of these models, some loan applicants are better credit risks than others, applicants know their own types, and are willing to misrepresent (say they're good when they're bad). FIs do not know the applicants' types, although it is conventional to assume that everyone knows the underlying distribution of applicant types. The FI's objective is to accept (reject) good (bad) applicants where possible. In some but not in all cases, it is possible to adroitly choose terms of lending such that good applicants voluntarily sign up, and bad applicants withdraw. In other cases, the best strategy is simply to accept (reject) all applicants.

Another important aspect of lending, and an aspect at which FIs excel, is monitoring borrowers after they have received the money. This '*ex post* monitoring' has also been heavily studied in the FI literature. Once they have the money, borrowers may take actions that reduce their probability of repaying, or events beyond their control may have the same effect. To protect their interests lenders normally pre-specify loan covenants that state what happens in such cases, and they monitor borrowers to enforce these covenants. An example that homeowners will understand is a residential mortgage: to protect its interests, the lender must be sure that property taxes are being paid, and that the house is fully insured. Now, it is often the case that loans are large relative to the wealth of individual agents in the economy. This naturally occurs because many production technologies exhibit economies of scale. For example, an automobile plant must be of a particular size to be efficient, and few if any agents can fund such an investment with their own wealth. Therefore, to fund a loan often requires obtaining financing from several agents simultaneously. Unless FIs are present there is a coordination problem among the several lenders, and it is a problem first studied by Diamond (1984) and Williamson (1986).

Monitoring of borrowers is costly, and no one wants to do it if they don't have to. Now, for simplicity, assume that there are just two lenders for a given loan, lender A and lender B. Now, A (B) may assume that B (A) will monitor, in which case neither lender actually does. This is obviously undesirable because their interests are not being protected. Alternatively, lender A and lender B might both be conservative, assume the other is unreliable, and monitor themselves. In that case there would be redundant monitoring which is unnecessary and wasteful. Clearly, what is needed is an arrangement in which all lenders agree to have *ex post* monitoring done by a single, efficient 'delegated monitor'. What is critical, if such an arrangement is to work, is that the delegated monitor finds it in its own interests (incentive compatible) to actually do the work as promised. Otherwise, it might be necessary to monitor the monitor, which obviously would be inefficient, too. Diamond (1984) and Williamson (1986) showed that efficient *ex post* monitoring can be achieve by a bank that pools funds from many depositors and uses the proceeds to make many loans.

Summary
In a world in which different agents have different information sets FIs earn a positive interest spread between their average asset returns and average liability costs, in return for providing valuable services. They are brokers between ultimate borrowers and ultimate lenders, and they provide payments services. They transform ultimate financial claims in the sense that their liabilities have different attributes from their assets. Typically, their liabilities are shorter in maturity, more liquid and less risky; thus, such liabilities are more desirable to savers. This process of 'asset transformation' is not without risk. FIs are exposed to interest rate risk and particularly vulnerable to

unexpected interest rate increases. We discussed the case of the US savings and loan industry and its devastating exposure to interest rate increases. Due to their liquidity provision, banks are exposed to the risk of bank runs. Bank runs have been common historically, and still have occurred with some frequency in the modern wave of banking crises. Finally, all FIs are exposed to default risk when their loans or other investments do not pay off in a timely manner.

4. An aside on equilibrium credit rationing

When economists began studying intermediation environments with private information, in which agents could withhold the facts, intentionally deceive one another, and so on, all manner of new and interesting results were obtained. One seminal model of financial intermediation featured an outcome called 'equilibrium credit rationing' (Stiglitz and Weiss, 1981). In such cases, at the equilibrium rate of interest there is excess demand in the sense that some would-be borrowers are denied access to credit. This is quite at odds with a classical market equilibrium, and immediately raises the question, 'why don't lenders just increase the rate of interest to a level at which demand equals supply?' A variety of answers to this question can be found in the literature, reflecting the different environments that have been shown to produce equilibrium credit rationing. For one example, assume that credit applicants are of two types, good and bad, and that lenders take account of borrower heterogeneity in their rate setting. Then, it can be the case that for sufficiently low interest rates both good and bad will borrow, but above some threshold rate r^* good types become unwilling to borrow. In such cases lenders may find it optimal to set the rate at r^* even though there is excess demand at that rate. A second example is an environment with moral hazard in the form of a bad action that borrowers may take *ex post* (such as increasing the risk of their investment project). For some parameterizations, when rates are below a threshold r^+, borrowers will not take the bad action, but above r^+ they will. As in the case above, it may be optimal for lenders to set the rate at r^+, thus avoiding the bad action, and resorting to credit rationing.

These first two environments are with private information; however, a third one can result in equilibrium credit rationing even when all information is public. Imagine that default by borrowers results in a deadweight loss – for example, an out-of-pocket bankruptcy cost. Then, the probability of costly default directly depends on the rate of interest, and the higher that rate is the higher the default probability is. Increasing the rate of interest increases the expected rate of return to lenders in good (non-default) states, but also increases the probability of default which is costly to both parties. Depending on the distribution of possible returns facing borrowers, it may be that raising the rate beyond some threshold r^- is futile in the sense that the marginal cost exceeds the marginal benefit. In these cases, rates above r^- are harmful to both parties and will never be observed in equilibrium. Yet it may also be true that r-plus is too low to clear the market, and equilibrium credit rationing will again be observed (Williamson, 1986).

Arguably, equilibrium credit rationing is a topic where theory leads measurement. There has not been a lot of good empirical work on credit rationing per se, primarily because it is so hard to do right. Credit rationing equilibria are off the usual demand and supply curves that econometricians like to estimate, and they may exhibit nasty jumps, discontinuities, and so on. If the theorists are right, however, and credit rationing is popping up all over, more empirical work would be useful, especially in the area of finance and development.

5. Regulation

Banks and other FIs are, almost without exception, rather heavily regulated. This is true in virtually all countries and has been true for centuries. There are at least three reasons for this special and obtrusive regulatory treatment. First, banks are the conduit for monetary policy, and problems in banking are likely to interfere with monetary policy conduct. Second, it is widely believed that bank failures may result in negative externalities (social costs). And third, governments may find it irresistible to control a critical industry that creates money and allocates a large fraction of investment capital. Some recent work has emphasized the importance of political economy issues for regulation, in particular arguing that it is unlikely that bank regulation can contribute positively to social welfare in economies with weak and/or corrupt governments (Barth, Caprio and Levine, 2006).

The Great Depression was a difficult time for banks in the United States and many other countries, and during the late 1920s and early 1930s there were literally thousands of bank failures worldwide. Many of these were associated with bank runs and panics. In response, many nations substantially beefed up their regulation of FIs and put in mechanisms such as deposit insurance to reduce or eliminate the prevalence of bank runs. For example, the Federal Deposit Insurance Corporation was created by US federal legislation in 1933. Beginning in the mid-1930s, the industry stabilized (at least in developed nations), and went through a period of relative calm that lasted for about three decades. Many observers believed that these policy interventions had solved the problem of instability in banking; but that was not to be. Beginning in roughly the mid-1960s, a new wave of banking crises affected well over 100 nations. Banking crises – some of them severe – have been recently experienced in developing and developed economies alike.

No one knows for sure what has caused this interesting historical sequence of events in banking, but many scholars have emphasized that *policy interventions intended to stabilize the industry may have actually had opposite effect.* In most countries, banks have access to emergency borrowing from the government (a Discount Window), and have some form of government insurance to protect depositors. Additionally, there is a common practice known as 'too big to fail' whereby governments will prop up their very largest FIs if they get into trouble. This package of interventions is widely referred to as 'the safety net', and it has been very heavily studied. Most of the literature on this topic concludes that, whatever the benefits of a safety net, it also distorts bank incentives in a perverse way. Depositors and other bank creditors don't care how much risk the bank takes (they are protected by government), and normal market risk-constraining mechanisms become ineffective.

In the presence of a safety net, banks may have an incentive to take on more risk *ceteris paribus* than otherwise; indeed, they may even become risk lovers who intentionally seek out investments with low expected returns and high variance. It's not hard to see why this is so. If an FI has very risky investments and these payoff, all the profits go to FI shareholders. If they don't payoff the FI goes broke, but the resulting losses are mostly absorbed by government. In essence, this is a 'heads I win tails you lose' gamble. Perhaps the most dramatic evidence of this distortion turned up during the U.S. S&L crisis. At that time, many S&Ls were obviously bankrupt but could not be closed down since their federal deposit insurer, the FSLIC, had run out of money. Many such institutions gambled for redemption by taking extreme risks. If they were lucky enough they might survive, and if not ... well, they were already broke.

As of 2007, solving the problems associated with the safety net is arguably the most vexing policy issue facing FI regulators and scholars of that industry. Many regulatory interventions, such as restrictions on asset holdings, attempt to control FIs' behaviour but do not deal with the fundamental distortion of risk incentives. Other regulatory interventions such as capital regulation are intended to reduce FIs' distortion of risk incentives, but may not be effective (Hellmann, Murdoch and Stiglitz, 2000). FIs have a natural tendency to try to get around all these regulations, pursuing strategies that render the regulations ineffective. On the other hand, getting rid of the safety net would have its own risks, and it is far from obvious how governments could ever credibly commit to a policy of no FI bailouts. This issue is probably best described as important but unfinished business.

6. Trends in recent research, and open research questions

1. As discussed earlier, the modelling of financial intermediaries has come a long way since the mid-1980s, and most modern macroeconomic models reflect that reality. Even so, there is still recent work that reflects old ways of thinking about FIs. To make this point I provide just one example: the ongoing discussions of the so-called 'Friedman Rule'. This rule, in simplest form, calls for a monetary policy that produces a rate of *deflation* such that the real rate of return on bank reserves equals the rate of interest on real investment. Then, it is argued, banks will voluntarily hold all their assets in the form of reserves, and bank runs, crises, and so on will never happen. Bruce Smith (whose death in 2003 was a great loss to economics) makes it beautifully clear that this once-beguiling idea should be relegated to the history of economic thought (Smith, 2002). Application of the Friedman rule may indeed result in risk-free banks. However, except for the provision of payments services, it precludes banks from making any of their valuable economic contributions detailed by Diamond (1984), Diamond and Dybvig (1986) and others, and as discussed earlier.

2. Boyd and Prescott (1986) have a theorem that financial intermediary coalitions composed of large numbers of agents can support allocations that cannot be supported with decentralized markets, and are efficient subject to resource and incentive constraints. As lamented by Green and Zhou (2001), virtually all subsequent theoretical research on FIs has studied decentralized (market) environments. Now, this could be just a matter of preferences amongst theorists as to the most interesting and tractable environment in which to study FIs. It's not, in my opinion, and this topic is of more than theoretical interest. Boyd–Prescott financial intermediary coalitions look (at some high level of abstraction) like mutual or cooperative FIs. It is fact that over several continents and many centuries mutual FIs seem to endogenously spring up with great regularity. When a class of arrangements is 'revealed preferred' so often, there is probably a good reason for it. There has been some theoretical research on this topic, but arguably not enough.

3. Virtually all of our general equilibrium models with FIs force agents into discrete silos: for example, an agent must choose to become a producer (borrower), a consumer (lender), or an FI. In reality we often observe organizations that are both producers and financial intermediaries at the same time (for example, General Electric or Cargill). Moreover, we sometimes see firms radically change their blend of activities. For example, in a few years Enron evolved from a production firm to a financial intermediary. I am aware of only one study (Bhanot and Mello, 2006) that allows, in a serious way, for endogenous choice of FI *and* non-FI activities in the same organization. More work along these lines could be useful.

4. As discussed, banks, even very simple ones, perform a number of economic functions *simultaneously*: brokerage, payments service provision, maturity transformation, liquidity provision, and default risk reduction. This is what we observe in reality and there is undoubtedly a reason. Yet our theoretical models tend to isolate these economic functions and look at them one at a time. Only a few studies have seriously looked at the jointness in providing even two services simultaneously (Kasyap, Rajan and Stein, 2002). This separation of functions is done for tractability, and even then our models can become complex. Putting all of these features in a model simultaneously becomes technically daunting, but it needs to be done. There are undoubtedly interesting interactions or synergisms among these activities, and we cannot learn about those by studying them individually.

J.H. BOYD

Bibliography

Barth, J., Caprio, G. and Levine, R. 2006. *Rethinking Bank Regulation: Till Angels Govern.* Cambridge: Cambridge University Press.
Bhanot, K. and Mello, A. 2006. Should production and trading activities be separated? Working paper, University of Wisconsin.
Board of Governors of the Federal Reserve System. 2005. *Flow of Funds Accounts.* Online. Available at http://www.federalreserve.gov/RELEASES/z1/, accessed 16 January 2007.

Boyd, J.H. and Prescott, E.C. 1986. Financial intermediary coalitions. *Journal of Economic Theory* 2, 211–32.

Bureau of Economic Analysis. 2006. *Industry Economic Accounts*. Online. Available at http://bea.gov/bea/dn2/home/annual_industry.htm, accessed 3 February 2007.

De Nicolò, G., Bartholomew, P., Zaman, J. and Zephirin, M. 2004. Bank consolidation, internationalization and conglomeration: trends and implications for financial risk. *Financial Markets, Institutions & Instruments* 13(4), 173–217.

Diamond, D. 1984. Financial intermediation and delegated monitoring. *Review of Economic Studies* 51, 393–414.

Diamond, D. and Dybvig, P. 1986. Banking theory, deposit insurance, and bank regulation. *Journal of Business* 59, 55–68.

Gorton, G. and Winton, A. 2003. Financial intermediation. In *Handbooks in the Economics of Finance, Volume 1A: Corporate Finance*, ed. G. Constantinides, M. Harris and R. Stulz. Amsterdam: North-Holland.

Green, E. and Zhou, R. 2001. Financial intermediation regime and efficiency in a Boyd–Prescott economy. *Carnegie-Rochester Series on Public Policy* 54, 117–29.

Hellmann, T., Murdoch, K. and Stiglitz, J. 2000. Liberalization, moral hazard in banking and prudential regulation: are capital requirements enough? *American Economic Review* 90, 147–65.

Kasyap, A., Rajan, R. and Stein, J. 2002. Banks as liquidity providers: an explanation of the coexistence of lending and deposit-taking. *Journal of Finance* 57, 33–74.

Levine, R. 2005. Finance and growth: theory and evidence. In *Handbook of Economic Growth*, ed. P. Aghion and S. Durlauf. Amsterdam: North-Holland.

McKinnon, R. 1973. *Money and Capital in Economic Development*. Washington, DC: Brookings Institution.

Smith, B.D. 2002. Monetary policy, banking crises and the Friedman rule. *American Economic Review* 92, 128–34.

Stiglitz, J. and Weiss, A. 1981. Credit rationing in markets with imperfect information. *American Economic Review* 71, 393–410.

Tobin, J. 1969. A general equilibrium approach to monetary theory. *Journal of Money, Credit, and Banking* 2, 461–72.

Williamson 1986. Costly monitoring, financial intermediation, and equilibrium credit rationing. *Journal of Monetary Economics* 18, 159–79.

free banking era

Imagine the US economy without Federal Reserve notes, that is, without a uniform currency. Instead, imagine that the currency consists of notes issued by privately owned banks and that are redeemable in specie on demand. And imagine that to enter the banking business is relatively easy, so that the notes of hundreds of banks exist. And imagine as you travel around the country, notes of out-of-town banks are not readily accepted as means of payment at par because the solvency of such banks is difficult to ascertain.

How well would such a banking system function? In particular, with free entry into banking, would banks not have an incentive to over-issue their notes, leaving the public holding worthless pieces of paper when the banks failed? And would trade not be difficult without the existence of a uniform currency? Indeed, a reading of historical accounts of the so-called free banking era – the 26 years from 1837 to 1863, a period when entry into banking was relatively free and banks issued their own notes – would lead to this conclusion. The prevailing view of this period, at least until the mid-1970s, was that allowing such freedom in banking was a mistake. However, a more recent examination of the era reveals that while the free banking system was not without its problems, free banks and their noteholders fared much better than has often been portrayed.

The beginning of free banking

Prior to 1837, to establish a bank in the United States was a very cumbersome, and at times political, process. Individuals who wanted to start a bank had to obtain a charter from the legislature of the state in which they wanted to operate. Beginning in 1837, some states reformed their bank-chartering systems so that entry into the banking industry would be easier. States tempered the goal of easy entry with another goal: to provide the public with a safe bank currency. Most states attempted to reach these goals by enacting what were called *free banking laws*.

The first free banking law was proposed in New York. Its provisions openly aimed at both easy entry and safety. The law allowed anyone to operate a bank as long as two basic requirements were met: (*a*) all notes the bank issued had to be backed by state bonds deposited at the state auditor's office and (*b*) all notes had to be redeemable on demand at par, or face, value. If the bank failed to redeem notes presented for payment, however, the auditor would close the bank, sell the bonds, and pay off the noteholders. If the bond sale did not generate enough specie to redeem the bank's notes at par, noteholders had additional protection by having first legal claim to the bank's other assets. Thus, free banking meant free *entry* into banking; it did not mean laissez-faire banking.

New York's proposed free banking law became the basic blueprint for the free banking laws in other states. (Michigan actually passed a free banking law modelled on the New York proposal a year before the legislation was passed there.) Table 1 shows which states passed free banking laws and when the laws passed. Note that of the states that passed such legislation, most did so in the 1850s.

The experience

One effect of the free banking laws was to increase the number of banks. In Michigan, for example, the number of banks rose from ten before the law was passed in March 1837 to 33 one year later. In New York the number of banks rose from 97 before the law was passed in March 1838 to 162 three years later. And Indiana, Illinois, and Wisconsin, which each had only one bank in existence when their free banking laws were passed, saw 13, 41, and 15 new banks established respectively within two years. Minnesota had no banks when its free banking law was passed; it saw 16 banks established within one year. In total, of the almost 2,300 banks that existed in the United States prior to the Civil War, slightly more than three-eighths were established or operated under a free banking law (Weber, 2006).

Free banking, however, must also be judged by the laws' second objective – by how many banks survived and provided their communities with a stable source of banking

Table 1   US states with and without free banking laws by 1860

States with free banking laws	Year law passed	States without free banking laws
Michigan	1837[a]	Arkansas
Georgia	1838[b]	California
New York	1838	Delaware
Alabama	1849[b]	Kentucky
New Jersey	1850	Maine
Illinois	1851	Maryland
Massachusetts	1851[b]	Mississippi
Ohio	1851[c]	Missouri
Vermont	1851[b]	New Hampshire
Connecticut	1852	North Carolina
Indiana	1852	Oregon
Tennessee	1852[b]	Rhode Island
Wisconsin	1852	South Carolina
Florida	1853[b]	Texas
Louisiana	1853	Virginia
Iowa	1858[b]	
Minnesota	1858	
Pennsylvania	1860[b]	

[a]Michigan prohibited free banking after 1839 and then passed a new free banking law in 1857.
[b]According to Rockoff, very little free banking was done under the laws of these states.
[c]In 1845, Ohio passed a law that provided for the establishment of 'independent banks' with a bond-secured note issue.
Source: Rockoff (1975, pp. 3, 125–30).

services, especially a safe currency. Measured by this criterion, free banking is generally considered a failure.

Michigan's disastrous experience with free banking is probably the most famous. By the end of 1839, less than two years after its free banking law was passed, all but four of Michigan's free banks closed (Rockoff, 1975, p. 96). Although explicit loss data do not exist, it has been estimated that the total loss to Michigan's noteholders was as high as four million dollars. This would have been nearly 45 per cent of Michigan's annual income in 1840 (Rockoff, 1975, pp. 17–48). Other states' experiences with free banking, while not as famous as Michigan's, were almost as bad. Of the 16 free banks that opened under Minnesota's 1858 law, for example, 11 closed by 1863. And many that closed left their noteholders with very little.

However, some states had positive experiences with free banking. New York had very few free bank failures and noteholder losses after 1843. Indiana had much the same record after 1854. And all the failures and losses experienced by Wisconsin free banks occurred in 1861 after the Civil War had begun and the bonds issued by Southern states had greatly depreciated in value.

Free banking was not wildcat banking

According to some historians and economists writing about this period (see, for example, Hammond, 1985, p. 618; Knox, 1903, p. 747; and Luckett, 1980, p. 242), the losses experienced under free banking were due to fraudulent banking practices by so-called wildcat banks. These were banks that purportedly located redemption offices in remote areas, issued notes far in excess of what they planned to redeem, and then disappeared, leaving the public with notes worth considerably less than their original value.

Although some wildcat banking may have occurred, this explanation is not appropriate for most free banking experience because the data do not support it. Wildcat banks supposedly stayed in business for only a few months, after which time their noteholders sustained losses. However, in New York, Indiana, Wisconsin, and Minnesota – four states that were supposed to have had many wildcats – free banks were generally not short-lived.

Most losses to the holders of free bank notes were due not to fraud, but to capital losses suffered by the banks because of several substantial drops in the prices of the state bonds that were required to back the notes they issued. Moreover, while these declines in bond prices may have been induced by any number of economic developments, they were not induced by wildcat banks.

Summary and conclusion

The free banking era was a time when entry into banking was virtually unrestrained, when banks could issue their own currency and when the government did not insure banks. It was also a time when many banks closed and many noteholders reportedly suffered. An early view of this period is that free entry led to banks over-issuing notes, resulting in large losses for noteholders. More recent research has shown that this view is not correct. Although free bank failures and noteholder losses did occur, these were generally due to capital losses banks suffered when the prices of the state bonds backing their notes fell. In general, they were not due to note over-issuance or fraudulent banking practices.

ARTHUR J. ROLNICK AND WARREN E. WEBER

See also **monetary economics, history of.**

Bibliography

Hammond, B. 1985. *Banks and Politics in America*. Princeton: Princeton University Press.
Knox, J.J. 1903. *A History of Banking in the United States*. New York: Bradford Rhodes.
Luckett, D.G. 1980. *Money and Banking*. New York: McGraw-Hill.
Rockoff, H. 1974. The free banking era: a reexamination. *Journal of Money, Credit and Banking* 6, 141–67.
Rockoff, H. 1975. *The Free Banking Era: A Re-examination*. Dissertations in American History. New York: Arno Press. Ph.D. dissertation, University of Chicago, 1972.
Rolnick, A.J. and Weber, W.E. 1983. New evidence on the free banking era. *American Economic Review* 73, 1080–91.
Rolnick, A.J. and Weber, W.E. 1984. The causes of free bank failures: a detailed examination. *Journal of Monetary Economics* 14, 267–91.
Weber, W.E. 2006. Early state banks in the United States: how many were there and when did they exist? *Journal of Economic History* 66, 433–55.

German hyperinflation

German hyperinflation after the First World War originated in the decision of July/ August 1914 to suspend the gold convertibility of the mark and associated gold-reserve requirements. As with other hyperinflations, this one was irregular. German wholesale prices slightly more than doubled during the First World War. By February 1920 the ratio to 1913 prices was about 17, but then fell, irregularly, to a ratio of 13 in May 1921. After May 1921 inflation resumed and between then and June 1922 average monthly inflation was 13.5 per cent; in the following 12 months it reached 60 per cent (including a short cessation in early 1923 as the Reichsbank temporarily pegged the exchange rate), and 32,700 per cent or about 20 per cent per day between June and November 1923. The mark was stabilized in later November 1923 at one million millionth of its 1913 dollar exchange rate. Although only the period from June 1922 was 'hyperinflationary' (above 50 per cent per month), this period cannot be studied independently of the preceding inflationary history (Holtfrerich, 1986).

Contemporary explanation was highly politicized (Kindleberger, 1984a). The 'quantity theory' was adopted, especially by the French, to prove the agency of the German authorities in causing the inflation, allegedly in order to undermine the reparations regime. The official German counter-explanation was a variant of the 'quantity theory' known as the 'balance of payments' theory, whereby a budget deficit and its monetization followed inexorably from the exchange-rate collapse, which they blamed on the Treaty of Versailles and its reparations demands (see Williams, 1922). The quantity theory presumed a constant velocity of circulation, which was at variance with the facts (Graham, 1930; Bresciani-Turroni, 1931); an intellectually satisfying resolution of this puzzle awaited Cagan's (1956) embodiment of 'expected inflation' as an argument in the demand-for-money function. The rational expectations' revolution, however, argued that Cagan's formulation of price expectations as a weighted average of past inflation was rational only if the money supply were endogenously determined (Sargent and Wallace, 1973).

The question whether German hyperinflation was a 'bubble' divorced from monetary 'fundamentals' continues to be discussed, but the evidence remains inconclusive (for example, Chan, Lee and Woo, 2003). The centrality of fiscal policy and seigniorage to the generation of the German hyperinflation is generally agreed. It is the starting point of Webb's (1989) analysis. The Reichsbank, considering Germany still effectively in a state of war, subordinated its monetary policy to the financing of the Reich's expenditure. Though scarcely stable, a real deficit persisted throughout the inflation, albeit with some tendency to decline as inflation accelerated. The private sector's real investment in debt diminished as its belief weakened in the sufficiency of future budget surpluses to meet the state's contractual debt-servicing obligations (including reparations). The private sector inferred from this insufficiency that prices would rise to reduce the real value of this debt-servicing, and converted its non-monetary debt into money and money into goods. This forced greater monetization of the budget deficit; and the conjuncture of the declining real demand for money with rising nominal supply made the public expectation of inflation self-realizing. 'Unpleasant monetarist arithmetic' would probably have produced an analogous result even with Reichsbank independence (Holtferich, 1986, pp. 172 ff.).

Frenkel (1977) sought direct evidence of inflationary expectations from the forward discount on the mark in the London foreign exchange market; but, awkwardly from an analytical point of view, until July 1922 the mark sold at a forward *premium*. Webb argued that this reflected the animal spirits of – mainly foreign – speculators with their diversified portfolios, rather than inflationary expectations; these he inferred from the rate of shrinkage of the real value of government debt. On this basis he could link the major shifts in the rate of inflation with announcements of fiscal 'news' that prompted state debt-holders into revising their previous estimates of future real budget surpluses. Plausible connexions of this sort can be made for November 1918 (the Armistice), May 1919 (publication of the Treaty of Versailles), May 1921 (announcement of the Allies' London Reparations Plan) and June 1922 (refusal of a bankers' committee headed by J.P. Morgan Jr. to recommend a loan to Germany except on the – at that point unlikely – condition of a reduction in Allied reparations claims).

Webb explained the sudden cessation of inflation in March 1920 by a conjectural calculation that the expected revenues from the new federal direct taxation introduced by Finance Minister M. Erzberger in 1919 now harmonized with debt obligations (though the reparations obligation was still undefined). He explained the stabilization in November 1923 with reference to the cessation, in late September, of state-subsidized 'passive resistance' against the Franco-Belgian occupation of the Ruhr; to the imposition of indexed tax liabilities from October (see Franco, 1990); to the appointment of the Dawes Committee to propose a temporary rescheduling of reparations; possibly to awareness that the Reichsbank was at last threatening to use the independence granted it in May 1922 to cease monetizing the deficit from the end of 1923; and to the successful pegging of the exchange rate against the dollar in mid-November. These developments have to be assumed to have influenced the minds of state debt-holders more than the evidence of the disintegration of the Reich, the collapse of the majority coalition on 3 November, and the lack of clarity, in the hour of France's triumph, over what level of reparations' revision would actually be agreed. Perhaps, after the trauma of hyperinflation, the 'credibility bar' over which stabilization policy had to jump was much lowered (Horsman, 1988, p. 33).

The 'Structural School' (Kindleberger, 1984b; see Alesina and Drazen, 1991) argues that domestic social conflict, especially on the labour market and partly operating through non-budgetary channels, was central to the hyperinflation. Burdekin and Burkitt (1996) focus on the hugely increased discounting of private-sector bills at the Reichsbank from mid-1922, in order (in their view) to pre-finance inflationary wage settlements. Prior to this, foreign speculation in the mark had financed bank lending to business at negative real rates of interest, so that domestic distributional conflicts could be assuaged out of the wealth of foreigners (Holtfrerich, 1986, pp. 279 ff.). However, once the forward exchange rate flipped over to discount in July 1922, in the absence of Reichsbank accommodation business would have had to pay positive real interest rates, with a correspondingly deflationary effect.

Webb (1989, p. 42) denied that inflation was deliberate government policy. The only reason that the stabilization after March 1920 did not 'stick' was that the Allies' 'London Plan' of May 1921 derailed it; without this element, the Erzberger fiscal reforms were propelling the budget towards surplus. It was irrational to operate in a hyperinflationary zone when, according to the theoretical consensus, real seigniorage revenues would have been greater at a lower rate of inflation. Webb also accepted the 'structural' case that parliamentary conditions and civil-service wage pressure prevented further fiscal reform before autumn 1923 (see Kunz, 1986). Cukierman (1988), however, argued for government agency in the inflationary process on the grounds that, due to increasing lags of inflationary expectations behind actual inflation, it could temporarily increase its seigniorage by increasing inflation, even if at the expense of lower seigniorage in the longer run. The foreshortened time preference of the Reich during its acute diplomatic crisis with the Allies made this rational. Only when expected inflation entered the zone where seigniorage revenues declined – partly due to substitution of other currencies (Bernholz, 1995) – did the government stabilize. Cukierman combines this with an argument that the government and the electorate in any case preferred lower long-run seigniorage revenues as these curbed the reparations rapacity of the Allies.

Holtfrerich (1986, pp. 203–05) argued that the inflation counterfactually raised output by neutralizing the effects of the global post-war slump, and equalized income and wealth (but see Kindleberger, 1994). However, the ultra-low unemployment of the period was also partly due to vast labour hoarding by public enterprises, dating from the demobilization, and to a trough in participation rates. Bresciani-Turroni (1931, pp. 197–203, 403) argued that the inflation caused misallocation of investment; but Holtfrerich argued (1986, pp. 205–06) that not this misallocation but the deflationary gold-standard regime from 1924 caused the low-capacity utilization of the later 1920s. However, Lindenlaub's (1985) archival investigation concluded that, except for industries receiving government compensation for treaty losses, real fixed investment was minimal (see Fischer, Sahay and Végh, 2002).

Sargent (1986, pp. 40 ff.) argued that the credibility of the German stabilization made it virtually costless. But Dornbusch (1987) regarded the willingness to make monetary policy hurt from November 1923 to June 1924 as necessary to establishing credibility. The 'stabilization boom' of the second half of 1924 and the delayed but sharp year-long recession from June 1925 may roughly replicate recent high-inflationary experience (Fischer, Sahay and Végh, 2002).

THEO BALDERSTON

See also **hyperinflation; quantity theory of money.**

Bibliography

Alesina, A. and Drazen, A. 1991. Why are stabilizations delayed? *American Economic Review* 81, 1170–88.

Bernholz, P. 1995. Currency competition, inflation, Gresham's law and exchange rate. In *Great Inflations of the 20th Century. Theories, Polices, Evidence*, ed. P. Siklos. Aldershot: Edward Elgar.

Bresciani-Turroni, C. 1931. *The Economics of Inflation: A Study of Currency Depreciation in Post-War Germany*. London: Allen & Unwin, 1937.

Burdekin, R.C.K. and Burkitt, P. 1996. *Distributional Conflict and Inflation: Theoretical and Historical Perspectives*. Basingstoke: Macmillan.

Cagan, P. 1956. The monetary dynamics of hyperinflation. In *Studies in the Quantity Theory of Money*, ed. M. Friedman. Chicago: University of Chicago Press.

Chan, H.L., Lee, S.K. and Woo, K.-Y. 2003. An empirical investigation of price and exchange-rate bubbles during the interwar European hyperinflations. *International Review of Economics* 12, 327–44.

Cukierman, A. 1988. Rapid inflation: deliberate policy or miscalculation? *Carnegie-Rochester Series on Public Policy* 29, 11–76.

Dornbusch, R. 1987. Lessons from the German inflation experience of the 1920s. In *Macroeconomics and Finance. Essays in Honour of Franco Modigliani*, ed. R. Dornbusch, S. Fischer and J. Bossons. Cambridge, MA: MIT Press.

Fischer, S., Sahay, R. and Végh, C.A. 2002. Modern hyper- and high inflations. *Journal of Economic Literature* 40, 837–80.

Franco, G.H.B. 1990. Fiscal reforms and stabilisation: four hyperinflation cases examined. *Economic Journal* 100, 176–87.

Frenkel, J.A. 1977. The forward exchange rate, expectations, and the demand for money: the German hyperinflation. *American Economic Review* 67, 653–70.

Graham, F.D. 1930. *Exchange, Prices, and Production in Hyper-Inflation: Germany 1920–23*. Princeton: Princeton University Press.

Holtfrerich, C.-L. 1986. *The German Inflation 1924–23: Causes and Effects in International Perspective*. Berlin: De Gruyter. German original, 1980.

Horsman, G. 1988. *Inflation in the Twentieth Century: Evidence from Europe and North America*. Hemel Hempstead: Harvester Wheatsheaf.

Kindleberger, C.P. 1984a. *A Financial History of Western Europe*. London: Allen & Unwin.

Kindleberger, C.P. 1984b. A structural view of the German inflation. In *The Experience of Inflation*, ed. G.D. Feldman, C.-L. Holtfreich and G.A. Ritter. Berlin: De Gruyter.

Kindleberger, C.P. 1994. Review: the great disorder: a review of the book of that title by Gerald D. Feldman. *Journal of Economic Literature* 32, 1216–25.

Kunz, A. 1986. *Civil Servants and the Politics of Inflation in Germany 1914–1924*. Berlin: De Gruyter.

Lindenlaub, D. 1985. *Maschinenbauunternehmen in der deutschen Inflation*. Berlin: De Gruyter.

Sargent, T.J. 1986. *Rational Expectations and Inflation*. New York: Harper & Row.

Sargent, T.J. and Wallace, N. 1973. Rational expectations and the dynamics of hyperinflation. *International Economic Review* 14, 328–50.

Webb, S.B. 1989. *Hyperinflation and Stabilization in Weimar Germany*. New York: Oxford University Press.

Williams, J.H. 1922. German foreign trade and reparations payments. *Quarterly Journal of Economics* 36, 482–503.

gold standard

The classical gold standard (which ended in 1914) and the interwar gold standard are examined within the same framework, but their experiences are vastly different.

Types of gold standard

All gold standards involve (*a*) a fixed gold content of the domestic monetary unit, and (*b*) the monetary authority both buying and selling gold at the mint price (the inverse of the gold content of the monetary unit), whereupon the mint price governs in the marketplace. A 'coin' standard has gold coin circulating as money. Privately owned bullion (gold in form other than domestic coin) is convertible into gold coin, at (approximately) the mint price, at the government mint or central bank. Private parties may melt domestic coin into bullion – the effect is as if coin were sold to the monetary authority for bullion. The authority could sell gold bars directly for coin, saving the cost of coining.

Under a pure coin standard, gold is the only money. Under a mixed standard, there are also notes issued by the government, central bank, or commercial banks, and possibly demand deposits. Government or central-bank notes (and central-bank deposit liabilities) are directly convertible into gold coin at the fixed price on demand. Commercial-bank notes and demand deposits are convertible into gold or into gold-convertible government or central-bank currency. Gold coin is always exchangeable for paper currency or deposits at the mint price. Two-way transactions again fix the currency price of gold at the mint price.

The coin standard, naturally 'domestic', becomes 'international' with freedom of international gold flows and of foreign-exchange transactions. Then the fixed mint prices of countries on the gold standard imply a fixed exchange rate (mint parity) between their currencies.

A 'bullion' standard is purely international. Gold coin is not money; the monetary authority buys or sells gold bars for its notes. Similarly, a 'gold-exchange' standard involves the monetary authority buying and selling not gold but rather gold-convertible foreign exchange (the currency of a country on a gold coin or bullion standard).

For countries on an international gold standard, costs of importing and exporting gold give rise to 'gold points', and therefore a 'gold-point spread', around the mint parity. If the exchange rate, number of units of domestic per unit of foreign currency, is greater (less) than the gold export (import) point, arbitrageurs sell (purchase) foreign currency at the exchange rate and also obtain (relinquish) foreign currency by exporting (importing) gold. The domestic-currency cost of the transaction per unit of foreign currency is the gold export (import) point; so the 'gold-point arbitrageurs' receive a profit proportional to the exchange-rate/gold-point divergence. However, the arbitrageurs' supply of (demand for) foreign currency returns the exchange rate to below (above) the gold export (import) point. Therefore perfect arbitrage would keep the exchange rate within the gold-point spread. What induces gold-point arbitrage is the profit motive and *the credibility of the monetary-authorities' commitment* to (*a*) the fixed gold price and (*b*) freedom of gold and foreign-exchange transactions.

A country can be effectively on a gold standard even though its legal standard is bimetallism. This happens if the gold–silver mint-price ratio is greater than the world price ratio. In contrast, even though a country is legally on a gold standard, its government and banks could 'suspend specie payments', that is, refuse to convert their notes into gold; so that the country is in fact on a 'paper standard'.

Countries on the classical gold standard

Britain, France, Germany and the United States were the 'core countries' of the gold standard. Britain was the 'centre country', indispensable to the spread and functioning of the standard. Legally bimetallic from the mid-13th century, Britain switched to an effective gold standard early in the 18th century. The gold standard was formally adopted in 1816, ironically during a paper-standard regime (Bank Restriction Period). The United States was legally bimetallic from 1786 and on an effective gold standard from 1834, with a legal gold standard established in 1873 1 – also during a paper standard (the greenback period). In 1879 the United States went back to gold, and by that year not only the core countries but also some British dominions and non-core western European countries were on the gold standard. As time went on, a large number of other countries throughout the globe adopted gold; but they (along with the dominions) were in 'the periphery' – acted on rather than actors – and generally (except for the dominions) not as committed to the gold standard.

Almost all countries were on a mixed coin standard. Some periphery countries were on a gold-exchange standard, usually because they were colonies or territories of a country on a coin standard.

In 1913, the only countries not on gold were traditional silver-standard countries (Abyssinia, China, French Indochina, Hong Kong, Honduras, Morocco, Persia, Salvador), some Latin American paper-standard countries (Chile, Colombia, Guatemala, Haiti, Paraguay), and Portugal and Italy (which had left gold but 'shadowed' the gold standard, pursuing policies as if they were gold-standard countries, keeping the exchange rate relatively stable).

Elements of instability in classical gold standard

Three factors made for instability of the classical gold standard. First, the use of foreign exchange as official reserves increased as the gold standard progressed. While by 1913 only Germany among the core countries held any measurable amount of foreign exchange, the percentage for the rest of the world was double that for Germany. If there were a rush to cash in foreign exchange for gold, reduction of the gold of reserve-currency countries would place the gold standard in jeopardy.

Second, Britain was in a particularly sensitive situation. In 1913, almost half of world foreign-exchange reserves was in sterling, but the Bank of England had only three per cent of gold reserves. The Bank of England's 'reserve ratio' (ratio of 'official reserves' to 'liabilities to foreign monetary authorities held in London financial institutions') was only 31 per cent, far lower than those of the monetary authorities of the other core countries. An official run on sterling could force Britain off the gold standard. Private foreigners also held considerable liquid assets in London, and could themselves initiate a run on sterling.

Third, the United States was a source of instability to the gold standard. Its Treasury held a high percentage of world gold reserves (in 1913, more than that of the three other core countries combined). With no central bank and a decentralized banking system, financial crises were more frequent and more severe than in the other core countries. Far from the United States assisting Britain, gold often flowed from the Bank of England to the United States, to satisfy increases in US demand for money. In many years the United States was a net importer rather than exporter of capital to the rest of the world – the opposite of the other core countries. The political power of silver interests and recurrent financial panics led to imperfect credibility in the US commitment to the gold standard. Indeed, runs on banks and on the Treasury gold reserve placed the US gold standard near collapse in the 1890s. The credibility of the Treasury's commitment to the gold standard was shaken; twice the US gold standard was saved only by cooperative action of the Treasury and a bankers' syndicate, which stemmed gold exports.

Automatic force for stability: price specie-flow mechanism

The money supply is the product of the money multiplier and the monetary base. The monetary authority alters the monetary base by changing its gold holdings and domestic assets (loans, discounts, and securities). However, the level of its domestic assets is dependent on its gold reserves, because the authority generates demand liabilities (notes and deposits) by increasing its assets, and convertibility of these liabilities must be supported by a gold reserve. Therefore the gold standard provides a constraint on the level (or growth) of the money supply.

Further, balance-of-payments surpluses (deficits) are settled by gold imports (exports) at the gold import (export) point. The change in the money supply is the product of the money multiplier and the gold flow, providing the monetary authority does not change its domestic assets. For a country on a gold-exchange standard, holdings of foreign exchange (a reserve currency) take the place of gold.

A country experiencing a balance-of-payments deficit loses gold and its money supply decreases *automatically*. Money income contracts and the price level falls, thereby increasing exports and decreasing imports. Similarly, a surplus country gains gold, exports decrease, and imports increase. In each case, balance-of-payments equilibrium is restored via the current account, the 'price specie-flow mechanism'. To the extent that wages and prices are inflexible, movements of real income in the same direction as money income occur; the deficit country suffers unemployment, while the payments imbalance is corrected.

The capital account also acts to restore balance, via interest-rate increases in the deficit country inducing a net inflow of capital. The interest-rate increases also reduce real investment and thence real income and imports. The opposite occurs in the surplus country.

Rules of the game

Central banks were supposed to reinforce (rather than 'sterilize') the effect of gold flows on the monetary base, thereby enhancing the price specie-flow mechanism. A gold outflow decreases the international assets of the central bank and the money supply. The central-bank's 'proper' response is: (1) decrease lending and sell securities, thereby decreasing domestic assets and the monetary base; (2) raise its 'discount rate', which induces commercial banks to adopt a higher reserves–deposit ratio, thereby reducing the money multiplier. On both counts, the money supply is further decreased. Should the central bank increase its domestic assets when it loses gold, it engages in sterilization of the gold flow, violating the 'rules of the game'. The argument also holds for gold inflow, with sterilization involving the central bank decreasing its domestic assets when it gains gold.

Monetarist theory suggests the 'rules' were inconsequential. Under fixed exchange rates, gold flows adjust money supply to money demand; the money supply is not determined by policy. Also, prices, interest rates, and incomes are determined worldwide. Even core countries can influence these variables domestically only to the extent that they help determine them in the global marketplace. Therefore the price-specie flow and like mechanisms cannot occur. Historical data support this conclusion: gold flows were too small to be suggestive of these processes; and, at least among the core countries, prices, incomes, and interest rates moved closely in correspondence, contradicting the specie-flow mechanism and rules of the game.

Rather than rule (1), central-bank domestic and international assets moving in the same direction, the opposite behaviour – sterilization – was dominant, both in core and non-core European countries. The Bank of England followed the rule more than any other central bank, but even so violated it more often than not!

The Bank of England did, in effect, manage its discount rate ('Bank Rate') in accordance with rule (2). The Bank's primary objective was to maintain convertibility of its notes into gold, and its principal tool was Bank Rate. When the Bank's 'liquidity ratio' (ratio of gold reserves to outstanding note liabilities) decreased, it usually increased Bank Rate. The increase in Bank Rate carried with it market short-term interest rates, inducing a short-term capital inflow and thereby moving the exchange rate away from the gold-export point. The converse also held, with a rise in the liquidity ratio generating a Bank Rate decrease. The Bank was constantly monitoring its liquidity ratio, and in response altered Bank Rate almost 200 times over 1880–1913.

While the Reichsbank also generally moved its discount rate inversely to its liquidity ratio, other central banks often violated rule (2). Discount-rate changes were of inappropriate direction, or of insufficient magnitude or frequency. The Bank of France kept its discount rate stable, choosing to have large gold reserves, with payments imbalances accommodated by fluctuations in its gold rather than financed by short-term capital flows. The United States, lacking a central bank, had no discount rate to use as a policy instrument.

Reason for stability: credible commitment to convertibility

From the late 1870s onward, there was absolute private-sector credibility in the commitment to the fixed domestic-currency price of gold on the part of Britain, France, Germany, and other important European countries. For the United States, this absolute credibility applied from about 1900. That commitment had a contingency aspect: convertibility could be suspended in the event of dire emergency; but, after normal conditions were restored, convertibility and honouring of gold contracts would be re-established at the pre-existing mint price – even if substantial deflation was required to do so. The Bank Restriction and greenback periods were applications of the contingency. From 1879, the 'contingency clause' was exercised by none of these countries.

The absolute credibility in countries' commitment to convertibility at the existing mint price implied that there was zero 'convertibility risk' (Treasury or central-bank notes non-redeemable in gold at the established mint price) and zero 'exchange risk' (alteration of mint parity, institution of exchange control, or prohibition of gold export).

Why was the commitment to credibility so credible?

1. Contracts were expressed in gold; abandonment of convertibility meant violation of contracts – anathema to monetary authorities.
2. Shocks to economies were infrequent and generally mild.
3. The London capital market was the largest, most open, most diversified in the world, and its gold market was also dominant. A high proportion of world trade was financed in sterling, London was the most important reserve-currency centre, and payments imbalances were often settled by transferring sterling assets rather than gold. Sterling was an international currency – a boon to other countries, because sterling involved positive interest return, and its transfer costs were much less than those of gold. Advantages to Britain were the charges for services as an international banker, differential interest return on its financial intermediation, and the practice of countries on a sterling (gold-exchange) standard of financing payments surpluses with Britain by piling up short-term sterling assets rather than demanding Bank gold.
4. 'Orthodox metallism' – authorities' commitment to an anti-inflation, balanced-budget, stable-money policy – reigned. This ideology implied low government spending, low taxes, and limited monetization of government debt. Therefore, it was not expected that a country's price level would get out of line with that of other countries.

5. Politically, gold had won over paper and silver, and stable-money interests (bankers, manufacturers, merchants, professionals, creditors, urban groups) over inflationary interests (farmers, landowners, miners, debtors, rural groups).

6. There was a competitive environment and freedom from government regulation. Prices and wages were flexible. The core countries had virtually no capital controls, Britain had adopted free trade, and the other core countries had only moderate tariffs. Balance-of-payments financing and adjustment were without serious impediments.

7. With internal balance an unimportant goal of policy, preservation of convertibility of paper currency into gold was the primary policy objective. Sterilization of gold flows, though frequent, was more 'meeting the needs of trade' (passive monetary policy) than fighting unemployment (active monetary policy).

8. The gradual establishment of mint prices over time ensured that mint parities were in line with relative price levels; so countries joined the gold standard with exchange rates in equilibrium.

9. Current-account and capital-account imbalances tended to be offsetting for the core countries. A trade deficit induced a gold loss and a higher interest rate, attracting a capital inflow and reducing capital outflow. The capital-exporting core countries could stop a gold loss simply by reducing lending abroad.

Implications of credible commitment

Private parties reduced the need for balance-of-payments adjustment, via both gold-point arbitrage and stabilizing speculation. When the exchange rate was outside the spread, gold-point arbitrage quickly returned it to the spread. Within the spread, as the exchange value of a currency weakened, the exchange rate approaching the gold-export point, speculators had an ever greater incentive to purchase domestic with foreign currency (a capital inflow). They believed that the exchange rate would move in the opposite direction, enabling reversal of their transaction at a profit. Similarly, a strengthened currency involved a capital outflow. The further the exchange rate moved toward a gold point, the greater the potential profit opportunity in betting on a reversal of direction; for there was a decreased distance to that gold point and an increased distance from the other point. This 'stabilizing speculation' increased the exchange value of depreciating currencies, and thus gold loss could be prevented. Absence of controls meant such private capital flows were highly responsive to exchange-rate changes.

Government policies that enhanced stability

Specific government policies enhanced gold-standard stability. First, by the turn of the 20th century, South Africa – the main world gold producer – was selling all its gold output in London, either to private parties or to the Bank of England. Thus the Bank had the means to replenish its gold reserves. Second, the orthodox-metallism ideology and the leadership of the Bank of England kept countries' monetary policies disciplined and in harmony. Third, the US Treasury and the central banks of the other core countries manipulated gold points, to stem gold outflow. The cost of exporting gold was artificially increased (for example, by increasing selling prices for bars and foreign coin) and/or the cost of importing gold artificially decreased (for example, by providing interest-free loans to gold importers).

Fourth, central-bank cooperation was forthcoming during financial crises. The precarious liquidity position of the Bank of England meant that it was more often the recipient than the provider of financial assistance. In crises, the Bank would obtain loans from other central banks, and the Bank of France would sometimes purchase sterling to support that currency. When needed, assistance went from the Bank of England to other central banks. Also, private bankers unhesitatingly made loans to central banks in difficulty.

Thus, 'virtuous' interactions were responsible for the stability of the gold standard. The credible commitment to convertibility of paper money at the established mint price, and therefore to fixed mint parities, were both a cause and an effect of the stable environment in which the gold standard operated, the stabilizing behaviour of arbitrageurs and speculators, and the responsible policies of the authorities – and these three elements interacted positively among themselves.

Experience of periphery

An important reason for periphery countries to join and maintain the gold standard was the fostering of access to core-countries' capital markets. Adherence to the gold standard connoted that the peripheral country would follow responsible macro-economic policies and repay debt. This 'seal of approval', by reducing the risk premium, involved a lower interest rate on the country's bonds sold abroad, and very likely a higher volume of borrowing, thereby enhancing economic development.

However, periphery countries bore the brunt of the burden of adjustment of payments imbalances with the core (and other western European) countries. First, when the gold-exchange-standard periphery countries ran a surplus (deficit), they increased (decreased) their liquid balances in the United Kingdom (or other reserve-currency country) rather than withdraw gold from (lose gold to) the reserve-currency country. The monetary base of the periphery country increased (decreased), but that of the reserve-currency country remained unchanged. Therefore, changes in domestic variables – prices, incomes, interest rates, portfolios – that occurred to correct the imbalance were primarily in the periphery.

Second, when Bank Rate increased, London drew funds from France and Germany, which attracted funds from other European countries, which drew capital from the periphery. Also, it was easy for a core country to correct a deficit by reducing lending to, or bringing capital home from, the periphery. While the periphery was better off with access to capital, its welfare gain was reduced by the instability of capital import. Third, periphery-countries' exports were largely primary products, sensitive to world market conditions. This feature made adjustment in the periphery take the form more of real than financial correction.

The experience of adherence to the gold standard differed among periphery groups. The important British dominions and colonies successfully maintained the gold standard. They paid the price of serving as an economic cushion to the Bank of England's financial situation; but, compared with the rest of the periphery, gained a stable long-term capital inflow. In southern Europe and Latin America, adherence to the gold standard was fragile. The commitment to convertibility lacked credibility, and resort to a paper standard occurred. Many of the reasons for credible commitment that applied to the core countries were absent. There were powerful inflationary interests, strong balance-of-payments shocks, and rudimentary banking sectors. The cost of adhering to the gold standard was apparent: loss of the ability to depreciate the currency to counter reductions in exports. Yet the gain, in terms of a steady capital inflow from the core countries, was not as stable or reliable as for the British dominions and colonies.

Breakdown of classical gold standard

The classical gold standard was at its height at the end of 1913, ironically just before it came to an end. The proximate cause of the breakdown of the classical gold standard was the First World War. However, it was the gold-exchange standard and the Bank of England's precarious liquidity position that were the underlying cause. With the outbreak of war, a run on sterling led Britain to impose extreme exchange control – a postponement of both domestic and international payments – making the international gold standard inoperative. Convertibility was not suspended legally; but moral suasion, legalistic action, and regulation had the same effect. The Bank of England commandeered gold imports and applied moral suasion to bankers and bullion brokers to restrict gold exports.

The other gold-standard countries undertook similar policies – the United States not until 1917, when it adopted extra-legal restrictions on convertibility and restricted gold exports. Commercial banks converted their notes and deposits only into currency. Currency convertibility made mint parities ineffective; floating exchange rates resulted.

Return to the gold standard

After the First World War, a general return to gold occurred; but the interwar gold standard differed institutionally from the classical gold standard. First, the new gold standard was led by the United States, not Britain. The US embargo on gold exports was removed in 1919, and currency convertibility at the pre-war mint price was restored in 1922. The gold value of the dollar rather than pound sterling was the typical reference point around which other currencies were aligned and stabilized. The core now had two central countries, the United Kingdom (which restored gold in 1925) and the United States.

Second, for many countries there was a time lag between stabilizing the currency in the foreign-exchange market (fixing the exchange rate or mint parity) and resuming currency convertibility. The interwar gold standard was at its height at the end of 1928, after all core countries were fully on the standard and before the Great Depression began. The only countries that never joined the interwar gold standard were the USSR, silver–standard countries (China, Hong Kong, Indochina, Persia, Eritrea), and some minor Asian and African countries.

Third, the 'contingency clause' of convertibility conversion, that required restoration of convertibility at the mint price that existed prior to the emergency (the First World War), was *broken* by various countries, and even core countries. While some countries (including the United States and United Kingdom) stabilized their currencies at the pre-war mint price, others (including France) established a gold content of their currency that was a fraction of the pre-war level: the currency was devalued in terms of gold, the mint price was higher than pre-war. Still others (including Germany) stabilized new currencies adopted after hyperinflation.

Fourth, the gold coin standard, dominant in the classical period, was far less prevalent in the interwar period. All four core countries had been on coin in the classical gold standard; but only the United States was on coin interwar. The gold-bullion standard, non-existent pre-war, was adopted by the United Kingdom and France. Germany and most non-core countries were on a gold-exchange standard.

Instability of interwar gold standard

The interwar gold standard was replete with forces making for *instability*.

1. The process of establishing fixed exchange rates was piecemeal and haphazard, resulting in disequilibrium exchange rates. Among core countries, the United Kingdom restored convertibility at the pre-war mint price without sufficient deflation, and had an overvalued currency of about ten per cent. France and Germany had undervalued currencies.
2. Wages and prices were less flexible than in the pre-war period.
3. Higher trade barriers than pre-war also restrained adjustment.
4. The gold-exchange standard economized on total world gold via the gold of the United Kingdom and United States in their reserves role for countries on the gold-exchange standard and also for countries on a coin or bullion standard that elected to hold part of their reserves in London or New York. However, the gold-exchange standard was unstable, with a conflict between (*a*) the expansion of sterling and dollar liabilities to foreign central banks, to expand world liquidity, and (*b*) the resulting deterioration in the reserve ratio of US and UK authorities.

    This instability was particularly severe, for several reasons. First, France was now a large official holder of sterling, and France was resentful of the United Kingdom. Second, many more countries were on the gold-exchange standard than pre-war. Third, the gold-exchange standard, associated with colonies in the classical period, was considered a system inferior to a coin standard.
5. In the classical period, London was the one dominant financial centre; in the interwar period it was joined by New York and, in the late 1920s, Paris. Private and

official holdings of foreign currency could shift among the two or three centres, as interest-rate differentials and confidence levels changed.

6. There was maldistribution of gold. In 1928, official reserve-currency liabilities were much more concentrated than in 1913, British pounds accounting for 77 per cent of world foreign-exchange reserves and French francs less than two per cent (versus 47 and 30 per cent in 1913). Yet the United Kingdom held only seven per cent of world official gold and France 13 per cent. France also possessed 39 per cent of world official foreign exchange. The United States held 37 per cent of world official gold.

7. Britain's financial position was even more precarious than in the classical period. In 1928, the gold and dollar reserves of the Bank of England covered only one-third of London's liquid liabilities to official foreigners, a ratio hardly greater than in 1913. UK liquid liabilities were concentrated on stronger countries (France, United States), whereas UK liquid assets were predominantly in weaker countries (Germany). There was ongoing tension with France, which resented the sterling-dominated gold-exchange standard and desired to cash in its sterling holding for gold, to aid its objective of achieving first-class financial status for Paris.

8. Internal balance was an important goal of policy, which hindered balance-of-payments adjustment, and monetary policy was influenced by domestic politics rather than geared to preservation of currency convertibility.

9. Credibility in authorities' commitment to the gold standard was not absolute. Convertibility risk and exchange risk could be high, and currency speculation could be destabilizing rather than stabilizing. When a country's currency approached or reached its gold-export point, speculators might anticipate that currency convertibility would not be maintained and that the currency would be devalued.

10. The 'rules of the game' were violated even more often than in the classical gold standard. Sterilization of gold inflows by the Bank of England can be viewed as an attempt to correct the overvalued pound by means of deflation. However, the US and French sterilization of their persistent gold inflows reflected exclusive concern for the domestic economy and placed the burden of adjustment (deflation) on other countries.

11. The Bank of England did not provide a leadership role in any important way, and central-bank cooperation was insufficient to establish credibility in the commitment to currency convertibility. The Federal Reserve had three targets for its discount-rate policy: strengthen the pound, combat speculation in the New York stock market, and achieve internal balance – and the first target was of lowest priority. Although, for the sake of external balance, the Bank of England kept Bank Rate higher than internal considerations would dictate, it was understandably reluctant to abdicate Bank Rate policy entirely to the balance of payments, with little help from the Federal Reserve. To keep the pound strong, substantial international cooperation was required, but was not forthcoming.

Breakdown of interwar gold standard

The Great Depression triggered the unravelling of the gold standard. The depression began in the periphery. Low export prices and debt-service requirements created insurmountable balance-of-payments difficulties for gold-standard commodity producers. However, US monetary policy was an important catalyst. In 1927 the Federal Reserve favoured easy money, which supported foreign currencies but also fed the New York stock-market boom. Reversing policy to tame the boom, higher interest rates attracted monies to New York, weakening sterling in particular. The crash of October 1929, while helping sterling, was followed by the US depression. This spread worldwide, with declines in US trade and lending. In 1929 and 1930 a number of periphery countries –both dominions and Latin American countries – either formally suspended currency convertibility or restricted it so that currencies violated the gold-export point.

It was destabilizing speculation, emanating from lack of confidence in authorities' commitment to currency convertibility, which ended the interwar gold standard. In May 1931 there was a run on Austria's largest commercial bank, and the bank failed. The run spread to other eastern European countries and to Germany, where an important bank also collapsed. The countries' central banks lost substantial reserves; international financial assistance was too late; and in July 1931 Germany adopted exchange control, followed by Austria in October. These countries were definitively off the gold standard.

The Austrian and German experiences, as well as British budgetary and political difficulties, were among the factors that destroyed confidence in sterling, which occurred in mid-July 1931. Runs on sterling ensued, and the Bank of England lost much of its reserves. Loans from abroad were insufficient, and in any event taken as a sign of weakness. The gold standard was abandoned in September, and the pound quickly and sharply depreciated on the foreign-exchange market, as overvaluation of the pound would imply.

Following the UK abandonment of the gold standard, many countries followed, some to maintain their competitiveness via currency devaluation, others in response to destabilizing capital flows. The United States held on until 1933, when both domestic and foreign demands for gold, manifested in runs on US commercial banks, became intolerable. 'Gold bloc' countries (France, Belgium, Netherlands, Switzerland, Italy, Poland), with their currencies now overvalued and susceptible to destabilizing speculation, succumbed to the inevitable by the end of 1936.

The Great Depression was worsened by the gold standard: gold-standard countries hesitated to inflate their economies, for fear of suffering loss of gold and foreign-exchange reserves, and being forced to abandon convertibility or the gold parity. The gold standard involved 'golden fetters', which inhibited monetary and fiscal policy to fight the Depression. As countries left the gold standard, removal of monetary and fiscal policy from their 'gold fetters' enabled their use in expanding real output, providing the political will existed.

In contrast to the interwar gold standard, the classical gold standard functioned well because of a confluence of 'virtuous' interactions, involving government policies, credible commitment to the standard, private arbitrage and speculation, and fostering economic and political environment. We will not see its like again.

LAWRENCE H. OFFICER

See also **banking crises; Bank of England; commodity money; silver standard.**

Bibliography

Bayoumi, T., Eichengreen, B. and Taylor, M.P., eds. 1996. *Modern Perspectives on the Gold Standard.* Cambridge: Cambridge University Press.

Bordo, M.D. and Kydland, F.E. 1995. The gold standard as a rule: an essay in exploration. *Explorations in Economic History* 32, 423–64.

Bordo, M.D. and Rockoff, H. 1996. The gold standard as a 'Good Housekeeping Seal of Approval'. *Journal of Economic History* 56, 389–428.

Bordo, M.D. and Schwartz, A.J., eds. 1984. *A Retrospective on the Classical Gold Standard, 1821–1931.* Chicago: University of Chicago Press.

De Macedo, J.B., Eichengreen, B. and Reis, J., eds. 1996. *Currency Convertibility: The Gold Standard and Beyond.* London: Routledge.

Eichengreen, B. 1992. *Golden Fetters: The Gold Standard and the Great Depression, 1919–1939.* New York: Oxford University Press.

Eichengreen, B. and Flandreau, M. 1997. *The Gold Standard in Theory and History,* 2nd edn. London: Routledge.

Gallarotti, G.M. 1995. *The Anatomy of an International Monetary Regime: The Classical Gold Standard, 1880–1914.* New York: Oxford University Press.

Officer, L.H. 1996. *Between the Dollar–Sterling Gold Points.* Cambridge: Cambridge University Press.

Officer, L.H. 2001. Gold standard. *EH. Net Encyclopedia,* ed. R. Whaples. Online. Available at http://eh.net/encyclopedia/article/officer.gold.standard, accessed 20 October 2006.

government budget constraint

The government budget constraint is an accounting identity linking the monetary authority's choices of money growth or nominal interest rate and the fiscal authority's choices of spending, taxation, and borrowing at a point in time. Whenever borrowing is the source of some fiscal financing, the government budget constraint also serves to link current monetary and fiscal choices to expected future monetary and fiscal policy variables. This intertemporal dimension creates a rich set of possible impacts of routine macro policy actions, as current or future policies can be expected to adjust to satisfy the government budget, along with other equilibrium conditions. Taking the government budget constraint seriously can overturn some widely held beliefs about policy effects.

The notion that current government policy has intertemporal implications goes back to Barro (1974), who revived ideas associated with Ricardo (1821). Traditional Keynesian models, in contrast, mostly ignored the impact of the government budget constraint on allocations and prices until the work of Christ (1967, 1968), see Sims (1998) for a review and extensions). Hansen, Roberds and Sargent (1991) show that identification of the responses of allocations and prices to changes in the government budget constraint require specification of the economic primitives of preferences, technology and market structure.

The modern treatment of the government budget constraint begins with Sargent and Wallace (1981). They show that, when the primary fiscal surplus is fixed, an open-market sale of debt, and contraction of base money, produces higher future inflation. This stunning result arises because, with fiscal policy fixed, faster money supply growth is the only policy expected to balance future government budget constraints. A related but different mechanism by which the government budget constraint can restrict the equilibrium price level, namely, the 'fiscal theory of the price level', is developed by Leeper (1991), Sims (1994), Woodford (1995; 2001) and Cochrane (1999), among others. That theory demonstrates that, under certain assumptions on policy behaviour, debt-financed cuts in lump-sum taxes can stimulate aggregate demand, in apparent contradiction of Ricardian equivalence.

This article uses endowment and growth economies to study the restrictions the government budget constraint imposes on the intertemporal trade-offs between current and future monetary and fiscal policies. The endowment economy allows us to depict the policy trade-offs associated with a bond-financed tax cut, holding government spending fixed. We show that the effects of policy changes depend on current and expected future monetary and fiscal policies that are consistent with the government budget constraint at each date. Although we illustrate these points for a bond-financed tax cut, analogous results hold for an open-market operation. Implicit in the analyses is that the expected discounted value of real government debt has no value at the infinite horizon; that is, a transversality condition for government debt holds at the infinite horizon. This is a sufficient condition for an equilibrium to exist.

Model primitives

The models are variations of Sidrauski (1967) and share the following features: perfect foresight, a representative, infinitely lived household with utility defined over consumption, c_t, and real balances, M_t/P_t, $U(c_t, M_t/P_t) = u(c_t) + v(M_t/P_t)$, and nominal one-period government bonds, B, paying net nominal interest of i. The models also have in common two equilibrium conditions that stem from optimal household choices: a portfolio balance expression

$$\frac{v'(M_t/P_t)}{u'(c_t)} = \frac{i_t}{1+i_t},\tag{1}$$

and optimality of bond choices, a Fisher relation, represented by the Euler equation

$$1 = \beta(1+i_t)\left[\frac{u'(c_{t+1})}{u'(c_t)}\frac{P_t}{P_{t+1}}\right],\tag{2}$$

where $0 < \beta < 1$ is the household's discount factor.

The structure of the government balance sheet, revenue sources, and expenditure process is also common across the models we examine. The government chooses sequences of $\{M_t, B_t, T_t, z_t\}$ to finance purchases of goods and services, g_t, and transfer payments, z_t, to satisfy the government budget constraint

$$g_t + z_t = T_t + \frac{M_t - M_{t-1}}{P_t} + \frac{B_t - (1 + i_{t-1})B_{t-1}}{P_t},\tag{3}$$

where T_t denotes total tax revenues. Government spending is specified as shares of output: $g_t = s_t^g y_t$ and $z_t = s_t^z y_t$. The government budget constraint (3) has the present value form

$$\frac{B_{t-1}}{P_{t-1}} - E_t \sum_{j=0}^{\infty} \prod_{l=0}^{j}\left(\frac{\pi_{t+l}}{1+i_{t-1+l}}\right)\left[T_{t+j} - g_{t\mid j} - z_{t+j} + s_{t+j}\right],\tag{4}$$

where $s_t = (M_t - M_{t-1})/P_t$ is seigniorage revenues. To arrive at (4), the infinite-horizon transversality condition for debt from the household's optimization problem has been imposed: $\lim_{q \to \infty} E_t \beta^q u'(c_{t+q}) \prod_{j=0}^{q}\left(\frac{\pi_{t+j}}{1+i_{t+j+1}}\right)\frac{B_{t+q}}{P_{t+q}} = 0$. This is the relevant sufficient condition because it forces the household to expect that it cannot postpone consumption, hold government bonds for ever, and raise lifetime utility (see Becker and Boyd, 1997, for good economic intuition). It is important to note that in stochastic models the transversality condition need not hold always and everywhere along equilibrium paths, as it does in perfect foresight equilibria. Rather, it holds only in *expectation* (see Kamihigashi, 2005, for discussion and examples).

Endowment economy

It is useful to study an endowment economy because it draws out the role of the government budget constraint in macroeconomic analyses. The household budget constraint is

$$c_t + \frac{M_t + B_t}{P_t} \le y_t + z_t + \frac{M_{t-1} + (1 + i_{t-1})B_{t-1}}{P_t}, \tag{5}$$

where y is the endowment of goods each period and we have set $T_t = 0$, for all t, so $z^t > 0$ (< 0) represents lump-sum transfers (taxes). Output and government purchases are constant, so $y_t = y$ and $g_t = s^g y$, which implies that in equilibrium consumption is a constant share of GDP, $c_t = c = (1 - s^g)y$. Thus, the equilibrium real interest rate equals a constant, $1/\beta$, the Fisher relation reduces to $1 + i_t = \beta^{-1}\pi_{t+1}$ (where $\pi_{t+1} = P_{t+1}/P_t$), and money demand varies only with the nominal interest rate, $v'(M_t/P_t) = u'(c)[i_t/(1 + i_t)]$.

We focus on circumstances in which the economy is in a stationary equilibrium at dates $s > t$, but starts from a different equilibrium at date t. Denote money growth by $\rho_t = M_t/M_{t-1}$. Assume tax and monetary policies are fixed in the future stationary equilibrium: $s_s^z = s^z$ and $\rho_s = \rho$ for $s > t$; at date t, however, policies may be different: $s_t^z \ne s^z$ and $\rho_t \ne \rho$.

In the stationary equilibrium with constant real money balances, inflation depends only on money growth, $\pi = \rho$, which implies the Fisher relation is $1 + i_s = \beta^{-1}\rho_{s+1}$, $s \ge t$. Stationary real money balances become $M_s/P_s = h(\rho_{s+1})$, for dates $s \ge t$.

We derive two versions of the government budget constraint that describe the trade-offs among current and future monetary and fiscal policies that arise in equilibrium. By imposing equilibrium prices on the government budget constraint (3), we obtain

$$\frac{h(\rho)}{y}\left[1 - \frac{1}{\rho_t} + \frac{B_t}{M_t} - \frac{1 + i_{t-1}}{\rho_t}\frac{B_{t-1}}{M_{t-1}}\right] = s^g + s_t^z. \tag{6}$$

For given future expected policies, expression (6) reports the feasible trade-offs among current (date t) policies, when initial liabilities are $(M_{t-1}, (1 + i_{t-1})B_{t-1})$. On the assumption that future policy is anticipated (i.e., $1 + i = \beta^{-1}\rho$), the government budget constraint is

$$\frac{h(\rho)}{y}\left[1 - \frac{1}{\rho} + \left(1 - \frac{1}{\beta}\right)\frac{B}{M}\right] = s^g + s^z, \tag{7}$$

along the equilibrium path for dates $s > t$, given $B_t/M_t = B/M$. Note that the bond–money ratio is constant in the stationary equilibrium. Conditional on the state of government indebtedness, equation (7) describes the trade-offs among future policies that are consistent with equilibrium.

Policy analysis

In the policy experiments we consider, government purchases, s^g, are held fixed. The experiments take the form of an initial cut in taxes at date t (negative s_t^z becomes larger in absolute value), which is financed by sales of nominal bonds. We consider three alternative responses of current and future policies that satisfy (6) and (7). The analysis traces the effects of each specification of policy behaviour on the price level and inflation.

Policy 1

For policy experiment 1, suppose current and future money growth, (ρ_t, ρ), are held fixed. This policy, together with the money demand relation, (1), and Fisher relation, (2), peg the nominal interest rate at $1 + i = \rho/\beta$ and fix equilibrium real balances at $h(\rho)$. Neither the initial price level, P_t, nor the stationary inflation rate, π, changes. A reduction in taxes today is consistent with equilibrium if nominal debt expands to satisfy the government budget constraint (6) with fixed money growth. This raises B_t/M_t, which, by the government budget constraint (7), forces future taxes to rise sufficiently to service the new, higher level of government indebtedness. This mix of policies yields Ricardian equivalence: the timing of taxes and debt is irrelevant for equilibrium allocations and prices. The policies also imply monetary policy is independent of fiscal considerations, as the quantity theory of money maintains. Of course, as this exercise illustrates, the quantity theory requires specific fiscal behaviour.

Policy 2

In the second experiment, the central bank credibly pegs the nominal interest rate by fixing future money growth, ρ, and the fiscal authority credibly fixes future taxes. Can this be an equilibrium? With future policies fixed, the anticipated budget constraint (7) implies current policies cannot alter government indebtedness in the future, which is summarized by B/M. Since the expansion in nominal debt cannot be transformed into future higher real debt, P_t must rise in proportion to B_t. However, a pegged nominal interest rate fixes real money balances. The result is that the current money stock must expand in proportion to the increase in prices, which ensures B_t/M_t is unchanged in the date t budget constraint (6).

The central bank loses control of the current money stock and the price level in this experiment. Changes in these variables are governed by fiscal needs that are beyond the central bank's direct control. A pegged nominal rate subordinates current monetary policy to fiscal needs, but this is not 'monetization of deficits' in the usual sense of printing money to purchase newly issued government debt. Instead, the expansion in money is a passive adjustment of the money supply to clear the money market at the prevailing interest rate and price level. The monetary expansion is given by $dM_t = dB_t/(B_t/M_t)$, making clear that monetary accommodation varies inversely with the level of indebtedness. This exercise corresponds to the fiscal theory of the price level as described by Leeper (1991), Sims (1994), and Woodford (1995). The precise result relies on government debt being sold at par, as Cochrane (2001) observes. If government debt is sold at a discount, bond prices may absorb some of the adjustment to equilibrium, which pushes the price level effects into the future.

Policy 3

The third experiment has the central bank fix current money growth, ρ_t, while the fiscal authority continues to hold future taxes, s^z, constant. It remains feasible for current policy to imply more debt in the future because the anticipated increase in debt service forces future money growth and inflation to rise. The date t response is seen in a higher nominal interest rate and reduced real money balances driven by an increase in P_t to clear the money market, which follows from a fixed M_t. Beyond date t, debt service is financed by higher inflation and seigniorage – 'inflation tax' on nominal assets – revenues. Again, with future net-of-interest fiscal deficits held fixed at $s^g + s^z$, monetary policy is constrained by fiscal needs. In this case, the central bank loses control of future inflation. Sargent and Wallace (1981) employ these assumptions about policy in their classic 'unpleasant monetarist arithmetic' example.

A growth economy

A growth model with elastic capital supply, inelastic labour supply, and a distorting income tax extends the analysis by adding interesting intertemporal margins. The model consists of a representative household, a firm that produces the single consumption good, and a government (see , Gordon and Leeper (2006) for related analysis). Assume physical capital depreciates completely after one period. Output is allocated to consumption, capital, k_t, and government purchases of goods, with the technology $f(k_{t-1})$ generating output, y_t, where $f(0) = 0$, $f'(k_{t-1}) > 0$, and $0 \geq f''(k_{t-1})$. Capital share's of production is denoted by σ. The economy is closed with the aggregate resource constraint

$$c_t + k_t + g_t = f(k_{t-1}). \tag{8}$$

A competitive firm rents capital at rate r from the household and pays taxes levied against sales of goods, which determine the profit function, $D_t = (1 - \tau_t) y_t - (1 + r_t)k_{t-1}$. Profit maximization yields the after-tax factor price $1 + r_t = (1 - \tau_t)f'(k_{t-1})$.

The household supplies labour inelastically, owns the firm, and receives factor payments. Subject to the budget constraint

$$c_t + k_t + \frac{M_t + B_t}{P_t} \leq (1 + r_t)k_{t-1} + D_t + z_t + \frac{M_{t-1} + (1 + i_{t-1})B_{t-1}}{P_t}, \tag{9}$$

the household maximizes the expected discounted value of its infinite horizon utility function, given P_t, i_t, τ_t, and the initial conditions $(k_{-1} > 0, M_{-1} + (1 + i_{-1})B_{-1} > 0)$. Government behaviour is unchanged from the endowment economy, but tax revenue is $T_t = \tau_t(1 + r_t)k_{t-1}$.

Equilibrium

We recover an explicit characterization of the model's equilibrium with $u(c_t) = \ln(c_t)$ and $v(M_t/P_t) = \ln(M_t/P_t)$. After imposing transversality conditions for capital, debt and money, equate the supply and demand for capital to find the solution

$$k_t = \left(1 - \frac{1}{\eta_t}\right)\left(1 - s_t^g\right)f(k_{t-1}),$$ (10)

where $\eta_t \equiv E_t \sum_{i=0}^{\infty}(\sigma\beta)^i\prod_{j=0}^{i-1}(\frac{1-\tau_{t+j+1}}{1-s_{t+j+1}^g})$. Money market equilibrium sets money supply to money demand to yield

$$\frac{M_t}{P_t} = c_t\mu_t,$$ (11)

where $\mu_t \equiv E_t \sum_{i=0}^{\infty} \beta^i\prod_{j=0}^{i-1}\frac{1}{\rho_{t+j+1}}$. Note that μ and η completely summarize what agents need to know to form rational expectations. Since eqs. (8) and (10) imply a decision rule for consumption, equilibrium real balances can be expressed in terms of their opportunity cost, $1/\mu_t = i_t/(1 + i_t)$, the transactions they help finance, $c_t + k_t$, and expected fiscal policies:

$$\frac{M_t}{P_t} = \frac{1}{\eta_t}\left(\frac{i_t}{1+i_t}\right)^{-1}c_t + k_t.$$ (12)

With $c + k$ serving as a scale variable, expression (12) is a conventional money demand function except for the dependence on expected fiscal policies. Expectations about future fiscal policies are essential to tie down the equilibrium. This is a key to the dynamics of the growth model and the impacts of fiscal policy on the current equilibrium.

Equilibrium requires that current and future policies satisfy the government's budget constraint and that agents' expectations of policy are consistent with equilibrium. This creates interactions between current and future policies. As before, we distill the analysis down to two periods – now and the future. Fix current and future government spending shares, $\{s_t^g, s_t^z\}$, for all t, and assume future money growth and tax rates are constant $\rho_s = \rho, \tau_s = \tau, s > t$. Current policies, however, may differ: $\rho_t \neq \rho, \tau_t \neq \tau$.

The government budget constraint can be expressed entirely in terms of current and expected policies. In period t, the constraint is

$$\left[\frac{\rho_t - 1}{\rho_t} + \frac{B_t}{M_t} - \frac{1+i_{t-1}}{\rho_t}\frac{B_{t-1}}{M_{t-1}}\right]\frac{\mu_t}{\eta_t} = \frac{s_t^g + s_t^z - \tau_t}{1 - s_t^g}.$$ (13)

Given policy expectations are embedded in μ_t/η_t and initial government indebtedness is summarized by $(1 + i_{t-1})B_{t-1}/M_{t-1}$, expression (13) reports the equilibrium trade-offs among current policies.

Equilibrium trade-offs between current and future policies are given by the state of government indebtedness. We use the budget constraint (13) to develop this idea for the growth model. Shift the timing of eq. (13) forward one period and assume future interest liabilities are correctly anticipated at t by substituting the expression for the equilibrium nominal return $1 + i_t$. Given the bond–money ratio is constant at $B/M = B_t/M_t$ in the stationary equilibrium, there can be no net additions to debt in the future. Dropping the time subscript for variables dated $t + 1$ and imposing equilibrium yields

$$\frac{\mu}{\eta}\left[\left(1 - \frac{1}{\beta}\right)\frac{B}{M} + \left(\frac{\rho - 1}{\rho}\right)\right] = \frac{s^g + s^z - \tau}{1 - s^g}. \tag{14}$$

Equation (14) describes the trade-offs among future policies that are consistent with fixed μ_t/η_t being an equilibrium. The trade-offs represented by eqs. (13) and (14) tie together current policies and expectations of future policies. Any change in policy at date t that requires a change in μ_t/η_t must be accompanied by a change in policy in the future that is consistent with revised values of μ_t/η_t, conditional on the level of government debt B/M.

Policy analysis
As for the endowment economy, we study the current and future responses of fiscal and monetary policy to a date t debt finance tax cut in the analysis that follows.

Policy 1
Hold current and future money growth fixed at (ρ_t, ρ). This policy pegs the nominal interest rate by fixing μ_t but it does not fix real money balances unless η_t is also constant. Since new debt issued to finance the tax reduction raises B_t/M_t, a higher level of debt is carried into the future. To clear the government budget constraint in the future, budget constraint (14) implies future taxes must rise. Higher taxes reduce the return on capital (a lower η) and induce substitution from real to nominal assets, which includes money. Equilibrium in the money market requires the current price level to fall. The source of the non-Keynesian reduction in inflation is the link between current policy (that is, the fiscal expansion) and the expectation that future policy will expand government debt.

Policy 2
Fix both future money growth and future taxes at (ρ, τ). By assumption, all future policies are constant in the face of the current tax cut. Current policies must adjust to ensure the real value of debt in the future is unchanged, as was true when this policy was applied to the endowment economy. The real value of debt remains unchanged because the current money stock rises by the amount that the current budget constraint (13) dictates is needed to maintain the pre-tax cut level of B_t/M_t. The monetary expansion necessary to maintain equilibrium is sufficient to produce additional future seigniorage (that is, the level of the money supply rises). Since the fixed rate of money growth is just enough to pay for the increased debt service and with equilibrium real money balances fixed by constant future policies, (12) predicts the current price level rises in proportion to the increase in M_t. Gordon and Leeper (2006) label this 'the canonical fiscal theory exercise'.

The implications of the fiscal theory contrast with the tax cut of policy 1. The bond-financed tax cut is pure fiscal policy in the sense that it is *independent* of the path of the money stock. It also reduces nominal spending and the price level. An essential aspect of the fiscal theory is that the current money stock adjusts passively to clear the money market, raising nominal demand and the price level. If the policy authorities peg the nominal interest rate and fix future taxes without reference to the rest of the economy, higher prices are inevitable consequences of a tax cut. This is an illustration of the fiscal theory.

Policy 3

The fiscal authority holds future taxes constant and the central bank fixes current money growth. If future money growth rises sufficiently to generate the seigniorage revenue to service the new debt, an expansion in current debt can be carried into the future. Expected inflation increases, which lowers the expected return on money (that is, μ falls), decreases money demand, raises the price level, and contributes to higher future inflation. The change in future money growth depends, of course, on future B/M, which drives the change in debt service.

Concluding remarks

The equilibria described in this article can easily be couched in terms of arbitrary sequences of policy variables. It has become increasingly popular, however, to endow policy authorities with simple rules that make the policy instrument a time-invariant function of only a few variables that are not directly related to the actions of other policy institutions (that is, the interest rate–monetary policy rules studied in Taylor, 1999). Although this approach has the advantages of being interpretable and tractable, it runs the risk of oversimplifying policy behaviour. For example, it is difficult to square simple time-invariant policy functions with the observation that policy regimes can, and do, change, sometimes because of the interactions of different policymakers.

A natural extension of simple rules allows feedback parameters to take on finitely many values ('regimes') whose evolution is governed by a Markov process. Relative to simple rules, this extension produces a far richer set of expectations of future policy variables, a generalization that can overturn some of the principles guiding macro policy research that have been obtained from simple rules (see Davig, Leeper and Chung, 2004, and Davig and Leeper, 2005).

Markov switching of policy rules has also generalized the test of the long-run sustainability of fiscal policy proposed by Hamilton and Flavin (1986). Davig (2005) finds expansionary and contractionary regimes in US government debt that nonetheless yield a stochastic process for discounted debt with an unconditional expected value equal to zero in the long run.

Theoretical work that takes seriously the restrictions imposed by the government budget constraint has established some important and surprising results. In light of these theoretical findings, it is remarkable how little applied work on monetary and fiscal policy treats the government budget constraint with equal seriousness. This is an open area of research.

ERIC M. LEEPER AND JAMES M. NASON

See also **hyperinflation; monetary and fiscal policy overview; optimal fiscal and monetary policy (with commitment); optimal fiscal and monetary policy (without commitment).**

Bibliography

Barro, R. 1974. Are government bonds net wealth? *Journal of Political Economy* 82, 1095–117.

Becker, R. and Boyd, J., III 1997. *Capital Theory, Equilibrium Analysis, and Recursive Utility.* Malden, MA: Blackwell.

Christ, C. 1967. A short-run aggregate-demand model of the interdependence and effects of monetary and fiscal policies with Keynesian and classical interest elasticities. *American Economic Review* 57, 434–43.

Christ, C. 1968. A simple macroeconomic model with a government budget restraint. *Journal of Political Economy* 76, 53–67.

Cochrane, J. 1999. A frictionless view of U.S. inflation. In *NBER Macroeconomics Annual 1998,* ed. B. Bernanke and J. Rotemberg. Cambridge, MA: MIT Press.

Cochrane, J. 2001. Long-term debt and optimal policy in the fiscal theory of the price level. *Econometrica* 69, 69–116.

Davig, T. 2005. Periodically expanding discounted debt: a threat to fiscal policy sustainability? *Journal of Applied Econometrics* 20, 829–40.

Davig, T. and Leeper, E. 2005. Fluctuating macro policies and the fiscal theory. Working Paper No. 11212. Cambridge, MA: NBER.

Davig, T., Leeper, E. and Chung, H. 2004. *Monetary and fiscal policy switching.* Working Paper No. 10362. Cambridge, MA: NBER.

Gordon, D. and Leeper, E. 2006. The price level, the quantity theory of money, and the fiscal theory of the price level. *Scottish Journal of Political Economy* 53, 4–27.

Hamilton, J. and Flavin, M. 1986. On the limitations of government borrowing: a framework for empirical testing. *American Economic Review* 76, 808–19.

Hansen, L., Roberds, W. and Sargent, T. 1991. Time series implications of present value budget balance and of martingale models of consumption and taxes. In *Rational Expectations Econometrics,* ed. L. Hansen and T. Sargent. Boulder, CO: Westview Press.

Kamihigashi, T. 2005. Necessity of the transversality condition for stochastic models with bounded or CRRA utility. *Journal of Economic Dynamics and Control* 29, 1313–29.

Leeper, E. 1991. Equilibria under 'active' and 'passive' monetary and fiscal policies. *Journal of Monetary Economics* 27, 129–47.

Ricardo, D. 1821. *On the Principles of Political Economy and Taxation.* 3rd edn. London: John Murray.

Sargent, T. and Wallace, N. 1981. Some unpleasant monetarist arithmetic. *Federal Reserve Bank of Minneapolis Quarterly Review* 5, 1–17.

Sidrauski, M. 1967. Rational choice and patterns of growth in a monetary economy. *American Economic Review Papers and Proceedings* 57, 534–44.

Sims, C. 1994. A simple model for study of the determination of the price level and the interaction of monetary and fiscal policy. *Economic Theory* 4, 381–99.

Sims, C. 1998. Econometric implications of the government budget constraint. *Journal of Econometrics* 83, 9–19.

Taylor, J. 1999. *Monetary Policy Rules.* Chicago: University of Chicago Press.

Woodford, M. 1995. Price-level determinacy without control of a monetary aggregate. In *Carnegie-Rochester Conference Series on Public Policy*, ed. B. McCallum and C. Plosser, 43, 1–46.

Woodford, M. 2001. Fiscal requirements for price stability. *Journal of Money, Credit, and Banking* 33, 669–728.

Great Depression, monetary and financial forces in

What caused the worldwide collapse in output from 1929 to 1933? Why was the recovery from the trough of 1933 so protracted for the United States? How costly was the decline in terms of welfare? Was the decline preventable? These are some of the questions that have motivated economists to study the Great Depression.

Cole and Ohanian (1999) document that US per capita GNP fell 38 per cent below its long-run trend path (of two per cent per annum growth) from 1929 to 1933. Real per capita non-durables consumption fell nearly 30 per cent, durables consumption fell over 55 per cent, and business investment fell nearly 80 per cent. On the input side, total employment fell 24 per cent and total factor productivity (TFP) fell 14 per cent. On the nominal and financial side, the GNP deflator fell 24 per cent; per capita M1 (currency plus deposits) fell 30 per cent; M1 velocity fell 32 per cent; the per capita monetary base rose 9 per cent; the currency–deposit ratio rose over 160 per cent (Friedman and Schwartz, 1963, Table B3); the loan–deposit ratio fell 30 per cent (Bernanke, 1983, Table 1); and *ex post* real commercial paper rates rose from six per cent in 1929 to a peak of 13.8 per cent in 1932.

What caused the Depression? For the United States, Friedman and Schwartz (1963, p. 300) argued that it was the decline in the stock of M1 – a consequence of Fed tightening and of a fall in the money multiplier induced by banking panics. According to Eichengreen (1992), international adherence to the gold standard transmitted the US monetary contraction to other industrialized countries. Specifically, high interest rates and low prices in the United States attracted foreign inflows of gold (in 1932 the United States and France held over 70 per cent of the world gold reserves), which the Fed largely sterilized (that is, sold domestic government debt and bought money). The outflow of gold from foreign countries implied that gold-backed money supplies of those countries had to decline in order to meet their cover ratios. Further evidence (see Bernanke and James, 1991, Table 4) of the importance of the gold standard in transmitting the contraction comes from the experience of countries like Britain, which suspended the gold standard in 1931 and recovered by 1932; from Spain, which never was on it and had a much less severe contraction than those on the gold standard; and from France, which was one of the last major countries to leave it and still faced declining industrial production past the 1933 trough. As Bernanke (1995, p. 3) puts it: 'The new gold-standard research allows us to assert with considerable confidence that *monetary factors played an important causal role*, both in the worldwide decline in prices and output and in their eventual recovery.'

However, much of this evidence is problematic in that it is in the nature of correlations between *endogenous* variables – a fact that makes it challenging to establish causality. Did the decline in M1 *cause* the decline in aggregate output or – as

Temin (1976) argued early on – did M1 and aggregate output decline in response to some other common shock? If the 'monetary-cum-exchange- rate-policy' explanation is indeed correct, we ought to be able to demonstrate its correctness in a reasonably calibrated, dynamic stochastic general equilibrium (DSGE) model. To paraphrase Lucas (1993, p. 271): 'If we know what a depression is, we ought to be able to *make* one.' The challenge of 'making' a depression has been taken up by various researchers and constitutes a noteworthy recent development in depression research.

The conventional explanation of why money affected output is sticky nominal wages – goods prices fell as a result of the monetary contraction but nominal wages adjusted slowly and the ensuing increase in the real wage depressed the demand for labour. One significant contribution to evaluating this conventional explanation is by Bordo, Erceg and Evans (2000). They calibrate a one-sector stochastic macro model with four-quarter nominal wage rigidity and find that 70 per cent of the output decline from 1929 to 1933 can be accounted for by feeding in the negative innovations to the actual M1 money supply process during that period.

Although the findings of Bordo, Erceg and Evans are striking, there are some unresolved issues. One is that the real-wage rise in the model was chosen to mimic the actual real-wage rise in the manufacturing sector while there is some indirect evidence that non-manufacturing real wages actually fell during the 1929–33 downturn. Cole and Ohanian (2000) re-examine the sticky-wage hypothesis in a multisector model and find much less support for it.

A second unresolved issue is that Bordo, Erceg and Evans do not take into account the evidence on aggregate labour productivity and TFP, both of which declined between 1929 and 1933. Ohanian (2002) argues that only about a third of the decline in labour productivity and/or TFP can be plausibly accounted for by mismeasurement of factor inputs. By itself, a decline in TFP could account for a substantial fall in aggregate output, consumption and investment. Unless a decline in TFP can be viewed as an endogenous response to the monetary shock (through, for example, aggregate increasing returns), the decline leaves less scope for a purely monetary explanation. Using a DSGE model where money is non-neutral due to imperfect information, Cole, Ohanian and Leung (2005) show that the decline in M1 accounts for only one-third of the decline in output from 1929 to 1933, while the effect of an exogenous decline in TFP accounts for two-thirds. They use a misperceptions model of monetary non-neutrality because such a model generates less of a counterfactual movement in labour productivity than a model with nominal wage rigidities.

Sticky wages and monetary misperceptions are not the only mechanisms through which money can affect real output. Irving Fisher (1933) pointed out that the unanticipated fall in prices during 1929–33 led to bankruptcies because it increased the real value of nominal debt of households, firms, and financial intermediaries. This 'debt-deflation' hypothesis was analysed by Mishkin (1978) for households and formalized by Bernanke and Gertler (1989) for firms. More generally, Bernanke (1983) argued that the reduction in borrower net worth increased the cost of obtaining external finance, while bank failures and tightened credit standards hampered the efficient allocation of capital. However, a quantitative DSGE model featuring this mechanism has yet to be implemented for the Great Depression. Such a model holds out the promise of explaining some portion of the puzzling decline in TFP during 1929–33 as an endogenous response to a misallocation of capital.

One of the most striking facts of the Depression was the reduction in the money multiplier from 1929 to 1933 associated with the flight from bank deposits to currency. Cooper and Corbae (2002) construct a model in which households have the option of saving in the form of currency or bank deposits, and in which bank deposits ultimately fund working capital for businesses. Because of increasing returns in the intermediation technology associated with fixed verification costs, their model admits multiple equilibria. In the good equilibrium the return on bank deposits is high, households hold small amounts of currency, and output is high. In the bad equilibrium, the return on bank deposits is low, households substitute into currency, and output is low. A shift from the good to the bad equilibrium replicates many of the salient nominal changes that occurred between 1929 and 1933. Although not quantitative, their work formalizes the idea that output, credit and money supply responded negatively to a loss in confidence – much as Irving Fisher (1933, p. 343) suggested it did.

Why was the recovery from the trough of 1933 so protracted for the United States? As noted by Cole and Ohanian (1999), aggregate US output was still below trend in 1939. The answer cannot be the gold standard or M1 because the United States left the gold standard in 1933 and the US money stock recovered rapidly thereafter. One explanation offered is that the National Industrial Recovery Act (NIRA) encouraged businesses to accept high real wages of industrial workers. Cole and Ohanian (2004) embed labour bargaining into a DSGE model and quantitatively explore the effect of the NIRA, giving more weight to workers in the bargaining process post 1933. Their model is reasonably successful in producing a slow recovery. Adverse labour market interventions also appear to have played a role in other industrialized countries such as Germany, France, the UK and Italy (Kehoe and Prescott, 2002).

How costly was the Depression in terms of welfare? Real per capita consumption of non-durables fell 30 per cent in the United States but it is not known how this decline was distributed across households. Chatterjee and Corbae (2006) analyse how households that can self-insure against uninsured earnings losses would fare through a depression. They found that the welfare cost of living in a world with a small likelihood of a Depression-like event is quite large – somewhere between one and seven per cent of consumption in perpetuity depending on the completeness of asset markets. Much of this cost is associated with the increased variability of individual consumption streams.

Was the Depression preventable? First, if the 'monetary-cum-exchange-rate-policy' explanation is correct, the right monetary policy could have prevented the decline. Christiano, Motto and Restagno (2003) estimate a DSGE model with many shocks but find that a liquidity preference shock inducing households to hold currency instead of deposits played the most important role in the contraction phase of the Depression.

They then specify a policy rule that raises the monetary base as a function of liquidity shocks, and run a counterfactual experiment where they find that output would have declined only six per cent if such a reaction function had been in place. Second, if a portion of the decline in output was the result of a banking collapse stemming from a shock to confidence, then – as shown by Cooper and Corbae (2002) – an announcement by the monetary authority that it stands ready to supply liquidity to the banking system might have moderated the decline. Finally, with regard to the slow recovery in the United States, the only credible explanation offered is adverse labour market intervention. If this explanation is correct, we know what *not* to do to prolong a severe decline in output.

SATYAJIT CHATTERJEE, P. DEAN CORBAE

Bibliography

Bernanke, B. 1983. Nonmonetary effects of the financial crisis in the propagation of the Great Depression. *American Economic Review* 73, 257–76.

Bernanke, B. 1995. The macroeconomics of the Great Depression: a comparative approach. *Journal of Money, Credit and Banking* 27, 1–28.

Bernanke, B. and Gertler, M. 1989. Agency costs, net worth, and economic performance. *American Economic Review* 79, 14–31.

Bernanke, B. and James, H. 1991. The gold standard, deflation, and financial crisis in the Great Depression: an international comparison. In *Financial Markets and Financial Crises*, ed. R. Glenn Hubbard. Chicago: University of Chicago Press.

Bordo, M., Erceg, C. and Evans, C. 2000. Money, sticky wages, and the Great Depression. *American Economic Review* 90, 1447–63.

Chatterjee, S. and Corbae, D. 2007. On the aggregate welfare cost of Great Depression unemployment. *Journal of Monetary Economics* 54, 1529–1544.

Christiano, L., Motto, R. and Rostagno, M. 2003. The Great Depression and the Friedman–Schwartz hypothesis. *Journal of Money, Credit, and Banking* 35, 1119–97.

Cole, H. and Ohanian, L. 1999. The Great Depression in the United States from a neoclassical perspective. *Federal Reserve Bank of Minneapolis Quarterly Review* 23(1), 25–31.

Cole, H. and Ohanian, L. 2000. Re-examining the contributions of money and banking shocks to the U.S. Great Depression. *NBER Macroeconomics Annual* 15(1), 183–227.

Cole, H. and Ohanian, L. 2004. New Deal policies and the persistence of the Great Depression: a general equilibrium analysis. *Journal of Political Economy* 112, 779–816.

Cole, H. Ohanian, L. and Leung, R. 2005. Deflation and the international Great Depression: a productivity puzzle. Working Paper No. 11237. Cambridge, MA: NBER.

Cooper, R. and Corbae, D. 2002. Financial collapse: a lesson from the Great Depression. *Journal of Economic Theory* 107, 159–90.

Eichengreen, B. 1992. *Golden Fetters: The Gold Standard and the Great Depression 1919–1939.* New York: Oxford University Press.

Fisher, I. 1933. The debt–deflation theory of Great Depressions. *Econometrica* 1, 337–57.

Friedman, M. and Schwartz, A. 1963. *A Monetary History of the United States, 1867–1960.* Princeton: Princeton University Press.

Kehoe, T. and Prescott, E.C. 2002. *Great Depressions of the Twentieth Century.* Special Issue of the *Review of Economic Dynamics* 5(1).

Lucas, R. 1993. Making a miracle. *Econometrica* 61, 251–72.

Mishkin, F. 1978. The household balance sheet and the Great Depression. *Journal of Economic History* 38, 918–37.

Ohanian, L. 2002. Why did productivity fall so much during the Great Depression? *Federal Reserve Bank of Minneapolis Quarterly Review* 26(2), 12–17.

Temin, P. 1976. *Did Monetary Forces Cause the Great Depression?* New York: W.W. Norton and Company.

hyperinflation

Price stability shares with a healthy knee a particular feature: both are precious, but you do not realize how much until you miss them. When you run, your knees perform amazing functions, without you even being aware of them. That is price stability. Under some circumstances, one of your knees may be under some stress and you may be forced to use medication to be able to run well. While you run, you are aware of your knee. That is inflation. Eventually, your knee hurts so much you can only walk. That is high inflation. Finally, in the worst case, your knee is broken and you must lie in bed. That is hyperinflation.

Money – that is, a commodity that is widely used as a medium of exchange – has been in use in the world since commerce became a social activity. However, to the extent that money was a particular commodity or was paper money but pegged to a commodity like silver or gold, there was no risk of long-run inflation.

From the point of view of the theory, this premise comes from the quantity equation that was first formalized by Irving Fisher (1934). He argued that the general level of prices was a constant proportion to the ratio of the supply of currency and some index of the total quantity of goods that are traded in a year. Thus, there cannot be long-run inflation without long-run growth of the net supply of the commodity that serves as money or that backs the paper money in circulation, where by 'net supply' I mean the rate of growth of money in excess of the growth rate of the index of total goods.

The first known example of inflation occurred during the 16th century in Europe, precisely because of the increase in the supply of gold and silver that came from South America after the Spanish conquest. It is interesting to recall, however, that this first inflation was roughly 100 per cent during the whole century or, equivalently, 0.7 per cent a year. According to the theory, this means that the net supply of gold and silver doubled in 100 years. (The ability of Fisher's quantity framework to explain low inflation events during relatively short periods of time like a few years has been rightly called into question. However, for the kind of episodes that I discuss here, which involve very high inflation rates, this conceptual framework is perfectly suitable. See Marcet and Nicolini, 2005, and all references therein.)

By 1900 paper money was the norm, but all economies were functioning under some form of commodity standard in the sense that money was backed by some commodity, typically gold. Governments would suspend convertibility in some circumstances, like wars, but would eventually restore it. Thus, the ability to increase the net supply of paper money depended on the ability of the issuer to accumulate the commodity that backed it. As a consequence, the economic history of the world does not have records of persistent increases in the general level of prices up to the

20th century, except for the cases of the exceptional gold and silver inflows after the Spanish conquest of America mentioned above.

In a seminal paper, Cagan (1956) defined monthly inflation rates that exceed 50 per cent a month as hyperinflations. To generate a hyperinflation according to this definition, Columbus would have had to double Europe's net supply of gold and silver in a little less than two months!

The 20th century witnessed, among other things, a key change in the functioning of our monetary systems. Today, almost without exception, all modern economies function under fiat money arrangements in the sense that paper money circulates, is widely accepted and used in transactions, and is not backed to any particular commodity. Thus, the size of its net supply depends only on the will of the issuer.

All episodes of hyperinflation we observed during the 20th century, no matter how we define them, and with absolutely no exception, occurred during periods of unbacked paper money. All of them, no matter how we define them and with absolutely no exception, occurred during periods in which the net supply of paper money increased at enormous rates. And all of them occurred in times of substantial fiscal imbalances, represented by excessive government expenditures, inadequate government revenues or a huge government debt burden – or a combination of these.

The first burst of hyperinflations occurred in the 1920s in countries that lost the First World War, most notably Germany and Hungary. Sargent (1992) provides a very neat description of the causes and remedies for each of the cases. It is remarkable that the only cases registered in the first half of the century were highly concentrated in time and space: all occurred between 1922 and 1923 and in central Europe. A common story can be told about those episodes: political instability, large fiscal imbalances due, in part, to war and huge increases in the money supply.

It is also interesting to note that the first half of the century was still characterized mainly by convertible monetary systems. The four hyperinflationary experiences described by Sargent occurred during temporary suspensions of the gold standard. By the mid-1970s, however, after the fall of the Bretton Woods arrangement, the world moved to a fiat money system, in which no commodity serves as backing.

The second half of the century also witnessed hyperinflationary episodes. Somewhat surprisingly, the second wave of hyperinflationary episodes was concentrated in the period 1985–94. And they were concentrated in two regions; it would appear, though, that the temporal coincidence was just random. The countries involved were Argentina, Brazil, Bolivia and Peru in Latin America, and Yugoslavia and Poland in central Europe. Again, a common story could be told: in the first years of the 1980s, the four Latin American countries experienced major financial crises, including default in international debt markets. As a consequence, the ability of the governments to smooth temporary fiscal shocks via credit markets was severely restricted. The four countries had experienced in the previous decade substantial political instability, including military dictatorships and weak democratic governments. On the other hand, both Poland and Yugoslavia were undergoing substantial political and economic transformation after the fall of the USSR. In all cases, there were major fiscal imbalances: government deficits were chronic and volatile. As consequence, money printing became the only source of revenues and major bursts in inflation rates occurred.

It is interesting to note that other Latin American countries (Colombia, Uruguay, Mexico) also suffered financial and debt crises, but did not experience inflation rates of this magnitude, and other central European countries underwent major political and economic transformation and did not have hyperinflations.

Indeed, what we have learned (see Bruno et al., 1988; 1991) is that major political and economic crises are a necessary condition for hyperinflations to occur. But crisis will lead to hyperinflation if, and only if, the crisis manifests itself in serious fiscal imbalances that are financed by the central bank issuing unbacked paper money. There is a wide consensus in the literature about this.

Although we know very precisely the conditions under which hyperinflations are almost unavoidable, it is difficult to tell exactly when the burst will start and how large it will be.

The subtlety of hyperinflationary dynamics has been explored in a sequence of papers (Eckstein and Leiderman, 1992; Zarazaga, 1993; Marcet and Nicolini, 2003) that can be seen as complementary. All these models share the property, supported by evidence, that hyperinflations can occur only in economies with large and persistent fiscal deficits that are purely financed by printing money, or seigniorage. In all the models, the problem arises because the required seigniorage is close to the maximum revenue that can be raised, given the demand for real money, that is, the maximum of the Laffer curve. Eckstein and Leiderman (1992) argue that if the elasticity of money demand with respect to the inflation rate approaches one form above, when average seigniorage is very high, very small shocks to it can generate drastic changes in the required inflation rate.

Zarazaga (1993) introduces a decentralized government with a common pool of resources and private information on the shock to the spending opportunities of each member of the government. Hyperinflations occur when there are too many positive expenditure shocks, there is too much demand for resources, and the required seigniorage is too high. When this happens, a price war-type strategy follows in which all agencies become excessively demanding and the central bank ends up issuing enormous amounts of currency. Finally, Marcet and Nicolini (2003) introduce very small departures from rationality and show that the dynamics of the most simple seigniorage model change in a way that fits the evidence surprisingly well.

From the point of view of inflation stabilization policies, the debate has taken three routes. The first claims that the key for a successful stabilization policy is to correct the fundamentals, this is, to make a drastic and permanent change in fiscal policy so as to eliminate the need to print money. This kind of policy is called 'orthodox'. The second puts the emphasis on 'heterodox' policies, that is, a combination of nominal anchors like fixing the nominal exchange rate – eventually moving towards a gold or strong currency standard – and price and wage controls. Finally, a third approach points to the need to combine the other two policies. From the point of view of experience and the theory, it is clear that no attempt to stabilize the economy without orthodox policies has any chance of success in the medium term. And it appears from experience that in most successful cases (although there has been some debate on whether this was true in all of them), some type of nominal anchor, typically the exchange rate, was also important. While not all theoretical models put much weight on the nominal anchor (Marcet and Nicolini, 2003, is the most notable exception), in all of the models these policies are either harmless or good for the success of the stabilization effort.

A final word regarding Cagan's (1956) definition: as with any definition, it is arbitrary. Had we taken a lower inflation rate per month, like 25 per cent, the number of experiences would have been greater, and many more countries would have been involved in our discussion. However, the general lessons one learns are essentially the same. Quantity theory predictions work extremely well, and the most appropriate policies to deal with these experiences are the same.

JUAN PABLO NICOLINI

See also **German hyperinflation.**

Bibliography

Bruno, M., Di Tella, G., Dornbusch, R. and Fisher, S. 1988. *Inflation Stabilization: The Experience of Argentina, Brazil, Israel and Mexico.* Cambridge, MA: MIT Press.
Bruno, M., Fisher, S., Helpman, E. and Liviatan, N. 1991. *Lessons of Economic Stabililzation and its Aftermath.* Cambridge, MA: MIT Press.
Cagan, P. 1956. The monetary dynamics of hyperinflation. In *Studies in the Quantity Theory of Money*, ed. M. Friedman. Chicago: University of Chicago Press.
Eckstein, Z. and Leiderman, L. 1992. Seigniorage and the welfare cost of inflation. *Journal of Monetary Economics* 29, 389–410.
Fisher, I. 1934. *Stable Money: A History of the Movement.* New York: Adelphi.
Marcet, A. and Nicolini, J. 2003. Recurrent hyperinflations and learning. *American Economic Review* 93, 1476–98.
Marcet, A. and Nicolini, J. 2005. Money and prices in models of bounded rationality in high-inflation economies. *Review of Economic Dynamics* 8, 452–79.
Sargent, T. 1992. The ends of four big inflations. In *Rational Expectations and Inflation*, 2nd edn. New York: Harper and Row.
Zarazaga, C. 1993. Hyperinflation and moral hazard in the appropriation of seigniorage. Working paper, Federal Reserve Bank of Philadelphia.

inflation targeting

Inflation targeting is a monetary-policy strategy that was introduced in New Zealand in 1990, has been very successful, and as of 2007 had been adopted by more than 20 industrialized and non-industrialized countries. It is characterized by (*a*) an announced numerical inflation target, (*b*) an implementation of monetary policy that gives a major role to an inflation forecast and has been called 'inflation-forecast targeting', and (*c*) a high degree of transparency and accountability.

The *numerical inflation target* is typically around two per cent at an annual rate for the Consumer Price Index (CPI) or a core CPI, in the form of a range, such as one to three per cent in New Zealand; or a point target with a range, such as a two per cent point target with a range/tolerance interval of plus/minus one percentage points in Canada and Sweden; or a point target without any explicit range, such as two per cent in the UK and 2.5 per cent in Norway. The difference between these forms does not seem to matter in practice: a central bank with a target range seems to aim for the middle of the range, and the edges of the range are normally interpreted as 'soft edges' in the sense that they do not trigger discrete policy changes, and being just outside the range is not considered much different from being just inside.

In practice, inflation targeting is never 'strict' inflation targeting but always 'flexible' inflation targeting, in the sense that all inflation-targeting central banks ('central bank' is used as the generic name for monetary authority) not only aim at stabilizing inflation around the inflation target but also put some weight on stabilizing the real economy, for instance, implicitly or explicitly stabilizing a measure of resource utilization such as the output gap between actual output and 'potential' output. Thus, the 'target variables' of the central bank include not only inflation but other variables as well, such as the output gap. The objectives under flexible inflation targeting seem well approximated by a quadratic loss function consisting of the sum of the square of inflation deviations from target and a weight times the square of the output gap, and possibly also a weight times the square of instrument-rate changes (the last part corresponding to a preference for interest-rate smoothing). (The instrument rate is the short nominal interest rate that the central bank sets to implement monetary policy.) However, for new inflation-targeting regimes, where the establishment of 'credibility' is a priority, stabilizing the real economy probably has less weight than when credibility has been established (more on credibility below).

Because there is a lag between monetary-policy actions (such an instrument-rate change) and its impact on the central bank's target variables, monetary policy is more effective if it is guided by forecasts. The implementation of inflation targeting therefore gives a main role to forecasts of inflation and other target variables. It can be described as *forecast targeting*, that is, setting the instrument rate (more precisely, deciding on an instrument-rate path) such that the forecasts of the target variables conditional on that instrument-rate path 'look good', where 'look good', for instance, means that the inflation forecast approaches the inflation target and the output-gap forecast approaches zero at an appropriate pace.

Inflation targeting is characterized by a high degree of *transparency*. Typically, an inflation-targeting central bank publishes a regular monetary-policy report which includes the bank's forecast of inflation and other variables, a summary of its analysis behind the forecasts, and the motivation for its policy decisions. Some inflation-targeting central banks also provide some information on, or even forecasts of, their likely future policy decisions.

This high degree of transparency is exceptional in view of the history of central banking. Traditionally, central-bank objectives, deliberations, and even policy decisions have been subject to considerable secrecy. It is difficult to find any reasons for that secrecy beyond central bankers' desire not to be subject to public scrutiny (including scrutiny and possible pressure from governments or legislative bodies). The current emphasis on transparency is based on the insight that monetary policy to a very large extent is 'management of expectations'. Monetary policy has an impact on the economy mostly through the private-sector expectations that current monetary-policy actions and announcements give rise to. The level of the instrument rate for the next few weeks matter very little to most economic agents. What matters is the expectations of future instrument settings, which expectations affect longer interest rates that do matter for economic decisions and activity.

Furthermore, private-sector expectations of inflation for the next one or two years affect current pricing decisions and inflation for the next few quarters. Therefore, the anchoring of private-sector inflation expectations on the inflation target is a crucial precondition for the stability of actual inflation. The proximity of private-sector inflation expectations to the inflation target is often referred to as the 'credibility' of the inflation-targeting regime. Inflation-targeting central banks sometimes appear to be obsessed by such credibility, there are good reasons for this obsession. If a central bank succeeds in achieving credibility, a good part of the battle to control inflation is already won. A high degree of transparency and high-quality and convincing monetary-policy reports are often considered essential to establishing and maintaining credibility. Furthermore, a high degree of credibility gives the central bank more freedom to be 'flexible' and also stabilize the real economy.

Whereas many central banks in the past seem to have actively avoided *accountability*, for instance by not having explicit objectives and by being very secretive, inflation targeting is normally associated with a high degree of accountability. A high degree of accountability is now considered generic to inflation targeting and an important component in strengthening the incentives faced by inflation-targeting central banks to achieve their objectives. The explicit objectives and the transparency of monetary-policy reporting contribute to increased public scrutiny of monetary policy. In several countries inflation-targeting central banks are subject to more explicit accountability. In New Zealand, the Governor of the Reserve Bank of New Zealand is subject to a Policy Target Agreement, an explicit agreement between the Governor and the government on the Governor's responsibilities. In the UK, the Chancellor of the Exchequer's remit to the Bank of England instructs the Bank to write a public letter explaining any deviation from the target larger than one percentage point and what actions the Bank is taking in response to the deviation. In several countries, central-bank officials are subject to public hearings in the Parliament where monetary policy is scrutinized; and in several countries, monetary policy is regularly or occasionally subject to extensive reviews by independent experts (for instance, New Zealand, the UK, Norway, and Sweden).

So far, since its inception in the early 1990s, inflation targeting has been a considerable *success*, as measured by the stability of inflation and the stability of the real economy. There is no evidence that inflation targeting has been detrimental to growth, productivity, employment, or other measures of economic performance. The success is both absolute and relative to alternative monetary-policy strategies, such as exchange-rate targeting or money-growth targeting. No country has so far abandoned inflation targeting after adopting it, or even expressed any regrets. For both industrial and non-industrial countries, inflation targeting has proved to be a most flexible and resilient monetary-policy regime, and has succeeded in surviving a number of large shocks and disturbances. As of 2007, a long list of non-industrial countries were asking the International Monetary Fund for assistance in introducing inflation targeting. Although inflation targeting has been an unqualified success in all the small- and medium-sized industrial countries that have introduced it, the United States, the eurozone and Japan have not yet adopted all the explicit characteristics of inflation targeting, but they are all moving in that direction. Reservations about inflation targeting have mainly suggested that it might give too much weight on inflation stabilization to the detriment of the stability of the real economy or other possible monetary-policy objectives; the fact that real-world inflation targeting is flexible rather than strict and the empirical success of inflation targeting in the countries where it has been implemented seem to confound those reservations.

A possible alternative to inflation targeting is *money-growth targeting*, whereby the central bank has an explicit target for the growth of the money supply. Money-growth targeting has been tried in several countries but been abandoned, since practical experience has consistently shown that the relation between money growth and inflation is too unstable and unreliable for money-growth targeting to provide successful inflation stabilization. Although Germany's Bundesbank paid lip service to money-growth targeting for many years, it often deliberately missed its money-growth target in order to achieve its inflation target, and is therefore arguably better described as an implicit inflation targeter. Many small and medium-sized countries have tried exchange-rate targeting in the form of a *fixed exchange rate*, that is, fixing the exchange rate relative to a centre country with an independent monetary policy. For several reasons, including increased international capital flows and difficulties defending misaligned fixed exchange rates against speculative attacks, fixed exchange rates have become less viable and less successful in stabilizing inflation. This has led many countries to instead pursue inflation targeting with flexible exchange rates.

A current much-debated issue concerning the further development of inflation targeting is the appropriate *assumption about the instrument-rate path* that underlies the forecasts of inflation and other target variables and the *information provided about future policy actions*. Traditionally, inflation-targeting central banks have assumed a constant interest rate underlying its inflation forecasts, with the implication that a constant-interest-rate inflation forecasts that overshoots (undershoots) the inflation target at some horizon such as two years indicates that the instrument rate needs to increased (decreased). Increasingly, central banks have become aware of a number of serious problems with the assumption of constant interest rates. These problems include that the assumption may often be unrealistic and therefore imply biased forecasts, imply either explosive or indeterminate behaviour of standard models of the transmission mechanism of monetary policy, and on closer scrutiny be shown to combine inconsistent inputs in the forecasting process (such as some inputs such as asset prices that are conditional on market expectations of future interest rates rather than constant interest rates) and therefore produce inconsistent and difficult-to-interpret forecasts. Some central banks have moved to an instrument-rate assumption equal to market expectations at some recent date of future interest rates, as they can be extracted from the yield curve. This reduces the number of problems mentioned above but does not eliminate them. For instance, the central bank may have a view about the appropriate future interest-rate path that differs from the market's view. A few central banks (notably in New Zealand, Norway, and Sweden – the last probably within the next few months) have moved to deciding on and announcing an optimal instrument-rate path; this approach solves all the above problems, is the most consistent way of implementing inflation targeting, and provides the best information for the private sector. The practice of deciding on and announcing optimal instrument-rate paths is now likely to be gradually adopted by other central banks in other countries, in spite of being considered more or less impossible, or even dangerous, only a few years ago.

Another issue is whether flexible inflation targeting should eventually be transformed into flexible *price-level targeting*. Inflation targeting as practised implies that past deviations of inflation from target are not undone. This introduces a unit root in the price level and makes the price level non-stationary. That is, the conditional variance of the future price level increases without bound with the horizon. In spite of this, inflation targeting with a low inflation rate is referred to as 'price stability'. An alternative monetary-policy regime would be 'price-level targeting', where the objective is to stabilize the price level around a price-level target. That price-level target need not be constant but could follow a deterministic path corresponding to a steady inflation of two per cent, for instance. Stability of the price level around such a price-level target would imply that the price level becomes trend stationary, that is, the conditional variance of the price level becomes constant and independent of the horizon. One benefit of this compared with inflation targeting is that long-run uncertainty about the price level is smaller. Another benefit is that, if the price level falls below a credible price-level target, inflation expectations would rise and reduce the real interest rate even if the nominal interest rate is unchanged. The reduced real interest rate would stimulate the economy and bring the price level back to the target. Thus, price-level targeting may imply some automatic stabilization. This may be highly desirable, especially in situations when the zero lower bound on nominal interest rates is binding, the nominal interest rate cannot be further reduced, and the economy is in a liquidity trap, as has been the case for several years until recently in Japan. Whether price-level targeting would have any negative effects on the real economy remains a topic for current debate and research.

LARS E.O. SVENSSON

See also **central bank independence; hyperinflation.**

Bibliography

Roger, S. and Stone, M. 2005. On target? The international experience with achieving inflation targets. Working Paper No. 05/163. Washington, DC: International Monetary Fund.

Svensson, L.E.O. 2002. Monetary policy and real stabilization. In *Rethinking Stabilization Policy: A Symposium Sponsored by the Federal Reserve Bank of Kansas City*. Kansas City, MO: Federal Reserve Bank for Kansas City.

Svensson, L.E.O. 2007. Optimal inflation targeting: further developments of inflation targeting. In *Monetary Policy Under Inflation Targeting*, ed. F. Mishkin and K. Schmidt-Hebbel. Santiago, Chile: Banco Central de Chile.

Woodford, M. 2005. Central-bank communication and policy effectiveness. In *The Greenspan Era: Lessons for the Future – A Symposium Sponsored by the Federal Reserve Bank of Kansas City*. Kansas City, MO: Federal Reserve Bank for Kansas City.

inside and outside money

Money is an asset that serves as a medium of exchange.

Outside money is money that is either of a fiat nature (unbacked) or backed by some asset that is not in zero net supply within the private sector of the economy. Thus, outside money is a net asset for the private sector. The qualifier 'outside' is short for '(coming from) outside the private sector'.

Inside money is an asset representing, or backed by, any form of private credit that circulates as a medium of exchange. Since it is one private agent's liability and at the same time some other agent's asset, inside money is in zero net supply within the private sector. The qualifier 'inside' is short for '(backed by debt from) inside the private sector'.

Background

In 1960, John G. Gurley and Edward S. Shaw published *Money in a Theory of Finance*, in which they attempted to develop a theory of finance that encompasses the theory of money and a theory of financial institutions that includes banking theory.

Consider a simple economy similar to the one considered by Gurley and Shaw. The economy has fiat money – an intrinsically useless asset with no backing whatsoever – that is generally accepted as a means of payment. A monetary authority or 'government' has the monopoly over issuing this asset. The economy is closed and consists of three sectors: households, firms and government. Firms issue debt in the form of homogeneous, perfectly safe nominal bonds. (For example, think of these bonds as being promises to pay one dollar at some future date.)

Table 1 shows hypothetical sectoral balance sheets for this economy. In this example, households hold only financial wealth (that is, no real wealth such as houses), in particular money, equity in firms, and the bonds issued by the firms. Here households have no liabilities, so their net worth (NW) is just the sum of the value of their assets. The assets owned by firms consist of cash and physical capital. A part of these assets has been financed with debt (bonds), and another part by issuing equity.

Table 1

Households				Firms				Government		
Assets		Liabilities		Assets		Liabilities		Assets	Liabilities	
Money	50			Money	100	Bonds	25		Money	150
Bonds	25			Capital	200	Equity	275			
Equity	275									
		NW	350			NW	0		NW	−150

The former represent the firms' liabilities toward the bond holders, and the latter represent the firms' liabilities towards share holders. The firms' net worth (net of equity) is zero. The government has no real assets, but at some point in the past it issued financial assets – money – to pay for expenditures, and from an accounting point of view these outstanding government-issued pieces of paper constitute liabilities. (If the money was backed by a real asset, for example gold, and also fully convertible, then the value of the gold would show up on the government's Assets column. In this case, the money issued is literally a liability representing the government's commitment to redeem the money for gold. In the case of fiat money, there need not be a counterpart on the Assets column of the government's balance sheet.)

Table 2 shows what happens if we consolidate the balance sheets of the private sector. The bonds are debts from private agents (in this example the firms) to other private agents (in this example the households), so they have cancelled out. The only assets left in the balance sheet of the public sector are physical capital and the money issued by the government. Money can be thought of as a 'claim' held by consumers and firms against the government. From the standpoint of the private sector, it is a net external, or outside, claim: it is *outside money*.

Gurley and Shaw (1960) were interested in considering the effects of 'open market operations' whereby the government issues money to purchase private bonds. Suppose, for example, that they purchase $15 worth of private bonds. The resulting balance sheets are those in Table 3, which should be compared with those in Table 1. The government now has $15 worth of assets (the private bonds it purchased), and its liabilities have increased by $15 because of the money issued to pay for these bonds. Households still hold $350 worth of assets, but the composition of their portfolio has changed: they now hold $65 in money and $10 in bonds, as opposed to the $50 in money and $25 in bonds of Table 1. The additional $15 in money holdings comes from the new issue of money, backed by private bonds. These $15 are government debt, but they are issued in payment for government purchases of private securities. They are a claim of consumers and firms against the world outside the private sector, but they are counterbalanced by private debt to the world outside, that is, to the government. These additional cash balances are based on internal debt, so Gurley and Shaw referred to these $15 as *inside money*.

Table 2

Combined private sector			Government		
Assets		Liabilities	Assets		Liabilities
Money	150			Money	150
Capital	200				
		NW	350		NW	−150

Table 3

Households			Firms				Government			
Assets		Liabilities	Assets		Liabilities		Assets		Liabilities	
Money	65		Money	100	Bonds	25	Bonds	15	Money	165
Bonds	10		Capital	200	Equity	275				
Equity	275									
	NW	350			NW	0			NW	−150

To use the terminology of Gurley and Shaw, the $165 stock of money in the economy of Table 3 consists of $150 of outside money and $15 of inside money. Both types of money are really the same physical object, for example, green pieces of paper: The qualifiers *inside* and *outside* refer to the asset counterpart of the money. Inside money is backed by private domestic debt. Outside money is of a fiat nature (or backed by some other asset that is not in zero net supply within the private sector, such as gold). Note that, if we consolidate the balance sheets of the private sector in Table 3, the net worth of the private sector is still $350, just as in Table 2. Also, note that inside money is 'endogenous' in that if, for example, firms pay off their whole debt, *ceteris paribus* the money supply would shrink by $15. Most likely, Gurley and Shaw were led to stress the distinction between inside and outside money because they viewed money and private debt as assets that played distinct roles in exchange, so that an economy with the balance sheets of Table 1, where households hold $50 in cash and $25 in private bonds, would function differently from an economy with the balance sheets of Table 3, where households hold $65 in cash and $10 in private bonds. (See Gurley and Shaw, 1960, pp. 82–8, the section titled 'Monetary Policy in a Modified Second Model'.) The theoretical analysis throughout the book is predominantly verbal, so it is not clear which are the precise trade-offs that agents consider when making a portfolio decision between money and bonds. The fact that households treat them as different assets is explicit in the Mathematical Appendix, where Alain C. Enthoven assumes distinct reduced-form demand functions for the two financial assets. Note that, since bonds are nominal and riskless in this set-up, it is not obvious why households would not treat them as perfect substitutes for money.)

The contemporary literature on monetary theory in general, and the subfield that deals with inside and outside money in particular, does not take it as given that money and bonds play different roles. Instead, it seeks to understand whether they indeed do, and whether they ought to. The recent emphasis has been on trying to gain a deeper understanding of the precise roles that fiat money and private debt play and ought to play, both as media of exchange and as vehicles to channel resources across economic agents, towards their most efficient use. This change of emphasis has led to a slightly different definition of inside money. The more modern use of the concept does not rely on the type of open market operations of Gurley and Shaw. Inside money need not be defined narrowly as circulating fiat money backed by private debt; the private debt *itself* is regarded as inside money if it circulates as means of payment among the private agents. The more modern definition given at the beginning of this article encompasses both the case where private debt circulates directly and Gurley and Shaw's original example. To illustrate, consider again the economy of Table 1. According to the modern use of the term, there is not enough information in that table to decide how much inside money there is in the economy; there are $25 of inside assets, that is, assets that are in zero net supply within the private sector, but whether these assets constitute inside money depends on whether they circulate as means of payment. If they do not – for example if lenders merely hold the bonds until maturity to redeem them – then these bonds are not inside money.

Contemporary perspectives

Gurley and Shaw (1960) simply asserted that agents would want to hold government-issued fiat money (this weakness was stressed by Patinkin, 1961), and for their purposes the distinction between inside and outside money was relevant because they implicitly regarded them as imperfect substitutes. The modern literature on monetary theory seeks to identify the fundamental features of the basic economic environment that can make fiat money, or, more generally, any asset that serves as a medium of exchange, valuable and socially beneficial. Modern theory also focuses on the differences and similarities between inside and outside money. When is outside money valued? Under which circumstances does inside money arise? Are inside and outside money substitutes or complements? Under which circumstances can they coexist? Are they *both* needed to achieve efficient outcomes?

Inside money is private debt that also circulates as a tangible medium of exchange. Thus, an economy with inside money must perform a delicate balancing act. On the one hand, it must have enough commitment or enforcement for credit to be feasible, but at the same time credit must not function too well, for otherwise a tangible medium of exchange would be inessential. For example, Kocherlakota (1998) shows that a tangible medium of exchange is not essential if agents can commit to future actions or if their trading histories are public. Starting from this observation, Cavalcanti and Wallace (1999a) consider an environment where trading histories are public for a subset of agents but private for the rest, and show that a social optimum requires note issue by those agents with public trading histories. In addition, those notes are in turn used in trade among the agents whose trading histories are private. Thus, in their environment an optimum requires inside money.

Kiyotaki and Moore (2002a) instead consider an environment where everyone is anonymous, and emphasize the importance of the agents' ability to make bilateral and multilateral commitments. The degree of (bilateral) commitment a borrower can make to an initial lender when selling a paper claim places a bound on the entire stock of private debt. The degree of (multilateral) commitment a borrower can make to repay any bearer determines the extent to which the borrower's debt can circulate in equilibrium. Kiyotaki and Moore find that only outside money circulates in economies with very low degrees of bilateral commitment. For higher, but still low, degrees of bilateral commitment, outside and inside money circulate alongside each other in equilibrium. For yet higher degrees, only inside money circulates, and, when the agents' ability to make bilateral commitments is large enough, the economy can manage without any money, inside or outside.

RICARDO LAGOS

I thank Narayana Kocherlakota and Warren Weber for comments. I also thank the C.V. Starr Center for Applied Economics at New York University for financial support. The views expressed herein are those of the author and not necessarily those of the Federal Reserve Bank of Minneapolis or the Federal Reserve System.

Bibliography

Cavalcanti, R. de O., Erosa, A. and Temzelides, T. 1999. Private money and reserve management in a random-matching model. *Journal of Political Economy* 107, 929–45.

Cavalcanti, R. de, O. and Wallace, N. 1999a. A model of private bank-note issue. *Review of Economic Dynamics* 2, 104–36.

Cavalcanti, R. de O. and Wallace, N. 1999b. Inside and outside money as alternative media of exchange. *Journal of Money, Credit, and Banking* 31, 443–57.

Gurley, J. and Shaw, E. 1960. *Money in a Theory of Finance*. Washington, DC: Brookings Institution.

Kiyotaki, N. and Moore, J. 2002a. Inside money and liquidity. Mimeo, London School of Economics.

Kiyotaki, N. and Moore, J. 2002b. Evil is the root of all money. *American Economic Review* 92(2), 62–6.

Kiyotaki, N. and Moore, J. 2005. Financial deepening. *Journal of the European Economic Association* 3, 701–13.

Kocherlakota, N. 1998. Money is memory. *Journal of Economic Theory* 81, 232–51.

Patinkin, D. 1961. Financial intermediaries and the logical structure of monetary theory: a review article. *American Economic Review* 51(1), 95–116.

Wallace, N. 2000. Knowledge of individual histories and optimal payment arrangements. *Federal Reserve Bank of Minneapolis Quarterly Review* 24(3), 11–21.

liquidity trap

A liquidity trap is defined as a situation in which the short-term nominal interest rate is zero. In this case, many argue, increasing money in circulation has no effect on either output or prices. The liquidity trap is originally a Keynesian idea and was contrasted with the quantity theory of money, which maintains that prices and output are, roughly speaking, proportional to the money supply.

According to the Keynesian theory, money supply has its effects on prices and output through the nominal interest rate. Increasing money supply reduces the interest rate through a money demand equation. Lower interest rates stimulate output and spending. The short-term nominal interest rate, however, cannot be less than zero, based on a basic arbitrage argument: no one will lend 100 dollars unless she gets at least 100 dollars back. This is often referred to as the 'zero bound' on the short-term nominal interest rate. Hence, the Keynesian argument goes, once the money supply has been increased to a level where the short-term interest rate is zero, there will be no further effect on either output or prices, no matter by how much money supply is increased.

The ideas that underlie the liquidity trap were conceived during the Great Depression. In that period the short-term nominal interest rate was close to zero. At the beginning of 1933, for example, the short-term nominal interest rate in the United States – as measured by three-month Treasuries – was only 0.05 per cent. As the memory of the Great Depression faded and several authors challenged the liquidity trap, many economists begun to regard it as a theoretical curiosity.

The liquidity trap received much more attention again in the late 1990s with the arrival of new data. The short-term nominal interest rate in Japan collapsed to zero in the second half of the 1990s. Furthermore, the Bank of Japan (BoJ) more than doubled the monetary base through traditional and non-traditional measures to increase prices and stimulate demand. The BoJ policy of 'quantitative easing' from 2001 to 2006, for example, increased the monetary base by over 70 per cent in that period. By most accounts, however, the effect on prices was sluggish at best. (As long as five years after the beginning of quantitative easing, the changes in the CPI and the GDP deflator were still only starting to approach positive territory.)

The modern view of the liquidity trap

The modern view of the liquidity trap is more subtle than the traditional Keynesian one. It relies on an intertemporal stochastic general equilibrium model whereby aggregate demand depends on current and expected future real interest rates rather than simply the current rate as in the old Keynesian models. In the modern framework, the liquidity trap arises when the zero bound on the short-term nominal interest rate prevents the central bank from fully accommodating sufficiently large deflationary shocks by interest rate cuts.

The aggregate demand relationship that underlies the model is usually expressed by a consumption Euler equation, derived from the maximization problem of a representative household. On the assumption that all output is consumed, that equation can be approximated as:

$$Y_t = E_t Y_{t+1} - \sigma(i_t - E_t \pi_{t+1} - r_t^e) \tag{1}$$

where Y_t is the deviation of output from steady state, i_t is the short-term nominal interest rate, π_t is inflation, E_t is an expectation operator and r_t^e is an exogenous shock process (which can be due to host of factors). This equation says that current demand depends on expectations of future output (because spending depends on expected future income) and the real interest rate which is the difference between the nominal interest rate and expected future inflation (because lower real interest rates make spending today relatively cheaper than future spending). This equation can be forwarded to yield

$$Y_t = E_t Y_{T+1} - \sigma \sum_{s=t}^{T} E_t(i_s - \pi_{s+1} - r_s^e)$$

which illustrates that demand depends not only on the current short-term interest rate but on the entire expected path for future interest rates and expected inflation. Because long-term interest rates depend on expectations about current and future short-term rates, this equation can also be interpreted as saying that demand depends on long-term interest rates. Monetary policy works through the short-term nominal interest rate in the model, and is constrained by the fact that it cannot be set below zero,

$$i_t \geq 0. \tag{2}$$

In contrast to the static Keynesian framework, monetary policy can still be effective in this model even when the current short-term nominal interest rate is zero. In order to be effective, however, expansionary monetary policy must change the public's expectations about future interest rates at the point in time when the zero bound will no longer be binding. For example, this may be the period in which the deflationary shocks are expected to subside. Thus, successful monetary easing in a liquidity trap involves committing to maintaining lower future nominal interest rates for any given price level in the future once deflationary pressures have subsided (see, for example, Reifschneider and Williams, 2000; Jung, Teranishi and Watanabe, 2005; Eggertsson and Woodford, 2003; Adam and Billi, 2006).

This was the rationale for the BoJ's announcement in the autumn of 2003 that it promised to keep the interest rate low until deflationary pressures had subsided and CPI inflation was projected to be in positive territory. It also underlay the logic of the Federal Reserve announcement in mid-2003 that it would keep interest rates low for a 'considerable period'. At that time, there was some fear of deflation in the United States (the short-term interest rates reached one per cent in the spring of 2003, its lowest level since the Great Depression, and some analysts voiced fears of deflation).

There is a direct correspondence between the nominal interest rate and the money supply in the model reviewed above. There is an underlying demand equation for real money balances derived from a representative household maximization problem (like the consumption Euler equation 1). This demand equation can be expressed as a relationship between the nominal interest rate and money supply

$$\frac{M_t}{P_t} \geq L(Y_t, i_t) \tag{3}$$

where M_t is the nominal stock of money and P_t is a price level. On the assumption that both consumption and liquidity services are normal goods, this inequality says that the demand for money increases with lower interest rates and higher output. As the interest rate declines to zero, however, the demand for money is indeterminate because at that point households do not care whether they hold money or one-period riskless government bonds. The two are perfect substitutes: a government liability that has nominal value but pays no interest rate. Another way of stating the result discussed above is that a successful monetary easing (committing to lower *future* nominal interest rate for a given price level) involves committing to higher money supply *in the future* once interest rates have become positive again (see, for example, Eggertsson, 2006a).

Irrelevance results

According to the modern view outlined above, monetary policy will increase demand at zero interest rates only if it changes expectations about the future money supply or, equivalently, the path of future interest rates. The Keynesian liquidity trap is therefore only a true trap if the central bank cannot to stir expectations. There are several interesting conditions under which this is the case, so that monetary easing is ineffective. These 'irrelevance' results help explain why BoJ's increase in the monetary base in Japan through 'quantitative easing' in 2001–6 may have had a somewhat more limited effect on inflation and inflation expectations in that period than some proponents of the quantity theory of money expected.

Krugman (1998), for example, shows that at zero interest rates if the public expects the money supply in the future to revert to some constant value as soon as the interest rate is positive, quantitative easing will be ineffective. Any increase in the money supply in this case is expected to be reversed, and output and prices are unchanged.

Eggertsson and Woodford (2003) show that the same result applies if the public expects the central bank to follow a 'Taylor rule', which may indeed summarize behaviour of a number of central banks in industrial countries. A central bank following a Taylor rule raises interest rates in response to above-target inflation and above-trend output. Conversely, unless the zero bound is binding, the central bank reduces the interest rate if inflation is below target or output is below trend (an output gap). If the public expects the central bank to follow the Taylor rule, it anticipates an interest rate hike as soon as there are inflationary pressures in excess of the implicit inflation target. If the target is perceived to be price stability, this implies that quantitative easing has no effect, because a commitment to the Taylor rule implies that any increase in the monetary base is reversed as soon as deflationary pressures subside.

Eggertsson (2006a) demonstrates that, if a central bank is discretionary, that is, unable to commit to future policy, and minimizes a standard loss function that depends on inflation and the output gap, it will also be unable to increase inflationary expectations at the zero bound, because it will always have an incentive to renege on an inflation promise or extended 'quantitative easing' in order to achieve low *ex post* inflation. This deflation bias has the same implication as the previous two irrelevance propositions, namely, that the public will expect any increase in the monetary base to be reversed as soon as deflationary pressures subside. The deflation bias can be illustrated by the aid of a few additional equations, as illustrated in the next section.

The deflation bias and the optimal commitment

The deflation bias can be illustrated by completing the model that gave rise to (1), (2) and (3). In the model prices are not flexible because firms reset their price at random intervals. This gives rise to an aggregate supply equation which is often referred to as the 'New Keynesian' Phillips curve. It can be derived from the Euler equation of the firm's maximization problem (see, for example, Woodford, 2003)

$$\pi_t = \kappa(Y_t - Y_t^n) + \beta E_t \pi_{t+1} \tag{4}$$

where Y_t^n is the natural rate of output (in deviation from steady state), which is the 'hypothetical' output produced if prices were perfectly flexible, β is the discount factor of the household in the model and the parameter $\kappa > 0$ is a function of preferences and technology parameters. This equation implies that inflation can increase output above its natural level because not all firms reset their prices instantaneously.

If the government's objective is to maximize the utility of the representative household, it can be approximated by

$$\sum_{t=0}^{\infty} \beta^t \{\pi_t^2 + \lambda_y (Y_t - Y_t^e)^2\} \tag{5}$$

where the term Y_t^e is the target level of output. It is also referred to as the 'efficient level' or 'first-best level' of output. The standard 'inflation bias' first illustrated by Kydland and Prescott (1977) arises when the natural level of output is lower than the efficient level of output, that is, $Y_t^n < Y_t^e$.

Eggertsson (2006a) shows that there is also a deflation bias under certain circumstances. While the inflation bias is a steady state phenomenon, the deflation bias arises to temporary shocks. Consider the implied solution for the nominal interest rate when there is an inflation bias of π. It is

$$i_t = \pi + r_t^e.$$

This equation cannot be satisfied in the presence of sufficiently large deflationary shocks, that is, a negative r_t^e. In particular if $r_t^e < -\pi$ this solution would imply a negative nominal interest rate. It can be shown (Eggertsson, 2006a) that a discretionary policymaker will in this case set the nominal interest rate to zero but set inflation equal to the 'inflation bias' solution π as soon as the deflationary pressures have subsided (that is, when the shock is $r_t^e \geq -\pi_t$). If the disturbance r_t^e is low enough, the zero bound frustrates the central bank's ability to achieve its 'inflation target' π which can in turn lead to excessive deflation. (While deflation and zero interest rates are due to real shocks in the literature discussed above, an alternative way of modelling the liquidity trap is that it is the result of self-fulfilling deflationary expectations; see, for example, Benhabib, Schmitt-Grohe and Uribe, 2001.)

To illustrate this consider the following experiment. Suppose the term r_t^e is unexpectedly negative in period 0 ($r_t^e = r_L < 0$) and then reverts back to its steady state value $r > 0$ with a fixed probability α in every period. For simplicity assume that $\pi = 0$. Then it is easy to verify from eqs. (1), (4), the behaviour of the central bank described above and the assumed process for r_t^e that the solution for output and inflation is given by (see Eggertsson, 2006a, for details)

$$\pi_t = \frac{1}{\alpha(1 - \beta(1 - \alpha)) - \sigma\kappa(1 - \alpha)}\kappa\sigma r_L^e \text{ if } r_t^e = r_L^e \text{ and } \pi_t = 0 \text{ otherwise} \quad (6)$$

$$Y_t = \frac{1 - \beta(1 - \alpha)}{\alpha(1 - \beta(1 - \alpha)) - \sigma\kappa(1 - \alpha)}\sigma r_L^e \text{ if } r_t^e = r_L^e \text{ and } Y_t = 0 \text{ otherwise} \quad (7)$$

Figure 1 shows the solution in a calibrated example for numerical values of the model taken from Eggertsson and Woodford (2003). (Under this calibration $\alpha = 0.1$, $\kappa = 0.02$, $\beta = 0.99$ and $r_L = -\frac{0.02}{4}$ but the model is calibrated in quarterly frequencies.) The dashed line shows the solution under the contingency that the natural rate of interest reverts to positive level in 15 periods. The inability of the central bank to set negative nominal interest rate results in a 14 per cent output collapse and 10 per cent annual deflation. The fact that in each quarter there is a 90 per cent chance of the exogenous disturbance to remaining negative for the next quarter creates the expectation of future deflation and a continued output depression, which creates even further depression and deflation. Even if the central bank lowers the short-term nominal interest rate to zero, the real rate of interest is positive, because the private sector expects deflation. The same results applies when there is an inflation bias, that is, $\pi > 0$, but in this case the disturbance r_t^e needs to be correspondingly more negative to lead to an output collapse.

The solution illustrated in Figure 1 is what Eggertsson (2006a) calls the deflation bias of monetary policy under discretion. The reason why this solution indicates a deflation bias is that the deflation and depression can largely be avoided by the correct *commitment* to optimal policy. The solid line shows the solution in the case that the central bank can commit to optimal future policy. In this case the deflation and the

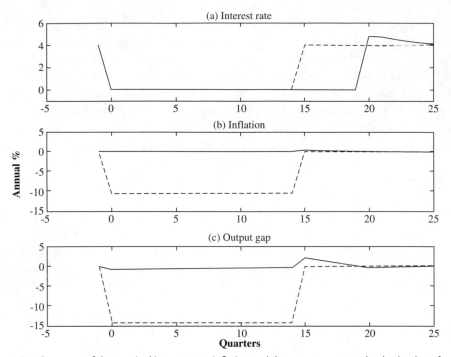

Figure 1   Response of the nominal interest rate, inflation and the output gap to a shocks that lasts for 15 quarters. *Note*: The dashed line shows the solution under policy discretion, the solid line the solution under the optimal policy commitment.

output contraction are largely avoided. In the optimal solution the central bank commits to keeping the nominal interest at zero for a considerable period beyond what is implied by the discretionary solution; that is, interest rates are kept at zero even if the deflationary shock r_t^e has subsided. Similarly, the central bank allows for an output boom once the deflationary shock subsides and accommodates mild inflation. Such commitment stimulates demand and reduces deflation through several channels. The expectation of future inflation lowers the real interest rate, even if the nominal interest rate cannot be reduced further, thus stimulating spending. Similarly, a commitment to lower future nominal interest rate (once the deflationary pressures have subsided) stimulates demand for the same reason. Finally, the expectation of higher future income, as manifested by the expected output boom, stimulates current spending, in accordance with the permanent income hypothesis (see Eggertsson and Woodford, 2003, for the derivation underlying this figures. The optimal commitment is also derived in Jung, Teranishi and Watanabe, 2005, and Adam and Billi, 2006, for alternative processes for the deflationary disturbance).

The discretionary solution indicates that this optimal commitment, however desirable, is not feasible if the central bank cannot commit to future policy. The discretionary policymaker is cursed by the deflation bias. To understand the logic of this curse, observe that the government's objective (5) involves minimizing deviations of inflation and output from their targets. Both these targets can be achieved at time $t = 15$ when the optimal commitment implies targeting positive inflation and generating an output boom. Hence the central bank has an incentive to renege on its previous commitment and achieve zero inflation and keep output at its optimal target. The private sector anticipates this, so that the solution under discretion is the one given in (6) and (7); this is the deflation bias of discretionary policy.

Shaping expectations

The lesson of the irrelevance results is that monetary policy is ineffective if it cannot stir expectations. The previous section illustrated, however, that shaping expectations in the correct way can be very important for minimizing the output contraction and deflation associated with deflationary shocks. This, however, may be difficult for a government that is expected to behave in a discretionary manner. How can the correct set of expectations be generated?

Perhaps the simplest solution is for the government to make clear *announcements* about its future policy through the appropriate 'policy rule'. This was the lesson of the 'rules vs. discretion' literature started by Kydland and Prescott (1977) to solve the inflation bias, and the same logic applies here even if the nature of the 'dynamic inconsistency' that gives rise to the deflation bias is different from the standard one. To the extent that announcements about future policy are believed, they can have a very big effect. There is a large literature on the different policy rules that minimize the distortions associated with deflationary shocks. One example is found in both Eggertsson and Woodford (2003) and Wolman (2005). They show that, if the government follows a form of price level targeting, the optimal commitment solution can be closely or even completely replicated, depending on the sophistication of the targeting regime. Under the proposed policy rule the central bank commits to keep the interest rate at zero until a particular price level is hit, which happens well after the deflationary shocks have subsided.

If the central bank, and the government as a whole, has a very low level of credibility, a mere announcement of future policy intentions through a new 'policy rule' may not be sufficient. This is especially true in a deflationary environment, for at least three reasons. First, the deflation bias implies that the government has an incentive to promise to deliver future expansion and higher inflation, and then to renege on this promise. Second, the deflationary shocks that give rise to this commitment problem are rare, and it is therefore harder for a central bank to build up a reputation for dealing with them well. Third, this problem is even further aggravated at zero interest rates because then the central bank cannot take any direct actions (that is, cutting interest rate) to show its new commitment to reflation. This has led many authors to consider other policy options for the government as a whole that make a reflation credible, that is, make the optimal commitment described in the previous section 'incentive compatible'.

Perhaps the most straightforward way to make a reflation credible is for the government to issue debt, for example by deficit spending. It is well known in the literature that government debt creates an inflationary incentive (see, for example, Calvo, 1978). Suppose the government promises future inflation and in addition prints one dollar of debt. If the government later reneges on its promised inflation, the real value of this one dollar of debt will increase by the same amount. Then the government will need to raise taxes to compensate for the increase in the real debt. To the extent that taxation is costly, it will no longer be in the interest of the government to renege on its promises to inflate the price level, even after deflationary pressures have subsided in the example above. This commitment device is explored in Eggertsson (2006a), which shows that this is an effective tool to battle deflation.

Jeanne and Svensson (2007) and Eggertsson (2006a) show that foreign exchange interventions also have this effect, for very similar reasons. The reason is that foreign exchange interventions change the balance sheet of the government so that a policy of reflation is incentive compatible. The reason is that, if the government prints nominal liabilities (such as government bonds or money) and purchases foreign exchange, it will incur balance-sheet losses if it reneges on an inflation promise because this would imply an exchange rate appreciation and thus a portfolio loss.

There are many other tools in the arsenal of the government to battle deflation. Real government spending, that is, government purchases of real goods and services, can also be effective to this end (Eggertsson, 2005). Perhaps the most surprising one is that policies that temporarily reduce the natural level of output, Y_t^n, can be shown to increase equilibrium output (Eggertsson, 2006b). The reason is that policies that suppress the natural level of output create actual and expected reflation in the price level and this effect is strong enough to generate recovery because of the impact on real interest rates.

Conclusion: the Great Depression and the liquidity trap

As mentioned in the introduction, the old literature on the liquidity trap was motivated by the Great Depression. The modern literature on the liquidity trap not only sheds light on recent events in Japan and the United States (as discussed above) but also provides new insights into the US recovery from the Great Depression. This article has reviewed theoretical results that indicate that a policy of reflation can induce a substantial increase in output when there are deflationary shocks (compare the solid line and the dashed line in Figure 1: moving from one equilibrium to the other implies a substantial increase in output). Interestingly, Franklin Delano Roosevelt (FDR) announced a policy of reflating the price level in 1933 to its pre-Depression level when he became President in 1933. To achieve reflation FDR not only announced an explicit objective of reflation but also implemented several policies which made this objective credible. These policies include all those reviewed in the previous section, such as massive deficit spending, higher real government spending, foreign exchange interventions, and even policies that reduced the natural level of output (the National Industrial Recovery Act and the Agricultural Adjustment Act: see Eggertsson, 2006b, for discussion). As discussed in Eggertsson (2005; 2006b) these policies may greatly have contributed to the end of the depression. Output increased by 39 per cent during 1933–7, with the turning point occurring immediately after

FDR's inauguration, when he announced the policy objective of reflation. In 1937, however, the administration moved away from reflation and the stimulative policies that supported it – prematurely declaring victory over the depression – which helps explaining the downturn in 1937–8, when monthly industrial production fell by 30 per cent in less than a year. The recovery resumed once the administration recommitted to reflation (see Eggertsson and Puglsey, 2006). The modern analysis of the liquidity trap indicates that, while zero short-term interest rates made static changes in the money supply irrelevant during this period, expectations about the future evolution of the money supply and the interest rate were key factors determining aggregate demand. Thus, recent research indicates that monetary policy was far from being ineffective during the Great Depression, but it worked mainly through expectations.

GAUTI B. EGGERTSSON

See also **optimal fiscal and monetary policy (with commitment); optimal fiscal and monetary policy (without commitment).**

Bibliography

Adam, K. and Billi, R. 2006. Optimal monetary policy under commitment with a zero bound on nominal interest rates. *Journal of Money, Credit and Banking* (forthcoming).

Benhabib, J., Schmitt-Grohe, S. and Uribe, M. 2001. Monetary policy and multiple equilibria. *American Economic Review* 91, 167–86.

Calvo, G. 1978. On the time consistency of optimal policy in a monetary economy. *Econometrica* 46, 1411–28.

Eggertsson, G. 2005. Great expectations and the end of the depression. Staff Report No. 234. Federal Reserve Bank of New York.

Eggertsson, G. 2006a. The deflation bias and committing to being irresponsible. *Journal of Money, Credit and Banking* 38, 283–322.

Eggertsson, G. 2006b. Was the New Deal contractionary? Working paper, Federal Reserve Bank of New York.

Eggertsson, G. and Pugsley, B. 2006. The mistake of 1937: a general equilibrium analysis. *Monetary and Economic Studies* 24(SI), 151–90.

Eggertsson, G. and Woodford, M. 2003. The zero bound on interest rates and optimal monetary policy. *Brookings Papers on Economic Activity* 2003(1), 212–19.

Jeanne, O. and Svensson, L. 2007. Credible commitment to optimal escape from a liquidity trap: the role of the balance sheet of an independent central bank. *American Economic Review* 97, 474–90.

Jung, T., Teranishi, Y. and Watanabe, T. 2005. Zero bound on nominal interest rates and optimal monetary policy. *Journal of Money, Credit and Banking* 37, 813–36.

Krugman, P. 1998. It's baaack! Japan's slump and the return of the liquidity trap. *Brookings Papers on Economic Activity* 1998(2), 137–87.

Kydland, F. and Prescott, E. 1977. Rules rather than discretion: the inconsistency of optimal plans. *Journal of Political Economy* 85, 473–91.

Reifschneider, D. and Williams, J. 2000. Three lessons for monetary policy in a low inflation era. *Journal of Money, Credit and Banking* 32, 936–66.

Wolman, A. 2005. Real implications of the zero bound on nominal interest rates. *Journal of Money, Credit and Banking* 37, 273–96.

Woodford, M. 2003. *Interest and Prices: Foundations of a Theory of Monetary Policy.* Princeton: Princeton University Press.

monetarism

Monetarism is the view that the quantity of money has a major influence on economic activity and the price level and that the objectives of monetary policy are best achieved by targeting the rate of growth of the money supply.

Background and initial development

Monetarism is most closely associated with the writings of Milton Friedman who advocated control of the money supply as superior to Keynesian fiscal measures for stabilizing aggregate demand. Friedman (1948) had proposed that the government finance budget deficits by issuing new money and use budget surpluses to retire money. The resulting countercyclical variations in the money stock would stabilize the economy, provided that the government set its expenditures and tax rates to balance the budget at full employment. In his *A Program for Monetary Stability* (1960), however, Friedman proposed that constant growth of the money stock, divorced from the government budget, would be simpler and equally effective for stabilizing the economy.

In their emphasis on the importance of money, these proposals followed a tradition of the Chicago School of economics. Preceding Friedman at the University of Chicago, Henry Simons (1936) had advocated control of the money stock to achieve a stable price level, and Lloyd Mints (1950) laid out a specific monetary programme for stabilizing an index of the price level. These writers rejected reliance on the gold standard because it had failed in practice to stabilize the price level or economic activity. Such views were not confined to the University of Chicago. In the 1930s James Angell of Columbia University (1933) advocated constant monetary growth, and in the post-Second World War period Karl Brunner and Allan Meltzer were influential proponents of monetarism. The term 'monetarism' was first used by Brunner (1968). He and Meltzer founded the 'Shadow Open Market Committee' in the 1970s to publicize monetarist views on how the Federal Reserve should conduct monetary policy. Monetarism gradually gained adherents not only in the United States but also in Britain (Laidler, 1978) and other Western European countries, and subsequently around the world. The growing prominence of monetarism led to intense controversy among economists over the desirability of a policy of targeting monetary growth.

The roots of monetarism lie in the quantity theory of money which formed the basis of classical monetary economics from at least the 18th century. The quantity theory explains changes in nominal aggregate expenditures – reflecting changes in both the physical volume of output and the price level – in terms of changes in the money stock and in the velocity of circulation of money (the ratio of aggregate expenditures to the money stock). Over the long run changes in velocity are usually smaller than those in the money stock and in part are a result of prior changes in the money stock, so that aggregate expenditures are determined largely by the latter.

Moreover, over the long run growth in the physical volume of output is determined mainly by real (that is, non-monetary) factors, so that monetary changes mainly influence the price level. The observed long-run association between money and prices confirms that inflation results from monetary overexpansion and can be prevented by proper control of the money supply. This is the basis for Friedman's oft-repeated statement that inflation is always and everywhere a monetary phenomenon.

The importance of monetary effects on price movements had been supported in empirical studies by classical and neoclassical economists such as Cairnes, Jevons and Cassel. But these studies suffered from limited data, and the widespread misinterpretation of monetary influences in the Great Depression of the 1930s fostered doubts about their importance in business cycles. As Keynesian theory revolutionized thinking in the late 1930s and 1940s, it offered an influential alternative to monetary interpretations of business cycles.

The first solid empirical support for a monetary interpretation of business cycles came in a series of studies of the United States by Clark Warburton (for example, 1946). Subsequently Friedman and Anna J. Schwartz compiled new data at the National Bureau of Economic Research in an extension of Warburton's work. In 1962 they demonstrated that fluctuations in monetary growth preceded peaks and troughs of all US business cycles since the Civil War. Their dates for significant steps to higher or lower rates of monetary growth showed a lead over corresponding business cycle turns on the average by about a half year at peaks and by about a quarter year at troughs, but the lags varied considerably. Other studies have found that monetary changes take one to two years or more to affect the price level.

In *A Monetary History of the United States, 1867–1960* (1963b) Friedman and Schwartz detailed the role of money in business cycles and argued in particular that severe business contractions like that of 1929–33 were directly attributable to unusually large monetary contractions. Their monetary studies were continued in *Monetary Statistics of the United States* (1970) and *Monetary Trends in the United States and the United Kingdom* (1982). A companion National Bureau study *Determinants and Effects of Changes in the Stock of Money* (1965) by Phillip Cagan presented evidence that the reverse effect of economic activity and prices on money did not account for the major part of their observed correlation, which therefore pointed to an important causal role of money.

The monetarist proposition that monetary changes are responsible for business cycles was widely contested, but by the end of the 1960s the view that monetary policy had important effects on aggregate activity was generally accepted. The obvious importance of monetary growth in the inflation of the 1970s restored money to the centre of macroeconomics.

Monetarism versus Keynesianism
Monetarism and Keynesianism differ sharply in their research strategies and theories of aggregate expenditures. The Keynesian theory focuses on the determinants of the components of aggregate expenditures and assigns a minor role to money holdings.

In monetarist theory money demand and supply are paramount in explaining aggregate expenditures.

To contrast the Keynesian and monetarist theories, Friedman and David Meiselman (1963) focused on the basic hypothesis about economic behaviour underlying each theory: for the Keynesian theory the consumption multiplier posits a stable relationship between consumption and income, and for the monetarist theory the velocity of circulation of money posits a stable demand function for money. Friedman and Meiselman tested the two theories empirically using US data for various periods by relating consumption expenditures in one regression to investment expenditures, assuming a constant consumption multiplier, and in a second regression to the money stock, assuming a constant velocity. They reported that the monetarist regression generally fitted the data much better. These dramatic results were not accepted by Keynesians, who argued that the Keynesian theory was not adequately represented by a one-equation regression and that econometric models of the entire economy, based on Keynesian theory, were superior to small-scale models based solely on monetary changes.

The alleged superiority of Keynesian models was contested by economists at the Federal Reserve Bank of St Louis (see Andersen and Jordan, 1968). They tested a 'St Louis equation' in which changes in nominal GNP depended on current and lagged changes in the money stock, current and lagged changes in government expenditures, and a constant term reflecting the trend in monetary velocity. When fitted to historical US data, the equation showed a strong permanent effect of money on GNP and a weak transitory (and in later work, non-existent) effect of the fiscal variables, contradicting the Keynesian claim of the greater importance of fiscal than monetary policies. Although the St Louis equation was widely criticized on econometric issues, it was fairly accurate when first used in the late 1960s to forecast GNP, which influenced academic opinion and helped bring monetarism to the attention of the business world.

Although budget deficits and surpluses change interest rates and thus can affect the demand for money, monetarists believe that fiscal effects on aggregate demand are small because of the low interest elasticity of money demand. Government borrowing crowds out private borrowing and associated spending, and so deficits have little net effect on aggregate demand. The empirical results of the St Louis equation are taken as confirmation of weak transitory effects. The debate over the effectiveness of fiscal policy as a stabilization tool has produced a large literature.

In their analysis of the transmission of monetary changes through the economy, Brunner and Meltzer (1976) compare the effects of government issues of money and bonds. If the government finances increased expenditures in a way that raises the money supply, aggregate expenditures increase and nominal income rises. Moreover, the increased supply of money adds to the public's wealth, and greater wealth increases the demand for goods and services. This too raises nominal income. The rise in nominal income is at first mainly a rise in real income and later a rise in prices. They compare this result with one in which the government finances its increased expenditures by issuing bonds rather than money. Again wealth increases, and this raises aggregate expenditures. As long as the government issues either money or bonds to finance a deficit, nominal income must rise due to the increase in wealth. Brunner and Meltzer therefore agree with Keynesians that in principle a deficit financed by bonds as well as by new money is expansionary. However, they show that the empirical magnitudes of the economy are such that national income rises more from issuing a dollar of money than a dollar of bonds.

Policy implications of monetarism
Because monetary effects have variable lags of one to several quarters or more, countercyclical monetary policy actions are difficult to time properly. Friedman as well as Brunner and Meltzer argued that an active monetary policy, in the absence of an impossibly ideal foresight, tends to exacerbate, rather than smooth, economic fluctuations. In their view a stable monetary growth rate would avoid monetary sources of economic disturbances, and could be set to produce an approximately constant price level over the long run. Remaining instabilities in economic activity would be minor and, in any event, were beyond the capabilities of policy to prevent. A commitment by the monetary authorities to stable monetary growth would also help deflect constant political pressures for short-run monetary stimulus and would remove the uncertainty for investors of the unexpected effects of discretionary monetary policies.

A constant monetary growth policy can be contrasted with central bank practices that impart pro-cyclical variations to the money supply. It is common for central banks to lend freely to banks at times of rising credit demand in order to avoid increases in interest rates. Although such interest-rate targeting helps to stabilize financial markets, the targeting often fails to allow rates to change sufficiently to counter fluctuations in credit demands. By preventing interest rates from rising when credit demands increase, for example, the policy leads to monetary expansion that generates higher expenditures and inflationary pressures. Such mistakes of interest-rate targeting were clearly demonstrated in the 1970s, when for some time increases in nominal interest rates did not match increases in the inflation rate, and the resulting low rates of interest in real terms (that is, adjusted for inflation) overstimulated investment and aggregate demand.

The same accommodation of market demands for bank credit results from the common practice of targeting the volume of borrowing from the central bank. Attempts to keep this volume at some designated level require the central bank to supply reserves through open market operations as an alternative to borrowing by banks when rising market credit demands tighten bank reserve positions, and to withdraw reserves in the opposite situation. The resulting procyclical behaviour of the money supply could be avoided by operations designed to maintain a constant growth rate of money.

Brunner and Meltzer (1964a) developed an analytic framework describing how monetary policy should aim at certain intermediate targets as a way of influencing aggregate expenditures. The intermediate targets are such variables as the money supply or interest rates. (Since the Federal Reserve does not control long-term interest rates or the money stock directly, it operates through instrumental variables, such as bank reserves or the federal funds rate, which it can affect directly.) The question of the appropriate intermediate targets of monetary policy soon became the most widely discussed issue in monetary policy.

In recognition of the deficiencies of interest-rate targeting, some countries turned during the 1970s to a modified monetary targeting in which annual growth ranges were announced and adhered to, though with frequent exceptions to allow for departures deemed appropriate because of disturbances from foreign trade and other sources. Major countries adopting some form of monetary targeting included the Federal Republic of Germany, Japan, and Switzerland, all of which kept inflation rates low and thus advertised by example the anti-inflationary virtues of monetarism. In the United States the Federal Reserve also began to set monetary target ranges during the 1970s but generally did not meet them and continued to target interest rates. In October 1979, when inflation was escalating sharply, the Federal Reserve announced a more stringent targeting procedure for reducing monetary growth. Although the average growth rate was reduced, the large short-run fluctuations in monetary growth were criticized by monetarists. In late 1982 the Federal Reserve relaxed its pursuit of monetary targets.

By the mid-1980s the US and numerous other countries were following a partial form of monetary targeting, in which relatively broad bands of annual growth rates are pursued but still subject to major departures when deemed appropriate. These policies are monetarist only in the sense that one or more monetary aggregates are an important indicator of policy objectives; they fall short of a firm commitment to a steady, let alone a non-inflationary, monetary growth rate.

Monetarist theory
Monetarist theory of aggregate expenditures is based on a demand function for monetary assets that is claimed to be stable in the sense that successive residual errors are generally offsetting and do not accumulate. Given the present inconvertible-money systems, the stock of money is treated as under the control of the government. Although a distinction is made in theory between the determinants of household and business holdings of money, money demand is usually formulated for households and applied to the total. In these formulations the demand for money depends on the volume of transactions, the fractions of income and of wealth the public wishes to hold in the form of money balances, and the opportunity costs of holding money rather than other income-producing assets (that is, the difference between yields on money and on alternative assets). The alternative assets are viewed broadly to include not only financial instruments but also such physical assets as durable consumer goods, real property, and business plant and equipment. The public is presumed to respond to changes in the amount of money supplied by undertaking transactions to bring actual holdings of both money and other assets into equilibrium with desired

holdings. As a result of substitutions between money and assets, starting with close substitutes, yields change on a broad range of assets, including consumer durables and capital goods, in widening ripples that affect borrowing, investment, consumption, and production throughout the economy.

The end result is reflected in *aggregate* expenditures and the average level of prices. Independently of this monetary influence on aggregate expenditures and the price level, developments specific to particular sectors determine the distribution of expenditures among goods and services and relative prices. Thus monetarist theory rejects the common technique for forecasting aggregate output by adding up the forecasts for individual industries or the common practice of explaining changes in the price level in terms of price changes for particular goods and services.

Monetarists were early critics of the once influential Keynesian theory of a highly elastic demand for money with respect to short-run changes in the interest rate on liquid short-term assets, which in extreme form became a 'liquidity trap'. Empirical studies have found instead that interest rates on savings deposits and on short-term market securities have elasticities smaller even than the $\frac{-1}{2}$ implied by the simple Baumol–Tobin cash balance theory (Baumol, 1952; Tobin, 1956).

In empirical work a common form of the demand function for money includes one or two interest rates and real GNP as a proxy for real income. A gradual adjustment of actual to desired money balances is allowed for, implying that a full adjustment to a change in the stock is spread over several quarters. The lagged adjustment is subject to an alternative interpretation in which money demand reflects 'permanent' instead of current levels of income and interest rates. This interpretation de-emphasizes the volume of transactions as the major determinant of money demand in favour of the monetarist view of money as a capital asset yielding a stream of particular services and dependent on 'permanent' values of wealth, income, and interest rates (in most studies captured empirically by a lagged adjustment). Treatment of the demand for money as similar to demands for other assets stocks is now standard practice.

The monetarist view of money as a capital asset suggests that the demand for it depends on a variety of characteristics, and not uniquely on its transactions services. The definition of money for policy purposes depends on two considerations: the ability of the monetary authorities to control its quantity, and the empirical stability of a function describing the demand for it. In their study of the United States Friedman and Schwartz used an early version of M2, which included time and savings deposits at commercial banks, but they argued that minor changes in coverage would not greatly affect their findings. Subsequently the quantity of transaction balances M1 has become the most widely used definition of money for most countries, though many central banks claim to pay attention also to broader aggregates in conducting monetary policy.

In view of the wide range of assets into which the public may shift any excess money balances, the transmission of monetary changes through the economy to affect aggregate expenditures and other variables can follow a variety of paths. Monetarists doubt that these effects can be adequately captured by a detailed econometric model which prescribes a fixed transmission path. Instead they prefer models that dispense with detailed transmission paths and focus on a stable overall relationship between changes in money and in aggregate expenditures.

In both the monetarist model and large-scale econometric models, changes in the money stock are usually treated as exogenous (that is, as determined outside the model). It is clear that money approaches a strict exogeneity only in the long run. The US studies by Friedman and Schwartz and by Cagan established that the money supply not only influences economic activity but also is influenced by it in turn. This creates difficulties in testing empirically for the monetary effects on activity because allowance must be made for the feedback effect of economic activity on the money supply. Econometric models of the money supply can allow for feedback through the banking system (Brunner and Meltzer, 1964b). Under modern systems of inconvertible money, however, the feedback is dominated by monetary policies of the central banks, and attempts to model central bank behaviour have been less than satisfactory. Statistical tests of the exogeneity of the money supply using the Granger–Sims methodology have given mixed results. Although the concurrent mutual interaction between money and economic activity remains difficult to disentangle, the longer the lag in monetary effects the less likely that the feedback from activity to money can account for the observed association. In the St Louis equation, for example, while the correlation between changes in GNP and in money concurrently could largely reflect feedback from GNP to money, the correlation between changes in GNP and lagged changes in money are less likely to be dominated by such feedback.

Opposition to monetary targeting
While monetarism has refocused attention on money and monetary policy, there is widespread doubt that velocity is sufficiently stable to make targeting of monetary growth desirable. Movements in velocity when monetary growth is held constant produce expansionary and contractionary effects on the economy. In the United States the trend of velocity was fairly stable and predictable from the early 1950s to the mid-1970s, but money demand equations based on that period showed large over-predictions after the mid-1970s (Judd and Scadding, 1982). Financial innovations providing new ways of making payments and close substitutes for holding money were changing the appropriate definition of money and the parameters of the demand function. In the United States the gradual removal of ceilings on interest rates banks could pay on deposits played a major role in these developments by increasing competition in banking. In Great Britain the removal of domestic controls over international financial transactions led to unusual movements in money holdings in 1979–80. Germany and Switzerland also found growing international capital inflows at certain times a disruptive influence on their monetary policies.

The 'monetary theory of the balance of payments' (Frenkel and Johnson, 1976) is an extension of monetarism to open economies where money supply and demand are interrelated among countries through international payments. A debated issue is whether individual countries, even under flexible exchange rates, can pursue largely independent monetary policies. The growing internationalization of capital markets is often cited as an argument against the monetarist presumption that velocity and the domestic money supply under flexible foreign exchange rates are largely independent of foreign influences.

Uncertainties over the proper definition of money and instability in the velocity of money as variously defined led to monetarist proposals to target the monetary liabilities of the central bank, that is, the 'monetary base' consisting of currency outstanding and bank reserves. The monetary base has the advantage of not being directly affected by market innovations and so of not needing redefinitions when innovations occur. Monetarists have proposed maintaining a constant growth rate of the base also because it would simplify – indirectly virtually eliminate – the monetary policy function of central banks and governments. Some of the European central banks have found targeting the monetary base preferable to targeting the money supply, though not without important discretionary departures from the target.

Yet financial market developments can also produce instabilities in the relationship between the monetary base and aggregate expenditures. Economists opposed to monetarism propose instead that stable growth of aggregate expenditures be the target of monetary policy and that it be pursued by making discretionary changes as deemed appropriate in growth of the base. This contrasts sharply with the monetarist opposition to discretion in the conduct of policy.

The Phillips curve trade-off

The inflationary outcome of discretionary monetary policy since the Second World War can be explained in terms of the Phillips curve trade-off between inflation and unemployment. Along the Phillips curve lower and lower unemployment levels are associated with higher and higher inflation rates. Such a relationship, first found in historical British data, was shown to fit US data for the 1950s and 1960s and earlier. The trade-off depends on sticky wages and prices. As aggregate demand increases, the rise in wages and prices trails behind, inducing an expansion of output to absorb part of the increase in demand. US experience initially suggested that any desired position on the Phillips curve could be maintained by the management of aggregate demand. Thus a lower rate of unemployment could be achieved and maintained by tolerating an associated higher rate of inflation. Given this presumed trade-off, policymakers tended to favour lower unemployment at the cost of higher inflation.

In the 1970s, however, the Phillips curve shifted towards higher rates of inflation for given levels of unemployment. Friedman (1968) argued that the economy gravitates toward a 'natural rate of unemployment' which in the long run is largely independent of the inflation rate and cannot be changed by monetary policy. Wages and prices adjust sluggishly to unanticipated changes in aggregate demand but adjust more rapidly to maintained increases in demand and prices that are anticipated. Consequently, the only way to hold unemployment below the natural rate is to keep aggregate demand rising faster than the anticipated rate of inflation. Since the anticipated rate tends to follow the actual rate upward, this leads to faster and faster inflation. This 'acceleration principle' implies that there is no permanent trade-off between inflation and unemployment. The existence of a natural rate of unemployment also implies that price stability does not lead to higher unemployment in the long run.

Monetarist thought puts primary emphasis on the long-run consequences of policy actions and procedures. It rejects attempts to reduce short-run fluctuations in interest rates and economic activity as usually beyond the capabilities of monetary policy and as generally inimical to the otherwise achievable goals of long-run price stability and maximum economic growth. Monetarists believe that economic activity, apart from monetary disturbances, is inherently stable. Much of their disagreement with Keynesians can be traced to this issue.

Rational expectations
One version of the rational expectations theory goes beyond monetarism by contending that there is little or no Phillips curve trade-off between inflation and unemployment even in the short run, since markets are allegedly able to anticipate any systematic countercyclical policy pursued to stabilize the economy. Only unanticipated departures from such stabilization policies affect output; all anticipated monetary changes are fully absorbed by price changes. Since unsystematic policies would have little countercyclical effectiveness or purpose, the best policy is to minimize uncertainty with a predictable monetary growth.

This theory shares the monetarist view that unpredictable fluctuations in monetary growth are an undesirable source of uncertainty with little benefit. But the two views disagree on the speed of price adjustments to predictable monetary measures and on the associated effects on economic activity. Monetarists do not claim that countercyclical policies have no real effects, but they are sceptical of our ability to use them effectively. It is the ill-timing of countercyclical policies as a result of variable lags in monetary effects that underlies the monetarist preference for constant monetary growth to avoid uncertainty and inflation bias.

Interest in private money supplies
Monetarism is the fountainhead of a renewed interest in a subject neglected during the Keynesian Revolution: the design of monetary systems that maintain price-level stability. Scepticism that price-level stability can be achieved even by a constant growth rate of money however defined or of the monetary base has led to proposals for a strict gold standard or for a monetary system in which money is supplied by the private sector under competitive pressures to maintain a stable value. While monetarists are sympathetic to proposals to eliminate discretionary monetary policies, they view such alternative systems as impractical and believe that a non-discretionary government policy of constant monetary growth is the best policy.

Associated views of the Monetarist School

Monetarism is associated with various related attitudes towards government (see Mayer, 1978). Monetarism shares with laissez-faire a belief in the long-run benefits of a competitive economic system and of limited government intervention in the economy. It opposes constraints on the free flow of credit and on movements of interest rates, such as the US ceilings on deposit interest rates (removed by the mid-1980s except on demand deposits). The disruptive potential of such ceilings became evident in the 1970s when financial innovations, partly undertaken to circumvent the ceilings, produced the transitional shifts in the traditional money-demand functions that created difficulties for the conduct of monetary policy. Government control over the quantity of money is viewed as a justifiable exception to laissez-faire, however, in order to ensure the stability of the value of money.

PHILLIP CAGAN

See also **monetary policy, history of; quantity theory of money.**

Bibliography

Anderson, L.C. and Jordan, J.L. 1968. Monetary and fiscal actions: a test of their relative importance in economic stabilization. *Federal Reserve Bank of St Louis Review* 50(November), 11–24.

Angell, J. 1933. Monetary control and general business stabilization. In *Economic Essays in Honour of Gustav Cassel*. London: Allen and Unwin.

Baumol, W.J. 1952. The transactions demand for cash: an inventory theoretic approach. *Quarterly Journal of Economics* 66, 545–56.

Brunner, K. 1968. The role of money and monetary policy. *Federal Reserve Bank of St Louis Review* 50(July), 8–24.

Brunner, K. and Meltzer, A. 1964a. The Federal Reserve's attachment to the free reserve concept. U.S. Congress House Committee on Banking and Currency, Subcommittee on Domestic Finance, April.

Brunner, K. and Meltzer, A. 1964b. Some further investigations of demand and supply functions for money. *Journal of Finance* 19, 240–83.

Brunner, K. and Meltzer, A. 1976. An aggregative theory for a closed economy. In *Studies in Monetarism*, ed. J. Stein. Amsterdam: North-Holland.

Cagan, P. 1965. *Determinants and Effects of Changes in the Stock of Money 1875–1960*. New York: Columbia University Press for the NBER.

Frenkel, J.A. and Johnson, H.G., eds. 1976. *The Monetary Approach to the Balance of Payments*. Toronto: University of Toronto Press.

Friedman, M. 1948. A monetary and fiscal framework for economic stability. *American Economic Review* 38, 256–64.

Friedman, M. 1960. *A Program for Monetary Stability*. New York: Fordham University Press.

Friedman, M. 1968. The role of monetary policy. *American Economic Review* 58, 1–17.

Friedman, M. and Meiselman, D. 1963. The relative stability of monetary velocity and the investment multiplier in the United States, 1897–1958. In Commission on Money and Credit, *Stabilization Policies*. Englewood Cliffs, NJ: Prentice–Hall.

Friedman, M. and Schwartz, A.J. 1963a. Money and business cycles. *Review of Economics and Statistics* 45(1), Part II, Supplement, 32–64.

Friedman, M. and Schwartz, A. 1963b. *A Monetary History of the United States 1867–1960.* Princeton: Princeton University Press for the NBER.

Friedman, M. and Schwartz, A. 1970. *Monetary Statistics of the United States Estimates, Sources, Methods.* New York: NBER.

Friedman, M. and Schwartz, A. 1982. *Monetary Trends in the United States and the United Kingdom Their Relation to Income, Prices and Interest Rates, 1867–1975.* Chicago: University of Chicago Press.

Judd, J.P. and Scadding, J.L. 1982. The search for a stable money demand function: a survey of the post-1973 literature. *Journal of Economic Literature* 20, 993–1023.

Laidler, D. 1978. Mayer on monetarism: comments from a British point of view. In *The Structure of Monetarism*, ed. T. Mayer. New York: Norton.

Mayer, T., ed. 1978. *The Structure of Monetarism.* New York: Norton.

Mints, L.W. 1950. *Monetary Policy for a Competitive Society.* New York: McGraw-Hill.

Simons, H. 1936. Rules versus authorities in monetary policy. *Journal of Political Economy* 44(February), 1–30.

Tobin, J. 1956. The interest elasticity of transactions demand for cash. *Review of Economics and Statistics* 38(August), 241–7.

Warburton, C. 1946. The misplaced emphasis in contemporary business-fluctuation theory. *Journal of Business* 19, 199–220.

monetary aggregation

Aggregation theory and index-number theory have been used to generate official governmental data since the 1920s. One exception still exists. The monetary quantity aggregates and interest rate aggregates supplied by many central banks are not based on index-number or aggregation theory, but rather are the simple unweighted sums of the component quantities and quantity-weighted or arithmetic averages of interest rates. The predictable consequence has been induced instability of money demand and supply functions, and a series of 'puzzles' in the resulting applied literature. In contrast, the Divisia monetary aggregates, originated by Barnett (1980), are derived directly from economic index-number theory. Financial aggregation and index number theory was first rigorously connected with the literature on microeconomic aggregation and index number theory by Barnett (1980; 1987). A collection of many of his contributions to that field is available in Barnett and Serletis (2000).

Data construction and measurement procedures imply the theory that can rationalize the procedure. The assumptions implicit in the data construction procedures must be consistent with the assumptions made in producing the models within which the data are to be used. Unless the theory is internally consistent, the data and its applications are incoherent. Without that coherence between aggregator function structure and the econometric models within which aggregates are embedded, stable structure can appear to be unstable. This phenomenon has been called the 'Barnett critique' by Chrystal and MacDonald (1994).

Aggregation theory versus index number theory

The exact aggregates of microeconomic aggregation theory depend on unknown aggregator functions, which typically are utility, production, cost, or distance functions. Such functions must first be econometrically estimated. Hence the resulting exact quantity and price indexes become estimator- and specification-dependent. This dependency is troublesome to governmental agencies, which therefore view aggregation theory as a research tool rather than a data construction procedure.

Statistical index-number theory, on the other hand, provides indexes which are computable directly from quantity and price data, without estimation of unknown parameters. Such index numbers depend jointly on prices and quantities, but not on unknown parameters. In a sense, index number theory trades joint dependency on prices and quantities for dependence on unknown parameters. Examples of such statistical index numbers are the Laspeyres, Paasche, Divisia, Fisher ideal, and Törnqvist indexes.

The loose link between index number theory and aggregation theory was tightened, when Diewert (1976) defined the class of second-order 'superlative' index numbers.

Statistical index number theory became part of microeconomic theory, as economic aggregation theory had been for decades, with statistical index numbers judged by their nonparametric tracking ability to the aggregator functions of aggregation theory.

For decades, the link between statistical index number theory and microeconomic aggregation theory was weaker for aggregating over monetary quantities than for aggregating over other goods and asset quantities. Once monetary assets began yielding interest, monetary assets became imperfect substitutes for each other, and the 'price' of monetary-asset services was no longer clearly defined. That problem was solved by Barnett (1978; 1980), who derived the formula for the user cost of demanded monetary services. Subsequently Barnett (1987) derived the formula for the user cost of supplied monetary services. A regulatory wedge can exist between the demand and supply-side user costs if non-payment of interest on required reserves imposes an implicit tax on banks.

Barnett's results on the user cost of the services of monetary assets set the stage for introducing index number theory into monetary economics.

The economic decision

Consider a decision problem over monetary assets that illustrates the capability of monetary aggregation theory. The decision problem will be defined so that the relevant literature on economic aggregation over goods is immediately applicable. Initially we shall assume perfect certainty.

Let $\mathbf{m}'_t = (m_{1t}, m_{2t}, \ldots m_{nt})$ be the vector of real balances of monetary assets during period t, let $\mathbf{r}_t$ be the vector of nominal holding-period yields for monetary assets during period t, and let R_t be the one-period holding yield on the benchmark asset during period t. The benchmark asset is defined to be a pure investment that provides no services other than its yield, R_t, so that the asset is held solely to accumulate wealth. Thus, R_t is the maximum holding period yield in the economy in period t.

Let y_t be the real value of total budgeted expenditure on monetary services during period t. Under simplifying assumptions for data within one country, the conversion between nominal and real expenditure on the monetary services of one or more assets is accomplished using the true cost of living index on consumer goods. But for multi-country data or data aggregated across heterogeneous regions, the correct deflator can be found in Barnett (2003; 2007). The optimal portfolio allocation decision is:

$$\text{maximize } u(\mathbf{m}_t) \tag{1}$$

$$\text{subject to } \boldsymbol{\pi}'_t \, \mathbf{m}_t = y_t,$$

where $\boldsymbol{\pi}'_t = (\pi_{1t}, \ldots, \pi_{nt})$ is the vector of monetary-asset real user costs, with

$$\pi_{it} = \frac{R_t - r_{it}}{1 + R_t}. \tag{2}$$

This function u is the decision maker's utility function, assumed to be monotonically increasing and strictly concave. The user cost formula (2), derived by Barnett (1978; 1980), measures the forgone interest or opportunity cost of holding monetary asset i, when the higher yielding benchmark asset could have been held.

To be an admissible quantity aggregator function, the function u must be weakly separable within the consumer's complete utility function over all goods and services. Producing a reliable test for weak separability is the subject of much intensive research by an international group of econometricians (see, for example, Jones, Dutkowsky and Elger, 2005; Fleissig and Whitney, 2003; De Peretti, 2005). Two approaches exist. One approach uses stochastic extensions of nonparametric revealed preference tests, while the other uses parametric econometric models.

Let $\mathbf{m}_t^*$ be derived by solving decision (1). Under the assumption of linearly homogeneous utility, the exact monetary aggregate of economic theory is the utility level associated with holding the portfolio, and hence is the optimized value of the decision's objective function:

$$M_t = u(\mathbf{m}_t^*). \tag{3}$$

The Divisia index

Although equation (3) is exactly correct, it depends upon the unknown function, u. Nevertheless, statistical index-number theory enables us to track M_t exactly without estimating the unknown function, u. In continuous time, the exact monetary aggregate, $M_t = u(\mathbf{m}_t^*)$, can be tracked exactly by the Divisia index, which solves the differential equation

$$\frac{d \log M_t}{dt} = \sum_i s_{it} \frac{d \log m_{it}^*}{dt} \tag{4}$$

for M_t, where

$$s_{it} = \frac{\pi_{it} m_{it}^*}{y_t}$$

is the i'th asset's share in expenditure on the total portfolio's service flow. In equation (4), it is understood that the result is in continuous time, so the time subscripts are a shorthand for functions of time. We use t to be the time period in discrete time, but the instant of time in continuous time. The dual user cost price aggregate $\Pi_t = \Pi(\boldsymbol{\pi}_t)$, can be tracked exactly by the Divisia price index, which solves the differential equation

$$\frac{d \log \Pi_t}{dt} = \sum_i s_{it} \frac{d \log \pi_{it}}{dt}. \tag{5}$$

The user cost dual satisfies Fisher's factor reversal in continuous time:

$$\Pi_t M_t = \boldsymbol{\pi}_t' \, \mathbf{m}_t. \tag{6}$$

As a formula for aggregating over quantities of perishable consumer goods, that index was first proposed by François Divisia (1925) with market prices of those goods inserted in place of the user costs in equation (4). In continuous time, the Divisia index, under conventional neoclassical assumptions, is exact. In discrete time, the Törnqvist approximation is:

$$\log M_t - \log M_{t-1} = \sum_i s_{it}(\log m_{it}^* - \log m_{i,t-1}^*), \tag{7}$$

where

$$s_{it} = \tfrac{1}{2}(s_{it} + s_{i,t-1}).$$

In discrete time, we often call equation (7) simply the Divisia quantity index. After the quantity index is computed from (7), the user cost aggregate most commonly is computed directly from equation (6).

Diewert (1976) defines a 'superlative index number' to be one that is exactly correct for a quadratic approximation to the aggregator function. The discretization (7) to the Divisia index is in the superlative class, since it is exact for the quadratic translog specification to an aggregator function. With weekly or monthly monetary data, Barnett (1980) has shown that the Divisia index growth rates, (7), are accurate to within three decimal places. In addition, the difference between the Fisher ideal index and the discrete Divisia index growth rates are third order and comparably small. That third-order differential error typically is smaller than the round-off error in the component data.

Prior applications
Divisia monetary aggregates were first constructed for the United States by Barnett (1980), when he was on the staff of the Special Studies Section of the Board of Governors of the Federal Reserve System, and are now maintained by the Federal Reserve Bank of Saint Louis in its data base, called FRED (see Anderson, Jones and Nesmith, 1997, who produced the Divisia data for FRED). A Divisia monetary-aggregates data base also has been produced for the United Kingdom by the Bank of England. An overview of Divisia data maintained by many central banks throughout the world can be found in Belongia and Binner (2000; 2005) and in Barnett, Fisher and Serletis (1992), along with a survey of empirical results with that data. The most extensive collection of relevant applied and theoretical research in that area is in Barnett and Serletis (2000) and Barnett and Binner (2004).

The state of the art
The European Central Bank is implementing a multilateral extension of the Divisia monetary aggregates for monetary quantity and interest rate aggregation within the euro area. This aggregation is multilateral in the recursive sense that it permits aggregation of monetary service flows first within countries, then over countries.

The resulting aggregation will be in a strictly nested, internally consistent manner. The multilateral extension of the theory was produced by Barnett (2003; 2007). This extension was produced under three increasingly strong sets of assumptions: (*a*) with the weakest being produced from heterogeneous agents theory, (*b*) followed by the somewhat stronger assumption of existence of a multilateral representative agent, and (*c*) finally with the strongest being the assumption of the existence of a unilateral representative agent. The intent is to move from the weakest towards the strongest assumptions, as progress is made within the European Monetary Union towards its harmonization and economic convergence goals. Since Barnett's three assumption structures are nested, construction of the data under the most general heterogeneous countries approach would continue to be valid, as the stronger assumptions become more reasonable and are attained within the euro area.

Extension of index number theory to the case of risk was introduced by Barnett, Liu and Jensen (2000), who derived the extended theory from Euler equations rather than from the perfect-certainty first-order conditions used in the earlier index number-theory literature. Since that extension is based upon the consumption capital-asset-pricing model (CCAPM), the extension is subject to the 'equity premium puzzle' of smaller than necessary adjustment for risk. We believe that the under-correction produced by CCAPM results from its assumption of intertemporal blockwise strong separability of goods and services within preferences. Barnett and Wu (2005) have extended Barnett, Liu, and Jensen's result to the case of risk aversion with intertemporally non-separable tastes.

The extension to risk is likely to be especially important to countries whose residents hold significant deposits in foreign denominated assets, since exchange rate risk can cause rates of return on monetary assets to be subject to non-negligible risk. With the recent trend towards financial integration in many parts of the world, exchange-rate risk is likely to grow in importance in monetary aggregation. In many countries, the largest holder of foreign-denominated deposits is the central bank itself. Within the United States, the extension to risk is highly relevant to the so called 'missing M2' episode of the early 1990s, when substitutability among small time deposits, stock funds, and bond funds produced 'puzzles'.

User cost aggregates are duals to monetary quantity aggregates. Either implies the other uniquely. In addition, user-cost aggregates imply the corresponding interest-rate aggregates uniquely. The interest-rate aggregate r_t implied by the user-cost aggregate Π_t is the solution for r_t to the equation:

$$\frac{R_t - r_t}{1 + R_t} = \Pi_t.$$

Accordingly, any monetary policy that operates through the opportunity cost of money (that is, interest rates) has a dual policy operating through the monetary quantity aggregate, and vice versa. Aggregation theory implies no preference for either of the two dual policy procedures or for any other approach to policy, so long as the policy does not violate principles of aggregation theory.

Conclusion

Aggregation theory is about measurement, and has little, if anything, to say about the choice of policy instrument, such as the funds rate or the base. But accurate measurement, through proper application of aggregation theory, has much to say about the transmission of policy, modelling of structure, and the measurement of intermediate targets (if any) and final targets.

Policies that violate aggregation theoretic principles include the following oversimplified approaches: (*a*) inflation targeting that targets one arbitrary consumer-good price as a final target, while ignoring all other consumer goods prices, rather than targeting the true cost-of-living index over all consumer goods prices; (*b*) interest rate targeting that analogously targets one arbitrary interest rate as an intermediate target while ignoring all other interest rates, rather than targeting the aggregation-theoretic interest-rate or user-cost aggregate over a weakly separable collection of monetary assets; (*c*) monetary quantity targeting that targets a simple-sum monetary aggregate as an intermediate target rather than the aggregator function over a weakly separable collection of monetary assets; and (*d*) policy simulations using money-demand or money-supply functions containing simple-sum monetary aggregates or quantity-weighted interest-rate aggregates. The measurement defects in the above four cases are unrelated to the choice of the funds rate or monetary base as an instrument of policy. Unlike intermediate targets, final targets, and variables in models, the chosen instruments of policy tend to be highly controllable, disaggregated variables, presenting few serious measurement problems.

The objective of the Divisia monetary aggregates is measurement of the economy's monetary service flow and its dual opportunity cost (user cost) and implied interest rate aggregate, not advocacy of any particular policy use of the correctly measured variables. But all uses of data are adversely affected by improper measurement, and a long series of 'puzzles' in monetary economics have been shown to have been produced by improper measurement (see, for example, Barnett and Serletis, 2000, ch. 24).

WILLIAM A. BARNETT

See also **Federal Reserve System; inflation targeting; monetary economics, history of; monetary and fiscal policy overview.**

Bibliography

Anderson, R., Jones, B. and Nesmith, T. 1997. Building new monetary services indexes: concepts, data and methods. *Federal Reserve Bank of St Louis Review* 79, 53–82.

Barnett, W. 1978. The user cost of money. *Economics Letters* 1, 145–49. Repinted in Barnett and Serletis (2000, ch. 1).

Barnett, W. 1980. Economic monetary aggregates: an application of aggregation and index number theory. *Journal of Econometrics* 14, 11–48. Reprinted in Barnett and Serletis (2000, ch. 2).

Barnett, W. 1987. The microeconomic theory of monetary aggregation. In *New Approaches in Monetary Economics*, ed. W. Barnett and K. Singleton. Cambridge: Cambridge University Press. Reprinted in Barnett and Serletis (2000, ch. 3).

Barnett, W. 2003. Aggregation-theoretic monetary aggregation over the euro area, when countries are heterogeneous. Working Paper No. 260. Frankfurt: European Central Bank.

Barnett, W. 2007. Multilateral aggregation-theoretic monetary aggregation over heterogeneous countries. *Journal of Econometrics* 136, 457–82.

Barnett, W. and Binner, J. 2004. *Functional Structure and Approximation in Econometrics.* Amsterdam: North-Holland.

Barnett, W., Fisher, D. and Serletis, A. 1992. Consumer theory and the demand for money. *Journal of Economic Literature* 30, 2086–119. Reprinted in Barnett and Serletis (2000, ch. 18).

Barnett, W., Liu, Y. and Jensen, M. 2000. CAPM risk adjustment for exact aggregation over financial assets. *Macroeconomic Dynamics* 1, 485–512.

Barnett, W. and Serletis, A., eds. 2000. *The Theory of Monetary Aggregation.* Amsterdam: North-Holland.

Barnett, W. and Wu, S. 2005. On user costs of risky monetary assets. *Annals of Finance* 1, 35–50.

Belongia, M. and Binner, J. 2000. *Divisia Monetary Aggregates: Theory and Practice.* Basingstoke: Palgrave.

Belongia, M. and Binner, J. 2005. *Money, Measurement, and Computation.* Basingstoke: Palgrave.

Chrystal, A. and MacDonald, R. 1994. Empirical evidence on the recent behaviour and usefulness of simple-sum and weighted measures of the money stock. *Federal Reserve Bank of St. Louis Review* 76, 73–109.

De Peretti, P. 2005. Testing the significance of the departures from utility maximization. *Macroeconomic Dynamics* 9(3), 373–97.

Diewert, W. 1976. Exact and superlative index numbers. *Journal of Econometrics* 4, 115–45.

Divisia, F. 1925. L'Indice monétaire et la théorie de la monnaie. *Revue d'Economie Politique* 39, 980–1008.

Fleissig, A. and Whitney, G. 2003. A new PC-based test for Varian's weak separability conditions. *Journal of Business and Economic Statistics* 21, 133–44.

Jones, B., Dutkowsky, D. and Elger, T. 2005. Sweep programs and optimal monetary aggregation. *Journal of Banking and Finance* 29, 483–508.

monetary and fiscal policy overview

In this article I provide an overview of economic thinking about monetary and fiscal policy. There are three terms that need to be defined in this sentence: policy, monetary, and fiscal. I begin by defining each in turn.

A government's *policy* is akin to a strategy in game theory. It specifies a function at each date that maps the government's information at that date into the government's actions. This information typically takes two forms. First, it includes *endogenous* variables such as past prices, past quantities or past actions of the government. For example, under the famous Taylor rule, a government's choice of current short-term interest rates is based on past observations of the consumer price index and gross domestic product. Second, the government's information includes *exogenous* variables, like the realizations of shocks to productivity or to money demand.

These sources of information may be public or they may be known only to the government. Thus, in the United States the Federal Reserve collects information about the state of the economy that it uses for making decisions but is kept confidential from households in the economy. Note, too, that the government's actions themselves may be private information to the government; for example, until recently, the Federal Open Market Committee publicly announced its decisions only with a lag.

In the popular press, the term 'policy' is commonly used in a different way, to refer only to the *current* choice of the government. However, as long as *some* economic actors (firms, households or the government itself) are forward-looking, such a specification of policy is intrinsically incomplete. Forward-looking decision-makers need to know not just the government's choice of policy today but also how the government will respond to new information in the future. (This is true even if these forward-looking actors have expectations that are far from rational.) Thus, if the government raises taxes today, my response to that increase depends crucially on whether I believe it will persist for a long time. To make that judgement, I need to know not just the government's choices today but also how its choices in the future depend on new information that the government receives.

Whether a policy is monetary or fiscal or neither depends on the nature of the actions specified by that policy. A policy is said to be *monetary* if the relevant actions are those generally undertaken by a central bank. These may include the size of monetary injections, reserve requirements, the discount rate, or the scale of interventions in bond or foreign exchange markets. A policy is said to be *fiscal* if the relevant actions are tax rates and/or expenditures on various commodities. Of course, many government policies (should Iran be invaded or not?) are neither fiscal nor monetary.

In the body of this article, I discuss several lessons from the study of monetary and fiscal policy. Before doing so, though, it is useful to understand the methodology that was used to learn those lessons (see Lucas, 1980, and Prescott, 2005, for a fuller discussion of this methodology). Any analysis of policy starts with the following question: on the assumption that no other exogenous variables change, how does the economy respond to a change in policy? This kind of question is really asking about the outcome of a controlled *experiment*. It would be best answered by constructing giant national or super-national laboratories in order to conduct these experiments. But it is clearly impossible to perform controlled experiments of this kind. How then do macroeconomists proceed?

The approach taken by macroeconomists is closely related to the methods used by other non-experimental sciences. Consider for example the issue of global warming. There have been no prior episodes in world history in which man has been able to generate such a large amount of CO_2 in such a short period of time. Hence, there is no way to use prior data to understand the impact of this build-up on climatic variables like temperature. Instead, climatologists rely on computer simulations of abstract models to understand the impact of greenhouse gases on the world's climate.

Similarly, macroeconomists build abstract computational models to answer questions about the impact of monetary and fiscal policy. It is well-understood from many years of computational experimentation that useful models must have certain elements to provide reliable answers to policy questions. The models need to be both dynamic and stochastic in nature. The models need to be explicit about aggregate resource constraints: the amount of goods consumed by governments and households cannot exceed the amount of goods produced. The models should feature households with well-defined objectives and budget constraints. The households and firms in the models should be forward-looking (although they may or may not be fully informed about the state of the economy).

To provide a quantitative answer about the impact of a particular policy, macroeconomists need to be specific about many other elements of the computational model (preferences of households, shocks hitting the economy, and so on). Again, it is useful to refer to the natural sciences as a way to understand how macroeconomists proceed. Consider a biologist that wants to understand the impact of a new drug on human beings. At least initially, she experiments on animals. For some kinds of drugs, she may use mice. For others, she may use more expensive animals like monkeys or dogs. Her decision about which proxy to use is a complex one, grounded in theory, collective prior experience about other drugs and these animals, and individual judgement.

In the same fashion, macroeconomists do not use the same model for all policy questions. Instead, they choose the model based on the question at hand. Thus, for questions concerning the short-run impact of monetary policies, they may include adjustment costs in physical capital and/or prices. For other questions concerning the long-run impact of monetary policy, they may neglect these elements. Like the biologist, their decisions are based on theory, collective prior experience and judgement.

One aspect of this decision-making that receives particular attention in macroeconomics is how to quantify the various elements of the model. How risk-averse are the households in the model economy? What is the elasticity of substitution between capital and labour in the model economy? Fortunately, for many of these parameter choices, there is a profession-wide consensus, informed by many years of experience and discussion. For other parameters, new choices have to be made. Generally, macroeconomists use a mix of information from both microeconomic and macroeconomic sources to make these choices. There may well be a range of plausible choices for a given parameter, and then the answer to the policy question under consideration is really a set, not a single point.

In the remainder of this article, I discuss some of the conclusions about monetary and fiscal policy that macroeconomists have reached from using this methodology. I focus on results that are highly robust, in the sense that they occur across a wide class of models. I begin by looking at lessons from the *positive* approach to policy, which studies the response of the private sector to different specifications of policy. I then look at lessons from the *normative* approach, which looks at properties of *ex ante* optimal policies. Finally, I discuss some difficulties associated with modelling policy choices as being an endogenous response to economic conditions.

The positive approach to policy

There is a large amount of macroeconomic research that treats monetary and fiscal policy as wholly exogenous to the economy. It asks questions of the sort: how does some aspect of private sector economic behaviour respond to a given specification of monetary and fiscal policy? Macroeconomists have described the outcomes to many specific experiments of this kind. There is no useful way to summarize this knowledge. However, there are several general lessons that one can draw from this research. In what follows, I discuss three of these.

Lesson 1. fiscal vs. monetary policy

I have drawn a distinction between fiscal and monetary policy. However, this distinction is more than a little artificial for two reasons. First, in macroeconomic models households face budget constraints and aggregate resource constraints are satisfied. Together, these imply that the government itself must satisfy a budget constraint in equilibrium: the present value of the government's revenues must equal the present value of its expenditures. (There are overlapping-generations model economies in which this restriction need not be satisfied. However, these models are typically not thought to be empirically relevant; Abel et al., 1989.) This constraint implies a sharp linkage between fiscal and monetary policy. Changes in monetary policies affect the government's revenue from money creation. Hence, the two types of policies are inextricably linked, because they cannot be changed separately. (This fundamental linkage between fiscal and monetary policy was made especially clear by Sargent and Wallace, 1981.)

The second reason is that, in terms of its impact on the economy, monetary policy is merely fiscal policy by another name. People and firms who hold money are forgoing the interest that they could receive by holding bonds instead. They hold that money because it helps them buy goods and services that are difficult to purchase using bonds. Higher interest rates makes money more costly to hold, and makes those goods and services more costly to buy. The interest rate acts like a sales tax on those goods and services.

Monetary policy has still other distorting effects on the economy when some prices are more flexible than others. For example, suppose nominal wages do not respond rapidly to changes in inflation, but gas prices do. Then, the relative price of labour and gasoline may vary in response to variations in monetary instruments. Again, though, a particular kind of fiscal policy – variations in the gasoline tax – can affect the economy in exactly the same way. (This equivalence between fiscal and monetary policy is stressed by Correia, Nicolini and Teles, 2004.)

Lesson 2. Ricardian equivalence

I pointed out above that the present value of government expenditures must equal the present value of government revenues. This simple fact has surprising consequences. Consider two policies with the same government purchases. Suppose one policy generates lower tax revenue in the next ten years than the other policy. Obviously, under the first policy, the government must borrow more. This extra demand in loans puts upward pressure on interest rates.

However, the government's intertemporal budget constraint also implies that the first policy must necessarily generate *higher* tax revenue in the future. Forward-looking households anticipate this increase in their future tax burden. They respond by saving more to meet this tax burden. In a classic paper, Barro (1974) shows that, if households are sufficiently forward-looking, and markets are frictionless, then the households' extra demand for savings under the first policy is exactly equal to the government's extra demand for loans. Hence, even though the government is borrowing more, there is no extra pressure on interest rates; they should be the same under the two policies. This result is generally termed *Ricardian equivalence* (because of some antecedents in the work of David Ricardo).

The exact Ricardian equivalence result is not robust to adding plausible frictions like borrowing constraints on households. Nonetheless, there is a qualitative lesson that holds much more generally and is often forgotten in policy discussions: economics does not predict a stable relationship between current government debt or deficits and interest rates.

Lesson 3. Expectations matter

I have emphasized above that households' expectations about future government actions matter for current outcomes. However, in many macroeconomic models a given household's behaviour depends also on its expectations of other households' current and future actions. This feedback generates the possibility of multiple equilibrium outcomes for a given government policy.

Here's a simple example of this phenomenon. Suppose both government investment and household labour are necessary inputs into production – that is, either zero government investment or zero labour input leads to zero output. Suppose as well that the government collects resources to fund its investment by taxing output. In such a world, regardless of the government's policy, there is always an equilibrium in which households do not work at all. In this equilibrium, because other households are not working, a given household realizes that the government cannot fund any investment. Hence, it is individually optimal for that household not to provide any labour input.

This kind of multiplicity leads to the possibility of what are called *sunspot* fluctuations in macroeconomic variables. The idea here is that households use some arbitrary random variable to coordinate their behavior. Thus, if they all see rain in Peoria, they decide not to work. If they see sun in Peoria, they decide to work. Whether it is sunny or not in Peoria, of course, is irrelevant for economic fundamentals – but in this economy, this variable can still affect equilibrium outcomes. (For early expositions of the concept of sunspot equilibria, see Azariadis, 1981, and Cass and Shell, 1983.)

Note that this example is only an illustration of a much more general phenomenon. It is especially prevalent in monetary economies. In these settings, a household's decision about how many real balances to hold today depends crucially on the household's expectations about future inflation rates. Obstfeld and Rogoff (1983) demonstrate how this intertemporal feedback can generate a continuum of welfare-indexed possible inflation paths as equilibria, even if the money supply is fixed. Sargent and Wallace (1975) demonstrate how this intertemporal feedback can generate a continuum of welfare-indexed possible inflation paths as equilibria even if interest rates are fixed. (Pareto-ranked equilibria do not occur in all economies. In many economies – especially non-monetary ones – it may be possible to prove that any equilibrium allocation solves a maximization problem in which the objective is a weighted average of households' utilities. In such settings, equilibrium allocations are necessarily Pareto non-comparable. Without such a proof in hand, though, one has to be aware that there is the potential for sunspot fluctuations between Pareto-ranked outcomes. Many macroeconomists restrict attention to so-called recursive equilibria or Markov-perfect equilibria. Under these notions of equilibrium, outcomes have the property that they depend on the past only through a small number of state variables. This restriction is undoubtedly useful for simplifying computational or econometric work. However, the restriction may inadvertently rule out important sources of potential multiplicity. See, for example, Woodford's, 1994, analysis of Lucas and Stokey's, 1987, model economy.)

The normative approach to policy

I now turn to the second approach to studying macroeconomic policy. This approach posits a government that chooses a policy at the beginning of time; its objective is to maximize some weighted average of household utilities. Crucially, the government is able to commit to never change the policy. This kind of commitment power is clearly artificial; the goal of the second approach is to tell us what kinds of policies maximize *ex ante* social welfare, not what policies are actually adopted by governments. By construction, there is no requirement that the optimal policies be realistic: normative analyses tell us what the government should do, not what they actually do. Thus, economists use normative analyses to argue strongly in favour of free trade, which is a policy that has never been followed by any country at any time.

Everything in this approach hinges on what is assumed about the set of instruments available to the government. It is well-known that *lump-sum* taxes are a highly desirable taxation instrument. A lump-sum tax is a tax on a household or firm which is independent of their actions. Such a tax is desirable because it does not distort the choices of the household or the firm.

But lump-sum taxes are typically not used by governments. Once one notices this fact, there are at least two ways to proceed in thinking about optimal taxes. One can assume that the governments can only use a limited set of tax instruments that does not include lump-sum taxes. This approach is generally called the *Ramsey* approach. Alternatively, one can build model economies in which governments have access to all possible tax instruments, but *choose*, because of a particular private information friction, not to use lump-sum taxes. This approach is generally called the Mirrlees approach.

The Ramsey approach and its lessons

Suppose the government can impose a linear tax on capital income, a linear tax on labour income, and can print money. It must optimally choose these instruments so as to finance an optimally chosen process for government purchases. What are the properties of the optimal taxes? An enormous amount of work has been done on this question; see Chari and Kehoe (1999) for a survey. I first briefly describe the mathematical approach, and then turn to the properties of the optimal taxes.

One way to proceed here would be to solve for the households' and firms' response to all possible tax policies. Then, given this response function, we could solve the government's optimization problem. This problem turns out to be difficult in most circumstances.

Fortunately, there is a way to substitute out the tax schedules; we can instead think of the government directly choosing quantities subject to two types of restrictions. The first is the usual physical feasibility constraints. The other is a set of constraints called *implementability* constraints. These look like household budget constraints, except that we substitute the household marginal rates of substitution in for all prices; the constraints then contain only physical quantities. Somewhat remarkably, these simple implementability constraints turn out to capture exactly the seemingly complicated restriction that the government can use only linear taxes.

Of course, because it is couched only in terms of quantities, the solution to this problem does not contain direct information about optimal taxes. Once one solves the optimization problem, one sees that there are differences (commonly termed *wedges*) between marginal rates of substitution and marginal rates of transformation in the solution. The optimal taxes in equilibrium are equal to these wedges from the solution of the optimization problem. Note these wedges exist only because of the implementability constraints; without them, all wedges would be zero, and it would be optimal to set all taxes to zero.

What then are the properties of optimal taxes when we apply this kind of analysis? In general, the quantitative properties of the optimal taxes depend on many precise details of the specification of the environment. However, there are (at least) two remarkably robust properties of the optimal taxes. The first is that if the government can accumulate assets, the long-run optimal capital income tax rate is zero. (This result was originally derived by Chamley, 1986, and Judd, 1985.) Intuitively, suppose the long-run capital income tax is positive. This tax rate affects the rate of return in every period, and its impact cumulates as the horizon of the investment grows. Hence, the tax rate on accumulating capital between period t and period $t+s$ gets arbitrarily large as t, s get large. This arbitrarily large tax rate creates too much social waste, given that it is raising only a finite amount of revenue. The second property of optimal taxes is that, under very general conditions, the optimal nominal interest rate is zero (in all periods, not just in the long run) (see Chari, Christiano and Kehoe, 1996; Correia and Teles, 1999; Correia, Nicolini and Teles, 2004).

Here, the basic intuition is that any positive nominal interest rate is a tax on money holdings (as discussed above). But money is not a final good; it is only an intermediate input into production and consumption. A tax on intermediate inputs creates two distortions: people are deterred both from using the intermediate input and from consuming any final goods that use the intermediate input. It is generally optimal to eliminate this double distortion by simply taxing final goods and not taxing any intermediate inputs, including money.

Even though the nominal interest rate is zero, the real interest rate can still be positive as long as the price index is falling over time. If prices are fully flexible, then this consistent deflation has no real effects. However, if prices are sticky, this steady deflation may create inefficiencies in a world with sticky prices. In particular, if some prices are adjusted downward more frequently than others, then any consistent deflation creates distortions in relative prices.

Correia, Nicolini and Teles (2004) demonstrate that this kind of systematic distortion can be fixed by using *sales* taxes. Their key observation is that the nominal interest rate can be zero and the real interest rate can be positive as long as the *after-tax* price level is falling over time. Hence, if the government sets the sales tax to fall at the correct rate, firms will find it optimal to never change their prices even though the nominal interest rate is zero.

The Mirrlees approach and its lessons
The Ramsey approach simply assumes that governments cannot use lump-sum taxes. But why do governments not use lump-sum taxes? One problem is that, if the

government imposes a tax of, say, $10,000 per head, then some people will have the ability to generate this income and others will not. This is not a difficulty if the government can tell who is in which group – it can just exempt those who cannot pay.

Unfortunately, people can *pretend* to be unable to generate this level of income by pretending to have back pain, mental illness or other sources of disability. The government cannot figure out whom to exempt from the head tax.

This observation suggests that governments are deterred from using lump-sum taxes because people are privately informed about their abilities or skills. The Mirrlees approach starts with this informational restriction. The government is allowed to use any form of taxes that it wishes (linear, nonlinear, and so on) on any private sector choice. Because it is not restricted to linear taxes, the implementability constraint discussed above vanishes. Instead, the government faces an *incentive-compatibility constraint* that reflects the ability of people to pretend to be less able than they truly are.

Given this difference in constraints, one can proceed much as in the Ramsey approach. The first step is to set up a maximization problem in which the government maximizes *ex ante* welfare subject to feasibility constraints and incentive-compatibility constraints. This type of maximization problem is roughly equivalent to the kind of dynamic contracting problems originally considered by Green (1987). One considerable complication is that abilities may change over time due to health shocks. Dynamic contracting models with persistent shocks are highly challenging to solve even with a computer (see Fernandes and Phelan, 2000).

The next step is to design a tax system such that the optimal allocations emerge as equilibrium outcomes. These tax systems are complicated objects when abilities evolve over time. Nonetheless, we can draw remarkably strong conclusions about the structure of optimal capital income taxes. If preferences are additively separable between consumption and leisure, then one can show that there exists an optimal tax system which is *linear* in capital income. (Remember that the government is free to use an arbitrarily nonlinear system.) The optimal tax system *subsidizes* the capital income of surprisingly highly skilled people and *taxes* the capital income of surprisingly low-skilled people. While seemingly regressive, this tax system actually provides better social insurance. Intuitively, the tax system provides better incentives because it deters people from accumulating lots of wealth and then pretending to be low-skilled. These better incentives expand the scope for social insurance.

The heterogeneity in tax rates across people means that the Mirrlees prescription for optimal capital taxes differs from the Ramsey prescription for optimal capital tax rates. However, the two approaches do coincide in their recommendations for total and average capital income taxes. The Mirrlees approach recommends subsidies on some people and taxes on others. However, one can prove that, in the optimal tax system, both the average tax rate (across people) and the total tax revenue from capital income taxes are zero at every date. (See Kocherlakota, 2006, for a survey article on the Mirrlees approach.)

Making government endogenous

In both the positive approach and the normative approach, the government is a pre-programmed robot during the life of the economy. It would be useful to develop models in which the government is another economic actor (or, even more realistically, a collection of economic actors) that makes choices at intervals based on its information. Such models would allow us to understand what forces lead to the kinds of policy choices that we see in reality. (See Persson and Tabellini, 2000, for a much more complete discussion of these issues.)

These models need to capture at least two types of conflict. One source of conflict is heterogeneity. Households differ in their attributes and so in their preferences over policies. Old people have shorter horizons and typically prefer to set public investment to lower levels than young people. People with lots of capital prefer lower capital tax rates than do people with little capital. People with lots of nominal debt would like to raise nominal interest rates; their lenders prefer the opposite.

There is a great deal of research studying these kinds of conflicts. Unfortunately, it has been hard to generate the kind of robust answers that macroeconomists have obtained from the positive and normative approaches. There is no real consensus about how to model the games that get played by the different groups. Some researchers use voting games, while others use bargaining games. Some researchers treat conflicts in isolation, while others model conflicts as being resolved in bundles. These different modelling choices generate substantially different predictions about policy formation.

In a classic article, Kydland and Prescott (1977) set forth a second source of conflict. Suppose the world lasts two periods, and a government wants to raise taxes to finance purchases using capital income taxes and labour income taxes. Assume that all households are identical – so that the first type of conflict is removed – and that the government cares only about maximizing household welfare. It would seem that all sources of conflict have been removed in this situation.

But this is not true. The period 1 government's preferences over period 2 capital taxes are fundamentally different from the period 2 government's preferences. In period 2, the amount of capital in the economy is fixed – there is no way to get any more. The period 2 government would like to set a high tax rate on this fixed tax base to raise as much revenue as possible.

In period 1, though, the amount of capital in period 2 has yet to be determined. The period 1 government has to consider how the tax rate in period 2 affects the size of the period 2 tax base. Its preferred period 2 tax rate is much smaller than the tax rate that the period 1 government likes.

Thus, even if governments at different dates are all benevolent, there is a dynamic conflict between them. How this conflict gets resolved is, again, a non-trivial matter. The dynamic game does have a unique equilibrium in a finite horizon. Unfortunately, this unique equilibrium is unrealistic in most countries: capital tax rates are set very high in every period. On the other hand, if the game has an infinite horizon, then there are an infinite number of equilibrium outcomes, including ones with high capital tax rates, low capital tax rates, and paths that vary between the two (see Chari and Kehoe, 1990). The predictive power of the model is then quite limited.

Conclusions

There is an old joke to the effect that if you ask 10 macroeconomists about a policy question, you'll get 11 different answers. This joke provided a disturbingly accurate picture of the state of the field in the 1970s and 1980s. To a remarkable extent, it was no longer applicable as of 2005. There is a profession-wide consensus on methods that simply did not exist in the early 1980s. This consensus has led to a set of results about monetary and fiscal policy that are sharp, robust and surprising.

NARAYANA R. KOCHERLAKOTA

I thank Barbara McCutcheon for her comments. The opinions expressed herein are mine and not necessarily those of the Federal Reserve Bank of Minneapolis or the Federal Reserve System.

Bibliography

Abel, A., Mankiw, N.G., Summers, L. and Zeckhauser, R. 1989. Assessing dynamic efficiency: theory and evidence. *Review of Economic Studies* 56, 1–19.
Azariadis, C. 1981. Self-fulfilling prophecies. *Journal of Economic Theory* 25, 380–96.
Barro, R. 1974. Are government bonds net wealth? *Journal of Political Economy* 82, 1095–117.
Cass, D. and Shell, K. 1983. Do sunspots matter? *Journal of Political Economy* 91, 193–227.
Chamley, C. 1986. Optimal taxation of capital income in general equilibrium with infinite lives. *Econometrica* 54, 607–22.
Chari, V.V., Christiano, L. and Kehoe, P. 1996. Optimality of the Friedman rule in economies with distorting taxes. *Journal of Monetary Economics* 37, 203–23.
Chari, V.V. and Kehoe, P. 1990. Sustainable plans. *Journal of Political Economy* 98, 783–802.
Chari, V.V. and Kehoe, P. 1999. Optimal fiscal and monetary policy. In *Handbook of Macroeconomics*, vol. 1C, ed. J.B. Taylor and M. Woodford. Amsterdam: North-Holland.
Correia, I. and Teles, P. 1999. The optimal inflation tax. *Review of Economic Dynamics* 2, 325–46.
Correia, I., Nicolini, J.-P. and Teles, P. 2004. Optimal fiscal and monetary policy: equivalence results. Working paper, Centre for Economic Performance, London School of Economic.
Fernandes, A. and Phelan, C. 2000. A recursive formulation for repeated agency with history dependence. *Journal of Economic Theory* 91, 223–47.
Green, E. 1987. Lending and smoothing of uninsurable income. In *Contractual Agreements for Intertemporal Trade*, ed. E. Prescott and N. Wallace. Minneapolis: University of Minnesota Press.
Judd, K. 1985. Redistributive taxation in a perfect foresight model. *Journal of Public Economics* 28, 59–84.
Kocherlakota, N. 2006. Advances in dynamic optimal taxation. *Advances in Economics and Econometrics: Theory and Applications: Ninth World Congress of the Econometric Society*, vol. 1, ed. R. Blundell, W. K. Newey and T. Persson. Cambridge: Cambridge University Press.
Kydland, F. and Prescott, E. 1977. Rules rather than discretion: the inconsistency of optimal plans. *Journal of Political Economy* 85, 473–91.
Lucas, R.E., Jr. 1980. Methods and problems in business cycle theory. *Journal of Money, Credit, and Banking* 12, 696–715.

Lucas, R.E., Jr. and Stokey, N. 1987. Money and interest in a cash-in-advance economy. *Econometrica* 55, 491–513.

Obstfeld, M. and Rogoff, K. 1983. Speculative hyperinflations in maximizing models: can we rule them out? *Journal of Political Economy* 91, 675–87.

Persson, T. and Tabellini, G. 2000. *Political Economics, Explaining Economic Policy.* Cambridge, MA: MIT Press.

Prescott, E. 2005. The transformation of macroeconomic policy and research. In *Les Prix Nobel. The Nobel Prizes 2004*, ed. T. Frängsmyr. Stockholm: Nobel Foundation. Online. Available at http://nobelprize.org/nobel_prizes/economics/laureates/2004/prescott-lecture.pdf, accessed 18 October 2006.

Sargent, T. and Wallace, N. 1975. Rational expectations, the optimal monetary instrument and the optimal money supply rule. *Journal of Political Economy* 83, 241–54.

Sargent, T. and Wallace, N. 1981. Some unpleasant monetarist arithmetic. *Federal Reserve Bank of Minneapolis Quarterly Review* 5(3), 1–18.

Woodford, M. 1994. Monetary policy and price level determinacy in a cash-in-advance economy. *Economic Theory* 4, 345–80.

monetary business cycle models (sticky prices and wages)

Since the earliest analysis of the monetary transmission mechanism by pre-eminent classical economists of the 18th and early 19th century, sticky prices and wages have been identified as playing a central role (Humphrey, 2004). The classical economists believed that prices adjusted gradually to a change in the nominal money stock, so that monetary changes could exert substantial short-run effects on output. Nominal wages were regarded as particularly slow to change, and thus helped account for gradual price adjustment by mitigating short-run pressures on factor costs.

The classical economists and their successors used this framework both to guide recommendations about policy and to evaluate alternative monetary regimes. For example, the belief that prices would respond slowly to a monetary contraction led Thornton and Ricardo to recommend a gradualist approach to deflation.

Early Keynesian models, and some critiques

A major contribution of Keynes (1936) and prominent successors such as Hicks to understanding the monetary transmission mechanism consisted in developing an explicit theoretical framework expressed in terms of equilibrium conditions in goods and asset markets. This IS–LM framework was of great value in illuminating the channels through which monetary shocks affected interest rates and output. However, the assumption of fixed prices and wages was a major shortcoming. It was eventually supplanted by the famous 'Phillips curve' relation linking nominal wage inflation to the unemployment rate, or variants relating price inflation to the output gap:

$$p(t) - p(t-1) = b * (y(t) - y(t)^*) b > 0 \tag{1}$$

where $p(t)$ is (the log of) the price level, $y(t)$ output, $y(t)*$ potential output, and b is a parameter. The Phillips curve filled a missing link in earlier 'fixed price' IS–LM analysis by making it feasible to trace the dynamic effects of a monetary shock on prices and output. Thus, an initial rise in output following a monetary expansion boosts prices via (1), which in turn causes real balances and output to revert gradually to pre-shock levels. However, the Phillips curve had weak theoretical underpinnings, so that there was little economic rationale for what determined the sensitivity of prices to the output gap (that is, 'b' in (1)), for the activity variable(s) driving price dynamics, and for how inflation might be influenced by expectations.

A series of remarkable critiques beginning with the analysis of Friedman (1968) and Phelps (1968) provided impetus for developing more theoretically coherent models of price and wage dynamics. These authors argued that the Phillips curve should be augmented so that actual inflation depended directly on inflation expectations in addition to real activity. In this framework, output could be pushed above potential only through surprising private agents by keeping inflation above the level that they had forecast in previous periods. Since such surprises could not continue indefinitely, there could be no long-run trade-off between inflation and output: expansionary monetary policy would eventually raise expected inflation, resulting in higher inflation with no output stimulus.

Shortly thereafter, Lucas (1972) derived an 'expectations-augmented' Phillips curve in a clearly specified rational expectations model. Lucas adopted a signal extraction framework in which agents partly misinterpreted aggregate nominal shocks as shocks to the relative price of their own output good (due to limited information), and responded by adjusting their supply. Consistent with Friedman and Phelps, Lucas's model implied that aggregate output varied positively with the unanticipated component of inflation (with anticipated inflation exerting no real effects). But because unanticipated inflation was linked explicitly to a 'rational expectations' forecast error in Lucas's model – which would be expected to die away quickly as agents learned about the nature of underlying shocks – monetary shocks could exert only transient effects on output. This posed a serious challenge to traditional Keynesian models by suggesting that their ability to derive persistent effects in response to a monetary injection relied on ad hoc assumptions about price dynamics or expectations formation. Moreover, because only unanticipated changes in inflation affected output, Lucas's supply relation implied that any predictable policy was as good as any other (the 'policy ineffectiveness' proposition). This point, emphasized by Sargent and Wallace (1975), contrasted sharply with the activist policy stance that emerged from typical Keynesian models.

Monetary transmission in optimization-based MBC models
Since the mid-1990s a new generation of optimization-based MBC models has emerged that can generate 'traditional' Keynesian implications, but in a framework consistent with rational expectations and rigorous microfoundations. Roughly speaking, these new MBC models graft features that can induce sluggish price and/or wage adjustment onto an underlying real business cycle (RBC) model. (Blanchard, 2000, and Taylor, 1999, provide comprehensive surveys of the foundations of modern optimization-based MBC models, which were laid in a series of important contributions spanning several decades.)

To highlight salient features of the modern approach, it is helpful to examine a specific characterization of price-setting that has been utilized extensively in the literature. This relation, often called the 'New Keynesian Phillips curve (NKPC)', takes the form

$$p(t) - p(t-1) = B * E(t) [p(t+1) - p(t)] + b * (y(t) - y(t)^*) \tag{2}$$

where $E(t)$ is the conditional expectation operator, and B is the discount factor.

Following Calvo (1983) and Yun (1996), the NKPC can be derived in a framework consistent with intertemporal optimization. Firms are assumed to behave as monopolistic competitors in the output market, and face downward-sloping demand curves for their distinctive products. Firms face a dynamic decision problem, because they are constrained to set a price that remains fixed in nominal terms over some random duration of time (referred to as the 'contract period', since firms are assumed to meet all demand at this fixed price until allowed to adjust). When a firm receives a signal enabling it to adjust its price, the firm resets it based on estimates of current and future marginal costs expected to prevail over the contract period. Because not all firms can change their price in a given period, price-setting is staggered – similar to the decentralized price-setting in actual economies. (For a discussion of the staggered contracts model.)

From a qualitative perspective, an MBC model in which prices are determined by the NKPC provides a conventional Keynesian account of the monetary transmission mechanism. Thus, a monetary shock increases nominal spending and, since the price level adjusts gradually, real output exhibits a persistent increase (in contrast to the transient real effects in Lucas's model). But as time passes, a larger proportion of firms receive a signal that allows them to raise their price in response to higher projected marginal costs. At an aggregate level, these relative price adjustments translate into a higher price level, which eventually restores real balances and output to pre shock levels.

A major virtue of the microfounded approach is that it illuminates how the monetary policy rule and various structural features of the economy affect the transmission of nominal (and real) shocks. First, given that price adjustment is influenced directly by inflation expectations (as in (2)), monetary surprises have smaller effects on current inflation to the extent that the policy rule is expected to keep future inflation near target (that is, 'anchors' inflation expectations). Second, while the sensitivity of price inflation to the output gap ('b') clearly plays a key role in determining how quickly prices and output adjust to a monetary injection, this parameter is itself determined by features of the microeconomic environment. Quite intuitively, the parameter 'b' varies inversely with the mean duration of price contracts, so that longer contracts imply slower price adjustment and more persistent effects on output. But 'b' also depends on the responsiveness of firm-level marginal costs to the aggregate output gap, which in turn hinges on features of the specific microeconomic environment, including assumptions about factor mobility, capital utilization, and preferences. While some assumptions constrain 'b' to be large, a considerable literature has emerged showing how various 'real rigidities' such as firm-specific capital and labour can account for a low 'b' (even with fairly short-lived contracts); an insightful overview is provided in Woodford (2003). Such real rigidities appear important in allowing macro models to account for persistent output effects, while remaining consistent with disaggregate price data suggesting that firms change prices frequently (Bils and Klenow, 2004).

The NKPC in (2), in which the output gap enters as the activity variable, is derived under the assumption that wages are fully flexible. But, as noted above, there is a long precedent in macroeconomics suggesting that sticky wages play an important role in the transmission process. As shown by Erceg, Henderson and Levin (2000), wage rigidity may be modelled in a framework isomorphic to that rationalizing price rigidity, with households acting as monopolistic suppliers of differentiated labour services. Christiano, Eichenbaum and Evans (2005) have shown that a model that incorporates both wage and price rigidity can account remarkably well for the estimated dynamic effects of a monetary shock on output, prices, and interest rates. The presence of wage rigidity damps the rise in marginal cost due to a positive monetary injection, helping account for estimated persistence in the response of output. Moreover, a model including both types of rigidities can help account for the observed acyclicality of the real wage. By contrast, sticky prices alone imply too much procyclicality in the real wage, while sticky wages alone (in the spirit of the classical economists and Keynes) imply too much counter-cyclicality.

Real shocks and alternative policies in MBC models

Given that monetary policy is widely perceived to have been much more stable since the mid-1980s, the literature has focused greater attention on how policy should respond to real shocks. Modern optimization-based MBC models are useful in this regard, because they provide a coherent framework for examining the transmission of real shocks in the presence of sticky wages and prices, and for assessing the role of monetary policy in affecting the economy's responses.

The presence of nominal rigidities can markedly affect the economy's responses to real shocks. Following Gali (1999), this can be illustrated by contrasting the effects of a persistent rise in technology in an RBC model (in which prices and wages are flexible) with the effects in an MBC model in which prices adjust according to eq. (2). For simplicity, it is assumed that money demand takes the interest-inelastic form $M = P^*Y$, and that the monetary authority holds the nominal money stock constant. In either model, money market equilibrium implies that output can expand only if prices fall proportionally. But as prices can drop instantaneously in the RBC model, the money supply rule is irrelevant in determining the real effects of the shock. Thus, the technology shock immediately boosts employment (as the substitution effect dominates the income effect), and the (percentage) jump in output exceeds the magnitude of the shock. By contrast, prices fall gradually in the MBC model, so that output is constrained to rise slowly given the fixed money stock. With prices determined by the NKPC, negative output gaps are required to induce prices to fall, consistent with employment remaining persistently below its pre-shock level.

As in the case of nominal shocks, the effects of real shocks may be highly sensitive to underlying features of the microeconomic framework, including those that determine the speed of price or wage adjustment. Thus, features that affect 'b' in the NKPC can markedly change how real shocks impact the economy. In the case of the technology shock, additional price sluggishness would translate into a smaller short-run expansion in output and greater employment contraction. Similarly, the inclusion of wage stickiness can markedly affect the responses to technology shocks. For example, while the NKPC derived under the assumption of flexible wages (eq. (2))

implies that price inflation stabilization also keeps output at potential, the same policy could generate large output gap fluctuations if wages were sticky as well as prices.

Modern MBC models have also been applied fruitfully to normative issues. Optimal policy is derived by maximizing an objective function subject to the model's behavioural equations. Importantly, the objective function used in ranking alternative policies is typically derived from the utility functions of the economy's households (Woodford provides an extensive treatment).

A compelling message of this normative literature is that a well-designed policy must take account of its ability to influence inflation through an expectations channel. Thus, a policymaker acting 'under discretion' in an environment where inflation was determined by (2) would act as if the only margin on which to trade in devising a policy involved current inflation and output. However, such a 'discretionary' policy is suboptimal, because it fails to take account of its influence on the expected inflation term in (2). The analysis of Clarida, Gali and Gertler (1999) and Woodford shows that rules that are devised to take account of their influence on future expected inflation can perform much better in maximizing social welfare than discretionary policies that take future inflation as outside the central bank's control. For example, these authors show that well-designed policies can reduce substantially the impact of an adverse cost-push shock on current inflation (relative to the effects under discretion) by creating the perception that future policy will bring inflation back quickly to baseline.

Woodford emphasizes that the optimal monetary policy rule in an environment with forward-looking price-setting exhibits history dependence, so that current monetary policy actions depend on past inflation and activity. This inertial character reflects that the optimal policy rule is derived in a framework in which future policy is expected to take full account of its influence on inflation expectations at earlier dates, much as optimal tax rules recognize their impact on previous investment decisions. Consistent with this history dependence, Woodford shows that it is generally optimal for monetary policy to reverse spikes in inflation above its target value, rather than follow the conventional wisdom of allowing 'bygones to be bygones'. Interestingly, this analysis provides strong support for some form of price level targeting – as recommended by Fisher and Keynes nearly a century ago – with the twist that the modern justification highlights the role it can play in optimally anchoring inflation expectations.

CHRISTOPHER J. ERCEG

See also **monetary transmission mechanism.**

Bibliography

Bils, M. and Klenow, P. 2004. Some evidence on the importance of sticky prices. *Journal of Political Economy* 112, 947–85.

Blanchard, O. 2000. What do we know about macroeconomics that Fisher and Wicksell did not? *Quarterly Journal of Economics* 115, 1375–409.

Calvo, G. 1983. Staggered prices in a utility-maximizing framework. *Journal of Monetary Economics* 12, 383–98.

Christiano, L., Eichenbaum, M. and Evans, C. 2005. Nominal rigidities and the dynamic effects of shocks to monetary policy. *Journal of Political Economy* 113, 1–45.

Clarida, R., Gali, J. and Gertler, M. 1999. The science of monetary policy: a new Keynesian perspective. *Journal of Economic Literature* 37, 1661–707.

Erceg, C., Henderson, D. and Levin, A. 2000. Optimal monetary policy with staggered wage and price contracts. *Journal of Monetary Economics* 46, 281–313.

Fisher, I. 1920. *Stabilizing the Dollar*. Norwood, MA: Norwood Press.

Friedman, M. 1968. The role of monetary policy. *American Economic Review* 58(1), 1–17.

Gali, J. 1999. Technology, employment, and the business cycle: do technology shocks explain aggregate fluctuations? *American Economic Review* 89, 249–71.

Humphrey, T. 2004. Classical deflation theory. *Federal Bank of Richmond Economic Quarterly* 90, 11–32.

Keynes, J. 1936. *The General Theory of Interest, Employment, and Money*. London: Macmillan.

Lucas, R. 1972. Expectations and the neutrality of money. *Journal of Economic Theory* 4, 103–24.

Phelps, E. 1968. Money–wage dynamics and labor market equilibrium. *Journal of Political Economy* 76, 678–711.

Sargent, T. and Wallace, N. 1975. Rational expectations, the optimal monetary instrument, and the optimal money supply rule. *Journal of Political Economy* 83, 169–83.

Taylor, J. 1999. Staggered wage and price setting in macroeconomics. In *Handbook of Macroeconomics*, ed. J.B. Taylor and M. Woodford. Amsterdam: North-Holland.

Woodford, M. 2003. *Interest and Prices*. Princeton: Princeton University Press.

Yun, T. 1996. Nominal price rigidity, money supply endogeneity, and business cycles. *Journal of Monetary Economics* 37, 345–70.

monetary business cycles (imperfect information)

Business cycle theories based on incomplete information start from the premise that key economic decisions on pricing, investment or production are often made on the basis of incomplete knowledge of constantly changing aggregate economic conditions. As a result, decisions tend to respond slowly to changes in economic fundamentals, and small or temporary economic shocks may have large and long-lasting effects on macroeconomic aggregates.

Incomplete information theories have been popular in particular for explaining sluggish price or wage adjustment in response to monetary shocks. At the heart of this theory lies the assumption that firms or households only pay attention to a relatively small number of indicators regarding conditions in markets relevant to their own activities, but they may not acquire information more broadly about aggregate economic activity. With imprecise information about these aggregate conditions, it takes the firms some time to sort out temporary from permanent changes, or nominal from real disturbances. Prices then respond with a delay to changes in nominal spending, and monetary shocks may have significant effects on real economic activity in the intervening periods – despite the fact that firms have the opportunity to constantly readjust their decisions.

This basic idea was proposed first by Phelps (1970) and formalized by Lucas (1972). In Lucas (1972), economic agents produce in localized markets, in which they observe the market-clearing price at which they can sell their output. This price is affected both by aggregate spending shocks and by market-specific supply shocks. Under perfect information, quantities adjust in response to local supply shocks, but not prices, and prices respond to aggregate spending shocks, but not quantities. With imperfect information, agents are unable to filter out the magnitudes of the aggregate and market-specific shocks from the observed prices in the short run. Output then responds positively to price changes and spending shocks in the short run, but not in the long run, once agents have been able to sort out the spending shocks from the market-specific supply shocks.

Lucas (1972) formulated this idea in a rational expectations market equilibrium model, in which agents' expectations are fully Bayesian, and the resulting output responses are optimal. His model also includes stark assumptions about the nature of local versus aggregate market interactions, as well as the nature of shocks (monetary versus real, demand versus supply, aggregate versus market-specific) and the information to which firms have access.

Importantly, the model lacks a natural internal amplification mechanism: the extent of incomplete nominal adjustment depends almost entirely on the degree of informational incompleteness. Subsequent work has tried to address these issues, for example by introducing richer information structures. Townsend (1983) considers an investment model in which firms get to observe how much some of the other firms invest. Therefore, they need to form forecasts about each others' beliefs – forecasting the forecasts of others. This leads to a complicated infinite regress problem, whereby a firm's current investment level depends on its observation of other firms' past investment, which in turn depended on observations about past investment… Townsend showed that this type of problem does not admit a simple finite-dimensional recursive structure. As a result, firms must draw inference about all past realizations of shocks simultaneously, leading to an infinite-dimensional filtering and fixed point problem, with no easily characterized solution.

These and other important technical and computational hurdles effectively imposed limitations on the complexity and economic realism of the early incomplete information models. Moreover, the model is open to the criticism that if incomplete information is a major source of business cycle fluctuations, then there seems to be an important societal benefit to making the relevant information publicly available to everyone. In part because of these difficulties, economists have, from the mid-1980s, turned their attention to New Keynesian sticky price theories that emphasize the role of adjustment and coordination frictions in price-setting. (Among others, see Calvo, 1983; Blanchard and Kiyotaki, 1987.)

Recently, the incomplete information theories have made a comeback, which can be traced to two factors. First, technological progress has made models such as Townsend (1983) computationally tractable. Second, new game-theoretic results regarding equilibrium analysis with a lack of common knowledge and heterogeneity in beliefs, as well as insights borrowed from the sticky price literature regarding the role of real rigidities and pricing complementarities (Ball and Romer, 1990) have enabled us to paint a much richer picture of the adjustment dynamics resulting from incomplete information models. The empirical performance of these new incomplete information models, however, still remains to be seen.

In the remainder of this article I provide a unified exposition of the main ideas behind the incomplete information theories, from the original contributions to the more recent renewal. I also attempt to chart out some of the challenges that lie ahead. This is a lively and active area of research, with many open questions and few definite answers.

A canonical framework

Consider the following model, which is based on the New Keynesian models of monopolistic competition. There is a large number of firms, indexed by $i \in [0,1]$. In each period, each firm sets its (log-)price $p_t(i)$ equal to its expectation of a target price p_t^*, $p_t(i) = E(p_t^*|\mathscr{I}_t^i)$, where $\mathscr{I}_t^i$ denotes the information set of firm i at date t, that is all signals on which it can condition its pricing decision. p_t^* is characterized as

$$p_t^* = ky_t + p_t, \tag{1}$$

where $p_t = \int p_t(i)di$ denotes the average of the firms' pricing decisions, y_t denotes the aggregate real output in period t, relative to its trend level that would prevail with complete information, and $k > 0$ measures the response of optimal pricing decisions to real output. A firm's ideal relative price $p_t^* - p_t$ is determined by real output deviations from trend.

We augment this pricing rule by a quantity equation, $y_t + p_t = m_t$, where m_t denotes nominal spending. Combining the two, we find

$$p_t^* = km_t + (1 - k)p_t. \tag{2}$$

Nominal spending m_t is driven by exogenous shocks; for simplicity, assume that $m_t = m_{t-1} + \varepsilon_t$, where $\{\varepsilon_t\}$ is i.i.d. white noise.

Each firm's target price is therefore a linear combination of the exogenous shocks and the prices set by the other firms. If $k \in (0,1)$, prices are complementary, that is, an increase in the average price level implies that each firm has an incentive to raise its own price. The parameter value of k depends on the substitution elasticity between the firms' products, the firms' returns to scale parameter in the technology, and the Frisch elasticity of labour supply.

To complete the model description, we need to specify each firm's information set $\mathscr{I}_t^i$ – this is where different incomplete information theories vary. An equilibrium of this model requires that prices satisfy the optimality condition $p_t(i) = E(p_t^*|\mathscr{I}_t^i)$, taking into account that p_t^* itself depends on the aggregate price level.

Common information

Suppose first that all firms have identical information sets, $\mathscr{I}_t^i = \mathscr{I}_t$. Then, they will set identical prices, equal to $p_t(i) = p_t = E(m_t|\mathscr{I}_t)$. This reflects the implications of the original Lucas model that prices adjust to the common expectation of the underlying shocks. When information is incomplete, firms will only learn gradually about m_t, prices adjust slowly, and monetary surprises have real effects: y_t is determined directly by the discrepancy between the realized and the expected value of m_t. However, if the available information on which these expectations are based is sufficiently precise, then $E(m_t|\mathscr{I}_t)$ cannot be far from the true value of m_t. As discussed above, the real effects of monetary shocks are bounded by the degree of informational incompleteness – as firms have better information, their prices track m_t more closely, and monetary shocks have smaller real effects.

Heterogeneous beliefs, but independent strategies

A similar conclusion emerges when firms have different information sets, but their target prices do not respond to the other firms' decisions ($k = 1$). Each firm's price is set equal to its expectation of the spending shock $p_t(i) = E(m_t|\mathscr{I}_t^i)$, and the average price adjusts according to the average expectation $p_t = \bar{E}(m_t) = \int E(m_t|\mathscr{I}_t^i)\, di$ of the spending shock. Once again, if firms are sufficiently well informed, their pricing decisions will on average not be far from the nominal spending shock, which implies little delay in price adjustment and only small real output effects.

Heterogeneous beliefs and complementary strategies

Suppose now that instead $k \in (0, 1)$, so that there are complementarities in pricing decisions. Averaging the pricing equation, and substituting forward, firm i's equilibrium price is given by

$$p_t(i) = k \sum_{s=0}^{\infty} (1 - k)^s E\left[\bar{E}^{(s)}(m_t) | \mathscr{I}_t^i \right] \tag{3}$$

where $\bar{E}^{(s)}(m_t)$ denotes the s-order average expectation of m_t, or the average expectation of the average expectation of ... (repeat s times) ... of m_t. A firm's optimal price is therefore given as a geometrically weighted average of higher-order expectations – a firm needs to forecast not only the realized shock but also the other firms' expectations of the shock, the other firms' expectations of the other firms' expectations of the shock, and so on.

If the firms all had identical information, the law of iterated expectations would simply collapse the right-hand side above into the common first-order expectation of m_t. The model thus derives its interest from the fact that with heterogeneous information, higher-order expectations respond differently to new information than first-order expectations about m_t.

The following example illustrates this point and serves also to derive the main results of this model. Suppose that all firms observe m_{t-1} exactly, but only a fraction λ (the *informed*) gets to observe m_t. Then, $E(m_t) = \lambda m_t + (1 - \lambda)m_{t-1}$, but the second order average expectation is $E^{(2)}(m_t) = \lambda[\lambda m_t + (1 - \lambda)m_{t-1}] + (1 - \lambda)m_{t-1} = \lambda^2 m_t + (1 - \lambda^2)m_{t-1}$. By iteration, the s-order average expectation of m_t is $E^{(s)}(m_t) = \lambda^s m_t + (1 - \lambda^s)m_{t-1}$. The average price is

$$p_t = k \sum_{s=0}^{\infty} (1 - k)^s E^{(s+1)}(m_t) = m_{t-1} + \frac{k\lambda}{1 - (1 - k)\lambda}(m_t - m_{t-1}). \tag{4}$$

Two important conclusions emerge. First, note that $\frac{k\lambda}{1-(1-k)\lambda} < \lambda$. The informed firms whose prices may react to m_t take into account that the uninformed firms won't respond, which in turn reduces their incentives to adjust prices. Therefore, while incomplete information serves as the initial source of sluggish price adjustment, the complementarity and the heterogeneity in beliefs dampen the response of prices far beyond what the initial degree of informational incompleteness would suggest. To illustrate the strength of this amplification effect, consider the following numerical example: suppose that $k = 0.15$ (as in standard parametrizations of New Keynesian sticky price models), and that half the firms are informed. Then, the contemporaneous response of average prices is $\frac{k\lambda}{1-(1-k)\lambda} \approx 0.13$, that is a one per cent increase in nominal spending leads to only a 0.13 per cent increase in prices, and a 0.87 per cent increase in real output – despite the fact that half of the firms actually observe the increase in nominal spending and are hence able to respond to it!

Second, this amplification can be large, even if the degree of informational incompleteness is small. If λ is close to 1, almost all firms exactly observe the current realization m_t. Nevertheless, if k is close to 0, that is if there is a strong pricing complementarity, they still won't respond to the monetary shock. The presence of only a few uninformed firms is therefore enough to radically overturn the conclusions of the complete information model.

These two observations apply quite generally, once firms have heterogeneous beliefs. They form the central insight of the new incomplete information theories. In Mankiw and Reis (2002), heterogeneous beliefs result because, in any given period, only a fraction of firms observe new information. This generalizes the above example to allow for richer adjustment dynamics. In Woodford (2002), all firms observe a conditionally independent idiosyncratic signal x_t^i of the current realization of m_t in each period. The resulting inference problem is more complicated but can be solved numerically. Again, the response of prices to monetary shocks is significantly dampened by the fact that firms do not share in common information, yet their pricing decisions are complementary.

The role of public information

Hellwig (2002) provides a simplified version of Woodford (2002), providing closed-form solutions to a general class of information structures. This simplified model also accommodates the presence of additional public sources of information such as central bank announcements. Besides dampening the response to idiosyncratic private signals, the complementarity in prices generates overreaction to public news. Public announcements thus speed up price adjustment and reduce the real effects of monetary shocks, but the noise in public news creates an additional source of volatility, which in some cases may increase rather than decrease real output fluctuations. (Similar results are derived by Amato and Shin, 2003, for Woodford's model, and by Ui, 2003, in the original Lucas island model.)

Looking ahead

These new contributions have provided promising insights into the amplification and propagation mechanisms of incomplete information models. But they also abstract from important modelling issues that need to be addressed before a comprehensive quantitative evaluation becomes possible.

So far, much of the analysis is based on a stylized price-setting model that captures the essence of pricing complementarities as described above, without deriving them within a fully specified dynamic general equilibrium model. This short-cut is not without problems. First, the lack of a proper context of markets makes it difficult to interpret these propagation results. Presumably in a market firms obtain some information about price and quantity variables – so far, this is not formally modelled.

Second, the assumption that firms are heterogeneously informed implies that other frictions must be present – in particular, the extent to which information about fundamental shocks can be inferred from publicly observable prices must be limited, implying that the asset market must be incomplete. But then, one faces the problem of isolating the effects of informational heterogeneity from the effects of other market imperfections. In Lorenzoni, (2006) for instance, a precautionary savings motive generates a multiplier effect in household spending, which is further amplified by the presence of heterogeneous information.

Third, there is an issue of interpretation. At this point, there exist several different interpretations regarding the source of the differences in beliefs across firms, and they may lead to radically different model conclusions. In Mankiw and Reis (2002), firms update their information only infrequently, and in the intervening periods set prices on the basis of outdated information; Reis (2006) further develops this idea on the basis of menu costs in updating decisions. Woodford (2002) instead bases his model on the notion of 'rational inattention', developed by Sims (2003; 2006a). Sims argues that decision makers only have a finite capacity to process new information, which constrains the quality of the signals they observe in any given period. Heterogeneity in beliefs then arises naturally through the idiosyncratic noise in each individual's information processing channel (see Sims, 2006b, for further discussion of the resulting conceptual and modelling issues). A third interpretation suggests that individuals are Bayesian, but access to information is limited – for example, firms observe the demand for their own products, but not the demand for competitors' products. If each firm is subject to idiosyncratic, as well as common shocks, then an information structure much like the above with idiosyncratic private signals emerges. On the other hand, firms also observe market prices, which generates a source of common information.

Finally, all these models treat the information structure as an exogenous primitive. In reality, firms and households have access to overwhelming amounts of information, and information processing becomes a matter of choice, given the existing constraints and trade-offs. By and large, the effects of information costs and choices and the strategic interaction that results from these choices remains unexplored. Preliminary developments in this direction include Mackowiak and Wiederholt (2005) and Hellwig and Veldkamp (2005). In Mackowiak and Wiederholt, firms need to allocate a fixed information processing capacity between firm-specific and aggregate variables. Hellwig and Veldkamp explore how the pricing complementarities that are relevant for business cycle implications also shape incentives for information acquisition.

In summary, the most important issue that remains to be resolved is the grounding of new incomplete information theories within a fully specified model of goods and asset markets, with special emphasis on the origins of the informational frictions. Beyond that, the new incomplete information theories raise many intriguing questions, which merit further attention, or have already been addressed to some extent: for example, Ball, Mankiw and Reis (2005) reconsider the role of monetary policy, and Morris and Shin (2002), Hellwig (2005) and Angeletos and Pavan (2004; 2007) discuss the welfare effects of information disclosures. Finally, the combination of new evidence on the cross-sectional and business cycle properties of expectations (Mankiw, Reis and Wolfers, 2004) and new micro-level data on price adjustments (Bils and Klenow, 2004) promises to provide an interesting avenue for evaluating the empirical performance of the model's cross-sectional and business cycle implications.

CHRISTIAN HELLWIG

See also **monetary business cycles models (sticky prices and wages); monetary transmission mechanism.**

Bibliography

Amato, J. and Shin, H.S. 2003. Public and private information in monetary policy models. Working Paper No. 138, Bank of International Settlements.

Angeletos, G.-M. and Pavan, A. 2004. Transparency of information and coordination in economies with investment complementarities. *American Economic Review* 94, 91–8.

Angeletos, G.-M. and Pavan, A. 2007. Efficient use of information and social value of information. *Econometrica* 75, 1103–42.

Ball, L., Mankiw, G. and Reis, R. 2005. Monetary policy for inattentive economies. *Journal of Monetary Economics* 52, 703–25.

Ball, L. and Romer, D. 1990. Real rigidities and the non-neutrality of money. *Review of Economic Studies* 57, 183–203.

Bils, M. and Klenow, P. 2004. Some evidence on the importance of sticky prices. *Journal of Political Economy* 112, 947–85.

Blanchard, O. and Kiyotaki, N. 1987. Monopolistic competition and the effects of aggregate demand. *American Economic Review* 77, 647–66.

Calvo, G. 1983. Staggered prices in a utility maximizing framework. *Journal of Monetary Economics* 12, 383–98.

Hellwig, C. 2002. Public announcements, adjustment delays and the business cycle. Discussion paper, University of California, Los Angeles.

Hellwig, C. 2005. Heterogeneous information and the welfare effects of public information disclosures. Discussion paper, University of California, Los Angeles.

Hellwig, C. and Veldkamp, L. 2005. Knowing what others know: coordination motives in information acquisition. Discussion paper, University of California, Los Angeles and New York University.

Lorenzoni, G. 2006. A theory of demand shocks. Discussion paper, Massachusetts Institute of Technology.

Lucas, R. 1972. Expectations and the neutrality of money. *Journal of Economic Theory* 4, 103–24.

Mackowiak, B. and Wiederholt, M. 2005. Optimal sticky prices under rational inattention. Discussion paper, Humboldt University Berlin.

Mankiw, G. and Reis, R. 2002. Sticky information versus sticky prices: a proposal to replace the new Kaynesian Phillips curve. *Quarterly Journal of Economics* 117, 1295–328.

Mankiw, G., Reis, R. and Wolfers, J. 2004. Disagreement about inflation expectations. In *NBER Macroeconomics Annual 2003*. Cambridge, MA: MIT Press.

Morris, S. and Shin, H.S. 2002. The social value of public information. *American Economic Review* 92, 1521–34.

Phelps, E. 1970. Introduction: the new microeconomics in employment and inflation theory. In *Microeconomic Foundations of Employment and Inflation Theory*. New York: Norton.

Reis, R. 2006. Inattentive producers. *Review of Economic Studies* 73, 1–29.

Sims, C. 2003. Implications of rational inattention. *Journal of Monetary Economics* 50, 665–90.

Sims, C. 2006a. Rational inattention: beyond the linear-quadratic case. *American Economic Review* 96, 158–63.

Sims, C. 2006b. Rational inattention: a research agenda. Discussion paper, Princeton University.

Townsend, R. 1983. Forecasting the forecasts of others. *Journal of Political Economy* 91, 546–88.

Ui, T. 2003. A note on the Lucas model: iterated expectations and the non-neutrality of money. Discussion paper, Yokohama National University.

Woodford, M. 2002. Imperfect common knowledge and the effects of monetary policy. In *Knowledge, Information and Expectations in Modern Macroeconomics*, ed. P. Aghion. et al. Princeton: Princeton University Press.

monetary economics, history of

Origins of monetary economics

As with so much else in the Western tradition, theorizing about the role of money can be traced back to Plato and Aristotle in the fourth century BCE, although they may have drawn on pre-Socratic philosophers whose works survive, if at all, only in fragments. In his *Republic* (1974), Plato remarked that money was a symbol devised to make exchange easier. He disapproved of gold and silver as money, preferring a currency that would have value only internally, not in external commerce. The analysis in Aristotle's *Nicomachean Ethics* (1996) and *Politics* (1984) of what constitutes just exchange led Aristotle to a more systematic discussion of a medium of exchange. His account of the functions of money, and of the properties that suit a commodity such as gold or silver to be the medium of exchange, as well as his use of the myth of Midas to distinguish between gold and wealth, influenced comparable presentations by Nicolas Oresme in about 1360 (Oresme, de Sassoferrato and Buridan, 1989), Adam Smith (1776), and, through Smith, any number of 19th-century textbooks (see Menger, 1892; Monroe, 1923). Barter might be the most basic form of exchange, but it involves accepting goods one does not wish to consume in order to make a further exchange for what is desired. Aristotle noted the convenience of a generally accepted medium of exchange in reducing the number of transactions required. He saw the convenience of stating prices in terms of the medium of exchange, and that, if a commodity is to serve as a medium of exchange, it must also be a store of value, retaining purchasing power between being received and being spent (but he did not mention the function of money as a standard of deferred payment). Precious metals provided a suitable medium of exchange because of being homogenous, divisible, portable, and sufficiently scarce to a have a high value relative to their weight, although that value could change. Unlike Plato, Aristotle viewed the weight and purity of the precious metals as the source of the purchasing power of money, with coinage just saving the inconvenience of having to weigh and assay the metals at every transaction.

The quantity theory of money, described by David Laidler (1991b) as 'always and everywhere controversial' and by Mark Blaug as 'the oldest surviving theory in economics' (Blaug et al., 1995), holds that the price level (the inverse of the purchasing power of money) depends on how large the stock of money is compared with the demand for real money balances, with the direction of causation running from money to prices (Hegeland, 1951). The quantity theory originated in the 16th century, when Martin de Azpilcueta Navarro in Salamanca in 1556 and Jean Bodin in France in 1568 identified the inflow of silver from the Spanish colonies of Mexico and Upper Peru as the cause of the rise in prices and depreciation of silver throughout Europe, a phenomenon now known as the 'price revolution' (Grice-Hutchinson, 1952; O'Brien, 2000). In contrast to the recognition by Navarro and Bodin of the inverse relationship between the quantity of the precious metals and their purchasing power, contemporaries such as the Seigneur de Malestroit had attributed rising prices of commodities to the debasement of various national coinages. The astronomer Copernicus had remarked earlier that money usually depreciates when it is too abundant (Grice-Hutchinson, 1952, p. 34), but Navarro and Bodin went beyond such passing insights to formulate a theory they could use to explain the observed trend of commodity prices. Later research has shown that the 16th century quadrupling of prices was also due in part to the growing output of central European silver mines and to an increase in the velocity of circulation of money as systems of payment and communication evolved, notably the use of bills of exchange.

Mercantilists also took note of the inflow of precious metals from Spain's conquest in the New World, viewing this gold and silver as the 'sinews of war' with which Spain could pay armies in Europe. Although both alchemy and seizure of the Spanish treasure fleet were attempted (the physicist Isaac Newton was both Master of the Royal Mint and an avid alchemist), mercantilists such as Thomas Mun advocated interventionist government policies to achieve a surplus of exports over imports as the way to bring gold and silver into a country that lacked its own mines. Mercantilists held that increased circulation of gold and silver in a country would both increase national power and stimulate real economic activity (Viner, 1937; Vickers, 1959). Isaac Gervaise (1720), Richard Cantillon (2001, written c. 1730 and published post-humously in 1755), and, most fully and forcefully, David Hume (1752) used the quantity theory of money to develop the specie-flow mechanism of international payments adjustment that rendered such mercantilist schemes futile. An increase in gold and silver circulating in a country, whether due to colonial conquests, discovery of new mines, or a trade surplus engineered by tariffs on imports and bounties on exports, would increase spending. Although Hume recognized that one immediate, temporary effect of such increased spending would be to stimulate production (see Humphrey, 1993) in due course prices and wages would rise, making domestic goods more expensive in relation to foreign goods. This would reduce exports and increase imports, eliminating the trade surplus, so that the only lasting result would be the misallocation of resources caused by tariffs, bounties and quotas. For Adam Smith (1776), a small open economy such as that of Scotland took prices under the gold standard as given by the world market, so the balance of payments adjustment would take place without any change in the relative price of foreign and domestic goods. An excess supply of money in a country would directly cause more imports and more exportable goods to be purchased domestically (and the contrary in a country with an excess demand for money) unless the world's supply of monetary metal was distributed across countries in proportion to their demand for money. Humphrey (1993) and Laidler (2003, ch. 1) show that Smith's analysis bore a closer resemblance than that of Hume to the modern monetary approach to the balance of payments.

From Aristotle and the Bible onwards, payment of interest on loans had been condemned as usury on the grounds that it was unnatural for gold ('barren metal') to breed and that interest violated justice (exchange of equal values), as the amount of money repaid exceeded the initial loan. Cantillon, Hume, A.R.J. Turgot, and Jeremy Bentham argued for the legitimacy of an interest rate set by market forces of supply and demand, with Turgot invoking time preference to point out that the amount of money lent and the larger amount of money repaid represented the same present value. Contrary to his general stand against government intervention, Adam Smith (1776) endorsed legal limits on interest to prevent high-risk lending for speculation and reckless consumption, and was rebuked for inconsistency by the young Bentham (West, 1997).

Monetary controversies in classical economics

Monetary theory was advanced by two British debates, the Bullionist Controversy, which surrounded the suspension of the convertibility of Bank of England notes into gold from 1797 to 1821, and the clash between the Banking School and the Currency School in the 1840s leading up to and following the Bank Act revision that separated and regulated the Bank of England's Issue Department (whose liabilities were bank notes, with gold held in reserve) and Banking Department (whose liabilities were deposits, with Bank of England notes held in reserve). During the suspension of convertibility during the Napoleonic Wars, Henry Thornton (1802) and, from 1809 onwards, David Ricardo (1810) argued the high price of bullion and foreign exchange showed that the Bank of England had engaged in over-issue of bank notes, raising commodity prices and depreciating the pound sterling (Fetter, 1965; Marcuzzo and Rosselli, 1991). Christiernin (1761) had made a similar argument in Sweden, but appears not to have been known in Britain. Thornton was the leading figure on a House of Commons Select Committee on the High Price of Gold Bullion in 1810 that adopted this view in the Bullion Report, but the directors of the Bank of England persuaded the full House not to act on the committee's report. The directors, invoking the authority of Adam Smith, held that they could not have been guilty of any inflationary overissue of notes beyond what the needs of trade required as long as they issued notes only by discounting bills of exchange created by genuine commercial transactions, rather than financial speculation. This version of the real bills doctrine ignored Smith's assumption that bank notes were convertible into gold upon demand, so that any increase in the quantity of notes sufficient to depress their value below their gold par would cause the excess notes to be redeemed. Without convertibility as a constraint on overissue, the demand for bills would be unbounded as long as the discount rate was less than the prevailing rate of profit. The distinction between real and fictitious bills also failed to recognize that the length of time a bill was discounted need not correspond to the length of time goods were in process (Mints, 1945; Laidler, 2003; Davis, 2005).

The depression that accompanied the end of the Napoleonic Wars and Britain's subsequent return to the gold standard stimulated a debate over the possibility of a general glut of commodities. Thomas Robert Malthus and J.C.L. Simonde de Sismondi attributed the depression to an insufficiency of effective demand. Malthus's argument was acclaimed by John Maynard Keynes a century later, although, unlike Keynes, Malthus did not distinguish between a decision to save and a decision to invest (see Keynes's 1933 essay on Malthus). Ricardo and Jean-Baptiste Say upheld Say's (or James Mill's) Law of Markets, denying the possibility of a general glut of commodities or an insufficiency of aggregate effective demand, since a commodity was offered for sale only with the intention of acquiring the means to purchase some other commodity, not with intent to hoard money, which is only a medium of exchange (Say was not quite as unambiguous as James Mill). Ricardo and Say recognized that unemployment would occur during the adjustment to a major change in the mix of commodities demanded, as the end of the Napoleonic Wars curtailed military and naval spending and as the purchasing power of money changed: Ricardo was prepared to accept restoration of gold convertibility at the depreciated parity, to avoid the price deflation associated with going back to the pre-war parity, and Say endorsed public works to employ those who would otherwise be jobless during the transition period. But, according to Ricardo, Say and James Mill, such distress resulted from a temporary mismatch between the mix of commodities produced and those demanded, with excess supply in some markets and excess demand in others, not from generalized excess supply.

Throughout the 19th century, classical economists such as John Stuart Mill struggled to formulate an acceptable version of the law of markets that would be stronger than what Oskar Lange later labelled Say's Equality but weaker than what Lange called Say's Identity (Corry, 1962; Sowell, 1972; Baumol, 1977; 1999; Davis, 2005). Say's equality, which held that at equilibrium prices the value of excess demand sums to zero across all markets except that for money, is a trivial implication of the market-clearing equilibrium condition that at market-clearing prices supply equals demand in each market. Say's identity, which held that at any prices the value of excess demand always sums to zero across all markets except money, implies (when combined with the summation of individual budget constraints) that money demand always equals the money supply at any prices, which leaves the absolute price level (the inverse of the purchasing power of money) indeterminate. In the 1870s, Leon Walras reformulated Say's Law as what Lange termed Walras's Law: the value of aggregate excess demand summed over all markets (including money) is identically zero, from the summation of individual budget constraints (the net value of each individual's transactions is at most zero, since people must pay for their purchases) plus local non-satiation (so that no one is willing to throw away purchasing power). Robert Clower (1984), seeking to understand Keynes's rejection of Say's Law of Markets, argued that Walras's Law only applies to notional demands, not to quantity-constrained effective demands when markets do not clear (in Keynes's case, the labour market): if workers cannot sell all the labour they wish at the prevailing wage rate, then the quantity of labour they cannot sell multiplied by the wage rate that they would have received should not be included in their budget constraint for demanding goods.

Currency School adherents (for example, J.R. McCulloch, G.W. Norman and Lord Overstone), whose ideas shaped Sir Robert Peel's Bank Act of 1844, urged that, beyond maintaining convertibility, the Bank of England should conduct its operations so that a mixed metallic and paper currency would fluctuate in the same way that a purely metallic currency would. Building on Ricardo's presentation of the quantity theory of money and the price specie-flow mechanism, the Currency School wished the central bank to follow a stabilizing policy that would prevent gold outflows, rather than waiting for such international cash drains to bring about adjustment. The Currency School attributed the banking crises of 1825, 1832 and 1836–37 to monetary mismanagement by the Bank of England, which could have regulated the volume of coin and notes in circulation so as to stabilize prices. In contrast, Banking School writers such as Thomas Tooke and John Fullarton, drawing on Thornton, emphasized the endogeneity of the total volume of credit (financial instruments convertible into gold), of which bank notes were only a small part (Fullarton, 1836; 1845; Fetter, 1965; Arnon, 1991; Cassidy, 1998; Skaggs, 1999). Karl Marx also held that the volume of money adjusted to satisfy the equation of exchange (de Brunhoff, 1976). Elements of both Currency School and Banking School positions appeared in the writings of John Stuart Mill. The Banking School thought that the volume of credit was as likely to respond to changes in prices as to cause them, and so did not share the Currency School view of the banking system as the initiator of credit cycles. The Banking School prescription was for the Bank of England to hold a bullion reserve large enough to ride out temporary disturbances in credit and international payments. While the Currency and Banking Schools differed on the appropriate policy for a central bank, another group of writers, including Henry Dunning Macleod (1855), James Wilson of *The Economist* and Jean-Gustave Courcelle-Seneuil, opposed having a central bank with a legally protected dominant position and special privileges. Instead, they advocated a system of free banking, with the market valuing the notes of competing banks, a proposal revived by Vera Smith (1936) and later by Friedrich Hayek (1976), who had been her dissertation adviser. Walter Bagehot's *Lombard Street* (1873) established the monetary orthodoxy, emerging from the Currency School–Banking School debates, on how the central bank should manage the discount rate to maintain convertibility and its role as a lender of last resort to preserve the liquidity of the banking system, rather than simply acting in the interests of its shareholders.

The golden age of the quantity theory

In studies collected posthumously in Jevons (1884), William Stanley Jevons used index numbers, with equal weights on different commodities, to show the rise in prices following the gold rushes in California in 1849 and Australia in 1851, as did John Elliot Cairnes. Commodity prices tended downwards from 1873 to 1896 as the world's demand for real money balances grew faster than its money supply, a decline halted by the introduction of the cyanide process for extracting gold from low-grade ores and by gold discoveries in South Africa and the Klondike. Together with the return of the

United States to gold convertibility of the dollar in 1873 after the issue of inconvertible greenbacks during the Civil War, this deflation contributed to bimetallist agitation that reached its peak in William Jennings Bryan's presidential campaign in 1896, in which Bryan spoke against 'crucifying mankind on a cross of gold'. The bimetallists argued that monetizing silver as well as gold would raise the price by increasing the quantity of money, and this would have lasting real benefits. This led hard-money, classical economists such as J. Laurence Laughlin of the University of Chicago to associate the quantity theory of money with claims of long-run non-neutrality (Skaggs, 1995). In place of the quantity theory, Laughlin (1903) derived the value of money from the convertibility into gold, whose value depended on its cost of production, a view which David Glasner (1985; 2000) shows had figured alongside the quantity theory in classical political economy. The quantity theorists David Kinley (1904), Edwin Kemmerer (1907) and Irving Fisher (with Harry G. Brown, *The Purchasing Power of Money*, 1911, in Fisher, 1997, vol. 4) responded by seeking to show, contrary to Laughlin and his Chicago associates, that exogenous changes in the quantity of money explained the behaviour of prices (given the trend in money demand), and, contrary to the bimetallists, that money is neutral in the long run. These quantity theorists extended earlier statements of the equation of exchange by Simon Newcomb (to whom Fisher dedicated his 1911 book) and Sir John Lubbock. Fisher allowed currency (M) and bank deposits (M') to have different velocities of circulation, restating the equation of exchange as $MV + M'V' = PT$, where T is an index of the volume of transactions and P is the price level. To use the equation of exchange to make the case that the changing money supply explained the observed movements of US prices (rather than just having the equation as a tautology defining the velocity of circulation) required independent measures of the velocity of circulation. To estimate V, Fisher persuaded 116 people at Yale (including 113 male undergraduates) to keep daily records of their spending and cash balances. For V', the velocity of circulation of bank deposits, Fisher used linear interpolation between the estimates from two empirical studies by David Kinley counting all bank clearings in the United States for a day in 1896 (for the Comptroller of the Currency) and a day in 1910 (for the National Monetary Commission). From an Austrian perspective, Ludwig von Mises (1935) objected to the aggregative reasoning of the quantity theorists, arguing that an index number of the price level gives a distorted picture of how agents respond to prices.

Systematically developing earlier remarks by John Stuart Mill and Alfred Marshall and an article by Jacob de Haas, Irving Fisher argued in *Appreciation and Interest* (1896, in Fisher, 1997, vol. 1) that that nominal interest is the sum of real interest and the expected rate of inflation, so that only unanticipated changes in the purchasing power of money change the real interest rate and redistribute wealth. Contrary to bimetallist claims, expected inflation or deflation would have no real effects. Fisher's 1896 analysis included uncovered interest arbitrage parity (the difference between nominal interest rates in two currencies is the expected rate of change of the exchange rate) and the expectations theory of the term structure of interest rates (variations in nominal interest on loans of different duration reflects expectations of the time-path of prices). But from *The Purchasing Power of Money* onwards, while continuing to insist on the long-run neutrality of money, Fisher argued that money was not neutral during transition periods (of up to ten years), as nominal interest adjusted only slowly to monetary shocks, and that the 'so-called "business cycle"' was really a 'dance of the dollar'. While Ralph Hawtrey (1919) and Fisher advanced monetary theories of economic fluctuations, many economists in the late 19th and early 20th centuries, from Jevons on sunspot cycles to Joseph Schumpeter on clusters of innovations, emphasized real shocks and truly periodic cycles of varying lengths such as Juglar, Kondratiev and Kitchin cycles. Fisher's article, 'A Statistical Relationship between Unemployment and Price Level Changes' (1926) correlated unemployment with a distributed lag of past price level changes and was reprinted in the *Journal of Political Economy* in 1973 as 'Lost and Found: I Discovered the Phillips Curve'. Fisher correlated nominal interest with a distributed lag of price changes (a version of adaptive expectations) to show the slow adjustment of nominal interest and inflation expectations (*The Theory of Interest*, 1930), resulting from what he termed *The Money Illusion* (the title of his 1928 book), the widespread tendency to think in nominal rather than real terms.

Bimetallism foundered on its insistence on fixing the relative price of gold and silver, at 15 or 16 ounces of silver per ounce of gold. As the relative market valuation changed, due to changing marginal costs of production or shifts in non-monetary demand for precious metals, one of the two metals would disappear from circulation and its coins be melted down. Alfred Marshall's (1887) suggestion of symmetallism, a unit of value consisting of a quantity of gold plus a quantity of silver (reprinted in Pigou, 1925), was more practical, but did not seem so to bimetallists or the general public. Marshall's tentative proposal to peg the monetary value of a basket of two commodities instead of just one (gold) marked a step towards a monetary policy of targeting the price level (or its rate of change) rather than the exchange rate with gold. Like Jevons (1884), Marshall suggested voluntary indexation, with contracts made in terms of a 'standard unit of purchasing power', which Marshall argued would reduce cyclical fluctuations (Laidler, 1991a, pp. 172–8). Irving Fisher and Senator Robert Owen attempted unsuccessfully to get such a price level target into the Federal Reserve Act of 1913. The Federal Reserve Act, influenced by J.L. Laughlin and his student H. Parker Willis, instead adopted a fixed price of gold and, inconsistent with that goal, a version of the real bills doctrine that the volume of currency and bank credit should vary pro-cyclically with the needs of trade. As Knut Wicksell (1915) and others objected, Fisher compromised his compensated dollar plan by disguising it as a version of the gold standard, with the gold weight of the dollar changed periodically to peg the dollar price of a basket of commodities, a system vulnerable to speculative attacks. By 1935, when Fisher endorsed open market operations under a floating exchange rate to achieve a price-level target, he had lost his audience.

While Fisher distinguished nominal and real interest rates, Knut Wicksell (1898; 1915) stressed the distinction between the market rate of interest, set by the banking system, and the natural rate of interest that would equilibrate desired investment and saving (Laidler, 1991a; Humphrey, 1993). As long as the market rate is less than the natural rate, entrepreneurs can profit by borrowing and investing, causing total spending to increase and prices to rise. Such a cumulative inflation would continue until the growth of loans and deposits and a drain of cash out of the banking system reduced the ratio of reserves to bank deposits, forcing banks to raise the market rate to restore their liquidity. Wicksell pointed out that in a cashless economy, with only bank money used for transactions and no reserves held by banks, there would be no such force to automatically halt a cumulative inflation or deflation, and stability would depend on deliberate action by the monetary authority to match the market rate to the changing natural rate. To explain observed price movements, Wicksell emphasized real shocks that changed the natural rate as initiating fluctuations. Wicksell's two-rate model greatly influenced the Stockholm School (Karin Kock, Erik Lindahl, Erik Lundberg, Gunnar Myrdal, Bertil Ohlin) and John Maynard Keynes's *Treatise on Money* (1930). Recent financial innovations, diminishing the role of money as a means of payment and as an asset, have renewed attention to Wicksell's analysis of a cashless economy in which the monetary authority pursues stabilization by setting the interest rate rather than the quantity of money. The title of Michael Woodford's (2003) *Interest and Prices* deliberately echoes the title of Wicksell's (1898) *Interest and Prices* and a change of emphasis from Don Patinkin's (1965) *Money, Interest and Prices*. The 'Taylor rule', the influential monetary policy rule proposed by John Taylor, amounts to an attempt to set the market rate of interest equal to a Wicksellian natural rate that changes over time and is not directly observable.

Cambridge monetary theory and the Keynesian revolution

In his lectures at Cambridge, evidence to official inquiries (collected by Keynes after Marshall's death as Marshall, 1926), and manuscripts from the 1870s that half a century later formed the basis of Marshall (1923), Alfred Marshall expounded the quantity theory of money in a version that emphasized that desired cash balances are proportional to nominal income, $M = kPY$ (see Robertson, 1922; Marget, 1938–42; Eshag, 1963; Bridel, 1987; Laidler, 1999 on Cambridge monetary economics). The Cambridge coefficient k is the reciprocal of V, the income velocity of circulation of money in the equation of exchange, so that the two versions of the quantity theory are formally equivalent, although Marshall's disciples A.C. Pigou and J.M. Keynes claimed that Cambridge discussions of the determinants of k were more choice-theoretic and less mechanical than Fisher's discussion of the determinants of velocity. Related contributions emerged from both traditions: Fisher was the first to correctly state the marginal opportunity cost of holding real money balances (1930), Keynes the first to explicitly write money demand as a function of income and nominal interest (*General Theory*, 1936). Writing in a time of floating exchange rates and Continental European hyperinflations after the First World War, the young Keynes, in *A Tract on Monetary Reform* (1923), extended Marshall's monetary economics to analyse inflation as a tax on holding money and government bonds, the social costs of inflation (both distortions from incorrectly anticipated inflation and higher transactions costs as expected inflation reduces the demand for real money balances), and covered interest arbitrage parity (the spread between spot and forward exchange rates is the difference between nominal interest in two currencies). Keynes opposed Britain's return to the gold standard at the pre-war parity in 1925 as entailing domestic deflation and, until wages declined, unemployment. Keynes's position recalled Ricardo's preference for restoring convertibility as a depreciated parity after the Napoleonic Wars. D.H. Robertson (1926), deeply Marshallian although a student of Keynes and Pigou rather than directly of Marshall, examined the effect of price level changes on saving and investment, notably how an increase in the price level causes forced saving ('induced lacking') to restore real money balances (Laidler, 1999).

Reflecting on Britain's stagnation after the return to gold and on the worldwide Great Depression of the 1930s, Keynes's *General Theory of Employment, Interest and Money* (1936) denied the automatic restoration of full employment in a monetary economy after a negative demand shock. Keynes lumped together economists from Ricardo to Marshall and Pigou as 'classical' economists who accepted Say's Law (summarized by Keynes as 'supply creates its own demand'). Keynes subsequently clarified that he did not regard Fisher, Hawtrey, Robertson or Wicksell's Swedish followers as classical (but he did think that Wicksell himself was trying to be classical), and, as Ellis (1934) showed, German monetary theorists such as Joseph Schumpeter and L. Albert Hahn were far from classical about the real effects of an expansion of the banking system. In contrast to von Mises (1935) and Hayek (1931), who viewed depressions as necessary corrections of earlier overinvestment, Keynes held that depressions were calamities that the government and monetary authority could overcome by increasing aggregate demand, rather than relying on wage and price deflation to restore full employment. Keynes considered it crucial that wage bargains are made in money terms, so that workers concerned about relative wages might accept a price level increase to clear the labour market while quite rationally opposing money wage cuts as staggered contracts came up for renegotiation (1936, ch. 2). Wage cuts, and the associated deflation of prices, would increase demand for real money balances, exerting a contractionary effect on aggregate demand (1936, ch. 19). Keynes identified volatile private investment, resulting from fundamental uncertainty about future profitability, as the source of economic fluctuations, and, like the generations of Keynesian, New Keynesian and Post Keynesian economists after him, saw a need for management of aggregate demand to stabilize the economy.

The revival of the quantity theory of money

While Keynes was arguing the case for stabilization policy, Henry Simons of the University of Chicago made the case for rules rather than discretion in monetary policy (Simons, 1936). Keynes saw a role for government to counteract the instability resulting from volatile private spending, but Chicago quantity theorists (later called monetarists) such as Simons (1936) and Milton Friedman and his students (Friedman, 1956) blamed volatile, unpredictable monetary policy for economic instability. Keynesians invoked the Great Depression of the 1930s as demonstrating the need for government stabilization of an unstable private sector in a monetary economy, but Friedman and Anna J. Schwartz (1963) blamed the depression on a misguided Federal Reserve system that permitted a 'great contraction' of the money supply. Misled by the real bills doctrine, the Federal Reserve Board had not paid sufficient attention to the quantity of money. Where Keynes had emphasized the fundamental uncertainty underlying long-period expectations of profitability, Friedman (like Fisher) stressed the endogeneity of expectations of inflation: people cannot be fooled indefinitely by inflation into working more for a lower real wage that they think they are getting, because they will learn from experience (see Friedman and his critics in Gordon, 1974). Keynes worried about involuntary unemployment – an excess supply of labour because the labour market did not clear – while Friedman held that at any correctly anticipated inflation rate unemployment would be at its natural rate, reflecting voluntary investment in search and consumption of leisure. Friedman claimed in 1956 to be following a Chicago oral tradition of monetary theory taught by Frank Knight, Jacob Viner, Henry Simons and Lloyd Mints that had replaced J. Laurence Laughlin's opposition to the quantity theory. Don Patinkin (1981) and David Laidler (2003), who both held Chicago Ph.D.s, argued that Friedman overstated the purely Chicago sources of his monetarism: Friedman's teachers had taught the works of non-Chicago quantity theorists such as Fisher as well as Keynes's earlier Marshallian *Tract on Monetary Reform* (1923) and his Wicksell-influenced *Treatise on Money* (1930). Friedman took a course in which the main textbook was Keynes's *Treatise*, which Keynes's detailed and extensive contribution to monetary analysis. Fisher had advocated a monetary policy rule (a price level target, rather than the constant of money growth proposed by Friedman), while Keynes's *Tract* was as attentive as any Chicago monetarist to the social costs of inflation. A key element of Friedman's monetarism, money demand as a function of a small list of variables, had first appeared in Keynes's *General Theory*. There were also parallel, independent revivals of the quantity theory of money far from Chicago, such as that associated with Marius Holtrop, longtime president of the Netherlands central bank (De Jong, 1973).

Integrating the theory of money into general economic theory

Rationalizing the use of money has been a problem in the development of general equilibrium theory: if markets are complete, or all debts will be repaid with certainty, there is no need for a particular asset to be singled out as a generally accepted means of payment. Irving Fisher's 1892 dissertation introduced general equilibrium analysis in North America, but he did not integrate his later monetary economics into a general equilibrium framework. Leon Walras, the founder of general equilibrium theory, wrote on the theory of money (for example, Walras, 1886), starting with the equation of exchange and later discussing desired cash balances, *encaisse désirée*, but simply assumed that monetary exchange is superior to barter, rather than demonstrating that the use of money reduces transactions costs: 'In Walras's economy, agents hold money not out of choice but of a technological necessity' (Bridel, 1997, p. 119; see also Patinkin, 1965, pp. 531–72). In Walras's analysis, prices were stated in terms of a particular commodity, the *numéraire*, but it was not clear why transactions should use that commodity. The idea that money is only a veil over the real side of the economy long predates the introduction of the term 'veil of money' in English by Dennis Robertson (1922) and of 'neutrality of money' by Hayek (1931): (see Pigou, 1949; Patinkin and Steiger, 1989). Don Patinkin (1965) argued that a long list of classical and neoclassical economists postulated, at least implicitly, an invalid dichotomy between the real and nominal sides of the economy, in which an equi-proportional change in all money prices (so that no relative prices changed) would not affect the excess demands for commodities. Such a dichotomy would exclude the real balance effect that would bring the general price level to equilibrium. The valid dichotomy would hold that an equi-proportional change in all money prices, the quantity of money, and any exogenous nominal variables (such as quantities of government bonds) would have no real effects.

John Hicks (1935) set the agenda for much later work integrating the theory of money into the more general theory of value, seeking choice-theoretic explanations of why fiat money, not backed by convertibility into a commodity such as gold or silver, has a positive purchasing power, and why people choose to hold part of their wealth in money (either non-interest-bearing high-powered money or highly liquid close substitutes paying low rates of interest) rather than in alternative assets that pay a higher rate of return. Following Hicks's argument for treating the decision to hold money as part of the allocation of wealth across a portfolio of assets, James Tobin (1958) introduced money as a riskless asset (at least in nominal terms) into Harry Markowitz's theory of portfolio choice. Risk-averse individuals would divide their wealth between money (zero return, zero risk) and a portfolio of risky assets with positive expected return. Each investor would combine risky assets in the same proportions, differing from other investors only in the fraction of wealth held in the riskless asset. If returns were normally distributed or investors had quadratic loss functions, this portfolio choice could be conveniently captured by a two-dimensional diagram (the mean and standard distribution of portfolio returns), and if investors had constant relative risk aversion, the share of wealth held in each asset (including money) would be independent of the level of wealth (see Tobin, 1958; 1969; Tobin and Golub, 1998). However, money is a risky asset in real terms, as its purchasing power may be eroded by inflation, and is dominated in rate of return by such short-term, highly liquid assets as Treasury bills, which, like money, have no default risk. While Treasury bills have some nominal risk, since a rise in nominal interest would lower their market price, this risk is limited by the short maturity of the bills. Tobin (1969) extended his portfolio approach to a 'general equilibrium approach to monetary theory' that treated money as one of a range of imperfectly substitutable assets whose rates of return are determined simultaneously, with an adding-up constraint that asset demands sum to total wealth, but without assuming continuous clearing of non-financial markets (Tobin, 1971; Tobin and Golub, 1998).

Another approach to a choice-theoretic explanation of demand for fiat money assumes that money must be used as a means of payment and that it is costly to trade between money and interest-bearing assets, so that individuals trade off the interest forgone by holding money against the transaction costs (including the value of one's time spent going to the bank) incurred by having to liquidate interest-bearing assets when having to make payments. Maurice Allais in 1947, William Baumol in 1952, and James Tobin in 1956 independently derived the square-root rule for this inventory approach to the transactions demand for money by minimizing the total cost of cash management, forgone interest plus transactions costs (see Allais, 1947, pp. 238–41; Tobin and Golub, 1998), unaware that Francis Ysidro Edgeworth (1888), followed by Wicksell (1898, pp. 57–8), had derived a similar square-root rule for the demand for reserves by banks given randomness in withdrawals of deposits.

Another explanation for a positive value of fiat money is provided by overlapping generations (OLG) models, pioneered independently by Allais (1947) and Paul Samuelson (1958). In OLG models, agents live for two periods, but produce consumption goods only when young. The young trade goods to the old in return for money in anticipation of being able to exchange that money for goods in the next period when they themselves are old. Such models explain the existence of positive-valued fiat money on the assumption that no other assets exist. Other efforts to provide microeconomic foundations for fiat money emphasize monitoring costs and default risks, so that liabilities of a single, more easily monitored monetary authority are less risky than private promissory notes and therefore more acceptable as means of payments.

The long history of monetary economics reveals several recurring issues: why fiat money has value, how the real and monetary sides of the economy are related, whether a central bank should follow a rule (and if so which rule) or have discretion (or whether a central bank should even exist), is the lender of last resort function consistent with a policy rule, whether money has a special role or is just one of many assets and forms of credit, how should monetary exchange be incorporated in the general theory of value. Monetary analysis has also been focused and stimulated by external events and current policy issues: the 'price revolution' of the 16th century, the high price of bullion while the convertibility of Bank of England notes was suspended during the Napoleonic Wars, the Bank of England's charter coming up for renewal in 1844 after several banking crises, the decline in the purchasing power of gold following the California and Australian gold rushes and its appreciation from 1873 to 1896, the Continental European hyperinflations after the First World War, Britain's return to the gold exchange standard at the pre-war parity in 1925, and the Great Depression.

ROBERT W. DIMAND

See also **quantity theory of money; real bills doctrine versus the quantity theory.**

Bibliography

Allais, M. 1947. *Économie et intérêt*. Paris: Librairie des Publications Officieles.

Aristotle. 1984. *The Politics*, tr. Carnes Lord. Chicago: University of Chicago Press.

Aristotle. 1996. *The Nicomachean Ethics*, tr. Harris Rackham Ware, Herts., UK: Wordsworth Editions.

Arnon, A. 1991. *Thomas Tooke, Pioneer of Monetary Theory*. Aldershot, UK, and Brookfield, VT: Edward Elgar.

Bagehot, W. 1873. *Lombard Street*. In Bagehot (1974–86).

Bagehot, W. 1974–86. *The Collected Works of Walter Bagehot*. London: The Economist.

Baumol, W.J. 1977. Say's (at least) eight laws, or what Say and James Mill may really have meant. *Economica* NS 44, 145–62.

Baumol, W.J. 1999. Retrospectives: Say's law. *Journal of Economic Perspectives* 13, 195–204.

Blaug, M., Eltis, W., O'Brien, D., Patinkin, D., Skidelsky, R. and Wood, G.E. 1995. *The Quantity Theory of Money from Locke to Keynes and Friedman*. Aldershot, UK, and Brookfield, VT: Edward Elgar.

Boyer, J.de. 2003. *La pensée monétaire: Histoire et analyse*. Paris: Éditions Les Solos.

Bridel, P. 1987. *Cambridge Monetary Thought: The Development of Saving-Investment Analysis*. Basingstoke: Macmillan.

Bridel, P. 1997. *Money and General Equilibrium Theory: From Walras to Pareto (1870–1923)*. Cheltenham: Edward Elgar.

Brunhoff, S. de 1976. *Marx on Money*, tr. M. Goldbloom. New York: Urizen.

Cantillon, R. 2001. *Essay on the Nature of Commerce in General*, tr. H. Higgs. New Brunswick, NJ: Transaction.

Cassidy, M. 1998. The development of John Fullarton's monetary thought. *European Journal of the History of Economic Thought* 5, 509–36.

Christiernin, P.N. 1761. *Lectures on the High Price of Foreign Exchange in Sweden*, tr. in R.V. Eagly, ed., *The Swedish Bullionist Controversy*. Philadelphia: American Philosophical Society, 1967.

Clower, R.W. 1984. *Money and Markets: Essays by Robert W. Clower*, ed. Donald A. Walker. Cambridge: Cambridge University Press.

Corry, B. 1962. *Money, Saving and Investment in English Economics 1800–1850*. London: Macmillan.

Davis, T. 2005. *Ricardo's Macroeconomics: Money, Trade Cycles and Growth*. Cambridge: Cambridge University Press.

De Jong, F.J. 1973. *Developments of Monetary Theory in the Netherlands*. Rotterdam: Rotterdam University Press.

Edgeworth, F.Y. 1888. Mathematical theory of banking. *Journal of the Royal Statistical Society* 51, 113–27.

Ellis, H.S. 1934. *German Monetary Theory 1905–1933*. Cambridge, MA: Harvard University Press.

Eshag, E. 1963. *From Marshall to Keynes: An Essay on the Monetary Theory of the Cambridge School*. Oxford: Basil Blackwell.

Fetter, F.W. 1965. *The Development of British Monetary Orthodoxy 1797–1875*. Cambridge, MA: Harvard University Press.

Fisher, I. 1892. *Mathematical Investigations in the Theory and Value of Prices*. New York: Macmillan In Fisher (1997), vol. 1.

Fisher, I. 1896. *Appreciation and Interest*. In Fisher (1997), vol. 1.

Fisher, I. and Brown, H. 1911. *The Purchasing Power of Money*. In Fisher (1997), vol. 4.

Fisher, I. 1926. 'A statistical relationship between unemployment and price level changes'. In *International Labour Review* 13, 785–92. Repr. 1973 as 'Lost and found: I discovered the Phillips curve', *Journal of Political Economy* 81, 496–502. Also in Fisher (1997), vol. 8.

Fisher, I. 1928. *The Money Illusion*. In Fisher (1997), vol. 8.

Fisher, I. 1930. *The Theory of Interest*. In Fisher (1997), vol. 9.

Fisher, I. 1997. *The Works of Irving Fisher*, 14 vols. ed. W.J. Barber, assisted R.W. Dimand and K. Foster. London: Pickering & Chatto.

Friedman, M. 1956. *Studies in the Quantity Theory of Money*. Chicago: University of Chicago Press.

Friedman, M. and Schwartz, A.J. 1963. *A Monetary History of the United States 1867–1960*. Princeton, NJ: Princeton University Press for the NBER.

Fullarton, J. 1836. Response to a proposal for a bank of India. Repr. 1998 in *European Journal of the History of Economic Thought* 5, 480–508.

Fullarton, J. 1845. *Regulation of Currencies of the Bank of England*. New York: Augustus M. Kelley, 1969.

Gervaise, I. 1720. *The System or Theory of Trade of the World*. London: J. Roberts; repr. Baltimore: Johns Hopkins Press, 1954.

Glasner, D. 1985. A reinterpretation of classical monetary theory. *Southern Economic Journal* 52, 46–68.

Glasner, D. 2000. Classical monetary theory and the quantity theory. *History of Political Economy* 32, 39–59.

Gonnard, R. 1936. *Histoire des doctrines monétaires, dans ses rapports avec l'histoire des monnaies*, 2 vols. Paris: Sirey.

Gordon, R.J. 1974. *Milton Friedman's Monetary Framework: A Debate with his Critics*. Chicago: University of Chicago Press.

Grice-Hutchinson, M. 1952. *The Salamanca School: Readings in Spanish Monetary Theory 1544–1605*. Oxford: Clarendon Press.

Guggenheim, T. 1989. *Preclassical Monetary Theories*. London and New York: Pinter.

Hawtrey, R.G. 1919. *Currency and Credit*. London: Longmans, Green, 3rd edn. 1934.

Hayek, F.A. 1931. *Prices and Production*. London: Routledge.

Hayek, F.A. 1976. *The Denationalisation of Money*. London: Institute of Economic Affairs.

Hegeland, H. 1951. *The Quantity Theory of Money*. Göteborg: Elanders Boktryckeri; New York: Augustus M. Kelley, 1969.

Hicks, J.R. 1935. A suggestion for simplifying the theory of money. *Economica* NS 2, 1–19.

Hume, D. 1752. *Writings on Economics*, ed. E. Rotwein. Madison: University of Wisconsin Press, 1955.

Humphrey, T.M. 1993. *Money, Banking, and Inflation: Essays in the History of Economic Thought*. Aldershot, UK, and Brookfield, VT: Edward Elgar.

Jevons, W.S. 1875. *Money and the Mechanism of Exchange*. New York: D. Appleton, 1897.

Jevons, W.S. 1884. *Investigations in Credit and Prices*, ed. H.S. Foxwell. London: Macmillan.

Kemmerer, E.W. 1907. *Money and Credit Instruments in their Relation to General Prices*. New York: Henry Holt.

Keynes, J.M. 1923. *A Tract on Monetary Reform*. In Keynes (1971–89), vol. 4.

Keynes, J.M. 1930. *Treatise on Money*. In Keynes (1971–89), vols 5 and 6.

Keynes, J.M. 1933. Robert Malthus: the first of the Cambridge economists. In J.M. Keynes, *Essays in Biography*, London: Macmillan. Repr. in Keynes (1971–89), vol. 9.

Keynes, J.M. 1936. *General Theory of Employment, Interest and Money*. In Keynes (1971–89), vol. 7.

Keynes, J.M. 1971–89. *Collected Writings of John Maynard Keynes*, 30 vols. ed. D.E. Moggridge and E.A.G. Robinson. London: Macmillan, and New York: Cambridge University Press, for the Royal Economic Society.

Kinley, D. 1904. *Money, a Study of the Theory of the Medium of Exchange*. New York: Macmillan.

Laidler, D. 1991a. *The Golden Age of the Quantity Theory*. Princeton, NJ: Princeton University Press.

Laidler, D. 1991b. The quantity is always and everywhere controversial – why? *Economic Record* 67, 289–306.

Laidler, D. 1999. *Fabricating the Keynesian Revolution*. Cambridge: Cambridge University Press.

Laidler, D. 2003. *Macroeconomics in Retrospect: Selected Essays*. Cheltenham: Edward Elgar.

Laughlin, J.L. 1903. *The Principles of Money*. New York: Scribner.

Lowry, S. Todd. 1987. *The Archaeology of Economic Ideas: The Classical Greek Tradition*. Durham, NC: Duke University Press.

Macleod, H.D. 1855. *The Theory and Practice of Banking*, 5th edn. London: Longmans, Green, 1893.

Marcuzzo, M.C. and Rosselli, A. 1991. *Ricardo and the Gold Standard: The Foundations of the International Monetary Order*. London: Macmillan.

Marget, A.W. 1938–42. *The Theory of Prices: A Re-examination of the Central Problems of a Monetary Theory*, 2 vols. New York: Augustus M. Kelley, 1966.

Marshall, A. 1887. Remedies for fluctuations in general prices. *Contemporary Review*, reprinted in *Memorials of Alfred Marshall*, ed. A.C. Pigou. London: Macmillan, 1925.

Marshall, A. 1923. *Money, Credit and Commerce*. London: Macmillan.

Marshall, A. 1926. *Official Papers*, ed. J.M. Keynes. London: Macmillan.

Menger, C. 1892. On the origin of money. *Economic Journal* 2, 239–55.

Mints, L. 1945. *A History of Banking Theory in Great Britain and the United States*, 5th edn. Chicago: University of Chicago Press, 1970.

Mises, L. Von. 1935. *The Theory of Money and Credit*, tr. H. Batson. London: Cape.

Monroe, A.E. 1923. *Monetary Theory before Adam Smith*. New York: Augustus M. Kelley, 1969.

O'Brien, D.P. 2000. Bodin's analysis of inflation. *History of Political Economy* 32, 267–92.

Oresme, N., de Sassoferrato, B. and Buridan, J. 1989. *Traité des monnaies et autres écrits monétaires du XIVe siècle*, ed. C. Dupuy, tr. F. Chartrain. Lyon: La Manufacture.

Patinkin, D. 1965. *Money, Interest and Prices*, 2nd edn. New York: Harper & Row.

Patinkin, D. 1981. *Essays on and in the Chicago Tradition*. Durham, NC: Duke University Press.

Patinkin, D. and Steiger, O. 1989. In search of the 'Veil of Money' and the 'Neutrality of Money': a note on the origin of terms. *Scandinavian Journal of Economics* 91, 131–46.

Pigou, A.C. 1925. *Memorials of Alfred Marshall*. London: Macmillan.

Pigou, A.C. 1949. *The Veil of Money*. London: Macmillan.

Plato. 1974. *The Republic*, tr. G.M.A. Grube. Indianapolis: Hackett Publishing.

Ricardo, D. 1810. *The High Price of Bullion, a Proof of the Depreciation of Bank Notes*. London: John Murray, 4th edn 1811. Repr. in Ricardo (1951–73), vol. 3.

Ricardo, D. 1951–73. *Works and Correspondence of David Ricardo*, Cambridge: Cambridge University Press 11 vols, ed. P. Sraffa and M.H. Dobb.

Rist, C. 1938. *Histoire des doctrines relative au crédit et à la monnaie depuis John Law jusqu'à nos jours*. Paris: Sirey. Tr. as *History of Monetary and Credit Theory from John Law to the Present Day*, New York: Augustus M. Kelley, 1966.

Robertson, D.H. 1922. *Money*. Cambridge: Cambridge Economic Handbooks.

Robertson, D.H. 1926. *Banking Policy and the Price Level*. London: P.S. King.

Samuelson, P.A. 1958. An exact consumption-loan model of interest with or without the social contrivance of money. *Journal of Political Economy* 66, 467–82.

Simons, H.C. 1936. Rules versus authorities in monetary policy. *Journal of Political Economy* 44, 1–30.

Skaggs, N.T. 1995. The methodological roots of J. Laurence Laughlin's anti-quantity theory of money and prices. *Journal of the History of Economic Thought* 17, 1–20.

Skaggs, N.T. 1999. Changing views: twentieth-century opinion on the banking school-currency school controversy. *History of Political Economy* 31, 361–91.

Smith, A. 1776. *An Inquiry into the Nature and Causes of the Wealth of Nations*, ed. E. Cannan. New York: Random House, 1937.

Smith, V.C. 1936. *The Rationale of Central Banking*. London: P.S. King.

Sowell, T. 1972. *Say's Law: An Historical Analysis*. Princeton, NJ: Princeton University Press.

Thornton, H. 1802. *An Enquiry into the Nature and Effects of the Paper Credit of Great Britain*, with an introduction by F.A. Hayek. London: George Allen & Unwin, 1939. New York: Augustus M. Kelley, 1965.

Tobin, J. 1958. Liquidity preference as behavior towards risk. *Review of Economic Studies* 25, 65–86.

Tobin, J. 1969. A general equilibrium approach to monetary theory. *Journal of Money, Credit and Banking* 1, 15–29.

Tobin, J. 1971. *Essays in Economics*, vol. 1, *Macroeconomics*. Chicago: Markham.

Tobin, J. and Golub, S. 1998. *Money, Credit, and Capital*. New York: McGraw-Hill.

Vickers, D. 1959. *Studies in the Theory of Money 1690–1776*. New York: Chilton.

Viner, J. 1937. *Studies in the Theory of International Trade*. London: George Allen & Unwin.

Walker, D.A. 1984. *Money and Markets: Selected Essays of Robert Clower*. Cambridge: Cambridge University Press.

Walras, L. 1886. *Théorie de la monnaie*. Paris: Éditions Larose et Forcel.

West, E.G. 1997. Adam Smith's support for money and banking regulation: a case of inconsistency. *Journal of Money, Credit and Banking* 29, 127–35.

Wicksell, K.G. 1898. *Interest and Prices*, tr. R.F. Kahn. London: Macmillan, 1936.

Wicksell, K.G. 1915. *Lectures on Political Economy*, vol. 2, *Money*, tr. E. Claasen. London: Routledge, 1935.

Woodford, M. 2003. *Interest and Prices: Foundations of a Theory of Monetary Policy*. Princeton, NJ: Princeton University Press.

monetary policy, history of

Today monetary policy is the principle way in which governments influence the macroeconomy. To implement monetary policy the monetary authority uses its policy instruments (short-term interest rates or the monetary base) to achieve its desired goals of low inflation and real output close to potential. Monetary policy has evolved over the centuries, along with the development of the money economy.

The origins

Debate swirls between historians, economists, anthropologists and numismatists over the origins of money. In the West it is commonly believed that coins first appeared in ancient Lydia in the eighth century BC. Some date the origins to ancient China.

Money evolved as a medium of exchange, a store of value and unit of account. According to one authority – Hicks (1969), following Menger (1892) – its rise was associated with the growth of commerce. Traders would hold stocks of another good, in addition to the goods they traded in, which was easily stored, widely recognized, and divisible, with precious metals evolving as the best example. This good would serve as the unit of account and then as a medium of exchange. According to this story money first emerged from market activity.

Governments became involved when the monarch realized that it was easier to pay his soldiers in terms of generalized purchasing power than with particular goods. This led to the origin of seigniorage or the government's prerogative in the coining of money. Seigniorage originally represented the fee that the royal mint collected from the public to convert their holdings of bullion into coin. Governments generally since ancient times had a monopoly over the issue of coins (either licensing their production or producing them themselves).

The earliest predecessors to monetary policy seem to be those of debasement, where the government would call in the coins, melt them down and mix them with cheaper metals. They would alter either the weight or the quality of the coins (fineness). An alternative method used was to alter the unit of account (see Redish, 2000; Sussman, 1993; Sargent and Velde, 2002). The practice of debasement was widespread in the later years of the Roman Empire (Schwartz, 1973), but reached its perfection in western Europe in the late Middle Ages. Sussman (1993) describes how the French monarchs of the 15th century, unable to collect more normal forms of taxes, used debasement as a form of inflation tax to finance the ongoing Hundred Years War with the English. Debasement was really a form of fiscal rather than monetary policy, but it set the stage for the later development of monetary policy using fiduciary money.

Fiduciary or paper money evolved from the operations of early commercial banks in Italy (Cipolla, 1967) to economize on the precious metals used in coins (although there is evidence that paper money was issued by imperial decree in China centuries earlier: see Chown, 1994). This development has its origins in the practice of goldsmiths who would issue warehouse receipts as evidence of their storing gold coins and bullion for their clients. Eventually these certificates circulated as media of exchange. Once the goldsmiths learned that not all the claims were redeemed at the same time, they were able to circulate claims of value greater than their specie reserves. Thus was borne fiduciary money (money not fully backed by specie) and fractional reserve banking. The goldsmiths and early commercial bankers learned by experience to hold a precautionary reserve sufficient to meet the demands for redemption in the normal course of business.

Governments began issuing paper money in Europe only in the 18th century. An early example was Sweden's note issue, initiated to finance its participation in the Seven Years War (Eagly, 1969). Fiat money reached its maturity during the American Revolutionary Wars when the Congress issued continentals to finance military expenditures. These were promissory notes to be convertible into specie; but the promise was not kept. They were issued in massive quantities. However, the rate of issue and the average inflation rate of 65 per cent per annum (Rockoff, 1984) was not far removed from the revenue-maximizing rate of issue by a monopoly fiat money issuing central bank of the 20th century (Bailey, 1956). During the French Revolution the overissue of paper money, the *assignats*, which were based initially on the value of seized Church lands, led to hyperinflation (White, 1995).

An early predecessor of monetary policy was John Law's system. In 1719 Law persuaded the Regent of France to convert the French national debt into stock in his Compagnie des Indes. He then used the stock as backing for the issue of notes in his Banque Royale. Note issue could then support and finance the issue of further shares. Law then conducted a proto typical form of monetary policy in 1720 to save his system when he attempted both to peg the exchange rate of notes in terms of specie and provide a support price to stem the collapse in the price of shares (Bordo, 1987; Velde, 2007).

Central banks

Monetary policy is conducted by the monetary authority. It is the issuer of national currency and the source of the monetary base. Usually we think of central banks as fulfilling these functions, but in many countries, until well into the 20th century, in the absence of a central bank, these were performed by the Treasury or in some cases (Australia, Canada, New Zealand) by a large commercial bank entrusted with the government's tax revenues (Goodhart, 1989). The earliest central banks were established in the 17th century (the Swedish Riksbank founded in 1664, the Bank of England founded in 1694, the Banque de France, founded in 1800, and the Netherlands Bank in 1814) to aid the fisc of the newly emerging nation states.

In the case of the Bank of England a group of private investors was granted a royal charter to set up a bank to purchase and help market government debt.

The establishment of the bank helped ensure the creation of a deep and liquid government debt market which served as the base of growing financial system (Dickson, 1969; Rousseau and Sylla, 2003. The bank eventually evolved into a bankers' bank by taking deposits from other nascent commercial banks. Its large gold reserves and monopoly privilege eventually allowed it to become a lender of last resort, that is, to provide liquidity to its correspondents in the face of a banking panic – a scramble by the public for liquidity.

Monetary policy as we know it today began by the bank discounting the paper of other financial institutions, both government debt and commercial paper. The interest rate at which the bank would lend, based on this collateral became known as bank rate (in other countries as the discount rate). By altering this rate the bank could influence credit conditions in the British economy. It could also influence credit conditions in the rest of the world by attracting or repelling short-term funds (Sayers, 1957).

A second wave of central banks was initiated at the end of the 19th century. This was not based explicitly on the fiscal revenue motive as had been the case with the first wave, but on following the rules of the gold standard and ironing out swings in interest rates induced by seasonal forces and by the business cycle. Included in this group are the Swiss National Bank founded in 1907 (Bordo and James, 2007) and the Federal Reserve founded in 1913 (Meltzer, 2003). Subsequent waves of new central banks followed in the interwar period as countries in the British Empire, the new states of central Europe and Latin America attempted to emulate the experiences of the advanced countries (Capie et al., 1994).

Central bank independence

Although the early central banks had public charters, they were privately owned and they had policy independence. A problem that plagued the Bank of England in its early years was that it placed primary weight on its commercial activities and on several occasions of financial distress was criticized for neglecting the public good. Walter Bagehot formulated the responsibility doctrine in 1873 according to which the bank was to place primary importance on its public role as lender of last resort (Bagehot, 1873).

From the First World War onwards central banks focused entirely on public objectives, and many fell under public control. Their objectives also changed from emphasis on maintaining specie convertibility towards shielding the domestic economy from external shocks and stabilizing real output and prices. This trend continued in the 1930s and after the Second World War. Moreover, the Great Depression led to a major reaction against central banks, which were accused of creating and exacerbating the depression. In virtually every country monetary policy was placed under the control of the Treasury and fiscal policy became dominant. In every country central banks followed a low interest peg to both stimulate the economy and aid the Treasury in marketing its debt.

Monetary policy was restored to the central banks in the 1950s (for example, in the United States, after the Treasury–Federal Reserve Accord of 1951), and there followed a brief period of price stability until the mid-1960s. This was followed by a significant run up in inflation worldwide. The inflation was broken in the early 1980s by concerted tight monetary policies in the United States, the United Kingdom and other countries and a new emphasis placed on the importance of low inflation based on credible monetary policies. Central banks in many countries were granted goal independence and were given a mandate to keep inflation low.

Classical monetary policy

The true origin of modern monetary policy occurred under the classical gold standard, which prevailed from 1880 to 1914. The gold standard evolved from the earlier bimetallic regime. Under the gold standard all countries would define their currencies in terms of a fixed weight of gold and then all fiduciary money would be convertible into gold. The key role of central banks was to maintain gold convertibility. Central banks were also supposed to use their discount rates to speed up the adjustment to external shocks to the balance of payments, that is, they were supposed to follow the 'rules of the game' (Keynes, 1930). In the case of a balance of payments deficit, gold would tend to flow abroad and reduce a central bank's gold reserves. According to the rules, the central bank would raise its discount rate. This would serve to depress aggregate demand and offset the deficit. At the same time the rise in rates would stimulate a capital inflow. The opposite set of policies was to be followed in the case of a surplus.

There is considerable debate on whether the rules were actually followed (Bordo and MacDonald, 2005). There is evidence that central banks sterilized gold flows and prevented the adjustment mechanism from working (Bloomfield, 1959). Others paid attention to the domestic objectives of price stability or stable interest rates or stabilizing output (Goodfriend, 1988). There is also evidence that because the major central banks were credibly committed to maintaining gold convertibility they had some policy independence to let their interest rates depart from interest rate parity and to pursue domestic objectives (Bordo and MacDonald, 2005).

After the First World War the gold standard was restored, but in the face of a changing political economy – the extension of suffrage and organized labour (Eichengreen, 1992) – greater emphasis was placed by central banks on the domestic objectives of price stability and stable output and employment than on external convertibility. Thus for example the newly created Federal Reserve sterilized gold flows and followed countercyclical policies to offset two recessions in the 1920s (Meltzer, 2003).

The depression beginning in 1929 was probably caused by inappropriate monetary policy. The Federal Reserve followed the flawed real bills doctrine, which exacerbated the downturn, and the gold sterilization policies followed by the Fed and the Banque de France greatly weakened the adjustment mechanism of the gold standard. As mentioned above, the central banks were blamed for the depression and monetary policy was downgraded until the mid-1950s.

The goals of monetary policy

The goals of monetary policy have changed across monetary regimes. Until 1914, the dominant monetary regime was the gold standard. Since then the world has gradually shifted to a fiat money regime. Under the classical gold standard the key goal was gold convertibility with limited focus on the domestic economy. By the interwar period gold convertibility was being overshadowed by emphasis on domestic price level and output stability, and the regime shifted towards fiat money. This continued after the Second World War. Under the 1944 Bretton Woods Articles of Agreement, member countries were to maintain pegged exchange rates and central banks were to intervene in the foreign exchange market to do this, but the goal of domestic full employment was also given predominance. The Bretton Woods system evolved into a dollar gold exchange standard in which member currencies were convertible on a current account basis into dollars and the dollar was convertible into gold (Bordo, 1993). A continued conflict between the dictates of internal and external balance was a dominant theme from 1959 to 1971 as was the concern over global imbalance because the United States, as centre country of the system, would provide through its balance of payments deficits and its role as a financial intermediary more dollars than could be safely backed by its gold reserves (Triffin, 1960).

The collapse of Bretton Woods between 1971 and 1973 was brought about largely because the United States followed an inflationary policy to finance both the Vietnam War and expanded social welfare programmes like Medicare under President Johnson's Great Society, thus ending any connection of the monetary regime to gold and propelling the world to a pure fiat regime. In this new environment the balance was largely tipped in favour of domestic stability and was coupled with the now dominant belief by central bankers in the Phillips curve trade-off between unemployment and inflation (Phillips, 1958): this led to a focus on maintaining full employment at the expense of inflation.

The resulting 'great inflation' of the 1970s finally came to an end in the early 1980s by central banks following tight monetary policies. Since then the pendulum has again swung towards the goal of low inflation and the belief that central banks should eschew control of real variables (Friedman, 1968; Phelps, 1968).

The instruments of monetary policy

The original policy instrument was the use of the discount rate and rediscounting. Open market operations (the buying and selling of government securities) was first developed in the 1870s and 1880s by the Bank of England in order to make bank rate effective, that is to force financial institutions to borrow (Sayers, 1957). Other countries with less developed money markets than those of Britain used credit rationing (France) and gold policy operations to alter the gold points and impede the normal flow of gold (Sayers, 1936).

In the interwar period the newly established Federal Reserve initially used the discount rate as its principal tool, but after heavy criticism for its use in rolling back the post-First World War inflation and thereby creating one of the worst recessions of the 20th century in 1920–1 (Meltzer, 2003), the Fed shifted to open market policy, its principal tool ever since. In the 1930s it also began changing reserve requirements. Its policy of doubling reserve requirements in 1936 was later blamed as the cause for the recession of 1937–8 (Friedman and Schwartz, 1963). In the 1930s and 1940s, along with the downgrading of monetary policy, came an increased use of various types of controls and regulations such as margin requirements on stock purchases, selective credit controls on consumer durables and interest rate ceilings. Similar policies were adopted elsewhere. The return to traditional monetary policy in the 1950s restored open market operations to the position of predominance.

Intermediate targets

Traditionally, central banks altered interest rates as the mechanism to influence aggregate spending, prices and output. In the 1950s, the monetarists revived the quantity theory of money and posited the case for using money supply as the intermediate target (Friedman, 1956; Brunner and Meltzer, 1993). The case for money was based on evidence of a stable relationship between the growth of money supply, on the one hand, and nominal income and the price level, on the other hand, and the evidence that, by focusing on interest rates, the Fed and other central banks aggravated the business cycle, and then – in part because of their inability to distinguish between real and nominal rates – generated the great inflation of the 1970s (Brunner and Meltzer, 1993).

By the 1970s most central banks had monetary aggregate targets. However, the rise in inflation in the 1970s (which was followed by disinflation) as well as continuous financial innovation (which was in turn exacerbated by inflation uncertainty) made the demand for money function less predictable (Laidler, 1980; Judd and Scadding, 1982). This meant that central banks had difficulty in meeting their money growth targets. In addition, the issue was raised as to which monetary aggregate to target (Goodhart, 1984). By the late 1980s most countries had abandoned monetary aggregates and returned to interest rates. But since the early 1990s monetary policy in many countries has been based on pursuing an inflation target (implicit or explicit) with the policy rate set to allow inflation to hit the target, a policy which seems to be successful.

Theories of monetary policy

The development of the practice of monetary policy described above was embedded in major advances in monetary theory that began in the first quarter of the 19th century. A major controversy in England, the Currency Banking School debate, has shaped subsequent thinking on monetary policy ever since. That debate evolved out of the Bullionist debate during the Napoleonic wars over whether inflation in Britain was caused by monetary or real forces (Viner, 1937). In a later debate, Currency School advocates emphasized the importance for the Bank of England to change its monetary liabilities in accordance with changes in its gold reserves – that is, according to the currency principle, which advocated a rule tying money supply to the balance of payments. The opposing Banking School emphasized the importance of disturbances in the domestic economy and the domestic financial system as the key variables the Bank of England should react to. They advocated that the bank directors should use their discretion rather than being constrained by a rigid rule. The controversy still rages.

Later in the 19th century, the two principles became embedded in central banking lore (Meltzer, 2003, ch. 2). The Federal Reserve and other central banks (including the Swiss National Bank) were founded on two pillars that evolved from this debate – the gold standard and the real bills doctrine.

The latter evolved from 19th-century practice and the Banking School theory. The basic premise of real bills is that as long as commercial banks lend on the basis of self-liquidating short-term real bills they will be sound. Moreover, as long as central banks discount only eligible real bills the economy will always have the correct amount of money and credit. Adherence to real bills sometimes clashed with the first pillar, gold adherence, for example when the economy was expanding and real bills dictated ease while the balance of payments was deteriorating, which dictated tightening. This conflict erupted in the United States on a number of occasions in the 1920s (Friedman and Schwartz, 1963).

Adherence to the two pillars led to disaster in the 1930s. The Fed made a serious policy error by following real bills. A corollary of that theory urged the Fed to defuse the stock market boom because it was believed that speculation would lead to inflation, which would ultimately lead to deflation (Meltzer, 2003). According to Friedman and Schwartz, Meltzer and others, the Fed's tight policy triggered a recession in 1929 and its inability to stem the banking panics that followed in the early 1930s led to the Great Depression. The depression was spread globally by the fixed exchange rate gold standard. In addition, the gold standard served as 'golden fetters' for most countries because, lacking the credibility they had before 1914, they could not use monetary policy to allay banking panics or stimulate the economy lest it trigger a speculative attack (Eichengreen, 1992).

The Great Depression gave rise to the Keynesian view that monetary policy was impotent. This led to the dominance of fiscal policy over monetary policy for the next two decades. The return to traditional monetary policy in the 1950s was influenced by Keynesian monetary theory. According to this approach monetary policy should influence short-term rates and then by a substitution process across the financial portfolio would affect the real rate of return on capital. This money market approach dominated policy until the 1960s.

The monetarists criticized the Fed for failing to stabilize the business cycle, for still adhering to vestiges of real bills (for example, free reserves: Calomiris and Wheelock, 1998), and for its belief in a stable Phillips curve – that unemployment could be permanently reduced at the expense of inflation. This, they argued, led to an acceleration of inflation as market agents' expectations adjusted to the higher inflation rate, which produced the great inflation of the 1970s. As mentioned above, the subsequent adoption of monetary aggregate targeting was short lived because of unpredictable shifts in velocity.

The approach to monetary policy followed since the early 1990s has learned the basic lesson from the monetarists of the primacy of price stability. It also learned about the distinction between nominal and real interest rates (Fisher, 1922). Moreover, it has adopted a principle from the earlier gold standard literature, Wicksell's (1898) distinction between the natural rate of interest and the bank rate (Woodford, 2003). In Wicksell's theory, central banks should gear their lending rate to the natural rate (the real rate of return on capital). If it keeps bank rate too low, inflation will ensue, which under the gold standard will lead to gold outflows and upward market pressure on the bank rate. Today's central banks, dedicated to low inflation, can be viewed as following the Taylor rule, according to which they set the nominal policy interest rate relative to the natural interest rate as a function of the deviation of inflation forecasts from their targets and real output from its potential (Taylor, 1999).

Rules versus discretion

A key theme in the monetary policy debate is the issue of rules versus discretion. The question that followed the Currency Banking School debate was whether monetary policy should be entrusted to well meaning authorities with limited knowledge or to a rule that cannot be designed to deal with unknown shocks (Simons, 1936; Friedman, 1960).

A more recent approach focuses on the role of time inconsistency. According to this approach a rule is a credible commitment mechanism that ties the hands of policymakers and prevents them from following time-inconsistent policies – policies that take past policy commitments as given and react to the present circumstances by changing policy (Kydland and Prescott, 1977; Barro and Gordon, 1983). In this vein, today's central bankers place great emphasis on accountability and transparency to support the credibility of their commitments to maintain interest rates geared towards low inflation (Svensson, 1999).

Conclusion

Monetary policy has evolved since the early 19th century. It played a relatively minor role before 1914, although it was then that many of its tools and principles were developed. The role of monetary policy in stabilizing prices and output came to fruition in the 1920s, but for the Federal Reserve, which used a flawed model – the real bills doctrine – and adhered to a less than credible gold standard, the policy was a recipe for disaster and led to the great contraction of 1929–33. When monetary policy was restored in the 1950s in the United States, it still was influenced by real bills (Calomiris and Wheelock, 1998), which may have led to the policy mistakes that created the great inflation. The rest of the world was tied to the United States by the pegged exchange rates of Bretton Woods. Since the early 1990s monetary policy in many countries has returned back to a key principle of the gold standard era – price stability based on a credible nominal anchor (Bordo and Schwartz, 1999) and to Wicksell's distinction between real and nominal interest rates. Yet it is based on a fiat regime and the commitment of central banks to follow credible and predictable policies.

MICHAEL D. BORDO

See also **Bank of England; central bank independence; fiat money; gold standard; inflation targeting; monetary and fiscal policy overview.**

Bibliography

Barro, R.I. and Gordon, D.B. 1983. Rules, discretion and reputation in a model of monetary policy. *Journal of Monetary Economics* 12, 101–21.

Bloomfield, A.I. 1959. *Monetary Policy under the International Gold Standard.* New York: Federal Reserve Bank of New York.

Bagehot, W. 1873. *Lombard Street: A Description of the Money Market.* Reprint edn. London: John Murray, 1917.

Bailey, M.J. 1956. The welfare costs of inflationary finance. *Journal of Political Economy* 64, 93–110.

Bordo, M.D. 1987. John Law. In *The New Palgrave: A Dictionary of Economic Theory and Doctrine,* ed. J. Eatwell and M. Milgate. London: Macmillan.

Bordo, M.D. 1993. The Bretton Woods international monetary system: a historical overview. In *A Retrospective on the Bretton Woods System: Lessons for International Monetary Reform,* ed. M.D. Bordo and B. Eichengreen. Chicago: University of Chicago Press.

Bordo, M.D. and James, H. 2007. The SNB 1907–1946: a happy childhood or a troubled adolescence? In Swiss National Bank. Centenary Conference volume, Zurich.

Bordo, M.D. and MacDonald, R. 2005. Interest rate interactions in the classical gold standard: 1880–1914: was there monetary independence? *Journal of Monetary Economics* 52, 307–27.

Bordo, M.D. and Schwartz, A.J. 1999. Monetary policy regimes and economic performance: the historical record. In *Handbook of Macroeconomics,* ed. J.B. Taylor and M. Woolford. New York: North-Holland.

Brunner, K. and Meltzer, A.H. 1993. *Money and the Economy: Issues in Monetary Analysis.* Cambridge: Cambridge University Press.

Calomiris, C.W. and Wheelock, D.C. 1998. Was the great depression a watershed for American monetary policy? In *The Defining Moment: The Great Depression and the American Economy in the Twentieth Century,* ed. M.D. Bordo, C. Goldin and E.N. White. Chicago: University of Chicago Press.

Capie, F., Goodhart, C., Fischer, S. and Schnadt, N. 1994. *The Future of Central Banking.* Cambridge: Cambridge University Press.

Chown, J.F. 1994. *The History of Money from AD 800.* London: Routledge.

Cipolla, C.M. 1967. *Money, Prices, and Civilization in the Mediterranean World, Fifth to Seventeenth Century.* New York: Gordian Press.

Dickson, P.M. 1969. *The Financial Revolution in England: A Study in the Development of Public Credit, 1688–1756.* London: Macmillan.

Eagly, R.U. 1969. Monetary policy and politics in mid-eighteenth century Sweden. *Journal of Economic History* 29, 739–57.

Eichengreen, B. 1992. *Golden Fetters.* New York: Oxford University Press.

Fisher, I. 1922. *The Purchasing Power of Money.* New York: Augustus M. Kelley, 1965.

Friedman, M. 1956. Quantity theory of money: a restatement. In *Studies in the Quality Theory of Money,* ed. M. Friedman. Chicago: University of Chicago Press.

Friedman, M. 1960. *A Program for Monetary Stability.* New York: Fordham University Press.

Friedman, M. 1968. The role of monetary policy. *American Economic Review* 58, 1–17.

Friedman, M. and Schwartz, A.J. 1963. *A Monetary History of the United States, 1867–1960.* Princeton: Princeton University Press.

Goodfriend, M. 1988. Central banking under the gold standard. *Carnegie Rochester Conference Series on Public Policy* 19, 85–124.

Goodhart, C.A.E. 1984. Chapter 3 problems of monetary management. In *Monetary Theory and Practice. The UK Experience.* London: Macmillan.

Goodhart, C. 1989. *The Evolution of Central Banks.* Cambridge, MA: MIT Press.

Hicks, J.R. 1969. *A Theory of Economic History.* Oxford: Clarendon Press.

Judd, J.P. and Scadding, J.L. 1982. The search for a stable money demand function: a survey of the post-1973 literature. *Journal of Economic Literature* 20, 993–1023.

Keynes, J.M. 1930. *A Treatise on Money*, vol. 2: *The Applied Theory of Money.* Repr. in *The Collected Writings of John Maynard Keynes.* 30 vols, ed. A. Robinson and D. Moggridge, vol. 6. London: Macmillan for the Royal Economic Society, 1971.

Kydland, F.E. and Prescott, E.C. 1977. Rules rather than discretion: the inconsistency of optimal plans. *Journal of Political Economy* 85, 473–92.

Laidler, D. 1980. The demand for money in the United States – yet again. In *The State of Macro-Economics, Carnegie-Rochester Conference Series on Public Policy*, vol. 12, ed. K. Brunner and A.H. Meltzer. New York: North-Holland.

Meltzer, A.H. 2003. *A History of the Federal Reserve*, vol. 1. Chicago: University of Chicago Press.

Menger, K. 1892. On the origins of money. *Economic Journal* 2, 238–58.

Phillips, A.W. 1958. The relation between unemployment and the rate of change of money wage rates in the United Kingdom 1861–1957. *Economica* 25, 283–99.

Phelps, E.S. 1968. Money-wage dynamics and labor market equilibrium. *Journal of Political Economy* 76, 678–711.

Redish, A. 2000. *Bimetallism: An Economic and Historical Analysis.* Cambridge: Cambridge University Press.

Ricardo, D. 1811. High price of bullion: a proof of the depreciation of bank notes. In *The Works and Correspondence of David Ricardo*, ed. P. Sraffa. Cambridge: Cambridge University Press.

Rockoff, H. 1984. *Drastic Measures: A History of Wage and Price Controls in the United States.* New York: Cambridge University Press.

Rousseau, P. and Sylla, R. 2003. Financial systems ,economic growth and globalization. In *Globalization in Historical Perspective*, ed. M.D. Bordo, A. Taylor and J. Williamson. Chicago: University of Chicago Press.

Sargent, T. and Velde, F. 2002. *The Big Problem of Small Change.* Princeton: Princeton University Press.

Sayers, R.S. 1936. *Bank of England Operations, 1890–1914.* London: P.S. King & Son.

Sayers, R.S. 1957. *Central Banking after Bagehot.* Oxford: Oxford University Press.

Schwartz, A.J. 1973. Secular price change in historical perspective. *Journal of Money, Credit and Banking* 5, 243–69.

Simons, H.C. 1936. Rule versus authorities in monetary policy. *Journal of Political Economy* 44, 1–30.

Sussman, N. 1993. Debasement, royal reviews and inflation in France during the second stage of the Hundred Years War. *Journal of Economic History* 56, 789–808.

Svensson, L.E.O. 1999. Inflation targeting as a monetary policy rule. *Journal of Monetary Economics* 43, 607–54.

Taylor, J.B. 1999. A historical analysis of monetary policy rules. In *Monetary Policy Rule*, ed. J.B. Taylor. Chicago: University of Chicago Press.

Thornton, H. 1802. *An Inquiry into the National Effects of the Paper Credit of Great Britain.* Fairfield, NJ: Augustus M. Kelley, 1978.

Triffin, R. 1960. *Gold and the Dollar Crisis.* New Haven: Yale University Press.

Velde, F. 2007. *Government Equity and Money: John Laws System in 1720 France.* Princeton: Princeton University Press.

Viner, J. 1937. *Studies in the Theory of International Trade.* New York: Augustus M. Kelley, 1975.

Woodford, M. 2003. *Interest and Prices: Foundations of a Theory of Monetary Policy.* Princeton: Princeton University Press.

Wicksell, K. 1898. *Interest and Prices.* New York: Augustus M. Kelley, 1965.

White, E.N. 1995. The French Revolution and the politics of government finance, 1770–1815. *Journal of Economic History* 55, 227–55.

monetary transmission mechanism

The monetary transmission mechanism describes how policy-induced changes in the nominal money stock or the short-term nominal interest rate impact on real variables such as aggregate output and employment.

Key assumptions

Central bank liabilities include both components of the monetary base: currency and bank reserves. Hence, the central bank controls the monetary base. Indeed, monetary policy actions typically begin when the central bank changes the monetary base through an open market operation, purchasing other securities – most frequently, government bonds – to increase the monetary base or selling securities to decrease the monetary base.

If these policy-induced movements in the monetary base are to have any impact beyond their immediate effects on the central bank's balance sheet, other agents must lack the ability to offset them exactly by changing the quantity or composition of their own liabilities. Thus, any theory or model of the monetary transmission mechanism must assume that there exist no privately issued securities that substitute perfectly for the components of the monetary base. This assumption holds if, for instance, legal restrictions prevent private agents from issuing liabilities having one or more characteristics of currency and bank reserves.

Both currency and bank reserves are nominally denominated, their quantities measured in terms of the economy's unit of account. Hence, if policy-induced movements in the nominal monetary base are to have real effects, nominal prices must not be able to respond immediately to those movements in a way that leaves the real value of the monetary base unchanged. Thus, any theory or model of the monetary transmission mechanism must also assume that some friction in the economy works to prevent nominal prices from adjusting immediately and proportionally to at least some changes in the monetary base.

The monetary base and the short-term nominal interest rate

If, as in the US economy today, neither component of the monetary base pays interest or if, more generally, the components of the monetary base pay interest at a rate that is below the market rate on other highly liquid assets such as short-term government bonds, then private agents' demand for real base money M/P can be described as a decreasing function of the short-term nominal interest rate i: $M/P = \mathrm{L}(i)$. This function L summarizes how, as the nominal interest rate rises, other highly liquid assets become more attractive as short-term stores of value, providing stronger incentives for households and firms to economize on their holdings of currency and banks to economize on their holdings of reserves. Thus, when the price level P cannot adjust fully in the short run, the central bank's monopolistic control over the nominal quantity of base money M also allows it to influence the short-term nominal interest rate i, with a policy-induced increase in M leading to whatever decline in i is necessary to make private agents willing to hold the additional volume of real base money and, conversely, a policy-induced decrease in M leading to a rise in i. In the simplest model where changes in M represent the only source of uncertainty, the deterministic relationship that links M and i implies that monetary policy actions can be described equivalently in terms of their effects on either the monetary base or the short-term nominal interest rate.

Poole's (1970) analysis shows, however, that the economy's response to random shocks of other kinds can depend importantly on whether the central bank operates by setting the nominal quantity of base money and then allowing the market to determine the short-term nominal interest rate or by setting the short-term nominal interest rate and then supplying whatever quantity of nominal base money is demanded at that interest rate. More specifically, Poole's analysis reveals that central bank policy insulates output and prices from the effects of large and unpredictable disturbances to the money demand relationship by setting a target for i rather than M. Perhaps reflecting the widespread belief that money demand shocks are large and unpredictable, most central banks around the world today – including the Federal Reserve in the United States – choose to conduct monetary policy with reference to a target for the short-term nominal interest rate as opposed to any measure of the money supply. Hence, in practice, monetary policy actions are almost always described in terms of their impact on a short-term nominal interest rate – such as the federal funds rate in the United States – even though, strictly speaking, those actions still begin with open market operations that change the monetary base.

The channels of monetary transmission

Mishkin (1995) usefully describes the various channels through which monetary policy actions, as summarized by changes in either the nominal money stock or the short-term nominal interest rate, impact on real variables such as aggregate output and employment.

According to the traditional Keynesian *interest rate channel*, a policy-induced increase in the short-term nominal interest rate leads first to an increase in longer-term nominal interest rates, as investors act to arbitrage away differences in risk-adjusted expected returns on debt instruments of various maturities as described by the expectations hypothesis of the term structure. When nominal prices are slow to adjust, these movements in nominal interest rates translate into movements in real interest rates as well. Firms, finding that their real cost of borrowing over all horizons has increased, cut back on their investment expenditures. Likewise, households facing higher real borrowing costs scale back on their purchases of homes, automobiles and other durable goods. Aggregate output and employment fall. This interest rate channel lies at the heart of the traditional Keynesian textbook IS–LM model, due originally to

Hicks (1937), and also appears in the more recent New Keynesian models described below.

In open economies, additional real effects of a policy-induced increase in the short-term interest rate come about through the *exchange rate channel*. When the domestic nominal interest rate rises above its foreign counterpart, equilibrium in the foreign exchange market requires that the domestic currency gradually depreciate at a rate that, again, serves to equate the risk-adjusted returns on various debt instruments, in this case debt instruments denominated in each of the two currencies – this is the condition of uncovered interest parity. Both in traditional Keynesian models that build on Fleming (1962), Mundell (1963), and Dornbusch (1976) and in the New Keynesian models described below, this expected future depreciation requires an initial appreciation of the domestic currency that, when prices are slow to adjust, makes domestically produced goods more expensive than foreign-produced goods. Net exports fall; domestic output and employment fall as well.

Additional *asset price channels* are highlighted by Tobin's (1969) q-theory of investment and Ando and Modigliani's (1963) life-cycle theory of consumption. Tobin's q measures the ratio of the stock market value of a firm to the replacement cost of the physical capital that is owned by that firm. All else equal, a policy-induced increase in the short-term nominal interest rate makes debt instruments more attractive than equities in the eyes of investors; hence, following a monetary tightening, equilibrium across securities markets must be re-established in part through a fall in equity prices. Facing a lower value of q, each firm must issue more new shares of stock in order to finance any new investment project; in this sense, investment becomes more costly for the firm. In the aggregate across all firms, therefore, investment projects that were only marginally profitable before the monetary tightening go unfunded after the fall in q, leading output and employment to decline as well. Meanwhile, Ando and Modigliani's life-cycle theory of consumption assigns a role to wealth as well as income as key determinants of consumer spending. Hence, this theory also identifies a channel of monetary transmission: if stock prices fall after a monetary tightening, household financial wealth declines, leading to a fall in consumption, output and employment.

According to Meltzer (1995), asset price movements beyond those reflected in interest rates alone also play a central role in *monetarist* descriptions of the transmission mechanism. Indeed, monetarist critiques of the traditional Keynesian model often start by questioning the view that the full thrust of monetary policy actions is completely summarized by movements in the short-term nominal interest rate. Monetarists argue instead that monetary policy actions impact on prices simultaneously across a wide variety of markets for financial assets and durable goods, but especially in the markets for equities and real estate, and that those asset price movements are all capable of generating important wealth effects that impact, through spending, on output and employment.

Two distinct *credit channels*, the *bank lending channel* and the *balance sheet channel*, also allow the effects of monetary policy actions to propagate through the real economy. Kashyap and Stein (1994) trace the origins of thought on the bank lending channel back to Roosa (1951) and also highlight Blinder and Stiglitz's (1983) resurrection of the loanable funds theory and Bernanke and Blinder's (1988) extension of the IS–LM model as two approaches that account for this additional source of monetary non-neutrality. According to this lending view, banks play a special role in the economy not just by issuing liabilities – bank deposits – that contribute to the broad monetary aggregates but also by holding assets – bank loans – for which few close substitutes exist. More specifically, theories and models of the bank lending channel emphasize that for many banks, particularly small banks, deposits represent the principal source of funds for lending and that for many firms, particularly small firms, bank loans represent the principal source of funds for investment. Hence, an open market operation that leads first to a contraction in the supply of bank reserves and then to a contraction in bank deposits requires banks that are especially dependent on deposits to cut back on their lending, and firms that are especially dependent on bank loans to cut back on their investment spending. Financial market imperfections confronting individual banks and firms thereby contribute, in the aggregate, to the decline in output and employment that follows a monetary tightening.

Bernanke and Gertler (1995) describe a broader credit channel, the balance sheet channel, where financial market imperfections also play a key role. Bernanke and Gertler emphasize that, in the presence of financial market imperfections, a firm's cost of credit, whether from banks or any other external source, rises when the strength of its balance sheet deteriorates. A direct effect of monetary policy on the firm's balance sheet comes about when an increase in interest rates works to increase the payments that the firm must make to service its floating rate debt. An indirect effect arises, too, when the same increase in interest rates works to reduce the capitalized value of the firm's long-lived assets. Hence, a policy-induced increase in the short-term interest rate not only acts immediately to depress spending through the traditional interest rate channel, it also acts, possibly with a lag, to raise each firm's cost of capital through the balance sheet channel, deepening and extending the initial decline in output and employment.

Recent developments

Recent theoretical work on the monetary transmission mechanism seeks to understand how the traditional Keynesian interest rate channel operates within the context of dynamic, stochastic, general equilibrium models. This recent work builds on early attempts by Fischer (1977) and Phelps and Taylor (1977) to combine the key assumption of nominal price or wage rigidity with the assumption that all agents have rational expectations so as to overturn the policy ineffectiveness result that McCallum (1979) associates with Lucas (1972) and Sargent and Wallace (1975). This recent work builds on those earlier studies by deriving the key behavioural equations of the New Keynesian model from more detailed descriptions of the objectives and constraints faced by optimizing households and firms.

More specifically, the basic New Keynesian model consists of three equations involving three variables: output y_t, inflation π_t, and the short-term nominal interest rate i_t. The first equation, which Kerr and King (1996) and McCallum and Nelson (1999) dub the expectational IS curve, links output today to its expected future value and to the *ex ante* real interest rate, computed in the usual way by subtracting the expected rate of inflation from the nominal interest rate:

$$y_t = E_t y_{t+1} - \sigma(i_t - E_t \pi_{t+1}),$$

where σ, like all of the other parameters to be introduced below, is strictly positive. This equation corresponds to a log-linearized version of the Euler equation linking an optimizing household's intertemporal marginal rate of substitution to the inflation-adjusted return on bonds, that is, to the real interest rate. The second equation, the New Keynesian Phillips curve, takes the form

$$\pi_t = \beta E_t \pi_{t+1} + \gamma y_t$$

and corresponds to a log-linearized version of the first-order condition describing the optimal behavior of monopolistically competitive firms that either face explicit costs of nominal price adjustment, as suggested by Rotemberg (1982), or set their nominal prices in randomly staggered fashion, as suggested by Calvo (1983). The third and final equation is an interest rate rule for monetary policy of the type proposed by Taylor (1993),

$$i_t = \alpha \pi_t + \psi y_t,$$

according to which the central bank systematically adjusts the short-term nominal interest in response to movements in inflation and output. This description of monetary policy in terms of interest rates reflects the observation, noted above, that most central banks today conduct monetary policy using targets for the interest rate as opposed to any of the monetary aggregates. A money demand equation could be appended to this three-equation model, but that additional equation would serve only to determine the amount of money that the central bank and the banking system would need to supply to clear markets, given the setting for the central bank's interest rate target (see Ireland, 2004, for a detailed discussion of this last point).

In this benchmark New Keynesian model, monetary policy operates through the traditional Keynesian interest rate channel. A monetary tightening in the form of a shock to the Taylor rule that increases the short-term nominal interest rate translates into an increase in the real interest rate as well when nominal prices move sluggishly due to costly or staggered price setting. This rise in the real interest rate then causes households to cut back on their spending, as summarized by the IS curve. Finally, through the Phillips curve, the decline in output puts downward pressure on inflation, which adjusts only gradually after the shock.

Importantly, however, the expectational terms that enter into the IS and Phillips curves displayed above imply that policy actions will differ in their quantitative effects depending on whether these actions are anticipated or unanticipated; hence, this

New Keynesian model follows the earlier rational expectations models of Lucas and Sargent and Wallace by stressing the role of expectations in the monetary transmission mechanism. And, as emphasized by Kimball (1995), by deriving these expectational forms for the IS and Phillips curves from completely spelled-out descriptions of the optimizing behaviour of households and firms, the New Keynesian model takes advantage of the powerful microeconomic foundations introduced into macroeconomics through Kydland and Prescott's (1982) real business cycle model while also drawing on insights from earlier work in New Keynesian economics as exemplified, for instance, by the articles collected in Mankiw and Romer's (1991) two-volume set.

Clarida, Gali and Gertler (1999) and Woodford (2003) trace out the New Keynesian model's policy implications in much greater detail. Obstfeld and Rogoff (1995) develop an open-economy extension in which the exchange rate channel operates together with the interest rate channel of monetary transmission. Andres, Lopez-Salido and Nelson (2004) enrich the New Keynesian specification to open up a broader range of asset price channels and, similarly, Bernanke, Gertler and Gilchrist (1999) extend the basic model to account for the balance sheet channel of monetary transmission. Hence, all of these papers contribute to a large and still growing body of literature that examines the workings of various channels of monetary transmission within dynamic, stochastic, general equilibrium models.

Other recent research on the monetary transmission mechanism focuses on the problem of the zero lower bound on nominal interest rates – a problem that appears most starkly in the basic New Keynesian model sketched out above, in which monetary policy affects the economy exclusively through the Keynesian interest rate channel. Private agents always have the option of using currency as a store of value; hence, equilibrium in the bond market requires a non-negative nominal interest rate. In a low-inflation environment where nominal interest rates are also low on average, the central bank may bump up against this zero lower bound and find itself unable to provide further monetary stimulus after the economy is hit by a series of adverse shocks. Interest in the zero lower bound grew during the late 1990s and early 2000s when, in fact, nominal interest rates approached zero in Japan, the United States and a number of other countries. Among recent studies, Summers (1991) and Fuhrer and Madigan (1997) rank among the first to call for renewed attention to the problem of the zero lower bound; Krugman (1998) draws parallels between the zero lower bound and the traditional Keynesian liquidity trap; and Eggertsson and Woodford (2003), Svensson (2003), and Bernanke, Reinhart and Sack (2004) propose and evaluate alternative monetary policy strategies for coping with the zero lower bound.

Finally, on the empirical front, quite a bit of recent work looks for evidence of quantitatively important credit channels of monetary transmission. Kashyap and Stein (1994) and Bernanke, Gertler and Gilchrist (1996) survey this branch of the literature. Also, the striking rise in equity and real estate prices that began in the mid-1990s in the United States, the United Kingdom, and elsewhere has sparked renewed interest in quantifying the importance of the asset price channels described above. Noteworthy contributions along these lines include Lettau and Ludvigson (2004) and Case, Quigley and Shiller (2005).

PETER N. IRELAND

See also **liquidity trap; monetary business cycles (imperfect information); monetary business cycle models (sticky prices and wages); money supply; Taylor Rules.**

I would like to thank Steven Durlauf and Jeffrey Fuhrer for extremely helpful comments and suggestions.

Bibliography

Ando, A. and Modigliani, F. 1963. The 'life cycle' hypothesis of saving: aggregate implications and tests. *American Economic Review* 53, 55–84.

Andres, J., Lopez-Salido, J. and Nelson, E. 2004. Tobin's imperfect asset substitution in optimizing general equilibrium. *Journal of Money, Credit, and Banking* 36, 665–90.

Bernanke, B. and Blinder, A. 1988. Credit, money, and aggregate demand. *American Economic Review* 78, 435–39.

Bernanke, B. and Gertler, M. 1995. Inside the black box: the credit channel of monetary policy transmission. *Journal of Economic Perspectives* 9(4), 27–48.

Bernanke, B., Gertler, M. and Gilchrist, S. 1996. The financial accelerator and the flight to quality. *Review of Economics and Statistics* 78, 1–15.

Bernanke, B., Gertler, M. and Gilchrist, S. 1999. The financial accelerator in a quantitative business cycle framework. In *Handbook of Macroeconomics*, ed. J. Taylor and M. Woodford. Amsterdam: North-Holland.

Bernanke, B., Reinhart, V. and Sack, B. 2004. Monetary policy alternatives at the zero bound: an empirical assessment. *Brookings Papers on Economic Activity* 2004(2), 1–78.

Blinder, A. and Stiglitz, J. 1983. Money, credit constraints, and economic activity. *American Economic Review* 73, 297–302.

Calvo, G. 1983. Staggered prices in a utility-maximizing framework. *Journal of Monetary Economics* 12, 383–98.

Case, K., Quigley, J. and Shiller, R. 2005. Comparing wealth effects: the stock market versus the housing market. *Advances in Macroeconomics* 5 . http://www.bepress.com/bejm/advances/vol5/iss1/art1/.

Clarida, R., Gali, J. and Gertler, M. 1999. The science of monetary policy: a New Keynesian perspective. *Journal of Economic Literature* 37, 1661–707.

Dornbusch, R. 1976. Expectations and exchange rate dynamics. *Journal of Political Economy* 84, 1161–76.

Eggertsson, G. and Woodford, M. 2003. The zero bound on interest rates and optimal monetary policy. *Brookings Papers on Economic Activity* 2003(1), 139–211.

Fischer, S. 1977. Long-term contracts, rational expectations, and the optimal money supply rule. *Journal of Political Economy* 85, 191–205.

Fleming, J. 1962. Domestic financial polices under fixed and under floating exchange rates. *International Monetary Fund Staff Papers* 9, 369–79.

Fuhrer, J. and Madigan, B. 1997. Monetary policy when interest rates are bounded at zero. *Review of Economics and Statistics* 79, 573–85.

Hicks, J. 1937. Mr. Keynes and the 'Classics': a suggested interpretation. *Econometrica* 5, 147–59.

Ireland, P. 2004. Money's role in the monetary business cycle. *Journal of Money, Credit, and Banking* 36, 969–83.

Kashyap, A. and Stein, J. 1994. Monetary policy and bank lending. In *Monetary Policy*, ed. N. Mankiw. Chicago: University of Chicago Press.

Kerr, W. and King, R. 1996. Limits on interest rate rules in the IS model. *Federal Reserve Bank of Richmond Economic Quarterly* 82, 47–75.

Kimball, M. 1995. The quantitative analytics of the basic neomonetarist model. *Journal of Money, Credit, and Banking* 27, 1241–77.

Krugman, P. 1998. It's baaack: Japan's slump and the return of the liquidity trap. *Brookings Papers on Economic Activity* 1998(2), 137–87.

Kydland, F. and Prescott, E. 1982. Time to build and aggregate fluctuations. *Econometrica* 50, 1345–70.

Lettau, M. and Ludvigson, S. 2004. Understanding trend and cycle in asset values: reevaluating the wealth effect on consumption. *American Economic Review* 94, 276–99.

Lucas Jr., R. 1972. Expectations and the neutrality of money. *Journal of Economic Theory* 4, 103–24.

Mankiw, N. and Romer, D. 1991. *New Keynesian Economics. Volume 1: Imperfect Competition and Sticky Prices. Volume 2: Coordination Failures and Real Rigidities.* Cambridge, MA: MIT Press.

McCallum, B. 1979. The current state of the policy-ineffectiveness debate. *American Economic Review* 69, 240–5.

McCallum, B. and Nelson, E. 1999. An optimizing IS–LM specification for monetary policy and business cycle analysis. *Journal of Money, Credit, and Banking* 31, 296–316.

Meltzer, A. 1995. Monetary, credit and (other) transmission processes: a monetarist perspective. *Journal of Economic Perspectives* 9, 49–72.

Mishkin, F. 1995. Symposium on the monetary transmission mechanism. *Journal of Economic Perspectives* 9(4), 3–10.

Mundell, R. 1963. Capital mobility and stabilization policy under fixed and flexible exchange rates. *Canadian Journal of Economics and Political Science* 29, 475–85.

Obstfeld, M. and Rogoff, K. 1995. Exchange rate dynamics redux. *Journal of Political Economy* 103, 624–60.

Phelps, E. and Taylor, J. 1977. Stabilizing powers of monetary policy under rational expectations. *Journal of Political Economy* 85, 163–90.

Poole, W. 1970. Optimal choice of monetary policy instruments in a simple stochastic macro model. *Quarterly Journal of Economics* 84, 197–216.

Roosa, R. 1951. Interest rates and the central bank. In *Money, Trade, and Economic Growth: Essays in Honor of John Henry Williams.* New York: Macmillan.

Rotemberg, J. 1982. Sticky prices in the United States. *Journal of Political Economy* 90, 1187–211.

Sargent, T. and Wallace, N. 1975. 'Rational' expectations, the optimal monetary instrument, and the optimal money supply rule. *Journal of Political Economy* 83, 241–54.

Summers, L. 1991. How should long-term monetary policy be determined? *Journal of Money, Credit, and Banking* 23, 625–31.

Svensson, L. 2003. Escaping from a liquidity trap and deflation: the foolproof way and others. *Journal of Economic Perspectives* 17(4), 145–66.

Taylor, J. 1993. Discretion versus policy rules in practice. *Carnegie-Rochester Conference Series on Public Policy* 39, 195–214.

Tobin, J. 1969. A general equilibrium approach to monetary theory. *Journal of Money, Credit, and Banking* 1, 15–29.

Woodford, M. 2003. *Interest and Prices: Foundations of a Theory of Monetary Policy.* Princeton: Princeton University Press.

money

Money as a social institution and public good

Among the conventions of almost every human society of historical record has been the use of *money*, that is, particular commodities or tokens as measures of value and media of exchange in economic transactions. Somehow the members of a society agree on what will be acceptable tender in making payments and settling debts among themselves. General agreement to the convention, not the particular media agreed upon, is the source of money's immense value to the society. In this respect money is similar to language, standard time, or the convention designating the side of the road for passing.

The reason for the universality of money as a social institution is that it facilitates trade. Trade among individuals enables them to achieve much higher standards of living than if each person or family were restricted to autarchic subsistence. Because of economies of scale, division of labour among specialists yields enormous gains. Of course, trades have always taken place by barter, and even in modern economies many exchanges occur without money. Barter is usually bilateral, thus in Jevons's famous phrase it requires 'a double coincidence [of wants], which will rarely happen' (1875: 3). Multilateral trade is much more efficient, permitting each trader bilateral imbalances provided her trade in aggregate is balanced. Imagine, for example, that for lack of double coincidences no bilateral trades are possible among A, B and C because A wants C's goods, B wants A's and C wants B's. Obviously three-way exchange would benefit everyone.

Multilateral barter is conceivable. It could be arranged by putting participants in simultaneous communication with each other – in person as at a village market or a commodity or stock exchange, or by modern telecommunications. But any multi-participant multi-commodity market would need a clearing mechanism. A trader would not have to be balanced with every other trader. But in the absence of a money each trader would have to be balanced in every commodity. This would be awkward and inefficient. Participants would need to come to market with inventories of many goods. A natural conclusion of any one market session would be intertemporal deals, commodities acquired today in exchange for promised future deliveries of the same or other commodities. Without money, this too would be awkward: a typical trader would end up with debts to or claims on other traders in many specific commodities.

One could imagine using intrinsically valueless tokens during a market session to lubricate barter – like poker chips for scorekeeping in a stakeless poker game. The tokens would make it possible to price each commodity in a common *numéraire* rather than in each of numerous other commodities. But if the tokens became worthless at the end of the session, each participant would have to be required to return as many tokens as he or she started with. Otherwise no one would sell useful goods for tokens, for fear of leaving the market with them rather than with commodities of value. If instead the tokens will be acceptable tenders in this and other markets in future – well, then they are money (on these issues see Hawtrey, 1927, ch. 1; Starr, 1972; Shubik, 1984; Kareken and Wallace, 1980).

The social convention makes a society's money generally acceptable within it, and the practice of general acceptability reinforces the convention. Y accepts money from X in exchange for goods and services and other things of value because Y is confident that Z, A, B, . . . , and indeed X will in turn accept that same money. Moreover, money is accepted from the bearer immediately and impersonally – without delay, without identification. Since an economic agent's purchases and sales, outlays and receipts, are not perfectly synchronous, each agent's inventory of money fluctuates in size as money circulates throughout the economy. These fluctuations in individual money holdings enable essential intertemporal exchanges to take place. Workers are paid for their labour today, and next week they buy the food and clothing that are the truly desired proceeds of their work. The farmer and the tailor accumulate money from those sales; on payday they pay it out to their hired hands.

The moneys chosen by societies have varied tremendously over human history. So have their languages. In each case, what is universal and important is that something is chosen, not what is chosen. The variety of choice defies generalizations about the intrinsic properties of moneys. Livestock, salt, glass beads and seashells have served as money. Major grain crops were natural media for payments of wages and rents, and therefore in other transactions and accounts. Cigarettes were money in prisoner-of-war camps. On the island of Yap debts were settled by changing the ownership of large immovable stone wheels. The practice continued after the sea flooded their site and the stones were invisible at the bottom of a lagoon. (Similarly when gold was international money in the twentieth-century title to it often changed while the gold itself, safe in underground vaults, never moved.)

Some moneys have been commodities valued independently of their monetary role, intrinsically useful in production or consumption. Others have been tokens of no intrinsic utility and negligible cost of production, coins or pieces of paper. Commodity moneys derive their value partly, and token moneys wholly, from the social convention that designates them as money.

In modern nation-states the sovereign government can generally determine the society's money. For example, the United States constitution assigns to the federal government (thus, not to the states) the power 'to coin money, regulate the value thereof, and of foreign coin'. The central government defines the monetary unit, decides in what media taxes and other debts to the government itself may be paid, and defines what media are legal tender in the settlement of other debts and contracts (Starr, 1974).

Precious metals as money

Gold and silver have histories going back many centuries as the moneys of choice of many societies and as international media of exchange. Copper coinage antedates them, but copper became too abundant and was relegated to subsidiary coins. The precious metals are durable. They are divisible into convenient denominations. They can be made into ingots, bars and coins of standard weights. When used as moneys, they have been sufficiently scarce – relative to the non-monetary demands for them – as to pack considerable value into convenient portable forms. They glitter. They have long been prized for ornament and display. Gold and silver, one or the other or both, were the basic moneys of Europe and of European dominions and settlements throughout the world from the 17th century, or before, until recently. In modern times gold, in particular, acquired awesome mystique (Keynes, 1930).

Sovereigns minted these precious metals on demand into coins of their own realms, with their own names. In addition to minting *full-bodied* coins for public circulation, sovereigns commonly provided *token* coins made of metals, convenient for retail transactions, negligible in intrinsic value but convertible into the basic money of the realm. Many full-bodied coins circulated across national boundaries with values equivalent to their weight. For example, the original monetary unit of the United States was the silver dollar of Spanish America.

Until the late nineteenth century silver was more prevalent than gold as a monetary commodity. From medieval times silver was the English money of account; the pound sterling was initially a weight of silver. England and many other countries coined both silver and gold, but there were frequent periods when bimetallism degenerated *de facto* into one standard or the other. This happened when their prices at the mint diverged enough from their relative values in other countries or in commerce to offset the costs of arbitrage. Then 'Gresham's law' would take over, and the metal undervalued at the mint, the 'good money', would disappear from monetary circulation, 'driven out' by the 'bad money' overpriced at the mint (Hawtrey, 1927: 202–4, 283).

In England in 1717 Isaac Newton, Master of the Mint, unintentionally overvalued gold, pushing silver out of circulation and in effect putting England on a gold standard. The switch was formalized in 1816. During the nineteenth century other European countries and the United States likewise gravitated from bimetallism to gold. Alexander Hamilton, America's first Secretary of the Treasury, complemented the silver dollar with gold coins. But it was not until the late nineteenth century that gold overtook silver as the basic money of the United States. The values of sterling and dollars in gold set by Newton and Hamilton, implying an exchange rate of $4.86 per pound, lasted until 1931, with several wartime interruptions.

The heyday of the international gold standard was 1880–1914, when all major national currencies were convertible into gold at fixed rates. Silver, like copper before it, was eventually demoted to token coin status (Hawtrey, 1927, chs 16–20).

Functions of money

A triad long familiar to students of introductory economics lists the functions of money: (1) unit of account, or *numéraire*, (2) means of payment, or medium of exchange, and (3) store of value.

The US dollar, for example, is the unit of account in the United States. Prices of everything are quoted in dollars, and accounts are kept in dollars. The various media that change hands in transactions – coins, paper currency, deposits – are denominated in dollars. That does not prevent anyone who cares to do so from quoting prices in a foreign currency or in bushels of wheat, or from finding sellers who will accept them in payment for other things. It just would not be very efficient as a general practice.

To be sure, some societies have used, and kept accounts in, more than one money – in both gold and silver or, for example, in Japan two centuries ago, both in coins and in standard weights of rice. Today some national currencies may be acceptable means of payment in other jurisdictions – dollars in Russia, Israel and Canada, yen in Hawaii, Deutschemarks in Eastern Europe. The reason may be the frequency of cross-border tourism and trade. Or it may be that as a consequence of hyperinflation people turn to a 'hard' foreign currency as unit of account. For still a different reason, a new European currency, the ecu, may become a *numéraire* parallel to national currencies like pounds, francs and Deutschemarks during the period of transition to a common currency.

A society's money is necessarily a store of value. Otherwise it could not be an acceptable means of payment. (New York subway tokens cannot be generally acceptable money; they can become valueless any day, even for use as subway fare. US food stamps, intended to be in-kind welfare benefits, are exchanged with cash at par, while grocery brands' discount coupons are disqualified by their expiration dates.)

Money is the principal means of payment of a society, but it is only one of many stores of value – and quantitatively a minor one at that. Through most of human history land has been the major form of wealth, increasingly augmented by livestock and reproducible capital – buildings, tools, machines and durable goods of all kinds. Claims to much of this wealth today take the form of bonds and shares and other securities. In the United States, basic money is only 6 per cent of total privately owned wealth.

Even though a particular commodity or token is established as the generally acceptable medium for discharging debts denominated in the unit of account, it need not be and generally is not the sole means of payment in use. Derivative media, often termed *representative* money, arise and circulate as media of exchange. They are promises to pay the *basic*, sometimes called *definitive*, money on demand. In the commercial city states of northern Italy, merchants left gold with goldsmiths for safekeeping. They then found it convenient to circulate the 'warehouse' receipts in place of the gold. Those payable to bearers were precursors of paper currency and banknotes. Those payable to named persons, and on their order to third parties, were precursors of cheques. Indeed, once the goldsmiths realized that they need not keep 100 percent gold reserves against the outstanding claims upon them, and that they could lend their certificates to merchants promising to deliver gold later, they became banks.

Besides providing token coins, states issued paper currency redeemable in gold or silver, or delegated the privilege to a private bank chartered to serve the state, like the

Bank of England, founded in 1694. In addition, ordinary private banks issued their own notes, backed only by their own promises to pay basic money, gold or silver. In the nineteenth and twentieth centuries, governments and their central banks came to monopolize the issue of paper currency. This was not a catastrophe for banks. In modern economies, demand deposits in banks, transferable to third parties by cheque or wire or other order, have become the most important derivative media of exchange.

Whether derivative moneys were officially or privately issued, the ability of the issuers to carry out their promises to redeem them in basic money, gold or silver, was a recurrent problem. In wars and other emergencies governments often suspended these promises and issued irredeemable paper money. The trend in the twentieth century was to dispense with commodity money and to replace it with fiat money of no intrinsic value. Within each nation, the official derivative money, government currency, became the basic money. In 1933 United States paper dollars became inconvertible into gold except by foreign governments or central banks.

Internationally, gold was dethroned in 1971 as the medium for settlement of imbalances of payments between countries. Governments are no longer prepared to buy or sell gold at prices fixed in their own currencies. Gold is traded freely in private markets all over the world. Its price fluctuates as people speculate about its future. In the United States there is still an official weight of gold that theoretically corresponds to the dollar – 0.0231 oz, that is a gold price of $43.22, about one eighth of the free market price. But the US government is not prepared to sell any gold for dollars at the official price – or at the free market price, for that matter.

The US monetary base (M0) is the amount of fiat currency the government, mainly its central bank, the Federal Reserve System, has issued. It is a 'debt' to the public on which the government pays no interest and against which the government holds virtually no assets (other than its remaining gold stock, $11 billion at the official price, and its drawing rights at the International Monetary Fund, $19 billion). Derivative promises to pay dollars are now, directly or indirectly, commitments to pay this fiat money. Those promises include bank deposits and all other debts, private and public, denominated in dollars and payable at specified future times, tomorrow or 30 years hence.

In the United States in the fourth quarter of 1991 the stock of *transactions money* (M1) held by economic agents other than the federal government and banks averaged $890 billion, $265 of currency (paper and coin) and $617 of chequable deposits available on demand. The banks held reserves of $53 billion in currency in their vaults or on deposit in the 12 Federal Reserve Banks, collectively the American central bank. The sum of the currency in public circulation and the currency or equivalent held as bank reserves is the *monetary base* (M0), $318 billion. It is often called *high-powered* money: every dollar of M0 was supporting $2.80 of Ml, and GNP transactions of $18.20 a year.

Sovereigns have long profited from their money monopolies. Their mints charged 'seigniorage' fees – and sometimes they cheated. Likewise, issue of currency bearing zero interest is a way for a government to pay its bills, easier than taxation and cheaper than interest-bearing debt. By regularly issuing base money to keep up with economic growth and inflation, the sovereign collects seigniorage year after year. In the United States today seigniorage is a minor source of revenue. Since base money is only 6 per cent of GNP, growth of dollar GNP at 7 per cent a year means new issue of base money of only 0.42 per cent of GNP, 1.68 per cent of the federal budget. But for many less developed countries printing money is a major way of financing public expenditures; seigniorage is a major source of revenue, because implicit taxation by inflation is politically easier than explicit taxation.

Commodity money vs fiat money

The age of fiat money, first in one nation after another and finally internationally as well, has been more inflationary than the century of silver and gold standards between the Napoleonic wars and the First World War. During and following the 1914–18 war the gold standard broke down, and attempts to re-establish it during the Great Depression did not succeed. The Bretton Woods regime established in 1945 linked the world's currencies to gold via their fixed parities with the US dollar, because foreign governments could convert dollars into gold at a fixed price. But this system differed radically from the pre-1914 gold standard in that currency exchange rates could be and were frequently changed. The discipline imposed on a government and economy by an exchange parity fixed for a long time was diluted. In 1971, when this discipline became too much for the US itself, the gold–dollar parity gave way, and the international monetary system was wholly a regime of fiat money.

Discontent with inflation since the Second World War, and with the volatility of currency exchange rates since 1971, has led to agitation for return to the gold standard or some other commodity money. A commodity standard, if adhered to, provides a real anchor for nominal prices; its discipline prevents hyperinflation.

However, although the long-run trend of prices during the gold standard period was flat, there were violent inflationary and deflationary fluctuations around it. More important, real economic activity was highly volatile, to a degree that would be politically unacceptable nowadays (Cooper, 1982, 1991).

Irving Fisher, writing during the gold standard era, was greatly concerned by the instability of prices. He was complaining, in effect, about the volatility of the relative price of gold. Ideally, he would define the dollar in terms of a representative package of goods and services, the bundle priced in a comprehensive index number. Thus he revived the idea of a 'tabular standard', proposed by several early-nineteenth-century writers, and described with approval by Jevons (1875, ch. 25). But exchange between paper currency and such bundles is impractical. Fisher proposed instead to make periodic adjustments of the gold content of the dollar, raising or lowering it in proportion to the rise or fall in the price index since the previous adjustment. In effect, the Treasury would be selling gold for dollars to fight inflation and buying gold for dollars to fight deflation (Fisher, 1920).

A recent proposal by Robert Hall (1982) would tie the dollar to a composite commodity 'ANCAP' of ammonium nitrate, copper, aluminium and plywood.

Because ANCAP's prices have historically mirrored general indices, it is meant to be a feasible proxy for the economy's aggregate market basket (other proposals for commodity standards are described in Cooper, 1991).

The Fisher strategy could be followed, even imposed as a nondiscretionary rule on the central bank, in a regime of fiat money. The market operations to implement it would be carried out in securities rather than in gold. The fundamental issue is not the monetary standard but whether stabilizing a price index should be the exclusive objective of monetary policy, to the exclusion of stabilization of real output growth and employment.

Free market money?

Would it be possible to privatize money? Certainly it is possible to privatize derivative issues of money, promises to pay fixed amounts of base money on demand. But United States experience suggests that the supply of money, even derivative 'low-powered' money, cannot safely be left to free market competition.

Before the establishment of the national banking system in 1864, private banknotes were the only paper currency of the United States. The several states freely chartered banks, and those banks freely issued their own banknotes. These were promises to pay silver dollars, but so-called 'wildcat' banks contrived to make it tough for noteholders to find them. There was no central bank to control the aggregate issue of banknotes. The notes circulated at varying discounts from par and often became worthless, stranding innocent holders.

As a result, Congress established a system of nationally chartered banks in 1864, and taxed state banknotes out of existence. Only nationally chartered banks could issue notes, and these had to be fully backed by US Treasury debt securities. In effect, they were Treasury currency, supplementing various direct issues of Treasury currency (including the inconvertible 'greenbacks' the union government issued during the 1861–5 Civil War, which were made convertible into specie in 1879). Central banking did not begin in the United States until the Federal Reserve Act of 1914, which confined the issue of banknotes to Federal Reserve Banks.

Although private banks, state and national, were out of the business of issuing demand notes, they were still in the business of accepting demand deposits, the increasingly prevalent form of derivative money. Banks' balance sheets were regulated, but depositors were at risk. Their banks might not be able to pay in gold or equivalent on demand. After the epidemic bank failures of the 1920s and 1930s, Congress initiated a system of federal deposit insurance. Deposits in banks and other financial institutions became governmentally guaranteed, like banknotes after 1864. In the 1980s, these deposit guarantees became an expensive burden on federal taxpayers.

Could government get out of the money business altogether? It seems barely possible with commodity money and not possible with fiat money. If the government defined the *dollar* as a certain weight of gold or ANCAP or some other commodity or bundle, then private entrepreneurs could issue 'dollars', either chequable deposits or paper notes. They would be promises to pay the bearer the equivalent in the chosen commodities. The commodities themselves would not necessarily circulate on their own; indeed ANCAP and other composites could not.

The money entrepreneurs would have to keep inventories of the commodity as reserves. If one hundred per cent reserves were required, the currency would be like goldsmiths' warehouse receipts, and the private issuers would earn just a small fee for 'minting' the commodity into paper. Left to themselves, they would become banks, acquiring risky and illiquid assets while incurring demand liabilities. *Caveat emptor* would reign. The rates various banks would have to pay to attract funds would reflect depositors' appraisals of the risks. Notes and cheques of risky banks would not be honoured at par. In short, the very problems that resulted in consensus that issue of money cannot safely be left to unregulated free markets would recur.

Could the government's role be confined to defining the unit of account, the commodity equivalent of a dollar, in the same way that the government – through the Bureau of Standards in the United States – defines weights and measures? Could the system operate without any government-owned or government-issued base money? In its absence, clearings among private banks would require awkward transfers of ownership of the commodities kept as reserves against their liabilities. Very probably some one bank or consortium would arise as an unofficial central bank, and its liabilities would play the role of base money, the medium in which clearing imbalances among other banks are settled. The central bank, official or unofficial, would have to hold inventories of the standard commodity, gold or ANCAP or whatever, and be prepared to convert currency into the commodity and vice versa. That institution, history also suggests, would eventually be nationalized.

A fortiori, if there is neither an official definition of the 'dollar' nor any issue of dollars by the government or a quasi-governmental institution, there would be no standard commodity for private banks to compete in supplying to the public. Barter trading would be the rule, and the public-good advantages of social agreement on money would be lost. Since the institution of money is a public good, it is not surprising that its advantages cannot be realized by private market competition unassisted and uncontrolled.

How can money have positive value in exchange?

Economists have long regarded the theory of value as the central question of their discipline. What determines the prices at which goods and services are traded for each other? The prices in question include the wages of labour in terms of consumer goods, the rent of land in terms of its produce, and many other relative prices. They encompass interest rates and asset prices, thus the terms of trade of commodities to be delivered in future for commodities available today. They cover interregional and international trade, where the prices of concern are the terms on which imports can be obtained by exports.

Money, however, is an embarrassment to value theory. According to standard theory, something can have positive value only if it generates positive marginal utility in individuals' consumption or positive marginal productivity in the making of goods and services that do generate marginal utility. The embarrassing puzzle is sharpest for fiat money. All of its value comes from the fiat that makes it money. Fiat money has no intrinsic non-monetary source of value. It cannot be eaten or worn or be used in any other way that generates utility for consumers, except a few numismatists. Nor can it contribute to the production of things that consumers do value. It can be produced at zero social cost. Yet it is a scarce commodity for any individual agent. Why is it worth anything at all? That the institution of money is of value to the society as a whole as a public good does not automatically give it value to individuals in market exchanges.

The uphill struggle of modern economic theorists to cope with these challenges is exhibited in the proceedings of a recent conference (Kareken and Wallace, 1980). Their solutions relied principally on the overlapping generations model, which unrealistically assigns to money the function of being the sole or the principal store of value that links one generation to the next. The most careful, thoughtful and perceptive formal models of the roles of credit and money in transactions and strategies, in partial equilibrium and general equilibrium systems, are those of the game theorist Martin Shubik (1984).

It was argued at the beginning that a condition for fiat money to be held and valued today is that it will be acceptable in exchange for intrinsically useful commodities tomorrow. But this bootstrap story may not work. Suppose the world itself is known to be finite; its end will come at a definite future time. In the last period, one minute before midnight so to speak, you may need money to buy whatever consumer goods might generate utility, at least solace. Otherwise you will be confined to your own resources. But who will sell you anything, knowing that the money will be worthless while the goods might be a source of some utility? Thus money is worthless one minute before midnight, and by iterations of the same argument, it is worthless today. Even if the institution of money had public-good value between now and the end of the world, the money itself would have no market value to individuals.

The escape from this logical impasse is that we do not all and will not all expect with certainty the end of the world at any definite time. We always do, always will, assign some probability to its continuation. Since there are many other paradoxes involved in thinking about human behaviour in a world with no chance of a future beyond a definite time, it is best not to take that prospect seriously in economic modelling.

Formal general equilibrium theory, which describes the imaginary world of frictionless barter, does of course express the prices of goods and services in a *numéraire*. It is tempting to identify *numéraire* prices as money prices. But the *numéraire* is just a mathematical normalization convenient for handling the fact that the supply equals-demand equations for N commodities determine only the $N - 1$ relative prices. Those relative prices are, by construction, independent of the scalar arbitrarily attached to the *numéraire*.

Standard value theory does, of course, have something to say about the value of commodity money in terms of other goods and services. In a gold standard regime, the relative prices of gold in other commodities have to be the same at the mint and in the market; they cannot depend on whether the gold is circulating in coins or being used in jewellery, dentistry or rocketry. That is simply a condition of the absence of arbitrage profits. It definitely does not say that under the gold standard the relative price of gold is the same as it would be if gold were not money. As argued above, gold's role as money must increase the demand for it, and that must affect its price unless it is supplied perfectly elastically. The same will be true of any other commodity or bundle of commodities chosen as the monetary standard. A substantial part of the value of any commodity used as money arises from the convention or the fiat that makes it money. The distinction between commodity money and fiat money is not absolute.

The neutrality of money

Although business managers, financiers, politicians and workers worry a great deal about monetary institutions and policies and their consequences for economic activity and well-being, pure economic theory minimizes these consequences. Theory puts the burden of proof on anyone who contends that money and monetary inflations or deflations do much good or much ill.

Classical economists liked to insist that money is a veil, obscuring but not altering the real economic scenario (Robertson, [1922] 1959:7). Their modern descendants expound 'real business cycle theory', premised on the view that economic developments that matter to societies and individuals are independent of monetary events and policies (Prescott, 1986). It is true that economic fluctuations and trends are frequently misinterpreted by stressing superficial monetary phenomena to the neglect of resources, technologies and tastes. But money does matter, really.

Does an economy arrive at the same *real* outcomes (in variables like volumes of production, consumption and employment, and in relative prices such as the purchasing power of wages and the price of oil relative to that of bread) as it would without the institution of money? Clearly not. Without money, confined to barter, the economy would produce a different menu of products, less of most things. People would spend more time searching for trades and less in actual production, consumption and leisure.

That is not the comparison the classical economists, old and new, intend by the 'veil' metaphor. Their fantasy is a frictionless, costless system of multilateral barter, in which relative prices and the allocations of labour and capital among various productive activities are determined in competitive markets. Their proposition is that the outcomes of an economy with money are the same as those that would arise from their ideal barter model. The corollary is that real economic outcomes are independent of the particular nature of the monetary institutions (Dillard, 1988).

These propositions cannot be true of commodity money. Real economic outcomes with commodity money will differ from those with fiat money, and will also depend on what commodity is selected as money. Inventories of the chosen commodity have to be held for exchange purposes and for governmental and bank reserves, beyond the stocks held in connection with the commodity's non-monetary uses in production and consumption. In growing economies demands for monetary inventories will be steadily increasing. The relative demands for monetary and non-monetary inventories are bound to change with economic and technological developments that alter the incentives to produce the commodity and change its prices in terms of other goods and services. Examples are discoveries or exhaustions of gold and silver deposits and innovations in mining and processing technologies. Since the monetary commodity's price is fixed in money, its output will decline when there is general inflation and rise when there is deflation. Intertemporal choices involving the monetary commodity, as well as contemporaneous choices, will be significantly affected by its monetary use.

The availability of moneys, whether commodity or fiat, whether basic or derivative, as stores of value necessarily brings about significant deviations in real outcomes from the hypothetical regime of frictionless barter. This is true even though that regime is postulated to include markets in state-contingent commodity futures, 'Arrow–Debreu' contracts (Arrow and Debreu, 1954). Holding monetary assets gives agents more flexibility: they can convert them into consumption of any kind at any time in any 'state of nature', though not at predictable prices. The flexibility is a convenience to individual agents. But, as Keynes saw, it opens the door to 'coordination failures' which are the essence of macroeconomics – demand for goods and services may at times diverge seriously from supplies (Keynes, 1936, chs 16, 17).

The classical dichotomy

It is possible to recognize that an economy with monetary institutions is different in real outcomes from a barter economy, even from an ideal frictionless barter economy, and still to argue that its real outcomes are independent of the purely nominal parameters of those institutions. It would be terribly convenient if the determination of the absolute price level, the reciprocal of the value of the monetary unit in a representative bundle of consumer goods, could be split off from the determination of relative prices and the associated real quantities.

Don Patinkin (1956) called this separation the *classical dichotomy*. Only monetary shocks would affect the general price level, and those shocks would raise or lower the nominal prices of all commodities in the same proportions. Only real shocks – to tastes, technologies and resource supplies – would affect relative prices and real quantities. This proposition would not exclude the fact that the monetary institutions themselves matter. The choice between commodity money and fiat money, the choice among possible commodity standards, and the arrangements for derivative moneys might well affect the social efficiency of markets and trade.

What are the nominal parameters whose settings, according to the classical dichotomy, would make no real difference? For a commodity money, such a parameter is the definition of the monetary unit in terms of the standard commodity, for example the weight in gold of a dollar. For fiat money, the key nominal parameter is the quantity of money – base money, all transactions money, or some even more inclusive aggregate.

Why should cutting the gold content of the dollar from 0.0484 ounces to 0.0286 ounces, raising the dollar price of gold from $20.67 to $35.00 (as Franklin Roosevelt did in 1933), make any real difference? The dollar values of existing public and private stocks of gold, and of monetary claims to gold would rise in the same proportion. Will not all other commodity prices do likewise? Then all relative prices and real quantities, including those of gold, will be the same as before.

For fiat money systems, and for commodity standards where issues of derivative moneys have become essentially independent of the commodity, the *quantity theory of money* achieved similar dichotomization. According to the theory, which might more accurately be called the quantity-of-money theory of prices, an increase in the nominal quantity of money would raise all nominal commodity prices in the same proportion, leaving relative prices and real quantities unchanged. Quantity theorists argue that an increase in the quantity of money is equivalent to a change in the monetary unit. A hundred-fold increase in the stock of French francs would be – would it not? – the same as De Gaulle's decree changing the unit of account to a new franc equivalent to 100 old francs. Since the units change could make no real difference, the other way of multiplying the money stock could not either.

These analogies fail, for several related reasons. In most economies money is by no means the only asset denominated in the monetary unit. There are many promises to pay base money on demand or at specified dates. If there is a thorough units change, like De Gaulle's, all these assets are automatically converted to the new unit of account. Roosevelt's devaluation of the dollar relative to gold was not a pure units change. He did not scale up the dollar values of outstanding currency or even of Treasury bonds with provisions for such revaluation. Naturally private assets and debts expressed in dollars were not scaled up either. Likewise, when the quantity of money is changed by normal operations of governments or central banks or by other events, the outstanding amounts of other nominally denominated assets are not scaled up or down in the same proportion. They may remain constant, as when money is printed to finance government expenditures. They may move in the opposite direction, as when central banks engage in open-market operations, which typically increase the amount of base money outstanding by buying bills or bonds, thus reducing the quantities of them in the hands of the public.

The quantity theory

The quantity theory goes back to David Hume, probably farther, but its major and most effective protagonists have been Irving Fisher (1911) and Milton Friedman (1956).

In its crudest form, the quantity theory is a mechanistic proposition strangely alien to the assumptions of rational maximizing behaviour on which classical and neoclassical economic theories generally rely, as J.R. Hicks eloquently pointed out in a famous article (1935). Specifically, it ignores the effects of the returns to holding money on the amounts economic agents choose to hold. The technology of monetary circulation fixes the annual turnover of a unit of money. Suppose that every dollar 'sitting' supports just V dollars per year 'on the wing', to use D.H. Robertson's famous terms ([1922] 1959: 30). Suppose, further, that the economy is assumed to be in real equilibrium and the supply of money is doubled. The public will not wish to hold the additional money until the dollar value of transactions is doubled, and this requires prices to double.

Surely the demand for money to hold is not so mechanical. The velocity of money can be speeded up if people put up with more inconvenience and risk more illiquidity in managing their transactions. Money holdings depend, therefore, on the opportunity costs, the expected changes in the value of money and the real yields of other assets into which the same funds could be placed. Fisher and Friedman would agree.

The quantity theory can still be rationalized, as a proposition in comparative statics. Compare, for example, two stationary situations of a given economy, in each of which the money supply and price level are constant over time. Let the money supply in the second situation be twice that in the first. Then an equilibrium in the second situation will be the equilibrium of the first with a nominal price level twice as high. This will be true even if the demand for money is modelled as behavioural, not mechanical, and is allowed to depend on interest rates, expected inflation and other variables.

However, it is not sufficient to double solely the quantity of money, narrowly defined. All exogenous nominal quantities, including outstanding stocks of debts and assets, must also be doubled. Or the second equilibrium must be interpreted as a stationary state that will be reached only when all these other nominal stocks have had time to adjust endogenously to the new quantity of money. This quantity theory does not apply to short-run changes in monetary quantities engineered by central banks, for the same reasons that render the 'units change' metaphor inapplicable.

In its interpretation as a proposition in long-run comparative statics, the quantity theory supports 'neutrality' as asserted in the classical dichotomy. Neutrality has come to have two meanings in monetary economics. Simple *neutrality* means that real economic outcomes are independent of the levels of nominal prices. *Superneutrality* means that those outcomes are also independent of the rates of change of nominal prices.

The case for superneutrality appeals to, and depends upon, the 'Fisher equation'. Early on, Fisher (1896) saw the importance of distinguishing between nominal and real rates of interest on assets and debts denominated in monetary units. *Ex post*, the algebraic difference between them is by definition the rate of inflation or deflation. This is a tautology. But Fisher (1911) is also credited with a meaningful proposition: anticipation of inflation (deflation) raises (lowers) nominal rates of interest but does not alter real rates of interest. The corollary is that whatever is the time path of money stocks that determines the path of prices, the paths of real economic variables are the same. Fisher himself was enough of a classical economist to believe this as a long-run theoretical truth, but enough of a pragmatic empiricist to find that nominal rates were very slow to incorporate adjustments for ongoing inflations and deflations.

The price of money

A 1975 conference on monetarism at Brown University is remembered for a pithy observation by Milton Friedman, offered only half in jest:

> For the monetarist/non-monetarist dichotomy, I suspect that the simplest litmus test would be the conditioned reflex to the question, 'What is the price of money?' The monetarist will answer, 'The inverse of the price level'; the non-monetarist (Keynesian or central banker) will answer, 'the interest rate'. The key difference is whether the stress is on money viewed as an asset with special characteristics, or on credit and credit markets, which leads to the analysis of monetary policy and monetary change operating through organized 'money', i.e. 'credit', markets, rather than through actual and desired cash balances. Though not so obvious, the answer given also affects attitudes toward prices: whether their adjustment is regarded as an integral part of the economic process analyzed, or as an institutional datum to which the rest of the system will adjust (Stein, 1976: 316).

'What am I', asked the chairman of the session, George Borts, 'if I answer "one"?'

Any durable good has at least two 'prices', the price at which it can be bought or sold, and the price of the services it renders per unit time. The price of the good itself is the present value of the expected, though uncertain, values of the services it will render in future. For money, the first price is its purchasing power. Its services come in two forms: as a store of value, the capital gain or loss from changes in its purchasing power, and, as a medium of exchange, the benefits it yields in convenience, effort-saving and risk reduction. Without cash on hand, an economic agent may find it costly to make desirable transactions, or to forgo them. The marginal productivity of holding money is the value of an additional dollar in reducing those costs.

What is the marginal opportunity cost to which agents will equate the marginal productivity of holding money? It depends on what alternatives are available. If money proper were the only store of value in the economy, the opportunity cost of holding money would be the marginal utility of immediate consumption relative to future consumption. Although this set-up is all too common in the literature, it confuses theories of money and of saving. Acknowledging the availability of other stores of value makes the cost of holding money the difference between the real capital gain or loss on money and the real rate of return on the non-money assets in which a marginal dollar could be invested.

If money proper were the only store of value in the monetary unit of account, though not the only one in the economy at large, the relevant opportunity cost would be the return on real capital, that is storable or durable commodities. In modern economies, however, the immediate substitutes for money are promises to pay money in future. Since money and these substitutes are affected equally by price level changes, the opportunity cost is simply the nominal interest rate on those non-money substitutes. (This assumes zero nominal interest on money itself.)

Friedman's Keynesian is careless if he calls any of these opportunity cost concepts the price of money. These are prices of the services of money. Friedman's monetarist is right, therefore, to say that the price of money is the reciprocal of the commodity price level – the real price, that is, for Borts was right about money's nominal price. Of course, there are as many relative prices as there are non-monetary commodities, and any average value of money requires using an arbitrary commodity price index.

To implement Friedman's asset valuation approach to the price of money, suppose that the nominal supply of money per capita, real per capita output and the real interest rate all follow arbitrary variable paths, anticipated in advance. Assume, at least for illustrative purposes, the Allais–Baumol–Tobin model of the demand for money (Baumol and Tobin, 1989). The marginal productivity of nominal cash holdings for a representative agent is the reduction in the frequency and cost of exchanges back and forth between money and dollar-denominated interest-bearing substitutes. It is, by the usual approximation equal to $a(t)y(t)/(2\,m(t)^2v(t))$, where a is the real cost of one of those exchanges, y is the agent's real income per period, m is the agent's average nominal cash holding, and v is the value of money, the reciprocal of the price level. Of these, a, y and m are arbitrary exogenous functions of time, while the valuation v is a function of time to be determined. Let $r(t)$ be the exogenous path of the real interest rate. The value of money at any time T is the discounted value of its future marginal productivities:

$$v(T) = a(T) \int_T^\infty \exp\left(- \int_T^t r(s)\mathrm{d}s\right) y(t)/(2m(t)^2v(t))\mathrm{d}t, \tag{1}$$

$$v'(T) = r(T)v(T) - a(T)y(T)/(2m(T)^2v(T)), \tag{2}$$

$$r(T) - v'(T)/v(T) = a(t)y(T)/(2m(T)^2v(T)^2). \tag{3}$$

Equation (3), with the nominal interest rate on the left, is the familiar equation for optimal *real* cash holdings. It involves the stronger Fisher equation, because the real rate has been taken as exogenous.

Interpreted as the price dynamics of the economy, these equations describe the time path of the 'price of money'. The level of prices at each time converts the autonomous nominal money supply into the real quantity on which its marginal productivity depends. The price path itself generates the rates of price change which, added to the autonomous real interest rates, give the nominal rates. The marginal productivity of money at each point in time is equated to the nominal interest rate. Future as well as current values of money supplies, as well as other variables, affect current prices. An expected increase in future money supply raises prices today, and so does an expected future increase in real rates of interest. The Fisher equation is essential to maintain the assumed dichotomy between the paths of real and nominal variables (for a calculation in this same spirit, see Sargent and Wallace 1981).

Money and macroeconomics
In the above scenario, a key institutional fact is that the nominal interest rate on money proper is fixed, at zero. Expected inflation makes money's real interest rate

negative and reduces the attraction of holding money compared to assets bearing the economy's real interest rate. For the same reason, an increase in that real interest rate is a disincentive to hold money.

However, the same institution – the fixed nominal interest rate on money – threatens the classical dichotomy. It calls into question the Fisher equation, which is central to the independence from monetary influence of the real rate of interest and related real variables. It calls it into question in principle, in long runs and short, in equilibrium and in disequilibrium. If expected inflation diminishes demand for money, it by the same token increases demands for other assets, both interest-bearing promises to pay money and real capital. These substitutions will reduce the real interest rates on those assets; their nominal interest rates will rise less than the full inflation premium. This effect – associated in the literature with the names of Mundell (1963) and Tobin (1965, 1969) – refutes superneutrality, which is essential to neutrality in any general dynamic meaning. That is to say, it is not possible to determine the real interest rate and related real variables independently of the money equation, or to determine the value of money from the demand = supply equation for money by itself.

This is true whether the economy is assumed to be classical, with full employment assured by flexibility of nominal interest rates and prices, or Keynesian, with aggregate demand short of full employment. However, the real effects of expected price inflation and deflation are a reason for doubting the efficacy of price flexibility in sustaining or restoring full employment equilibrium in the face of aggregate demand shocks (Fisher, 1933; Keynes, 1936, ch. 19; Tobin, 1975).

Irving Fisher, Alfred Marshall and other monetary economists of the early twentieth century regarded neutrality in any sense as properties of long-run static equilibrium, not of the dynamic transitions that dominate empirical observations of monetary and real variables. According to them, people are slow in translating experience of inflation into their expectations of the future. This is how Fisher interpreted the strong positive correlations he found between inflation rates and real output (Fisher, 1911). However, the Mundell–Tobin effect suggests a still stronger conclusion, since it calls into question the Fisher equation even when inflation expectations are correct and people are not victims of 'money illusion'.

In Friedman's litmus test there is much more at stake than meets the eye. The issue is how the price level, whose reciprocal is the 'price of money', is determined. The monetarist's trained instinct is to think of it as determined by the demand = supply equation for money 'as an asset with special characteristics'. With the absolute price level thus determined, the function of markets for goods and services is to generate real, relative prices, just as in Walrasian general equilibrium theory. Those real variables, in turn, are exogenous to the path of the 'price of money'.

The Keynesian's trained instinct, on the other hand, is to think of the price level as an index of nominal prices of goods and services. As Keynes (1936, Book I) emphasized – for labour markets especially – markets in our monetary economies determine in the first instance nominal prices, not real prices. The price 'level' is a synthetic aggregate of multitudes of individual prices determined in diverse imperfect markets, often decided by administrative decisions or by negotiations. For price determination the most relevant equations of a macroeconomic model are price and wage equations, often members of the Phillips curve family. These specify inertia of varying degrees in nominal prices and relate their changes to measures of real excess demand or supply. As a result, price indices move smoothly and sluggishly over time, not 'jumping' like the price of a financial asset sensitive to market views of the future.

With the price level determined in goods markets, the function of the money demand = supply equation is to generate interest rates. That explains the Keynesian's instinctive response to the test question. Of course, the Keynesian recognizes that the endogenous variables of a simultaneous equations system are determined jointly, not equation by equation. That real variables are among those endogenous variables can be attributed to the fact that there is usually a non-zero discrepancy between the price path determined by the full system and the path that would be generated by the monetarist's asset price of money. The non-monetarist view does not take prices 'as an institutional datum to which the rest of the system will adjust', but it does rely on variables besides prices to equate 'actual and desired cash balances'.

The equation of money demand and supply is just one of many relations in a theoretical or econometric macroeconomic model. The small tail cannot wag the big dog. That was too much to expect. The price level is a factor common to the valuation of many assets denominated in the monetary unit, many of them close substitutes for transactions money. Their quantities now and in future must make a difference. Of course monetary policies and supplies, current and prospective, are important determinants of the price level, and so are credit markets. But the channels of these influences run through demands and supplies in markets for goods and services. Understanding the process belongs to the messy subject of macroeconomics. Finance theory, however elegant, cannot provide a shortcut.

Monetary events and policies are not a sideshow to the main performance. The real variables of a monetary economy are hopelessly entangled with monetary phenomena. They do not behave as if an economy enjoying the societal advantages of money were a frictionless multilateral barter economy seen through a veil. That barter economy would never have business cycles characterized by economy-wide excess demands and supplies of labour and other goods and services. The public-good advantages of the institution of money do not come so cheap. Among their costs are fluctuations in business activity and in the value of money itself. Pragmatic monetary economics is a central part of macroeconomics in general.

JAMES TOBIN

See also **fiat money; financial intermediation; gold standard; monetarism; quantity theory of money.**

Bibliography

Arrow, K.J. and Debreu, G. 1954. Existence of equilibrium for a competitive economy. *Econometrica* 22, 265–90.

Baumol, W.J. and Tobin, J. 1989. The optimal cash balance proposition: Maurice Allais's priority. *Journal of Economic Literature* 27 , 1160–62.

Cooper, R.N. 1982. The gold standard: historical facts and future prospects. *Brookings Papers on Economic Activity* 1982(1), 1–45.

Cooper, R.N. 1991. Toward an international commodity standard? In *Money, Macroeconomics, and Economic Policy*. ed. W.C. Brainard, W.D. Nordhaus and H.W. Watts. Cambridge, MA: MIT Press.

Dillard, D. 1988. The barter illusion in classical and neoclassical economics. *Eastern Economic Journal* 14 , 299–318.

Fisher, I. 1896. *Appreciation and Interest*. Publications of the American Economic Association, 3rd series 11(4); reprinted, Fairfield, NJ: A.M. Kelley, 1991.

Fisher, I. 1906. *The Nature of Capital and Income*. New York: Macmillan.

Fisher, I. 1911. *The Purchasing Power of Money*. New York: Macmillan.

Fisher, I. 1920. *Stabilizing the Dollar*. New York: Macmillan.

Fisher, I. 1933. The debt-deflation theory of great depressions. *Econometrica* 1, 337–57.

Friedman, M. 1956. *Studies in the Quantity Theory of Money*. Chicago: University of Chicago Press.

Hall, R.E. 1982. Explorations in the gold standard and related policies for stabilizing the dollar. In *Inflation: Causes and Effects*, ed. R.E. Hall. Chicago: University of Chicago Press.

Hawtrey, R.G. 1927. *Currency and Credit*. 3rd edn. London: Longmans, Green & Co.

Hicks, J.R. 1935. A suggestion for simplifying the theory of money. *Economica*, NS 2(1), 1–19.

Jevons, W.S. 1875. *Money and the Mechanism of Exchange*. London: King.

Kareken, J.H. and Wallace, N., eds. 1980. *Models of Monetary Economics*. Minneapolis, MN: Federal Reserve Bank.

Keynes, J.M. 1930. Auri sacra fames. In *Essays in Persuasion*, reprinted in *The Collected Writings of John Maynard Keynes*, vol. 9, London: Macmillan, 1972; New York: Harcourt Brace.

Keynes, J.M. 1936. *The General Theory of Employment, Interest, and Money*. Reprinted in *The Collected Writings of John Maynard Keynes*, vol. 7. London: Macmillan, 1973; New York: Harcourt Brace.

Mundell, R.A. 1963. Inflation and real interest. *Journal of Political Economy* 71, 280–83.

Patinkin, D. 1956. *Money, Interest, and Prices*. New York: Harper and Row; 2nd edn, 1965.

Prescott, E. 1986. Theory ahead of business cycle measurement. *Federal Reserve Bank of Minneapolis Quarterly Review* 10(4), 9–22.

Robertson, D.H. 1922. *Money*. Cambridge Economic Handbook, 4th edn, Chicago: University of Chicago Press, 1959.

Sargent, T.J. and Wallace, N. 1981. Some unpleasant monetarist arithmetic. *Federal Reserve Bank of Minneapolis Quarterly Review* 5(3), 1–17.

Shubik, M. 1984. *A Game-Theoretic Approach to Political Economy*. Cambridge, MA: MIT Press.

Starr, R.M. 1972. The structure of exchange in barter and monetary economies. *Quarterly Journal of Economics* 86, 290–302.

Starr, R.M. 1974. The price of money in a pure exchange economy with taxation. *Econometrica* 42, 45–54.

Stein, J.L., ed. 1976. *Monetarism*. Amsterdam: North-Holland.

Tobin, J. 1965. Money and economic growth. *Econometrica* 33, 671–84.

Tobin, J. 1969. A general equilibrium approach to monetary theory. *Journal of Money, Credit, and Banking* 1(1), 15–29.

Tobin, J. 1975. Keynesian models of recession and depression. *American Economic Review* 65, 195–202.

money and general equilibrium

The general equilibrium theory of value, as developed by Walras (1874–77) and his followers, determines the relative prices of goods in terms of non-monetary factors such as technology, preferences, and endowments. Monetary factors are used to determine the nominal price level once relative prices have been determined. Relative prices are determined by the market-clearing conditions for goods whereas the general price level is determined by the market-clearing condition for money. Given a vector of nominal prices $p = (p_1, \ldots, p_\ell)$, the market excess demand functions can be denoted by $f(p) = (f_1(p), \ldots, f_\ell(p))$, where p_h denotes the nominal price of good h and $f_h(p)$ denotes the market excess demand for good h. The functions $f(p)$ are assumed to be homogeneous of degree zero in nominal prices:

$$f(p) = f(tp),$$

for any positive scalar $t > 0$. The market-clearing conditions for goods require that the excess demand for each good vanishes at the equilibrium price vector p^*, that is $f(p^*) = 0$. These conditions can at most determine relative prices, because if p^* is an equilibrium price vector, then so is tp^*, for any positive scalar $t > 0$.

To determine the nominal price level, a demand function for money is introduced. The aggregate demand for money is assumed to be a function of prices $M(p)$. Money demand is homogeneous of degree one in prices:

$$M(tp) = tM(p),$$

for any price vector p and any scalar $t > 0$. For any vector of nominal prices p^* satisfying the goods market-clearing condition $f(p^*) = 0$, there is a unique value of $t > 0$ such that

$$M(tp^*) = M,$$

where $M > 0$ is the exogenous money supply. Thus, once relative prices have been determined by the real factors, the level of nominal prices is determined by monetary factors. This doctrine, which became known as the classical dichotomy, characterized the classical (pre-Keynesian) thinking about monetary economics (see Fisher, 1963, for example).

The integration of monetary theory and the theory of value was stimulated by the appearance of Keynes's General Theory (Keynes, 1936). Pigou (1943) argued that the demand for goods could not be homogeneous of degree zero in prices, because a general fall in prices would increase the real value of money and the wealth effect would in turn increase demand for goods. The Pigou effect (the effect of a general fall in prices on the aggregate demand for goods) is a special case of the real balance effect: that is, the effect of any change in real balances on the aggregate demand for goods. In an attempt to make sense of Keynes's short period analysis, Hicks (1946) introduced the concept of temporary equilibrium, in which prices adjust to clear markets in a particular time period, taking as given expectations about prices in future periods. Building on the work of Hicks and Pigou, Patinkin (1965) argued that the real balance effect is essential for the existence and stability of equilibrium. The classical writers assumed that the market excess demand functions satisfy Say's Law, that is, the value of excess demands for goods sum to zero or

$$p \cdot f(p) = 0,$$

for any price vector p. However, Patinkin pointed out that Walras's Law should also be satisfied: that is, the value of the excess demands for goods and money should sum to zero, or

$$p \cdot f(p) + M(p) - M = 0,$$

for any price vector p. Say's Law and Walras's Law together imply that

$$M(p) = M,$$

for any price vector p. Then homogeneity of the excess demand function $f(p)$ once again implies that, if p^* is a market-clearing price vector, so is tp^* for any $t > 0$ and the price level is once again undetermined. To avoid this indeterminacy, Patinkin argued that there must be a real balance effect: a change in the general price level implies a change in real balances, and hence a change in wealth which must change the demand for commodities. Thus, in a monetary economy the excess demand for goods $f(p, M)$ is a (homogeneous of degree zero) function of nominal prices and the money supply.

Hahn (1965) pointed out another problem in the theory of monetary equilibrium, viewed from the Walrasian perspective. The problem was the lack of a proof that money has positive value in equilibrium. Hahn observed that the uses of money that might be expected to give rise to a positive demand for money all require money to have positive value in exchange. If the value of money were zero, the economy would be identical to a barter economy. Under the usual assumptions on the excess demand functions, such a non-monetary economy would possess an equilibrium, but it would not be a monetary equilibrium, because money would have no role in exchange.

Grandmont (1983) provided an elegant solution to the problem posed by Hahn (1965). He showed that, while the real balance effect might be necessary, it was not sufficient for the existence of an equilibrium in which the value of money is positive. A strong intertemporal substitution effect is needed as well. Consider an economy in which there are two periods (the present and the future). In the first period, agents buy and sell goods for immediate consumption. They also demand money as a store of value, which they hold until the following period. The value of money is given by an indirect utility function $v(m, p')$, where $m > 0$ is the amount of money held until the future and p' is the vector of future nominal prices. An agent's expectations are represented by a probability measure μ on the space of price vectors. Expectations of future prices depend on current prices p via the expectation function $\mu = \psi(p)$. Then the expected utility associated with the cash balance m is simply the expected value of

$\tilde{v}(m, p')$, conditional on the current price vector p:

$$v(m, p) = \int \tilde{v}(m, p') d\psi(p).$$

Let $u(x)$ denote the utility associated with the consumption of a vector of current goods x. Then the agent seeks to maximize

$$u(x) + v(m, p)$$

subject to the budget constraint

$$p \cdot x + m \le p \cdot e + m,$$

where e is the agent's endowment of goods and $\bar{m}$ his endowment of money. The crucial assumption (sufficient condition) for the existence of an equilibrium in which money has a positive value is that the expectation function $\psi(p)$ satisfies the uniform tightness property: for any number $\varepsilon > 0$ and for every current price vector p, there is a compact set K in the space of positive prices such that $\psi(p)$ assigns probability at least $1 - \varepsilon$ to the event that the future price vector p' belongs to K.

While the classical dichotomy cannot hold in the short run, Archibald and Lipsey (1958) argued that it would hold in the long run because the allocation of money balances is endogenous in the long run. This gave rise to the study of stationary states (see Grandmont, 1983).

The cash-in-advance constraint

Introduced by Clower (1967), the cash-in-advance constraint provides a simple motivation for the use of money as a medium of exchange. Lucas (1980) derives the cash-in-advance constraint as follows. Every household is assumed to consist of two agents, one of whom is responsible for selling the household's endowment of goods (for example, supplying labour) and the other is responsible for purchasing goods. At the beginning of each day, the seller sets off for the market with a bundle of goods to sell, while the buyer sets of for a different set of markets to buy the goods they need. Following Clower's dictum that 'money buys goods and goods buy money but goods do not buy goods', the buyer needs to have a stock of money at the beginning of the day. The money earned by the seller is not available until the end of the day, so the buyer's purchases are constrained by the amount of money she has at the beginning of the day. The money brought home by the seller must be held until the next day. If m is the amount of money held initially and $\bar{m}$ is the amount carried forward to the next day, the budget constraint can be written as

$$p \cdot x + m \le p \cdot e + \bar{m}$$

and the cash-in-advance constraint can be written as

$$p \cdot (x - e)^{+} \le \bar{m},$$

where ξ^{+} denotes the vector consisting of the non-negative part of the vector ξ.

Grandmont and Younes (1973) used a cash-in-advance constraint to study the efficiency of monetary equilibrium. They considered stationary equilibria of an infinite-horizon, pure-exchange economy in which a finite number of individuals $i = 1,\ldots, I$ maximize the discounted sum of utilities $\sum_{s=t}^{\infty} \delta^{s-t} u_i(x_i(s))$ subject to a sequence of budget constraints and a cash-in-advance constraint in the form

$$p(t) \cdot (x_i(t) - e_i)^+ + kp \cdot (x_i(t) - e)^- \leq m(t-1),$$

where $0 \leq k \leq 1$. For $k = 0$ this constraint reduces to the Clower–Lucas version. Grandmont and Younes established Friedman's optimum quantity of money result: any laissez-faire, stationary equilibrium of this economy is Pareto inefficient but, if the rate of price deflation equals the subjective rate as time preference, this is sufficient to guarantee that equilibrium is efficient. Grandmont and Laroque (1975) also showed that the payment of interest on money has no effect on efficiency. More precisely, it is the gap between the inflation rate and the interest rate which has an effect, and this is attributable to the lump-sum taxes rather than the interest payments.

The cash-in-advance constraint has played an important role in macroeconomics, particularly in the study of the effect of fiscal and monetary policy (see, for example, Lucas and Stokey, 1983; 1987; Sargent, 1987).

Financial securities
The classical model of general competitive equilibrium assumes that markets are complete. Hart (1975) showed that, with incomplete markets, the existence of equilibrium is no longer guaranteed and the fundamental theorems of welfare economics no longer hold. In Hart's model, incomplete markets are represented by trade in real securities, which are promises to deliver bundles of commodities at some future date and event. Cass (2006) and Werner (1985) introduced financial securities, whose payoffs are denominated in units of money, and showed that this resolved the existence problem. However, as Balasko and Cass (1989) and Geanakoplos and Mas-Colell (1989) showed, financial securities also introduced indeterminacy of equilibrium. The problem is that a change in the price level in some state changes the real purchasing power of money and hence changes the real payoffs of the financial securities. Magill and Quinzii (1992) pointed out that the indeterminacy arises from the fact that 'money' serves only as a unit of account in the Cass–Werner model. Money has no role in exchange or savings and investment, and hence there is no well defined demand for money.

To address this problem, Magill and Quinzii introduce a cash-in-advance constraint in the spirit of Clower (1967). There are two dates, $t = 0$, 1, and S states of nature, $s = 1,\ldots, S$. The state is unknown at date 0; the true state is revealed at date 1. It is convenient to treat the situation at date 0 as another state, denoted $s = 0$. Then each period s is divided into three sub-periods, denoted s_1, s_2, and s_3. In sub-period s_1, agents sell their entire endowment of money to a central exchange and receive money instead. In sub-period s_2, they invest in financial securities (at date 0) and receive dividends (at date 1). In sub-period s_3, they use money to purchase goods from the central exchange. The separation of the sale and purchase of goods between sub-periods s_1 and s_3 forces agents to hold money in equilibrium. Money can also be used to store wealth between periods 0 and 1, but agents will do this only if they anticipate deflation. The supply of money is determined exogenously by the government.

Three main results were established by Magill and Quinzii. First, they showed that, *generically in endowments and money supply, an economy has a finite number of locally unique monetary equilibria*. This means that equilibrium is locally determinate: the well-defined demand for money has eliminated the indeterminacy of the price level. Second, *if money is used as a medium of exchange only, local changes in the money supply have no real effects if the asset markets are complete* – changes in the money supply will change the price level but this will have no effect on the real allocation as long as markets are complete – *whereas, if markets are incomplete, local changes in money supply translate into an S−1 dimensional submanifold of real allocations*. When markets are incomplete, any change in the price level implies a change in the real payoffs of the securities, and this translates into a real change in the allocation. Finally, *if money is used as a store of value, local changes in the money supply translate into an S-dimensional submanifold of real allocations in the case of both complete and incomplete markets*. This follows because the use of money as a store of value to transfer wealth between periods implies that the real allocation is directly impacted by changes in the real payoffs from holding money.

A related study by Geanakoplos and Dubey (1992) addresses a similar set of questions, but does so in the context of a model with a banking system.

Market games

To provide microeconomic foundations for monetary equilibrium, Shubik (1972) introduced a game that integrates the use of money as a medium of exchange with a generalized Nash–Cournot model of markets. The generalization by Shapley and Shubik (1977) can be summarized as follows. There is an exchange economy with ℓ commodities, indexed by $h = 1, \ldots, \ell$, and I traders, indexed by $I = 1, \ldots, I$. Each trader is characterized by a consumption set $\mathbf{R}_+^\ell$, an endowment $e_i \in \mathbf{R}_+^\ell$, and a utility function $u_i : \mathbf{R}_+^\ell \to \mathbf{R}$. The utility functions are assumed to be C^1, non-decreasing and concave. We assume that each commodity has a positive aggregate endowment $e_h > 0$ and that each individual has a non-zero endowment $e_i > 0$.

For simplicity, we assume that traders offer their entire endowment of assets for sale and then bid for the assets they want to hold using fiat money as a means of payment. Each trader i has an endowment of fiat money $m_i > 0$. The amount of money he bids for asset h is denoted by $b_{ih} \geq 0$ and the vector consisting of his bids is denoted by $b_i \in \mathbf{R}_+^\ell$.

A trader cannot bid more money than he holds, so the bid vector chosen by trader i must satisfy the cash-in-advance constraint

$$\sum_{h=1}^{\ell} b_{ih} \leq m_i.$$

The set of bid vectors satisfying the cash-in-advance constraint for trader i is denoted by B_i, where it is understood that the initial balance m_i is exogenously given.

For any strategy profile $b = (b_1, \ldots, b_I)$, define an attainable allocation of commodities as follows. Let the price of commodity h be denoted by $p_h(b)$ and defined by

$$p_h(b) = \frac{b_h}{e_h},$$

where $b_h \equiv \sum_{i=1}^{I} b_{ih}$ and $e_h = \sum_{i=1}^{I} e_{ih}$. Then let the quantity of commodity h received by trader i be denoted by $\xi_{ih}(b)$ and defined by

$$\xi_{ih}(b) = \begin{cases} b_{ih}/p_h & \text{if } p_h > 0 \\ 0 & \text{if } p_h = 0. \end{cases}$$

Then the commodity bundle achieved by i for any strategy profile b is denoted by $\xi_i(b)$. It is easy to see that the I-tuple $\{\xi_i(b)\}$ is an attainable allocation for any $b \in B$.

The traders must return their initial balances of fiat money to the government at the end of the game. This means that trader i must end the trading period with at least m_i units of money. We assume that any choice of b_i resulting in end-of-period money balances that are lower than m_i will yield a payoff of $-\infty$. The terminal balance for trader i equals his initial balance m_i minus the sum of his bids $\sum_{h=1}^{\ell} b_{ih}$ plus the revenue from the sale of his initial portfolio $p(b) \cdot e_i$. It is easy to show that the terminal balance satisfies

$$m_i - \sum_{h=1}^{\ell} b_{ih} + p(b) \cdot e_i = m_i - p(b) \cdot (\xi_i(b) - e_i),$$

so the terminal constraint is satisfied if and only if $p(b) \cdot (\xi_i(b) - e_i) \leq 0$. For any strategy profile b, let trader i's payoff be denoted by $\pi_i(b)$ and defined by

$$\pi_i(b) = \begin{cases} u_i(\xi_i(b)) & \text{if } p(b) \cdot (\xi_i(b) - e_i) \leq 0, \\ -\infty & \text{if } p(b) \cdot (\xi_i(b) - e_i) > 0. \end{cases}$$

Shapley and Shubik (1977) demonstrate the existence of a Nash equilibrium for this game under the additional assumption that for each commodity h there are at least two individuals whose utility is increasing in that commodity. They also provide conditions under which the equilibrium allocation converges to a competitive equilibrium as the number of traders increases without bound.

Concluding remarks

As Joseph Ostroy wrote in the first edition of *The New Palgrave* (1987, p. 515),

> We shall argue that the incorporation of monetary exchange tests the limits of general equilibrium theory, exposing its implicitly centralized conception of trade and calling for more decentralized models of exchange.

That comment is just as true today as it was then, and remains the great challenge for economists who want to develop more satisfactory models of the process of monetary exchange at the level of the economy as a whole.

DOUGLAS GALE

See also **monetary policy, history of; money supply.**

Bibliography

Archibald, G. and Lipsey, R. 1958. Monetary and value theory: a critique of Patinkin and Lange. *Review of Economic Studies* 26, 1–22.

Balasko, Y. and Cass, D. 1989. The structure of financial equilibrium: I. exogenous yields and unrestricted participation. *Econometrica* 57, 135–62.

Cass, D. 2006. Competitive equilibrium with incomplete financial markets. *Journal of Mathematical Economics* 42, 384–405.

Clower, R. 1967. A reconsideration of the microfoundations of monetary theory. *Economic Inquiry* 6, 1–8.

Fisher, I. 1963. *The Purchasing Power of Money*, rev. edn. New York: Kelley.

Geanakoplos, J. and Mas-Colell, A. 1989. Real indeterminacy with financial assets. *Journal of Economic Theory* 47, 22–38.

Geanakoplos, J. and Dubey, P. 1992. The value of money in a finite-horizon economy: a role for banks. In *Economic Analysis of Markets and Games*, ed. P. Dasgupta et al. Cambridge, MA: MIT Press.

Grandmont, J.-M. 1983. *Money and Value: A Reconsideration of Classical and Neoclassical Monetary Theories*. Cambridge: Cambridge University Press; Paris: Maison des Sciences de l'Homme.

Grandmont, J.-M. and Laroque, G. 1975. On money and banking. *Review of Economic Studies* 42, 207–36.

Grandmont, J.-M. and Younes, Y. 1973. On the efficiency of monetary equilibrium. *Review of Economic Studies* 40, 149–65.

Hahn, F. 1965. On some problems of proving the existence of an equilibrium in a monetary economy. In *The Theory of Interest Rates*, ed. F. Hahn and F. Brechling. London: Macmillan.

Hart, O. 1975. On the optimality of equilibrium when the market structure is incomplete. *Journal of Economic Theory* 11, 418–43.

Hicks, J. 1946. *Value and Capital: An Inquiry into Some Fundamental Principles of Economic Theory*, 2nd edn. Oxford: Clarendon.

Keynes, J. 1936. *The General Theory of Employment, Interest and Money*. London: Macmillan.

Lucas, R. 1980. Equilibrium in a pure currency economy. *Economic Enquiry* 18, 203–20.

Lucas, R. and Stokey, N. 1983. Optimal fiscal and monetary policy in an economy without capital. *Journal of Monetary Economics* 12, 55–93.

Lucas, R. and Stokey, N. 1987. Money and interest in a cash-in-advance economy. *Econometrica* 55, 491–513.

Magill, M. and Quinzii, M. 1992. Real effects of money in general equilibrium. *Journal of Mathematical Economics* 21, 301–42.

Ostroy, J.M. 1987. Money and general equilibrium. In *The New Palgrave: A Dictionary of Economics*, vol. 3, ed. J. Eatwell, M. Milgate and P. Newman. London: Macmillan.

Patinkin, D. 1965. *Money, Interest, and Prices: An Integration of Monetary and Value Theory*, 2nd edn. New York: Harper and Row.

Pigou, A.C. 1943. The classical stationary state. *Economic Journal* 53, 343–51.

Sargent, T. 1987. *Dynamic Macroeconomic Theory*. Cambridge, MA: Harvard University Press.

Shapley, L. and Shubik, M. 1977. Trade using one commodity as a means of payment. *Journal of Political Economy* 85, 937–68.

Shubik, M. 1972. Commodity money, oligopoly, credit and bankruptcy in a general equilibrium model. *Western Economic Journal* 10, 24–38.

Werner, J. 1985. Equilibrium in economies with incomplete financial markets. *Journal of Economic Theory* 36, 110–19.

money supply

Supplying money for use in everyday transactions, so as to obviate the need for cumbersome barter, has been a function of governments for more than 2,000 years. Not surprisingly, government-issued money, once in existence, rapidly became a store of value as well. As an aspect of the history of human society and institutions, the process by which governments supply money has naturally attracted substantial attention. But the primary interest in money supply within the discipline of economics has stemmed from the proposition that movements in money are an important – according to some views, the most important – determinant of movements in prices, in output and employment, and in other economic phenomena of well-established interest on their own account.

Two analytical frameworks that rose to prominence in the latter half of the 20th century – indeed, that dominated macroeconomic thinking during much of that period – attached just this importance to money: quantity-theory monetarism, and IS–LM Keynesianism. Both these frameworks, however, took for granted that governments conduct their affairs (specifically in this context, that central banks conduct monetary policy) in such a way as to create independent movements in the supply of money, as opposed to merely passive movements in response to changes in money demand that therefore could not plausibly be the cause of movements in either prices or real economic activity. As of the outset of the 21st century, however, the number of central banks that in fact carry out their responsibilities in such a way is small and shrinking. Instead, most central banks implement monetary policy by setting some designated short-term interest rate.

As a result, interest in how money is supplied has sharply diminished among economists, and the details of the money supply process are now often omitted from the standard economics curriculum. (Examples at the graduate level are the instructional text by David Romer, 2006, and the theoretical treatise by Michael Woodford, 2003.) In the absence of some substantive knowledge of how money is supplied, however, just how a central bank can set 'the interest rate' would remain mysterious. Even if the number of central banks that actively seek to influence money supply as an element of the conduct of monetary policy shrinks to zero, therefore, money supply is unlikely to disappear from the purview of economics altogether.

The analytical basics

The first recognized monies supplied by governments for ordinary economic use mostly consisted of precious metals. The authorities' role was to provide standardized units, together with what amounted to stamped certification that the amount of metal in the coin or other object conformed. Apart from the certification, therefore, anyone who had an adequate quantity of the chosen metal could supply money along with the government.

In the more modern conception of money supply, relevant only since the 19th century, money is a form of debt. Most government-issued money consists of currency, which represents the liability of a partly or wholly government-owned central bank. Currency is typically not interest-bearing, and so the motives for holding it do not stem from its role as an earning asset. And although it is the government's (the central bank's) liability, in modern times it usually does not represent an obligation on the government's part to pay the bearer in some other form. Instead, both private citizens and businesses hold these government liabilities for their convenient use in everyday transactions, normally enforced by their statutory status as legal tender.

The fact that government issued money is supplied as the liability of the central bank, and the presumption that the central bank has control over its balance sheet, together create the conceptual foundation for viewing the supply of money as a tool of economic policy. Indeed, much of the initial interest in this subject in the modern era arose from the experience of countries where the central bank had lost control of its balance sheet for some period of time, often in the aftermath of war or under other circumstances that prevented the government from raising ordinary revenues to cover its ongoing expenditures. The observation that such episodes often led to spiralling hyperinflation, with rising prices requiring the government to issue more money (in the absence of other revenues) and the larger supply of money leading to further increases in prices, immediately suggested a connection between money supply and prices, if not real economic activity as well.

Apart from situations of runaway money supply and hyperinflation, however, the issuance of currency is usually not the focus of economists' interest in how the supply of money relates to economic activity. While the great majority of government-issued money in the economically advanced countries now consists of currency held by the public (as of 2006, 69 per cent in the United Kingdom, and 95 per cent in the United States), currency is nonetheless only a small part of the money that individuals and firms use for savings and to execute everyday economic transactions. The money that individuals and firms use mostly consists of deposits issued by banks and other financial institutions. In the United Kingdom, deposit money outweighs currency by more than 30 to 1. Even in the United States, where the country's currency is also commonly used in both legal and illegal transactions around the world, the ratio is more than 8 to 1. Moreover, although in principle a central bank could seek to influence the economy by manipulating how much currency it supplies, in practice most central banks supply currency passively to accommodate whatever demands the public may have. (The role of currency issuance as a source of government finance – the heart of most examples of hyperinflation – is likewise limited in most economically advanced countries. Even in the United States, with demand for the currency enlarged by the use of US dollars in other countries, issuance of currency in a typical year amounts to only one to two per cent of the federal government's spending.) The simple construct of an economy in which the public depends entirely on government-issued currency to execute economic transactions, and the central bank exerts its economic influence by expanding or contracting the supply of that currency, is a textbook instructional device with limited relevance to most actual economies.

From the perspective of any active connection to either nonfinancial economic activity or the pricing of assets in the financial markets, therefore, what matters is the larger money supply issued by banks and other depository institutions (hereafter simply 'banks' for short). And in most modern banking systems, what gives the central bank the ability to influence the volume of deposits that banks in the aggregate create is its control over the amount of its own liabilities that it supplies for banks to hold. While most of the central bank's liabilities consist of currency held by the public, the remainder (31 per cent in the United Kingdom, and only five per cent in the United States, as of 2006) are held as assets – normally called 'reserves' – by the banks. The link between the banks' creation of deposits for the public to hold and their own holdings of reserves at the central bank constitutes the heart of the money supply process for purposes of a connection to most matters of concern to monetary policy.

Banks hold central bank reserves – and, importantly, hold more reserves as they have more deposits outstanding (all other things equal) – for several reasons. First, in traditional 'fractional reserve' banking systems, banks are required by law to hold such reserves in amounts equal to at least some fixed percentage of their outstanding deposits. Hence a larger supply of reserves makes it possible for the banks to do more lending (or buy more securities) and therefore create more money. Conversely, contracting the supply of reserves requires banks to shrink the amount of deposits they have outstanding, normally by not extending new loans to replace existing credits that mature or are otherwise repaid, or by selling securities.

Second, banks need a supply of currency to satisfy customers who draw on their accounts or present checks or other negotiable instruments for payment. In some banking systems, currency held by banks (as opposed to currency held by the public) is counted as part of banks' reserves. When a customer cashes a check, therefore, bank reserves fall and there is a corresponding increase in currency held by the public. (Because the central bank is not a party to the transaction, the total amount of central bank liabilities remains unchanged.) But banks cannot satisfy such demands unless they are holding an adequate amount of currency to begin with. And the greater the bank's volume of business, including in particular the amount of deposits it has outstanding against which its customers may want to draw, the more currency – hence the more reserves, if bank-held currency counts as reserves – the bank will ordinarily hold.

Third, banks also need to settle transactions with one another. If a customer of one bank deposits a check written against an account at another bank, the two banks must transfer some asset from one to the other. The same is true if one bank sells a security to another. Although banks in most countries have various mechanisms, like private clearing houses, for effecting such transfers without involving the central bank, some inter-bank transactions do normally settle by transferring reserves at the central bank from the paying bank to the receiving bank. In order to participate in that process, banks therefore need to hold at least some amount of reserves; and the more deposits the bank has outstanding, the more inter-bank transactions it may have to settle on a given day, and so the more reserves it will ordinarily hold. Moreover, in some banking systems the central bank reinforces the demand for its reserves by requiring banks to settle certain classes of inter-bank transactions in this way. Especially in systems where there are no reserve requirements in the traditional form of a stated minimum percentage of outstanding deposits, requiring the banks to settle inter-bank transactions in this way reinforces the banks' need to hold central bank reserves.

Banks' demand for reserves, therefore, is in many ways analogous to the public's demand for money. Reserves provide banks with an ability to do business, just as the money that individuals and nonfinancial firms hold enables them carry out their everyday economic affairs. That ability has value, but not infinite value. Hence the more expensive it is for banks to hold reserves, in terms of interest forgone by holding reserves instead of some other asset, the more banks will seek to economize on their reserve holdings in relation to their outstanding volume of deposits. For a given amount of deposits, therefore, banks' demand for reserves is negatively elastic with respect to the interest rate on alternative assets (typically loans or securities), just as the public's demand for money is negatively interest elastic for a given amount of income being earned or transacting being done. If reserves at the central bank bear an interest rate that varies in close step with what banks can get from holding other earning assets, this negative interest elasticity is likely to be small, or even trivial. But if the interest rate that the central bank pays on reserves is fixed (in the United States, for example, it is fixed at zero), or even if it varies together with market returns but only imperfectly, the negative interest elasticity in banks' reserve demand is likely to be significant. (The classic paper making this point is Dewald, 1963.)

The analytical mirror image of banks' negatively elastic demand for reserves, for a given volume of deposits outstanding, is their positively elastic willingness to create deposits for a given amount of reserves that they hold. The higher are market interest rates on earning assets, compared to whatever rate the central bank pays on reserves, the greater is the incentive for banks to stretch their reserves further by making more loans and buying more securities – and in the process creating more deposits – rather than leaving an increasingly expensive cushion of reserves that may provide benefits (less risk of having to take abrupt action in the event of a shortfall, for example) but are costly nonetheless.

The result is a positively interest-elastic supply of money, representing the behaviour of banks, to go along with the usual negatively interest elastic demand for money representing the behaviour of the households and firms that hold bank deposits, together with currency, as the money that they use for economic purposes. In the absence of some pathology, the intersection of this positively interest-elastic money supply and negatively interest-elastic money demand determines the equilibrium quantity of money created and held, for a given supply of reserves and a given level of income, together with the interest rate at which the market clears. (And, because the positively interest-elastic supply of money is simply the mirror image of the negatively interest-elastic demand for reserves – both represent the same aspect of banks' behaviour – the market for reserves is likewise in equilibrium, with demand equal to whatever quantity of reserves the central bank is supplying, at the same interest rate.) Integrating this partial equilibrium of the money market (and the reserves market) with the demand for goods and services then completes a simple representation of the economy's aggregate demand. Further integrating that aggregate demand representation with aggregate supply, importantly including the labour market, in turn completes the economy's short-run general equilibrium (short-run in that such dynamic elements as the stocks of capital, technology, and other relevant factors are still unaccounted for).

In some treatments of money supply within the economics literature, this explicit supply–demand equilibrium in the markets for money and reserves is, instead, implicitly represented by a simple 'money multiplier' stating the relationship between the total liabilities supplied by the central bank – often called the 'monetary base' – and the resulting amount of money, including bank deposits as well as currency. Purely as a matter of arithmetic, specifying the ratio of reserves to deposits that the banks choose to hold (influenced in part by whatever reserve requirements and other institutional strictures banks face), and the ratio of currency to deposits that the public chooses within its holdings of money, is sufficient to determine the quantity of money that goes along with any given monetary base set by the central bank. But the banks' reserve-to-deposit ratio depends in part on interest rates as well, and the public's demand for currency often varies with a host of factors (confidence in the banking system, use of currency abroad or for purposes of illegal transactions, and so on), so that the 'money multiplier' representation is really just a short-hand simplification that works well or badly depending on the strength of the relevant interest elasticities and the extent of variation in interest rates and the many other factors involved. (See, for example, Cagan, 1965. A brief statement of the central ideas appeared in Friedman and Schwartz, 1963, ch. 2, sec. 4.) Underneath, the supply–demand equilibrium established by the central bank's supply of reserves, banks' behaviour in demanding reserves and supplying deposits, and the public's behaviour in demanding both deposits and currency, is what establishes an economy's money supply. (For a fully articulated treatment, see Modigliani, Rasche, and Cooper, 1970.)

The link to monetary policy

The logical starting point in this process is the central bank's supply of its own liabilities, and it is the central bank's control over the liabilities it issues that gives the supply of money its place in economic policy. Until fairly recently – well into the 19th century – governments issued either coins or paper currency mostly as a means of payment for goods and services they purchased. Such actions were, in effect, a combination of what have come to be known as fiscal and monetary policies. In the modern era, however, especially with the advent of central banks as distinct and often quasi-independent governmental institutions, economists have thought of fiscal and monetary policies as likewise distinct.

In the absence of a securities market, or some similar set of financial institutions, it is difficult to conceive of how monetary policy would operate independently of fiscal policy: how could the government, in such a setting, increase the amount of money outstanding without simultaneously making either a purchase or at least a transfer payment? One metaphor sometimes used in the theoretical economics literature to represent such an action – and which only serves to indicate how far-fetched such a situation is – is to picture the government dropping money from a helicopter. While monetary and fiscal policies are distinguishable in most modern economies, central banks, of course, do not drop money from helicopters. The reason is that the economies in which they operate in fact have securities markets.

The primary means by which central banks in most modern economies change the amount of their liabilities outstanding is to purchase, or sell, securities – actions typically called 'open market operations'. When the central bank buys a security, it makes payment by increasing the amount of reserves credited to the seller's bank. (In systems in which bank-held currency is counted as part of reserves, the consequence is the same even if the central bank makes payment by delivering currency to the seller's bank.) When the central bank sells a security, it correspondingly receives payment by reducing the amount of reserves credited to the buyer's bank. In either case, the central bank's assets, consisting mostly of the securities it holds, and its liabilities, consisting partly of the reserves credited to banks, rise or fall in lockstep. But because of the ways in which banks' ability to create deposits depends on their holdings of reserves, the change is not economically irrelevant. Changes in the supply of reserves, effected via open market operations, shift a key underpinning of the equilibrium in the reserves market and the money market, thereby changing not only the resulting quantity of money but the yields and prices of non-money assets and ultimately the equilibrium of the nonfinancial economy as well.

Not all open market operations carried out by central banks change the quantity of reserves. Most importantly, the central bank also needs to accommodate the public's changing demand for currency. In a growing economy with rising prices, the demand for currency is usually increasing. When individuals and businesses go to their banks to get more currency, their doing so increases the amount of currency in public circulation but reduces the amount of the banks' reserves (as long as bank-held currency is counted as reserves). As a part of their normal ongoing procedures, therefore, most central banks routinely purchase securities – that is, carry out open market operations – in order to offset such reductions in reserves due to increasing public demand for currency. Central banks also regularly carry out open market purchases or sales in order to prevent short-run fluctuation in other technical factors, such as international transactions and variations in the amount of checks currently in the clearing process, from affecting the supply of reserves.

Central banks can also create reserves by lending to banks, rather than buying earning assets from them, and in some countries' systems the lending of reserves is more important for purposes of carrying out monetary policy than open market operations. Whether banks distinguish between reserves that they have borrowed from the central bank and reserves that they simply own outright (often called 'nonborrowed reserves' to distinguish the two) depends on the specifics of the individual system's institutions. Most obviously, borrowed reserves are a liability of the bank, on which it presumably has to pay interest, while its nonborrowed reserves are an asset on which it may or may not earn interest. In addition, in some systems (the United States, for example), borrowing reserves from the central bank exposes a bank to regulatory oversight with implicit costs well beyond what the interest rate paid would suggest.

Whether reserves are borrowed or nonborrowed, however, the essence of monetary policy is the central bank's provision of reserves to the banking system. The recognition of the way in which that role played by the central bank potentially affects an economy's money supply, interest rates, asset prices, nonfinancial activity, and prices and wages, in turn sets the stage for both normative and positive consideration of monetary policy. The ensuing economics literature has become vast. In most countries the corresponding public discussion is likewise active and intense.

The modern economist most identified with emphasizing the role of money supply in the conduct of monetary policy – as opposed to focusing on interest rates, or measures of reserves in the banking system, or other relevant indicators of what a central bank is doing in this respect – is Milton Friedman. At the most fundamental normative level, Friedman advocated a long-run policy of shrinking the supply of money (by which he meant government-issued money) at a rate adequate to render nominal interest rates on assets closely substitutable for money equal to zero on average over time. The basic logic was that, since the government could create such money at essentially no cost, it should be costless for the public to hold; the public's effort to economize on holdings of money balances, when market interest rates on money substitutes are positive, represents a deadweight loss to the economy (see Friedman, 1969). Given the demonstrated dangers of deflation, however – with a positive real rate of interest, negative inflation would be necessary to achieve a zero average nominal interest rate – this recommendation had little impact on actual monetary policy.

At a more practical level, however, over short- and medium-run horizons Friedman advocated keeping the supply of money (by which he meant the deposits and currency held by the public) growing at a constant rate. Here the argument was that the influence of monetary policy on both prices and real economic activity operates with lengthy delays, subject to unpredictable variation, and that active attempts by the central bank to use monetary policy to offset nonmonetary influences on the economy were likely to be destabilizing (see Friedman, 1953; 1956). Many other economists, more optimistic about the prospects for using active variation in monetary policy to blunt the influence on the economy of factors that the central bank could either foresee or at least recognize quickly once they had occurred, followed Friedman in advocating the use of growth in the money supply as the way to gauge whether the central bank was exerting a stimulative or a contractionary force on economic activity. Beginning in the 1960s, but more so in the 1970s, many central banks around the world implemented these recommendations by adopting one or another form of explicit target for the growth of its money supply.

The role of empirical evidence

The crucial empirical underpinning of such policy frameworks, whether they involved constant money growth or attempts at active stabilization nonetheless benchmarked by money growth, was the observation that movements in money bore a reliable relationship to movements in income and prices. Early in the post-Second World War period, Philip Cagan documented such a relationship between money growth and price inflation in several well-known episodes of hyperinflation in Europe that had followed each of the two world wars (Cagan, 1956). But hyperinflation in the context of post-war chaos (especially for the war's losers) bore only limited implications for the conduct of monetary policy under more normal circumstances. In a massive historical study, Milton Friedman and Anna J. Schwartz documented the relationships between money and prices, and also money and income, for the United States during the period 1867–1960 – including the Great Depression of the 1930s but also many more ordinary business fluctuations as well – and following their work many other empirical researchers attempted similar (though mostly smaller-scale) studies for other countries and other time periods (Friedman and Schwartz, 1963).

At the conceptual level, the central idea linking this empirical research to the implied role of money supply in conducting monetary policy was that, if fluctuations in money growth and fluctuations in income and/or prices are systematically related, and if the observed fluctuations in money growth within those relationships represent independent movements of money supply, then the central bank can exploit those relationships by purposefully steering the money supply along an optimally chosen course (which may or may not be a simply constant-growth path). Following the work of Friedman and Schwartz, and the many other researchers who applied ever more sophisticated empirical methodologies to the same line of enquiry, questions about each of these two underlying issues – how strong the observed relationships are, and whether they result from independent movements of money supply – generated a similarly large literature.

One immediate difficulty, recognized early on, is that, since money supply necessarily equals money demand, inferences about the money–income or money–price relationship on the basis of observed movements in money are subject to the usual problem of statistical identification. (An early paper making this point was Teigen, 1964. Another, addressed more explicitly to the work of Friedman and Schwartz, was Tobin, 1970.) Hence what may look like a relationship between movements of prices and income induced by movements in money supply may in reality be movements in money demand induced by movements in prices and income. Further, unless the central bank takes its decisions affecting money supply with no regard for the behaviour of prices and income, the observed relationships may also represent the reactive behaviour of the central bank itself. Indeed, under some plausible accounts of how central banks make monetary policy, relationships of the kind observed in the data would spuriously emerge. (An early paper making this point was Goldfeld and Blinder, 1972.) Still more fundamentally, even if the relationships observed between money and either income or prices actually did represent exactly the kind of causal influence of money supply that was claimed, the attempt by the central bank to exploit such a relationship for policy purposes, once widely recognized, could cause the relationship to change or even break down altogether. (The classic statement of this proposition in a general context is Lucas, 1976. For a formulation in the specific context of monetary policy, see Goodhart, 1984; the original formulation of 'Goodhart's Law' dates to 1975 when this paper was first presented.)

Starting in the mid-1970s, however, and then increasingly so over the next two decades, these questions became moot. Fluctuations in money growth no longer appeared to bear much observed relation to fluctuations in either income or prices over time horizons that were useful for conducting monetary policy, especially after controlling for other obvious information like past movements of income and prices themselves. In parallel, the evidence indicated that money demand was unstable. The presumption of a stable functional relationship between money demand and income or prices had always been central to the claim that money supply was a useful tool for purposes of monetary policy. But now evidence for a stable money demand gave way, in one country after another, to evidence of instability.

The reasons for the disappearance of stable money demand were many, and, at a qualitative level, straightforward to understand. (The empirical money demand literature is a separate subject; for a survey, see Goldfeld and Sichel, 1990. For an earlier survey, written before the instability became so widespread or so evident, see Laidler, 1977, ch. 7.) One reason was changing regulation (in the United States, for example, the removal of the prohibition against banks' paying interest on checkable deposits, and also of the ceilings limiting the interest that banks could pay on interest-bearing savings deposits). Another, in part prompted by regulatory changes, was innovation in the kinds of deposits and deposit-like instruments that banks and other financial institutions offered their customers (for example, money market mutual funds). A third was the electronic revolution, which made various forms of financial transactions ever easier and less costly (for example, shifting funds between checkable and noncheckable accounts). A fourth was rapid globalization, which made businesses in particular, but many individuals as well, increasingly willing to hold assets, and to borrow, in multiple currencies, and to substitute readily among them. But regardless of the precise reasons, which presumably varied from one country to another, money demand no longer appeared to be stable. Nor, in parallel, did the relationships of a simpler form between money and either income or prices that had spurred policy interest in money supply in the first place.

The decline of money supply as a tool of monetary policy

In the absence of empirical evidence of stable money demand, the rationale for the role of money supply as a tool of monetary policy collapsed as well. If money demand is unstable, then even perfectly stable money supply introduces into income and prices the influence of whatever disturbances to the public's money-holding behaviour occur. Under those circumstances, the central bank can do a better job of stabilizing either prices or income, over the short or medium run, by fixing some interest rate and thereby allowing fluctuations in money supply to accommodate fluctuations in money demand that occur for reasons unrelated to movements of income and prices. (The classic paper making this point is Poole, 1970; for a survey of the optimal monetary policy literature along these lines, including the role of money supply behaviour along with money demand, see Friedman, 1990. In the long run, however, there must be at least some absolute nominal element in the policy mechanism to anchor the price level; the interest rate is a relative price, not an absolute price.) Following the increasing evidence of money demand instability, and the collapse of money–price and money–income relationships, that is precisely what an increasing number of central banks have done.

The experience in the Unites States is illustrative. The Federal Reserve System, the US central bank, first began to take explicit note of money supply movements in formulating its monetary policy in 1970. In 1975 the US Congress adopted a resolution requiring the Federal Reserve to announce, in advance, quantitative targets for the growth of key money (and credit) aggregates and, after the fact, to report to the relevant Congressional oversight committees on its success or failure in meeting these targets. In 1979 the Federal Reserve publicly declared an intensified dedication to controlling money growth, with the main focus on the narrow M1 aggregate (consisting primarily of currency and checkable deposits), and adopted new day-to-day operating procedures, centred on the supply of nonborrowed reserves, designed to enhance its ability to achieve control of M1.

The movement towards ever greater emphasis on money supply in US monetary policy took less than a decade; unwinding it took only a little longer. In 1982, the Federal Reserve recognized the increasing instability of demand for M1 and shifted its focus to the broader M2 (including not only currency and demand deposits but also most forms of time and savings deposits). Soon thereafter, it abandoned its operating system based on nonborrowed reserves, in favour of simply setting the federal funds rate (the overnight interest rate on bank reserves) at the level most likely to achieve the desired M2 growth. After 1986 the Federal Reserve stopped setting a target for M1 growth, but continued to do so for M2 and M3 (a still broader aggregate). In the late 1980s evidence based on how the Federal Reserve changed the federal funds rate in response to observed movements of money suggested that the M2 growth target still bore significant influence on US monetary policy. (See, for example, Friedman, 1997; but the empirical literature on this issue is voluminous.)

That influence had mostly dissipated by 1990, and in 1993 the Federal Reserve publicly 'downgraded' the role of its M2 target. Thereafter it continued to set 'ranges' for M2 and M3 growth, but it made clear that these were not actual money growth targets; they were merely 'intended to communicate its expectation as to the growth of these monetary aggregates that would result' under specified assumed conditions. In 1998 the Federal Reserve further confirmed that these ranges were not 'guides to policy'. In 2001 it stopped setting such ranges altogether.

The pattern in most other countries was roughly parallel. By 1980 the use of money supply targets for monetary policy was an idea whose time had come. Most of the major central banks had put such targets at the core of their policymaking process. By 1990 money growth targets were already largely a thing of the past. By the mid-1990s most central banks had either de-emphasized such targets or dropped them altogether. By 2000 it had become standard that central banks carry out monetary policy by setting some short-term interest rate. Money supply mostly disappeared from public discussion, and the professional economics literature largely dispensed with the now-unnecessary apparatus of money demand, money supply, and likewise demand and supply in the market for reserves. (See, for example, Clarida, Gali and Gertler, 1999.)

Implicitly, however, that conceptual apparatus nonetheless stands behind the ability of central banks to set the designated interest rate in the first place. In principle, a central bank – or anyone else with large enough resources, for that matter – could fix the price or yield on any asset simply by buying or selling that asset in sufficient volume to shift the entire market equilibrium, ultimately including the real returns established by the fundamental economic forces of thrift and productivity. (Given the lags with which monetary policy influences price inflation, in the short run the interest rate the central bank is setting is a real interest rate.) But in fact most central banks normally move the interest rate they use for monetary policy purposes by executing only very small transactions, and in an increasing number of cases they do so without executing any transactions at all; often the mere announcement of what the central bank would like the designated rate to be is sufficient.

What gives a central bank the ability to do so is, presumably, market participants' knowledge that the interest rate being set is closely tied to that on the central bank's own liabilities (in systems like that in the United States, it is exactly that rate), and that the central bank can make the supply of those liabilities whatever it chooses. But market equilibrium requires that the demand for those liabilities equal the supply, and the demand for central bank liabilities in turn is an aspect of the same behavioural process that determines the supply of money. Hence money supply remains a part of the story, even if now mostly a hidden one.

BENJAMIN M. FRIEDMAN

See also **inside and outside money; monetary and fiscal policy overview; monetary policy, history of; monetary transmission mechanism; money.**

Bibliography

Cagan, P. 1956. The monetary dynamics of hyperinflation. In *Studies in the Quantity Theory of Money*, ed. M. Friedman. Chicago: University of Chicago Press.

Cagan, P. 1965. *Determinants and Effects of Changes in the Stock of Money, 1875–1960*. New York: NBER.

Clarida, R., Gali, J. and Gertler, M. 1999. The science of monetary policy: a new Keynesian perspective. *Journal of Economic Literature* 37, 1661–1707.

Dewald, W.G. 1963. Free reserves, total reserves and monetary control. *Journal of Political Economy* 71, 141–53.

Friedman, B.M. 1990. Targets and instruments of monetary policy. In *Handbook of Monetary Economics*, vol. 2, ed. B.M. Friedman and F. Hahn. Amsterdam: North-Holland.

Friedman, B.M. 1997. The rise and fall of money growth targets as guidelines for U.S. monetary policy. In *Towards More Effective Monetary Policy*, ed. I. Kuroda. London: Macmillan.

Friedman, M. 1953. The effects of a full-employment policy on economic stability: a formal analysis. In *Essays in Positive Economics*. Chicago: University of Chicago Press.

Friedman, M. 1956. The quantity theory of money: a restatement. In *Studies in the Quantity Theory of Money*. Chicago: University of Chicago Press.

Friedman, M. 1969. The optimum quantity of money. In *The Optimum Quantity of Money and Other Essays*. Chicago: Aldine.

Friedman, M. and Schwartz, A.J. 1963. *A Monetary History of the United States, 1867–1960*. Princeton: Princeton University Press.

Goldfeld, S.M. and Blinder, A.S. 1972. Some implications of endogenous stabilization policy. *Brookings Papers on Economic Activity* 1972(3), 585–644.

Goldfeld, S.M. and Sichel, D.E. 1990. The demand for money. In *Handbook of Monetary Economics*, vol. 2, ed. B.M. Friedman and F. Hahn. Amsterdam: North-Holland.

Goodhart, C. 1984. Problems of monetary management: the U.K. experience. In *Monetary Theory and Practice: The U.K. Experience*. London: Macmillan.

Laidler, D.E. 1977. *The Demand for Money: Theories and Evidence*, 2nd edn. New York: Harper & Row.

Lucas, R.E., Jr. 1976. Econometric policy evaluation: a critique. In *The Phillips Curve and Labor Markets*, ed. K. Brunner and A.H. Meltzer. Amsterdam: North Holland.

Modigliani, F., Rasche, R. and Cooper, J.P. 1970. Central bank policy, the money supply and the short-term rate of interest. *Journal of Money, Credit and Banking* 2, 166–218.

Poole, W. 1970. Optimal choice of monetary policy instruments in a simple stochastic macro model. *Quarterly Journal of Economics* 84, 197–216.

Romer, D. 2006. *Advanced Macroeconomics*, 3rd edn. Boston: McGraw-Hill/Irwin.

Teigen, R.L. 1964. Demand and supply functions for money in the Unites States: some structural estimates. *Econometrica* 32, 467–509.

Tobin, J. 1970. Money and income: post hoc ergo propter hoc? *Quarterly Journal of Economics* 84, 301–17.

Woodford, M. 2003. *Interest and Prices: Foundations of a Theory of Monetary Policy*. Princeton: Princeton University Press.

neutrality of money

'Neutrality of money' is a shorthand expression for the basic quantity-theory proposition that it is only the level of prices in an economy, and not the level of its real outputs, that is affected by the quantity of money which circulates in it. Thus the notion – though not the term – goes back to early statements of the quantity theory, such as the classic one by David Hume in his 1752 essays 'Of Money', 'Of Interest' and 'Of the Balance of Trade'. At that time the notion also served as one of the arguments against the mercantilist doctrine that the wealth of a nation was to be measured by the quantity of gold (which in 18th-century England constituted a – if not the – major form of metallic money: Feaveryear, 1963, p. 158) that it possessed. The term itself is much more recent. Though attributed by Hayek (1935, pp. 129–31) to Wicksell, it is actually due to continental economists in the late 1920s and early 1930s to whom Hayek also refers (see 1935, pp. 129–31; see also Patinkin and Steiger, 1988).

1. The rigorous demonstration of, the neutrality of money is based on the critical assumption that individuals are free of 'money illusion'. An individual is said to suffer from such an illusion if he changes his economic behaviour when a currency conversion takes place: when, for example (as in Israel in 1985), a new monetary unit – the 'new shekel' – is introduced in circulation and declared to be equivalent to 1,000 old shekels.

It can be shown (Patinkin, 1965) that an illusion-free individual in an economy with borrowing who maximizes utility subject to his budget constraint will have demand functions which depend on relative prices, the rate of interest, and the real value of his initial wealth – which consists of physical capital, bond holdings, and money balances. That is, the demand of this representative individual for the jth good, d_j, is described by the function

$$d_j = f_j(p_1/p, \ldots, p_{n-2}/p, r, K_0 + B_0/p + M_0/p)(j = 1, \ldots, n - 2),$$

where the p_j are the respective money (or absolute) prices of the $n - 2$ goods; p is the average price level as defined by $p = \sum_j w_j p_j$ where the w_j are fixed weights; r is the rate of interest; K_0 is physical capital, B_0 is the initial nominal value of bond holdings (which, for a debtor, is negative), and M_0 is the initial quantity of money. Thus when the new shekel is introduced in circulation, the price of each good in terms of this shekel (and hence the general price level), the terms of indebtedness, and the nominal quantity of initial money holdings are respectively reduced to 1/1,000th of what they were before; hence relative prices and the real value of initial wealth are unaffected; hence so are the amounts demanded of each good.

Mathematically, the foregoing property of the demand functions is described by the statement that these functions are homogeneous of degree zero in the money prices *and* in the initial quantity of financial assets, including money. Accordingly, the absence of money illusion is sometimes referred to as the homogeneity property of the demand functions. (For the necessary and sufficient conditions that must be satisfied by the utility function in order to generate such illusion-free demand functions, see Howitt and Patinkin, 1980.) This homogeneity property is to be sharply distinguished from what the earlier literature denoted as the 'homogeneity postulate', by which it meant the invariance of demand functions with respect to an equiproportionate change in money prices alone, and which invariance it erroneously regarded as the condition for the absence of money illusion and hence for the neutrality of money (Leontief, 1936, p. 192; Modigliani, 1944, pp. 214–15): for even in the case of an individual who is neither debtor nor creditor, such a change affects the real value of his initial money balances, hence is not analogous to a change in the monetary unit, and hence – by virtue of the real-balance effect – will generally lead him to change the amounts he demands of the various goods.

For a closed economy, the aggregate value of B_0 is obviously zero, for to each creditor there corresponds a debtor. For simplicity, we can also consider the amount of physical capital, K_0, to remain constant. Disregarding distribution effects, the demand functions of the economy as a whole for the $n-2$ goods can then be represented by

$$D_j = F_j(p_1/p, \ldots, p_{n-2}/p, r, M_0/p)(j = 1, \ldots, n-2)$$

and the corresponding supply functions by

$$S_j = G_j(p_1/p, \ldots, p_{n-2}/p, r).$$

The general-equilibrium system of the economy is then

$$
\begin{vmatrix}
F_1(p_1/p, \ldots, p_{n-2}/p, r, M_0/p) = G_1(p_1/p, \ldots, p_{n-2}/p, r) \\
\vdots \qquad \vdots \qquad \vdots \\
F_{n-2}(p_1/p, \ldots, p_{n-2}/p, r, M_0/p) = G_{n-2}(p_1/p, \ldots, p_{n-2}/p, r) \\
F_{n-1}(p_1/p, \ldots, p_{n-2}/p, r, M_0/p) = 0 \\
F_n(p_1/p, \ldots, p_{n-2}/p, r, M_0/p) = M_0/p.
\end{vmatrix}
$$

The $(n-1)$st equation is for real bond holdings, whose aggregate net value is (as already noted) zero; and the nth equation is for real money balances. Assume that this system has a unique equilibrium solution with money prices $p_1^0, \ldots, p_{n-2}^0, p^0$ and the rate of interest r^0, and that the economy is initially at this position. Let the quantity of money now be changed to kM_0, where k is some positive constant. From the preceding system of equations we can immediately see that (on the further assumption that the system is stable) the economy will reach a new equilibrium position with money prices $kp_1^0, \ldots, kp_{n-2}^0, kp^0$ and an unchanged rate of interest r^0. (Clearly, this conclusion would continue to hold if the supply functions $G_j(\ )$ were also dependent on M_0/p.) Thus the increased quantity of money does not affect any of the real variables of the system, namely, relative prices, the rate of interest, the real value of money balances, and hence the respective outputs of the $n-2$ goods. In brief, money is neutral: or in the picturesque phrase which Robertson (1922, p. 1) apparently coined, money is a veil. (For empirical studies, see Lucas, 1980, and Lothian, 1985.)

Furthermore, Archibald and Lipsey (1958) have shown that if the initial equilibrium exists not only with respect to the economy as a whole, but also with respect to each and every individual in it (which, inter alia, means that each individual was initially holding his optimum quantity of money), then this neutrality will obtain in the long run even if one does take account of distribution effects. That is, even if one takes account of differences in tastes, endowments, and hence individual demand functions, an increase in the quantity of money, no matter how distributed among individuals, will in the long run cause an equiproportionate increase in prices and leave the rate of interest invariant. This conclusion in turn follows from the fact that the sequence of short-run equilibria generated by the increase in the quantity of money will in the long run redistribute this quantity in a way that results in an equiproportionate increase in the money holdings of each individual, relative to his holdings in the initial equilibrium position (see also Patinkin, 1965, pp. 50–9).

It should also be noted that the preceding analysis has implicitly assumed a unitary elasticity of expectations with respect to future prices, so that neutrality is not disturbed by substitution between present and future commodities.

2. The conclusions of the foregoing analysis are clearly those of long-run comparative-statics analysis. It was this fact that led Keynes – even in his quantity-theory period as represented by his *Tract on Monetary Reform* (1923) – to disparage their policy implications with the famous remark that *'in the long run* we are all dead' (1923, p. 80, italics in original). It should therefore be emphasized that at the same time they demonstrated the long-run neutrality of money, quantity theorists (including Keynes of the *Tract*) also emphasized its non-neutrality in the short run (Patinkin, 1972a). Thus Hume emphasized that prices do not immediately rise proportionately to the increased quantity of money and that in the intervening period this stimulates production. In Hume's words:

> it is of no manner of consequence, with regard to the domestic happiness of a state, whether money be in a greater or less quantity. The good policy of the magistrate consists only in keeping it, if possible, still increasing; because, by that means, he keeps alive a spirit of industry in the nation … (1752, pp. 39–40)

Hume's emphasis on the irrelevance of the absolute level of the money supply (and hence of money prices) in contrast with the significance of the rate of change of this level was also made by later quantity-theorists. Some of them stressed the stimulating effects of rising prices on 'business confidence' and hence economic activity. A more frequent explanation of the short-run non-neutrality of money was in terms of the shift in the distribution of real income as between creditors and debtors generated by a changing price level. Of particular importance was the danger that a sharply declining price level would increase the number of bankruptcies among debtors, with all its adverse repercussions on the economy. Another source of non-neutrality was the fact that individual prices do not change at the same rate in response to a monetary change. Thus if after a monetary decrease, wage rigidities cause the decline in wages to lag behind that of product prices, the resulting increase in the real wage rate would generate unemployment; conversely, the lag of wages in the case of an inflation would increase profits and hence stimulate production. This consideration led some quantity-theorists to deny even the long-run neutrality of money on the grounds that profit-recipients had a higher tendency to save than wage-earners, so that the shift in income in favour of profits would increase savings, and that these would lead to an increase in the real stock of physical capital in the economy, and hence to a decline in the long-run rate of interest.

For Irving Fisher, the important lag was that of the nominal rate of interest behind the rate of (say) inflation generated by a monetary increase. In particular, because of the lack of perfect foresight on the part of savers (who are the lenders), the nominal rate does not rise sufficiently to offset this inflation; and the resulting decline in the real rate of interest causes entrepreneurs to increase their borrowings, hence investments and economic activity in general. Conversely, when prices decline, corresponding misperceptions cause an increase in the real rate of interest and hence a decline in economic activity. Indeed, Fisher (1913, ch. 4) based his whole theory of the business cycle on this process: the cycle was for him 'the dance of the dollar' (Fisher, 1923).

The greatly increased importance of income and capital-gains taxation since Fisher's time is the background of the present-day view – much stressed by Feldstein (1982, and references there cited) – that inflation would have real effects on the economy even if there were perfect foresight, so that the nominal rate fully adjusted itself to the rate of inflation, leaving the real rate of interest unchanged. This is particularly true for the taxation of income from capital, with the simplest example being the increased tax burden on corporations generated by the calculation of depreciation expenses on the basis of historical (as distinct from replacement) costs in an inflationary economy (see also Birati and Cukierman, 1979). This is a specific instance of the short-run non-neutrality of money generated by the existence of a tax structure formulated in nominal terms (as is the case with, for example, specific taxes and income-tax brackets) which are generally adjusted to the rate of inflation only after a lag.

Short-run non-neutrality is a basic feature of Keynesian monetary theory and stems from the contention that in a situation of unemployment, prices will not rise proportionately to the increased quantity of money, and that the resulting increase in the real quantity of money will cause a decline in the rate of interest and hence an increase in the volume of investment and the level of national income. The short-run non-neutrality of money is, however, also a basic tenet of today's monetarists, who contend that though the long-run effect of a change in the quantity of money is primarily on prices, its short-run effect is primarily on output. In Friedman's words: 'In the short run, which may be as much as five or ten years, monetary changes affect primarily output. Over decades, on the other hand, the rate of monetary growth affects primarily prices' (Friedman, 1970, pp. 23–4).

This non-neutrality has been rationalized by Lucas (1972) in terms of the individual's inability to determine whether a change in the price of a good with which he is particularly concerned (for example labour, in the case of a wage-earner) is a change only in the price of that good (in which case it represents a change in its relative price, which calls for a quantity adjustment) or is part of a general change in prices which does not affect relative prices. In accordance with this approach, and under the assumption that markets always clear, it has also been claimed that only an unanticipated change in the quantity of money will have real effects; for an anticipated one will be expected by the individual to affect all prices proportionately (Lucas, 1975; Barro, 1976). A far-reaching corollary of this claim is that if, in accordance with the assumption of rational expectations, the public anticipates the actions that government will carry out within the framework of its proclaimed monetary policy, then this policy too will be neutral: that is, the systematic component of monetary policy will not affect any of the real variables of the system (cf. McCallum, 1980 and references there cited). Thus under these circumstances even the short-run Phillips curve is – from the viewpoint of systematic monetary policy – vertical.

Empirical support for the claim that only unanticipated monetary changes will have real effects was at first provided by Sargent (1976) and Barro (1978). Contrary conclusions were, however, reached in subsequent empirical studies by Fischer (1980), Boschen and Grossman (1982), Gordon (1982), Mishkin (1982; 1983) and Cecchetti (1986). These differing conclusions stem from different views about the respective ways to estimate (1) that part of a monetary change that is anticipated and/or (2) the extent of the time lags that must be taken account of in measuring the effects of a monetary change on output. In any event, the weight of opinion today is that both anticipated and unanticipated changes in the money supply have short-term real effects. To the extent that anticipated changes have such effects, this can be interpreted either as reflecting the influence of nominally formulated elements (for example the aforementioned tax structure, or long-term wage contracts – Fischer, 1977) in an economy functioning in accordance with the hypothesis of rational expectations cum market-clearing; or, alternatively, it can be interpreted as a refutation of this hypothesis in part or in whole. Thus once again we are confronted with *la condition scientifique* of our discipline: its inability in all too many cases to reach definitive conclusions about theoretical questions on the basis of empirical studies, an inability which increases directly with the political significance of the question at issue.

3. Neoclassical quantity-theorists contended that a shift in the demand curve for money would also have a long-run neutral effect on the economy. Thus consider the Cambridge cash-balance equation, $M = KPY$, where Y is the real volume of expenditures and K is that proportion of his planned money expenditures, PY, which the individual wishes to hold in the form of money. Assume that the economy is in equilibrium with a fixed quantity of money M_0 and price level P_0. Let there now take place a positive shift in the demand for money – that is, an increase in K. Because of the budget constraint, this must be accompanied by a negative shift in the demand for goods. Consequently, the price level P will decline until equilibrium is reestablished

with the same nominal quantity of money, M_0, but at a lower price level, $P_1 < P_0$. Thus the automatic functioning of the market will in the long run generate the additional quantity of real balances that individuals wish to hold, without affecting the output of goods.

This neutrality can also be demonstrated in terms of the general-equilibrium system presented above. In particular, if we assume that the increased demand for money is accompanied by a symmetric decrease in the demand for all other goods and for bonds, then a new equilibrium will be established with all money prices reduced in the same proportion, and with an unchanged rate of interest; correspondingly, the respective outputs of goods are also unchanged. In Keynesian monetary theory, however, the increased demand for money is assumed to be solely at the expense of bond holdings: this, after all, is an implication of Keynes's theory of liquidity preference. Such a shift in liquidity preference will accordingly not be neutral in its effects; instead, it will cause an increase in the rate of interest with consequent effects on investment and other real variables of the system (Patinkin, 1965, chs VIII:5 and X:4).

In an analogous manner, a change in the proportions between inside and outside money generated by a change in the currency/deposit ratio and/or the bank-reserve/deposit ratio will not be neutral in its effects (Gurley and Shaw, 1960, pp. 231–6). It should, however, be emphasized that if the demand and supply functions of the financial sector are also characterized by absence of money illusion, then an increase in outside money will leave these ratios unchanged and hence be neutral (Patinkin, 1965, ch. XII: 5–6).

So far, our concern has implicitly been an increase in the quantity of money generated by a one-time government deficit, after which the government returns to a balanced budget. This results in an initial net increase in the total of financial assets in the economy and is thus the real-world analytical counterpart of an increase in the quantity of money generated by the proverbial helicopter dropping down money from the skies. If, however, the monetary increase is generated by an open-market purchase of government bonds (so that initially there is no change in total financial assets), and if there is a real-balance effect in the commodity market, then, as Metzler (1951) showed in a classic article, the equilibrium rate of interest will decline, so that money will not be neutral in its effects. If, however, individuals fully anticipate and discount the future stream of tax payments needed to service the government bonds (in which case these bonds are not part of net wealth), neutrality will obtain in this case too (Patinkin, 1965, ch. XII:4).

4. The discussion until this point has dealt almost entirely with the neutrality of a once-and-for-all increase in the quantity of money in a stationary economy. An analogous question arises with reference to the long-run neutrality of a change in the rate of growth of the money supply in a growing economy – in which context the notion is referred to as 'superneutrality'. Thus consider an economy in steady-state equilibrium whose population is growing at the rate n. Assume that the nominal quantity of money is growing at a faster rate, $\mu = \dot{M}/M$ so that (in order to maintain the constant level of per-capita real money balances that is one of the characteristics of

such a steady state) prices rise at the constant rate $\pi = \mu - n$. Money is said to be superneutral if (say) an increase in the steady-state rate of its expansion, and hence in the corresponding rate of inflation, will not affect any of the steady-state real variables in the system, with the exception of per-capita real-balances: that is, per-capita capital, k; per-capita output, y; and the real rate of interest, r; equal to the marginal productivity of capital. On the other hand, because of the higher costs of holding real balances – in terms of loss of purchasing power, or, alternatively, in terms of the forgone higher nominal rate of interest, i, generated by the increased rate of inflation – the steady-state per capita real value of these balances, m, should generally be expected to decrease.

As already indicated, for Irving Fisher (1907, ch. 5; 1913, pp. 59–60; 1930, pp. 43–4) it was only the absence of perfect foresight which prevented such superneutrality from obtaining: for were such foresight to exist, the nominal rate of interest would simply increase so as to compensate for the inflation and thus leave the real rate of interest (which, under the assumption of continuous compounding, equals $i - \pi$) unchanged. Fisher, however, did not take account of the possible effects of the way the increased amount of money is injected into the economy and/or the possible effects of the resulting decrease in real balances on other markets. Thus by assuming that the government increases the quantity of money in the economy by distributing it to households and thereby increasing their disposable income, Tobin (1965; 1967) – in a generalization of the Solow (1956) growth model to a money economy – showed that a higher rate of inflation will generally cause individuals to change the composition of their asset portfolios by shifting out of real money balances and into physical capital, thus increasing the steady-state values of k and y – and hence (by the law of diminishing returns) decreasing that of r – so that superneutrality does not obtain.

Tobin's analysis assumes a constant savings ratio. In a critique of this analysis, Levhari and Patinkin (1968) showed inter alia that if instead this ratio is assumed to depend positively on the respective rates of return on capital and on real money balances – that is, on the real rate of interest and on the rate of deflation – then an increase in the rate of inflation might decrease steady-state savings and hence k, thus causing an increase in the real rate of interest. Similarly, if real money balances were explicitly introduced into the production function, an increase in the rate of inflation might so decrease these balances as to decrease steady-state per-capita output and hence savings sufficiently to offset the positive substitution effect on k, thus generating a decrease in the latter.

Patinkin (1972b) analysed superneutrality by means of an IS–LM model generalized to a full employment economy with a real-balance effect in the commodity market (the following largely reproduces the relevant material in this reference). As in Solow (1956), the economy is assumed to have a linearly homogeneous production function, $Y = F(K, L)$, where Y is output, K capital, and L labour, with the labour force assumed to be growing at the exogenous rate n. The intensive form of this function is then $y = f(k)$ and its derivative, $f'(k)$ is accordingly the marginal productivity of capital, so that the equilibrium real rate of interest is

$r = f'(k)$ Following Mundell (1963; 1965), the crucial assumption of this model is that whereas investment and saving (and hence consumption) decisions depend upon the real rate of interest, $r = i - \pi$, the decision with respect to the amount of real money balances to hold depends on the nominal rate of interest, $i-$ for the alternative cost of holding money instead of a bond is precisely this rate. The same is true if we measure this cost in terms of the alternative of holding physical capital: for the total yield on this capital is its marginal product (equal in equilibrium to the real rate of interest) *plus* the capital gain generated by the price change (π): that is, it is $r + \pi = i$. Alternatively, if we measure rates of return in real terms, the rate of return on money balances is $-\pi$ and that on physical capital r; hence the alternative cost of holding money is the difference between these two rates, or $r - (-\pi) = i$.

Consider now the commodity market. Let E represent the aggregate real demand for consumption and investment commodities combined. For simplicity, assume that this demand is a certain proportion, α, of total real income, Y. Assume further that this proportion depends inversely on the real rate of interest and directly on the ratio of real money balances, M/p, to physical capital, K. The second dependence is a type of real-balance effect, reflecting the assumption that the greater the ratio of real money balances to physical capital in the portfolios of individuals, the more they will tend (for any given level of income) to shift out of money and into commodities. The equilibrium condition in the commodity market is then represented by

$$\alpha(i - \pi, (M/p)/K) \cdot Y = Y. \tag{1}$$

By assumption, $\alpha_1(\cdot)$ is negative and $\alpha_2(\cdot)$ positive, where $\alpha_1(\alpha_2)$ is the partial derivative of $\alpha(\cdot)$ with respect to its first (second) argument.

Consider now the money market. Following Tobin (1965, p. 679), assume that the demand in this market depends on the volume of physical capital and the nominal rate of interest. More specifically, assume that the demand for money is a certain proportion, λ of physical capital. Thus the larger K, the greater (other things equal) the total portfolio of the individuals, hence the greater the demand for money: this can be designated as the scale or wealth effect of the portfolio. Assume further that the proportion λ depends inversely on the nominal rate of interest. That is, the higher this rate, the smaller the proportion of money relative to physical capital which individuals wish to hold in their portfolios: this can be designated as the composition or substitution effect. The equilibrium condition in the money market is then

$$\lambda(i) \cdot K = M/p \tag{2}$$

where by assumption the derivative $\lambda'(\cdot)$ is negative.

Dividing equations (1) and (2) through by Y and K, respectively – and transforming them into per capita form – we then obtain the equations

$$\alpha(i - \pi, m/k) = 1 \tag{3}$$

$$\lambda(i) = m/k. \tag{4}$$

In the steady state,

$$\mu = \pi + n. \tag{5}$$

Since μ and n are both assumed to be exogenously determined, the same can be said for the steady-state value of π. Thus in steady states, equations (3) and (4) can be considered as a system of two equations in the two endogenous variables i and m/k, and in the exogenous variable π. On the assumption of the solubility of these equations, the specific value of k (and hence m) can then be determined by making use of the additional equilibrium condition that the marginal productivity of capital equals the real rate of interest, or,

$$f'(k) = i - \pi. \tag{6}$$

In accordance with the usual assumption of diminishing marginal productivity, we also have

$$f''(k) < 0. \tag{7}$$

The solution of system (3)–(4) can be presented diagrammatically in terms of Figure 1. The curve CC represents the locus of points of equilibrium in the commodity market for a given value of π. Its positive slope reflects the assumption made above about the respective influences of the real rate of interest $(i-\pi)$ and of the real-balance effect (as represented by m/k) on α. Namely, a (say) increase in i increases the real rate of interest and thus tends to decrease α: hence the ratio m/k must increase in order to generate a compensating increase in α and thus restore equilibrium to the commodity

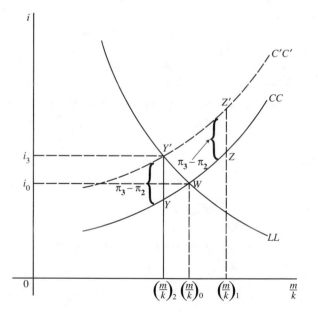

Figure 1

market. On the other hand, LL – the locus of points of equilibriums in the money market – must be negatively sloped: an increase in the supply of money and hence in m/k must be offset by a corresponding increase in the demand for money, which means that i must decline. The intersection of the two curves at W thus determines the steady-state position of the economy.

Assume for simplicity that the given value of π for which CC and LL are drawn is $\pi = \pi_2 > 0$, corresponding to the rate of monetary expansion μ_2. Assume now that this rate is exogenously increased to $\mu = \mu_3$, so that (by (5)) the steady-state value of π is increased accordingly to $\pi_3 = \mu_3 - n > \pi_2$. From the fact that π does not appear in (4), it is clear that LL remains invariant under this change. On the other hand, the curve CC must shift upwards in a parallel fashion by the distance $\pi_3 - \pi_2$: for at (say) the point Z' on the curve $C'C'$ so constructed, the money/capital ratio m/k and the real rate of interest $i - \pi$ are the same as they were at point Z on the original curve CC; hence Z' too must be a position of equilibrium in the commodity market.

We can therefore conclude from Figure 1 that the increase in the rate of monetary expansion (and hence rate of inflation) shifts the steady-state position of the economy from W to Y'. From the construction of $C'C'$ it is also clear that the real rate of interest at Y' is $r_3 = i_3 - \pi_3$ which is less than the real rate at W, namely, $r_0 = i_0 - \pi_2$. Thus the policy of increasing the rate of inflation decreases the steady-state value of the real rate of interest, and also the money/capital ratio.

Because of the diminishing marginal productivity of capital, the decline in r implies that k has increased. Thus the fact that m/k has declined does not necessarily imply that m has declined. This indeterminacy reflects the two opposing influences operating on m reflected in eq. (2), rewritten here in the per capita form as

$$\lambda(i) \cdot k = m. \tag{8}$$

To use the terminology indicated above, the increased inflation increases the steady-state stock of physical capital, and thus exerts a positive wealth effect on the quantity of real-money balances demanded. At the same time, the increased inflation means that the alternative cost of holding money balances (for a given level of k and hence r) has increased, and this exerts a negative substitution effect on the demand for these balances; that is, individuals will tend to shift out of money and into capital. Thus the final effect on m depends on the relative strength of these two forces. As is, however, generally assumed in economic theory, we shall assume that the substitution effect dominates, so that an increase in π decreases m.

We now note that the only exogenous variable which appears in system (3)–(5) is the rate of change of the money supply, as represented by its steady-state surrogate, $\pi = \mu - n$. In contrast, the absolute quantity of money, M, does not appear. It follows that once-and-for-all changes in M (after which the money supply continues to grow at the same rate) will not affect the steady-state values of m, k, and i as determined by the foregoing system for a given value of π. In brief, system (3)–(5) continues to reflect the neutrality of money. On the other hand, because of the Keynesian-like interdependence between the commodity and money markets, the system is not superneutral.

Note that in the absence of this interdependence, the system would also be superneutral. This would be the case either if the demand for commodities depended only on the real rate of interest, and not on m/k (that is if there were no real-balance effect); or if the demand for money depended only on k, and not on the nominal rate of interest – an unrealistic assumption, particularly in inflationary situations which cause this rate to increase greatly.

The first of these cases is analogous to the dichotimized case of stationary macroeconomic models (cf. Patinkin, 1965, pp. 242, 251 (n.19), and 297–8). It would be represented in Figure 1 by a CC curve which was horizontal to the abscissa. Correspondingly, the upward shift generated by the rate of inflation would cause the new CC curve to intersect the unchanged LL curve at a money rate of interest which was $\pi_3 - \pi_2$ greater than the original one, and hence at a real rate of interest (and hence value of k) which was unchanged; the value of m, however, would unequivocally decline. The second of these cases would be represented by a vertical LL curve. Hence the upward parallel shift in the CC curve generated by inflation would once again shift the intersection point to one which represented an unchanged real rate of interest. In this case (which, as already noted, is an unrealistic one) the value of m also remains unchanged.

5. A common characteristic of the foregoing money-and-growth models is that their respective savings functions are postulated and not derived from utility maximization. An analysis which does derive consumption (and hence savings) behaviour from such maximization was presented by Sidrauski (1967) in an influential article. As before, consider an economy growing at the constant rate n with a linearly homogeneous production function having the intensive form $y = f(k)$. Assume now that the representative individual of this economy is infinitely lived with a utility function which depends on consumption and real balances, and that he maximizes the discounted value of this function over infinite time, using the constant subjective rate of time preference, q. Under these assumptions, Sidrauski shows that money is superneutral.

As Sidrauski is fully aware, this conclusion follows from the form of his production function together with his assumption of a constant rate of time preference; for this fixes the steady-state real rate of interest at $r = q + n = f'(k)$, which determines the steady-state value of k and hence of r. If, however, the production function depends also on real balances – say, $y = g(k, m)$ – then this superneutrality no longer obtains. For the necessary equality between the marginal productivity of capital and $q + n$ in this case is expressed by the equation $g_k(k, m) = q + n$ (where $g_k(k, m)$ is the partial derivative with respect to k), which no longer fixes the value of k (Levhari and Patinkin, 1968, p. 234). In an analogous argument, Brock (1974) showed that if the individual's utility function depends also on leisure, then an increase in the rate of inflation will affect his demand for leisure, which means that it will affect his supply of labour (that is, labour *per capita*). Hence even though (in accordance with Sidrauski's argument) the increased rate of inflation will not affect the steady-state values of r, k (that is, capital per *labour-input*), and y (that is output per *labour-input*), it will affect the respective amounts of labour and capital *per capita* and hence output *per capita* – so that it will not be superneutral. Needless to say, Sidrauski's results will also not obtain if the rate of time preference is not constant.

6. The conclusion that can be drawn from this discussion is that whereas there is a firm theoretical basis for attributing long-run neutrality to money (but see Gale, 1982, pp. 7–58, and Grandmont, 1983, pp. 38–45, 91–5), there is no such basis for long-run superneutrality: for changes in the rate of growth of the nominal money supply and hence in the rate of inflation generally cause changes in the long-run equilibrium level of real balances; and if there are enough avenues of substitution between these balances and other real variables in the system (viz., commodities, physical capital, leisure), then the long-run equilibrium levels of these variables will also be affected. An exception to this generalization would obtain if money were to earn a rate of interest which varied one-to-one with the rate of inflation, so that the alternative cost of holding money balances would not be affected by changes in the latter rate; but though it is generally true that interest (though not necessarily at the foregoing rate) will eventually be paid on the inside money (that is bank deposits) of economies characterized by significant long-run inflation, this is not the case for the outside money which is a necessary (though in modern times quantitatively relatively small) component of any monetary system.

The discussion to this point has treated the economy's output as a single homogeneous quantity. A more detailed analysis which considers the sectoral composition of this output yields another manifestation of the absence of superneutrality. In particular, it is a commonplace that the higher the rate of inflation, the higher the so-called 'shoe-leather costs' of running to and from the banks and other financial institutions in order to carry out economic activity with smaller real money balances. In the case of households, the resulting loss of leisure is denoted as the 'welfare costs of inflation' as measured by the loss of consumers' surplus: that is, by the reduction in the triangular area under the demand curve for real money balances (cf. Bailey, 1956). In the case of businesses, the costs of inflation take the concrete form of the costs of the additional time and efforts devoted to managing the cash flow. What must now be emphasized is that the obverse side of the additional efforts of both households and businesses is the additional resources that must be diverted to the financial sector of the economy in order to enable it to meet the increased demand for its services. Thus the higher the rate of inflation, the higher (say) the proportion of the labour force of an economy employed in its financial sector as opposed to its 'real' sectors, and hence the smaller its 'real' output. This is a phenomenon that has been observed in economies with two- and especially three-digit inflation (cf. Kleiman, 1984 on the Israeli experience). Viewing the phenomenon in this way implicitly assumes that the services of the financial sector are not final products (which are a component of net national product) but 'intermediate products', whose function it is 'to eliminate friction in the productive system' and which accordingly are 'not net contributions to ultimate consumption' (Kuznets, 1951, p. 162; see also Kuznets, 1941, pp. 34–45).

DON PATINKIN

See also **quantity theory of money.**

Bibliography

Archibald, G.C. and Lipsey, R.G. 1958. Monetary and value theory: a critique of Lange and Patinkin. *Review of Economic Studies* 28, 50–6.

Bailey, M.J. 1956. The welfare cost of inflationary finance. *Journal of Political Economy* 64, 93–110.

Barro, R.J. 1976. Rational expectations and the role of monetary policy. *Journal of Monetary Economics* 2, 1–32.

Barro, R.J. 1978. Unanticipated money, output, and the price level in the United States. *Journal of Political Economy* 86, 549–80.

Birati, A. and Cukierman, A. 1979. The redistributive effects of inflation and of the introduction of a real tax system in the US bond market. *Journal of Public Economics* 12, 125–39.

Boschen, J.F. and Grossman, H.I. 1982. Tests of equilibrium macroeconomics using contemporaneous monetary data. *Journal of Monetary Economics* 10, 309–33.

Brock, W.A. 1974. Money and growth: the case of long run perfect foresight. *International Economic Review* 15, 750–77.

Cecchetti, S.G. 1986. Testing short-run neutrality. *Journal of Monetary Economics* 17, 409–23.

Feaveryear, A. 1963. *The Pound Sterling: A History of English Money.* 2nd edn, revised by E.V. Morgan. Oxford: Clarendon Press.

Feldstein, M. 1982. Inflation, capital taxation, and monetary policy. In *Inflation: Causes and Effects*, ed. R.E. Hall. Chicago: University of Chicago Press.

Fischer, S. 1977. Long-term contracts, rational expectations, and the optimal money supply rule. *Journal of Political Economy* 85, 191–205.

Fischer, S. 1980. On activist monetary policy with rational expectations. In *Rational Expectations and Economic Policy*, ed. S. Fischer. Chicago: University of Chicago Press.

Fisher, I. 1907. *The Rate of Interest.* New York: Macmillan.

Fisher, I. 1913. *The Purchasing Power of Money: Its Determination and Relation to Credit Interest and Crises.* Rev. edn. New York: Macmillan. Reprinted, New York: Augustus M. Kelley, 1963.

Fisher, I. 1923. The business cycle largely a 'Dance of the Dollar'. *Journal of the American Statistical Association* 18, 1024–8.

Fisher, I. 1930. *The Theory of Interest.* New York: Macmillan. Reprinted, New York: Kelley and Millman, 1954.

Friedman, M. 1970. *The Counter-Revolution in Monetary Theory.* London: Institute of Economic Affairs.

Gale, D. 1982. *Money: in Equilibrium.* Cambridge: Cambridge University Press.

Gordon, R.J. 1982. Price inertia and policy ineffectiveness in the United States, 1890–1980. *Journal of Political Economy* 90, 1087–117.

Grandmont, J.-M. 1983. *Money and Value: a Reconsideration of Classical and Neoclassical Monetary Theories.* New York: Cambridge University Press.

Gurley, J.G. and Shaw, E.S. 1960. *Money in a Theory of Finance.* Washington, DC: Brookings Institution.

Hayek, F.A. 1935. *Prices and Production.* 2nd edn. London: Routledge and Kegan Paul.

Howitt, P. and Patinkin, D. 1980. Utility function transformations and money illusion: comments. *American Economic Review* 70, 819–22, 826–8.

Hume, D. 1752. 'Of money', 'Of interest' and 'Of the balance of trade'. As reprinted in D. Hume, *Writings on Economics*, ed. E. Rotwein, Wisconsin: University of Wisconsin Press, 1970.

Keynes, J.M. 1923. *A Tract on Monetary Reform*. London: Macmillan.

Kleiman, E. 1984. Alut ha-inflatzya [The costs of inflation]. *Rivon Le-kalkalah* [Economic Quarterly] 30, 859–64.

Kuznets, S. 1941. *National Income and its Composition, 1919–1938*. New York: National Bureau of Economic Research.

Kuznets, S. 1951. National income and industrial structure. *Proceedings of the International Statistical Conferences 1947* 5, 205–39. As reprinted in S. Kuznets, *Economic Change*, London: William Heinemann, 1954.

Leontief, W. 1936. The fundamental assumption of Mr Keynes' monetary theory of unemployment. *Quarterly Journal of Economics* 51, 192–7.

Levhari, D. and Patinkin, D. 1968. The role of money in a simple growth model. *American Economic Review* 58, 713–53. As reprinted in Patinkin (1972c), 205–42.

Lothian, J.R. 1985. Equilibrium relationships between money and other economic variables. *American Economic Review* 75, 828–35.

Lucas, R.E., Jr. 1972. Expectations and the neutrality of money. *Journal of Economic Theory* 4, 103–24. As reprinted in Lucas (1981), 66–89.

Lucas, R.E., Jr. 1975. An equilibrium model of the business cycle. *Journal of Political Economy* 83, 1113–44. As reprinted in Lucas (1981), 179–214.

Lucas, R.E., Jr. 1980. Two illustrations of the quantity theory of money. *American Economic Review* 70, 1005–14.

Lucas, R.E., Jr. 1981. *Studies in Business Cycle Theory*. Cambridge, MA: MIT Press.

McCallum, B.T. 1980. Rational expectations and macroeconomic stabilization policy: an overview. *Journal of Money, Credit, and Banking* 12, 716–46.

Metzler, L.A. 1951. Wealth, saving and the rate of interest. *Journal of Political Economy* 59, 93–116.

Mishkin, F.S. 1982. Does anticipated monetary policy matter? An econometric investigation. *Journal of Political Economy* 90, 22–51.

Mishkin, F.S. 1983. *A Rational Expectations Approach to Macroeconometrics*. Chicago: University of Chicago Press.

Modigliani, F. 1944. Liquidity preference and the theory of interest and money. *Econometrica* 12, 45–88. As reprinted in American Economic Association, *Readings in Monetary Theory*, Philadelphia: Blakiston for the American Economic Association, 1951.

Mundell, R.A. 1963. Inflation and real interest. *Journal of Political Economy* 71, 280–3.

Mundell, R.A. 1965. A fallacy in the interpretation of macroeconomic equilibrium. *Journal of Political Economy* 73, 61–6.

Patinkin, D. 1965. *Money, Interest, and Prices*. 2nd edn. New York: Harper & Row.

Patinkin, D. 1972a. On the short-run non-neutrality of money in the quantity theory. *Banca Nazionale del Lavoro Quarterly Review* 100, 3–22.

Patinkin, D. 1972b. Money and growth in a Keynesian full-employment model. In Patinkin (1972c).

Patinkin, D. 1972c. *Studies in Monetary Economics*. New York: Harper & Row.

Patinkin, D. and Steiger, O. 1988. On the terms 'neutrality of money' and 'veil of money'. *Scandinavian Journal of Economics* 90.

Robertson, D.H. 1922. *Money*. Cambridge: Cambridge University Press.

Sargent, T.J. 1976. A classical macroeconometric model for the United States. *Journal of Political Economy* 84, 207–37.

Sidrauski, M. 1967. Rational choice and patterns of growth in a monetary economy. *American Economic Review* 57, 534–44.

Solow, R.M. 1956. A contribution to the theory of economic growth. *Quarterly Journal of Economics* 70, 65–94.

Tobin, J. 1965. Money and economic growth. *Econometrica* 33, 671–84.

Tobin, J. 1967. The neutrality of money in growth models: a comment. *Economica* 34, 69–72.

optimal fiscal and monetary policy (with commitment)

The Ramsey approach to the optimal taxation

'Ramsey approach to optimal taxation' is the solution to the problem of choosing optimal taxes and transfers given that only distortionary tax instruments are available.

A starting point of a Ramsey problem is postulating tax instruments. Usually, it is assumed that only linear taxes are allowed. Importantly, lump sum taxation is prohibited. Another assumption crucial to this approach is that all activities of agents are observable.

Given the set taxes, a social planner (government) maximizes its objective function given that agents (firms and consumers) are in a competitive equilibrium. Usually, it is assumed that government's objective is to finance an exogenously given level of expenditures. It is important to note that if the lump sum taxes were allowed than the first welfare theorem would hold, and the unconstrained optimum would be achieved.

There are two common approaches to solving Ramsey problems. The first is the *primal* approach, which characterizes a set of allocations that can be implemented as a competitive equilibrium with taxes. By 'implementation we mean' the following: for a set of taxes find a set of (consumption and labour) allocations and equilibrium prices such that these allocations are a competitive equilibrium given taxes. Conversely, a set of (consumption and labour) allocations is implementable if it is possible to find taxes and equilibrium prices such that these allocations are a competitive equilibrium given these prices and taxes. Implementation often makes it possible to simplify a Ramsey problem by reformulating a problem of finding optimal taxes as the problem of finding implementable allocations. This reformulation is referred to as the *primal approach* to Ramsey taxation.

Main lessons of Ramsey taxation: uniform commodity taxation, zero capital tax in the long run, and tax smoothing

One of the central results of the literature on Ramsey taxation is *uniform commodity taxation* (Atkinson and Stiglitz, 1972). Consider a model with a finite set of consumption goods that can be allocated between government and private consumption. All of these goods are produced with labour. Assume that each consumption good can be taxed at a linear rate. Then, under certain separability and homotheticity assumptions, commodity taxation is uniform, that is, the optimal taxes are equated across consumption goods.

Ramsey taxation provides a compelling argument against taxing capital income in the long run in a model of infinitely lived households. The *Chamley–Judd result* (Chamley 1986; Judd 1985) states that in a steady state there should be no wedge between the intertemporal rate of substitution and the marginal rate of transformation, or, alternatively, that the optimal tax on capital is zero. The intuition for the result is that even a small intertemporal distortion implies increasing taxation of goods in future periods in contrast to the prescription of the uniform commodity taxation. Therefore, distorting the intertemporal margin is very costly for the planner. Jones, Manuelli and Rossi (1997) extend the applicability of the Chamley–Judd result by showing that the return to human capital should not be taxed in the long run. Chari, Christiano and Kehoe (1994) provide the state-of-the art numerical treatment for optimal Ramsey taxation over the business cycle and conclude that the *ex ante* capital tax rate is approximately zero.

There has been a long debate on the optimal composition of taxation and borrowing to finance government expenditures. Barro (1979) considers a partial equilibrium economy and argues that it is optimal to smooth distortions from taxation over time, a policy referred as *tax smoothing*. The implication of this analysis is that optimal taxes should follow a random walk. Lucas and Stokey (1983) consider an optimal policy in a general equilibrium economy without capital, and show that, if government has access to state-contingent bonds, optimal taxes inherit the stochastic process of the shocks to government purchases. Chari, Christiano and Kehoe (1994) extend this analysis to an economy with capital and show the Lucas and Stokey results remain valid in that set-up with or without state contingent debt, as long as the government can use taxes on capital to effectively vary the *ex post* after-tax rate of return on bonds. Finally, Aiyagari et al. (2002) show that, if *ex post* taxation of returns is impossible, the optimal taxes follow a process similar to a random walk. They also show the conditions under which the tax smoothing hypothesis is valid.

The Mirrlees approach to optimal taxation

The Mirrlees approach to optimal taxation is built on a different foundation from Ramsey taxation. Rather than stating an ad hoc restricted set of tax instruments as in Ramsey taxation, Mirrlees (1971) assumed that an informational friction endogenously restricted the set of taxes that implement the optimal allocation. This set-up allows arbitrary nonlinear taxes, including lump-sum taxes.

The informational friction posed in those models is unobservability of agents' skills: only labour income of agents can be observed. Therefore, from a given level of labour income it cannot be determined whether a high-skill agent provides a low amount of labour or effort, or whether a low-skill agent works a prescribed amount. The objective of the social planner (government) is to maximize *ex ante*, before the realization of the shocks, utility of an agent. This objective can be interpreted as either insurance against adverse shocks or as *ex post* redistribution across agents of various skills. An informational friction imposes *incentive compatibility* constraints on the planner's problem: allocations of consumption and effective labour must be selected such that an agent chooses not to misrepresent its type.

In summary, the objective of the Mirrlees approach is to find the optimal incentive–insurance trade-off: how to provide the best insurance against adverse events (low realizations of skills) while providing incentives for the agents to reveal their types (provide high amount of labour).

Main lessons of the Mirrlees approach in a static framework

Theoretical results providing general characterization of the optimal taxes in the static Mirrlees environment are limited. The central result is that the consumption–leisure margin of an agent with the highest skill is undistorted, implying that the marginal income tax at the top of the distribution should be optimally set equal to zero. Saez (2001) is a state-of-the art treatment of the static Mirrlees model in which he derives a link between the optimal tax formulas and elasticities of income. Mirrlees (1971) was also able to establish broad conditions that would ensure that the optimal marginal tax rate on labour income was between zero and 100 per cent.

Main lessons of dynamic Mirrlees literature: distorted intertemporal margin

Recent literature starting with Golosov, Kocherlakota, and Tsyvinski (2003) and Werning (2001) extends the static Mirrlees (1971) framework to dynamic settings. Golosov, Kocherlakota, and Tsyvinski (2003) consider an environment with general dynamic stochastically evolving skills. An example of a large unobservable skill shock is disability that is often difficult to observe (classical example is back pain or mental illness). Golosov, Kocherlakota, and Tsyvinski (2003) show for arbitrary evolution of skills that, as long as the probability of agent's skill changing is positive, any optimal allocation includes a positive intertemporal wedge: a marginal rate of substitution across periods is lower than marginal rate of transformation. The reason for this is that this wedge improves the intertemporal provision of incentives by implicitly discouraging savings. This result holds even away from the steady state and sharply contrasts with the Chamley–Judd result that stems from the exogenous restriction on tax instruments. Golosov, Kocherlakota, and Tsyvinski (2003) and Werning (2001) show that in a case of constant types a version of uniform commodity taxation holds and the intertemporal margin is not distorted.

Implementation of dynamic Mirrlees models is more complicated than implementation of either static Mirrlees models, which are implemented with an income tax, or Ramsey models of linear taxation. By 'implementation' we mean finding tax instruments such that the optimal allocation is a competitive equilibrium with taxes. One possible implementation is a direct mechanism that mandates consumption and labour menus for each date. However, such a mechanism can include taxes and transfers never used in practice. Three types of implementations have been proposed. In Albanesi and Sleet (2006), wealth summarizes agents' past histories of shocks that are assumed to be i.i.d. and allows us to define a recursive tax system that depends only on current wealth and effective labour. Golosov and Tsyvinski (2006) implement an optimal disability insurance system with asset-tested transfers that are paid to agents with wealth below a certain limit. Kocherlakota (2005) allows for a general process for skill shocks and derives an implementation with linear taxes on wealth and arbitrarily nonlinear taxes on the history of effective labour.

Optimal monetary policy

The theory of the optimal monetary policy is closely related to the theory of optimal taxation. Phelps (1973) argues that the inflation tax is similar to any other tax, and therefore should be used to finance government expenditures. Although intuitively appealing, this argument is misleading. Chari, Christiano and Kehoe (1996) extend the Ramsey approach to analyse optimal fiscal and monetary policy jointly in several monetary models, and find that typically it is optimal to set the nominal interest rate to be equal to zero. Such a policy is called a 'Friedman rule', after Milton Friedman, who was one of the first proponents of zero nominal interest rates (Friedman, 1969). To understand intuition for the optimality of Friedman rule, it is useful to think about the distinctive the features that distinguish money from other goods and assets. In most models money plays a special role of providing liquidity services to households that cannot be obtained by using other assets such as bonds. Inefficiency arises if the rates of return on bonds and money are different, since by holding money balances households lose the interest rate. When a nominal interest rate is equal to zero, which in a deterministic economy implies that inflation is negative, with nominal prices declining with the rate of households' time preferences, the real rates of return on money and bonds are equalized and this inefficiency is eliminated.

The optimality of the Friedman rule stands in a direct contrast with Phelps' arguments for use of the inflationary tax together with other distortionary taxes such as taxes on consumption or labour income. The reason for this is that money, unlike consumption or leisure, is not valued by households directly but only indirectly, as long as it facilitates transactions and provides liquidity. Therefore, it is more appropriate to think of money as an intermediate good in acquiring final goods consumed by households. Diamond and Mirrlees (1971) established very general results about the undesirability of distortion of the intermediate goods sector, which in monetary models implies that the inflationary tax should not be used despite the distortions caused by taxes on the final goods and services.

The intuition developed above is valid under the assumption that nominal prices are fully flexible, and firms adjust to them immediately in response to changes in market conditions. However, even casual observation suggests that many prices remain unchanged over long periods of time, and Bils and Klenow (2004) document inflexibility of prices for a wide variety of goods. Inflexible or *sticky prices* lead to additional inefficiencies in the economy that could be mitigated by monetary policy. For example, an economy-wide shock, such as an aggregate productivity shock or change in government spending, may call for readjustment of real prices. If adjustment of nominal prices is sluggish, the central bank can increase welfare by adjusting nominal interest rates and affecting real prices.

It is important to recognize that the government is also able to affect real (after-tax) prices using fiscal instruments instead. In fact, Correia, Nicolini and Teles (2002) show that, if fiscal policy is sufficiently flexible and can respond to aggregate shocks quickly, then the Friedman rule continues to be optimal even with sticky prices, with fiscal instruments being preferred to monetary ones. In current practice, however, it appears that it takes a long time to enact changes in tax rates, while monetary policy can be adjusted quickly. Schmitt-Grohe and Uribe (2004) show that, as long as tax levels are fixed or the government is not able to levy some of the taxes on goods or firms' profits, then the optimal interest rate is positive and variable.

Most of the applied literature on the monetary policy is based on the joint assumption of sticky prices and inflexible fiscal policy. Woodford (2003) provides a comprehensive study of the optimal policy in such settings. This analysis examines how central bank response should depend on the type of the shock affecting the economy, the degree of additional imperfections in the economy, and the choice of policies that would rule out indeterminacy of equilibria. Two common policy recommendations for central banks share many of the features of the optimal policy responses in this analysis. One of such recommendations – a *Taylor rule* (see Taylor, 1993) – calls for the interest rates to be increased in response to an increase in the output gap (the difference between actual and a target level of GDP) or inflation. Another recommendation, *inflation forecast targeting*, requires that the central bank commits to adjust interest rate to ensure that the projected future path of inflation or other target variables does not deviate from the pre-specified targets.

In addition to the analysis set out above, several new, conceptually different approaches to the analysis of monetary policy have emerged in the recent years. For example, da Costa and Werning (2005) re-examine optimal monetary policy with flexible prices in Mirrleesian settings and confirm the optimality of the Friedman rule there. Seminal work by Kiyotaki and Wright (1989) has given rise to a large search-theoretic literature seeking to understand the fundamental reasons that money differs from other goods and assets in the economy. Lagos and Wright (2005) provide a framework for the analysis of optimal monetary policy in such settings.

MIKHAIL GOLOSOV AND ALEH TSYVINSKI

See also **monetary and fiscal policy overview; optimal fiscal and monetary policy (without commitment); Taylor rules.**

Bibliography

Aiyagari, S., Marcet, A., Sargent, T. and Seppala, J. 2002. Optimal taxation without state-contingent debt. *Journal of Political Economy* 110, 1220–54.

Albanesi, S. and Sleet, C. 2006. Dynamic optimal taxation with private information. *Review of Economic Studies* 73, 1–30.

Atkinson, A. and Stiglitz, J. 1972. The structure of indirect taxation and economic efficiency. *Journal of Public Economics* 1, 97–119.

Barro, R. 1979. On the determination of the public debt. *Journal of Political Economy* 87, 940–71.

Bils, M. and Klenow, P. 2004. Some evidence on the importance of sticky prices. *Journal of Political Economy* 112, 947–85.

Chamley, C. 1986. Optimal taxation of capital income in general equilibrium with infinite lives. *Econometrica* 54, 607–22.

Chari, V., Christiano, L. and Kehoe, P. 1994. Optimal fiscal policy in a business cycle model. *Journal of Political Economy* 102, 617–52.

Chari, V., Christiano, L. and Kehoe, P. 1996. Optimality of the Friedman rule in economies with distorting taxes. *Journal of Monetary Economics* 37, 203–23.

Correia, I., Nicolini, J.-P. and Teles, P. 2002. Optimal fiscal and monetary policy: equivalence results. Working Paper No. WP-02-16, Federal Reserve Bank of Chicago.

da Costa, C. and Werning, I. 2005. On the optimality of the Friedman rule with heterogeneous agents and non-linear income taxation. Working paper, MIT.

Diamond, P. and Mirrlees, J. 1971. Optimal taxation and public production I: production efficiency. *American Economic Review* 61, 8–27.

Friedman, M. 1969. The optimum quantity of money. In *The Optimum Quantity of Money and Other Essays*. Chicago: Aldine.

Golosov, M., Kocherlakota, N. and Tsyvinski, A. 2003. Optimal indirect and capital taxation. *Review of Economic Studies* 70, 569–87.

Golosov, M. and Tsyvinski, A. 2006. Designing optimal disability insurance: a case for asset testing. *Journal of Political Economy* 114, 257–79.

Jones, L., Manuelli, R. and Rossi, P. 1997. On the optimal taxation of capital income. *Journal of Economic Theory* 73, 93–117.

Judd, Kenneth L. 1985. Redistributive taxation in a simple perfect foresight model. *Journal of Public Economics* 28, 59–83.

Kiyotaki, N. and Wright, R. 1989. On money as a medium of exchange. *Journal of Political Economy* 97, 927–54.

Kocherlakota, N. 2005. Zero expected wealth taxes: a Mirrlees approach to dynamic optimal taxation. *Econometrica* 73, 1587–622.

Lagos, R. and Wright, R. 2005. A unified framework for monetary theory and policy analysis. *Journal of Political Economy* 113, 463–84.

Lucas, R. and Stokey, N. 1983. Optimal fiscal and monetary policy in an economy without capital. *Journal of Monetary Economics* 12, 55–93.

Mirrlees, J. 1971. An exploration in the theory of optimum income taxation. *Review of Economic Studies* 38, 175–208.

Phelps, E. 1973. Inflation in the theory of public finance. *Swedish Journal of Economics* 75, 67–82.

Saez, E. 2001. Using elasticities to derive optimal income tax rates. *Review of Economic Studies* 68, 205–29.

Schmitt-Grohe, S. and Uribe, M. 2004. Optimal fiscal and monetary policy under sticky prices. *Journal of Economic Theory* 114, 183–209.

Taylor, J. 1993. Discretion versus policy rules in practice. *Carnegie-Rochester Conference Series in Public Policy* 39, 195–214.

Werning, I. 2001. Optimal unemployment insurance with hidden savings. Mimeo, University of Chicago.

Woodford, M. 2003. *Interest and Prices*. Princeton: Princeton University Press.

optimal fiscal and monetary policy (without commitment)

Most of the results of optimal taxation literature in the Ramsey framework are derived under the assumption of commitment. *Commitment* is usually defined as ability of a government to bind future policy choices. This assumption is restrictive. A government, even a benevolent one, may choose to change its policies from those promised at an earlier date. The first formalization of the notion of time inconsistency is due to Kydland and Prescott (1977), who showed how timing of government policy may change economic outcomes. Furthermore, equilibrium without commitment can lead to lower welfare for society than when a government can bind its future choices.

An example that clarifies the notion of time inconsistency in fiscal policy is taxation of capital. A classical result due to Chamley (1986) and Judd (1985) states that capital should be taxed at zero in the long run. One of the main assumptions underlying this result is that a government can commit to a sequence of capital taxes. However, a benevolent government will choose to deviate from the prescribed sequence of taxes. The reason is that, once capital is accumulated, it is sunk, and taxing capital is no longer distortionary. A benevolent government would choose high capital taxes once capital is accumulated.

The reasoning above leads to the necessity of the analysis of time inconsistent policy as a game between a policymaker (government) and a continuum of economic agents (consumers). A formalization of such a game and an equilibrium concept is due to Chari and Kehoe (1990). They formulate a general equilibrium infinite-horizon model in which private agents are competitive, and the government maximizes the welfare of the agents. They define an equilibrium concept – sustainable equilibrium – which is a sequence of history-contingent policies that satisfy certain optimality criteria for the government and private agents.

Recent developments in solving for the set of sustainable government policies use the techniques of the analysis of repeated games due to Abreu (1986) and Abreu, Pearce and Stachetti (1990). Phelan and Stachetti (2001) extend these methods to analyse the equilibria of the Ramsey model of capital taxation. Their contribution is to provide a method in which the behaviour of consumers is summarized as a solution to the competitive equilibrium, thus significantly reducing the dimensionality of the problem. They provide a characterization of the whole set of sustainable equilibria of the game. Their methods are especially relevant for the environments in which the punishment to the deviator is difficult to characterize analytically.

Benhabib and Rusticchini (1997) and Marcet and Marimon (1994) provide an alternative method to solve policy games without commitment. They use the techniques of optimal control in which they explicitly impose additional constraints on the standard optimal tax problem such that a government does not deviate from the prescribed sequence of taxes. Their methods, while easier to use than those of Abreu (1986), Abreu, Pearce and Stachetti (1990) and Phelan and Stachetti (2001), are efficient only if the worst punishment to the deviating government can be easily determined.

Klein, Krusell and Rios-Rull (2004) numerically solve for equilibria where reputational mechanisms are not operative and characterize Markov-perfect equilibria of the dynamic game between successive governments in the context of optimal Ramsey taxation. For a calibrated economy, they find that the government still refrains from taxing at confiscatory rates.

Optimal monetary policy without commitment

The problem of time consistency also arises in monetary economics. Kydland and Prescott (1977) and Barro and Gordon (1983) analyse a reduced form economy with a trade-off between inflation and unemployment. Consider an economy where the growth rate of nominal wages is being set one period in advance. The government can decrease unemployment by having setting the inflation rate higher than the wage rate, thus reducing the real wage; but inflation is socially costly. Suppose that a monetary authority chooses the inflation rate *after* nominal wages were set in the economy to maximize social welfare. Such a rate would equalize the marginal benefits of reducing unemployment and the marginal costs of increasing inflation. But now consider wage determination in a rational-expectations equilibrium. In anticipation of the government's policy, agents will choose a positive growth rate of wages to avoid losses from inflation. Therefore, in equilibrium the monetary authority is not able to affect unemployment, but there is a positive rate of inflation. This outcome is inefficient since by committing not to inflate *ex ante* the monetary authority could achieve the same level of unemployment but with zero inflation. Therefore, the lack of commitment by the monetary authority will lead to *inflationary bias*, or an inefficiently high level of inflation.

Similar effects are present in many other monetary models. For example, Calvo (1978) shows time inconsistency of the optimal policy in a general equilibrium model. Chang (1998) considers a version of Calvo's model to find the optimal monetary policy without commitment. Similar to Phelan and Stacchetti (2001), he uses tools of repeated game theory to describe the best equilibrium in the game between the central bank and a large group of agents.

A substantial amount of work has been done in finding the ways to overcome time consistency problems. One of the first practical proposals is Rogoff's (1985) suggestion to appoint a 'conservative' central banker, whose private valuation of the costs of inflation is higher than the social valuation. Such a banker has less temptation to inflate, and the inflationary bias will be reduced.

Pre-specifying the rules of conduct for monetary policy reduces the discretionary actions a central bank can undertake and improves time consistency. For example, the commonly advocated Taylor rule prescribes that the central bank sets nominal interest rates as a linear function of inflation and the output gap with fixed coefficients (see, for example, Woodford, 2003). On the other hand, it may be desirable to leave some discretion to the central bank, particularly if it has access to information about economic conditions which is impossible or impractical to incorporate into predetermined rules. Athey, Atkeson and Kehoe (2005) consider an example of such an economy where the central bank has private information about the state of the economy, which is unavailable to others. They show that the optimal policy in such settings is an *inflationary cap* that allows discretion to the central bank as long as the inflation rate is below a certain bound.

Following Lucas and Stokey's (1983) analysis, substantial work has been done in determining conditions under which the government can eliminate the time consistency problem by optimally choosing debt of various maturities. Lucas and Stokey themselves point out the fundamental difficulty with this approach in monetary economies since, as long as the government holds a positive amount of nominal debt, it is tempted to inflate in order to reduce its real value. Two recent papers describe some of the conditions under which this problem can be overcome. Alvarez, Kehoe and Neumeyer (2004) consider several monetary models and show that if it is optimal to set nominal interest rates at zero (that is, the optimal monetary policy with commitment is to follow the *Friedman rule*), then the time consistency problem can be solved. By issuing a mixture of nominal and real (indexed) bonds in such a way that the present value of the nominal claims is zero, the temptation for inflation can be removed. Persson, Persson and Svensson (2006) consider a model where the Friedman rule is not optimal, but they still are able to characterize the optimal maturity structure of nominal and indexed bonds that achieve the social optimum with commitment even with time-inconsistent government.

MIKHAIL GOLOSOV AND ALEH TSYVINSKI

See also **monetary and fiscal policy overview; optimal fiscal and monetary policy (with commitment).**

Bibliography

Abreu, D. 1986. Extremal equilibria of oligopolistic supergames. *Journal of Economic Theory* 39, 191–225.

Abreu, D., Pearce, D. and Stacchetti, E. 1990. Toward a theory of discounted repeated games with imperfect monitoring. *Econometrica* 58, 1041–63.

Alvarez, F., Kehoe, P. and Neumeyer, P. 2004. The time consistence of optimal monetary and fiscal policies. *Econometrica* 72, 541–67.

Athey, S., Atkeson, A. and Kehoe, P. 2005. The optimal degree of monetary policy discretion. *Econometrica* 73, 1431–76.

Barro, R. and Gordon, D. 1983. A positive theory of monetary policy in a natural rate model. *Journal of Political Economy* 91, 589–610.

Benhabib, J. and Rustichini, A. 1997. Optimal taxes without commitment. *Journal of Economic Theory* 77, 231–59.

Calvo, G. 1978. On the time consistence of optimal policy in a monetary economy. *Econometrica* 46, 1411–28.

Chamley, C. 1986. Optimal taxation of capital income in general equilibrium with infinite lives. *Econometrica* 54, 607–22.

Chang, R. 1998. Credible monetary policy in an infinite horizon model: recursive approach. *Journal of Economic Theory* 81, 431–61.

Chari, V. and Kehoe, P. 1990. Sustainable plans. *Journal of Political Economy* 98, 783–802.

Judd, K. 1985. Redistributive taxation in a simple perfect foresight model. *Journal of Public Economics* 28, 59–83.

Klein, P., Krusell, P. and Ríos-Rull, J.-V. 2004. Time consistent public expenditures. Discussion Paper No. 4582. London: CEPR.

Kydland, F. and Prescott, E. 1977. Rules rather than discretion: the inconsistency of optimal plans. *Journal of Political Economy* 85, 473–92.

Lucas, R. and Stokey, N. 1983. Optimal fiscal and monetary policy in an economy without capital. *Journal of Monetary Economics* 12, 55–93.

Marcet, A. and Marimon, R. 1994. Recursive contracts. Working Paper No. 337, Department of Economics and Business, Universitat Pompeu Fabra.

Persson, M., Persson, T. and Svensson, L. 2006. Time consistency of fiscal and monetary policy: a solution. *Econometrica* 74, 193–212.

Phelan, C. and Stacchetti, E. 2001. Sequential equilibria in a Ramsey tax model. *Econometrica* 69, 1491–518.

Rogoff, K. 1985. The optimal degree of commitment to an intermediate monetary target. *Quarterly Journal of Economics* 100, 1169–90.

Woodford, M. 2003. *Interest and Prices*. Princeton: Princeton University Press.

optimum quantity of money

The optimum quantity of money is most famously associated with Milton Friedman (1969). The optimum is a normative policy conclusion drawn from the long-run properties of a theoretical model. Friedman posited an environment that abstracts from all exogenous shocks and nominal price and wage sluggishness. The basic logic is then straightforward. One criterion for Pareto efficiency is that the private cost of a good or service should be equated to the social cost of this good or service. The service in question is the transactions role of money. The social cost of producing fiat money is essentially zero. Since fiat money pays no interest, the private cost of using money is the nominal interest rate. Hence, one criterion for Pareto efficiency is that the nominal interest rate should equal zero. Since long-run real rates are positive, this implies that monetary policy should bring about a steady deflation in the general price level. This famous policy prescription is now commonly called the Friedman rule.

Although most closely associated with Friedman's (1969) bold statement of the policy conclusion, the basic idea of the optimum quantity can be found in Tolley (1957), who argues, on similar efficiency grounds, for paying interest on currency. Friedman (1960) credits Tolley with this suggestion, and further notes that an alternative policy would be a steady deflation. It is curious that Friedman (1960) dismisses the 'Friedman rule' deflation as not feasible for practical purposes. Finally, the optimum-quantity result is implicit, but never noted, in Bailey (1956) who examines the welfare cost of inflation but does not consider the welfare gain of deflations.

In practice, the optimum-quantity result has had remarkably little influence on monetary policy implementation. Although many central banks pursue low inflation rates with an eventual goal of price stability, no central bank has advocated a policy that would bring about a steady price deflation. There are likely several reasons, both judgemental and theoretical, that have led to this lack of influence. I will briefly review both types of objections.

One of the first theoretical objections to the optimum-quantity results was made by Phelps (1973), who argued that Friedman's first-best argument ignored the second-best fact that money growth produces seigniorage revenues for a government, and that all forms of taxation produce distortions of some kind. If 'money' or 'liquidity' is a good like any other, then familiar optimal taxation arguments would suggest that it should be taxed via a steady inflation. This argument seems all the more persuasive given empirical estimates of a fairly low money demand elasticity.

This public finance approach spawned a very large literature. Important contributions include Kimbrough (1986), Guidotti and Vegh (1993), Correia and Teles (1996; 1999), Chari, Christiano and Kehoe (1996), and Mulligan and Sala-i-Martin (1997). These analyses were much more explicit than Friedman (1969) and considered a fully dynamic theoretical environment with no nominal rigidities. A key relationship in all these models is the transactions or shopping function. The time spent by households shopping (s_t) is a function of the form: $s_t = \varphi(c_t, m_t)$, where c_t denotes real consumption and m_t denotes real cash balances. The function φ is assumed to be homogenous of degree k, increasing in consumption, and decreasing in real cash balances, the latter effect motivated by the transactions function of money. Money can be thought of as an intermediate good that facilitates consumption purchases. Now suppose a central government needs to finance an exogenous level of spending and can do so only with distortionary taxes on, say, labour income, or the inflation tax on money balances. In this case, is the Friedman rule still optimal?

Most of these papers were supportive of the Friedman rule, concluding that in such a second-best environment the optimal monetary policy is a zero nominal rate. Mulligan and Sala-i-Martin (1997) argued that the result was fragile as it depended on the degree of homogeneity in φ and the alternative tax instruments available to the government, for example, income taxes against consumption taxes. These conflicting results have been usefully explained in DeFiore and Teles (2003), who demonstrated that the reason for the divergent conclusions is an inappropriate specification of how consumption taxes are entered in the transactions cost function. They consider a more general environment in which the government has access to both consumption and income taxes. They also consider the case where money is costly to produce at a constant marginal cost of α. Further, they demonstrate that if φ is linearly homogenous (k = 1) then the optimal interest rate is equal to α. This is a modified Friedman rule in that the private cost and social cost of money are set equal to each other, and is analogous to the Diamond and Mirrlees (1971) optimal taxation result: intermediate goods should not be taxed when consumption taxes are available and the technology is constant returns to scale (k = 1). If φ is not linearly homogeneous, then the optimal policy involves a tax (or subsidy) on money proportional to α. Since money is essentially costless to produce ($\alpha = 0$) the optimal nominal interest rate is zero. DeFiore and Teles (2003) thus conclude that the Friedman rule is the optimal second-best policy for all homogeneous transactions technologies. Hence, the Phelps (1973) objection appears to be settled in Friedman's favour.

A second theoretical objection to the optimum-quantity result is that, in a world with nominal rigidities, a steady general price deflation would produce unwanted relative price movements since not all nominal prices would be adjusted simultaneously. Strictly speaking this is not a theoretical objection to Friedman (1969), as he assumed a world with perfectly flexible nominal prices and wages. But if one believes that nominal rigidities are important, and that they matter even in the long run, then this is a relevant objection to the Friedman rule. For example, in the dynamic new Keynesian (DNK) class of models (for example, Woodford, 2003) the assumed nominal rigidities have permanent effects so that any departure from price stability causes permanent movements in relative prices. Hence, these models typically suggest that optimal policy is a stable price level, and that a Friedman-rule deflation would be suboptimal. These DNK models typically abstract from the nominal interest rate distortions that are at the heart of the optimum-quantity result. A model that combined the DNK nominal rigidities with the nominal rate distortion would presumably result in a long-run optimal nominal interest rate somewhere between zero and the steady-state real rate.

The principle judgemental objection to the Friedman rule is historical. The instances in US history in which deflations occurred are associated with severe recessions, most famously in the 1929–33 period. A related judgemental concern deals with the zero bound. If the central bank's principal tool to stimulate the economy is a reduction in the nominal rate of interest, then the zero nominal rate prescribed by the Friedman rule apparently leaves no additional ammunition in the monetary policy arsenal (as nominal rates cannot be negative). This nervousness about the Friedman rule was enhanced by the experience of Japan during the 1990s. The Japanese economy performed poorly at a time in which general prices were falling and the short-term nominal rate was zero.

Since central banks have not followed Friedman's (1969) proposal to set the nominal rate to zero, a natural issue is to quantify the welfare costs of being away from Friedman's optimum quantity of money. Following in the footsteps of Bailey (1956), Lucas (2000) uses a theoretical environment similar to that of Correia and Teles (1996; 1999) to address this question. The welfare cost is approximately the area underneath the money demand curve between the optimal zero nominal rate and the interest rate under question. Lucas reports that the welfare cost of a four per cent nominal rate is between 0.2 per cent and one per cent of annual income, the difference depending upon the assumed behaviour of money demand as the nominal rate approaches zero. Since a zero nominal rate has not been observed in the United States in the post-Second World War period, the data cannot determine which estimate is more accurate. But either estimate suggests a fairly modest welfare cost.

Studies analysing the optimality of the Friedman rule have been reignited by the new class of search-theoretic monetary models. These models are micro-based, replacing the function φ in DeFiore and Teles (2003) with a search-based trading environment in which money improves the chances of successfully finding a suitable partner with whom to trade. In an innovative paper, Lagos and Wright (2005) use a search-theoretic environment to address the optimality of the Friedman rule and the welfare consequences of deviating from it. In search models of money the buyer and seller engage in a bargaining game to determine the transactions price at a given meeting. The buyer is carrying money and has thus postponed previous consumption. If sellers have some bargaining power, then there is a hold-up problem because part of the gain associated with the holding of money is received by the seller. This bargaining distortion leads the buyers to economize on money holdings so that they are below the socially efficient level. Lagos and Wright (2005) demonstrate that the optimal policy in this search environment is the Friedman rule (a similar conclusion is reached by Shi, 1997). But more interestingly, the welfare cost of being away from the Friedman rule, at say a four per cent nominal rate, is significantly higher than calculated by

Lucas (2000). This arises because the positive nominal rate exacerbates an already suboptimal level of real balances arising from the hold-up problem.

The search models of money have rekindled interest in the optimality of the Friedman rule at just the time when DeFiore and Teles (2003) appear to have settled the issue in the aggregative monetary models. The coming years will probably see further work on the Friedman rule from this search-theoretic perspective. A key issue is the nature of the bargaining process that arises at trading opportunities. These recent developments testify to the continued prominence of the optimum quantity of money in monetary theory, if not practice. The lasting contribution of the theory is to introduce explicit, utility-based welfare analysis into monetary economics.

TIMOTHY S. FUERST

See also **monetary policy, history of; money and general equilibrium; real bills doctrine versus the quantity theory.**

The author would like to thank Charles Carlstrom and John Hoag for their helpful comments.

Bibliography

Bailey, M.J. 1956. The welfare costs of inflationary finance. *Journal of Political Economy* 64, 93–110.

Chari, V.V., Christiano, L.J. and Kehoe, P. 1996. Optimality of the Friedman rule in economies with distorting taxes. *Journal of Monetary Economics* 37, 202–23.

Correia, I. and Teles, P. 1996. Is the Friedman rule optimal when money is an intermediate good. *Journal of Monetary Economics* 38, 223–44.

Correia, I. and Teles, P. 1999. The optimal inflation tax. *Review of Economic Dynamics* 2, 325–46.

DeFiore, F. and Teles, P. 2003. The optimal mix of taxes on money, consumption and income. *Journal of Monetary Economics* 50, 871–88.

Diamond, P.A. and Mirrlees, J.A. 1971. Optimal taxation and public production. *American Economic Review* 63, 8–27.

Friedman, M. 1960. *A Program for Monetary Stability*. New York: Fordham University Press.

Friedman, M. 1969. *The Optimum Quantity of Money and Other Essays*. Chicago: Aldine.

Guidotti, P.E. and Vegh, C.A. 1993. The optimal inflation tax when money reduces transactions costs. *Journal of Monetary Economics* 31, 189–205.

Kimbrough, K.P. 1986. The optimum quantity of money rule in the theory of public finance. *Journal of Monetary Economics* 18, 277–84.

Lagos, R. and Wright, R. 2005. A unified framework for monetary theory and policy analysis. *Journal of Political Economy* 46, 463–84.

Lucas, R.E. Jr. 2000. Inflation and welfare. *Econometrica* 68, 247–74.

Mulligan, C.B. and Sala-i-Martin, X. 1997. The optimum quantity of money: theory and evidence. *Journal of Money, Credit and Banking* 29, 687–715.

Phelps, E.S. 1973. Inflation in the theory of public finance. *Swedish Journal of Economics* 75, 37–54.

Shi, S. 1997. A divisible search model of fiat money. *Econometrica* 65, 75–102.

Tolley, G. 1957. Providing for growth of the money supply. *Journal of Political Economy* 65, 465–85.

Woodford, M. 2003. *Interest and Prices*. Princeton: Princeton University Press.

payment systems

A *payment* occurs when one party, the *payer*, transfers an asset to another party, the *payee*, for the purpose of discharging a debt incurred by the payer. Or, a payment may consist of the payer's instruction to a third party to make such a transfer, as is the case with a cheque payment. While in principle a payment may be made with any asset, in practice virtually all modern payments involve transfers of debt claims on either central banks (including 'outside money' in the form of both currency and deposits) or private banks ('inside money', today almost always in the form of deposits). Available evidence suggests that most payments are still made in cash, but these transactions tend to be for relatively small amounts. By value, the wide majority of payments involve transfer of bank deposits by various means.

A payment may or may not constitute *settlement*, a legal discharge of a debt. In most countries, for example, a payment by means of a transfer of claims on a central bank unconditionally settles a debt, whereas other types of payment settle a debt only after certain conditions have been fulfilled (for example, after a cheque has been honoured by the bank on which it is drawn).

A payment *system* is a collection of technologies, laws, and contracts that allow payments to occur and determine when a payment effects a settlement. Payment systems include currency, cheques, credit and debit cards, electronic funds transfers, and so on. Developed economies depend critically on the near-flawless operation of such systems. By offering debtors low-cost and trustworthy means of settling their debts, payment systems provide an important stimulus to the use of credit, and to economic activity more generally.

Some simple statistics illustrate these assertions: in the year 2003, 81 billion payments of $824 trillion were recorded in the United States, not counting payments made in currency (Committee on Payment and Settlement Systems, 2005). Another way of framing these numbers is to note that they imply, on average, $75 in non-cash payments for each dollar of final output produced in the United States in 2003. During the same year each US resident made 278 non-cash payments on average. All developed economies display similar levels of payments activity.

Theory of payments

Despite their ubiquity and their obviously central role in modern economies, payments have only recently begun to make their way into mainstream economic theory. Payment systems do not exist in Arrow–Debreu economies, where transfers may always be made in kind, and promises to transfer are enforced by a social planner. In these economies there is no need for specialized assets to allow for payments, technologies for transferring these assets, or rules concerning when such transfers settle a debt.

Even if the planner's ability to enforce promises is limited, payments may still be inessential. Agents will have incentives to honour their obligations so long as they have access to sufficient amounts of collateral that can be attached by creditors after a default. Payment systems become relevant when enforcement is limited and collateral is scarce. In such environments, payment systems serve as devices that allow for enforcement of debts while making efficient use of available collateral.

One commonly available type of collateral is, of course, outside fiat money, but a discussion of the comparative payment roles of inside and outside money is beyond the scope of this essay. Two influential papers in this area have been Freeman (1996; see especially its discussion in Green, 1999) and Cavalcanti and Wallace (1999). For the reminder of this article I will concentrate on payments in private debt.

An illustration

To demonstrate the function of payment systems, I consider some models of payment based on the celebrated 'Wicksell triangle' depicted in Figure 1. Each of the three agents is endowed with a unit of a generic numeraire good. Agent A has the possibility of converting this good into a 'customized' good that is (highly) desired by agent B, who can convert his numeraire into a good desired by agent C, who can produce a good that is desired by A. Barring difficulties in enforcement, efficiency would require each agent to produce the appropriate customized good and deliver it to the next agent. I call this allocation the *full-enforcement efficient* allocation.

The general goal of payment systems is to deliver an allocation that approximates this allocation, to the extent this is feasible under limited enforcement. I now consider to what extent various payment systems are able to do this. In each of these environments, any enforcement actions will occur through a fourth agent known as the *centre* or 'central counterparty', who has a restricted ability to punish agents who default on their obligations. Punishments may include limited fines, attachment of collateral, and public announcements of a default.

Payment model 1: 'netting'

Kahn, McAndrews and Roberds (2003) analyse the following version of the Wicksell-triangle environment. A, B, and C each consists of a buyer-seller pair who live at a

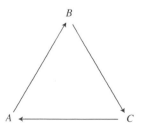

Figure 1   Wicksell triangle

separate 'location', meaning that trade occurs as bilateral encounters between buyer and seller. Agents are not particularly inclined to keep their promises, but may post some numeraire as collateral before trading begins. There is a single period during which sellers can visit buyers and transfers of customized goods can occur, and a subsequent period during which numeraire may be transferred. Prices of goods are given in numeraire and are determined through bilateral negotiations.

In this environment, it is easy to show that the amount of collateral required for trade can be minimized by the use of a payment system based on *net settlement*. However, as net settlement typically requires the diversion of resources in order to acquire and post costly collateral, its use will entail a welfare loss, relative to the full-enforcement efficient allocation.

Under net settlement, after trades have occurred, the central counterparty sums for each agent the amount the agent owes *to* the seller he bought from, minus the amount owed *from* the agent from the buyer sold to. If this sum is positive, the agent transfers numeraire to the central counterparty, and if the amount is negative, he receives numeraire from the central counterparty.

Payment in this environment simply consists of an agent's declaration of his intent to settle, and this occurs simultaneous with trade. *Settlement* is the two-stage process of (*a*) replacing gross obligations with net obligations and (*b*) discharging net obligations through transfer of numeraire.

A characteristic feature of net settlement is 'set-off,' under which a debt owed *by* party X is enforced by cancelling it ('setting it off') against its debt owed *to* party X. In this fashion, agent X's creditor may exercise a de facto prior claim against X, even when other means of exercising priority are costly (such as posting additional collateral). Payment systems incorporating net settlement allow set-off to occur in a regular and predictable fashion.

Netting of obligations is an ancient method of payment, dating at least to the 13th century fairs of Champagne (Kohn, 2001). It continues to be used extensively for settling high-value, recurring obligations such as those that arise between commercial banks (for example, the CHIPS system which operates in the United States). But there are certain limitations that prevent its more widespread use. The first is that there may be an inadequate legal basis for netting (Bliss, 2003). Second, netting works well only if all parties involved are of roughly equal creditworthiness (Kahn and Roberds, 2003). Finally, netting may require too much coordination in the sense that all parties must agree in advance to participate in the netting arrangement. These limitations have given rise to other forms of payment systems which, in effect, allow netting to occur in a more decentralized fashion.

Payment model 2: 'banknote'

Kiyotaki and Moore (2000) discuss a slightly different model from model 1 above. Suppose that preferences and endowments are the same as above, but that bilateral encounters between agents are separated in time: agent C first has an opportunity to buy his desired good from agent B, who then has an opportunity to buy from A, who can then buy from agent C. Agent C is known to be creditworthy but A and B are not.

In this model, the full-enforcement efficient allocation can be implemented if C's debt can 'circulate'. More specifically, B receives debt from C in return for a customized good. Agent B then trades C's debt to A, in return for A's customized good. A then presents C's debt to C for redemption. Finally, agent C completes the cycle of trade by transferring a customized good to A. *Payment* in this environment corresponds to either the issue (by C) or transfer (by B) of C's debt. If C is sufficiently creditworthy, B's transfer of C's debt will also constitute a *settlement*. Otherwise settlement may not occur until C redeems his debt.

Under this arrangement it is not necessary for all parties to be creditworthy for trade to occur. Agent C may enjoy some natural advantage in this regard. This advantage could take the form of ownership of attachable assets or, in a dynamic setting, it could be that people have better information on the actions of C than on the actions of other agents (Cavalcanti and Wallace, 1999). In this arrangement, C's debt becomes a form of specialized asset for use in payment, a 'banknote'.

This is the basic model for many transactions using not only privately issued banknotes (which are rarely observed nowadays) but also other means of transferring debt claims. A retail store may not be willing to accept a customer's IOU in exchange for merchandise but is perfectly willing to accept a debt (that is, deposit) claim on a bank, transferred by means of a credit or debit card.

This form of payment also has a long history. One of the most famous early examples is from 15th-century Genoa. There, payments were commonly made using claims on an institution responsible for managing the debt of the state (the *Casa di San Giorgio*; see Kohn, 1999). Under this arrangement agent C became, in effect, an agent of the state, whose creditworthiness derived from the taxation powers delegated to it. People owing taxes could use claims on the *Casa di San Giorgio* to discharge their own tax obligations, which generated a demand for these claims as payment instruments.

Note that model 2, like model 1, involves a form of netting. When a consumer purchases merchandise with, say, a debit card, the consumer is in effect netting out the debt he owes *to* the merchant against debt (deposits) owed him *by* his bank. In contrast to model 1, however, there need be no prior agreement between merchant and consumer, given sufficient trust in the banking system.

Payment model 3: 'bank loan'

Model 2 illustrates how payment systems allow netting to occur in a decentralized fashion. This model is inadequate for some situations, however, because it does not explain the simultaneous existence of both liquid and illiquid debt. In particular, this model is inappropriate for production economies where a producer may require prompt delivery of an intermediate good now in order to produce a final good that can be sold only later. In such situations, working capital is typically provided by the issue of debt.

To remedy this shortcoming, some studies have attempted to modify model 2 in order to incorporate both transferable ('liquid') and non-transferable ('illiquid') debt. Kiyotaki and Moore (2000) consider a model which maps into the following variation. Suppose that the timing of the first two transactions in the Wicksell triangle is reversed, so that that agent B first has an opportunity to buy from A, then C from B, and finally A from C. This timing is natural if B uses A's good as an intermediate good.

As in model 2, agent C is trustworthy but agents A and B may not be. In addition, Agent C enjoys a special privilege as a creditor, that is, an enhanced ability to enforce debts, and serves as 'banker' to agent B.

In this modified example, it is possible to show that the full-enforcement efficient allocation can sometimes be implemented through use of a combination of transferable and non-transferable debt. Specifically, suppose that B has an opportunity to meet with C before production of specialized goods can occur, and before trading begins. Agent B issues debt to C, and C in turn issues debt to B. When B then encounters A, he pays for A's specialized good by transferring C's debt to A. Agent B then has the opportunity to discharge his debt to agent C by transferring his specialized good to C. Finally, agent A presents C with his debt, and receives C's specialized good. *Payment* and *settlement* are defined as in model 2.

In short, in this model agent C is engaged in 'liquidity transformation', which consists of holding B's debt, which would be unenforceable by A, while issuing to B his own enforceable and therefore transferable debt. In practice, this liquidity transformation is usually provided by banks. This function of banks was already well established by the 14th century (Kohn, 2001).

Payment model 4: 'bill of exchange'

Model 3 allows for the coexistence of liquid and illiquid debt, but may not be appropriate for all circumstances. In some environments, there may be no agents with special enforcement abilities, such as agent C above. This is particularly true for economies with less developed legal and financial systems. Yet through the process of payment it may still be possible to economize on resources devoted to enforcement, by allowing for the discharge of one debt by the transfer of another.

Kahn and Roberds (2001) consider the following variation on model 2. The order of meetings is A with B, B with C, and C with A. The customized good produced by agent C is now valued by both A and B.

The full-enforcement efficient allocation can then be supported as follows. Suppose that agent B issues debt to A in the first transaction, and that agent C issues debt to B in the second transaction, which is subsequently passed to A. In the final transaction, A presents C's debt to C, and C redeems his debt by providing the appropriate good to A. *Payment* in this environment again corresponds to the passing of C's debt by B to A, and *settlement* occurs either simultaneously with payment, or when C redeems his debt.

The intuition behind the efficiency of this arrangement is as follows. Suppose that, instead of making use of transferable debt, trade is organized as a 'credit chain' (Kiyotaki and Moore, 1997), in which B issues debt to A, C issues debt to B, and B promises to discharge his debt with A once he has collected from C. If enforcement is less than perfect and B also values C's customized good, then B may collect C's debt then 'take the money and run', that is, abscond with C's good. But if A requires an 'early' payment from B in the form of a transfer of C's debt, B's default can be averted, provided that A can respond to a failure to pay at this stage by preventing B from collecting with C.

As in the models above, enforcement of B's obligation to A occurs through a form of netting. By requiring early payment from B in the form of C's transferable debt, A is in effect forcing B to cancel one debt with another. The key distinction between model 4 and earlier models is that this cancellation is no longer instantaneous. In other words, even potentially bad credits such as B are allowed to issue debts as long as they agree to punctually pay them off using the debt of another, possibly stronger credit.

The work of economic historians (see Ashtor, 1972) suggests that model 4 is also an ancient one. Its use in the West (in the form of bills of exchange and similar instruments) dates from the late 12th century, and likely arose from even earlier Middle Eastern precedents. Even in today's advanced economies, this model persists in the form of trade credit that is granted with the understanding it will be repaid in another form of debt, nowadays typically bank funds.

Payments and networks

Payment systems based on the models discussed above have been in use for some time. Successful application of these models, however, requires some information which may not always be present in practice. At a minimum, participants in these arrangements must be able to distinguish the identity of their counterparties, and have some notion of their counterparties' ability to honour their debts. Historically, these requirements have often worked to limit the use of many forms of non-cash payments to established businesses, wealthy individuals, or parties already well known to each other.

These constraints have become less onerous with improvements in information technology. In particular, the years since 1960 have seen rapid development of electronic payment systems based on the use of cards (Evans and Schmalensee, 1999). A noteworthy distinction between electronic systems and their paper-based counterparts is that the new systems require the use of specialized communications networks.

As is the case with other industries, the presence of 'network effects' in payment systems leads to complications (see Weinberg, 1997). Baxter (1983) was the first to point out the essentially 'two-sided' nature of the service provided by these networks: that is, that efficiency in these networks may depend critically on the allocation of their costs between buyers and sellers. This insight has been subsequently expanded on by many authors (an authoritative survey is given in Rochet and Tirole, 2004). Nonetheless, as of this writing, no consensus has emerged concerning efficient allocation of services provided by these systems (Evans and Schmalensee, 2005).

Conclusion

Payment systems are an important component of decentralized exchange. This article has illustrated how the fundamental role of these systems is the reduction of chains of obligations to a smaller and more readily enforceable set of obligations. Ongoing improvements in information technology have the potential to increase the scope and efficiency of payment systems, and this will require economists to provide more precise models of their function and essential nature.

WILLIAM ROBERDS

See also **inside and outside money; money and general equilibrium.**

Bibliography

Ashtor, E. 1972. Banking instruments between the Muslim East and Christian West. *Journal of European Economic History* 1, 553–73.

Baxter, W. 1983. Bank exchange of transactional paper: legal and economic perspectives. *Journal of Law and Economics* 26, 541–88.

Bliss, R. 2003. Bankruptcy law and large complex financial organizations: a primer. *Federal Reserve Bank of Chicago Economic Perspectives* 27(1), 48–58.

Cavalcanti, R. and Wallace, N. 1999. A model of private banknote issue. *Review of Economic Dynamics* 2, 104–36.

Committee on Payment and Settlement Systems. 2005. *Statistics on Payment and Settlement Systems: Figures for 2003*. Basel: Bank for International Settlements.

Evans, D. and Schmalensee, R. 1999. *Paying with Plastic: The Digital Revolution in Buying and Borrowing*. Cambridge, MA: MIT Press.

Evans, D. and Schmalensee, R. 2005. The economics of interchange fees and their regulation: an overview. Working Paper No. 18181. Cambridge, MA: Sloan School of Management, MIT.

Freeman, S. 1996. The payments system, liquidity, and rediscounting. *American Economic Review* 86, 1126–38.

Green, E. 1999. We need to think straight about electronic payments. *Journal of Money, Credit, and Banking* 31, 668–70.

Kahn, C. and Roberds, W. 2001. Transferability, finality, and debt settlement. Working paper. Federal Reserve Bank of Atlanta.

Kahn, C. and Roberds, W. 2003. Payments settlement under limited enforcement: public versus private systems. Working paper. Federal Reserve Bank of Atlanta.

Kahn, C., McAndrews, J. and Roberds, W. 2003. Settlement risk under net and gross settlement. *Journal of Money, Credit, and Banking* 47, 299–319.

Kiyotaki, N. and Moore, J. 1997. Credit chains. Mimeo. London School of Economics.

Kiyotaki, N. and Moore, J. 2000. Inside money and liquidity. Mimeo. London School of Economics.

Kohn, M. 1999. The capital market before 1600. Working Paper No. 99-06. Department of Economics, Dartmouth College.

Kohn, M. 2001. Payments and the development of finance in pre-industrial Europe. Working Paper No. 01-05. Department of Economics, Dartmouth College.

Rochet, J.C. and Tirole, J. 2004. Two-sided markets: an overview. Working Paper No. 275. IDEI, University of Toulouse.

Weinberg, J. 1997. The organization of private payment networks. *Federal Reserve Bank of Richmond Economic Quarterly* 83(2), 25–43.

quantity theory of money

Lowness of interest is generally ascribed to plenty of money. But ... augmentation [in the quantity of money] has no other effect than to heighten the price of labour and commodities ... In the progress toward these changes, the augmentation may have some influence, by exciting industry, but after the prices are settled ... it has no manner of influence.

> [T]hough the high price of commodities be a necessary consequence of the increase of gold and silver, yet it follows not immediately upon that increase; but some time is required before the money circulates through the whole state.... In my opinion, it is only in this interval of intermediate situation, between the acquisition of money and rise of prices, that the increasing quantity of gold and silver is favourable to industry.... [W]e may conclude that it is of no manner of consequence, with regard to the domestic happiness of a state, whether money be in greater or less quantity. The good policy of the magistrate consists only in keeping it, if possible, still increasing ...
> (David Hume, 1752).

In this survey, we shall first present a formal statement of the quantity theory, then consider the Keynesian challenge to the quantity theory, recent developments, and some empirical evidence. We shall conclude with a discussion of policy implications, giving special attention to the likely implications of the worldwide fiat money standard that has prevailed since 1971.

1. The formal theory

(a) Nominal versus real quantity of money

Implicit in the quotation from Hume, and central to all later versions of the quantity theory, is a distinction between the *nominal* quantity of money and the *real* quantity of money. The nominal quantity of money is the quantity expressed in whatever units are used to designate money – talents, shekels, pounds, francs, lira, drachmas, dollars, and so on. The real quantity of money is the quantity expressed in terms of the volume of goods and services the money will purchase.

There is no unique way to express either the nominal or the real quantity of money. With respect to the nominal quantity of money, the issue is what assets to include – whether only currency and coins, or also claims on financial institutions; and, if such claims are included, which ones should be, only deposits transferable by cheque, or also other categories of claims which in practice are close substitutes for deposits transferable by cheque. More recently, economists have been experimenting with the theoretically attractive idea of defining money not as the simple sum of various categories of claims but as a weighted aggregate of such claims, the weights being determined by one or another concept of the 'moneyness' of the various claims.

Despite continual controversy over the definition of 'money', and the lack of unanimity about relevant theoretical criteria, in practice, monetary economists have generally displayed wide agreement about the most useful counterpart, or set of counterparts, to the concept of 'money' at a particular times and places (Friedman and Schwartz, 1970, pp. 89–197; Barnett, Offenbacher and Spindt, 1984; Spindt, 1985).

The real quantity of money obviously depends on the particular definition chosen for the nominal quantity. In addition, for each such definition, it can vary according to the set of goods and services in terms of which it is expressed. One way to calculate the real quantity of money is by dividing the nominal quantity of money by a price index. The real quantity is then expressed in terms of the standard basket whose components are used as weights in computing the price index – generally, the basket purchased by some representative group in a base year.

A different way to express the real quantity of money is in terms of the time duration of the flow of goods and services the money could purchase. For a household, for example, the real quantity of money can be expressed in terms of the number of weeks of the household's average level of consumption its money balances could finance or, alternatively, in terms of the number of weeks of its average income to which its money balances are equal. For a business enterprise, the real quantity of money it holds can be expressed in terms of the number of weeks of its average purchases, or of its average sales, or of its average expenditures on final productive services (net value added) to which its money balances are equal. For the community as a whole, the real quantity of money can be expressed in terms of the number of weeks of aggregate transactions of the community, or aggregate net output of the community, to which its money balances are equal.

The reciprocal of any of this latter class of measures of the real quantity of money is a velocity of circulation for the corresponding unit or group of units. For example, the ratio of the annual transactions of the community to its stock of money is the 'transactions velocity of circulation of money', since it gives the number of times the stock of money would have to 'turn over' in a year to accomplish all transactions. Similarly, the ratio of annual income to the stock of money is termed 'income velocity'. In every case, the real quantity of money is calculated at the set of prices prevailing at the date to which the calculation refers. These prices are the bridge between the nominal and the real quantity of money.

The quantity theory of money takes for granted, first, that the real quantity rather than the nominal quantity of money is what ultimately matters to holders of money and, second, that in any given circumstances people wish to hold a fairly definite real quantity of money. Starting from a situation in which the nominal quantity that people hold at a particular moment of time happens to correspond at current prices to the real quantity that they wish to hold, suppose that the quantity of money unexpectedly increases so that individuals have larger cash balances than they wish to hold. They will then seek to dispose of what they regard as their excess money balances by paying out a larger sum for the purchase of securities, goods, and services, for the repayment of debts, and as gifts, than they are receiving from the corresponding sources. However, they cannot as a group succeed. One man's spending is another man's receipts. One man can reduce his nominal money balances only by persuading someone else to increase his. The community as a whole cannot in general spend more than it receives; it is playing a game of musical chairs.

The attempt to dispose of excess balances will nonetheless have important effects. If prices and incomes are free to change, the attempt to spend more will raise total spending and receipts, expressed in nominal units, which will lead to a bidding up of prices and perhaps also to an increase in output. If prices are fixed by custom or by government edict, the attempt to spend more will either be matched by an increase in goods and services or produce 'shortages' and 'queues'. These in turn will raise the effective price and are likely sooner or later to force changes in customary or official prices.

The initial excess of nominal balances will therefore tend to be eliminated, even though there is no change in the nominal quantity of money, by either a reduction in the real quantity available to hold through price rises or an increase in the real quantity desired through output increases. And conversely for an initial deficiency of nominal balances.

Changes in prices and nominal income can be produced either by changes in the real balances that people wish to hold or by changes in the nominal balances available for them to hold. Indeed, it is a tautology, summarized in the famous quantity equations, that all changes in nominal income can be attributed to one or the other – just as a change in the price of any good can always be attributed to a change in either demand or supply. The quantity theory is not, however, this tautology. On an analytical level, it has long been an analysis of the factors determining the quantity of money that the community wishes to hold; on an empirical level, it has increasingly become the generalization that changes in desired real balances (in the demand for money) tend to proceed slowly and gradually or to be the result of events set in train by prior changes in supply, whereas, in contrast, substantial changes in the supply of nominal balances can and frequently do occur independently of any changes in demand. The conclusion is that substantial changes in prices or nominal income are almost always the result of changes in the nominal supply of money.

(b) Quantity equations
Attempts to formulate mathematically the relations just presented verbally date back several centuries (Humphrey, 1984). They consist of creating identities equating a flow of money payments to a flow of exchanges of goods or services. The resulting quantity equations have proved a useful analytical device and have taken different forms as quantity theorists have stressed different variables.

The transactions form of the quantity equation
The most famous version of the quantity equation is doubtless the transactions version formulated by Simon Newcomb (1885) and popularized by Irving Fisher (1911):

$$MV = PT, \tag{1}$$

or

$$MV + M'V' = PT. \tag{2}$$

In this version the elementary event is a transaction – an exchange in which one economic actor transfers goods or services or securities to another actor and receives a transfer of money in return. The right-hand side of the equations corresponds to the transfer of goods, services, or securities; the left-hand side, to the matching transfer of money.

Each transfer of goods, services or securities is regarded as the product of a price and quantity; wage per week times number of weeks, price of a good times number of units of the good, dividend per share times number of shares, price per share times number of shares, and so on. The right-hand side of equations (1) and (2) is the aggregate of such payments during some interval, with P a suitably chosen *average* of the prices and T a suitably chosen *aggregate* of the quantities during that interval, so that PT is the total nominal value of the payments during the interval in question. The units of P are dollars (or other monetary unit) per unit of quantity; the units of T are number of unit quantities per period of time. We can convert the equation from an expression applying to an *interval* of time to one applying to a *point* in time by the usual limiting process of letting the interval for which we aggregate payments approach zero, and expressing T not as an aggregate but as a rate of flow. The magnitude T then has the dimension of quantity per unit time; the product of P and T, of dollars (or other monetary unit) per unit time.

T is clearly a rather special index of quantities: it includes service flows (man-hours, dwelling-years, kilowatt-hours) and also physical capital items yielding such flows (houses, electric-generating plants) and securities representing both physical capital items and such intangible capital items as 'goodwill'. Since each capital item or security is treated as if it disappeared from economic circulation once it is transferred, any such item that is transferred more than once in the period in question is implicitly weighted by the number of times it enters into transactions (its 'velocity of circulation', in strict analogy with the 'velocity of circulation' of money). Similarly, P is a rather special price index.

The monetary transfer analysed on the left-hand side of equations (1) and (2) is treated very differently. The money that changes hands is treated as retaining its identity, and all money, whether used in transactions during the time interval in question or not, is explicitly accounted for. Money is treated as a stock, not as a flow or a mixture of a flow and a stock. For a single transaction, the breakdown into M and V is trivial: the cash that is transferred is turned over once, or $V = 1$. For all transactions during an interval of time, we can, in principle, classify the existing stock of monetary units according as each monetary unit entered into 0, 1, 2, … transactions – that is, according as the monetary unit 'turned over' 0, 1, 2, … times. The weighted average of these numbers of turnover, weighted by the number of dollars that turned over that number of times, is the conceptual equivalent of V. The dimensions of M are dollars (or other monetary unit); of V, number of turnovers per unit time; so, of the product, dollars per unit time.

Equation (2) differs from equation (1) by dividing payments into two categories: those effected by the transfer of hand-to-hand currency (including coin) and those effected by the transfer of deposits. In equation (2) M stands for the volume of currency and V for the velocity of currency, M' for the volume of deposits, and V' for the velocity of deposits.

One reason for the emphasis on this particular division was the persistent dispute about whether the term *money* should include only currency or deposits as well. Another reason was the direct availability of data on $M'V'$ from bank records of clearings or of debits to deposit accounts. These data make it possible to calculate V' in a way that is not possible for V.

Equations (1) and (2), like the other quantity equations we shall discuss, are intended to be identities – a special application of double-entry bookkeeping, with each transaction simultaneously recorded on both sides of the equation. However, as with the national income identities with which we are all familiar, when the two sides, or the separate elements on the two sides, are estimated from independent sources of data, many differences between them emerge. This statistical defect has been less obvious for the quantity equations than for the national income identities – with their standard entry 'statistical discrepancy' – because of the difficulty of calculating V directly. As a result, V in equation (1) and V and V' in equation (2) have generally been calculated as the numbers having the property that they render the equations correct. These calculated numbers therefore embody the whole of the counterpart to the 'statistical discrepancy'.

Just as the left-hand side of equation (1) can be divided into several components, as in equation (2), so also can the right-hand side. The emphasis on transactions reflected in this version of the quantity equation suggests dividing total transactions into categories of payments for which payment periods or practices differ: for example, into capital transactions, purchases of final goods and services, purchases of intermediate goods, and payments for the use of resources, perhaps separated into wage and salary payments and other payments. The observed value of V might well depend on the distribution of total payments among categories. Alternatively, if the quantity equation is interpreted not as an identity but as a functional relation expressing desired velocity as a function of other variables, the distribution of payments may well be an important set of variables.

The income form of the quantity equation

Despite the large amount of empirical work done on the transactions equations, notably by Irving Fisher (1911, pp. 280–318; 1919, pp. 407–9) and Carl Snyder (1934, pp. 278–91), the ambiguities of the concepts of 'transactions' and the 'general price level' – particularly those arising from the mixture of current and capital transactions – have never been satisfactorily resolved. More recently, national or social accounting has stressed income transactions rather than gross transactions and has explicitly if not wholly satisfactorily dealt with the conceptual and statistical problems involved in distinguishing between changes in prices and changes in quantities. As a result, since at least the work of James Angell (1936), monetary economists have tended to express the quantity equation in terms of income transactions rather than gross transactions. Let Y = nominal income, P = the price index implicit in estimating national income at constant prices, N = the number of persons in the population, y = per capita national income in constant prices, and $y' = Ny$ = national income at constant prices, so that

$$Y = PNy = Py'. \tag{3}$$

Let M represent, as before, the stock of money; but define V as the average number of times per unit time that the money stock is used in making *income* transactions (that is, payment for final productive services or, alternatively, for final goods and services) rather than all transactions. We can then write the quantity equation in income form as

$$MV = PNy = Py'. \tag{4}$$

or, if we desire to distinguish currency from deposit transactions, as

$$MV + M'V' = PNy. \tag{5}$$

Although the symbols P, V, and V' are used both in equations (4) and (5) and in equations (1) and (2), they stand for different concepts in each pair of equations. (In practice, gross national product often replaces national income in calculating velocity even though the logic underlying the equation calls for national income. The reason is the widespread belief that estimates of GNP are subject to less statistical error than estimates of national income.)

In the transactions version of the quantity equation, each intermediate transaction – that is, purchase by one enterprise from another – is included at the total value of the transaction, so that the value of wheat, for example, is included once when it is sold by the farmer to the mill, a second time when the mill sells flour to the baker, a third time when the baker sells bread to the grocer, a fourth time when the grocer sells bread to the consumer. In the income version, only the net value added by each of these transactions is included. To put it differently in the transactions version, the elementary event is an isolated exchange of a physical item for money – an actual, clearly observable event. In the income version, the elementary event is a hypothetical event that can be inferred but is not directly observable. It is a complete series of transactions involving the exchange of productive services for final goods, via a sequence of money payments, with all the intermediate transactions in this income circuit netted out. The total value of all transactions is therefore a multiple of the value of income transactions only.

For a given flow of productive services or, alternatively, of final products (two of the multiple faces of income), the volume of transactions will be affected by vertical integration or disintegration of enterprises, which reduces or increases the number of transactions involved in a single income circuit, and by technological changes that lengthen or shorten the process of transforming productive services into final products. The volume of income will not be thus affected.

Similarly, the transactions version includes the purchase of an existing asset – a house or a piece of land or a share of equity stock – precisely on a par with an intermediate or final transaction. The income version excludes such transactions completely.

Are these differences an advantage or disadvantage of the income version? That clearly depends on what it is that determines the amount of money people want to hold. Do changes of the kind considered in the preceding paragraphs, changes that alter the ratio of intermediate and capital transactions to income, also alter in the same direction and by the same proportion the amount of money people want to hold? Or do they tend to leave this amount unaltered? Or do they have a more complex effect?

The transactions and income versions of the quantity theory involve very different conceptions of the role of money. For the transactions version, the most important thing about money is that it is transferred. For the income version, the most important thing is that it is held. This difference is even more obvious from the Cambridge cash-balance version of the quantity equation (Pigou, 1917). Indeed, the income version can perhaps best be regarded as a way station between the Fisher and the Cambridge version.

Cambridge cash-balance approach
The essential feature of a money economy is that an individual who has something to exchange need not seek out the double coincidence – someone who both wants what he has and offers in exchange what he wants. He need only find someone who wants what he has, sell it to him for general purchasing power, and then find someone who has what he wants and buy it with general purchasing power.

For the act of purchase to be separated from the act of sale, there must be something that everybody will accept in exchange as 'general purchasing power' – this aspect of money is emphasized in the transactions approach. But also there must be something that can serve as a temporary abode of purchasing power in the interim between sale and purchase. This aspect of money is emphasized in the cash-balance approach.

How much money will people or enterprises want to hold on the average as a temporary abode of purchasing power? As a first approximation, it has generally been supposed that the amount bears some relation to income, on the assumption that income affects the volume of potential purchases for which the individual or enterprise wishes to hold cash balances. We can therefore write

$$M = kPNy = kPy',$$ (6)

where M, N, P, y, and y' are defined as in equation (4) and k is the ratio of money stock to income – either the observed ratio so calculated as to make equation (6) an identity or the 'desired' ratio so that M is the 'desired' amount of money, which need not be equal to the actual amount. In either case, k is numerically equal to the reciprocal of the V in equation (4), the V being interpreted in one case as measured velocity and in the other as desired velocity.

Although equation (6) is simply a mathematical transformation of equation (4), it brings out sharply the difference between the aspect of money stressed by the transactions approach and that stressed by the cash-balance approach. This difference makes different definitions of money seem natural and leads to placing emphasis on different variables and analytical techniques.

The transactions approach makes it natural to define money in terms of whatever serves as the medium of exchange in discharging obligations. The cash-balance approach makes it seem entirely appropriate to include in addition such temporary abodes of purchasing power as demand and time deposits not transferable by check, although it clearly does not require their inclusion (Friedman and Schwartz, 1970, ch. 3).

Similarly, the transactions approach leads to emphasis on the mechanical aspect of the payments process; payments practices, financial and economic arrangements for effecting transactions, the speed of communication and transportation, and so on (Baumol, 1952; Tobin, 1956; Miller and Orr, 1966, 1968). The cash-balance approach, on the other hand, leads to emphasis on variables affecting the usefulness of money as an asset: the costs and returns from holding money instead of other assets, the uncertainty of the future, and so on (Friedman, 1956; Tobin, 1958).

Of course, neither approach enforces the exclusion of the variables stressed by the other. Portfolio considerations enter into the costs of effecting transactions and hence affect the most efficient payment arrangements; mechanical considerations enter into the returns from holding cash and hence affect the usefulness of cash in a portfolio.

Finally, with regard to analytical techniques, the cash-balance approach fits in much more readily with the general Marshallian demand-supply apparatus than does the transactions approach. Equation (6) can be regarded as a demand function for money, with P, N, and y on the right-hand side being three of the variables on which the quantity of money demanded depends and k symbolizing all the other variables, so that k is to be regarded not as a numerical constant but as itself a function of still other variables. For completion, the analysis requires another equation showing the supply of money as a function of these and other variables. The price level or the level of nominal income is then the resultant of the interaction of the demand and supply functions.

Levels versus rates of change

The several versions of the quantity equations have all been stated in terms of the levels of the variables involved. For the analysis of monetary change it is often more useful to express them in terms of rates of change. For example, take the logarithm of both sides of equation (4) and differentiate with respect to time. The result is

$$\frac{1}{M}\frac{dM}{dt} + \frac{1}{V}\frac{dV}{dt} = \frac{1}{P}\frac{dP}{dt} + \frac{1}{y'}\frac{dy'}{dt} \tag{7}$$

or, in simpler notation,

$$g_M + g_V = g_P + g_{y'} = g_{Y'}, \tag{8}$$

where g stands for the percentage rate of change (continuously compounded) of the variable denoted by its subscript. The same equation is implied by equation (6), with g_V replaced by $- g_k$.

The rate of change equations serve two very different purposes. First, they make explicit an important difference between a once-for-all change in the level of the quantity of money and a change in the rate of change of the quantity of money. The former is equivalent simply to a change of units – to substituting cents for dollars or pence for pounds – and hence, as is implicit in equations (4) and (6), would not be presumed to have any effect on real quantities, on neither V (nor k) nor y', but simply an offsetting effect on the price level, P. A change in the rate of change of money is a very different thing. It will tend, according to equations (7) and (8), to be accompanied by a change in the rate of inflation (g_P) which, as pointed out in section d below, affects the cost of holding money, and hence the desired real quantity of money. Such a change will therefore affect real quantities, V and g_V, y' and $g_{y'}$, as well as nominal and real interest rates.

The second purpose served by the rate of change equations is to make explicit the role of time, and thereby to facilitate the study of the effect of monetary change on the temporal pattern of response of the several variables involved. In recent decades, economists have devoted increasing attention to the short-term pattern of economic change, which has enhanced the importance of the rate of change versions of the quantity equations.

(c) The supply of money

The quantity theory in its cash-balance version suggests organizing an analysis of monetary phenomena in terms of (1) the conditions determining supply (this section); (2) the conditions determining demand (section d below); and (3) the reconciliation of demand with supply (section e below).

The factors determining the nominal supply of money available to be held depend critically on the monetary system. For systems like those that have prevailed in most major countries during the past two centuries, they can usefully be analysed under three main headings termed the proximate determinants of the quantity of money: (1) the amount of high-powered money – specie plus notes or deposit liabilities issued by the monetary authorities and used either as currency or as reserves by banks; (2) the ratio of bank deposits to bank holdings of high-powered money; and (3) the ratio of the public's deposits to its currency holdings (Friedman and Schwartz, 1963b, pp. 776–98; Cagan, 1965; Burger, 1971; Black, 1975).

It is an identity that

$$M = H \cdot \frac{\dfrac{D}{R}\left(1 + \dfrac{D}{C}\right)}{\dfrac{D}{R} + \dfrac{D}{C}}, \tag{9}$$

where H = high-powered money; D = deposits; R = bank reserves; C = currency in the hands of the public so that (D/R) is the deposit–reserve ratio; and (D/C) is the deposit–currency ratio. The fraction on the right-hand side of (9), i.e., the ratio of M to H, is termed the money multiplier, often a convenient summary of the effect of the two deposit ratios. The determinants are called proximate because their values are in turn determined by much more basic variables. Moreover, the same labels can refer to very different contents.

High-powered money is the clearest example. Until some time in the 18th or 19th century, the exact date varying from country to country, it consisted only of specie or its equivalent: gold, or silver, or cowrie shells, or any of a wide variety of commodities. Thereafter, until 1971, with some significant if temporary exceptions, it consisted of a mixture of specie and of government notes or deposit liabilities. The government notes and liabilities generally were themselves promises to pay specified amounts of specie on demand, though this promise weakened after World War I, when many countries promised to pay either specie or foreign currency. During the Bretton Woods periods after World War II, only the USA was obligated to pay gold, and only to foreign monetary agencies, not to individuals or other non-governmental entities; other countries obligated themselves to pay dollars.

Since 1971, the situation has been radically different. In every major country, high-powered money consists solely of fiat money – pieces of paper issued by the government and inscribed with the legend 'one dollar' or 'one pound' and the message 'legal tender for all debts public and private'; or book entries, labelled deposits, consisting of promises to pay such pieces of paper. Such a worldwide fiat (or irredeemable paper) standard has no precedent in history. The 'gold' central banks still record as an asset on their books is simply the grin of a Cheshire cat that has disappeared.

Under an international commodity standard, the total quantity of high-powered money in any one country – so long as it remains on the standard – is determined by the balance of payments. The division of high-powered money between physical specie and the fiduciary component of government-issued promises to pay is determined by the policies of the monetary authorities. For the world as a whole, the total quantity of high-powered money is determined both by the policies of the various monetary authorities and the physical conditions of supply of specie. The latter provide a physical anchor for the quantity of money and hence ultimately for the price level.

Under the current international fiat standard, the quantity of high-powered money is determined solely by the monetary authorities, consisting in most countries of a central bank plus the fiscal authorities. What happens to the quantity of high-powered money depends on their objectives, on the institutional and political arrangements under which they operate, and the operating procedures they adopt. These are likely to vary considerably from country to country. Some countries (e.g., Hong Kong, Panama) have chosen to link their currencies rigidly to some other currency by pegging the exchange rate. For them, the amount of high-powered money is determined in the same way as under an international commodity standard – by the balance of payments.

The current system is so new that it must be regarded as in a state of transition. Some substitute is almost sure to emerge to replace the supply of specie as a long-term anchor for the price level, but it is not yet clear what that substitute will be (see section 5 below).

The deposit–reserve ratio is determined by the banking system subject to any requirements that are imposed by law or the monetary authorities. In addition to any such requirements, it depends on such factors as the risk of calls for conversion of bank deposits to high-powered money; the cost of acquiring additional high-powered money in case of need; and the returns from loans and investments, that is, the structure of interest rates.

The deposit–currency ratio is determined by the public. It depends on the relative usefulness to holders of money of deposits and currency and the relative cost of holding the one or the other. The relative cost in turn depends on the rates of interest received on deposits, which may be subject to controls imposed by law or the monetary authorities.

These factors determine the *nominal*, but not the *real*, quantity of money. The real quantity of money is determined by the interaction between the *nominal* quantity supplied and the *real* quantity demanded. In the process, changes in demand for real balances have feedback effects on the variables determining the nominal quantity supplied, and changes in nominal supply have feedback effects on the variables determining the real quantity demanded. Quantity theorists have generally concluded that these feedback effects are relatively minor, so that the *nominal* supply can generally be regarded as determined by a set of variables distinct from those that affect the *real* quantity demanded. In this sense, the nominal quantity can be regarded as determined primarily by supply, the real quantity, primarily demand.

Instead of expressing the nominal supply in terms of the identity (9), it can also be expressed as a function of the variables that are regarded as affecting H, D/R, and D/C, such as the rate of inflation, interest rates, nominal income, the extent of uncertainty, perhaps also the variables that are regarded as determining the decisions of the monetary authorities. Such a supply function is frequently written as

$$M^S = h(R, Y, \ldots), \tag{10}$$

where R is an interest rate or set of interest rates, Y is nominal income, and the dots stand for other variables that are regarded as relevant.

(d) The demand for money

The cash-balance version of the quantity theory, by stressing the role of money as an asset, suggests treating the demand for money as part of capital or wealth theory, concerned with the composition of the balance sheet or portfolio of assets.

From this point of view, it is important to distinguish between ultimate wealth holders, to whom money is one form in which they choose to hold their wealth, and enterprises, to whom money is a producer's good like machinery or inventories (Friedman, 1956; Laidler, 1985; Friedman and Schwartz, 1982).

Demand by ultimate wealth holders

For ultimate wealth holders the demand for money, in real terms, may be expected to be a function primarily of the following variables:

1. *Total wealth*
   This is the analogue of the budget constraint in the usual theory of consumer choice. It is the total that must be divided among various forms of assets. In practice, estimates of total wealth are seldom available. Instead, income may serve as an index of wealth. However, it should be recognized that income as measured by statisticians may be a defective index of wealth because it is subject to erratic year-to-year fluctuations, and a longer-term concept, like the concept of permanent income developed in connection with the theory of consumption, may be more useful (Friedman, 1957, 1959).
   The emphasis on income as a surrogate for wealth, rather than as a measure of the 'work' to be done by money, is perhaps the basic conceptual difference between the more recent analyses of the demand for money and the earlier versions of the quantity theory.
2. *The division of wealth between human and non-human forms*
   The major asset of most wealth holders is personal earning capacity. However, the conversion of human into non-human wealth or the reverse is subject to narrow limits because of institutional constraints. It can be done by using current earnings to purchase non-human wealth or by using non-human wealth to finance the acquisition of skills, but not by purchase or sale of human wealth and to only a limited extent by borrowing on the collateral of earning power. Hence, the fraction of total wealth that is in the form of non-human wealth may be an additional important variable.
3. *The expected rates of return on money and other assets*
   These rates of return are the counterparts to the prices of a commodity and its substitutes and complements in the usual theory of consumer demand.

The nominal rate of return on money may be zero, as it generally is on currency, or negative, as it sometimes is on demand deposits subject to net service charges, or positive, as it sometimes is on demand deposits on which interest is paid and generally is on time deposits. The nominal rate of return on other assets consists of two parts: first, any currently paid yield, such as interest on bonds, dividends on equities, or cost, such as storage costs on physical assets, and, second, a change in the nominal price of the asset. The second part is especially important under conditions of inflation or deflation.

4. *Other variables determining the utility attached to the services rendered by money relative to those rendered by other assets – in Keynesian terminology, determining the value attached to liquidity proper*
One such variable may be one already considered – namely, real wealth or income, since the services rendered by money may, in principle, be regarded by wealth holders as a 'necessity', like bread, the consumption of which increases less than in proportion to any increase in income, or as a 'luxury', like recreation, the consumption of which increases more than in proportion.

Another variable that is important empirically is the degree of economic stability expected to prevail, since instability enhances the value wealth-holders attach to liquidity. This variable has proved difficult to express quantitatively although qualitative information often indicates the direction of change. For example, the outbreak of war clearly produces expectations of greater instability. That is one reason why a notable increase in real balances – that is, a notable decline in velocity – often accompanies the outbreak of war. Such a decline in velocity produced an initial *decline* in sensitive prices at the outset of both World War I and World War II – not the rise that later inflation would have justified.

The rate of inflation enters under item 3 as a factor affecting the cost of holding various assets, particularly currency. The variability of inflation enters here, as a major factor affecting the usefulness of money balances. Empirically, variability of inflation tends to increase with the level of inflation, reinforcing the negative effect of higher inflation on the quantity of money demanded.

Still another relevant variable may be the volume of trading in existing capital goods by ultimate wealth holders. The higher the turnover of capital assets, the larger the fraction of total assets people may find it useful to hold as cash. This variable corresponds to the class of transactions omitted in going from the transactions version of the quantity equation to the income version.

We can express this analysis in terms of the following demand function for money for an individual wealth holder:

$$M^D = P \cdot f(y, w, R_M^*, R_B^*, R_E^*; u), \tag{11}$$

where M, P, and y have the same meaning as in equation (6) except that they relate to a single wealth-holder (for whom $y = y'$); w is the fraction of wealth in non-human form (or, alternatively, the fraction of income derived from property); an asterisk denotes an expected value, so R_M^* is the expected nominal rate of return on money; R_B^* is the expected nominal rate of return on fixed-value securities, including expected changes in their prices; R_E^* is the expected nominal rate of return on physical assets, including expected changes in their prices; and u is a portmanteau symbol standing for other variables affecting the utility attached to the services of money. Though the expected rate of inflation is not explicit in equation (11), it is implicit because it affects the expected nominal returns on the various classes of assets, and is sometimes used as a proxy for R_E^*. For some purposes it may be important to classify assets still more finely – for example, to distinguish currency from deposits, long-term from short-term fixed-value securities, risky from relatively safe equities, and one kind of physical assets from another.

Furthermore, the several rates of return are not independent. Arbitrage tends to eliminate differences among them that do not correspond to differences in perceived risk or other nonpecuniary characteristics of the assets, such as liquidity. In particular, as Irving Fisher pointed out in 1896, arbitrage between real and nominal assets introduces an allowance for anticipated inflation into the nominal interest rate (Fischer, 1896; Friedman, 1956).

The usual problems of aggregation arise in passing from equation (11) to a corresponding equation for the economy as a whole – particular, from the possibility that the amount of money demanded may depend on the distribution among individuals of such variables as y and w and not merely on their aggregate or average value. If we neglect these distributional effects, equation (11) can be regarded as applying to the community as a whole, with M and y referring to per capital money holdings and per capital real income, respectively, and w to the fraction of aggregate wealth in non-human form.

Although the mathematical equation may be the same, its significance is very different for the individual wealth-holder and the community as a whole. For the individual, all the variables in the equation other than his own income and the disposition of his portfolio are outside his control. He takes them, as well as the structure of monetary institutions, as given, and adjusts his nominal balances accordingly. For the community as a whole, the situation is very different. In general, the nominal quantity of money available to be held is fixed and what adjusts are the variables on the right-hand side of the equation, including an implicit underlying variable, the structure of monetary institutions, which, in the longer run, at least, adjusts itself to the tastes and preferences of the holders of money. A dramatic example is provided by the restructuring of the financial system in the US in the 1970s and 1980s.

In practice, the major problems that arise in applying equation (11) are the precise definitions of y and w, the estimation of *expected* rates of return as contrasted with actual rates of return, and the quantitative specification of the variables designated by u.

Demand for business enterprises
Business enterprises are not subject to a constraint comparable to that imposed by total wealth of the ultimate wealth-holder. They can determine the total amount of

capital embodied in productive assets, including money, to maximize returns, since they can acquire additional capital through the capital market.

A similar variable defining the 'scale' of the enterprise may, however, be relevant as an index of the productive value of different quantities of money to the enterprise. Lack of data has meant that much less empirical work has been done on the business demand for money than on the aggregate demand enterprises. As a result, there are as yet only faint indications about the best variable to use: whether total transactions, net value added, net income, total capital in nonmoney form, or net worth.

The division of wealth between human and non-human form has no special relevance to business enterprises, since they are likely to buy the services of both forms on the market.

Rates of return on money and on alternative assets are, of course, highly relevant to business enterprises. These rates determine the net cost of holding money balances. However, the particular rates that are relevant may differ from those that are relevant for ultimate wealth-holders. For example, the rates banks charge on loans are of minor importance for wealth-holders yet may be extremely important for businesses, since bank loans may be a way in which they can acquire the capital embodied in money balances.

The counterpart for business enterprises of the variable u in equation (11) is the set of variables other than scale affecting the productivity of money balances. At least one subset of such variables – namely, expectations about economic stability and the variability of inflation – is likely to be common to business enterprises and ultimate wealth-holders.

With these interpretations of the variables, equation (11), with w excluded, can be regarded as symbolizing the business demand for money and, as it stands, symbolizing aggregate demand for money, although with even more serious qualifications about the ambiguities introduced by aggregation.

Buffer stock effects
In serving its basic function as a temporary abode of purchasing power, cash balances necessarily fluctuate, absorbing temporary discrepancies between the purchases and sales they mediate.

Though always recognized, this 'buffer stock' role of money has seldom been explicitly modelled. Recently, more explicit attention has been paid to the buffer stock notion in an attempt to explain anomalies that have arisen in econometric estimates of the short-run demand for money (Judd and Scadding, 1982; Laidler, 1984; Knoester, 1984).

(e) The reconciliation of demand with supply
Multiply equation (11) by N to convert it from a per capita to an aggregate demand function, and equate it to equation (10), omitting for simplicity the asterisks designating expected values, and letting R stand for a vector of interest rates:

$$M^S = h(R, Y, \ldots) = P \cdot N \cdot f(y, w, R, g_P, u). \tag{12}$$

The result is quantity equation (6) in an expanded form. In principle, a change in any of the underlying variables that produces a change in M^S and disturbs a pre-existing equilibrium can produce offsetting changes in any of the other variables. In practice, as already noted earlier, the initial impact is likely to be on y and R, the ultimate impact predominantly on P.

A frequent criticism of the quantity theory is that its proponents do not specify the transmission mechanism between a change in M^S and the offsetting changes in other variables, that they rely on a black box connecting the input – the nominal quantity of money – and the output – effects on prices and quantities.

This criticism is not justified insofar as it implies that the transmission mechanism for the quantity equation is fundamentally different from that for a demand–supply analysis of a particular product – shoes, or copper, or haircuts. In both cases the demand function for the community as a whole is the sum of demand functions for individual consumer or producer units, and the separate demand functions are determined by the tastes and opportunities of the units. In both cases, the supply function depends on production possibilities, institutional arrangements for organizing production, and the conditions of supply of resources. In both cases a shift in supply or in demand introduces a discrepancy between the amounts demanded and supplied *at the pre-existing price*. In both cases any discrepancy can be eliminated only by either a price change or some alternative rationing mechanism, explicit or implicit.

Two features of the demand–supply adjustment for money have concealed this parallelism. One is that demand–supply analysis for particular products typically deals with flows – number of pairs of shoes or number of haircuts per year – whereas the quantity equations deal with the stock of money at a point in time. In this respect the correct analogy is with the demand for, say, land, which, like money, derives its value from the flow of services it renders but has a purchase price and not merely a rental value. The second is the widespread tendency to confuse 'money' and 'credit', which has produced misunderstanding about the relevant price variable. The 'price' of money is the quantity of goods and services that must be given up to acquire a unit of money – the inverse of the price level. This is the price that is analogous to the price of land or of copper or of haircuts. The 'price' of money is not the interest rate, which is the 'price' of credit. The interest rate connects stocks with flows – the rental value of land with the price of land, the value of the service flow from a unit of money with the price of money. Of course, the interest rate may affect the quantity of money demanded – just as it may affect the quantity of land demanded – but so may a host of other variables.

The interest rate has received special attention in monetary analysis because, without quite realizing it, fractional reserve banks have created part of the stock of money in the course of serving as an intermediary between borrowers and lenders. Hence changes in the quantity of money have frequently occurred through the credit markets, in the process producing important transitory effects on interest rates.

On a more sophisticated level, the criticism about the transmission mechanism applies equally to money and to other goods and services. In all cases it is desirable to go beyond equality of demand and supply as defining a stationary equilibrium position and examine the variables that affect the quantities demanded and supplied and the dynamic temporal process whereby actual or potential discrepancies are eliminated. Examination of the variables affecting demand and supply has been carried farther for money than for most other goods or services. But for both, there is as yet no satisfactory and widely accepted description, in precise quantifiable terms, of the dynamic temporal process of adjustment. Much research has been devoted to this question in recent decades; yet it remains a challenging subject for research. (For surveys of some of the literature, see Laidler, 1985; Judd and Scadding, 1982.)

(f) First-round effects
Another frequent criticism of the quantity equations is that they neglect any effect on the outcome of the source of change in the quantity of money. In Tobin's words, the question is whether 'the genesis of new money makes a difference', in particular, whether 'an increase in the quantity of money has the same effect whether it is issued to purchase goods or to purchase bonds' (1974, p. 87).

Or, as John Stuart Mill put a very similar view in 1844, 'The issues of a *Government* paper, even when not permanent, will raise prices; because Governments usually issue their paper in purchases for consumption. If issued to pay off a portion of the national debt, we believe they would have no effect' (1844, p. 589).

Tobin and Mill are right that the way the quantity of money is increased affects the outcome in some measure or other. If one group of individuals receives the money on the first round, they will likely use it for different purposes than another group of individuals. If the newly printed money is spent on the first round for goods and services, it adds directly at that point to the demand for such goods and services, whereas if it is spent on purchasing debt, or simply held temporarily as a buffer stock, it has no immediate effect on the demand for goods and services. Such effects come later as the initial recipients of the 'new' money dispose of it. However, as the 'new' money spreads through the economy, any first-round effects tend to be dissipated. The 'new' money is merged with the old and is distributed in much the same way.

One way to characterize the Keynesian approach (see below) is that it gives almost exclusive importance to the first-round effect by putting primary emphasis on flows of spending rather than on stocks of assets. Similarly, one way to characterize the quantity-theory approach is to say that it gives almost no importance to first-round effects.

The empirical question is how important the first-round effects are compared with the ultimate effects. Theory cannot answer that question. The answer depends on how different are the reactions of the recipients of cash via alternative routes, on how rapidly a larger money stock is distributed through the economy, on how long it stays at each point in the economy, on how much the demand for money depends on the structure of government liabilities, and so on. Casual empiricism yields no decisive answer. Maybe the first-round effect is so strong that it dominates later effects; maybe it is highly transitory.

Despite repeated assertions by various authors that the first-round effect is significant, none, so far as I know, has presented any systematic empirical evidence to support that assertion. The apparently similar response of spending to changes in the quantity of money at widely separated dates in different countries and under diverse monetary systems establishes something of a presumption that the first-round effect is not highly significant. This presumption is also supported by several empirical studies designed to test the importance of the first-round effect (Cagan, 1972).

(g) The international transmission mechanism

From its very earliest days, the quantity theory was intimately connected with the analysis of the adjustment mechanism in international trade. A commodity standard, in which money is specie or its equivalent, was taken as the norm. Under such a standard, the supply of money in any one country is determined by the links between that country and other countries that use the same commodity as money. Under such a standard, the same theory explains links among money, prices, and nominal income in various parts of a single country – money, prices, and nominal income in Illinois and money, prices, and nominal income in the rest of the United States – and the corresponding links among various countries. The differences between interregional adjustment and international adjustment are empirical: greater mobility of people, goods, and capital among regions than among countries, and hence more rapid adjustment.

According to the specie-flow mechanism developed by Hume and elaborated by Henry Thornton, David Ricardo and their successors, 'too' high a money stock in country A tends to make prices in A high relative to prices in the rest of the world, encouraging imports and discouraging exports. The resulting deficit in the balance of trade is financed by shipment of specie, which reduces the quantity of money in country A and increases it in the rest of the world. These changes in the quantity of money tend to lower prices in country A and raise them in the rest of the world, correcting the original disequilibrium. The process continues until price levels in all countries are at a level at which balances of payments are in equilibrium (which may be consistent with a continuing movement of specie, for example, from gold- or silver-producing countries to non-gold- or silver-producing countries, or between countries growing at different secular rates).

Another strand of the classical analysis has recently been revived under the title 'the monetary theory of the balance of payments'. The specie-flow mechanism implicitly assumes that prices adjust only in response to changes in the quantity of money produced by specie flows. However, if markets are efficient and transportation costs are neglected, there can be only a single price expressed in a common currency for goods traded internationally. Speculation tends to assure this result. Internally, competition between traded and nontraded goods tends to keep their relative price in line with relative costs. If these adjustments are rapid, 'the law of one price' holds among countries. If the money stock is not distributed among countries in such a way as to be consistent with the equilibrium prices, excess demands and supplies of money will lead to specie flows. Domestic nominal demand in a country with 'too' high a quantity of money will exceed the value of domestic output and the excess will be met by imports, producing a balance of payments deficit financed by the export of specie; and conversely in a country with too 'low' a quantity of money. Specie flows are still the adjusting mechanism, but they are produced by differences between demand for output in nominal terms and the supply of output at world prices rather than by discrepancies in prices. Putative rather than actual price differences are the spur to adjustment. This description is highly oversimplified, primarily because it omits the important role assigned to short- and long-term capital flows by all theorists – those who stress the specie-flow mechanism and even more those who stress the single-price mechanism (Frenkel, 1976; Frenkel and Johnson, 1976).

In practice, few countries have had pure commodity standards. Most have had a mixture of commodity and fiduciary standards. Changes in the fiduciary component of the stock of money can replace specie flows as a means of adjusting the quantity of money.

The situation is still different for countries that do not share a unified currency, that is, a currency in which only the name assigned to a unit of currency differs among countries. Changes in the rates of exchange between national currencies then serve to keep prices in various countries in the appropriate relation when expressed in a common currency. Exchange rate adjustments replace specie flows or changes in the quantity of domestically created money. And exchange rate changes too may be produced by actual or putative price differences or by short- or long-term capital flows. Moreover, especially during the Bretton Woods period (1945–71), but more recently as well, governments have often tried to avoid changes in exchange rates by seeking adjustment through subsidies to exports, obstacles to imports, and direct controls over foreign exchange transactions. These measures involved either implicit or explicit multiple rate systems and were accompanied by government borrowing to finance balance-of-payments deficits, or governmental lending to offset surpluses. They sometimes led to severe financial crises and major exchange rate adjustments – one reason the Bretton Woods system finally broke down in 1971. Since then, exchange rates have supposedly been free to float and to be determined in private markets. In practice, however, governments still intervene in an attempt to affect the exchange rates of their currencies, either directly by buying or selling their currency on the market, or indirectly, by adopting monetary or fiscal or trade policies designed to alter the market exchange rate. However, most governments no longer announce fixed parities for their currencies.

2. Keynesian challenge to the quantity theory

The depression of the 1930s produced a wave of scepticism about the relevance and validity of the quantity theory of money. The central banks of the world – the Federal

Reserve in the forefront – proclaimed that, despite the teachings of the quantity theory, 'easy money' was proving to be ineffective in stemming the depression. They pointed to the low level of short-term interest rates as evidence of how 'easy' monetary policy was. Their claims seemed credible not only because of the confusion between 'lowness of interest' and 'plenty of money' pointed out by Hume but also because of the absence of readily available evidence on what was happening to the quantity of money. Most observers at the time did not know, as we do now, that the Federal Reserve permitted the quantity of money in the United States to decline by one-third between 1929 and 1933, and hence that the accompanying contraction in economic activity and deflation of prices was entirely consistent with the quantity theory. Monetary policy was incredibly 'tight' not 'easy'.

The scepticism about the quantity theory was further heightened by the publication of John Maynard Keynes's *The General Theory of Employment, Interest and Money* (Keynes, 1936) which offered an alternative interpretation of economic fluctuations in general and the depression in particular. Keynes emphasized spending on investment and the stability of the consumption function rather than the stock of money and the stability of the demand function for money. He relegated the forces embodied in the quantity theory to a minor role, and treated fiscal rather than monetary policy as the chief instrument for influencing the course of events. Received wisdom both inside and outside the economics profession became 'money does not matter'.

Keynes did not deny the validity of the quantity equation, in any of its forms – after all, he had been a major contributor to the quantity theory (Keynes, 1923). What he did was something very different. He argued that the demand for money, which he termed the liquidity-preference function, had a special form such that *under conditions of underemployment* the V in equation (4) and the k in equation (6) would be highly unstable and would passively adapt to whatever changes independently occurred in money income or the stock of money. Under such conditions, these equations, though entirely valid, were largely useless for policy or prediction. Moreover, he regarded such conditions as prevailing much, if not most of the time.

That possibility rested on two other key propositions. First, that, contrary to the teachings of classical and neoclassical economists, the *long-run equilibrium* position of an economy need not be characterized by 'full employment' of resources even if all prices are flexible. In his view, unemployment could be a deep-seated characteristic of an economy rather than simply a reflection of price and wage rigidity or transitory disturbances. This proposition has played an important role in promoting the acceptance of Keynesianism, especially by non-economists, even though, by now, it is widely accepted that, as a *theoretical* matter, the proposition is false. Keynes's error consisted in neglecting the role of wealth in the consumption function. There is no fundamental 'flaw in the price system' that makes persistent structural unemployment a possible or probable natural outcome of a fully operative market system (Haberler, 1941, pp. 242, 389, 403, 491–503; Pigou, 1947; Tobin, 1947; Patinkin, 1948; Johnson, 1961). The concept of 'underemployment equilibrium' has been replaced by the concept of a 'natural rate of unemployment' (see section 3 below).

Keynes's final key proposition was that, as an *empirical* matter, prices, especially wages, can be regarded as rigid – an institutional datum – for *short-run economic fluctuations*; in which case, the distinction between real and nominal magnitudes that is at the heart of the quantity theory is irrelevant for such fluctuations. This proposition, unlike the other two, did not conflict with the teachings of the quantity theory. Classical and neoclassical economists had long recognized that price and wage rigidity existed and contributed to unemployment during cyclical contractions, and to labour scarcity during cyclical booms. But to them, wage rigidity was a defect of the market; to Keynes, it was a rational response to the possibility of underemployment equilibrium (Keynes, 1936, pp. 269–71).

In his analysis of the demand for money (i.e., the form of equation (6) or (11)), Keynes treated the stock of money as if it were divided into two parts, one part, M_1, 'held to satisfy the transactions- and precautionary-motives', the other, M_2, 'held to satisfy the speculative-motive' (Keynes, 1936, p. 199). He regarded M_1 as a roughly constant fraction of income. He regarded the demand for M_2 as arising from '*uncertainty* as to the future course of the rate of interest' (Keynes, 1936, p. 168) and the amount demanded as depending on the relation between current rates of interest and the rates of interest expected to prevail in the future. Keynes, of course, recognized the existence of a whole complex of interest rates. However, for simplicity, he spoke in terms of 'the rate of interest', usually meaning by that the rate on long-term securities that were fixed in nominal value and that involved minimal risks of default – for example, government bonds. In a 'given state of expectations', the higher the current rate of interest, the lower would be the (real) amount of money that people would want to hold for speculative motives for two reasons: first, the greater would be the cost in terms of current earnings sacrificed by holding money instead of securities, and, second, the more likely it would be that interest rates would fall, and hence bond prices rise, and so the greater would be the cost in terms of capital gains sacrificed by holding money instead of securities.

To formalize Keynes's analysis in terms of the symbols we have used so far, we can write his demand (liquidity-preference) function as

$$M/P = M_1/P + M_2/P = k_1 y' + f(R - R^*, R^*) \qquad (13)$$

where R is the current rate of interest, R^* is the rate of interest expected to prevail, and k_1, the analogue to the inverse of the income velocity of circulation of money, is treated as determined by payment practices and hence as a constant at least in the short run. Later writers in this tradition have argued that k_1 too should be regarded as a function of interest rates (Baumol, 1952; Tobin, 1956).

Although expectations are given great prominence in developing the liquidity function expressing the demand for M_2, Keynes and his followers generally did not explicitly introduce an expected interest rate into that function as is done in equation (13). For the most part, in practice, they treated the amount of M_2 demanded as a function simply of the current interest rate, the emphasis on expectations serving only as a reason for attributing instability to the liquidity function. Moreover, for the most part, they omitted P (and replaced y' by Y) because of their assumption that prices were rigid.

Except for somewhat different language, the analysis up to this point differs from that of earlier quantity theorists, such as Fisher, only by its subtle analysis of the role of expectations about future interest rates, its greater emphasis on current interest rates, and its narrower restriction of the variables explicitly considered as affecting the amount of money demanded.

Keynes's special twist concerned the empirical form of the liquidity-preference function at the low interest rates that he believed would prevail under conditions of underemployment equilibrium. Let the interest rate fall sufficiently low, he argued, and money and bonds would become perfect substitutes for one another; liquidity preference, as he put it, would become absolute. The liquidity-preference function, expressing the quantity of M_2 demanded as a function of the rate of interest, would become horizontal at some low but finite rate of interest. Under such circumstances, an increase in the quantity of money by whatever means would lead holders of money to seek to convert their additional cash balances into bonds, which would tend to lower the rate of interest on bonds. Even the slightest lowering would lead speculators with firm expectations to absorb the additional money balances by selling any bonds demanded by the initial holders of the additional money. The result would simply be that the community as a whole would hold the increased quantity of money without any change in the interest rate; k would be higher and V lower. Conversely, a decrease in the quantity of money would lead holders of bonds to seek to restore their money balances by selling bonds, but this would tend to raise the rate of interest, and even the slightest rise would induce the speculators to absorb the bonds offered.

Or, again, suppose nominal income increases or decreases for whatever reason. That will require an increase or decrease in M_1, which can come out of or be transferred to M_2 without any further effects. The conclusion is that, *under circumstances of absolute liquidity preference*, income can change without a change in M and M can change without a change in income. The holders of money are in metastable equilibrium, like a tumbler on its side on a flat surface; they will be satisfied with whatever the quantity of money happens to be.

Keynes regarded absolute liquidity preference as a strictly 'limiting case' of which, though it 'might become practically important in future', he knew 'of no example ... hitherto' (1936, p. 207). However, he treated velocity as if in practice its behaviour frequently approximated that which would prevail in this limiting case.

Keynes's disciples went much farther than Keynes himself. They were readier than he was to accept absolute liquidity preference as the actual state of affairs. More important, many argued that when liquidity preference was not absolute, changes in the quantity of money would affect only the interest rate on bonds and that changes in this interest rate in turn would have little further effect. They argued that both consumption expenditures and investment expenditures were nearly completely insensitive to changes in interest rates, so that a change in M would merely be offset by an opposite and compensatory change in V (or a change in the same direction in k), leaving P and y almost completely unaffected. In essence their argument consists in asserting that only paper securities are substitutes for money balances – that real assets never are (see Hansen, 1957, p. 50; Tobin, 1961).

The apparent success during the 1950s and 1960s of governments committed to a Keynesian full-employment policy in achieving rapid economic growth, a high degree of economic stability, and relatively stable prices and interest rates, for a time strongly reinforced belief in the initial Keynesian views about the unimportance of variations in the nominal quantity of money.

The 1970s administered a decisive blow to these views and fostered a revival of belief in the quantity theory. Rapid monetary growth was accompanied not only by accelerated inflation but also by rising, not falling, average levels of unemployment (Friedman, 1977), and by rising, not declining, interest rates. As Robert Lucas put it in 1981,

> Keynesian orthodoxy ... appears to be giving seriously wrong answers to the most basic questions of macroeconomic policy. Proponents of a class of models which promised $3\frac{1}{2}$ to $4\frac{1}{2}$ percent unemployment to a society willing to tolerate annual inflation rates of 4 to 5 percent have some explaining to do after a decade [i.e., the 1970s] such as we have just come through. A forecast error of this magnitude and central importance to policy has consequences (pp. 559–60).

This experience undermined the belief that the price level could be regarded as rigid – or at any rate as determined by forces unrelated to the quantity of money; that the nominal quantity of money demanded could be regarded as a function primarily of the nominal interest rate, and that absolute liquidity preference was the normal state of affairs. No teacher of elementary economics since the late 1970s can, as so many did in the 1940s, 1950s, and 1960s, draw on the blackboard a downward sloping liquidity-preference diagram with the nominal quantity of money on the horizontal axis and a nominal interest rate on the vertical axis and confidently proclaim that the only important effect of an increase in the nominal quantity of money would be to lower the rate of interest. The distinction between the nominal interest rate and the real interest rate introduced by Irving Fisher in 1896 has entered – or re-entered – received wisdom (Fisher, 1896).

Despite its subsidence, the Keynesian attack on the quantity theory has left its mark. It has reinforced the tendency, already present in the Cambridge approach, to stress the role of money as an asset and hence to regard the analysis of the demand for money as part of capital or wealth theory, concerned with the composition of the balance sheet or portfolio of assets. The Keynesian stress on autonomous spending and hence on fiscal policy remains important in its own right but also has led to greater emphasis on the effect of government fiscal policies on the demand for money. Keynes's stress on expectations has contributed to the rapid growth in the analysis of the role and formation of expectations in a variety of economic contexts. Conversely, the revival of the quantity theory has led Keynesian economists to treat changes in the quantity of money as an essential element in the analysis of short-term change.

Finally, the controversy between Keynesians and quantity theorists has led both groups to distinguish more sharply between long-run and short-run effects of monetary changes; between 'static' or 'long-run equilibrium' theory and the dynamics of economic change.

As Franco Modigliani put it in his 1976 presidential address to the American Economic Association, there are currently 'no serious analytical disagreements between leading monetarists [i.e., quantity theorists] and leading nonmonetarists [i.e., Keynesians]' (1977, p. 1).

However, there still remain important differences on an empirical level. These all centre on the dynamics of short-run change – the process whereby a change in the quantity of money affects aggregate spending and the role of fiscal variables in the process.

The Keynesians regard a change in the quantity of money as affecting in the first instance 'the' interest rate, interpreted as a market rate on a fairly narrow class of financial liabilities. They regard spending as affected only 'indirectly' as the changed interest rate alters the profitability and amount of investment spending, again interpreted fairly narrowly, and as investment spending, through the multiplier, affects total spending. Hence the emphasis they give in their analysis to the interest elasticities of the demand for money and of investment spending.

The quantity theorists, on the other hand, stress a much broader and more 'direct' impact of spending, saying, as in section 1a above, that individuals will seek 'to dispose of what they regard as their excess money balances by paying out a larger sum for the purchase of securities, goods, and services, for the repayment of debts, and as gifts than they are receiving from the corresponding sources'.

The two approaches can be readily reconciled on a formal level. Quantity theorists can describe the transmission mechanism as operating 'through' the balance sheet and 'through' changes in interest rates. The attempt by holders of money to restore or attain a desired balance sheet after an unexpected increase in the quantity of money tends initially to raise the prices of assets and reduce interest rates, which encourages spending to produce new assets and also spending on current services rather than on purchasing existing assets. This is how an initial effect on balance sheets gets translated into an effect on income and spending. The resulting increase in spending tends to raise prices of goods and services which, in turn, by lowering the real value of the quantity of money and of nominal assets, tends to eliminate the initial decline in interest rates, even overshooting in the process.

The difference between the quantity theorists and the Keynesians is less in the nature of the process than in the range of assets considered. The Keynesians tend to concentrate on a narrow range of marketable assets and recorded interest rates. The quantity theorists insist that a far wider range of assets and interest rates must be taken into account – such assets as durable and semi-durable consumer goods, structures, and other real property. As a result, the quantity theorists regard the market rates stressed by the Keynesians as only a small part of the total spectrum of rates that are relevant.

This difference in the assumed transmission mechanism is largely a by-product of the different assumptions about price. The rejection of absolute liquidity preference forced Keynes's followers to let the interest rate be flexible. This chink in the key assumption that prices are an institutional datum was minimized by interpreting the 'interest rate' narrowly, and market institutions made it easy to do so. After all, it is most unusual to quote the 'interest rate' implicit in the sales and rental prices of houses and automobiles, let alone furniture, household appliances, clothes, and so on. Hence the prices of these items continued to be regarded as an institutional datum, which forced the transmission process to go through an extremely narrow channel. On the side of the quantity theorists there was no such inhibition. Since they regard prices as flexible, though not 'perfectly' flexible, it was natural for them to interpret the transmission mechanism in terms of relative price adjustments over a broad area rather than in terms of narrowly defined interest rates.

Less important differences are the tendency for Keynesians to stress the short-run as opposed to the long-run impact of changes to a far greater extent than the quantity theorists; and, a related difference, to give greater scope to the first-round effect of changes in the quantity of money.

3. The Phillips curve and the natural rate hypothesis

A major postwar development that contributed greatly to the revival of the quantity theory grew out of criticism by quantity theorists of the 'Phillips curve' – an allegedly stable inverse relation between unemployment and the rate of change of nominal wages such that a high level of unemployment was accompanied by declining wages, a low level by rising wages. Though not formally linked to the Keynesian theoretical system, the Phillips curve was widely welcomed by Keynesians as helping to fill a gap in the system created by the assumption of rigid wages. In addition, it appeared to offer an attractive trade-off possibility for economic policy: a permanent reduction in the level of unemployment at the cost of a moderate sustained increase in the rate of inflation. The Keynesian assumption that prices and wages could be regarded as institutionally determined made it easy for them to accept a relation between a nominal magnitude (the rate of change of wages) and a real magnitude (unemployment).

By contrast, the quantity theory distinction between real and nominal magnitudes implies that the Phillips curve is theoretically flawed. The quantity of labour demanded is a function of real not nominal wages; and so is the quantity supplied. Under any given set of circumstances, there is an equilibrium level of unemployment corresponding to an equilibrium structure of *real* wage rates. A higher level of unemployment will put downward pressure on real wage rates; a lower level will put upward pressure on real wage rates. The level of unemployment consistent with the equilibrium structure of real wage rates has been termed the 'natural rate of unemployment' and defined as

> the level that would be ground out by the Walrasian system of general equilibrium equations, provided there is imbedded in them the actual

structural characteristics of the labour and commodity markets, including market imperfections, stochastic variability in demands and supplies, the cost of gathering information about job vacancies and labour availabilities, the costs of mobility, and so on (Friedman, 1968, p. 8).

The nominal wage rate that corresponds to any given real wage rate depends on the level of prices. Whether that nominal wage rate is rising or falling depends on whether prices are rising or falling. If wages and prices change at the same rate, the real wage rate remains the same. Hence, in the long run, there need be no relation between the rate of change of *nominal* wages and the rate of change of *real* wages, and hence between the rate of change of nominal wages and the level of unemployment. In the long run, therefore, the Phillips curve will tend to be vertical at the natural rate of unemployment – a proposition that came to be termed the Natural Rate Hypothesis.

Over short periods, an *unanticipated* increase in inflation reduces real wages as viewed by employers, inducing them to offer higher nominal wages, which workers erroneously view as higher real wages. This discrepancy simultaneously encourages employers to offer more employment and workers to accept more employment, thereby reducing unemployment, which produces the inverse relation encapsulated in the Phillips curve. However, if the higher rate of inflation continues, the anticipations of workers and employers will converge and the decline in unemployment will be reversed. A negatively sloping Phillips curve is therefore a short-run phenomenon. Moreover, it will not be stable over time, since what matters is not the nominal rates of change of wages and prices but the difference between the actual and the *anticipated* rates of change. The emergence of stagflation in the 1970s quickly confirmed this analysis, leading to the widespread replacement of the original Phillips curve by an expectations-adjusted Phillips curve (Friedman, 1977).

Acceptance of the natural rate hypothesis has had far-reaching effects not only on received wisdom among economists but also on economic policy. It became widely recognized that expansionary monetary and fiscal policies at best gave only a temporary stimulus to output and employment and if long continued would be reflected primarily in inflation.

4. The theory of rational expectations

A subsequent theoretical development was the belated flowering of a seed planted in 1961 by John F. Muth, in a long-neglected article on 'Rational expectations and the theory of price movements' (Muth, 1961). The theory of rational expectations offers no special insight into stationary-state or long-run equilibrium analysis. Its contribution is to dynamics – short-run change, and hence potentially to stabilization policy.

It has long been recognized by writers of all persuasions that, as Abraham Lincoln put it over a century ago, 'you can't fool all of the people all of the time.' The tendency for the public to learn from experience and to adjust to it underlies David Hume's view that monetary expansion 'is favourable to industry' only in its initial stages, but that if it continues, it will come to be anticipated and will affect prices and nominal interest rates but not real magnitudes. It also underlies the companion view associated with the natural rate hypothesis that a 'full employment' policy in which monetary, or for that matter fiscal, measures are used to counteract any increase in unemployment will almost inevitably lead not simply to uneven inflation but to uneven inflation around a rising trend – a conclusion often illustrated by analogizing inflation to a drug of which the addict must take larger and larger doses to get the same kick.

Nonetheless, the importance of anticipations and how they are formed in determining the dynamic response to changes in money and other magnitudes remained largely implicit until Lucas and Sargent applied the Muth rational expectations idea explicitly to the reliability of econometric models of the economy and to stabilization policies (Fischer, 1980; Lucas, 1976; Lucas and Sargent, 1981).

The theory of rational expectations asserts that economic agents should be treated as if their anticipations fully incorporate both currently available information about the state of the world and a correct theory of the interrelationships among the variables. Anticipations formed in this way will on the average tend to be correct (a statement whose simplicity conceals fundamental problems of interpretation, Friedman and Schwartz, 1982, pp. 556–7).

The rational expectations hypothesis has far-reaching implications for the validity of econometric models. Suppose a statistician were able to construct a model that predicted highly accurately for a past period all relevant variables; also, that a monetary rule could be devised that if used during the past period with that model could have achieved a particular objective – say keeping unemployment between 4 and 5 per cent. Suppose now that that policy rule were adopted for the future. It would be nearly certain that the model for which the rule was developed would no longer work. The economic equivalent of the Heisenberg indeterminacy principle would take over. The model was for an economy without that monetary rule. Put the rule into effect and it will alter rational expectations and hence behaviour. Even without putting the rule into effect, the model would very likely continue to work only so long as its existence could be kept secret because if market participants learned about it they would use it in forming their rational expectations and thereby falsify it to a greater or lesser extent. Little wonder that every major econometric model is always being sent back to the drawing board as experience confounds it, or that their producers have reacted so strongly to the theory of rational expectations.

The implication of one variant of the theory that has received the most attention and generated the most controversy is the so-called neutrality hypothesis about stabilization policy – in particular, about discretionary monetary policy directed at promoting economic stability. Correct rational expectations of economic agents will include correct anticipation of any systematic monetary policy; hence such policy will be allowed for by economic agents in determining their behaviour. Given further the natural rate hypothesis, it follows that any systematic monetary policy will affect the behaviour only of nominal magnitudes and not of such real magnitudes as output and employment. The authorities can affect the course of events only by 'fooling' the participants, that is, by acting in an unpredictable, ad hoc way. But, in general, such strictly ad hoc intervention will destabilize the economy, not stabilize it, serving simply to introduce another series of random shocks into the economy to which participants must adapt and which reduce their ability to form precise and accurate expectations.

This is a highly oversimplified account of the rational expectations hypothesis and its implications. All otherwise valid models of the economy will not be falsified by being known. All real effects of systematic and announced governmental policies will not be rendered nugatory. Serious problems have arisen in formulating the hypothesis in a logically satisfactory way, and in giving it empirical content, especially in incorporating multi-valued rather than single-valued expectations and allowing for non-independence of events over time. Research in this area is exploding; rapid progress and many changes in received opinion can confidently be anticipated before the rational expectations revolution is fully domesticated.

5. Empirical evidence

There is perhaps no empirical regularity among economic phenomena that is based on so much evidence for so wide a range of circumstances as the connection between substantial changes in the quantity of money and in the level of prices. There are few if any instances in which a substantial change in the quantity of money per unit of output has occurred without a substantial change in the level of prices in the same direction. Conversely, there are few if any instances in which a substantial change in the level of prices has occurred without a substantial change in the quantity of money per unit of output in the same direction. And instances in which prices and the quantity of money have moved together are recorded for many centuries of history, for countries in every part of the globe, and for a wide diversity of monetary arrangements.

The statistical connection itself, however, tells nothing about direction of influence, and this is the question about which there has been the most controversy. A rise or fall in prices, occurring for whatever reason, could produce a corresponding rise or fall in the quantity of money, so that the monetary changes are a passive consequence. Alternatively, changes in the quantity of money could produce changes in prices in the same direction, so that control of the quantity of money implies control of prices. The second interpretation – that substantial changes in the quantity of money are both a necessary and a sufficient condition for substantial changes in the general level of prices – is strongly supported by the variety of monetary arrangements for which a connection between monetary and price movements has been observed. But of course this interpretation does not exclude a reflex influence of changes in prices on the quantity of money. The reflex influence is often important, almost always complex, and, depending on the monetary arrangements, may be in either direction.

Evidence from specie standards
Until modern times, money was mostly metallic – copper, brass, silver, gold. The most notable changes in its nominal quantity were produced by sweating and clipping, by

governmental edicts changing the nominal values attached to specified physical quantities of the metal, or by discoveries of new sources of specie. Economic history is replete with examples of the first two and their coincidence with corresponding changes in nominal prices (Cipolla, 1956; Feavearyear, 1931). The specie discoveries in the New World in the 16th century are the most important example of the third. The association between the resulting increase in the quantity of money and the price revolution of the 16th and 17th centuries has been well documented (Hamilton, 1934).

Despite the much greater development of deposit money and paper money, the gold discoveries in Australia and the United States in the 1840s were followed by substantial price rises in the 1850s (Cairnes, 1873; Jevons, 1863). When growth of the gold stock slowed, and especially when country after country shifted from silver to gold (Germany in 1871–3, the Latin Monetary Union in 1873, the Netherlands in 1875–6) or returned to gold (the United States in 1879), world prices in terms of gold fell slowly but fairly steadily for about three decades. New gold discoveries in the 1880s and 1890s, powerfully reinforced by improved methods of mining and refining, particularly commercially feasible methods of using the cyanide process to extract gold from low-grade ore, led to much more rapid growth of the world gold stock. Further, no additional important countries shifted to gold. As a result, world prices in terms of gold rose by 25 to 50 per cent from the mid-1890s to 1914 (Bordo and Schwartz, 1984).

Evidence from great inflations
Periods of great monetary disturbances provide the most dramatic evidence on the role of the quantity of money. The most striking such periods are the hyperinflations after World War I in Germany, Austria, and Russia, and after World War II in Hungary and Greece, and the rapid price rises, if not hyperinflations, in many South American and some other countries both before and after World War II. These 20th-century episodes have been studied more systematically than earlier ones. The studies demonstrate almost conclusively the critical role of changes in the quantity of money (Cagan, 1965; Meiselman, 1970; Sargent, 1982).

Substantial inflations following a period of relatively stable prices have often had their start in wartime, though recently they have become common under other circumstances. What is important is that something, generally the financing of extraordinary governmental expenditures, produces a more rapid growth of the quantity of money. Prices start to rise, but at a slower pace than the quantity of money, so that for a time the real quantity of money increases. The reason is twofold: first, it takes time for people to readjust their money balances; second, initially there is a general expectation that the rise in prices is temporary and will be followed by a decline. Such expectations make money a desirable form in which to hold assets, and therefore lead to an increase in desired money balances in real terms.

As prices continue to rise, expectations are revised. Holders of money come to expect prices to continue to rise, and reduce desired balances. They also take more active measures to eliminate the discrepancy between actual and desired balances. The result is that prices start to rise faster than the stock of money, and real balances start to decline (that is, velocity starts to rise). How far this process continues depends on the rate of rise in the quantity of money. If it remains fairly stable, real balances settle down at a level that is lower than the initial level but roughly constant – a constant expected rate of inflation implies a roughly constant level of desired real balances; in this case, prices ultimately rise at the same rate as the quantity of money. If the rate of money growth declines, inflation will follow suit, which will in turn lead to an increase in actual and desired real balances as people readjust their expectations; and conversely. Once the process is in full swing, changes in real balances follow with a lag changes in the rate of change of the stock of money. The lag reflects the fact that people apparently base their expectations of future rates of price change partly on an average of experience over the preceding several years, the period of averaging being shorter the more rapid the inflation.

In the extreme cases, those that have degenerated into hyperinflation and a complete breakdown of the medium of exchange, rates of price change have been so high and real balances have been driven down so low as to lead to the widespread introduction of substitute moneys, usually foreign currencies. At that point completely new monetary systems have had to be introduced.

A similar phenomenon has occurred when inflation has been effectively suppressed by price controls, so that there is a substantial gap between the prices that would prevail in the absence of controls and the legally permitted prices. This gap prevents money from functioning as an effective medium of exchange and also leads to the introduction of substitute moneys, sometimes rather bizarre ones like the cigarettes and cognac used in post-World War II Germany.

Other evidence

The past two decades have witnessed a literal flood of literature dealing with monetary phenomena. Expressed in broad terms, the literature has been of two overlapping types – qualitative and econometric – and has dealt with two overlapping sets of issues – static or long-term effects of monetary change and dynamic or cyclical effects.

Some broad findings are:

(1) For both long and short periods there is a consistent though not precise relation between the rate of growth of the quantity of money and the rate of growth of nominal income. If the quantity of money grows rapidly, so will nominal income, and conversely. This relation is much closer for long than for short periods.

Two recent econometric studies have tested the long-run effects using comparisons among countries for the post-World War II period. Lothian concludes his study for 20 countries for the period 1956–80:

> In this paper I have examined three sets of hypotheses associated with the quantity theory of money: the classical neutrality proposition [i.e., changes in the nominal quantity of money do not affect real magnitudes in the long run], the monetary approach to exchange rates [i.e., changes in exchange rates

between countries reflect primarily changes in money per unit of output in the several countries], and the Fisher equation [i.e., differences in sustained rates of inflation produce corresponding differences in nominal interest rates]. The data are completely consistent with the first two and moderately supportive of the last (1985, p. 835).

Duck concludes his study for 33 countries and the period 1962 to 1982 – which uses overlapping data but substantially different methods:

> Its [the study's] findings suggest that (i) the real demand for money is reasonably well explained by a small number of variables, principally real income and interest rates; (ii) nominal income is closely related to the quantity of money, but is also related to the behaviour of other variables, principally interest rates; (iii) most changes in nominal income or its determinants are absorbed by price increases; (iv) even over a 20-year period some nominal income growth is to a significant degree absorbed by real output growth; (v) the evidence that expectations are rational is weak (1985, p. 33).

(2) These findings for the long run reflect a long-run real demand function for money involving, as Duck notes, a small number of variables, that is highly stable and very similar for different countries. The elasticity of this function with respect to real income is close to unity, occasionally lower, generally higher, especially for countries that are growing rapidly and in which the scope of the money economy is expanding. The elasticity with respect to interest rates is, as expected, negative but relatively low in absolute value. The real quantity demanded is not affected by the price level (i.e., there is no 'monetary illusion') (Friedman and Schwartz, 1982; Laidler, 1985).

(3) Over short periods, the relation between growth in money and in nominal income is often concealed from the naked eye partly because the relation is less close for short than long periods but mostly because it takes time for changes in monetary growth to affect income, and how long it takes is itself variable. Today's income growth is not closely related to today's monetary growth; it depends on what has been happening to money in the past. What happens to money today affects what is going to happen to income in the future.

(4) For most major Western countries, a change in the rate of monetary growth produces a change in the rate of growth of nominal income about six to nine months later. This is an average that does not hold in every individual case. Sometimes the delay is longer, sometimes shorter. In particular, it tends to be shorter under conditions of high and highly variable rates of monetary growth and of inflation.

(5) In cyclical episodes the response of nominal income, allowing for the time delay, is greater in amplitude than the change in monetary growth, so that velocity tends to rise during the expansion phase of a business cycle and to fall during the contraction phase. This reaction appears to be partly a response to the pro-cyclical pattern of interest rates; partly to the linkage of desired cash balances to permanent rather than measured income.

(6) The changed rate of growth of nominal income typically shows up first in output and hardly at all in prices. If the rate of monetary growth increases or

decreases, the rate of growth of nominal income and also of physical output tends to increase or decrease about six to nine months later, but the rate of price rise is affected very little.

(7) The effect on prices, like that on income and output, is distributed over time, but comes some 12 to 18 months later, so that the total delay between a change in monetary growth and a change in the rate of inflation averages something like two years. That is why it is a long row to hoe to stop an inflation that has been allowed to start. It cannot be stopped overnight.

(8) Even after allowance for the delayed effect of monetary growth, the relation is far from perfect. There's many a slip over short periods 'twixt the monetary change and the income change.

(9) In the short run, which may be as long as three to ten years, monetary changes affect primarily output. Over decades, on the other hand, as already noted, the rate of monetary growth affects primarily prices. What happens to output depends on real factors: the enterprise, ingenuity and industry of the people; the extent of thrift; the structure of industry and government; the relations among nations, and so on. (In re points 3 to 9, Friedman and Schwartz, 1963a, 1963b; Friedman, 1961, 1977, 1984; Judd and Scadding, 1982.)

(10) One major finding has to do with severe depressions. There is strong evidence that a monetary crisis, involving a substantial decline in the quantity of money, is a necessary and sufficient condition for a major depression. Fluctuations in monetary growth are also systematically related to minor ups and downs in the economy, but do not play as dominant a role compared to other forces. As Friedman and Schwartz put it,

> Changes in the money stock are ... a consequence as well as an independent source of change in money income and prices, though, once they occur, they produce in their turn still further effects on income and prices. Mutual interaction, but with money rather clearly the senior partner in longer-run movements and in major cyclical movements, and more nearly an equal partner with money income and prices in shorter-run and milder movements – this is the generalization suggested by our evidence (1963b, p. 695; Friedman and Schwartz, 1963a; Cagan, 1965, pp. 296–8).

(11) A major unsettled issue is the short-run division of a change in nominal income between output and price. The division has varied widely over space and time and there exists no satisfactory theory that isolates the factors responsible for the variability (Gordon, 1980, 1981, 1982; Friedman and Schwartz, 1982, pp. 59–62).

(12) It follows from these propositions that *inflation is always and everywhere a monetary phenomenon* in the sense that it is and can be produced only by a more rapid increase in the quantity of money than in output. Many phenomena can produce temporary fluctuations in the rate of inflation, but they can have lasting effects only insofar as they affect the rate of monetary growth. However, there are many different possible reasons for monetary growth, including gold discoveries, financing of government spending, and financing of private spending. Hence, these propositions

are only the beginning of an answer to the causes and cures for inflation. The deeper question is why excessive monetary growth occurs.

(13) Government spending may or may not be inflationary. It clearly will be inflationary if it is financed by creating money, that is, by printing currency or creating bank deposits. If it is financed by taxes or by borrowing from the public, the main effect is that the government spends the funds instead of the taxpayer or instead of the lender or instead of the person who would otherwise have borrowed the funds. Fiscal policy is extremely important in determining what fraction of total national income is spent by government and who bears the burden of that expenditure. It is also extremely important in determining monetary policy and, via that route, inflation. Essentially all major inflations, especially hyperinflations, have resulted from resort by governments to the printing press to finance their expenditures under conditions of great stress such as defeat in war or internal revolution, circumstances that have limited the ability of governments to acquire resources through explicit taxation.

(14) A change in monetary growth affects interest rates in one direction at first but in the opposite direction later on. More rapid monetary growth at first tends to lower interest rates. But later on, the resulting acceleration in spending and still later in inflation produces a rise in the demand for loans which tends to raise interest rates. In addition, higher inflation widens the difference between real and nominal interest rates. As both lenders and borrowers come to anticipate inflation, lenders demand, and borrowers are willing to offer, higher nominal rates to offset the anticipated inflation. That is why interest rates are highest in countries that have had the most rapid growth in the quantity of money and also in prices – countries like Brazil, Chile, Israel, South Korea. In the opposite direction, a slower rate of monetary growth at first raises interest rates but later on, as it decelerates spending and inflation, lowers interest rates. That is why interest rates are lowest in countries that *have had* the slowest rate of growth in the quantity of money – countries like Switzerland, Germany, and Japan.

(15) In the major Western countries, the link to gold and the resultant long-term predictability of the price level meant that until some time after World War II, interest rates behaved as if prices were expected to be stable and both inflation and deflation were unanticipated; the so-called Fisher effect was almost completely absent. Nominal returns on nominal assets were relatively stable; real returns unstable, absorbing almost fully inflation and deflation.

(16) Beginning in the 1960s, and especially after the end of Bretton Woods in 1971, interest rates started to parallel rates of inflation. Nominal returns on nominal assets became more variable; real returns on nominal assets, less variable (Friedman and Schwartz, 1982, pp. 10–11).

6. Policy implications

On a very general level the implications of the quantity theory for economic policy are straightforward and clear. On a more precise and detailed level they are not.

Acceptance of the quantity theory means that the quantity of money is a key variable in policies directed at controlling the level of prices or of nominal income.

Inflation can be prevented if and only if the quantity of money per unit of output can be kept from increasing appreciably. Deflation can be prevented if and only if the quantity of money per unit of output can be kept from decreasing appreciably. This implication is by no means trivial. Monetary authorities have more frequently than not taken conditions in the credit market – rates of interest, availability of loans, and so on – as criteria of policy and have paid little or no attention to the quantity of money per se. The emphasis on credit as opposed to the quantity of money accounts both for the great contraction in the United States from 1929 to 1933, when the Federal Reserve System allowed the stock of money to decline by one-third, and for many of the post-World War II inflations.

The quantity theory has no such clear implication, even on this general level, about policies concerned with the growth of real income. Both inflation and deflation have proved consistent with growth, stagnation, or decline.

Passing from these general and vague statements to specific prescriptions for policy is difficult. It is tempting to conclude from the close average relation between changes in the quantity of money and in money income that control over the quantity of money can be used as a precision instrument for offsetting other forces making for instability in money income. Unfortunately the loose relation between money and income over short periods, the long and variable lag between changes in the quantity of money and other variables, and the often conflicting objectives of policy-makers precludes precise offsetting control.

An international specie standard leaves only limited scope for an independent monetary policy. Over any substantial period, the quantity of money is determined by the balance of payments. Capital movements plus time delays in the transmission of monetary and other impulses leave some leeway, which may be more or less extensive, depending on the importance of foreign transactions for a country and the sluggishness of response. As a result, monetary policy under an effective international specie standard has consisted primarily of banking policy, directed towards avoiding or relieving banking and liquidity crises (Bagehot, 1873).

Until 1971, departures from an international specie standard, at least by major countries, took place infrequently and only at times of crisis. Surveying such episodes, Fisher concluded in 1911 that 'irredeemable paper money has almost invariably proved a curse to the country employing it' (1911, p. 131), a generalization that has applied equally to most of the period since, certainly up to 1971, and that explains why such episodes were generally transitory.

The declining importance of the international specie standard and its final termination in 1971 have changed the situation drastically. 'Irredeemable paper money' is no longer an expedient grasped at in times of crisis; it is the normal state of affairs in countries at peace, facing no domestic crises, political or economic, and with governments fully capable of obtaining massive resources through explicit taxes. This is an unprecedented situation. We are in unexplored terrain.

As Keynes pointed out in 1923, monetary authorities cannot serve two masters: as he put it, 'we cannot keep *both* our own price level *and* our exchanges stable. And we are compelled to choose' (p. 126). Experience since has converted his dilemma into a trilemma. In principle, monetary authorities can achieve any two of the following three objectives: control of exchange rates, control of the price level, freedom from exchange controls. In practice, it has in fact proved impossible to achieve the first two by accepting exchange controls. Such controls have proved extremely costly and ultimately ineffective. The Bretton Woods system was ultimately wrecked on this trilemma. The attempts by many countries to pursue an independent monetary policy came into conflict with the attempt to maintain pegged exchange rates, leading to the imposition of exchange controls, repeated monetary crises, accompanied by large, discontinuous changes in exchange rates, and ultimately to the abandonment of the system in 1971.

Since then, most countries have had no formal commitment about exchange rates, which have been free to fluctuate and have fluctuated widely. Nonetheless, Keynes's dilemma is still alive and well. Monetary authorities have tried to influence the exchange rates of their currency and, at the same time, achieve internal objectives. The result has been what has been described as a system of managed floating.

One recent strand of policy discussions has consisted of attempts to devise a substitute for the Bretton Woods arrangements that would somehow combine the virtues of exchange rate stability with internal monetary stability. For example, one proposal, by McKinnon (1984), is for the USA, Germany, and Japan to fix exchange rates among their currencies and set a joint target for the rate of increase of the total quantity of money (or high-powered money) issued by the three countries together. So far, no such proposal has gained wide support among either economists or a wider public.

A different strand of policy discussions has been concerned with the instruments, targets, and objectives of monetary authorities. One element of the quantity theory approach that has had considerable influence is emphasis on the quantity of money as the appropriate intermediate target for monetary policy. Most major countries now (1985) follow the practice of announcing in advance their targets for monetary growth. That is so for the USA, Great Britain, Germany, Japan, Switzerland, and many others. The record of achievement of the announced targets varies greatly – from excellent to terrible. Recently, a considerable number of economists have favoured the use of nominal income (usually nominal gross national product) as the intermediate target. The common feature is the quantity theory emphasis on nominal magnitudes.

A more abstract strand of policy discussions has been concerned with the optimum quantity of money: what rate or pattern of monetary growth would in principle promote most effectively the long-run efficiency of the economic system – meaning by that a Pareto welfare optimum. This issue turns out to be closely related to a number of others, in particular the optimum behaviour of the price level; the optimum rate of interest; the optimum stock of capital, and the optimum structure of capital (Friedman, 1969, pp. 1–50).

One widely accepted answer is based on the observation that no real resource cost need be incurred in increasing the real quantity of money since that can be done by reducing the price level. The implication is that the optimum quantity of money is that at which the marginal benefit from increasing the real quantity is also zero. Various arrangements are possible that will achieve such an objective, of which perhaps the simplest, if money pays no interest, is a pattern of monetary growth involving a decline in the price level at a rate equal to the real interest rate (Mussa, 1977; Ihori, 1985).

This answer, despite its great theoretical interest, has had little practical consequence. Short-run considerations have understandably been given precedence to such a highly abstract long-run proposition.

Finally, there has been a literal explosion of discussion of the basic structure of the monetary system. One component derives from the belief that Fisher's generalization about irredeemable paper money will continue to hold for the present world fiat money system and that we are headed for a world monetary collapse ending in hyperinflation unless a specie (gold) standard is promptly restored. In the United States, this monetary belief was powerful enough to lead Congress to establish a Commission on the Role of Gold. In its final report, 'the Commission concludes that, under present circumstances, restoring a gold standard does not appear to be a fruitful method for dealing with the continuing problem of inflation. ... We favour no change in the flexible exchange rate system' (Commission, 1982, vol. 1, pp. 17, 20). The testimony before the Commission revealed that agreement on a 'gold standard' concealed wide differences in the precise meaning of the phrase, varying from a system in which money consisted of full-bodied gold or warehouse receipts for gold to one in which the monetary authorities were instructed to regard the price of gold as one factor affecting their policy.

A very different component of the discussion has to do with possible alternatives to gold as a long-term anchor to the price level. This include proposals for subjecting monetary authorities to more specific legislative or constitutional guidelines, varying from guidelines dealing with their objectives (price stability, rate of growth of nominal income, real interest rate, etc.) to guidelines specifying a specific rate of growth in money or high-powered money. Perhaps the most widely discussed proposal along this line is the proposal for imposing on the authorities the obligation to achieve a constant rate of growth in a specified monetary aggregate (Friedman, 1960, pp. 92–5; Commission, 1982, vol. 1, p. 17). Other proposals include freezing the stock of base money and eliminating discretionary monetary policy, and denationalizing money entirely, leaving it to the private market and a free banking system (Friedman, 1984; Friedman and Schwartz, 1986; Hayek, 1976; White, 1984a).

Finally, a still more radical series of proposals is that the unit of account be separated from the medium of exchange function, in the belief that financial innovation will establish an efficient payment system dispensing entirely with the use of cash. The specific proposals are highly sophisticated and complex, and have been sharply criticized. So far, their value has been primarily as a stimulus to a deeper analysis of the meaning and role of money. (For the proposals, see Black, 1970;

Fama, 1980; Hall, 1982a, 1982b; Greenfield and Yeager, 1983; for the criticisms, see White, 1984b; McCallum, 1985).

One thing is certain: the quantity theory of money will continue to generate agreement, controversy, repudiation, and scientific analysis, and will continue to play a role in government policy during the next century as it has for the past three.

MILTON FRIEDMAN

Bibliography

Angell, J.W. 1936. *The Behavior of Money.* New York: McGraw-Hill.

Bagehot, W. 1873. *Lambard Street.* London: Henry S. King.

Barnett, W.A., Offenbacher, E.K. and Spindt, P.A. 1984. The new Divisia monetary aggregates. *Journal of Political Economy* 92, 1049–85.

Baumol, W.J. 1952. The transactions demand for cash: an inventory theoretic approach. *Quarterly Journal of Economics* 66, 545–56.

Black, F. 1970. Banking and interest rates in a world without money: the effects of uncontrolled banking, *Journal of Bank Research* 1(3), 2–20.

Black, H. 1975. The relative importance of determinants of the money supply: the British case. *Journal of Monetary Economics* 1(2), 25–64.

Bordo, M.D. and Schwartz, A.J., eds. 1984. *A Retrospective on the Classical Gold Standard, 1821–1931.* Chicago: University of Chicago Press for the National Bureau of Economic Research.

Burger, A.E. 1971. *The Money Supply Process.* Belmont: Wadsworth.

Cagan, P. 1965. *Determinants and Effects of Changes in the Stock of Money, 1875–1960.* New York: Columbia University Press for the National Bureau of Economic Research.

Cagan, P. 1972. *The Channels of Monetary Effects on Interest Rates.* New York: National Bureau of Economic Research.

Cairnes, J.E. 1873. Essays on the gold question. In J.E. Cairnes, *Essays in Political Economy,* London: Macmillan.

Cipolla, C.M. 1956. *Money, Prices, and Civilization in the Mediterranean World, Fifth to Seventeenth Century.* Princeton: Princeton University Press.

Commission on the Role of Gold in the Domestic and International Monetary Systems. 1982. *Report to the Congress,* March. Washington, DC: The Commission.

Duck, N.W. 1985. Money, output and prices: an empirical study using long-term cross country data. Working Paper, University of Bristol, September.

Fama, E.F. 1980. Banking in the theory of finance. *Journal of Monetary Economics* 6(1), 39–57.

Feavearyear, A.E. 1931. *The Pound Sterling: a History of English Money.* 2nd edn., Oxford: Clarendon Press, 1963.

Fischer, S., ed. 1980. *Rational Expectations and Economic Policy.* Chicago: University of Chicago Press for the National Bureau of Economic Research.

Fischer, I. 1896. *Appreciation and Interest.* New York: American Economic Association.

Fisher, I. 1911. *The Purchasing Power of Money.* 2nd revised edn, 1926; reprinted New York: Kelley, 1963.

Fisher, I. 1919. Money, prices, credit and banking. *American Economic Review* 9, 407–9.

Frenkel, J.A. 1976. Adjustment mechanisms and the monetary approach to the balance of payments. In *Recent Issues in International Monetary Economics,* ed. E. Claassen and P. Salin. Amsterdam: North-Holland.

Frenkel, J.A. and Johnson, H.G. 1976. The monetary approach to the balance of payments: essential concepts and historical origins. In *The Monetary Approach to the Balance of Payments*, ed. J.A. Frenkel and H.G. Johnson. Toronto: University of Toronto Press.

Friedman, M. 1956. The quantity theory of money – a restatement. In *Studies in the Quantity Theory of Money*, ed. M. Friedman. Chicago: University of Chicago Press.

Friedman, M. 1957. *A Theory of the Consumption Function*. Princeton: Princeton University Press for the National Bureau of Economic Research.

Friedman, M. 1959. The demand for money: some theoretical and empirical results. *Journal of Political Economy* 67, August, 327–51. Reprinted as Occasional Paper No. 68, New York: National Bureau of Economic Research, and in Friedman (1969).

Friedman, M. 1960. *A Program for Monetary Stability*. New York: Fordham University Press.

Friedman, M. 1961. The lag in effect of monetary policy. *Journal of Political Economy* 69, 447–66. Reprinted in Friedman (1969).

Friedman, M. 1968. The role of monetary policy. *American Economic Review* 58, 1–17. Reprinted in Friedman (1969).

Friedman, M. 1969. *The Optimum Quantity of Money and Other Essays*. Chicago: Aldine.

Friedman, M. 1977. Inflation and unemployment (Nobel lecture). *Journal of Political Economy* 85, 451–72.

Friedman, M. 1984. Monetary policy for the 1980s. In *To Promote Prosperity: U.S. domestic policy in the mid-1980s*, ed. J.H. Moore. Stanford: Hoover Institution Press.

Friedman, M. and Schwartz, A.J. 1963a. Money and business cycles. *Review of Economics and Statistics* 45(1), Supplement, February, 32–64. Reprinted in Friedman (1969).

Friedman, M. and Schwartz, A.J. 1963b. *A Monetary History of the United States, 1867–1960*. Princeton: Princeton University Press for the National Bureau of Economic Research.

Friedman, M. and Schwartz, A.J. 1970. *Monetary Statistics of the United States*. New York: Columbia University Press for the National Bureau of Economic Research.

Friedman, M. and Schwartz, A.J. 1982. *Monetary Trends in the United States and the United Kingdom: Their Relation to Income, Prices, and Interest Rates, 1867–1975*. Chicago: University of Chicago Press for the National Bureau of Economic Research.

Friedman, M. and Schwartz, A.J. 1986. Has government any role in money? *Journal of Monetary Economics* 17(1), 37–62.

Gordon, R.J. 1980. A consistent characterization of a near-century of price behavior. *American Economic Review* 70, 243–49.

Gordon, R.J. 1981. Output fluctuations and gradual price adjustment. *Journal of Economic Literature* 19, 493–530.

Gordon, R.J. 1982. Price inertia and policy ineffectiveness in the United States, 1890–1980. *Journal of Political Economy* 90, 1087–117.

Greenfield, R.L. and Yeager, L.B. 1983. A laissez-faire approach to monetary stability. *Journal of Money, Credit, and Banking* 15, 302–15.

Haberler, G. 1941. *Prosperity and Depression*. 3rd edn., Geneva: League of Nations.

Hall, R.E. 1982a. Explorations in the gold standard and related policies for stabilizing the dollar. In *Inflation: Causes and Effects*, ed. R.E. Hall. Chicago: University of Chicago Press.

Hall, R.E. 1982b. 'Monetary trends in the United States and the United Kingdom': a review from the perspective of new developments in monetary economics. *Journal of Economic Literature* 20, 1552–6.

Hamilton, E.J. 1934. *American Treasure and the Price Revolution in Spain, 1501–1650*. Harvard Economic Studies, vol. 43, New York: Octagon, 1965.

Hansen, A. 1957. *The American Economy*. New York: McGraw-Hill.

Hayek, F.A. 1976. *Denationalization of Money*. 2nd extended edn., London: Institute of Economic Affairs, 1978.

Hume, D. 1752. Of interest; of money. In *Essays, Moral, Political and Literary*, vol. 1 of *Essays and Treatises*, a new edn, Edinburgh: Bell and Bradfute, Cadell and Davies, 1804.

Humphrey, T.M. 1984. Algebraic quantity equations before Fisher and Pigou. *Economic Review*, Federal Reserve Bank of Richmond 70(5), September–October, 13–22.

Ihori, T. 1985. On the welfare cost of permanent inflation. *Journal of Money, Credit, and Banking* 17(2), 220–31.

Jevons, W.S. 1863. A serious fall in the value of gold. In *Investigations in Currency and Finance*, 2nd edn. London: Macmillan, 1909.

Johnson, H.G. 1961. The General Theory after twenty-five years. *American Economic Association, Papers and Proceedings* 51, 1–17.

Judd, J.P. and Scadding, J.L. 1982. The search for a stable money demand function. *Journal of Economic Literature* 20, 993–1023.

Keynes, J.M. 1923. *A Tract on Monetary Reform*. Reprinted London: Macmillan for the Royal Economy Society, 1971.

Keynes, J.M. 1936. *The General Theory of Employment, Interest and Money*. Reprinted London: Macmillan for the Royal Economic Society, 1973.

Knoester, A. 1984. Pigou and buffer effects in monetary economics. Discussion Paper 8406 G/M, Institute for Economic Research, Erasmus University, Rotterdam.

Laidler, D. 1984. The 'buffer stock' notion in monetary economics. *Economic Journal* 94, Supplement, 17–34.

Laidler, D. 1985. *The Demand for Money: theories, evidence, and problems*. 3rd edn., New York: Harper & Row.

Lothian, J.R. 1985. Equilibrium relationships between money and other economic variables. *American Economic Review* 75, 828–35.

Lucas, R.E., Jr. 1976. Econometric policy evaluation: a critique. *Journal of Monetary Economics* supplementary series 1, 19–46.

Lucas, R.E., Jr. 1981. Tobin and monetarism: a review article. *Journal of Economic Literature* 19, 558–67.

Lucas, R.E., Jr. and Sargent, T.J., eds. 1981. *Rational Expectations and Economic Practice*. 2 vols, Minneapolis: University of Minnesota Press.

McCallum, B. 1985. Bank deregulation, accounting systems of exchange and the unit of account: a critical review. *Carnegie-Rochester Conference Series on Public Policy* 23, Autumn.

McKinnon, R. 1984. *An International Standard for Monetary Stabilization*. Cambridge, MA: MIT Press.

Meiselman, D., ed. 1970. *Varieties of Monetary Experience*. Chicago: University of Chicago Press.

Mill, J.S. 1844. Review of books by Thomas Tooke and R. Torrens. *Westminster Review*, June.

Miller, M.H. and Orr, D. 1966. A model of the demand for money by firms. *Quarterly Journal of Economics* 80, 413–35.

Miller, M.H. and Orr, D. 1968. The demand for money by firms: extensions of analytical results. *Journal of Finance* 23, 735–59.

Modigliani, F. 1977. The monetarist controversy, or should we forsake stabilization policies? *American Economic Review* 67, 1–19.

Mussa, M. 1977. The welfare cost of inflation and the role of money as a unit of account. *Journal of Money, Credit, and Banking* 9(2), 276–86.

Muth, J.F. 1961. Rational expectations and the theory of price movements. *Econometrica* 29, July, 315–35. Reprinted in Lucas and Sargent (1981).

Newcomb, S. 1885. *Principles of Political Economy.* New York: Harper & Brothers.

Patinkin, D. 1948. Price flexibility and full employment. *American Economic Review* 38, September, 543–64. Revised and reprinted in F.A. Lutz and L.W. Mints (American Economic Association), *Readings in Monetary Theory,* Homewood, IL: Irwin, 1951.

Phelps, E.S. 1967. Phillips curves, expectations of inflation, and optimal unemployment over time. *Economica* 34(135), 254–81.

Pigou, A.C. 1917. The value of money. *Quarterly Journal of Economics* 32, November, 38–65. Reprinted in F.A. Lutz and L.W. Mints (American Economic Association), *Readings in Monetary Theory,* Homewood, IL: Irwin, 1951.

Pigou, A.C. 1947. Economic progress in a stable environment. *Economica* 14(55), 180–88.

Sargent, T.J. 1982. The ends of four big inflations. In *Inflation: Causes and Effects,* ed. R.E. Hall. Chicago: University of Chicago Press.

Snyder, C. 1934. On the statistical relation of trade, credit, and prices. *Revue de l'Institut International de Statistique* 2, 278–91.

Spindt, P.A. 1985. Money is what money does: monetary aggregation and the equation of exchange. *Journal of Political Economy* 93, 1975–2204.

Tobin, J. 1947. Money wage rates and employment. In *The New Economics,* ed. S. Harris. New York: Knopf.

Tobin, J. 1956. The interest-elasticity of transactions demand for cash. *Review of Economics and Statistics* 38, 241–7.

Tobin, J. 1958. Liquidity preference as behavior toward risk. *Review of Economic Studies* 25, 65–86.

Tobin, J. 1961. Money, capital and other stores of value. *American Economic Review, Papers and Proceedings* 51, 26–37.

Tobin, J. 1974. Friedman's theoretical framework. In *Milton Friedman's Monetary Framework: a Debate with His Critics,* ed. R.J. Gordon. Chicago: University of Chicago Press.

White, L.H. 1984a. *Free Banking in Britain: Theory, Experience and Debate, 1800–1845.* New York: Cambridge University Press.

White, L.H. 1984b. Competitive payments systems and the unit of account. *American Economic Review* 74, 699–712.

real bills doctrine versus the quantity theory

Drawing on two very different hypotheses about the link between nominal money and economic activity, the real bills doctrine and the quantity theory of money represent sharply divergent advice on the conduct of monetary policy. The quantity theory has many prominent advocates, but the real bills doctrine has had a dominant influence in the history and practice of central banking. Further, the real bills doctrine was at the core of the Congressional act creating the US Federal Reserve System so that its importance echoes down to the current day.

The real bills doctrine views money as playing a decidedly passive role, calling for monetary expansion in line with economic activity. According to this view, economic activity is linked to business trade credit and the issuance of short-term debt instruments. Banks should freely purchase these 'real bills' with banknote issue, where the modifier 'real' refers to short-term debt instruments used to finance productive activity as opposed to speculation. The doctrine dates to at least 1705 with the publication of *Money and Trade Considered* by John Law, who suggested that banknote issue should be secured by and thus linked to the nominal value of land. The most famous statement of the doctrine is by Adam Smith, whose linkage of note issue to bills of exchange gave the doctrine its name:

> When a bank discounts to a merchant a real bill of exchange drawn by a real creditor upon a real debtor, and which, as soon as it becomes due, is really paid by that debtor; it only advances to him a part of the value which he would otherwise be obliged to keep by him unemployed, and in ready money for answering occasional demands. The payment of the bill, when it becomes due, replaces to the bank the value of what it had advanced, together with the interest. The coffers of the bank, so far as its dealings are confined to such customers, resemble a water pond, from which, though a stream is continually running out, yet another is continually running in, fully equal to that which runs out; so that, without any further care or attention, the pond keeps equally, or very nearly full. (1776, p. 304)

Smith's water-pond metaphor illustrates the real-bills view that note issue would be self-regulating when tied to economic activity, that is, money issue could never be excessive when issued against short-term commercial bills.

The fundamental criticism of the real bills doctrine is that the value of commercial bills (or, in Law's case, the value of land) is tied proportionately to the price level. A commercial bill necessarily includes the dollar value of the goods or services to which it is linked. Thus, under the real bills doctrine, nominal note issue is tied to the nominal price level. If the price level is influenced by the money supply, then we have a circularity problem: nominal prices determine note issue, and note issue affects prices. Henry Thornton first noted the danger of this inflationary circle in his 1802

An Enquiry into the Nature and Effects of the Paper Credit of Great Britain. (David Ricardo was also a prominent opponent of the doctrine.) The thrust of Thornton's criticism was that the real bills doctrine provided no limit on banknote issue. Smith seems to have avoided Thornton's criticism because in Smith's system the gold standard provided an overall restraint on note issue. An excessive banknote issue would result in a bank losing its gold holdings, and see a drain on its 'coffers'. (See Laidler, 1981; 1984, for a defence of Smith.) But in a world with an inconvertible paper currency Thornton's inflationary critique is devastating.

Humphrey (2001) provides an algebraic description of the real bills doctrine. Suppose that the needs for trade credit are proportional to nominal production, PY, where P denotes the price level and Y denotes real production. The real bills doctrine would imply that banknote issue and thus the money supply (M) should be proportionally linked to the needs of trade credit so that we have:

$$M = kPY$$

where k is the constant of proportionality between trade credit and nominal production. The Thornton inflationary critique is now obvious: even with an exogenous level of output (Y), there is no way of determining the two endogenous variables, the money supply (M) and price level (P). A real bills counter-argument would be that the price level is exogenous to money, that is, the money supply has no direct effect on prices. As discussed below, the quantity theory makes the exact opposite claim.

The real bills doctrine and the Great Depression

Remarkably, the real bills doctrine survived Thornton and Ricardo's withering 19th century criticism to find a central place in 20th century US monetary history. In a fascinating account, Meltzer (2003) and Humphrey (2001) trace the flowering of the real bills doctrine into the US Federal Reserve Act of 1913. US Federal Reserve Banks existed for the purpose of 'accommodating commerce and business' and were supposed to discount only 'eligible paper', which the Act defined as 'notes, drafts, and bills of exchange arising out of actual commercial transactions'. Although, like Adam Smith, the Act presumed the existence of the gold standard, the real bills doctrine was deemed sufficient even in the absence of a specie constraint. For example, in the *Tenth Annual Report* (1924) of the Board of Governors of the Federal Reserve System, it is noted that 'there is little danger that the credit created and distributed by the Federal Reserve Banks will be in excessive volume if restricted to productive issues' (1924, p. 28). The Report further suggested no link between money and prices: 'The interrelationship of prices and credit is too complex to admit of any simple statement' (1924, p. 32). Adolph Miller, a founding member of the Federal Reserve Board and co-author of the Report, rejected the notion that 'changes in the level of prices are caused by changes in the volume of credit and currency…or that changes in the volume of credit and currency are caused by Federal Reserve policy' (quoted in Meltzer, 2003, pp. 187–8).

Meltzer (2003) convincingly argues that it was this belief in the self-regulating nature of the real bills doctrine that led the Federal Reserve to stand idly by as the US economy spiralled into the Great Depression in the early 1930s. From a real-bills perspective, monetary policy was very loose during these years because Reserve Banks stood ready to discount bills at historically low nominal rates of interest. Meltzer (2003, p. 321) concludes that

> the real bills doctrine implied that the correct policy was a passive one. Most [Federal Reserve] governors had always held these views ... The economies of the United States and much of the rest of the world became victims of the Federal Reserve's adherence to an inappropriate theory and the absence of basic economic understanding such as that developed by [Henry] Thornton and [Irving] Fisher.

The quantity theory

In sharp contrast to the real bills doctrine, the quantity theory held as its fundamental principle that the quantity of nominal money (M) is largely exogenous and is the principal force determining the endogenous price level (P). This argument was first articulated by David Hume (1752). An immediate corollary is that changes in the price level, that is, inflation, are primarily determined by movements in the supply of money. In the words of the celebrated quantity theorist Milton Friedman (1956, pp. 20–1):

> there is perhaps no other empirical relation in economics that has been observed to recur so uniformly under so wide a variety of circumstances as the relation between substantial changes over short periods in the stock of money and in prices; the one is invariably linked with the other and is in the same direction; this uniformity is, I suspect, of the same order as many of the uniformities that form the basis of the physical sciences.

The quantity theory's causal link between M and P included the concept of long-run monetary neutrality: exogenous changes in M would eventually be exactly matched by proportional changes in P. This inference is grounded on the stability of real money demand. In the words of Friedman: 'The quantity theory is in the first instance a theory of the demand for money' (1956, p. 4); 'The quantity theorist accepts the empirical hypothesis that the demand for money is highly stable – more stable than functions such as the consumption function that are offered as alternative key relations' (1956, p. 16). If we let $L(R,Y)$ denote real money demand as a function of the nominal interest rate (R) and the level of real production (Y), we have a money market equilibrium condition given by:

$$L(R, Y) = \frac{M}{P}.$$

The proportionality hypothesis is then quite clear: for a stable level of L, exogenous changes in M must be matched by changes in P of the exact same magnitude.

The quantity theory also included the concept of short-run non-neutrality. In the words of Hume (1752, p. 38):

> When any quantity of money is imported into a nation, it is not at first disposed into many hands but is confined to the coffers of a few persons, who immediately seek to employ it to advantage ... It is easy to trace the money in its progress through the whole commonwealth, where we shall find that it must first quicken the diligence of every individual before it increase the price of labour.

'There is always an interval before matters be adjusted to their new situation' (1752, p. 40). Quantity theorists would argue that increases in M are initially met by increases in production (Y) and declines in interest rates (R), but that in the long run R and Y would return to their original levels and that P would thus fully reflect the new higher level of M.

The quantity theory is closely associated with the quantity equation which can be derived as follows. The previous money demand relationship can be re-written as

$$M\frac{Y}{L(R,Y)} = PY.$$

If we define the velocity of money as

$$V \equiv \frac{Y}{L(R,Y)}$$

then we can write this relationship as the celebrated quantity equation:

$$MV = PY.$$

This is Pigou's (1927) variant of Irving Fisher's (1922) classic equation of exchange. The quantity equation is a useful device for expositing the two central tenets of the quantity theory of money: (*a*) in the long run, output (Y) and velocity (V) are exogenous to money, so that exogenous movements in the money supply (M) are met by proportional movements in prices (P), and (*b*) in the short run, movements in the money supply are met by some combination of movements in velocity, prices and output, so that changes in M have non-neutral effects on output. The quantity equation can also be used to illustrate Thornton's inflationary critique of the real bills doctrine. For a given level of the nominal rate and an exogenous level of production, velocity is determined by the money demand function, but there is no restriction on the size of M or the size of P.

The contemporary policy debate

From the vantage point of the outset of the 21st century, there is a sense in which the quantity theory has won numerous intellectual battles but lost the war. Most economists subscribe to the principles of long-run monetary neutrality and short-run non-neutrality. Most would also agree that the quantity equation can be a useful intellectual organizing device. Finally, a standard result in any monetary theory course is the nominal indeterminacy that arises under an exogenous interest-rate operating procedure (for example, Sargent, 1987, ch. 4). This result is just the modern statement of Thornton's 1802 criticism of the real bills doctrine. Hence, it would appear that the quantity theory is in the ascendant.

But remnants of the real bills doctrine are pervasive in both monetary policy implementation and theoretical work. In terms of policy, essentially all central banks in the industrialized world typically ignore or downplay movements in monetary aggregates and instead conduct monetary policy according to an interest rate operating procedure, a close descendant of a real-bills policy. The rationale for such a policy choice is the assertion that the demand for money and thus velocity are unstable. Such a policy implies seasonal movements in monetary aggregates to accommodate movements in real activity, a passive money supply movement that is directly out of a real-bills playbook.

From a theoretical perspective, there have been two prominent recent contributions in favour of interest rate policy. First, Sargent and Wallace (1982) provide something of a rehabilitation of the real bills doctrine by developing a model in which fluctuating nominal interest rates are harmful, and in which a policy of pegging the nominal interest rate at zero is Pareto efficient. Second, Woodford (2003) has pioneered an effort to conduct monetary policy analysis in 'cashless' models – models in which the price level is well defined even though there is no money in the model and the central bank follows an interest-rate operating procedure. We review each of these contributions in turn.

Sargent and Wallace (1982) consider a two-period-lived overlapping-generations model in which fiat money is held even though nominal interest rates are positive because of a legal restriction on private real lending. There are three types of agents: poor savers, rich savers, and borrowers. Using their logarithmic preference specification, the two classes of savers have a constant desired level of savings, say, S^P for the poor and $S^R gg; S^P$ for the rich. The borrowers have a demand for loans given by

$$D^L = \frac{D}{1 + r}$$

where r is the real interest rate, and $D > S^R$. (Sargent and Wallace, 1982, consider the case in which the demand for loans fluctuates deterministically, but this is unimportant for their basic result.) The legal restriction is that borrowers cannot issue small-denomination notes. Hence, poor savers cannot lend directly to the borrowers, but can only save by accumulating fiat money. The equilibrium conditions for the money and credit markets are given by:

$$\text{Money market} : S^P = \frac{M_t}{P_t}$$

$$\text{Credit market}: S^R = \frac{D}{1+r_t}$$

where M_t and P_t denote the time-t money supply and price level, and r_t is the real rate of interest. Under what Sargent–Wallace call a 'quantity-theory' regime, the central bank keeps the money supply fixed at some $M_t = M$. In this case, the price level and the real interest rate are constant and calculated from the above equilibrium conditions. This equilibrium is clearly not Pareto optimal as agents do not face the same inter-temporal rate of return – that is, rich savers earn a return of $r > 0$, while poor savers earn a zero real return on currency holdings.

Under a 'real-bills' regime the central bank stands ready to lend cash at a zero nominal rate of interest so that

$$(1 + r_t) = \frac{P_t}{P_{t+1}}.$$

In particular, the central bank purchases the 'real bills' issued by the borrowers. To finance these purchases the central bank creates the new fiat money denoted by N_t. The borrowers can then use this cash to purchase goods from the poor savers. By purchasing the borrowers' bonds with fiat money, the central bank is effectively opening up an avenue by which poor savers can lend to borrowers. Without this central bank intervention, the positive nominal rates in the credit market are symptoms of a problem – the inability of a fixed money stock to promote proper credit allocation. The real bills equilibrium conditions are given by:

$$\text{Money market}: S^P = \frac{M_t + N_t}{P_t}$$

$$\text{Credit market}: \frac{N_t}{P_t} + S^R = \frac{D}{(P_t/P_{t+1})}.$$

Combining, we have that an equilibrium under the real-bills regime is defined by a price sequence that satisfies:

$$S^P + S^R = \frac{M_t}{P_t} + \frac{D}{(P_t/P_{t+1})}.$$

Solving, we have:

$$P_t = \left(\frac{D}{S^P + S^R}\right) P_{t+1} + \left(\frac{1}{S^P + S^R}\right) M_t.$$

Assuming $D < (S^P + S^R)$, the set of stationary equilibria are given by

$$P_t = \left(\frac{1}{S^P + S^R}\right) \sum_{j=0}^{\infty} \left(\frac{D}{S^P + S^R}\right)^j M_{t+j}$$

where the path of the money supply is free. In the special case in which the money supply grows at a constant rate g we have

$$P_t = \left(\frac{1}{S^P + S^R - D(1 + g)}\right) M_t.$$

Note that, if g becomes large enough, the monetary equilibrium disappears.

Sargent and Wallace restrict the analysis to a particular equilibrium in which the beginning-of-period money supply is held fixed, $M_t = M$ for $t = 0, 1, 2, 3 \ldots$. However, the money supply grows and contracts *within* each period as the central bank accommodates the supply of one-period bonds issued by the borrowers ('real bills') with the passive expansion of N_t. In this equilibrium the price level is constant and the real return on savings is zero. This equilibrium is Pareto efficient, in contrast to the Pareto inefficiency of the quantity-theory regime. This is an argument in favour of the real bills doctrine and represents Sargent and Wallace's rehabilitation of the doctrine.

There are difficulties with this conclusion. First, the real-bills equilibrium selected by Sargent and Wallace does not Pareto-dominate the quantity-theory regime (rich savers are worse off under the real-bills regime). Second, there is an infinite number of other real-bills equilibria, all defined by the behaviour of the money stock, and not all of these are Pareto efficient. For example, if the money supply grows at a constant rate $g > 0$ the real-bills equilibrium is not Pareto efficient. Finally, Thornton's inflationary critique of the real-bills regime endures: since the money supply is entirely free, there are no restrictions on the short-term and long-term price level.

The second body of recent theoretical work that has a real-bills flavour is provided by Woodford (2003). The title of Woodford's treatise is *Interest and Prices*, a title that makes clear a principal assertion in the work: the money supply is largely irrelevant to price-level determination. The key relationship in the work is the Fisher equation linking nominal rates (i_t) to inflation rates and real rates (r_t):

$$i_t = r_t + p_{t+1} - p_t$$

where p_t is the log of the price level. For simplicity let us suppose that the real rate is exogenous. If the central bank conducts policy according to an exogenous nominal interest rate policy, then the Fisher equation uniquely determines the growth rate of prices (the inflation rate), but not the level of prices. This is, again, the Thornton critique of the real bills doctrine. But Woodford assumes that the central bank follows an endogenous interest rate policy in which the nominal rate responds to movements in prices:

$$i_t = \alpha p_t.$$

Assuming that $\alpha > 0$, the unique stationary equilibrium is given by:

$$p_t = \sum_{j=0}^{\infty} \left(\frac{1}{1 + \alpha}\right)^{j+1} r_{t+j}.$$

From a quantity-theory perspective this is a remarkable conclusion: the price level is determined without any mention being made of the money supply. Where is the money demand curve? Either it does not matter (as the money supply moves passively to hit the interest rate target) or it does not even exist (a 'cashless' world). Woodford's (2003) analysis thus rejects the quantity theory as a useful guide for policy, and at the same time provides a 21st-century response to Thornton's 19th-century critique of the real bills doctrine: the money supply should be adjusted passively to hit the interest-rate target (as under a real-bills policy), but the interest-rate target should be moved endogenously to ensure price-level stability.

In the intellectual clash of ideas there are typically no clear winners or losers, but instead a synthesis of the combatants. This is surely true of the debate between the real-bills doctrine and the quantity theory of money. Current monetary policy practice and theory has a notable real-bills flavour in the near-universal use of interest rates as the operating target. To repeat, the advantage of such a policy is that it allows the money supply to respond automatically to and thus accommodate natural movements in real economic activity. But Thornton and the quantity theorists provide a cautionary critique: under an exogenous interest rate policy, there is no way of limiting the inflationary circle between note issue and the price level. To respond to this quantity-theory critique, Woodford (2003) and others have proposed an endogenous interest-rate policy of the form outlined above. This is just one manifestation of the synthesis of the two combatants in this intellectual debate.

TIMOTHY S. FUERST

See also **monetarism; quantity theory of money.**

Bibliography

Board of Governors of the Federal Reserve System. 1924. *Tenth Annual Report of the Federal Reserve Board: Covering Operations for the Year 1923*. Washington: Government Printing Office.

Fisher, I. 1922. *The Purchasing Power of Money*, Reprinted, 2nd edn. New York: August M. Kelley, 1963.

Friedman, M. 1956. The quantity theory of money: a restatement. In *Studies in the Quantity Theory of Money*. Chicago: University of Chicago Press.

Hume, D. 1752. Of interest; of money. In *Writings on Economics*, ed. E. Rotwein. Madison: University of Wisconsin Press, 1970.

Humphrey, T.M. 1974. The quantity theory of money: its historical evolution and role in policy debates. *Federal Reserve Bank of Richmond Economic Review* 1974(May/June), 2–19.

Humphrey, T.M. 1982. The real bills doctrine. *Federal Reserve Bank of Richmond Economic Review* 1982(September/October), 3–13.

Humphrey, T.M. 2001. Monetary policy frameworks and indicators for the federal reserve in the 1920s. *Federal Reserve Bank of Richmond Economic Quarterly* 87(1), 65–92.

Laidler, D. 1981. Adam Smith as a monetary economist. *Canadian Journal of Economics* 14, 185–200.

Laidler, D. 1984. Misconceptions about the real bills doctrine: a comment on Sargent and Wallace. *Journal of Political Economy* 92, 149–55.

Law, J. 1705. *Money and Trade Considered*. Edinburgh: Anderson.

Meltzer, A.H. 2003. *A History of the Federal Reserve, Volume I: 1913–1951*. Chicago: University of Chicago Press.

Pigou, A.C. 1917. The value of money. *Quarterly Journal of Economics* 32(November), 38–65.

Pigou, A.C. 1927. *Industrial Fluctuations*. London: Macmillan.

Sargent, T.J. 1987. *Macroeconomic Theory*, 2nd edn. Orlando, FL: Academic Press.

Sargent, T.J. and Wallace, N. 1982. The real-bills doctrine vs. the quantity theory: a reconsideration. *Journal of Political Economy* 90, 1212–36.

Smith, A. 1776. *An Inquiry into the Nature and Causes of the Wealth of Nations*. Indianapolis: Liberty Press, 1976.

Thornton, H. 1802. *An Enquiry into the Nature and Effects of the Paper Credit of Great Britain*. London: LSE Reprint Series, 1939.

Woodford, M. 2003. *Interest and Prices*. Princeton: Princeton University Press.

search-and-matching models of monetary exchange

In this article we review a class of equilibrium search (matching) models that can be used to study the trading process, and in particular to develop a formal theory of *money as a medium of exchange*. Developing such a theory is one of the longest-standing issues in economics, but it met with at best limited success prior to the development of search-based models, which provide a natural framework in which to formalize venerable stories about money helping to facilitate exchange.

These stories, going back to Smith, Jevons, Menger, Wicksell, and others – many of which are reprinted in Starr (1990) – concern a *double coincidence of wants problem* in bilateral exchange, as discussed below. Overlapping generations models (for example, Wallace, 1980) provide an alternative approach. Ostroy and Starr (1990) survey earlier attempts to develop microfoundations for monetary theory, including Jones (1976), which is similar in spirit if not detail to modern search models. There is not the space here to discuss the pros and cons of the various approaches, but it seems fair to say search and matching models now dominate the area.

Background

Diamond (1982) introduced a framework that, although it cannot be used directly, can be extended naturally to build microfoundations for monetary economics. In his model, a [0,1] continuum of infinitely lived agents interact in an economy where activity takes place in two distinct sectors: one for production and one for exchange. In the first sector, agents encounter potential production opportunities randomly over time according to a Poisson process with arrival rate α. Each opportunity yields a unit of output at cost $c \geq 0$, where c is random with CDF $F(c)$. Since c is observed before a production decision is made, given an opportunity, there is a reservation cost k such that agents produce if $c \leq k$. For now, these goods are indivisible, and agents can store at most one at a time.

All goods yield utility of consumption $u > 0$, except by assumption agents cannot consume their own output; hence they must trade. Traders with goods meet bilaterally in the exchange sector according to a Poisson process with arrival rate γ. Upon meeting they trade, consume, and return to production. Since all goods are the same, and indivisible, every meeting yields trade, and every trade is a one-for-one swap. Generally, $\gamma = \gamma(N)$ depends on the measure of agents in the exchange sector N. This is based on a matching technology that gives the number of agents who meet a partner per unit time as $m(N)$, with $m'(N) > 0$, implying $\gamma(N) = m(N)/N$ for all $N > 0$.

Let V_0 and V_1 be the value functions for producers and traders. The flow Bellman equation for a producer is

$$rV_0 = \alpha E \max\{V_1 - V_0 - c, 0\} = \alpha \int_0^k (k - c)dF(c),$$

where $k = V_1 - V_0$. Similarly, for a trader

$$rV_1 = \gamma(N)(u + V_0 - V_1) = \gamma(N)(u - k).$$

(We focus on steady states; for dynamics, see for example Diamond and Fudenberg, 1989.)

In words, the flow value rV_0 equals the arrival rate of opportunities times the expected option value of switching from production to exchange, while rV_1 equals the arrival rate of meetings times the gain from trading and switching back. Combining these equations,

$$rk = \gamma(N)(u - k) - \alpha \int_0^k (k - c)dF(c).$$

Given N this has a unique solution for k. Given k, in steady state, the flow of agents from production to exchange must equal the flow back,

$$(1 - N)\alpha F(k) = m(N).$$

An equilibrium is a pair (N, k) satisfying these last two equations. It is simple to derive results concerning existence, comparative statics, and so on. As Diamond emphasizes, under increasing returns in $m(N)$, if any non-degenerate equilibrium (one with production) exists then multiple such equilibria exist. Under constant returns, a unique non-degenerate equilibrium exists if parameters fall in a certain range – for example, u is not too low, r not too high, and so on. To complete our review of this basic model, notice that exchange is trivial, even though it is restricted to bilateral trade, because there is only one good (or, all goods are the same). To make money interesting we need to generalize this. (Diamond, 1984, took a short cut to getting money into the model with a cash-in-advance constraint. By changing the environment as we do below, we see this is not only uninteresting, it is unnecessary.)

To ease the presentation we first simplify the production process. Assume everyone is *always* in the exchange sector, and, instead of carrying goods around, they can produce whenever they meet someone, at deterministic cost $C \geq 0$. Now, following Kiyotaki and Wright (1991; 1993), assume goods come in varieties, say colours. Each agent produces a particular colour, but different agents like to consume different colours. The simplest specification assumes agents get $u = U > C$ from any good in some set, and $u = 0$ from other goods, and x is the probability output in the relevant set (that is, an agent wants what the other agent can produce) in any random meeting. Also, since agents can produce whenever they want, to simplify things we assume goods are non-storable.

When goods *are* storable, Kiyotaki and Wright (1989) determine endogenously which objects serve as media of exchange, potentially including commodity plus fiat money. That model illustrates the trade-off between fundamental properties like storability and equilibrium properties like acceptability. It has many implications – for example, there can be multiple equilibria with different monies, objects with bad fundamental properties may end up as money, and so on. Generalizations and applications of the model include Marimon, McGrattan and Sargent (1990); Aiyagari and Wallace (1991; 1992); Kehoe, Kiyotaki and Wright (1993); Wright (1995); and Duffy and Ochs (1999). Here, by making goods non-storable, we focus on determining how an economy operates when there is a single candidate medium of exchange, namely, fiat money.

On the assumption that exchange requires mutual agreement, which occurs when I want to consume your good and you want to consume mine, trade now occurs only in a meeting with probability x^2, at least if the event that I want your good is independent of the event that you want mine (see below). This captures nicely the famous *double coincidence problem* with direct barter: trade requires meeting someone who produces something you like – which would be a coincidence – and also likes what you produce – a double coincidence. Payoffs are given by $rV_B = \gamma x^2(U - C)$, where the subscript on V_B stands for 'barter'. If x is small, which is the case if there is a lot of specialization, double coincidence meetings are rare and V_B is very low.

But is it really necessarily the case that trade occurs iff both parties want to consume what the other produces? Following ideas in Kocherlakota (1998), suppose agents get together at the start of time and discuss when to trade. Clearly, they agree that whenever *either* agent wants what the other produces he should get it, since this maximizes *ex ante* welfare

$$rV_C = \gamma[x^2(U - C) + x(1 - x)U - (1 - x)xC] = \gamma x(U - C),$$

where the subscript on V_C stands for 'cooperation' (or perhaps 'commitment' or 'credit'). As long as $x < 1$, $V_C > V_B$. However, suppose agents cannot commit now to do things when they meet later that are not in their interest at that time. Then trades must satisfy incentive compatibility (IC), the binding condition being that you should be willing to produce in meetings where you do not consume.

If we can keep a public record of all agents' behaviour, we can try to use *trigger strategies* to support cooperative trade as follows: instruct agents to cooperate as long as everyone else does; but if anyone deviates, trigger to … 'something bad'. One can argue the worst trigger is 'autarky' which yields $V_A = 0$; or it may be 'barter' which yields V_B. In the former case the relevant IC condition is $-C + V_C \geq V_A$, which simplifies to $rC \leq \gamma x(U - C)$; in the latter case it is $-C + V_C \geq V_B$, which simplifies to $rC \leq \gamma x(1 - x)(U - C)$. In either case, if r is small we can sustain cooperative trade. Moreover, one can prove formally that money has no role here (Kocherlakota, 1998; Wallace, 2001); instead of proving this here we move to models where money does have a role.

First-generation search models of money

Suppose it is difficult to use triggers because, say, there is incomplete monitoring or record keeping, or, to take the simplest situation, suppose agents have no memory – they just cannot recall what happened in previous meetings! Kocherlakota (1998),

Kocherlakota and Wallace (1998), Wallace (2001), Corbae, Temzilides and Wright (2003), Araujo (2004), and Aliprantis, Camera and Puzzello (2007) explore less extreme variations, but our assumption allows us to make the point more easily. In our 'memoryless' world, your continuation payoff V_M cannot depend on what you do in a given meeting. Hence, the relevant constraint to get you to produce without consuming is $-C + V_M \geq V_M$, which is violated for any $C > 0$. There is no scope for using threats to sustain cooperation without memory (generally, there is limited scope when memory is imperfect, which is what we need; we use the starkest case merely for tractability).

Suppose we introduce into this world a new object called fiat *money*. By definition, a medium of exchange is an object that is accepted in trade not to be used for consumption – or production – but to be traded again later for something else. When an object serving as a medium of exchange is for some people at some times a consumption good, it is called commodity money. When an object with no consumption value serves as a medium of exchange it is fiat money. At the start of time, we endow a fraction M of the population each with $m = 1$ unit of money and the rest with $m = 0$. Initially, those with $m - 0$ can produce; after this, agents can produce after they consume but not before. This implies agents with money cannot produce, and at any point in time everyone either has $m = 1$ or $m = 0$. Now, even without memory, agents have an option other than pure barter: offer money for goods. Let Π be the probability a random producer accepts such an offer, and let π be your best response.

If V_m and V_p are the value functions of agents with and without money,

$$rV_p = \gamma(1 - M)x^2(U - C) + \gamma Mx\pi(V_m - V_p - C)rV_m$$
$$= \gamma(1 - M)x\Pi(U + V_p - V_m).$$

For example, rV_p equals the arrival rate of agents with goods $\gamma(1 - M)$, times the double coincidence probability x^2, times the gain from barter $U-C$; plus the arrival rate of agents with money γM, times the probability of trade $x\pi$, times the gain $V_m - V_p - C$. We restrict attention to pure strategies (mixed strategy equilibria are not robust here; see Shevchenko and Wright, 2004). Then the best response condition is $\pi = 0$ if $V_m - V_p < C$ and $\pi = 1$ if $V_m - V_p > C$. It is easy to see $\pi = 0$ is always an equilibrium, and $\pi = 1$ is an equilibrium iff

$$rC \leq \gamma(1 - M)x(1 - x)(U - C).$$

Naturally, $\pi = 0$ is an equilibrium – if no one else accepts money, why would you? It is more interesting that $\pi = 1$ can be an equilibrium, since then intrinsically worthless money is valued, as a medium of exchange. Given M, one can check $\pi = 1$ yields higher payoffs than $\pi = 0$. Alternatively, if we choose M to maximize welfare, one can check $M > 0$ iff x is not too big. Hence, introducing money can improve welfare, even given the assumption that money holders cannot produce. The convention of money as a medium of exchange is good because it eases trade. Now, $\pi = 1$ is only an equilibrium when r is not too high, and one can check the cutoff for r here is more stringent (and payoffs lower) than when we had memory and triggers – that is, money is not a perfect mechanism. One reason money is not as good as memory is the *random* nature of matching. The problem is that you might, for example, have two meetings in a row where you want a good from someone who does not want your good, and in the second one you will have run out of money (this can also happens with positive probability when we relax the upper bound of unity on money holdings). However, in an *endogenous* (rather than random) matching model this never happens – when you have no money you do not go to someone whose good you like, but to someone who likes your good; see Corbae, Temzilides and Wright (2003). Still, money can do pretty well here, and if we cannot use triggers it is the only way to improve on pure barter.

The model is obviously crude, yet it gets at the essence of money. To recap, the results assume the following explicit frictions: (*a*) a double coincidence problem (generated here by random bilateral matching, although there are other devices in the related literature); (*b*) imperfect commitment; and (*c*) imperfect memory (or anything else that makes it difficult to use triggers). These frictions are severe – but no one said it was going to be easy to get money into economic theory in an interesting way. There are many extensions and applications of this model (some of which are surveyed in Rupert et al., 2000), but in the interest of space, we now move on to models where prices are endogenous. We mention one extension to endogenous specialization in Kiyotaki and Wright, 1993, based on ideas in Adam Smith. Consider the case where the probability that someone accepts your good x is a *choice variable*: if you want a large fraction of the population to like your output, you cannot specialize too much, which reduces productivity. Thus, the arrival rate in the production sector – to return to Diamond's two sector set-up – is $\alpha(x)$, with $\alpha' < 0$. When choosing x, you take the average X as given, and in equilibrium $x = X$. Two results follow. First, monetary equilibria have lower x than non-monetary equilibria, so the use of money enhances specialization and productivity. Second, $x \to 0$ as $\gamma \to \infty$, so when frictions vanish, agents specialize completely, and since the double coincidence probability is x^2, barter completely disappears.

Second-generation models

Suppose that goods are no longer indivisible, but can be consumed and produced in any amount $q \geq 0$, which yields utility $U(q)$ and disutility $-C(q)$, respectively. These functions have all the usual properties, plus $C(0) = U(0) = 0$. We maintain for now the assumptions that money is indivisible, money holders cannot produce, and everyone holds $m \in \{0,1\}$. But we relax the assumption of independence in generating the double coincidence problem: the probability that I like your good is x, but now the probability that I like your good and you like mine is y, and not necessarily x^2, in general. (Consider N goods and N types, where type n produces good n, but likes good $n+1$ modulo N. If $N = 2$ then $x = y = 1/2$ (if I like your good you must like mine), while if $N \geq 3$ then $x = 1/N$ and $y = 0$ (if I like your good you cannot like mine). It is only under independence, which does not hold in these examples, that we necessarily have $y = x^2$.)

Conditional on money being accepted ($\pi = 1$), we have

$$rV_p = \gamma(1 - M)y[U(\hat{q}) - C\hat{q})] + \gamma Mx[V_m - V_p - C(q)]rV_m$$
$$= \gamma(1 - M)x[U(q) + V_p - V_m],$$

where $\hat{q}$ is the amount traded in barter and q the amount traded for money. It facilitates the presentation to start with the case $y = 0$ and then give general results. Now, to determine the equilibrium value of money, as in Shi (1995) or Trejos and Wright (1995), we say the following: when I meet you and want your good, if I have $m = 1$ while you have $m = 0$, we *bargain* over the q you produce for my money, taking as given q in all other meetings. Equilibrium is a fixed point, $q = q$, and the price level is $p = 1/q$.

One can use any bargaining solution, including generalized Nash

$$\max \; [U(q) + V_p - V_m]^{\theta}[V_m - V_p - C(q)]^{1-\theta},$$

for any $\theta \in (0,1)$; we use $\theta = 1$ because it is so easy. (See Rupert et al., 2001, for $\theta \in (0,1)$ and other generalizations. Alternatives to bargaining studied in versions of this model include posting – for example, Curtis and Wright, 2004 – and auctions – Julien, Kennes and King, 2007. Or, instead of imposing a particular pricing mechanism, one can study the entire set of incentive-feasible trades – Wallace, 2001.) When $\theta = 1$, agents with $m = 0$ get no gains from trade since they have no bargaining power (and $y = 0$). Hence $V_p = 0$, $V_m = C(q)$, and the Bellman equation for V_m reduces to

$$rC(q) = \gamma(1 - M)x[U(q) - C(q)].$$

This is 1 equation in q, with two solutions: 0 and a unique $q > 0$. Again, we get equilibrium where an intrinsically worthless object is valued as a medium of exchange. It is easy to do comparative statics, welfare analysis, and so on in this model (for example, it is immediate that q falls and p rises when M or r increase).

Once we reintroduce some barter – that is, once we allow $y > 0$ – one can show that, in addition to $q = 0$, generically there either exist two equilibria with $q > 0$ or no equilibrium with $q > 0$. If y is small then equilibrium with $q > 0$ always exists. It is not much harder to analyse the general case $\theta \in (0,1)$. This model has a large number of variations, extensions and applications – too many to review here (again see Rupert et al., 2000). Suffice it to say that the basic results of first-generation models more or less go through, with additional insights concerning prices.

Third-generation models

The approach sketched above provides a compelling microfoundation for monetary theory: it is based on sound economic thinking going back to some very famous economists, brought up to date with modern and rigorous methods and ideas.

Still, obviously those first- and second-generation models are quite abstract and quite special. In particular, the assumption that agents hold $m \in \{0,1\}$ is severe, and precludes using the models for much quantitative and policy analysis. The difficult part of relaxing this and allowing any $m \geq 0$ is that we need to keep track of the distribution of m across agents, which is complicated by the random nature of matching and the endogenous amount of money spent in each match. There are several ways to deal with this problem. Some analytic results are available in Green and Zhou (1998) and Camera and Corbae (1999) for example, while computation methods are used by Molico (2006).

Another approach is to amend the environment to get around this problem while hopefully maintaining the spirit and essence of the matching models outlined above. There are two main ways to do this, following either Shi (1997) or Lagos and Wright (2005). The Shi model assumes the fundamental decision makers are not individuals, but families, each with a large number of members. If the individual members experience independent random meetings, when they return to the household at the end of each period the total amount of money in the family is pinned down by the law of large numbers. Hence, each household starts the next period with the same (deterministic) amount of money. There are many extensions and applications of this framework (see Shi, 2006, for some references).

The Lagos–Wright model alternatively assumes that at the end of each round of decentralized trade agents go to a centralized market where they can (among other things) rebalance their money holdings. On the assumption of quasi-linear utility, all agents choose the same m for next period, independent of the amount with which they start. Again, agents enter each round of decentralized trade with the same m here, just as in the family model (although there are several interesting differences between the approaches). Versions of either model are easily used for quantitative and policy analysis. These models are perhaps still special, since they use 'tricks' to harness the distribution of m, but this is merely for technical convenience in deriving analytic results. If one is willing to use a computer, most of the special assumptions can be avoided (see, for example, Chiu and Molico, 2006).

Conclusion

We have reviewed several generations of search-and-matching models of the exchange process that can be used to provide microfoundations for monetary economics. While the literature is big, and growing fast, it is to be hoped that this article conveys some of the main ideas and models in an accessible fashion.

RANDALL WRIGHT

See also **fiat money; inside and outside money; money; money and general equilibrium.**

Bibliography

Aiyagari, S.R. and Wallace, N. 1991. Existence of steady states with positive consumption in the Kiyotaki Wright model. *Review of Economic Studies* 58, 901–16.

Aiyagari, S.R. and Wallace, N. 1992. Fiat money in the Kiyotaki Wright model. *Economic Theory* 2, 447–64.

Aliprantis, C.D., Camera, G. and Puzzello, D. 2007. Anonymous markets and monetary trading. *Journal of Monetary Economics* 54, 1905–28.

Araujo, L. 2004. Social norms and money. *Journal of Monetary Economics* 51, 241–56.

Camera, G. and Corbae, D. 1999. Monetary patterns of exchange with search. *International Economic Review* 40, 985–1008.

Chiu, J. and Molico, M. 2006. Liquidity, redistribution and the welfare cost of inflation. Mimeo, Bank of Canada.

Corbae, D., Temzilides, T. and Wright, R. 2003. Directed matching and monetary exchange. *Econometrica* 71, 731–56.

Curtis, E. and Wright, R. 2004. Price setting, price dispersion and the value of money, or the law of two prices. *Journal of Monetary Economics* 51, 1599–621.

Diamond, P.A. 1982. Aggregate demand management in search equilibrium. *Journal of Political Economy* 90, 881–94.

Diamond, P.A. 1984. Money in search equilibrium. *Econometrica* 52, 1–20.

Diamond, P.A. and Fudenberg, D. 1989. Rational expectations business cycles in search equilibrium. *Journal of Political Economy* 97, 606–19.

Duffy, J. and Ochs, J. 1999. Emergence of money as a medium of exchange: an experimental study. *American Economic Review* 89, 847–77.

Green, E. and Zhou, R. 1998. A rudimentary model of search with divisible money and prices. *Journal of Economic Theory* 81, 252–71.

Jones, R. 1976. The origin and development of media exchange. *Journal of Political Economy* 84, 757–75.

Julien, B., Kennes, J. and King, I. 2007. Bidding for money. *Journal of Economic Theory.*

Kehoe, T.J., Kiyotaki, N. and Wright, R. 1993. More on money as a medium of exchange. *Economic Theory* 3, 297–314.

Kiyotaki, N. and Wright, R. 1989. On money as a medium of exchange. *Journal of Political Economy* 97, 927–54.

Kiyotaki, N. and Wright, R. 1991. A contribution to the pure theory of money. *Journal of Economic Theory* 53, 215–35.

Kiyotaki, N. and Wright, R. 1993. A search theoretic approach to monetary economics. *American Economic Review* 83, 63–77.

Kocherlakota, N. 1998. Money is memory. *Journal of Economic Theory* 81, 232–51.

Kocherlakota, N. and Wallace, N. 1998. Optimal allocations with incomplete record keeping and no commitment. *Journal of Economic Theory* 81, 272–89.

Lagos, R. and Wright, R. 2005. A unified framework for monetary theory and policy analysis. *Journal of Political Economy* 113, 463–84.

Marimon, R., McGrattan, E.R. and Sargent, T.J. 1990. Money as a medium of exchange in an economy with artificially intelligent agents. *Journal of Economic Dynamics and Control* 14, 329–73.

Molico, M. 2006. The distribution of money and prices in search equilibrium. *International Economic Review* 47, 701–22.

Ostroy, J.M. and Starr, R.M. 1990. The transaction role of money. In *Handbook of Monetary Economics*, ed. B. Friedman and F. Hahn. Amsterdam: North-Holland.

Rupert, P., Schindler, M., Shevchenko, A. and Wright, R. 2000. The search-theoretic approach to monetary economics: a primer. *Federal Reserve Bank of Cleveland Review* 36, 10–28.

Rupert, P., Schindler, M. and Wright, R. 2001. Generalized search theoretic model of monetary exchange. *Journal of Monetary Economics* 48, 605–22.

Shevchenko, A. and Wright, R. 2004. A simple model of money with heterogeneous agents and partial acceptability. *Economic Theory* 24, 877–85.

Shi, S. 1995. Money and prices: a model of search and bargaining. *Journal of Economic Theory* 67, 467–96.

Shi, S. 1997. A divisible search model of fiat money. *Econometrica* 65, 75–102.

Shi, S. 2006. Viewpoint: a microfoundation of monetary economics. *Canadian Journal of Economics* 39, 643–88.

Starr, R.M. 1990. *General Equilibrium Models of Monetary Economics*. New York: Academic Press.

Trejos, A. and Wright, R. 1995. Search, bargaining, money and prices. *Journal of Political Economy* 103, 118–41.

Wallace, N. 1980. The overlapping generations model of fiat money. In *Models of Monetary Economies*, ed. J.H. Kareken and N. Wallace. Minneapolis: Federal Reserve Bank of Minneapolis.

Wallace, N. 2001. Whither monetary economics. *International Economic Review* 42, 847–70.

Wright, R. 1995. Search, evolution, and money. *Journal of Economic Dynamics and Control* 19, 181–206.

silver standard

The silver standard, the dominant monetary system for many centuries, lost much importance with the advent of the classical gold standard; and, due to US policy, residual monetary use of silver was virtually eliminated in the 1930s.

Definition of silver standard

A silver standard involves (*a*) a fixed silver content of the monetary unit, (*b*) 'free coinage' of silver, that is, privately owned silver in form other than domestic coin convertible into domestic silver coin at, or approximately at, the mint price (the inverse of the silver content of the monetary unit), (*c*) no restrictions on private parties (i) melting domestic coin into bullion, or (ii) importing or exporting silver in any form, and (*d*) full legal-tender status for domestic silver coin.

Other forms of money may exist, but silver is the primary money. Foreign silver coin may be given equal legal-tender status with domestic coin. Gold coin may be in circulation, but its value is in terms of the silver monetary unit and may fluctuate by weight, varying with the market gold–silver price ratio. Paper currency and deposits may exist, but, as liabilities of the issuer or bank, are payable in legal tender, that is, silver coin (or silver-convertible government or central-bank currency).

If silver (whether domestic or foreign coin, or both) constitutes the only money, then, even absent free coinage, the economy is clearly on a silver standard. This conclusion holds with gold coin circulating as well, providing it is circulating by weight or is a minor part of the money supply.

A silver standard might be effective even though the monetary system is legally bimetallic. If the coinage gold–silver price ratio is sufficiently below the market ratio, then gold, undervalued at the mint, will be sold on the world market (even in the form of melted domestic coin), while silver, overvalued, will be imported and coined. Ultimately, an effective silver standard may result.

Depreciation of the silver coinage involves an increased ratio of the legal (face) value of coins relative to silver content, usually by debasement (reducing the silver content, whether weight or fineness, of given-denomination coins) rather than by increasing the denomination of existing (given-weight-and-fineness) coins. In England, the penny (of sterling, 11/12th fineness) was steadily reduced in size from 24 grains in the eighth century to less than 1/3 that weight in 1601.

A silver standard, just as the gold standard, provides a constraint on the money stock. Depreciation of silver coinage was a way of escaping that constraint, even though the authority's objective typically was to increase government revenue (in the form of seigniorage) and/or to change the coinage ratio (under legal bimetallism).

Countries on silver standard to 1870

A silver standard first occurred in ancient Greece. Notwithstanding generally legal bimetallism, silver was everywhere the effective metallic standard – or at least the far-more-important coined metal in the money stock – well into the 18th century. Because of its relative scarcity and high density, gold was always much more valuable than silver on a per-ounce basis: coinage and market ratios were far above unity. So, with most transactions of low value compared with the unit of account, silver was better suited than gold to serve as a medium of exchange. In US history, 'one dollar' was both the smallest gold piece and the largest silver piece ever coined.

In England, from the Anglo-Saxon period until the late 13th century, the only coin in existence (with rare exceptions) was the silver penny, with 240 pence coined ideally from one pound of silver and later constituting one pound sterling (where 'sterling,' of course, denotes silver). This was a silver standard by default. With coinage of gold, in 1257, there was legal bimetallism; but the practice of denominating gold coins in (silver) shillings and pence was implicit recognition of an effective silver standard. Even the popular, consistently coined, (gold) guinea, first issued in 1663, was left to find its own market value in shillings and pence. However, by the turn of the 18th century, foreign gold–silver price ratios had been falling and, having been increased greatly in 1696, the British coinage ratio was not subsequently reduced enough to compensate. England went briefly on a bimetallic standard, and then on an effective gold standard, legalized in 1774 and 1816.

In the United States, since colonial times a silver standard was in effect, based on the Spanish dollar, the primary circulating silver coin, which varied much in weight and fineness. Yet the dollar was accepted everywhere at face value in terms of local (individual-state) pound–shilling–pence units of account. Gold coins were rated in dollars according to fine-metal content. The Coinage Act of 1792 placed the United States on a legal bimetallic standard; but the coinage ratio soon fell below the (increasing) world-market ratio. An effective silver standard resulted, until the coinage ratio was corrected in 1834.

In 1870, just before Germany united and established the gold standard (using as financing the French indemnity, emanating from the Franco–Prussian War), Netherlands, Denmark, Norway, Sweden, India, China, Straits Settlements, Hong Kong, Dutch East Indies, Mexico and some German states were on a silver standard. In the 1870s these European countries (and Dutch East Indies) abandoned silver in favour of gold. By 1885 almost all of western Europe – along with the United States, Britain, its dominions and various colonies – was on gold.

Asian abandonment of the silver standard prior to the First World War

Traditionally, Asian countries preferred silver to gold for both monetary and non-monetary use, and the low market ratios in the Far East reflected that fact. The silver standard continued after 1885 in the Asian countries listed above. Further, in the 1880s the Philippines and Japan went on de facto silver.

Until 1873, bimetallic France kept the world market gold–silver price ratio around a narrow band centred on the French coinage ratio of $15\frac{1}{2}$. When France ended bimetallism in 1873, the market ratio lost its anchor and escalated tremendously. The exchange rates between silver-standard and gold-standard currencies also lost their anchor. Following the market gold–silver price ratio, silver currencies depreciated greatly with respect to gold currencies. Exports were enhanced, imports were more expensive, debt and other obligations stated in terms of gold or gold currencies increased greatly in domestic currency, domestic inflation increased, and foreign investment was discouraged due to exchange-rate instability.

The problem of a depreciating currency was especially acute for India, which had the obligation of substantial recurring sterling-denominated 'home charges' to Britain (for debt service, pensions, military and other equipment, and so forth). In 1893 India abandoned the silver standard, and in 1898 went on the gold-exchange standard, pegging the (silver) rupee against the pound sterling.

In 1897 Japan switched from a de facto silver standard under legal bimetallism to a monometallic gold-coin standard, using as financing the indemnity received from defeated China in the Sino–Japanese War. In 1903 the Philippines adopted a gold-exchange standard, with the (silver) peso pegged to the US (gold) dollar. The impetus was transfer of the country from Spain to the United States, thanks to US victory in the Spanish–American War.

Mexico, a large silver producer, with both commodity exporters and silver producers in favour of a continued silver standard, finally adopted a gold-coin standard in 1905. At the beginning of the First World War, the silver standard encompassed only China, Hong Kong and a few minor countries.

Termination of the silver standard

The final blow to the silver standard was delivered by the United States, ironically after it left the gold standard. In December 1933, when the (fluctuating) market price of silver was 44 cents per ounce, President Roosevelt proclaimed that US mints should purchase all new domestically produced silver at a net price (to the depositor, or seller) of 64.65 cents per ounce (half the official, but inoperative, mint price of silver). In 1934 this policy was reinforced by the Silver Purchase Act, which directed the Treasury to purchase silver at home and abroad as long as (a) the Treasury stock of gold constituted less than one-quarter its total monetary stock, and (b) the market price did not exceed the US official mint price. Subsequently, the president ordered that all silver (with minor exceptions) then situated in the continental United States was to be delivered to US mints, at a net price of 50.01 cents per ounce. In 1935, in response to a higher foreign market price of silver (largely due to the US silver-purchase policy itself!), the president increased the net price for newly produced domestic silver to 71.11 cents.

The reason for the US silver-purchase policy was to provide a subsidy to the (politically powerful) domestic silver producers. Inadvertently, the policy effectively destroyed what remained of the silver standard. The last major country on the silver standard was China. As the gold-standard world suffered monetary and real deflation in 1929–30, the price of silver fell. The Chinese, silver-based, currency (yuan) therefore depreciated against the, gold-based, currencies of important trading partners (Britain, India, Japan). The enhanced competitiveness of export and import-competing industries, and resulting balance-of-payments surplus, prevented deflation. China lost some 'silver protection' in 1931, after Britain, India and Japan left the gold standard, as the yuan appreciated against the pound, rupee and yen; but the United States was still on the gold standard, and the yuan continued to fall, slightly, against the dollar. After the United States abandoned the gold standard, in 1933, the yuan appreciated against all four currencies.

While China had lost its 'silver protection' from the world depression, it nevertheless retained the silver standard and probably suffered less economically than its main trading partners. Disaster struck with the US silver policy of 1933–4. The huge increase in the US and market price of silver involved a corresponding appreciation of the yuan. Loss of competitiveness, balance-of-payments deficit, export of silver (and gold) to finance the deficit, and deflation followed. China had no choice but to leave the silver standard, effectively in 1934, and legally in 1935.

Other silver-standard, as well as silver-using, countries were also adversely affected by the US policy. Hong Kong followed China, and left the gold standard in 1935. Though not on the silver standard, various Latin American countries had a large silver coinage. These were token coins (face value higher than metallic-content value). Nevertheless, the high US price for silver encouraged the melting and export of these coins. The affected countries resorted to debasement and re-coining in order to retain their silver coinage.

Mexico was a special case. Silver coins constituted a high proportion of its money supply; but, as the world's largest producer of silver, Mexico benefited from a higher price for a major export. However, as other countries left the silver standard, the price of silver began to fall, and this advantage was reduced. Mexico prohibited melting or export of silver coins in 1935, and replaced the coins with paper money. Later, re-coinage occurred, and melting and export were again permitted. Yet the damage had been done, and Mexico was now on a 'managed paper standard', having lost the discipline provided by metallic money. In sum, in the 1930s, a US domestic-oriented policy reduced considerably such monetary use of silver as remained.

LAWRENCE H. OFFICER

See also **gold standard.**

Bibliography

Bojanic, A.N. 1994. The silver standard in two late adherents: Mexico and India. Ph.D. thesis, Auburn University.
Brandt, L. and Sargent, T.J. 1989. Interpreting new evidence about China and U.S. silver purchases. *Journal of Monetary Economics* 23, 31–51.

der Eng, P.V. 1993. *The Silver Standard and Asia's Integration into the World Economy, 1850–1914.* Canberra: Australian National University.

Eichengreen, B. and Flandreau, M. 1996. The geography of the gold standard. In *Currency Convertibility: The Gold Standard and Beyond*, ed. J.B. de Macedo, B. Eichengreen and J. Reis. London and New York: Routledge.

Einzig, P. 1970. *The History of Foreign Exchange*, 2nd edn. London: Macmillan.

Feavearyear, Sir A. 1963. *The Pound Sterling: A History of English Money,* 2nd edn. Oxford: Clarendon Press.

Friedman, M. 1992. *Money Mischief: Episodes in Monetary History.* New York: Harcourt Brace Jovanovich.

Lai, C. and Gau, J.J. 2003. The Chinese silver standard economy and the 1929 Great Depression. *Australian Economic History Review* 43, 155–68.

Leavens, D.H. *Silver Money.* Bloomington, IN: Principia Press.

Officer, L.H. 1996. *Between the Dollar–Sterling Gold Points.* Cambridge: Cambridge University Press.

Redish, A. 2000. *Bimetallism: An Economic and Historical Analysis.* Cambridge: Cambridge University Press.

Wilson, T. 2000. *Battles for the Standard: Bimetallism and the Spread of the Gold Standard in the Nineteenth Century.* Aldershot: Ashgate.

Taylor rules

Taylor rules are simple monetary policy rules that prescribe how a central bank should adjust its interest rate policy instrument in a systematic manner in response to developments in inflation and macroeconomic activity. They provide a useful framework for the analysis of historical policy and for the econometric evaluation of specific alternative strategies that a central bank can use as the basis for its interest rate decisions.

A perennial question in monetary economics has been how the monetary authority should formulate and implement its policy decisions so as to best foster ultimate policy objectives such as price stability and full employment over time. It is widely accepted that well-designed monetary policy can counteract macroeconomic disturbances and dampen cyclical fluctuations in prices and employment, thereby improving overall economic stability and welfare. In principle, when economic growth unexpectedly weakens below the economy's potential, accommodative monetary policy can stimulate aggregate demand and restore full employment. Likewise, when inflationary pressures develop, monetary restriction can restore the central bank's price stability objective. In practice, however, given the limited knowledge that economists have about the macroeconomy – for example, about macroeconomic dynamics, about the monetary transmission mechanism, and even about the measurement of fundamental concepts such as the natural rates of output, employment and interest – there is substantial disagreement about the scope of stabilization policy and about policy design.

One approach is to decide upon what seems to be the best policy on a period-by-period basis, without appeal to any specific policy guide. A seeming advantage of this approach is that it gives policymakers the discretion to use their judgement period by period. However, a basic tenet of modern research is that systematic policy – that is, policy based on a contingency plan or policy rule – has important advantages over a purely discretionary policy approach. By committing to follow a rule, policymakers can avoid the inefficiency associated with the time-inconsistency problem that arises when policy is formulated in a discretionary manner. Following a rule allows policymakers to communicate and explain their policy actions more effectively. Policy based on a well-understood rule enhances the accountability of the central bank and improves the credibility of future policy actions. Also, by making future policy decisions more predictable, rule-based policy facilitates forecasting by financial market participants, businesses, and households, thereby reducing uncertainty.

Various proposals for monetary policy rules have been made over time, and a vast literature continues to examine the relative advantages and drawbacks of alternatives in abstract theoretical terms, in the context of empirical macroeconometric models, and in terms of the practical experience accumulated from past policy practice.

To appreciate the appeal and limitations of Taylor rules, it is useful to relate their development to other proposals for systematic monetary policy.

Development of monetary policy rules

Some proposals suggest postulating a rule in terms of the main objectives of monetary policy, for example 'maintain economic stability' or 'maintain a constant aggregate price level'. (See Simons, 1936, for early arguments favouring price-level targeting over discretionary policy.) One important practical difficulty with these proposals, however, is that the concepts involved are not under the control of the central bank and thus the proposals are not operational. In essence, these proposals fail to draw a clear distinction between the objectives of monetary policy and the policy instruments that are at least under the approximate control of the central bank. As a result, the suggested rules are only implicit in nature and are difficult to monitor and to distinguish from discretionary policy in a meaningful manner.

To be useful in practice, policy rules must be simple and transparent to communicate, implement and verify. This requires a clear choice of what should serve as the policy instrument – for example the money supply, m, or the short-term interest rate, i – and clear guidance as to how any other information necessary to implement the rule   for instance recent readings or forecasts of inflation and economy activity – should be used to adjust the policy instrument.

Perhaps the simplest example of a policy rule is the proposal that the central bank maintain a constant rate of growth of the money supply – Milton Friedman's k-percent rule (Friedman, 1960). The rule draws on the equation of exchange expressed in growth rates:

$$\Delta m + \Delta v - \pi + \Delta q \tag{1}$$

where $\pi \equiv \Delta p$ is the rate of inflation and p, m, v, and q are (the logarithms of), respectively, the price level, money stock, money velocity, and real output. Selecting the constant growth of money, k, to correspond to the sum of a desired inflation target, π^*, and the economy's potential growth rate, Δq^*, and adjusting for any secular trend in the velocity of money, Δv^*, suggests a simple rule that can achieve, on average, the desired inflation target, π^*:

$$\Delta m = \pi^* + \Delta q^* - \Delta v^*. \tag{2}$$

Further, if the velocity of money were fairly stable this simple rule would also yield a high degree of economic stability. An early illustration of this rule appeared in 1935 in the work of Carl Snyder, a statistician at the Federal Reserve Bank of New York. After estimating that the normal rate of growth of trade in the United States was about four per cent per year at the time and observing that the velocity of money was stable, Snyder argued that 'the highest attainable degree of general industrial and economic stability will be gained by an expansion of currency and credit ... at this rate [four per cent]' (Snyder, 1935, p. 198). During the 1960s and early 1970s, Milton Friedman's recommendation that the Federal Reserve control the rate of money growth to equal four per cent per year was similarly based on the assumption that potential output growth in the Unites States roughly equalled four per cent – the prevailing estimate at that time.

Another way to interpret this policy rule is in terms of the growth of nominal income, $\Delta x = \pi + \Delta q$. With the economy's natural growth of nominal income defined as the sum of the natural growth rate of output and the central bank's inflation objective, $\Delta x^* = \pi^* + \Delta q^*$, a rule for constant money growth can be seen as targeting this natural growth rate. An advantage of a constant money growth rule is that very little information is required to implement it. If velocity does not exhibit a secular trend, the only required element for calibrating the rule is the economy's natural growth of output. In addition, while the calibration of this rule does not rest on the specification of any particular model, the rule is remarkably stable across alternative models of the economy. In this sense, the policy of maintaining a constant growth rate of money is arguably the ultimate example of a rule that is robust to possible model misspecification.

Simple modifications allowing for some automatic response of money growth to economic developments have also been proposed as simple rules that could deliver improved macroeconomic performance (see, for example, Cooper and Fischer, 1972). Among the simplest such alternatives is the rule associated with Bennett McCallum (1988; 1993):

$$\Delta m = \Delta x^* - \Delta v^* - \phi_{\Delta x}(\Delta x - \Delta x^*). \tag{3}$$

McCallum showed that, if a rule such as this (for example, with $\phi_{\Delta x} = 0.5$) had been followed, the performance of the US economy likely would have been considerably better than actual performance, especially during the 1930s and 1970s – the two periods of the worst monetary policy mistakes in the history of the Federal Reserve.

A factor that complicates the use of the money stock as a policy instrument is the potential for instability in the demand for money due either to temporary disturbances or to persistent changes resulting from financial innovation. In part for this reason, central banks generally prefer to adjust monetary policy using an interest rate instrument.

A policy rule quite as simple as Friedman's k-percent rule cannot be formulated with an interest rate instrument. As early as Wicksell's (1898) monumental treatise on *Interest and Prices*, it was recognized that attempting to peg the short-term nominal interest rate at a fixed value does not constitute a stable policy rule. (Indeed, this was one reason why Friedman, 1968, and others expressed a preference for rules with money as the policy instrument.) Wicksell argued that the central bank should aim to maintain price stability, which in theory could be achieved if the interest rate were always equal to the economy's natural rate of interest, r^*. Recognizing that the natural rate of interest is merely an abstract, unobservable concept, however, he noted: 'This does not mean that the bank ought actually to *ascertain* the natural rate before fixing their own rates of interest. That would, of course, be impracticable, and would also be quite unnecessary.' Rather, Wicksell pointed out that a simple policy rule that responded systematically to prices would be sufficient to achieve satisfactory, though imperfect, stability: 'If prices rise, the rate of interest is to be raised; and if prices fall, the rate of interest is to be lowered; and the rate of interest is henceforth to be maintained at its new level until a further movement in prices calls for a further change in one direction or the other' (Wicksell, 1898, p. 189, emphasis in the original). In algebraic terms, Wicksell proposed what is arguably the simplest reactive monetary rule with an interest rate instrument:

$$\Delta i = \theta \pi. \tag{4}$$

Wicksell's simple interest rate rule did not attract much attention in policy discussions, perhaps because of its exclusive focus on price stability and lack of explicit reference to developments in real economic activity.

The classic Taylor rule and its generalizations

The policy rules that are commonly referred to as Taylor rules are simple reactive rules that adjust the interest rate policy instrument in response to developments in both inflation and economic activity. An important advance in the development of these rules can be identified with the policy regime evaluation project reported in a volume published by the Brookings Institution (Bryant, Hooper and Mann, 1993). The objective of the project was to identify simple reactive interest rate rules that would deliver satisfactory economic performance for price stability and economic stability across a range of competing estimated models. The Brookings project examined rules that set deviations of the short-term nominal interest rate, i, from some baseline path, i^*, in proportion to deviations of target variables z, from their targets, z^*:

$$i - i^* = \theta(z - z^*). \tag{5}$$

The collective findings pointed to two alternatives as the most promising in delivering satisfactory economic performance across models. One targeted nominal income, while the other targeted inflation and real output:

$$i - i^* = \theta_\pi(\pi - \pi^*) + \theta_q(q - q^*). \tag{6}$$

The potential usefulness of this particular rule as a benchmark for setting monetary policy was further highlighted in the celebrated contribution by John B. Taylor at the Fall 1992 Carnegie-Rochester Conference on Public Policy. Taylor developed a 'hypothetical but representative policy rule' (1993, p. 214) by using the sum of the equilibrium or natural rate of interest, r^*, and inflation, π, for i^* and setting the inflation target and equilibrium real interest equal to two and the response parameters to one half. The result was what became known as the classic Taylor rule:

$$i = 2 + \pi + \frac{1}{2}(\pi - 2) + \frac{1}{2}(q - q^*). \tag{7}$$

Taylor noted that, if one used the deviation of real quarterly output from a linear trend to measure the output gap, $(q - q^*)$, and the year-over-year rate of change of the output deflator to measure inflation, π, this parameterization appeared to describe Federal Reserve behaviour well in the late 1980s and early 1990s.

The confluence of the econometric evaluation evidence supporting the stabilization properties of this rule and its usefulness for understanding historical monetary policy in a period generally accepted as having good policy performance generated tremendous interest, and numerous central banks began to monitor this policy rule or related variants to provide guidance in policy decisions. These developments also greatly influenced monetary policy research and teaching. By linking interest rate decisions directly to inflation and economic activity, Taylor rules offered a convenient tool for studying monetary policy while abstracting from a detailed analysis of the demand for and supply of money. This allowed the development of simpler models (see the survey in Clarida, Gali and Gertler, 1999, and papers in Taylor, 1999) and the replacement of the 'LM curve' with a Taylor rule in treatments of the Hicksian IS–LM apparatus. (It should be noted, however, that this abstraction is overly simplistic when the short-term interest rate approaches zero. At the zero bound, the stance of monetary policy can no longer be measured or communicated with a short-term interest rate instrument; see, for example, Orphanides and Wieland, 2000). Subsequent research (see Orphanides, 2003b, for a survey) suggested that a generalized form of Taylor's classic rule could provide a useful common basis both for econometric policy evaluation across diverse families of models and for historical monetary policy analysis over a broad range of experience:

$$i = (1 - \theta_i)(r^* + \pi^*) + \theta_i i_{-1} + \theta_\pi (\pi - \pi^*) + \theta_q (q - q^*) + \theta_{\Delta q}(\Delta q - \Delta q^*). \quad (8)$$

The generalized Taylor rule (8) nests rule (6) as a special case but introduces two additional elements. First, it allows for inertial behaviour in setting interest rates, $\theta_i > 0$, which proves particularly important for policy analysis in models with strong expectational channels (Woodford, 2003). Second, it allows the policy response to developments in economic activity to take two forms: a response to the level of the output gap, $(q - q^*)$, or its difference, which can also be restated as a response to the difference between output growth and its potential, $(\Delta q - \Delta q^*)$. The generalized Taylor rule also nests another simplification of special interest, $\theta_i = 1$ and $\theta_q = 0$, which yields a family of difference rules similar to Wicksell's original proposal:

$$\Delta i = \theta_\pi (\pi - \pi^*) + \theta_{\Delta q}(\Delta q - \Delta q^*). \quad (9)$$

These difference rules are also of interest because, like money-growth rules, their implementation does not require estimates of the natural rate of interest or the level of potential output (and the output gap) but only of the growth rate of potential output. Indeed, these rules may be viewed as a reformulation of money-growth rules in terms of an interest rate instrument. To see the relationship of (9) to money growth targeting, note that, by substituting the money growth in rule (3) into the equation of exchange, that rule can be stated in terms of the velocity of money:

$$\Delta v - \Delta v^* = (1 + \phi_{\Delta x})(\Delta x - \Delta x^*). \tag{10}$$

To reformulate this strategy in terms of an interest rate rule, consider the simplest formulation of money demand as a (log-) linear relationship between velocity deviations from its equilibrium and the rate of interest. In difference form this is

$$\Delta v - \Delta v^* = a\Delta i + e, \tag{11}$$

where $a > 0$ and e summarizes short-run money demand dynamics and temporary velocity disturbances. An interest-rate-based strategy that avoids the short-run velocity fluctuations, e, may be obtained by substituting the remaining part of (11) into (10). This yields

$$\Delta i = \theta((\pi - \pi^*) + (\Delta q - \Delta q^*)) \tag{12}$$

for some $\theta > 0$, which, as can be readily seen, has the same form as rule (9).

In light of this flexibility in nesting a wide range of alternative monetary policy strategies and the relative simplicity of the form (8), Taylor rules have been used to discuss a variety of policy regimes, from money growth targeting (see, for example, Clarida and Gertler, 1997) to inflation targeting (see, for example, Orphanides and Williams, 2007).

A crucial element for the design and operational implementation of a Taylor rule is the detailed description of its inputs. This requires specificity regarding the measures of inflation and economic activity that the policy rule should respond to, whether forecasts or recent outcomes of these variables are to be employed, and the source of these data or forecasts. In addition, the source of information and updating procedures regarding the unobservable concepts required for implementing the rule must be stipulated. Specificity in these dimensions is essential for practical analysis because there is often a multitude of competing alternatives and a lack of consensus about the appropriate concepts and sources of information that ought to be used for policy analysis. This situation is particularly vexing in regard to the treatment of unobservable concepts, such as the output gap. Unfortunately, econometric policy evaluation exercises suggest that inferences regarding the performance of a particular Taylor rule often depend sensitively on assumptions regarding the availability and reliability of these inputs. Differences in underlying assumptions complicate comparisons across studies and often explain differences in reported findings.

An illustrative example of this sensitivity relates to improper treatment of information regarding the current state of the economy. A common pitfall in theoretical policy evaluation exercises is to assume that the current state of the economy – for example, the current output gap – can be perfectly observed. Under this assumption, a Taylor rule with a vigorous response to the output gap is often recommended as 'optimal' in model-based policy evaluations. However, naive adoption of such recommendations would be counterproductive. Available real-time estimates of the output gap are imperfect, and historical experience suggests that the mismeasurement is often substantial. Under these circumstances, better stabilization outcomes would result if policy did not respond to the output gap at all or if it responded to output growth instead (Orphanides, 2003a). If the natural rate of interest is also unknown and its real-time estimates are subject to significant mismeasurement, the difference variant of the Taylor rule, (9), proves considerably more robust than the Brookings variant, (6), reversing the ranking of the two alternatives that is implied under perfect knowledge (Orphanides and Williams, 2002).

Another example of such sensitivity relates to the use of forecasts in the Taylor rule. Because of lags in the monetary policy transmission mechanism, pre-emptive policy reaction is generally recommended, especially with respect to inflation. But inferences regarding the performance of forecast-based policy are sensitive to the quality of the forecasts. In some models, Taylor rules responding to several-quarters-ahead forecasts of inflation appear more promising for stabilization than rules focusing only on near-term conditions. However, this conclusion is not robust and is overturned once the potential unreliability of longer-term forecasts due to model misspecification is factored into the analysis (Levin, Wieland and Williams, 2003).

As already noted, Taylor rules have proven valuable for historical policy analysis. Following Taylor (1993), numerous authors have examined historical monetary policy in the United States using either calibrated or estimated versions of Taylor rules (8). Studying the characteristics of policy in periods associated with good or bad economic performance helps identify aspects of policy that may be associated with such differences in performance. A complicating factor is the need for real-time data and forecasts for proper inference (Orphanides, 2001). The pitfall of using *ex post* revised data and retrospective estimates of unobserved concepts in estimating Taylor rules is not uncommon. However, interpretations of historical policy based on information that was unavailable to policymakers when policy decisions were made is of questionable value. Policy prescriptions from a fixed rule are distorted as the inputs to the rule are revised from those originally available to policymakers, and therefore counterfactual comparisons of alternative policy rules can be misleading when they are based on revised data.

Despite these challenges, some useful elements of policy design emerge from historical analysis of Taylor rules, (8). First, and arguably most important, good stabilization performance is associated with a strong reaction to inflation. Second, good performance is associated with policy rules that exhibit considerable inertia. Third, a strong reaction to mismeasured output gaps has historically proven counterproductive. Fourth, successful policy could still usefully incorporate information from real economic activity by focusing on the growth rate of the economy. To be sure, such broad principles provide insufficient guidance for identifying the precise policy rule that might be ideal in a specific context. But this is not the objective of policy design with Taylor rules. Rather, the goal is the identification of simple guides that are robust to misspecification and other sources of error experienced over history.

In summary, Taylor rules offer a simple and transparent framework with which to organize the discussion of systematic monetary policy. Their adoption as a tool for policy discussions has facilitated a welcome convergence between monetary policy practice and monetary policy research and proved an important advance for both positive and normative analysis.

ATHANASIOS ORPHANIDES

See also **inflation targeting.**

Bibliography

Bryant, R.C., Hooper, P. and Mann, C., eds. 1993. *Evaluating Policy Regimes: New Research in Empirical Macroeconomics.* Washington DC: Brookings.

Clarida, R., Gali, J. and Gertler, M. 1999. The science of monetary policy. *Journal of Economic Literature* 37, 1661–707.

Clarida, R. and Gertler, M. 1997. How the Bundesbank conducts monetary policy. In *Reducing Inflation: Motivation and Strategy*, ed. C. Romer and D. Romer. Chicago: University of Chicago Press.

Cooper, J.P. and Fischer, S. 1972. Simulations of monetary rules in the FRB–MIT–Penn model. *Journal of Money, Credit and Banking* 4, 384–96.

Friedman, M. 1960. *A Program for Monetary Stability.* New York: Fordham University Press.

Friedman, M. 1968. The role of monetary policy. *American Economic Review* 58, 1–17.

Levin, A., Wieland, V. and Williams, J.C. 2003. The performance of forecast-based monetary policy rules under model uncertainty. *American Economic Review* 93, 622–45.

McCallum, B.T. 1988. Robustness properties of a rule for monetary policy. *Carnegie Rochester Conference Series on Public Policy* 29, 173–203.

McCallum, B.T. 1993. Specification and analysis of a monetary policy rule for Japan. *Bank of Japan Monetary and Economic Studies* 11(2), 1–45.

Orphanides, A. 2001. Monetary policy rules based on real-time data. *American Economic Review* 91, 964–85.

Orphanides, A. 2003a. Monetary policy evaluation with noisy information. *Journal of Monetary Economics* 50, 605–31.

Orphanides, A. 2003b. Historical monetary policy analysis and the Taylor rule. *Journal of Monetary Economics* 50, 983–1022.

Orphanides, A. and Wieland, V. 2000. Efficient monetary policy design near price stability. *Journal of the Japanese and International Economies* 14, 327–65.

Orphanides, A. and Williams, J.C. 2002. Robust monetary policy rules with unknown natural rates. *Brookings Papers on Economic Activity* 2002(2), 63–145.

Orphanides, A. and Williams, J.C. 2007. Inflation targeting under imperfect knowledge. In *Monetary Policy under Inflation Targeting*, ed. F. Mishkin and K. Schmidt-Hebbel. Santiago: Central Bank of Chile.

Simons, H.C. 1936. Rules vs authorities in monetary policy. *Journal of Political Economy* 44, 1–30.

Snyder, C. 1935. The problem of monetary and economic stability. *Quarterly Journal of Economics* 49, 173–205.

Taylor, J.B. 1993. Discretion versus policy rules in practice. *Carnegie-Rochester Conference Series on Public Policy* 39, 195–214.

Taylor, J.B., ed. 1999. *Monetary Policy Rules.* Chicago: University of Chicago.

Wicksell, K. 1898. *Interest and Prices.* Trans. R.F. Kahn, London: Macmillan, 1936.

Woodford, M. 2003. *Interest and Prices: Foundations of a Theory of Monetary Policy.* Princeton: Princeton University Press.

time consistency of monetary and fiscal policy

A (possibly time- and state-contingent) strategy is said to be time inconsistent if an agent finds it optimal from the point of view of some initial period 0 but finds it suboptimal in some subsequent period t. Time inconsistency can obviously arise if the government has time-varying preferences because of alternations of government, as shown in Persson and Svensson (1989). However, as Kydland and Prescott (1977) discovered, the time-inconsistency problem is a pervasive feature of environments with a single benevolent policymaker taking decisions over time. This happens even though the policymaker has stable preferences and even in situations where there is no apparent conflict of interest – though the emphasis there should perhaps be on the word 'apparent'. This means that everyone in the economy can often be made better off if the policymaker gains access to a commitment technology – a mechanism that forces him or her to keep his or her promises.

As pointed out by Fischer (1980), what these environments have in common is (a) that the Pareto optimal allocation is not implementable, (b) that the behaviour of the private sector depends on its expectations about future government behaviour, and (c) that the government and a typical individual do not share the same preferences. The third of these sounds stronger than it is. It is consistent with the benevolence of the policymaker, that is, that she maximizes the utility of a representative individual. All that it requires is a minimal amount of selfishness on the part of a typical individual – for example, she doesn't internalize the government's budget constraint.

It is important to note that either (a) or (b) on its own is not problematic. If the Pareto optimum can be achieved and I declare a policy at the beginning of time that is consistent with this Pareto optimum, I have no reason to deviate in the future since nothing better is feasible. On the other hand, suppose the Pareto optimum cannot be achieved but current behaviour does not depend on future policy. Then the policymaker will make the right trade-off in each period and the second best will be achieved.

However, if both features are present at the same time, then the policy that achieves the second best will typically be time inconsistent: when choosing policy for period t, the policymaker faces different incentives in period 0 from the incentives faced in period t. In period 0 she rationally takes into account the effects on expectations; in period t it is no longer rational to do that, since expectations in the past are bygones. The temptation to bring the economy closer to the first-best renders the second-best solution time inconsistent, and rational expectations force the economy into a Pareto inferior third-best equilibrium.

The Phillips curve and inflation bias

The central example in Kydland and Prescott (1977) is a central bank setting inflation in an environment with an expectations-augmented Phillips curve. This environment has the feature that inflation surprises lead to deviations of output from its 'natural' rate. The authors then assume that a positive inflation surprise is good, since the 'natural' rate of output is suboptimal because of various (unspecified) distortions. However, in any rational expectations equilibrium, inflation expectations are fulfilled and output equals its natural rate. If inflation is bad in itself (other things being equal), then the best rational expectations equilibrium features zero expected and actual inflation. This is the second best: the best equilibrium that can be achieved subject to the constraint of rational expectations. The first best would be for output to be at some ideal level greater than its natural rate but with inflation maintained at zero. However, this ideal outcome is not consistent with rational expectations. Now suppose inflation policy can be revised after expectations are formed. Then the zero-inflation policy that gives rise to the best rational expectations equilibrium is not time consistent: when it is time to set inflation, the central bank would like to set an inflation rate above zero since a small rise in inflation has no first-order effect on the welfare cost of inflation but does have a first-order effect on the welfare cost of output being less than its ideal level. The result, under discretionary monetary policy, is a tendency for inflation to be above its desired level (inflation bias) with no (positive) effect on output or employment.

Overtaxation of capital and liquidity

Another early contribution is that of Fischer (1980), who discussed a situation where a fiscal authority decides on the levels of taxation on labour and capital and of public expenditure. There, the problem is that tomorrow's capital stock depends on today's investment. Meanwhile, today's investment depends on expectations about future capital income taxes. The result is that a government that sets taxes sequentially will typically overtax capital income. Similarly, Calvo (1978) described the time consistency problem in a monetary economy with money in the utility function. He found that, when lump-sum taxation is not available, the Friedman rule of optimal monetary policy is not time consistent; in general, the government wants to expand the money supply to relax the government budget constraint. This is because monetary expansion, like capital taxation, is distortionary only *ex ante*; it is the *expectation* of monetary expansion (and the consequent inflation) that leads people to economize on liquidity, a socially free resource.

Relation with game theoretic concepts

The relationship between time consistency, time inconsistency and various concepts in game theory have been much discussed. A common view, but by no means a consensus, has emerged, asserting that the best way to think about the situation is that the (Ramsey 1927) optimal policy, 'second best' or 'commitment solution' (these phrases are used interchangeably) is an equilibrium of one game, the time-consistent policy the equilibrium of another. The first game lets the government move before time starts, choosing a time- and state-contingent policy for the indefinite future. Thereafter it does not move again. The second game has the government moving sequentially, setting policy in each period as it arrives. When the policies implied by these equilibria differ, then we say that the Ramsey policy is time inconsistent. On the other hand, any equilibrium of the second game is time-consistent by construction. This view of course leaves open what the correct solution concept is for these various games. Chari and Kehoe (1990) and several successors discuss the appropriate solution concept for the second type of game. From this literature has emerged the concept of 'sustainable equilibrium' which roughly corresponds to the sequential equilibrium concept of Kreps and Wilson (1982) but modified to apply to economies with one large agent and many 'small' agents. A recent formulation can be found in Phelan and Stacchetti (2001).

Solving the time inconsistency problem

The literature on time consistency may usefully be divided into two parts: one attempts to characterize the equilibrium of the sequential-move game, the other tries to solve the time-inconsistency problem by somehow erasing the difference between the Ramsey policy and the time-consistent policy. A celebrated paper in the second category is Lucas and Stokey (1983), which discusses a dynamic monetary economy without capital. A price-taking representative agent chooses labour supply and the government sets labour taxes so as to minimize distortions subject to a government budget constraint. Government expenditure is exogenous. The government can issue state-contingent debt which it is committed to honouring. The main finding of the paper is that, if public debt has a sufficiently rich maturity structure, then the Ramsey optimal policy is time consistent. However, if only one-period state-contingent bonds are available, then the optimal policy is typically not time consistent. Persson, Persson and Svensson (1987) extend this result to monetary economies, showing how the government can render the optimal policy time consistent by accumulating nominal assets equal to the stock of money so that the outstanding stock of net nominal claims is zero. A minor mistake in that paper was pointed out by Calvo and Obstfeld (1990), but the basic result stands and applies quite generally, as explained in Alvarez, Kehoe and Neumayer (2001). The latter paper establishes a link between the optimality of the Friedman rule (zero nominal interest rates) and the possibility of rendering the Ramsey optimal policy time-consistent: for a wide class of economies they show that the Ramsey optimal policy can be made time-consistent if and only if the Friedman rule is optimal. Domínguez (2007) extends this result further for an economy with capital, showing that, if capital taxes are set one period in advance, then a sufficiently rich maturity structure of public debt is sufficient to render the optimal policy time consistent.

Another sub-literature in this category looks at reputational mechanisms that might render the optimal policy time consistent, or at least bring the time-consistent solution closer to the second-best optimum. In monetary policy, a key early contribution is Barro and Gordon (1983). In an environment with an expectations-augmented Phillips curve, it shows, using the well-known folk theorem from game theory, that the optimal monetary policy in the environment described by Kydland and Prescott (1977) can be sustained as a time-consistent equilibrium provided the policymaker is patient enough. A paper that analyses fiscal policy with a reputational-style approach is Kotlikoff, Persson and Svensson (1988). In this paper it is shown how the optimal tax scheme can be sustained in a two-period overlapping generations environment by threats of moving to the third-best equilibrium if any generation deviates.

Yet another set of solutions to the time-consistency problem of monetary policy is found in Rogoff (1985) and Persson and Tabellini (1993). The first, using an idea from industrial organization first published by Vickers (1985), shows that a monetary policymaker will typically be better off delegating monetary policy to a central banker that cares more about low inflation and less about output or employment than he or she does. Rogoff's result is aptly described as delegation to a 'conservative central banker'. This delegation improves welfare but does not achieve the second-best optimum. By contrast, the key result in Persson and Tabellini (1993) is that the second best can be achieved by signing a performance contract with the central banker.

Analysing what happens when the time inconsistency problem cannot be solved

The literature on characterizing time-consistent policy also divides into two parts: one focusing on a solution concept ('sustainable equilibrium') that is nearly always set-valued and the other on a refinement ('Markov perfect equilibrium') that often (but certainly not always) yields a unique equilibrium. The concept of Markov perfect equilibrium, whose purpose is essentially to rule out any reputational mechanisms, is defined in a game-theoretic setting in Maskin and Tirole (2001) and in a macroeconomic setting by, among several others, Klein, Krusell and Ríos-Rull (2006). In the latter paper, the authors find that in the Markov perfect equilibrium labour tends to be under-taxed even in an environment where no other taxes are available and the only other endogenous variable is government spending. That is, a government acting sequentially tends to exaggerate the distortionary effects of taxation. This is in marked contrast to the case of capital and inflation taxes. The reason is that the current labour income tax *encourages* labour supply in the previous period, by intertemporal substitution. This effect is ignored by a sequentially moving government that thus neglects a beneficial effect of raising the current labour income tax rate.

Other papers studying Markov perfect equilibrium in a fiscal policy setting include Klein and Ríos-Rull (2003), who look at time-consistent capital and labour income taxation where capital taxes are set one period in advance and the budget has to balance in each period. The main finding is that a calibrated model can replicate the capital and labour taxes that we observe in, say, the United States, reasonably well.

Krusell, Martin and Ríos-Rull (2004) consider public debt policy in an economy without capital and find that for positive initial debt there is a unique equilibrium but infinitely many steady states. For negative initial debt there are infinitely many equilibria, each associated with infinitely many steady states.

On the other hand, Phelan and Stacchetti (2001) study the set of sustainable equilibria in an economy with capital but without public debt. The methods used are similar to those in Abreu, Pearce and Stacchetti (1990). Fernandez-Villaverde and Tsyvinski (2002) consider all the sustainable equilibria in a stochastic environment with capital. They compare the best (from a welfare point of view) in that class with the Markov perfect equilibrium and the Ramsey equilibrium. Also, a literature is emerging on time-consistent policy under asymmetric information. Recent contributions include Sleet (2003) and Sleet and Yeltekin (2004).

A new departure in the study of time consistency of monetary policy is the consideration of the role of sticky prices. This introduces a new channel through which time inconsistency may arise: when prices are sticky and firms are bound to produce whatever is demanded at the given price, a surprise monetary expansion raises output. This is typically *ex post* welfare-improving in an economy suffering from some distortion, typically monopolistic rather than perfect competition. Important contributions include Albanesi, Chari and Christiano (2003a), who show that without commitment the economy can get stuck in an 'expectation trap' in the following sense. There are multiple, Pareto-ranked, equilibria. In the lower-ranked equilibria, the private sector expects high inflation. The measures the private sector takes to protect itself from high inflation create incentives for the policymaker to accommodate these expectations. On the other hand, in Albanesi, Chari and Christiano (2003b) the same authors show that optimal monetary policy is time consistent – and the Markov perfect equilibrium unique – in a wide class of models.

PAUL KLEIN

See also **central bank independence.**

Bibliography

Abreu, D., Pearce, D. and Stacchetti, E. 1990. Toward a theory of discounted repeated games with imperfect monitoring. *Econometrica* 58, 1041–63.

Albanesi, S., Chari, V.V. and Christiano, L. 2003a. Expectation traps and monetary policy. *Review of Economic Studies* 70, 715–41.

Albanesi, S., Chari, V.V. and Christiano, L. 2003b. How severe is the time inconsistency problem in monetary policy? *Federal Reserve Bank of Minneapolis Quarterly Review* 27(3), 17–33.

Alvarez, F., Kehoe, P.J. and Neumayer, P.A. 2001. The time consistency of fiscal and monetary policies. Staff Report No. 305, Federal Reserve Bank of Minneapolis.

Barro, R.J. and Gordon, D.B. 1983. Rules, discretion and reputation in a model of monetary policy. *Journal of Monetary Economics* 12, 101–21.

Calvo, G. 1978. On the time consistency of optimal policy in a monetary economy. *Econometrica* 46, 1411–28.

Calvo, G.A. and Obstfeld, M. 1990. Time consistency of fiscal and monetary policy: a comment. *Econometrica* 58, 1245–7.

Chari, V.V. and Kehoe, P.J. 1990. Sustainable plans. *Journal of Political Economy* 98, 784–802.
Domínguez, B. 2007. On the time-consistency of optimal capital taxes. *Journal of Monetary Economics* 54, 686–705.
Fernandez-Villaverde, J. and Tsyvinski, A. 2002. *Optimal fiscal policy in a business cycle model without commitment.* Mimeo: University of Pennsylvania.
Fischer, S. 1980. Dynamic inconsistency, cooperation and the benevolent dissembling government. *Journal of Economic Dynamics and Control* 2, 93–107.
Klein, P., Krusell, P. and Ríos-Rull, J.-V. 2006. *Time-consistent public expenditure.* Mimeo: Princeton University.
Klein, P. and Ríos-Rull, J.-V. 2003. Time-consistent optimal fiscal policy. *International Economic Review* 44, 1217–45.
Kotlikoff, L.J., Persson, T. and Svensson, L.E. 1988. Social contracts as assets: a possible solution to the time-consistency problem. *American Economic Review* 78, 662–77.
Kreps, D.M. and Wilson, R.B. 1982. Sequential equilibria. *Econometrica* 50, 863–94.
Krusell, P., Martin, F. and Ríos-Rull, J.-V. 2004. *On the determination of government debt.* Mimeo: Simon Fraser University.
Kydland, F.E. and Prescott, E.C. 1977. Rules rather than discretion: the inconsistency of optimal plans. *Journal of Political Economy* 85, 473–91.
Lucas, R.E. and Stokey, N.L. 1983. Optimal fiscal and monetary policy in an economy without capital. *Journal of Monetary Economics* 12, 55–93.
Maskin, E. and Tirole, J. 2001. Markov perfect equilibrium. *Journal of Economic Theory* 100, 191–219.
Persson, M., Persson, T. and Svensson, L. 1987. Time consistency of fiscal and monetary policy. *Econometrica* 55, 1419–31.
Persson, T. and Svensson, L.E. 1989. Why a stubborn conservative would run a deficit: policy with time-inconsistent preferences. *Quarterly Journal of Economics* 104, 325–45.
Persson, T. and Tabellini, G. 1993. Designing institutions for monetary stability. *Carnegie-Rochester Conference Series on Public Policy* 39, 53–84.
Phelan, C. and Stacchetti, E. 2001. Sequential equilibria in a Ramsey tax model. *Econometrica* 69, 1491–518.
Ramsey, F.P. 1927. A contribution to the theory of taxation. *Economic Journal* 37(145), 47–61.
Rogoff, K. 1985. The optimal degree of commitment to an intermediate monetary target. *Quarterly Journal of Economics* 100, 1169–90.
Sleet, C. 2003. Optimal taxation with private government information. *Review of Economic Studies* 71, 1217–39.
Sleet, C. and Yeltekin, S. 2004. *Credible social insurance.* Mimeo: University of Iowa.
Vickers, J. 1985. Delegation and the theory of the firm. *Economic Journal Supplement* 95, 138–47.

Index